The Organic Gardener's Handbook *of*
NATURAL PEST *and* DISEASE CONTROL

A Complete Guide to Maintaining a Healthy Garden and Yard the Earth-Friendly Way

Edited by FERN MARSHALL BRADLEY
BARBARA W. ELLIS, *and* DEBORAH L

RODALE

Writers
Helen Atthowe, Linda A. Gilkeson, Ph.D.,
L. Patricia Kite, Patricia S. Michalak, Barbara Pleasant,
Lee Reich, Ph.D., Alfred F. Scheider

Technical Reviewers
Whitney Cranshaw, Ph.D, Bioagricultural Sciences and Pest Management, Colorado State University
Margaret Skinner, Ph.D., Entomology Research Laboratory, University of Vermont
Beth K. Gugino, Ph.D., Department of Plant Pathology, Pennsylvania State University
and Leslie Doyle, The Sweet Tomato Test Garden, Las Vegas, Nevada

Library of Congress Cataloging-in-Publication Data
The organic gardener's handbook of natural pest and disease control : a complete guide to maintaining a healthy garden and yard the earth-friendly way /
edited by Fern Marshall Bradley, Barbara W. Ellis, and Deborah L. Martin.
    p.   cm.
Includes bibliographical references and index.
ISBN-13: 978–1–60529–542–8 (hardcover)
ISBN-13: 978–1–60529–677–7 (pbk.)
1. Organic gardening—Handbooks, manuals, etc.   2. Horticulture—Handbooks, manuals, etc.   3. Plants—Diseases and pests—Control.   I. Bradley,
Fern Marshall.   II. Ellis, Barbara W.   III. Martin, Deborah L.
SB453.5.0675 2010
632'.96—dc22   2009039996

Distributed to the trade by Macmillan
4 6 8 10 9 7 5 3 hardcover
4 6 8 10 9 7 5 3 paperback

CONTENTS

How to Use This Book

Whether it's spots on the tomatoes, hostas that mysteriously wilt and die, or worm-eaten apples, damage from pests and disease organisms is never welcome. How to manage these problems is a top concern of gardeners everywhere. This newly revised edition of a classic reference on organic solutions to pest and disease problems has been fully updated, and its quick-reference format will help you find the most up-to-date information for a wide range of common insect and disease problems.

HOW TO FIND IT

One look at the contents will illustrate that *The Organic Gardener's Handbook of Natural Pest and Disease Control* is really four books in one. Once you've paged through it to familiarize yourself with the format, flipping to the section you need will become second nature. And for quick and easy access to information, don't forget the index. Here's a rundown of what is included.

Part 1, Your Healthy Garden, is an overview of the basic practices of organic gardening to help you prevent problems before they ever get started. By learning how to build organically active soil, choose plants that are well adapted to conditions, and effectively tend your crops and ornamental plantings throughout the season, you'll create a balanced system in which problems are regulated naturally and there are few outbreaks of pests and diseases. This section is especially important for new gardeners and gardeners who have just switched to organic methods.

Part 2, Symptoms and Solutions, contains a plant encyclopedia with symptoms and solutions for the major problems suffered by popular plants—including fruits, vegetables, annuals, bulbs, perennials, and trees and shrubs. It also contains preventive information and general entries on the major plant groups.

Part 3, Identifying Pests and Diseases, features a photographic guide to garden pests and their natural enemies, and symptoms of diseases and disorders. It includes descriptions, life cycle information, and summaries of control options. With more than 225 color photographs, this section is an excellent starting point for diagnosing problems and deciding what to do about them.

Part 4, Organic Pest and Disease Management, is a thorough guide to nonchemical options for stopping insects in their tracks or curbing diseases before they overtake your yard. It begins with low-impact techniques that prevent problems by keeping pests and diseases from reaching your plants. There is a thorough discussion of biological controls, including naturally occurring biocontrols and commercial biocontrol products. To conclude, there's a rundown of homemade and commercial sprays and dusts that home gardeners can use to repel or kill pests and to prevent or lessen disease problems. Some of these products are offered as a last resort only—for the exceptional cases when the natural balance has been disturbed and pest problems threaten to ruin the harvest or kill your plants.

REMEMBERING THE BIG PICTURE

As you use this book, it's important that you not lose sight of the big picture of gardening organically. One of the principles at the heart of organic gardening is eliminating the need to use sprays and dusts at all. This may seem like a difficult—even unrealistic—goal to strive for, but organic gardeners everywhere will attest to the fact that it makes gardening more enjoyable—and safer—than ever. You'll be much more successful if you emphasize practices that promote garden health and management strategies that rely on nontoxic intervention methods.

So where do you start? Logically enough, at the beginning. Part 1 will set you on the path to creating the kind of garden environment that helps plants stay healthy naturally. You'll also find that the individual plant entries in Part 2 contain lots of helpful growing tips. Read and follow these to avoid many common garden problems.

While the individual plant, pest, and disease entries in Parts 2 and 3 do list some preventive measures, they are primarily designed to help you decide what to do once you've encountered specific problems in your garden. But keep in mind that preventive measures are the keys to successful organic gardening. To get the most out of this book—and to develop an effective management system for your garden—make sure you've implemented as many of the preventive methods discussed in Part 1 as possible.

When you do encounter a problem, then Part 4 will be your resource for making a plan to solve the problem.

You'll find that this revised edition is an invaluable reference for finding solutions to garden problems, with fully updated information throughout. When you follow a recommendation for controlling a specific insect or disease, always use the least-invasive method available.

Since some botanical poisons and copper and sulfur sprays are allowed for use (with restrictions) according to the National Organic Program regulations, we have included them in our recommendations throughout this book. (See "Organic and Natural" on page 3 for more information on the National Organic Program.) Thus, in total, the book includes hundreds of listings of pyrethrins, neem, sulfur, and copper as management options for specific pests or diseases. This does not mean we endorse widespread use of these substances. In your individual garden, you should opt to use one of these sprays or dusts only in *exceptional* cases.

If you do decide to use a botanical poison or a sulfur or copper product, remember that they can be dangerous to people as well as to plant pests and diseases. Never use them casually or carelessly. Whenever you use commercial products, always read and follow label directions.

In the big picture, we hope you gain a greater appreciation for just how well plants can keep themselves healthy, given the opportunity. Even in the middle of summer, when pest problems are more severe, bear in mind that the crisis will pass and your plants will get another chance with each new season. Plants have been making use of these second chances—devising their own self-defense tricks—since time began. Learning and using natural pest and disease management strategies gets you involved in these adventures, which are part of the fun and fascination of gardening.

PHOTO CREDITS

COVER PHOTOGRAPHS

© Photodisc (leaves)

© Rodale Images (cabbage, apples, blueberries)

© Robert Cardillo/Rodale Images (hornworm, flowers)

© Bill Beatty/Visuals Unlimited, Inc. (lacewing)

INTERIOR PHOTOGRAPHS

© Blickwinkel/Alamy: page 283 (pear slug)

© Nigel Cattlin/Alamy: pages 275 (rust mite damage), 280 (vine weevil damage), 282, 283 (cottony cushion scale), 298 (predatory mite), 316, 318 (nitrogen deficiency), 321 (verticillium wilt), 323 (curly top virus), 330 (powdery mildew), 333 (cane blight), 336 (fire blight), 340 (club root), 344 (damping-off)

© Custom Life Science Images/Alamy: page 301 (spider)

© Florida Images/Alamy: page 276 (mole cricket)

© Graphic Science/Alamy: page 289 (vinegar fly)

© B. Mete Uz/Alamy: page 269 (Japanese beetle)

© Wildlife GMBH/Alamy: pages 296 (mealybug destroyer), 297 (mealybug destroyer larva)

© Jack Clark/Animals Animals: page 277 (fruit moth larva)

© Breck P. Kent/Animals Animals: pages 267 (grasshopper), 299 (parasitized hornworm)

© PremaPhotos/Animals Animals: page 303

© James Robinson/Animals Animals: page 299 (cicada killer wasp)

© Richard Shiell/Animals Animals: page 287 (flower thrips)

© Donald Specker/Animals Animals: pages 265 (flea beetle damage), 271 (leafhopper), 286 (squash vine borer)

© Wild & Natural/Animals Animals: pages 273 (bean beetle damage), 293 (assassin bug)

© OSF/Konrad Wothe/Animals Animals: page 260 (potato beetle damage)

© Dr. Tristan Bantock: page 294

© Dr. Jeffrey K. Barnes: page 266 (fleahopper)

© W.R. Allen, Agriculture & Agri-Food Canada/Bugwood.org: page 336 (peach rosette)

© Gary Alpert, Harvard University/Bugwood.org: pages 292 (yellowjacket), 297 (yellowjacket)

© Robert L. Anderson, USDA Forest Service/Bugwood.org: pages 320 (sulfur dioxide injury), 337 (twig blight)

© Kevin D. Arvin/Bugwood.org: pages 261 (corn rootworm), 262

© Stephen Ausmus, USDA Agricultural Research Service/Bugwood.org: page 272 (leafroller)

© Paul Bachi, University of Kentucky Research & Education Center/Bugwood.org: page 323 (herbicide injury)

© Joseph Berger/Bugwood.org: page 270 (lace bug)

© Steve L. Brown, University of Georgia/Bugwood.org: page 261 (corn earworm moth)

© Elizabeth Bush, Virginia Polytechnic Institute & State University/Bugwood.org: page 317 (foliar nematodes)

© David Cappaert, Michigan State University/Bugwood.org: pages 252 (asparagus beetle larva), 265 (emerald ash borer)

© Clemson University–USDA Cooperative Extension Slide Series/Bugwood.org: pages 252 (asparagus beetle adult), 263 (cutworm feeding), 277 (fruit moth damage), 278 (plum curculio), 290 (sod webworm damage), 291 (June beetle larvae), 321 (winter injury), 327 (brown rot, flower blight), 329 (bacterial speck), 331 (sunscald), 339 (black knot)

© Whitney Cranshaw, Colorado State University/Bugwood.org: pages 251 (apple maggot damage), 258 (currant borer larva), 263 (cucumber beetle damage), 270 (lace bug damage), 277 (pear psylla damage), 279, 285 (squash bug), 286 (harlequin bug egg cluster), 296 (pink spotted lady beetle), 297 (pink spotted lady beetle, squash bug).

© Johnny N. Dell/Bugwood.org: page 254 (margined blister beetle)

© Division of Plant Industry Archive, Florida Department of Agriculture & Consumer Services/Bugwood.org: pages 273 (mealybug), 297 (mealybug), 331 (black rot)

© Jeffrey Eickwort, Florida Department of Agriculture & Consumer Services/Bugwood.org: page 253 (beetle damage)

© Michelle Grabowski, University of Minnesota Extension–Horticulture/Bugwood.org: page 312 (botrytis blight)

© Mary Ann Hansen, Virginia Polytechnic Institute & State University/Bugwood.org: pages 310, 319 (phosphorous deficiency), 329 (bacterial spot).

© Heinz USA Archive/Bugwood.org: page 329 (bacterial canker)

© William Jacobi, Colorado State University/Bugwood.org: pages 334 (lightning scar), 335 (slime flux)

© R.K. Jones, North Carolina State University/Bugwood.org: page 326 (botrytis blight)

© Brian Kunkel, University of Delaware/Bugwood.org: page 272 (birch leafminer damage)

© Joseph LaForest, University of Georgia/Bugwood.org: page 315 (salt injury)

© David B. Langston, University of Georgia/Bugwood.org: pages 311 (bacterial spot), 328 (anthracnose)

© H.J. Larsen/Bugwood.org: page 337 (verticillium wilt)

© Kenneth R. Law, USDA APHIS PPQ/Bugwood.org: page 281 (Asian long-horned beetle)

© Gerald J. Lenhard/Bugwood.org: page 281 (blackheaded pine sawfly)

© Minnesota Department of Natural Resources Archive, Minnesota Department of Natural Resources/Bugwood.org: page 333 (cytospora canker)

© Cheryl Moorehead/Bugwood.org: page 272 (birch leafminer)

© Joseph O'Brien, USDA Forest Service/Bugwood.org: pages 313 (cherry leaf spot), 314 (oak leaf blister), 323 (sooty mold), 333 (frost damage), 335 (dutch elm disease), 336 (oak wilt)

© Herbert A. Pase III, Texas Forest Service/Bugwood.org: page 281 (pine sawfly larvae)

© Frank Peairs, Colorado State University/Bugwood.org: page 291 (wireworms)

© Pennsylvania Department of Conservation & Natural Resources Forestry Archive/Bugwood.org: pages 253 (bagworm larva)

© R.J. Reynolds Tobacco Company Slide Set, R.J. Reynolds Tobacco Company/Bugwood.org: pages 255 (cabbage looper damage), 342 (root rot)

© Barry Rice, sarracenia.com/Bugwood.org: page 338 (dodder)

© Mike Schomaker, Colorado State Forest Service/Bugwood.org: page 314 (needlecast)

© Howard F. Schwartz, Colorado State University/Bugwood.org: pages 313 (early blight on plant), 318 (leaf scorch), 321 (aster yellows), 325 (fusarium wilt), 344 (mosaic virus)

© James Solomon, USDA Forest Service/Bugwood.org: pages 265 (apple tree borer), 281 (poplar borer)

© Alton N. Sparks, Jr., University of Georgia/Bugwood.org: pages 257 (carrot weevil damage), 276 (onion maggot damage)

© University of Georgia Archive, University of Georgia/Bugwood.org: page 276 (mole cricket damage)

PART 1

YOUR HEALTHY GARDEN

Everything you do in your garden to encourage healthy plant growth helps to prevent pest and disease problems. It's common sense—backed up by scientific research—that healthy plants are less likely to be attacked by insects or infected by disease. Promoting plant health is an integral part of organic gardening. From the moment you sketch out a planting scheme, prepare a bed for planting, or buy a pack of veggie seeds or a potted perennial, pest prevention should become a part of your gardening practices.

Preventing Problems by Promoting Plant Health

Prevention starts when you're paging through seed and plant catalogs: Look for cultivars that are described as pest tolerant or disease resistant. How and when you plant, how you water and fertilize, and ultimately, even how you clean up your gardens in fall can play a role in keeping plants healthy.

START WITH THE SOIL

Cultivating healthy soil is at the foundation of growing healthy plants. Good soil helps plants nurture themselves. Roots flourish in healthy soil. They're able to find and use nutrients as needed, which helps the plant grow strong and resilient.

When grown in poor, compacted soil that is low in nutrients, plants will grow weakly and be stressed by nutrient deficiencies. As a result, they'll be easy targets for insects and diseases. In contrast, soil that is fertile, well drained, and teeming with communities of diverse microbes greatly increases a plant's chance at a healthy, productive life. Also, since many pest and disease organisms spend part or all of their lives belowground, having a diverse community of organisms to keep them in check is important.

Healthy soil is an intricate mix of tiny rock particles, organic matter, water, air, microorganisms, and other animals. Living things abound in a robust, organically active soil—plant roots, animals, insects, bacteria, fungi, and other organisms. The more organic matter you provide, the livelier the life forms within your soil are likely to be. And, the livelier the soil life becomes, the more heated the competition becomes between beneficial soil microorganisms and plant pathogens.

All-Important Organic Matter

The single most important thing you can do to build soil health is to add organic matter. Over time, adding organic matter improves soil structure, which in turn improves the soil's ability to absorb and release both water and air. Obviously, without water plants cannot thrive, but too much water and too little air can also sabotage plant health. When soil becomes saturated, and water pools around plant roots, the roots may lose their ability to take up nutrients. Tiny root hairs may begin rotting away, followed by entire root branches. As organisms that cause root rot flourish, the plant may weaken. Aboveground, the plant may be simultaneously attacked by molds and mildews encouraged by damp conditions. In this way, plants can easily die from too much water.

There is tremendous variation in how much water plants can use, and here the question of natural resistance comes into play. Plants that are naturally adapted to wet conditions are resistant to many of the pathogens present in chronically wet soil; but plants that grow naturally in dry or very well-drained settings are easy prey to those same pathogens.

Local soil conditions have an important bearing on which plants are best for your garden. Soil pH affects the availability of certain nutrients to a plant, affecting its overall vigor, thus directly affecting its ability to maintain good health. Where soil tends to be very acidic, plants that like a low pH, such as blueberries and rhododendrons, will be much happier than plants such as asparagus and clematis, which are adapted to growing in soil that is close to a neutral pH. Although soil pH is easy to manipulate using organic matter, mineral fertilizers, and mulches, it's wise to consider the natural pH of your soil when choosing long-lived plants.

To help ensure that your soil is healthy and balanced, take the time to learn about its

Organic and Natural

When it comes to gardening and farming, what does the word *organic* mean? And what is natural pest control? The answer depends on who you ask.

Organic gardening and farming date back to the late 1800s and early 1900s as scientists began studying the life in the soil and some farmers developed a view of the farm as a living system that required recycling of organic wastes. These growers believed that the use of chemical fertilizers and pesticides (a relatively new innovation in farming at the time) would be harmful to the environment. Organic gardeners also adopted this viewpoint, and J. I. Rodale launched *Organic Farming and Gardening* magazine in 1942 to promote the organic method.

As interest in and demand for organic food increased in the late 20th century, the U.S. government adopted legislation called the Organic Foods Production Act (OFPA) to regulate organic

farming. As a result, the USDA created the National Organic Program (NOP), which wrote extensive regulations that include detailed guidelines on which fertilizers and pest and disease control substances are allowed, prohibited, or allowed with restrictions for use by certified organic farmers. A nonprofit organization called the Organic Materials Review Institute (OMRI) reviews applications from manufacturers of pest and disease control products to determine whether a product meets NOP standards. If it does, the manufacturer can include the OMRI logo on the product label to indicate that the product is suitable for use in organic production.

Certified organic farmers must write a detailed business plan that shows how their farm and growing practices conform to the NOP standards, and their farms must be periodically inspected by

representatives of certification agencies.

As a home gardener, you don't have to abide by NOP standards, but you may find them helpful in making choices. The standards will help educate you about some of the complex choices to be made when using commercial pest and disease control products. These are also discussed in Part 4 of this book.

At a simpler level, organic gardening is simply a method of gardening that uses our understanding of nature as a guide for growing plants without using synthetic chemical pesticides or synthetic fertilizers. Natural pest and disease control, it follows, is a method of managing pest and disease problems without the use of chemical pesticides and with an understanding that pests and disease are part of a living system that has an innate balance.

characteristics and fertility levels. If you're concerned that your soil is out of balance, have it tested by the Cooperative Extension Service or by a private laboratory (see listings on page 397). Use the results as a guide to bring your soil into balance by adding lime, compost, or organic soil amendments and fertilizers as needed. Maintain soil balance by growing green manure crops and adding organic matter each season.

Making and Using Compost

Adding high-quality compost to your soil is a simple way to build soil quality overall and also to help prevent problems with a variety of soil-dwelling pests. By improving the structure, moisture-holding capacity, and nutrient content of the soil, compost encourages healthy, balanced populations of soil organisms.

Compost piles are like "end-of-the-week soup"—they contain a little bit of everything. This also applies to the organisms that inhabit the compost community. Rarely is any one species or group predominant, because the type and number of organisms present change as materials decompose.

The microbial organisms, insects, spiders, earthworms, and related decomposers tend to work together to produce finished compost. Along the way, however, friends quickly become foes and food for one another. In addition, researchers have discovered that many beneficial microorganisms can outcompete pathogenic fungi. Still other microorganisms may produce toxic substances that inhibit or kill the pathogens surrounding them. In a successful compost pile, the resulting compost contains a balance of organisms, large and small, beneficial and pathogenic, so that no one organism occurs in sufficient quantities to cause damage.

This dynamic interplay among soil microbes is a fascinating area of ongoing research, and the more that is learned, the more evident it becomes that a biologically diverse soil is the best prescription for healthy plants. Some commercial biocontrol products contain beneficial microbes, and growers can help prevent diseases such as damping-off by applying these products to the soil (see page 370).

Foliar sprays made by soaking mature compost in water (sometimes with extra aeration involved) promote plant health by introducing a broad range of beneficial microorganisms to leaf surfaces when applied as a spray, and to the soil when applied as a drench. And compost tea can act as a natural fungicide against the early stages of leaf blights, powdery mildew, and similar diseases by introducing competitive, beneficial microorganisms to infected plants.

Sources of Compost

Compost is available for sale in bags or bulk at most garden centers. Many municipalities make compost and offer it to residents for free or for a low fee. You may find a commercial producer of compost in your area who will deliver it in bulk to your garden. Ask fellow gardeners or a knowledgeable nursery owner for sources of high-quality compost in your local area.

Although it can be hard to make enough compost to satisfy all your gardening needs, it's a great idea to make compost on-site in your garden, both for convenience and economy. You'll find it's easy to make a simple compost pile, even if you're new to gardening. You can find directions for making compost from a wide variety of sources, including many books on organic gardening or the *Organic Gardening* magazine Web site (www.organicgardening.com).

Applying Compost

Whether you buy it or make your own, make a habit of adding compost to your soil often. Here's how.

- Before planting, incorporate compost into the top inch or two of your veggie garden beds and places where you grow annual flowers.

- Use compost as mulch or a side-dressing in all your garden beds during the garden season.

- Spread compost as a mulch over the root zone area of established trees and shrubs.

- Spread a ¼- to ½-inch layer of fine compost over your lawn after aerating it.

Making Hot Compost

If you've already got a compost pile, chances are you're producing good-quality compost, whether you turn and tend it frequently or leave it alone to allow slow decomposition of materials. An advanced step in home composting that can add to your overall efforts to prevent pest and disease problems is to create a hot compost pile, one where the microbial populations expand so fast and furiously that they generate enough heat to kill many pathogens and pests.

As microbial activity increases, temperatures inside a compost pile increase until decomposition is complete. A pile is hottest at its center. Your goal should be to maintain the central pile temperature at between 130°F and 140°F for about a week. It may take a few days for temperatures to reach this range, and temperatures may exceed 140°F at times. If it rises above 150°F, you can add more carbon-rich materials to cool it down.

Follow these steps to create a hot compost pile.

1. **Collect materials.** Good raw materials for compost include garden wastes, grass clippings, kitchen scraps, newspapers, and sawdust. Avoid meat scraps and oils, both of which will attract foraging animals and will slow decomposition. Save the materials in a separate pile outdoors, or combine them indoors in a 5-gallon bucket with a tight-fitting lid; sprinkle sawdust or other absorbent material between layers of kitchen waste to control odors. Manure is a good material for starting a hot compost pile, but you must be sure that you know how to handle manure safely. Obtain it from a local organic farm if possible. Don't use manure from dogs, cats, or household pets—it can carry organisms that cause disease in humans. Wear gloves when you're working with manure and wash your hands and clothes thoroughly afterward. Don't leave manure piles sitting in spots where water will run off after rainfall.

2. **Shred or chop large pieces.** Shredding or chopping woody pruning debris, tree bark, and newspapers creates more surface area, which allows greater access by decomposer organisms.

3. **Combine the materials.** When you've collected enough wastes to fill a space measuring approximately 4 feet on each side, begin combining the materials. Your goal is to create a ratio of approximately 30 parts carbonaceous materials (dry, yellow or brown, plant-based) to 1 part nitrogenous materials (wet, green, or animal-based). This is achieved with roughly equal volumes of dry materials such as leaves, straw, sawdust, or paper, and wet materials, such as fresh grass clippings or manure.

4. **Add a compost starter.** While you build the pile, add several shovelfuls of soil or finished

compost—this serves to inoculate the pile with decomposer organisms naturally present in the soil. If no healthy soil or compost is available, a commercial compost starter can supply the necessary microorganisms. Keep the mixture damp but not soggy, sprinkling materials with water, as necessary. When finished, cover the pile to maintain the proper moisture level.

5. **Turn the pile.** Every few days, turn the pile with a garden fork, fluffing the materials as you go. If the pile seems dry, sprinkle with a little more water. Turning the pile works oxygen into the mix, which hastens decomposition. As microbial activity increases, the temperature will rise. Use a soil or compost thermometer to monitor your compost's progress. Frequent turning helps maintain the proper temperature. Hot compost can reach 170°F, but try to keep your pile below 150°F. Higher temperatures tend to kill the organisms important for continuing decomposition, while lower temperatures allow insect pests and disease organisms to survive the composting process.

You'll know your compost is finished when the temperature returns to normal and original ingredients are no longer recognizable. This can take as little as 2 weeks, if you turn the pile regularly and if adequate nitrogen is supplied. Hot composting is necessary to kill pests, and only does so when the pile is actively heating. If your piles are built slowly and remain on the cool to warm side, refrain from adding pest-ridden garden wastes, since temperatures won't be high enough to control the pests and the resulting compost might reintroduce pests and diseases to your garden.

Compost Tea

Old-fashioned compost tea is easy to make, and it offers lots of benefits for your garden. Some gardeners take the extra step of making aerated compost tea. And some landscape maintenance companies that have converted to organic methods brew aerated compost tea by the tankful for applying to athletic fields or large lawns. Before you begin making and using compost tea, however, be sure to educate yourself about proper brewing methods. Some studies show that compost tea brewed from compost with other added substances, such as molasses or humic acids, have the potential to contain *Escherichia coli* bacteria, which could be harmful to human health.

To make a traditional compost tea, also called compost extract, place 5 gallons of well-aged compost and 5 gallons of water in a small trash can or barrel. Put it in a place with steady temperature away from cold or heat. Stir it daily for at least 5 days. Filter the mixture through a screen or cloth, such as burlap or cheesecloth, and return the trapped solids to the compost pile or the garden. Apply the tea immediately to your garden. If the tea is bubbling or producing an unpleasant odor, do not use it.

You can also make or purchase aerated compost teas, which have air continuously bubbled through as they brew, to maintain aerobic conditions. Aerated teas are reputed to have even greater beneficial effects than regular compost tea. Garden suppliers offer brewing kits for making compost tea; follow the directions precisely and keep the container covered while the tea is brewing.

Apply aerated compost tea as a soil drench or as a foliar spray for ornamentals or lawns. For food crops, as a rule of thumb, allow at least 3 months between applying tea and harvesting tree fruits or other food crops that don't come in contact with soil; 4 months for crops that do contact soil (potatoes, beets, and other root crops). Do not spray leafy greens (kale, etc) or salad greens with compost tea.

Grow Cover Crops

Planting a cover crop is an excellent way to promote soil and plant health. A cover crop is one grown specifically to benefit the soil. You'll let the crop grow, then cut it and allow all the foliage and roots to be digested by earthworms and soil microorganisms. Buckwheat, white clover, and oats are three common cover crops that are easy for home gardeners to work with, but there are many other choices too.

Sowing a cover crop is simple. Start with an area prepared as you would for sowing vegetables or annual flowers. If possible, sow the seed just before it's supposed to rain. Use a small hand-operated seeder or broadcast the seed by hand. Check with seed suppliers for the proper sowing rate for the crop you're planting.

If you're sowing less than 1 pound of seed per 1,000 square feet, combine the seed with sand or finely screened soil first.

After you sow the seed, tamp the soil with the back of a rake or walk gently across the soil surface. Cover the area with (weed-free) grass clippings if you can, to help retain some surface moisture. The seed should come up well on its own after rain (if the rain doesn't materialize, set up a sprinkler to provide the necessary moisture).

Once the crop reaches the right stage of growth—just before flowering, in many cases—use a string trimmer, lawnmower, or other tool to cut

Plant Health Tonics

Like compost tea, applying seaweed sprays and kelp meal can help make plants more pest resistant by improving their overall health. Often described as growth enhancers, these products provide an extensive menu of nutrients such as iron and boron that plants need, in very small amounts, for proper growth and development. Plants can absorb these micronutrients through their leaves. Those products made with seaweed or kelp can also be categorized as growth regulators, since they contain amino acids and enzymes that promote stronger growth and increase plant yields.

If you know from experience that certain plants will face challenges from insects and diseases, you can apply seaweed spray to strengthen those plants and make them better able to defend themselves. Using seaweed spray, however, is not a substitute for good soil or nutrients taken up by plant roots.

If you have access to fresh seaweed, rinse it to remove the salt, then apply it to the garden as a mulch, or compost it.

Gardeners who don't have access to fresh seaweed can buy liquid seaweed extract. Before spraying it on your plants, dilute this concentrated product according to the directions on the label. Spray plants every 2 to 4 weeks, depending on the label directions. Remember: A little is good for your plants, but too much can be toxic, so don't be tempted to spray more frequently or use stronger solutions. Dried seaweed, sold as kelp meal, is a good long-term soil conditioner; apply 1 to 2 pounds per 100 square feet of soil.

the crop to ground level. You can let the cut crop break down in place, or you can lightly turn it into the top few inches of soil. In general, allow 3 to 4 weeks after cutting before you plant something new in the enriched bed.

Soil Tillage

It's not surprising that some pests raise their families in garden soil. When the larvae hatch from eggs or adults emerge from pupal cases, they're already seated at the dinner table. Sometimes, digging or tilling to expose these pests to heat and predators can break their life cycle and prevent problems. However, tilling can also be harmful to beneficial soil organisms.

Tilling or digging the soil is a traditional practice for combating soil-dwelling pests, but it's important to weigh the pros and cons before you act. The scale of disruption and, therefore, the level of pest control, depends on how deeply you work the soil and the equipment you use. Rotary tilling is the most destructive method. Using hand tools creates much less disturbance.

Tillage Tips

If you decide to till your soil, choose a day when the soil is fairly dry and crumbly. Maintaining soil structure is more important than tilling for pest control, so don't cultivate when the soil is too wet or too dry. Working the soil at these times can have disastrous effects on soil structure. When you till will depend on your local climate. If your area has lots of wet, overcast weather in fall, put off tilling until spring.

Review the following tilling tips and heed those that will help control pests that have been a problem in your garden.

■ Before planting, till to control weeds that may harbor armyworms, cutworms, and

tarnished plant bugs, and to disturb corn root aphids.

■ Leave a tilled, dry strip of soil around your garden to discourage entry by slugs and snails.

■ After harvest, till to control pea weevils, root maggots, and tomato hornworms and pinworms. Fall cultivation also destroys plant debris that can shelter overwintering European corn borers, flea beetles, squash bugs, and other pests.

As tillage decreases, most soil organisms, including insect pests, are favored. Organic matter and nutrients become concentrated at a shallow depth, providing more food and cover. Animal life cycles remain undisturbed. Pests of seedlings tend to increase in numbers, as do slugs and snails, but populations of natural enemies, such as predaceous ground beetles and spiders, increase as well.

CHOOSE PLANTS THAT FIGHT BACK

Some plants are naturally prone to diseases; others are like sparkling beacons to hungry insects. You can eliminate many problems in your garden by avoiding pest- or disease-prone plants. Instead, fill your property with dependable plants that can fend for themselves. In any climate, there are hundreds to choose from. With a solid collection of easy-to-grow plants in place, you can limit your pest-control activities to plants you consider indispensable. Tomatoes are prone to pest problems, but most gardeners agree that vine-ripened tomatoes are well worth the time and trouble it takes to create ideal soil conditions, research the best varieties, and patrol the tomato plot regularly for insect and disease activity.

Many diseases and even insects can be controlled by growing resistant or tolerant cultivars or species. By emphasizing disease resistance in your choice of cultivars, you can completely avoid some common pest problems. For example, some newer cultivars of shell pea, including 'Maestro', are resistant to mosaic virus as well as powdery mildew and Fusarium wilt. Similarly, 'Slicemaster' cucumber resists both downy mildew and powdery mildew, plus leaf spot, anthracnose, and mosaic virus.

For almost any popular type of landscape or food plant you can think of, plant breeders have developed select varieties that show resistance to damage caused by insects, diseases, and nematodes. Choosing resistant species and cultivars is a basic strategy for limiting pest problems. For example, instead of growing disease-prone hybrid tea roses, you can select from among the easier-to-satisfy cultivars of shrub roses, which require little care beyond occasional pruning. Keep in mind that, in general, plants native to your area may have more natural pest resistance than exotic species.

Disease resistance also varies among species within the same genus. Dogwood is a good example of this variability. Flowering dogwood (*Cornus florida*) is a favorite landscape tree in many areas, but it's highly subject to dogwood anthracnose and a syndrome known as dogwood decline, which causes foliage to turn yellow and become sparse. Branches may die and the trees become stunted. Kousa dogwood (*C. kousa*) suffers little from either of these problems. Whenever possible, get information (from extension agents, local nurseries, or fellow gardeners) about common pest and disease problems that occur in your area; use this knowledge to select plants that resist such problems.

Fit Plant to Place

You'll find many suggestions for disease- and insect-resistant cultivars throughout Part 2, beginning on page 23. Remember, though, even when you choose resistant plants, proper site selection and preparation are essential. For example, when azaleas or rhododendrons are grown in partial shade and acidic soil and are kept continuously mulched, they are more pest-resistant than when grown in full sun surrounded by moisture-grabbing grass. Take time to learn about the light, soil, and other site requirements of plants, especially nonnative plants, and try to find the best match of plant and site on your property.

Host Plant Resistance

Some plants have *true resistance,* which means they have an active physiological or mechanical means of fending off pests. Plants with physiological resistance produce antibiotics or other toxic compounds to inhibit pests. Plants with mechanical resistance have physical features that make pest attack difficult. Their defense may be a thick outer coating that resists penetration by a disease organism or a coat of long and stiff hairs that deters insect feeding. For example, shell beans and peas that have tough pods are more difficult for curculios to penetrate; corn that produces a husk that reaches past the tip of the ear is less likely to be bothered by corn earworms and birds.

Plants with *apparent resistance* can withstand attack by pests by growing rapidly, maturing early, or being very vigorous. Others are merely tolerant of invasion—they continue growing even when besieged by the enemy, as long as other conditions remain favorable. Some tolerate more damage than others. These types of disease-resistant plants may eventually show symptoms of the disease, but much later than susceptible crops will. For example, even when 'Straight Eight' cucumber (susceptible) develops downy mildew symptoms, a resistant variety such as 'Poinsett 76' growing nearby may not show any symptoms until several weeks later.

Grafting to Sidestep Disease

Developing resistant cultivars can be a lengthy process, but one shortcut that some commercial tomato growers are using is grafting tomato transplants onto resistant rootstocks, just as is done with many fruit trees. The growers choose a rootstock that is resistant or tolerant of soil-borne pathogens and nematodes. Onto that rootstock, they graft a susceptible tomato variety that has other desirable traits. For example, this technique is being used to produce good crops of heirloom tomatoes that are susceptible to Fusarium wilt, southern blight, and root-knot nematodes.

The grafted plants require pampering until the graft takes hold (growers use special "healing chambers" for this purpose). If you want to try grafting tomatoes, be sure you clean your work area and tools with alcohol before starting. Keep the grafted plants in a warm, humid place without light for the first several days, then gradually introduce light. If possible, move the plants into a green-house, and then transplant them to your garden. Be sure to keep the graft union above the soil line.

Resistance in the Garden

To maximize the benefit that pest and disease resistance can offer, keep these points in mind.

- When skimming through seed catalogs, select cultivars with resistance to the pests common in your garden. Seed suppliers indicate a cultivar's resistant characteristics with a series of abbreviated codes. Look for a key to the codes in each catalog for help in deciphering listings.

- When saving seed from your garden plants, collect seed only from the healthiest and most vigorous specimens. Select plants that seemed to naturally resist or tolerate pest attack, and those that were unattractive to your key pests.

- Keep records of the cultivars that were most successful in your garden. In subsequent seasons, include the same cultivars in your rotation for as long as they remain trouble free.

- Try new cultivars. Just as plants are constantly changing, so are the pests. Plants that were formerly resistant may become vulnerable to pests that have adapted in order to feed on them.

- Sample heirloom cultivars for resistance. Heirloom plants that have been carefully selected and cultivated for many generations also may contain high levels of pest resistance. Some heirloom tomato cultivars, for example, have been screened and selected by gardeners for such a long time that they are naturally resistant to diseases such as Verticillium and Fusarium wilts.

- Check with your local Cooperative Extension office for cultivar recommendations. Resistance for particular plants works better in some locations than in others.

PLANT SMART TO PREVENT PROBLEMS

When you plant and how you plant can actually help prevent pest and disease problems. For example, you can avoid certain pest problems by planting when the pest isn't around. Some pests, such as carrot rust flies, lay eggs only at a certain time in spring. By delaying planting, you reduce the chance that your crop will be infested by that pest.

Changing the planting site of crops from one year to the next in your vegetable garden—a technique known as crop rotation—can prevent pest populations from building up by denying them a food source from season to season. When practiced thoughtfully, crop rotation can help keep the populations of certain pests and diseases from reaching damaging thresholds. Possibilities include onion and cabbage root maggots, black rot of broccoli, and some diseases caused by soilborne bacteria.

Companion planting—planting two or more types of plants in close proximity—is a popular gardening technique that can reduce pest problems in a variety of ways. Some good companion plants, such as dill, fennel, and Queen Anne's lace, will attract beneficial insects. Other types of companion plants repel pests or confuse and confound insects or disease organisms in search of their preferred host plants.

Pay Attention to Timing

Adjusting the time that you plant or harvest a crop can be very effective in helping to prevent problems. Simply by planting (or harvesting) a crop earlier or later than usual, you can avoid the

Buying Healthy Plants

Sometimes you just won't manage to find a resistant variety for a plant or crop you want to grow. In that case, starting out with healthy plants is especially critical. But even when you are buying resistant varieties, always inspect potential purchases at nurseries and garden centers to make sure they're healthy. Otherwise, you'll be planting problems along with your new plants.

■ Look for a sales display where the plants are well cared for. Plants left out on hot, sunny sidewalks where they end up wilting frequently, are never a bargain, no matter how cheap.

■ Look at the entire group of plants being offered for sale. If some of the plants seem to be in poor health, shop somewhere else. Those that look healthy today may be diseased tomorrow.

■ Shop early in the season, when selection is good and plants are young.

■ Examine the roots. Gently shake a plant out of its container. Roots should be plentiful, but not wrapped into a tight spiral. With bareroot plants, look for fungi, lesions, and broken tissue; prune them off before planting.

■ Consider plant color. Pale overall color indicates a need for nutrients, which is easy to

correct. However, distinct yellow streaks or brown leaf spots often are symptoms of disease.

■ Buy perennials, trees, and deciduous shrubs when they are dormant or just beginning to bud out. Leaf emergence above ground is accompanied by rapid root growth below. Get plants situated before this growth spurt occurs.

■ If bedding plants are already in flower, pinch off the blossoms when you set them out. Pinching will help direct the plant's energy into growing roots, so it will be better able to support more flowers and fruit later in the season.

most damaging life stages of some common pests.

In earlier times, local gardeners passed on information from one generation to the next about which crops would benefit from timed planting. Nowadays, you can often find recommendations about timing of planting from your local extension agent or online. If you're gardening in a new area, or if you haven't tried timing your growing schedule before, try the approaches described below.

Planting by Degree Days

To a large extent, temperature regulates pest development. Scientists use units of measurement called degree days to track heat accumulation over time and predict the local appearance of various pests. The degree day formula assigns a value to each day's maximum and minimum temperature and compares that value—the degree day or heat unit—to the temperature at which a particular pest begins to develop. Units accumulate daily, starting from a known or readily determined point in the pest's life cycle. If the pest is a caterpillar, for example, degree day units might be calculated from the first day its adult stage (moth) appears.

Using this formula, entomologists predict when each pest will emerge from hibernation and begin laying eggs on your plants. If temperatures are lower than normal, degree days accumulate more slowly and pests develop later. If temperatures are higher than normal, pests develop more quickly and you can expect to see them earlier than usual. Your Cooperative Extension office or state forest department may be able to provide you with local pest emergence predictions for some pests. Use such information to schedule planting, harvesting, and preventive treatments.

Phenological Signals

Another way to tell time in the garden is by keeping track of local plant signals. Some gardeners can predict when a certain pest will emerge by watching the growth of flowering trees and shrubs and relating their development to that of the pest. This study of the timing of biological events and their relationship to one another is known as phenology. For example, you may observe that flea beetles appear when local lilacs begin to bloom. If you study and record these relationships over time, you may be able to use your observations to time plantings of crops to avoid pest attack.

Pheromone traps that mimic pests' own signals are useful tools for monitoring insect appearances. They can help you determine when the first pests arrive and when the population dwindles. The directions supplied with specific commercial traps explain how to interpret the population fluctuations. See "Pheromone Traps" on page 361 for details on using these traps.

Experiment for Success

To time planting dates accurately, begin collecting your own garden notes. Each season, review your notes to detect patterns, then adjust your garden schedule accordingly. Keep track of the first date on which a particular pest appears, the coinciding botanical signals, and the last date you see it. It also helps to note the relative abundance of a pest, and which life stage of the pest you saw on a particular date.

Experiment with successive plantings. Try several sowings of carrots, for example, to see which planting date is most effective for avoiding carrot rust fly infestation. Many gardeners find that delayed planting works best to control this pest. Growers of sweet corn often find that corn planted

The Transplant Solution

Sometimes, avoiding problems can be as simple as planting transplants instead of seeds. Seedlings that have just sprouted are particularly susceptible to attack by pests. So by growing plants indoors in a pest-free environment for the first several weeks of life (or by purchasing transplants), you can sidestep potentially lethal attacks by pests such as striped cucumber beetles, slugs, and earwigs. These pests may still feed on transplants, but they're less likely to do serious harm, and you're more likely to be able to spot and take action against the pests when they're feeding on larger plants.

One instance when transplanting is not the best choice is when "volunteer" seedlings turn up in your vegetable garden. For example, you may discover potatoes sprouting where you grew potatoes last year and missed a tuber while harvesting. And tomato seedlings tend to pop up in former tomato beds where fruits fell to the ground and left seeds in place. These volunteer plants may carry diseases that could spread to the rest of your crop, so don't transplant them. Instead, uproot and dispose of them.

early escapes attack by corn earworms or European corn borers.

When arranging your planting and harvesting schedule, include cultivars that mature earlier or later than your usual crop selections. Pests arrive to find their favorite plant hosts have already been harvested or are not mature enough to produce the fruit on which they feed. Either way, damage to your garden is reduced or eliminated and pest populations dwindle in the absence of the appropriate hosts.

In areas where nematodes are common in the soil, plant susceptible crops extra early or extra late to take advantage of lower soil temperatures. Most nematodes can't penetrate plant roots when soil temperatures are below 64°F.

Here are some other examples of crops and pests for which timed planting is effective.

- **Peas.** Cool, wet weather conditions encourage the development of many fungal diseases. In areas with cool, wet fall weather, plant peas only in spring. And if damping-off and root rot trouble your springtime seedlings, delay next spring's planting by a few weeks.

- **Tomatoes.** If your plants tend to succumb to late blight near the end of the season, choose cultivars that mature early.

- **Cabbage family crops.** In the North, plant radishes, broccoli, and other cabbage family crops early, to avoid cabbage maggot damage to roots. If cabbage maggots persist, grow these crops for fall harvest to avoid the pest.

- **Onions.** Plant them early to reduce damage caused by onion maggots. The first generation of adult flies usually appears as dandelions begin blooming. Onions that are already nearing maturity when pests arrive have greater resistance to injury than tiny seedlings do.

Companion Planting

The theory of companion planting is that growing a diverse group of plants side-by-side will help reduce the pest problems of one or more of the plants. Mixed planting mimics a natural ecosystem. Your garden is like a miniature forest in which hundreds of organisms interact among the trees, usually out of sight. While plants remain stationary, insects and microbial organisms are moving in and out of the forest daily. By planting a diversity of crops in your garden forest, you can tip the scale in favor of vigorous growth and minimum damage by selectively attracting certain organisms and repelling others.

Repellent Crops

Some plants make good companions because of the company they discourage. While these relationships remain more a part of gardening folklore than scientific fact, many gardeners are convinced of their usefulness. Both catnip and tansy, for example, reportedly repel green peach aphids and squash bugs from susceptible garden crops. Wormwood (*Artemisia absinthium*), southernwood (*A. abrotanum*), and tomatoes are said to repel flea beetles from cabbage family plants. Plant radishes amid hills of cucumbers and squash to repel cucumber beetles, and thereby limit the diseases spread by these pests.

Good Neighbors

Certain plant combinations succeed because of differences in nutritional needs, space requirements, or harvest times. These associations may not directly retard pest damage, but they do promote plant health.

Interplanting certain crops fills precious garden space efficiently without creating competition for light or nutrients. Corn and lettuce, for example, have different nutritional needs, rooting patterns, and pests. Lettuce fills the empty space between corn plants and is protected from the full glare of the summer sun by the towering corn stalks.

Other plants harmonize because they mature at different times. Radish and carrot seeds are often sown together; the larger radish seeds mark the row as you plant, and the quick-emerging radish seedlings hold the soil against rain for the slower-growing carrots. You'll harvest the radishes long before the carrots need the space to fatten.

Legumes such as alfalfa, clover, and vetch work with beneficial bacteria to convert atmospheric nitrogen gas into a form usable by plants, some of which is available to plants grown around them or after they are harvested. While often viewed as a weed in lawns, white clover actually helps supply nitrogen to the grass around it.

Still other plants seem to enhance the growth of plants growing near them. Basil is popular among gardeners who practice companion planting—they say that everything planted near it grows vigorously.

Patterns to Avoid

On the other hand, some crop combinations should be avoided in the interest of preventing pests. Crops that are closely related attract the same pests, and you may wish to separate them in your beds.

Some plants are allelopathic, which means they inhibit the growth of plants growing nearby. Their roots secrete substances that are toxic to a wide range of other plants. For example, a shallow-plowed cover crop of rye will inhibit the germination of small-seeded plants and weeds. Yellow and giant foxtail, nutsedge, quackgrass, sunflowers, and walnut trees all have allelopathic properties. Keep these relationships in mind if you're puzzling over a mysterious plant disorder that seems to be caused by invisible pests. The pest may actually be the large walnut tree growing nearby, or even a walnut tree that *used* to grow nearby. Tomatoes in particular are sensitive to the toxins that walnut roots secrete, and those toxins can persist in the soil long after the tree roots have died.

Crop Rotation

The theory of crop rotation is simple. Disease organisms, such as the fungi that cause leaf spot of cabbage, attack and grow in a crop during the growing season. During the winter, the fungi may overwinter as spores in the soil or in plant litter. The following year, they reinfest a new planting. So if you plant cabbage or its relatives in the same spot year after year, the pathogens can continue to build their populations and leaf spot will become an increasingly serious problem. However, if you plant cabbage in a bed one year, corn there the next, onions the third year, and beans the fourth year, many of the leaf spot fungi will die off due to the lack of food. When you plant cabbage there again, you'll have little problem with leaf spot.

If you have a small food garden, crop rotation may not be an option for you. If not, don't despair. Promoting plant health by amending your soil regularly with organic matter, keeping the soil covered, and making sure your plants don't suffer from water deprivation or other stresses should help you avoid most disease problems with most of your plants. If you have a large garden, though, initiating a crop rotation plan from the time you first establish the garden will help minimize problems with soilborne pathogens.

Fortunately, rotation generally isn't necessary for long-lived plants such as trees and shrubs, because they have developed their own pest-control strategies that enable them to live long, trouble-free lives. (Unless, of course, you lose a tree to a soilborne disease such as Verticillium wilt, in which case you should take care not to replace it with another susceptible species.) Below ground, trees and shrubs release substances into the soil that act as natural pesticides to soilborne fungi and bacteria. Aboveground, their tough, woody stems help resist bruising and insect attacks. When leaves are lost to disease, a shrub or tree has the ability to produce new leaves several times. When leaf-eating insects dine on tree leaves, the tree may respond by pumping more tannic acid into the leaves that remain, thus deterring further feeding.

Planning a Crop Rotation

In order to plan a rotation, you need some working knowledge of how botanical names of plants indicate relationships. All plants have a two-part botanical name, consisting of a genus name and a species name. For example, the botanical name of cucumber is *Cucumis sativus*. *Cucumis* is the genus name, *sativus* is the species epithet. Together these make up the species name, *Cucumis sativus*.

A genus is a group of fairly closely related organisms; a species is an individual organism in the group. Many disease organisms can attack more than one member of a genus. Following through with our example, muskmelons, *Cucumis melo,* belong to the same genus as cucumbers and are subject to many of the same pest problems.

Some pests attack an even broader spectrum of plants. Plant families are larger groupings of plants that contain several genera. Cucumbers and melons belong to the family Cucurbitaceae. This family also includes summer squash and winter squash, which belong to the genus *Cucurbita*. It's important to know and understand these relationships, because one of the basic principles in planning a crop rotation is to plant crops from different families in sequence in a particular location to prevent the buildup of pest populations in the soil.

Planning a rotation becomes more complex as the number of crops you wish to grow increases.

Here are some guidelines to keep in mind as you plan what to plant where, from year to year.

- Alternate crops in as many ways as possible. Grouping by families isn't the only choice. Alternately, you could choose to arrange your crops by the amount of space they require, by growth habit (root crops or vining crops), or by some other criterion.

- Leave as much time as you can spare between related crops. Placing related crops 3 to 6 years apart in a rotation is important to effectively break disease and insect cycles.

- Include soil-improving crops. Leave room for cover crops such as buckwheat, rye, or oats. With a little more space, you can grow clover or alfalfa, which remains in place for more than 1 year, enriching the soil and attracting beneficial insects. Sod crops, such as lawns, cover crops, or even weeds that are intact for several years, however, may harbor soil pests such as grubs or wireworms, which can damage root crops. Avoid crops such as potatoes and onions the first year after sod is plowed under.

- Grow legumes before grains. Nitrogen-fixing crops, including alfalfa, clover, beans, and peas, will boost the growth of most succeeding crops.

- Onions, lettuce, and squash seem to benefit any planting that follows them. By contrast, some crops grow poorly when planted after carrots, beets, and members of the cabbage family.

- Plant heavy-feeding crops such as corn, tomatoes, and cabbage the season before light feeders such as root vegetables, bulb crops, and herbs. Plant a soil-building crop in the third season.

- Make efficient use of garden space by planting overwintering annuals such as spinach, parsnips, and garlic after crops that are harvested in late summer.

- Although perennials such as asparagus and rhubarb remain in the same place each year, rotate the cover crops that surround them, or rotate different kinds of mulch.

- If you find it impossible to rotate crops, at least rotate cultivars.

- Certain soilborne diseases attack a broad spectrum of crops, and a more complex rotation is necessary to prevent infection. For example, the bacterium *Pseudomonas marginalis* can cause rots of lettuce, beans, cucumbers, and potatoes. If your garden is home to this disease organism, you may have to make it the sole focus of your rotation. Separate the susceptible crops by as much time as possible within your rotation.

- Be prepared to change your plans if this year's problems threaten crops planned for next season's rotation.

- Record your successes and failures, and review the list each time you plan a crop rotation.

GIVE GOOD CARE ALL SEASON LONG

Once you have planted your garden, the quality of care you provide throughout the season is important in keeping the garden healthy. Watering, fertilizing, weeding, and mowing are routine garden tasks, but taking a thoughtful approach to them will pay off in time saved dealing with pest and disease problems that develop if plants are neglected and stressed.

Water Wisely

Almost every garden needs watering now and then to keep plants growing strong. Plan ahead to be sure you have a watering system in place, whether it's a watering can for a small garden, or a set of soaker hoses laid under mulch for watering large beds and borders.

Keep in mind that water plays a key role in the development of bacterial and fungal diseases. Many soilborne fungal diseases become a problem in soils that are too wet. The fungi thrive in waterlogged conditions. And saturated conditions can actually damage plant roots, which leaves them more susceptible to infection. If you have wet soils, put in a drainage system, dig ditches to carry away excess water, or plant in raised beds to reduce problems with soilborne diseases, such as root rots and damping-off. Avoid overwatering, and when you do water, keep excess water from flooding around the trunks of woody plants.

How you water can be as important as how much you water. One advantage of drip irrigation over sprinklers is that it doesn't wet foliage. Thus, relative humidity is lower and fungal spores are less apt to germinate because there is no water on the leaves. There is also no splashing water to spread fungi and bacteria within or between plants. If you do water your plants by sprinkling, water early in the day, when the warming sun will dry the leaves quickly. (Leaves also dry quickly with afternoon watering, but much water may be wasted through evaporation.)

Most fungi and bacteria that attack the branches, fruit, and flowers of plants thrive in high humidity. Except for plants that need humid conditions, grow your outdoor plants where gentle breezes rapidly dry leaves and remove humid air hovering near them. Inside your home, especially in winter, the air is too dry for most aboveground diseases to develop. However, a home greenhouse can have the humid conditions that set the stage for such diseases as Botrytis on greenhouse geraniums. Use fans and vents to moderate humidity levels in greenhouses.

Help Air Circulate

Good air circulation will go a long way in discouraging disease development. Overcrowded plants do not dry rapidly after rain or watering, and the resulting high humidity can encourage disease. Don't sow seeds too densely, and thin emerged plants to an adequate spacing. Thin some stems from large clumps of multistemmed perennials, such as phlox and bee balm, to allow more air to flow through the plants.

Keep After the Weeds

It's easy to understand that weeds compete with our plants for nutrients and water, so therefore your garden will be healthier if weed competition is low. Whenever possible, deal with weeds when they're young. It's much faster and easier to use a hula hoe or a hand weeding tool to gently work the soil surface and kill weed seedlings than to dig or yank out large weeds. Plus, weeds can be hosts to insect pests and disease organisms, and dense weed growth can cause the air to stagnate around your plants. That's setting the stage for disease development. When possible, remove nearby wild or abandoned plants known to be susceptible to viruses that also attack your plants. Ragweed, nightshade, and milkweed, for example, are hosts of cucumber mosaic virus.

Mow High

Just as good pruning practices help maintain the health of trees, shrubs, and other garden plants, good mowing techniques encourage a healthy lawn. Mowing to the proper height and mowing less frequently when plants are stressed will help prevent a broad range of pest problems.

Each time you mow, a freshly cut surface is available for pathogens to colonize. Repeated short mowing, under stressful conditions, makes plants smaller and fewer and allows weeds to easily move in. When plants are stressed by heat and drought in midsummer, it's best to raise the height of the blade and mow less frequently.

Proper mowing height is the top priority for controlling lawn pest problems without pesticides. To control lawn diseases, adjust the height of your mower as high as possible and mow infrequently. Prostrate, low-growing grasses do well at a height of ¾ to 1 inch; fescues and ryegrasses should be maintained at 1½ to 3 inches.

Feed Judiciously

Although rich, well-fed soil is all many plants need to keep them growing vigorously, fertilizing them at the proper time is also beneficial and will help enhance their natural resistance to pests.

As a general rule, make sure annual vegetable and flower crops are well fed when they are young, and then give them a modest booster feeding when flowering and reproduction commences. Fertilize perennial vegetable and flower crops, along with trees and shrubs, during the first third of their active growth, which is just as they begin growing in spring. You can also fertilize during the second third of the plants' growing season, but not during the last third. Late fertilization can stress the plants by encouraging tender new growth that may be winterkilled. When you apply fertilizer, always keep in mind that more isn't necessarily better. Overfertilizing leads to rank, spindly growth and can even worsen problems with aphids and some other pests.

Handle with Care

One of the best ways to keep plants healthy and happy is to treat them with care. Bruised or torn leaves, damaged stems, and other plant wounds not only cause unnecessary stress that can weaken plants—wounds are also an open invitation to pests and disease organisms, which find it easy to enter plants through damaged tissue. Keep this in mind whenever you're in your garden, and avoid handling plants whenever possible. Whenever you do need to work in your garden—even when you walk down the rows between plants— touch the plants gently to keep damage to a minimum.

Never work around plants when they're wet. Many disease organisms (and some pests, too) travel easily on the film of water that covers foliage on damp days. When you work among wet plants, you're likely not only to help spread disease organisms, but also to provide them with easy access to your plants via bruised leaves. Tugging on plants when you harvest fruit or pick flowers can damage roots and stems: Always use a sharp knife or pruning shears to make a clean cut that will heal easily. The same goes for proper pruning.

Handling trees with care is one of the best ways to keep them healthy. Many tree pests can only invade through the exposed tissue at an injury site. For example, flowering dogwood is normally a very insect-resistant tree, its trunk protected by a thick, hard bark. But when bits of bark are broken away, as when you hit a young dogwood with a lawn mower or string trimmer, that injury becomes a point of entry for dogwood borer larvae— a very difficult-to-control pest that eats its way through living wood.

KEEP THINGS CLEAN

Keeping a clean garden means preventing pest-infested material from getting in, and doing as much as possible to get rid of plants or parts of plants that develop pest problems. Carefully inspect any plants you intend to buy for signs of insects or disease. See "Buying Healthy Plants" on page 11 for advice. And if pest problems do strike in your garden, use care in disposing of the diseased or infested material.

Good sanitation is a crucial step in preventing problems. Any pathogen that persists in soil from year to year, as do root-knot nematodes, Fusarium wilts, tobacco mosaic virus, and many others, can be spread via contaminated tools, infected or infested plant debris, or even your hands. Make thorough cleaning of shovels, digging forks, or the tines of your tiller part of your gardening routine, especially if soil-dwelling pests and pathogens are present in sections of your garden.

When the gardening season ends, you'll want to thoroughly clear any diseased plant material out of your garden beds. Otherwise, come the following spring, it can serve as a source of infection for new plants. In some cases, you can safely compost diseased plant material. In other cases, it's best to destroy it by burning or disposing of it in sealed containers with your household trash.

Before You Start Planting

The temptation to get a quick start in the spring may lead gardeners to skip sanitation efforts that help prevent later problems. Before you take your first steps onto the newly awakening soil, stop and remember these important rules.

Keep the gardener clean. Gardeners sometimes spread pest problems without realizing it. This can happen to you: When you visit a friend's garden or a nursery or farm, you could pick up spores on your clothing or shoes by walking in infested soil or brushing against infested plants. If you've been near potential sources of pathogens or insects, wash the clothing you were wearing as soon as possible afterward (and definitely before you enter your own garden). To sanitize your boots or shoes, rinse them with a 10 percent bleach solution (1 part bleach to 9 parts water).

Start with clean tools and supplies. And keep them that way. Especially when working among diseased plants, rinse your tools with isopropyl alcohol or a 10 percent bleach solution before moving on to another part of the garden. When pruning infected trees or shrubs, disinfect pruners between cuts. When your work is finished, clean your tools again and let them air dry, then coat them lightly with oil before storing.

At the end of the season, also disinfect any stakes, trellis wire, and cages that you plan to reuse. Exposure to winter cold isn't enough—bacteria can survive frigid temperatures in the cracks and crevices in wood and other materials.

Choose healthy plants. Inspect new plants before introducing them into your yard or garden. Look for signs of disease and insects, and reject any that look suspicious. If available, buy certified disease-free plants and seeds. Inquire about seed sterilization practices at your seed source. Buy from suppliers that use sanitation procedures and heat-sterilizing techniques instead of synthetic chemicals to control disease on nursery stock and seeds.

Don't be afraid to buy sight unseen from reputable mail-order nurseries. Most plants that are sold mail-order across state lines must be inspected and certified as disease free before they are packaged and shipped. Buy plants such as strawberries or raspberries, which often carry viral diseases, from a specialized producer. Such growers are most likely to offer a wide selection of disease-free plants and are more likely to back up their sales with guarantees should your new plants show disease symptoms.

Solarize the soil. If you anticipate pest problems in a garden section that must be planted, you can use the sun's heat to kill some pathogens and insects in the soil. Stretch a sheet of clear plastic tightly over a smooth, moist soil surface and leave it in place for as long as several weeks. The heat that builds up in the covered soil will kill most soilborne pathogens and weed seeds.

Start a compost pile. A well-managed hot compost pile can be the perfect destination for plant trimmings and other garden debris that may carry unseen pathogens and insect stages in waiting. See "Making and Using Compost" on page 4 for instructions on composting.

Remove winter mulches. As temperatures begin to rise and spring rains start falling, soggy winter mulch provides a harbor for disease pathogens and hungry slugs or snails. Pull the mulch from beds a little at a time; pay special attention to clearing it away from tree trunks, stems, and plant crowns.

As You Garden

Maintain your sanitation standards consistently throughout the growing season. Keep problems at bay by adding these sanitation techniques to your garden routine.

Stay away when it's wet. Some plant disease

Soil Solarization

If soilborne pests are a big problem in your garden, why waste your energy trying to combat them? Let the sun do it for you! This process, known as soil solarization, involves covering the soil with clear plastic so the heat can build up and destroy the soil organisms and weed seeds. Keep in mind that the high temperatures can also harm beneficial insects and organisms that live in the soil; only use this process when you have a serious pest or disease problem.

Soil solarization works best in midsummer, just before fall crops are planted. It is also most effective in areas that have long stretches of clear, hot weather. If you have a rainy or cool spell during the solarization period, soil temperatures may not stay high enough to kill off pathogens.

Prepare the site as you would for planting, removing old crop residues, working in any soil amendments, and raking soil into planting rows or beds. Water the site thoroughly, and dig a trench a few inches deep around the edges of the site. Cover the area with a sheet of 1 to 4 mil clear plastic, and bury the edges in the trench to anchor them. Leave in place for 1 to 2 months.

Remove the plastic and plant your crops, disturbing the soil as little as possible. Solarization can generate enough heat to kill organisms in the top 12 inches of the soil, but you can't be sure that your particular treatment worked. Assume that its effect penetrated only the top 3 to 5 inches of soil. Thus, deeper cultivation may bring up pathogens and seeds that can reinfest the newly treated plot. Since solarizing may also harm the microorganisms that help make soil organic matter available to plants, you may want to top-dress your crops with a microbe-rich material such as finished compost.

organisms are just waiting for a free ride on your clothing and hands. Don't cooperate! Most diseases need only a thin film of water to spread from one plant to the next. During warm rainy spells, disease transmission is at its greatest. Even morning dew provides enough moisture to allow spores to travel; wait until the dew dries to start your gardening chores.

Rogue and prune. Pull plants with symptoms of disease or heavy insect infestation and prune diseased sections from perennial plants. A hot compost pile will kill pathogenic fungi and bacteria. If you suspect viral infections, bury the prunings in an out-of-the-way area or put them in a sealed bag for disposal with the household trash. See "Pruning" on page 350 for specific suggestions on pest problems that you can combat by pruning.

Keep the site clean. Before planting a second crop, take the time to clean up and compost any plant remains. They'll be returned to the garden disease free.

End-of-Season Cleanup

Some of us lose steam over the season and are happy to let things lie until next year, but this is not the time to take it easy. End-of-season garden chores will make next year's garden that much healthier.

Prune perennial plants. It's time again for another round of pruning when growth has slowed and perennial plants have become dormant. Consult a pruning manual to help you determine the best time to trim and shape your plants.

Clean your equipment. Give tools a little tender loving care before storing them away. Clean them with a 10 percent bleach solution, wipe them dry, and coat them lightly with household oil to prevent rust.

Collect leaves and other plant residues. Garden cleanup should include composting plant residues and wastes that remain at the end of the season. Place debris that may carry pathogenic organisms in the center of the pile where temperatures are greatest. This also pertains to stalks, fruit, and leaves that may carry overwintering stages of insect pests and pathogens.

Continue adding to your compost pile for as long as you can. If temperatures dip low enough, decomposition will slow or stop, but will begin again when warmer temperatures return. Common fall compost ingredients include fruit you forgot to harvest, fallen leaves, and plant stems and flower stalks.

Remove row covers. If you're saving row covers for next season, dip them in a 10 percent bleach solution, then let them air dry before storage. This is particularly important for covers used on related plants and for most early spring crops that are susceptible to damping-off pathogens.

DEVELOP A SYSTEM

Keeping plants thriving, improving your soil, planting a variety of plants, and encouraging natural predators are all great ways to prevent pest and disease problems, but planning and record keeping are also essential weapons to add to your arsenal. A garden plan will help you develop a calendar of activities aimed at preventing problems. It will also help you set and achieve goals for your garden, such as eliminating or modifying problem-prone plantings or adding new gardens. Regular record keeping will help you identify the key pests in your area—the ones you see on a recurring basis. Once you've pinpointed key pests and diseases, you'll be able to anticipate them and get a head start on preventive measures.

Start your plan by finding out about the plants

you're growing as well as the ones you want to grow. Learn what conditions they prefer and which will grow best in your area. Next, draw a sketch of your garden. Mark down existing plantings, but also look for sites that might suit some plants but discourage others. For example, locate frost pockets, sites where air will circulate freely, areas with moist soil, and shady or sunny spots.

Then identify and list the problems you've had in the past or that are common in your area. Refer to the plant entries in Part 2 of this book to identify problems you've seen in your garden before. Learn about the life cycles of pests and diseases. How do they overwinter? When and how do they attack your plants?

Once you have all your options—and potential problems—in front of you, make a comprehensive plan. List the ways you could help control each of the problems on your list. Decide what gardening practices will help prevent problems and when they need to be done. Add biological controls and traps and barriers next, and make note of organic sprays and dusts for use as a last resort. Be sure to include the life-cycle stage at which each control is most effective. It may help to make a chart of the life cycle and control activities.

Use these notes to create a schedule of gardening activities. You'll find that certain chores, such as an annual fall cleanup, are well worth the effort because they'll prevent many types of pests. Planning ahead and following your schedule will enable you to make full use of preventive control measures, and they'll soon become second nature to you. You'll also know what tools and materials to have on hand to fight problems if they arise.

Learn to Look

All the planning in the world won't help if you don't keep an eye out for problems. Begin a garden journal for keeping records throughout the season. Make it a habit to walk through your garden at least once a week—daily is best. Look carefully at your plants, turning over leaves, and note overall appearance.

In your garden records, include pest appearance dates and details of insect behavior along with notes you make on the progress of various plants. This is the only way to discover useful facts, such as when birds are no longer effective cabbageworm predators on cabbage, cauliflower, or broccoli, or which members of the huge daisy family are first to be attacked by four-lined plant bugs.

If you notice plants that don't look healthy or aren't growing the way you'd expected, take time to examine them more closely. Look for signs of the problems you listed, and go over your plan to see what steps you need to take. Use the "Pest Patrol Checklist" on page 245 to gather the information you need to diagnose the problem. Once you've diagnosed the problem and identified the ways to control it, add the necessary information to your garden plan.

Keep notes on your program during the season. Write down what works and what doesn't, what controls you used, how much you used, and where. The more information you have, the better you'll be able to refine the plan for the next season.

The more time you spend in your garden, the better you will be able to recognize, understand, and treat pest problems. When you consider pest problems thoughtfully, you may be surprised at how little damage actually has occurred. Many plants can tolerate up to 30 percent less foliage without suffering serious cuts in productivity. And, although leaves with little holes in them don't look nice, they may actually help the plant defend itself by triggering the production of pest-repelling chemicals.

PART 2

SYMPTOMS AND SOLUTIONS

We've all experienced that "oh no!" reaction when we discover fat caterpillars devouring the leaves of our broccoli plants, wilted stem tips on a prized rhododendron, or nasty brown spots on the green tomatoes on our tomato vines. There's an urgency to take action, but the wise gardener knows to confirm a diagnosis before deciding what strategy to pursue. This encyclopedia of more than 220 popular garden plants is specially designed to help you figure out the specific identity of the pest or disease attacking your plants.

A Plant-by-Plant Problem-Solving Guide

The individual plant entries on the pages that follow include symptoms for the most common garden problems you may encounter, suggestions for gardening practices that help prevent problems, and options for managing specific pest and disease problems.

Food plants—vegetables, fruits, and herbs—are listed by common name. Ornamentals—annuals, bulbs, perennials, and trees, shrubs, and vines—are listed by botanical name. (If you don't know the botanical name of a particular plant, simply look up the common name in the index.)

The entries are designed to help you quickly zero in on specific plant problems. In the "Problems" section of each entry, you'll find short descriptions of symptoms in boldface type, such as "Leaves with yellow, V-shaped spots on margins." Scan these descriptions until you find the one that most closely matches the problem on your plant. You can then read that section to learn the cause of the problem and how to avoid or control it.

In addition to the individual plant entries, you'll also find separate general entries on flowers, herbs, lawns, and vegetables, along with a group entry on trees, shrubs, and vines. These general entries highlight problems that attack a wide variety of plants. You'll find them useful for solving some of the most common problems that attack your garden.

If you're using this guide to diagnose a specific plant problem, confirm your diagnosis before deciding on a control strategy. If you want more help in identifying a specific problem, you'll find photographs and descriptions of specific insects and diseases in the "Guide to Garden Pests and Their Natural Enemies," beginning on page 249, and in the "Guide to Disease Symptoms," beginning on page 309.

For more detailed information on how to safely and effectively apply particular strategies and products, refer to "Organic Pest and Disease Management," beginning on page 345. There you'll find information on the protection offered, toxicity to nonpest organisms, and any possible hazards related to strategy or product use.

ABIES Fir

Firs are cone-bearing evergreens with needle-like foliage and a symmetrical form, especially when young. They make impressive specimens or, in groups, effective dark backgrounds and tall screens.

Firs grow best under cool, moist conditions; they do not thrive in hot, dry climates. Set container-grown or balled-and-burlapped plants into acid, moist but well-drained soil, preferably in spring. Full sun is best, but firs will grow well (with a somewhat more open habit) in partial shade. Fir trees are seldom bothered by insects or diseases in the landscape. Planting healthy trees in the right conditions will prevent most potential pest problems.

Problems

Needles deformed. Cause: Balsam twig aphids. This ⅛-inch-long, greenish aphid has a white waxy coating. It feeds primarily on succulent new growth and exudes sticky honeydew, which covers the needles. Most of the damage occurs in late spring to early summer. Control with insecticidal soap. See "Leaves wrinkled and discolored" on page 211 for more controls.

Needles light gray or bronze. Cause: Spruce spider mites. These tiny, spiderlike pests damage needles as they feed; the injury weakens the plant and can kill young trees. Mites start feeding on lower, older needles and progress upward and outward; tiny webs may be visible on needles. Control in spring with horticultural oil at a dormant season dilution before growth starts. See "Leaves stippled with yellow; foliage webbed" on page 212 for more controls.

Branches defoliated. Cause: Hemlock loopers. The 1-inch-long, greenish yellow, black-spotted caterpillars usually begin feeding on the needles in June, starting from the branch tips and working toward the center of the plant. Handpick small populations; control large infestations with **Bacillus thuringiensis** var. **kurstaki** (BTK). See "Microbial Pest Control Products" on page 370.

Branches with brown tips. Cause: Spruce budworms. These brown, 1-inch caterpillars have white dots on their backs. They start tunneling into older needles and gradually migrate to opening buds. Damaged needles turn brown and drop; you may see tiny webs on shoot tips. Prune off affected branch tips or handpick if only a few pests are present. Spray severe infestations with BTK.

Plant defoliated; branches bear cocoonlike bags. Cause: Bagworms. See "Plant defoliated; branches bear cocoonlike bags" on page 212.

ACER Maple

Maples are a large group of easy-to-grow, 15- to 100-foot trees with opposite leaves and distinctive, two-winged fruit. They are popular as street or specimen trees.

In general, maples prefer rich, moist but well-drained, acidic soil and a sunny position. Some smaller species, such as Japanese maples (*Acer palmatum*), need at least partial shade. Set out maples in spring as container-grown or balled-and-burlapped plants.

Although they can host a range of pests, most maples survive nicely with little or no spraying. Note that oil sprays and insecticidal soaps may damage some maples; before using either product, note restrictions on the label and use with caution. Test on a few leaves before treating the whole plant.

Problems

Leaves with brown, dry edges. Cause: Leaf scorch. Caused by lack of water or reflected heat from surrounding pavement, this damage is often a problem on newly planted trees. Avoid by keeping soil around the tree evenly moist; a 2- to 3-inch-thick layer of mulch keeps roots cool and retains moisture. See "Leaf Scorch" on page 318 for more information.

Leaves yellow; whole plant weakened. Cause: Maple scales. Both maple phenacoccus and cottony maple scale produce small, fluffy, white egg masses. They feed on leaves and stems, weakening the plant. Spray the trunk and branches with horticultural oil: Use a dormant-season dilution before growth starts in spring or a growing-season dilution as buds begin to open. Or use insecticidal soap as buds begin to open. See "Scales, Armored" on page 282 for more controls.

Leaves and shoots blackened; leaves with moist or brown sunken spots. Cause: Anthracnose. See "Anthracnose" on page 310 for controls and more details on this disease.

Leaves distorted or bumpy. Cause: Mites. Several different mites attack maple leaves, causing pointed or wartlike swellings in various colors. Although they are unsightly, these galls don't seriously threaten tree health. Pick off damaged leaves, or apply horticultural oil at a dormant-season dilution in early spring, before growth starts.

Leaves, shoots, or seeds distorted. Cause: Boxelder bugs. These ½-inch-long bugs have charcoal-colored wings with red veins. They are a nuisance, but seldom cause serious problems. Spray plants with insecticidal soap or horticultural oil at a growing-season dilution when pests first appear.

Leaves skeletonized or with large holes. Cause: Caterpillars. See "Leaves skeletonized or with large holes; branches may be webbed" on page 212 for details.

Leaves with powdery white coating. Cause: Powdery mildew. See "Leaves with powdery white coating" on page 213 for controls.

Leaves with spots. Cause: Leaf spot. See "Leaves with spots" on page 213 for details.

Leaves wrinkled and discolored. Cause: Aphids. See "Leaves wrinkled and discolored" on page 211.

Branches wilt. Cause: Verticillium wilt. Parts of trees infected with this fungal disease may wilt suddenly or produce leaves that are yellow or smaller than normal. Cut and destroy or dispose of affected branches. Trees may recover if you provide extra water and fertilizer to promote strong, new, healthy growth. Remove severely infected trees; don't replant another maple in the same spot.

Trunk or branches with oozing lesions; branch tips die back. Cause: Canker. See "Trunk or branches with oozing lesions; branch tips die back" on page 214 for details.

Trunk or branches with small holes; limbs die or break off. Cause: Borers. See "Trunk or branches with small holes; limbs die or break off" on page 214 for controls.

ACHILLEA Yarrow

These hardy, easy-to-grow, drought-tolerant perennials prosper in well-drained soil in full sun. They thrive in heat and average to poor soil. Overly rich soil or excess fertilization yields poor, floppy growth and few flowers. Leaves are feathery and grayish green. Tiny yellow, red, or white flowers form dense, broadly flattened clusters from spring to midsummer. Plants form vigorous clumps that can spread; divide regularly for best performance.

Leaves of crowded plants in moist, humid, shady conditions may develop white or gray patches of powdery mildew. Thin afflicted plants to improve air circulation; avoid watering late in the day. See "Powdery Mildew" on page 322 for more controls.

ACTAEA (formerly Cimicifuga) Bugbane, snakeroot

The bugbanes are durable, 2- to 6-foot-tall natives that spread to 2 feet wide. Small, creamy white blooms appear in multiples to cover upright, slim spikes that tower above the dark green, fernlike leaves. Flowering occurs from late summer to early fall, depending on species. Flower aroma has been described as "sickly sweet" or "strange."

Bugbanes prosper in rich, moist, well-drained organic soil, similar to their native woodland habitat. These plants prefer light shade; bugbanes grown in deep shade bear fewer flowers. Plants can succeed in sunny areas with ample watering. Clumps expand outward slowly and can be divided in fall or spring, but bugbanes are deep-rooted and may suffer from division. Germination from seed is slow and inconsistent. Provide a winter mulch in colder areas, a protective summer mulch in warmer areas. Fertilize and water regularly. Few pests trouble bugbanes.

AESCULUS Horse chestnut

These deciduous plants have 3- to 10-inch-long, opposite, compound leaves with three to nine leaflets. The larger species are used as specimens or street trees; the shrubs are best in mass plantings or shrub borders.

All of these species thrive in moist, well-drained soil rich in organic matter. The tree forms do best in full sun, while the shrubs will flourish in conditions ranging from full sun to partial shade. Note that insecticidal soap sprays may damage some horse chestnuts, so read the label before applying and use with caution. Test spray on a few leaves before spraying the whole plant.

Problems

Leaves with irregular brown spots. Cause: Leaf blotch. Caused by a fungus, these spots may spread over leaves and lead to defoliation. Clean up and destroy fallen leaves to remove overwintering spores.

Leaves with brown, dry edges. Cause: Leaf scorch. This symptom indicates weak or damaged roots or poor soil conditions; it is caused by lack of water and/or heat reflected from surrounding pavement. Avoid by planting in rich, evenly moist soil and irrigating, if necessary, in very dry weather. See "Leaf Scorch" on page 318 for more information.

Leaves with powdery white coating. Cause: Powdery mildew. See "Leaves with powdery white coating" on page 213 for controls.

Leaves skeletonized or with large holes. Causes: Whitemarked tussock moths; Japanese beetles. See "Leaves skeletonized or with large holes; branches may be webbed" on page 212.

Leaves and shoots blackened; leaves with moist or brown sunken spots. Cause: Anthracnose. See "Leaves and shoots blackened; leaves with moist or brown sunken spots" on page 214 for details on this fungal disease.

Trunk or branches with oozing lesions; branch tips die back. Cause: Canker. See "Trunk or branches with oozing lesions; branch tips die back" on page 214 for details.

Plant defoliated; branches bear cocoonlike bags. Cause: Bagworms. See "Plant defoliated; branches bear cocoonlike bags" on page 212.

AGERATUM Ageratum, flossflower

The soft lavender, blue, or pink flower clusters of ageratums are lovely in flower gardens from early summer to first frost. Plants grow 6 to 36 inches high and about 1 foot wide. Ageratums also make good container plants.

For best germination, sow ageratum seeds indoors 8 weeks before the last frost. Seeds need light, so don't cover them; expect germination in about 10 days. Initial seedling growth is slow. Many gardeners prefer the ease of starting with nursery plants.

Ageratums grow best in fertile, well-drained soil on a sunny site with good air circulation. Poor soil and insufficient water cause plant browning. Too much shade causes decreased flowering and legginess. Remove spent flower heads to promote more blooms. Feed plants with a general-purpose fertilizer once a month. The first frost turns plants black.

Ageratums are seldom seriously troubled by pests. Whiteflies can cause weak plants with yellowed leaves. See "Whiteflies" on page 290 for controls. Leaves stippled with yellow and webby foliage and stem tips indicate spider mites. See "Mites, Spider" on page 275 for controls.

Finally, various fungi thrive in the moist, fertile soil ageratums require. They attack roots, causing plant stunting and wilting. Wilting may begin at lower leaves and progress toward the upper ones, or it may occur rapidly. If the plant is pulled up, you'll see the roots are dark brown and rotting. Discard infected plants. Improve drainage and lighten the soil with organic matter.

AJUGA Ajuga, bugleweed

These hardy groundcovers favor partial shade and moist, well-drained soil. Flower spikes appear from spring to summer over mats of dark green, bronze, or burgundy leaves. Common bugleweed (*Ajuga reptans*) spreads vigorously via stolons, desirable for a slope, less so in a lawn. Other species are more easily controlled. Set plants 6 inches apart for rapid coverage.

Excess moisture, especially in heavy, slow-draining soils, encourages crown and root rots

caused by soil-dwelling fungi. Dark spots appear on the crown and leaves of infected plants; roots blacken. Controls are cultural: Avoid planting ajuga in wet areas; cultivate to improve air circulation. Remove infected plants and surrounding soil; do not compost diseased plants. Clean up debris in fall to limit places where fungi overwinter.

ALBIZIA Albizia, mimosa, silk tree

Mimosas are deciduous trees growing to 40 feet high, with finely textured foliage and pink blooms. They are easy to transplant. Mimosas flower best in full sun and adapt to a range of soil conditions.

Because of their insect and disease problems, mimosas are usually short-lived. Mimosa web-worms, 1-inch brown caterpillars, bind leaves with webs and skeletonize foliage. Remove and destroy nests; spray leaves with BTK (see page 374). Mimosa wilt produces wilted leaves and dead branches. Remove and destroy infected trees.

ALCEA Hollyhock

Hardy hollyhocks create an excellent backdrop for a perennial border and offer blooms in shades of red, pink, purple, yellow, and white. They grow 5 to 9 feet tall, bearing midsummer spikes of single or double flowers, up to 4 inches wide.

Sun-loving and free-flowering, hollyhocks prosper in rich, heavy, moist, well-drained soils, but will thrive in ordinary soils, too. Plant 2 feet apart in a site sheltered from wind. Most cultivars require staking.

Problems

Leaf surfaces pale; powdery orange spots beneath. Cause: Rust. Hollyhock's most common disease also deforms leaves and stems and causes early leaf drop. The orange spots release fungal spores that spread via wind and rain. Grow resistant cultivars; keep leaves dry and encourage good air circulation. Remove and destroy infected plant parts. See "Rust" on page 315 for more controls.

Leaves skeletonized. Cause: Leaf-feeding beetles. Japanese beetles are prime suspects here, although other beetles, such as spotted cucumber beetles and rose chafers, may also attack. See "Japanese Beetle" on page 269 for controls.

Buds and leaves deformed or dwarfed. Cause: True bugs. Several of the true bugs injure hollyhocks with their piercing-sucking mouthparts and release a toxin that deforms plants. See "Buds and leaves deformed or dwarfed" on page 99 for control information.

ALLIUM Allium

Related to onions and garlic, but much prettier, ornamental alliums bloom in shades of blue, purple, pink, white, and yellow. Allium foliage may be rounded and hollow like onion leaves or straplike and solid; when bruised, the leaves release the pungent fragrance associated with culinary alliums. The blossoms, however, may have a pleasant floral smell. Small star- or bell-shaped flowers cluster in 2- to 9-inch globes atop leafless stems in early summer. Plants range from 6 inches to 5 feet tall.

Plant allium bulbs in fall at a depth roughly three times the bulbs' diameter. Select a site with full sun and well-drained soil; taller species may need some protection from wind. Water regularly throughout the growing season, but avoid excess moisture, which encourages rot. Allium foliage dies back shortly after flowering ends. If division is needed to reduce crowding, separate bulblets after foliage dies back; replant immediately.

Problems

Leaves with large, ragged holes. Cause: Slugs and snails. Slugs and snails may feed on foliage; see "Slugs/Snails" on page 284.

Leaves with silver-white streaks. Cause: Onion thrips. These $\frac{1}{50}$- to $\frac{1}{25}$-inch thrips suck sap from foliage; severe infestations stunt plants and may impair flowering. Thrips are hard to control because they burrow into plant tissue. Remove and destroy infested plant parts; encourage predators such as pirate bugs, lacewings, and lady beetles. Clean up debris where thrips may overwinter. Monitor and trap thrips with blue sticky traps. Apply insecticidal soap sprays regularly once pests appear on traps.

ALMOND *Prunus dulcis* (Rosaceae)

Almonds are deciduous trees that grow to about 20 feet and bloom in early spring. Nuts are borne on short-lived spurs—short branches that elongate only a fraction of an inch per year. Almonds are hardy in Zones 7–9.

Grow almonds where summers are hot and dry, in sunny sites, free from late spring frosts. To set nuts, most almond cultivars need cross-pollination; 'All-in-One' is self-pollinating. Almonds and peaches are closely related and are affected by similar pests and diseases; most almond trees are grafted onto peach rootstocks. For more information on problems and solutions, see the Peach entry beginning on page 153.

Problems

Blossoms shriveled, covered with fuzzy gray masses. Cause: Brown rot. Nut hulls also may rot. To control this fungal disease, harvest nuts early, just when hulls begin to split. Before spring growth begins, remove infected nuts and any twigs with sunken lesions (cankers). If brown rot has infected your trees in previous seasons, preventive sprays of sulfur just before blossoms open and again after blossoming may keep the fungus from affecting the nuts.

Nutmeats eaten; larvae, webbing, and insect excrement (frass) present in shells. Cause: Navel orangeworms. These moth larvae tunnel into almonds and feed on the nuts. Adults lay eggs on almonds around the time the husks begin to split; eggs hatch within 4 to 23 days. Eliminate this pest's overwintering sites by removing mummies (undeveloped nuts) from trees or on the ground. Harvest almonds promptly and completely before navel orangeworm activity begins. Spray BTK at hull split; repeat 1 week later.

Growing shoots wilted or dying. Causes: Oriental fruit moths; peach twig borers. Both pests tunnel into growing shoots and cause wilting. For controls, see "Oriental Fruit Moth" on page 276 and "Growing shoots wilted or dying" on page 155.

AMARANTHUS Amaranth

Their colorful leaves or drooping flower clusters make these plants ideal focal points in the garden. They grow from 1 to 6 feet tall, depending on the species and cultivar. The leaves or flowers also stand out in cut flower arrangements.

Amaranth seedlings do not transplant well, so direct-seed in early summer when night temperatures are consistently 60°F or above. Water and feed seedlings regularly only until their colors appear. Thin to 1 or 2 feet apart. Amaranth markedly prefers hot, dry, sunny areas and poor to average soil. Excess fertility causes dull foliage and

weak stems. Overwatering leads to root rot, causing stems, crowns, and roots to turn brown or black. Once it begins, there is no cure, so the best control is prevention.

ANEMONE Anemone, windflower

Tuberous species of anemone include low-growing Grecian windflower (*Anemone blanda*), a 6- to 8-inch plant with deeply divided leaves and daisylike blue, pink, or white flowers; and showy, 7- to 15-inch poppy anemone (*A. coronaria*), a more tender plant (Zone 8) with single or semidouble blooms in deep shades of red, blue, violet, and white. Both species bloom in early spring.

Soak tubers overnight in warm water before planting in fall. Plant tubers 3 inches deep in light shade in richly organic, neutral to slightly alkaline, well-drained soil. Windflower tubers often lack an obvious top and bottom; plant them on their sides, so stems grow up and roots grow down. Tubers planted sideways have a better chance of growing than those planted upside down. Poppy anemone tubers resemble claws; plant claw side down. Plantings expand slowly. Divide crowded clumps in late summer after foliage dies down, making sure each piece has a bud. Let dry for 2 days in a shady, airy spot before replanting. Dust with a copper-based fungicide or sulfur if rot has been a problem.

If anemone foliage disappears, suspect birds, rabbits, or other animal pests along with slugs and snails. See "Preventing Animal Damage" on page 304 and "Slugs/Snails" on page 284 for controls.

ANNUALS *See "Flowers" on page 96*

ANTIRRHINUM Snapdragon

These tender perennials are grown as annuals.

Most gardeners try snapdragons at least once, and many make them a garden mainstay. Bloom time is winter and spring in mild winter areas, and early summer to fall elsewhere. Snapdragons prefer cool weather but tolerate heat. Single or double upright flower spikes offer a variety of color choices, including red, white, yellow, orange, and pink. Height range is 4 to 48 inches. Plants may self-sow.

Start seeds indoors in late summer or early fall in mild climates and in early spring where frosts are common. Do not cover seeds; they require light and warmth for germination. Seedlings appear in 7 days. Move seedlings outside in spring when the planting bed can be worked. Direct-seeding outdoors is possible, but seeds dry out rapidly, so frequent sprinkling is necessary. Purchased bedding plants flower faster than home-grown plants because of the controlled growing conditions.

Place plants 6 to 12 inches apart in full sun and humus-rich, well-drained, somewhat sandy soil. To keep plants from becoming leggy or spindly, pinch them back when they are 3 to 6 inches high. Pinching may cause a slight flowering setback at first, but later, flower production will markedly increase. Give ample water from below. Fertilize once a month. Cut flower spikes frequently to maintain bloom. When flowering slows down, cut plants back severely and give liquid fertilizer. In windy areas, staking may be necessary.

Problems

Stems and leaf undersides with dusty, dark brown spots. Cause: Rust. This fungus develops quite rapidly, so leaves must be monitored for initial spotting. Rust-resistant snapdragons are now available; use them whenever possible, although they don't eliminate the problem.

Infections are less likely if snapdragons are grown rapidly and vigorously. Keeping the soil evenly moist encourages strong, healthy growth; water in the morning. If rust spotting appears, or if you have had rust problems in prior years, dust every 2 weeks with sulfur, beginning in very early spring. Fertilize and water regularly, but avoid overhead watering, which helps transfer rust spores. Remove and destroy badly infected plants. In severe situations, where rust appears in succeeding years despite controls, change planting locations.

Leaves, stems, and buds distorted. Cause: Aphids. See "Aphids" on page 250.

Leaves stippled with yellow; foliage webbed. Cause: Spider mites. For control measures, see "Mites, Spider" on page 275.

APPLE *Malus* spp. (Rosaceae)

Apples are deciduous trees that reach 6 feet to more than 30 feet, depending on soil, rootstock, and cultivar. The showy, pink-tinged white blossoms appear in spring mostly on spurs—short branches that elongate only a fraction of an inch per year. Apples are hardy in Zones 3–9, depending on the cultivar.

Culture

Plant in full sun in well-drained, moderately fertile, slightly acidic soil. Train trees to a framework of well-spaced, wide-angled branches. Prune bearing trees each winter to admit light into the tree and encourage good air circulation. As you prune, remove diseased and spindly wood and crossed branches. Where dense growth blocks out light, remove extra shoots at their bases. To develop growth on spindly shoots, remove the end of the shoot just above an outward-facing bud. For more pruning information, see "Pruning and Training" on page 104. For best results, choose cultivars resistant to the diseases prevalent in your area. Cultivars that resist a wide range of diseases include 'Goldrush', 'Jonafree', 'Liberty', 'Nova Easygro', 'Priscilla', 'Redfree', and 'William's Pride'.

To produce fruit, most cultivars need cross-pollination by a second compatible apple or crabapple planted within 40 to 50 feet. Some cultivars, such as 'Jonagold' and 'Mutsu', produce nonviable pollen and can't serve as pollinators. A few, like 'Golden Delicious', are self-pollinating. If you're planting one tree, improve fruit set by grafting a branch of a suitable pollinator onto the tree. For more information on setting fruit, see "Setting Fruit" on page 103.

Fruit Problems

Fruit with holes surrounded by brown, crumbly excrement. Cause: Codling moths. Adults appear in early spring and lay eggs in trees within 2 to 6 weeks of blossom time. Eggs hatch into larvae within 5 to 14 days. The fat, white or pinkish, $\frac{7}{8}$-inch caterpillars tunnel through fruit and may be gone by the time you find the holes, which may be filled with frass, waste material that resembles moist sawdust. Preventing codling moth damage on apples is most successful when cultural methods—such as destroying overwintering cocoons—are combined with traps to monitor pest activity, barriers, and the use of organic sprays when the moths are present. To see how controls can be tailored to the codling moth's life cycle, see "Meshing Your Management Methods" on page 348; for specific control methods, see "Codling Moth" on page 259.

Codling moths often produce several generations per growing season. Trapping the pupating caterpillars aids control. Remove loose bark and wrap the trunk with a band of corrugated cardboard or burlap. Periodically remove the band and destroy pupae. Inspect harvest containers for pupae.

Since codling moths prefer crowded fruit, you can discourage attack by thinning apples until no fruit touches. Infested apples may drop early; pick up and destroy dropped fruit before larvae emerge to pupate. If you have a single backyard tree and no other trees in your area, try trapping male moths with pheromones. Mating disruption pheromones are also available.

The effectiveness of other controls depends on local conditions. Introduced parasitic *Trichogramma* wasps control this pest in some orchards but not in others. Success depends on such factors as weather, optimum timing of parasite release, and using the correct species of wasp. If you try this technique, be sure to purchase a species of *Trichogramma* that parasitizes codling moths. BTK may also help with control, but you have to apply it during the 3 to 5 days between the time when the eggs hatch and the larvae enter the fruit. Once the larvae are in the fruit, BTK is ineffective. You may find that BTK is more effective when combined with a feeding attractant (also called an appetite stimulant), such as molasses.

Fruit dimpled; brown tunnels through flesh. Cause: Apple maggots. These $\frac{1}{4}$-inch larvae of the apple maggot fly ruin fruit by copious tunneling. Adult flies emerge from soil-dwelling pupae in late June and continue to appear until early autumn. Flies puncture fruit skin and deposit eggs, which hatch into fruit-tunneling maggots. Infested apples often drop. To prevent buildup of pupae around trees, collect and destroy dropped fruit at least weekly.

Apple maggot flies are attracted to fruit by sight. You can control them with traps made from dark red balls coated with a sticky coating, such as Tangle-Trap. Buy commercial traps or make your own from any apple-size red sphere. In mid-June hang one trap per dwarf tree or four to eight traps per full-size tree. Hang traps at eye level, 2 to 3 feet in from branch tips, near fruit but not completely hidden by leaves. Clean traps every few days and reapply the sticky coating. See "Apple Maggot" on page 251 for other control methods.

Young fruit with crescent-shaped scars. Cause: Plum curculios. This beetle, common east of the Rocky Mountains, leaves a characteristic crescent-shaped scar as it lays eggs in fruit. Damaged apples may drop, but frequently will remain on the tree. Since plum curculios cannot mature in hard apple flesh, fruit that doesn't drop will be superficially scarred but otherwise edible.

To control this pest without sprays, spread a dropcloth beneath the tree and tap the trunk and branches with a padded mallet. Collect and destroy curculios that fall onto the sheet. For best results, tap the tree twice a day, beginning as soon as you see the first scarred fruit. In addition, prevent hatching of some curculio eggs by picking up and discarding dropped fruit. Some apples ('Mutsu', for example) are more resistant to plum curculios than others. For more control information, see "Plum Curculio" on page 278.

Fruit with brown, velvety, or corky surface lesions. Cause: Apple scab. This serious, widespread disease begins when spring warmth and moisture promote the discharge of fungal spores from old, infested apple leaves into the air. These spores can infect the leaves and fruits of susceptible apples growing nearby. To prevent scab from spreading into the tree each spring, remove dropped leaves in fall.

Growing-season applications of sulfur or lime-sulfur sprays will help control scab. If you have susceptible cultivars or if the weather is very warm and wet, spray weekly, beginning with the appearance of the first green tips on the tree until disease pressure subsides. Pruning to encourage sunlight penetration and air circulation also helps with control. Many excellent scab-resistant cultivars are available, including 'Goldrush', 'Jonafree', 'Liberty', 'Redfree', and 'William's Pride'.

Fruit with rotting spots. Cause: Summer disease. Summer diseases are fungal diseases associated with hot weather. Dark spots with alternating black and brown rings indicate black rot. Other summer diseases include bitter rot (slightly sunken, tan spots) and white rot (watery decay). Black rot prevails where summers are milder; bitter rot and white rot, where summers are hot. Summer disease fungi overwinter in mummified fruit and in cankers on diseased wood. To control, remove and dispose of all cankered wood. Collect and destroy mummified fruit. Black rot and white rot attack weakened or wounded trees, so keep them healthy with good pruning and nutrition. Prune in early spring, when wounds heal most quickly. Sulfur sprays help control black rot. Resistance to summer rot disease varies, depending on the amount of fungi present and weather conditions. Cultivars least susceptible to summer disease infections are 'Enterprise', 'Golden Delicious', 'Goldrush', 'Gala Supreme', 'Braeburn', and 'Fuji'.

Fruit with yellow skin spots that later turn orange. Cause: Cedar-apple rust. Infected fruit is small, deformed, and may fall prematurely. For more information see "Leaves with pale yellow spots that enlarge and turn orange" on page 34.

Fruit with surface netting or russeting.
Cause: Powdery mildew. For more information,
see "Leaves with a pale powdery coating" below.

**Fruit with red skin spots bearing white
centers.** Cause: San Jose scale. For more information, see "Leaves yellow; death of whole branches"
on the opposite page.

**Fruit with raised black spots or brown
smudges on the surface.** Causes: Fly speck;
sooty blotch. Black spots are fly speck; brown
smudges are sooty blotch. Both of these blemishes
are fungal diseases and both can be controlled with
sulfur sprays. But since both are superficial, you
can just rub them off the fruit.

Leaf and Branch Problems

**Leaves with olive-brown, velvety spots that
become brown and corky.** Cause: Apple scab.
Infected leaves may turn yellow and drop prematurely, further weakening the tree. For controls, see
"Fruit with brown, velvety or corky surface
lesions" on page 33.

**New leaves twisted or curled and covered
with a sticky coating.** Cause: Aphids. You
may find these tiny green, black, gray, pink, or
white fluffy-coated insects on leaf undersides.
The leaves may be sticky and coated with black
sooty mold, a fungus that feeds on the honeydew
exuded by aphids. Aphids weaken trees by sucking sap, but they depart by midsummer. For a
light infestation, just wait it out. Grow nectar-
producing flowers, such as dill and buckwheat,
near your trees to provide food for aphid predators
(parasitic wasps, lady beetles, and hover flies).
Or attract aphid predators by spraying commercial
or homemade yeast-and-sugar mixtures on your
trees. For more information, see "Aphids" on
page 250.

**Leaves with pale yellow spots that enlarge
and turn orange.** Cause: Cedar-apple rust.
Leaves infected with cedar-apple rust may drop
prematurely. This fungal disease overwinters as a
gall on various juniper species—commonly on
Eastern red cedar (*Juniperus virginiana*). In spring
the galls swell, push out orange horns, and discharge disease spores that are borne on the wind
to infect apple trees. The leaf spots caused by
cedar-apple rust won't spread disease into the tree,
and you can't make them go away once they
appear.

Cedar-apple rust isn't a problem in areas with
few Eastern red cedars or other junipers (*Juniperus*
spp.). Removing nearby Eastern red cedars won't
prevent the arrival of windborne disease coming
from miles away. See "Cedar-Apple Rust" on page
312 for controls. Resistant cultivars include
'Arkansas Black', 'Baldwin', 'Empire', 'Granny
Smith', 'Gravenstein', 'Grimes Golden', 'Jerseymac',
'Liberty', 'McIntosh', 'Macoun', 'Redfree', and
'Winesap'.

Leaves with a pale powdery coating.
Cause: Powdery mildew. As this fungal disease
becomes more severe, leaves may curl lengthwise
and drop. Since it overwinters in dormant buds,
winter pruning of buds that show white fungal
growth aids control. See "Powdery Mildew" on
page 322 for controls. Resistant cultivars include
'Empire', 'Golden Delicious', 'Goldrush', 'Jonafree',
'McIntosh', 'Mutsu', 'Rhode Island Greening',
'Spigold', and 'William's Pride'.

**Leaves suddenly blacken, with tips of
growing shoots bent over.** Cause: Fire blight.
Don't confuse this disease with sooty mold, a black
fungus that rubs off easily. Fire blight bacteria may
travel to roots and kill the entire tree. For growing-season control, remove blighted parts at least 6
inches below the infected areas. Between cuts, dip
tools into isopropyl alcohol or 10 percent bleach

solution (1 part bleach to 9 parts water). Resistant cultivars include 'Empire', 'Jonafree', 'Goldrush', 'Liberty', 'Northwestern Greening', 'Nova Easygro', 'Prima', 'Red Delicious', 'Redfree', and 'Winesap'. For more information, see "Fire Blight" on page 336.

Whole Plant Problems

Leaves yellow; death of whole branches. Cause: San Jose scale. Clusters of these sucking insects cling to bark and appear as small gray bumps that can be easily scraped off with a fingernail. Use a late-winter application of horticultural oil at a dormant-season dilution to smother overwintering eggs. See "Scales, Armored" on page 282 for more information.

Fruit disappears; bark gnawed. Causes: Deer; rabbits; mice and voles. For information on identifying the damage caused by these pests and controls, see "Deer" on page 306, "Mice, Pocket Gophers, and Voles" on page 307, and "Rabbits" on page 308.

Tree declines; sawdustlike material on trunk near ground level. Cause: Roundheaded appletree borers. These creamy white, dark-headed beetle larvae bore into trunks near ground level, girdling the tree or tunneling into the heartwood. Kill borers by inserting a thin, flexible wire or by injecting parasite nematodes into their holes. See "Roundheaded Borers" on page 281 for more information.

APRICOT *Prunus armeniaca* (**Rosaceae**)

Apricots are deciduous trees growing 20 to 30 feet. The pink blossoms appear in spring on 1-year-old and older spurs—short branches that elongate only a fraction of an inch per year. Apricots are hardy in Zones 4–9.

Plant in a sunny site with well-drained, moderately fertile soil and protected from late frost. Most apricots are self-pollinating, but some cultivars bear more if cross-pollinated. For more information, see "Setting Fruit" on page 103. Apricots and peaches belong to the same genus and have similar problems. For more information on problems and solutions, see the Peach entry, beginning on page 153.

Problems

Young fruit with crescent-shaped scars. Cause: Plum curculios. These beetles, common east of the Rockies, leave characteristic scars as they lay eggs in fruit. Damaged fruit usually drops. For control information, see "Plum Curculio" on page 378.

Fruit with small brown spots that enlarge and grow fuzzy in humid weather. Cause: Brown rot. Blossoms attacked by this fungal disease also may wither, fruit may mummify (dry and shrivel) on the tree, and leaves may turn brown. Resistant cultivars include 'Harcot', 'Hargrand', 'Harlayne', and 'Harogem'. For more information, see "Brown Rot" on page 332.

Fruit with small, dark, sunken spots or cracks on skin. Cause: Bacterial leaf spot. This disease, common in the Southeast, is very difficult to control. Plant resistant cultivars, including 'Alfred', 'Curtis', 'Harcot', 'Hargrand', and 'Harlayne'. For more information, see "Fruit with small, dark, sunken spots or cracks on skin" on page 154.

Fruit with pinkish worms. Cause: Oriental fruit moth larvae. For more information on this pest, which also tunnels into growing shoots, see "Growing shoots wilted or dying" below.

Growing shoots wilted or dying. Causes:

Oriental fruit moths; peach twig borers. Both pests tunnel into growing shoots and cause wilting. For controls, see "Oriental Fruit Moth" on page 276 and "Growing shoots wilted or dying" on page 155.

Leaves with small purple spots, some spots with centers missing. Cause: Shothole disease. Centers of leaf spots often enlarge to about ¼ inch, then fall out. This fungal disease, common in the West, spreads rapidly on wet foliage. For more information, see "Leaves with small purple spots, some spots with centers missing" on page 156.

Tree declines; gummy exudates mixed with sawdustlike material on trunk near ground level. Cause: Peachtree borers. Inspect the trunk near or just below the ground; you may find holes and gummy exudates made by peachtree borers—the larvae of a clear-winged moth—that bore into the inner bark. For information on controls, see "Tree declines; gummy exudates mixed with sawdustlike material on trunk near ground" on page 156.

Branches wilting and dying, fail to leaf out in spring. Causes: Bacterial canker; Valsa canker. Both diseases may cause amber gum to exude from the bark. The cultivars 'Harcot', 'Hargrand', 'Harlayne', and 'Harogem' are resistant to Valsa. For more information, see "Cytospora Canker" on page 333.

AQUILEGIA Columbine

Columbines brighten spring and summer with blossoms of yellow, white, purple, red, or bicolor. Plants reach 1 to 3 feet and bear spurred, 1- to 4-inch flowers.

Plant these woodland natives in good, moist, well-drained, slightly acid soil. Overly rich soil causes weak, short-lived plants, lush growth, and

few flowers. Plants tolerate full sun if temperatures stay below 80°F but prefer light shade. Set plants 1 feet apart in spring after the last frost or in fall when plants are dormant, placing crowns at soil level. Columbines have long roots; only young plants transplant easily. To start from seed, sow outdoors in early summer or indoors in winter. Don't cover the seed; it needs light to germinate. Columbines self-seed, but seedlings may not match the parents. Mulch lightly in areas with cold winters.

Problems

Leaves with tan or brown blotches or serpentine tunnels. Cause: Leafminers. These tiny pale green fly larvae feed between the upper and lower leaf surfaces. Prune off and destroy infested leaves. Remove debris in fall to destroy overwintering leafminers. Attract parasitic wasps to control these pests. See "Leafmining Flies" on page 271 for more controls.

Stems blacken at base; leaves yellow; plant topples over. Cause: Fungal and/or bacterial rots. Prevent with cultural practices: Plant only in well-drained sites; avoid crown or root injuries from careless digging. Keep winter mulch away from crowns to prevent rotting during dormancy. Remove affected plants and surrounding soil; don't compost them.

ARABIS Rock cress

These low-growing, spreading plants are often used as groundcovers, in rock gardens, and as border edging; few species grow over 1 inch tall. Rock cresses prefer soil on the dry side, cool temperatures, and full sun. White, pink, or rose flowers appear in early spring.

Summer heat can cause clumps to die out in the center, a condition best prevented with good growing conditions. Divide mature plants in spring in most areas. Space plants 5 inches apart. Cut back after flowering to encourage dense growth. Apply a winter mulch in cold areas. If thrips, mites, or aphids cause leaf yellowing, knock them from plants with a strong water spray. Time watering so that plants have dried by nightfall; wait until soil is fairly dry before respraying. Overwatering encourages rot, as does poor drainage.

ARTEMISIA Artemisia, wormwood

This genus includes southernwood (*Artemisia abrotanum*), wormwood (*A. absinthium*), and tarragon (*A. dracunculus*). Durable and sometimes woody, most species are grown for their feathery, gray-green to silver foliage. Plants given full sun and average, well-drained soil suffer few problems. Rich soil promotes rangy growth; excess moisture encourages root rot. Mounding types such as silvermound artemisia (*A. schmidtiana*) often react to high temperatures by dying out in the center; cut stems back to about 1 inch to encourage overall new growth. Artemisia's aromatic oils repel most insects.

ASPARAGUS *Asparagus officinalis* (Liliaceae)

Asparagus is a long-lived perennial. Its tender young shoots are one of the first vegetables ready to harvest in spring.

Culture

Asparagus is hardy in Zones 2–9. It thrives in any area with winter ground freezes or a dry season to provide a dormant period each year. Asparagus does best in full sun and deep, well-drained soil. Select a permanent location carefully, since plants will produce for 20 years or more. Dig out all weeds and add plenty of compost to the soil before planting. Asparagus requires high levels of phosphorus, potassium, and nitrogen. Do a soil test and add amendments as necessary. If your soil is heavy or poorly drained, plant asparagus in raised beds.

Plant 1-year-old crowns from a reputable nursery that sells fresh, firm, disease-free roots, or start your plants from seed. Most seed-grown asparagus plants eventually outproduce those started from crowns. Soak seeds or crowns in compost tea for 5 minutes before planting to reduce disease problems. Choose all-male cultivars such as 'Jersey Giant', 'Jersey Prince', or 'Jersey Knight' for greater spear production. A bed of all male plants can produce as much as 30 percent more spears than a mixed bed of male and female plants.

Harvesting new plantings too soon can stress plants and make them more susceptible to pest problems. Harvest for 2 weeks the second season, 4 weeks the third season, and up to 8 weeks thereafter.

Mulch with high-nitrogen compost each spring before spears emerge, and again in fall. Leave winter-killed foliage, along with straw or other light mulch, on the bed to provide winter protection. Remove and destroy the old foliage before new growth appears in the spring; it can harbor diseases and pest eggs. Over the years, the crowns will push closer to the soil surface, resulting in smaller and less-tender spears. To remedy this, mound 6 inches of soil over the rows each spring.

Spear Problems

Spears small. Causes: Young plants; low soil fertility; overharvested plants. Harvest lightly the first few years so plants can grow strong roots. Reduce harvest if established plantings begin to lose vigor. Asparagus is a heavy feeder; add lots of compost to maintain high soil fertility.

Spears small with brown streaks or girdled at soil line. Cause: Asparagus miners.

Larvae are $\frac{3}{16}$-inch-long, white maggots. Adults are small black flies. Destroy infected spears to control.

Spears turn brown, may get soft or wither and dry. Cause: Cold injury. Cut and discard damaged spears. Cover spears with mulch or newspaper when freezing nights are predicted.

Spears small, with large lesions at or below soil line. Cause: Fusarium wilt. Leaves and stems yellow, plants wilt, seedlings die. There is no cure; remove and destroy infected plants. To avoid problems, don't put new plantings where asparagus or other Fusarium-susceptible plants have grown in the past 8 years. Plant disease-free seed and crowns or resistant cultivars such as 'Greenwich', 'Jersey Giant', 'Martha Washington', and 'Viking KB3'.

Spears turn brown near soil line. Cause: Crown rot. Remove and destroy diseased plants, including roots. Prevent crown rot by planting in raised beds and maintaining good drainage. Keep soil pH above 6.0. Wait 2 years before harvesting new plantings. Some research suggests that not harvesting the first spear of the spring on each plant may help prevent crown rot because the developing frond produces food for the plant.

Spears crooked and deformed, may be brown or scarred; leaves chewed or missing. Causes: Asparagus beetles; asparagus fern caterpillars; cucumber beetles; mechanical injury. Asparagus beetles are blue-black, $\frac{1}{4}$-inch-long insects with cream-colored spots and red borders on wing covers. Larvae are $\frac{1}{3}$-inch-long, humpbacked, gray grubs with black heads. They are most active in cool weather. Spotted asparagus beetles are reddish orange with 12 black spots on wing covers. Larvae are orange. Fertilize plants to encourage new leaf growth. Harvest spears promptly to remove eggs before they hatch into hungry grubs. Handpick beetles into a jar of soapy water. Use a broom to gently knock larvae off plants; often this kills them,

as they are unable to climb back onto the asparagus. Destroy plant tops in later winter to remove overwintering beetles.

Asparagus fern caterpillar (also known as the beet armyworm) feeds on leaves. It is a dull green, $1\frac{1}{2}$-inch-long caterpillar with a light-colored stripe along each side of its body. Handpick or spray with BTK to control.

Cucumber beetles also eat asparagus leaves. For description and controls, see "Cucumber Beetle, Spotted/Southern Corn Rootworm" on page 262.

Deep cultivation can damage developing spears. Cultivate shallowly or use mulch instead. In windy areas, blowing sand can scar spears; protect plantings with windbreaks.

Spears chewed at soil line. Cause: Cutworms. Check for cutworms at night with a flashlight. Control with BTK or parasitic nematodes. See "Cutworms" on page 263 for more controls.

Spear bracts open prematurely (feathering). Cause: Excessive heat. Harvest spears daily when they are about 8 inches high, especially when temperatures are above 95°F.

Leaf Problems

Leaves yellow; growth slow. Causes: Nitrogen deficiency; waterlogged soil. Spray foliage with fish-meal tea and side-dress with compost to correct nitrogen deficiency. Waterlogged soil will produce the same symptoms. Make sure soil is well-drained or plant in raised beds.

Leaves yellow; plant dwarfed or rosetted. Cause: Asparagus aphids. These soft-bodied, pale green, powdery-looking insects suck plant juices and cause plants to weaken. Knock aphids off plants with a strong blast of water, or spray with insecticidal soap. As a last resort, spray with neem (see page 387).

Leaves turn brown and drop; stems and branches have small reddish blisters. Cause: Rust. Clean up and dispose of tops in late winter to eliminate overwintering spores. Rust weakens plants by reducing the leaf area and the amount of food stored in the roots. Repeated attacks can kill plants. Plant resistant cultivars such as 'California 500', 'Jersey Giant', 'Martha Washington', 'Mary Washington', 'Viking KB3', and 'Waltham Washington'.

Leaves dull gray-green to brown. Cause: Thrips. Adults are tiny, pale, rapidly moving, winged insects. The larvae are smaller, wingless versions barely visible to the naked eye. See "Thrips" on page 287 for controls.

ASTER Aster, Michaelmas daisy

Daisylike aster flowers in shades of purple, pink, and white appear in late summer and fall on plants that range from 9 inches to 6 feet in height.

Asters require ample water—about 1 inch per week—but also need well-drained soil and a sunny location. Plants will self-sow with abandon if fading flowers are not removed; seedlings aren't usually true to parent type. Grow tall cultivars out of the wind and stake as needed. Divide in spring every 2 to 3 years.

Problems

Leaves, stems, and buds distorted, sticky; clusters of small insects. Cause: Aphids. For controls, see "Aphids" on page 250.

Leaves and/or flowers with holes. Cause: Japanese beetles. See "Japanese Beetle" on page 269 for controls.

Leaves covered with white powder. Cause: Powdery mildew. For controls, see "Powdery Mildew" on page 322.

Leaves and flowers deformed, yellowish; small, tarlike spots on undersides. Cause: Lace bugs. These small pests with lacy wings cause yellow-brown leaf spots. Dark brown droppings on lower leaf surfaces confirm their activity. Remove debris in spring and fall to deter overwintering. See "Lace Bugs" on page 270 for controls.

Leaves with pale areas on upper surfaces; downy patches underneath. Cause: Downy mildew. This fungus spreads quickly during cool, wet nights and warm, humid days, causing leaves to wilt and die. Remove and destroy infected plant parts, encourage air circulation, and water early in the day to allow plants to dry before nightfall.

ASTILBE Astilbe, false spirea

Astilbes have dark green to bronze, fernlike foliage that appears in spring, followed by pink, white, purple, or red plumelike flower spikes. These mid-border plants grow 1 to 3 feet tall with a similar spread.

Astilbes enjoy the soggy soil conditions shunned by most other perennials, although good drainage is needed if winters are wet. Use a 3-inch layer of mulch around plants to conserve water. Never let soil dry completely—this causes brown-edged leaves and poor growth. Set plants 1 foot apart in partial shade and rich soil. Astilbes benefit from spring fertilization and light feedings during the growing season. Divide every 3 to 5 years.

Grown under these conditions, astilbes suffer few pest or disease problems beyond those common to herbaceous perennials.

Problems

Leaves and/or flowers with holes. Cause: Japanese beetles. See "Japanese Beetle" on page 269 for controls.

Leaves covered with white powder. Cause: Powdery mildew. Crowding under moist conditions invites powdery mildew. For control information, see "Powdery Mildew" on page 322.

Plant wilts while soil is moist. Cause: Fusarium wilt. *Fusarium* spp. fungi sometimes infect astilbes, causing wilting unrelated to adequate soil moisture. Young plants wilt quickly, while older ones turn pale green and lower leaves wilt. Stems show brown streaks that darken gradually; grayish pink mold may appear. Remove and destroy infected plants and surrounding soil; do not compost diseased materials. Don't plant susceptible crops in sites where wilt has appeared. Sterilize tools after use around infected plants.

AVOCADO *Persea americana* (**Lauraceae**)

Avocado trees grow to about 60 feet and have long, drooping leaves. Though evergreen, some trees shed their leaves just before a growth flush. Each tree bears many thousands of flowers, but pollination of only a small percentage of flowers ensures a full crop. Avocados are mostly self-pollinating. They are hardy in Zones 9–10.

Avocados need full sunlight and well-drained soil. Pruning is only necessary to keep a tree within bounds and to remove diseased wood.

Problems

Fruit with brown or purplish, scablike lesions. Cause: Fruit scab. Scab is a superficial skin fungus and not otherwise harmful to the plant. No treatment is necessary unless infection is so severe that fruit is deformed. For severe infection, apply copper sprays in early May and twice more at 4- to 5-week intervals.

Fruit gnawed or eaten. Causes: Birds; squirrels; rats; other small animals. Use traps or physical barriers to get rid of rodents; netting may be necessary to deter birds.

Leaves skeletonized and webbed together. Causes: Avocado caterpillars; omnivorous leafroller caterpillars. The yellowish green avocado caterpillar (also called an amorbia) is the larva of a reddish brown moth. Omnivorous leafrollers, yellowish green caterpillars with a stripe down their backs, are the larvae of dark brown moths. Natural enemies, such as *Trichogramma* wasps, often keep these pests sufficiently in check. For heavy infestations, spray BTK. Also look for and crush caterpillars and masses of eggs.

Leaves wilt and yellow on an entire branch. Cause: Verticillium wilt. A soilborne fungus causes this disease, and there is no way to save a tree once it has this problem. Don't plant avocados in soil that has sustained other Verticillium-susceptible crops such as tomatoes, peppers, and eggplants. If you suspect *Verticillium* fungi may be in your soil, solarize it for 1 to 2 months over the summer before planting susceptible plants.

Leaves pale green to yellow and dropping. Cause: San Jose scale. Look for the small, ash-colored to sooty black bumps of San Jose scale clinging to the bark. Colonies of these immobile insects cling to bark and weaken trees by sucking sap. Control scale with a dormant-season dilution of horticultural oil spray applied in late winter.

Tree declines; stunted pale leaves; no new growth. Cause: Root rot. Root rot can be caused by overwatering or by poorly drained soil, but the disease may take years to develop. There is no cure. Replant in well-drained soil or on a raised mound of soil. 'Thomas' and 'Martin Grande' are rootstocks resistant to this problem.

BASIL *Ocimum basilicum* (**Labiatae**)

Basil is an annual herb grown for its aromatic leaves. To grow healthy, trouble-free plants, sow seed indoors in 70°F soil mix, or outdoors after the soil has warmed. Basil does best in rich, moist, well-drained soil with a pH between 5.0 and 8.0, and needs at least 4 hours of full sun per day for good growth.

Few pests or diseases regularly affect basil. Because it is a fast-growing annual, removing and replacing plants that are severely damaged by pests or diseases often is more practical than applying other controls. Protect plants with row covers when temperatures drop below 40°F, or dark spots caused by cold injury may appear on leaves. Fungal infections may also cause dark spots on foliage; downy mildew causes yellowing on upper leaf surfaces and "dirty" dark spots on the undersides of leaves. Remove affected leaves and spray remaining foliage with potassium bicarbonate if problem is severe. Keep soil evenly moist to prevent stress from weakening plants and avoid wetting foliage unnecessarily when watering. Other mint family plants, such as coleus, sage, and salvia, may also be affected. If leaves are mottled yellow with turned-down edges, plant may have cucumber mosaic virus. Destroy infected plants. See the Vegetables entry, beginning on page 219, for other problems that affect many food garden plants.

BEAN *Phaseolus* spp. (**Leguminosae**)

Beans are annual vegetables grown for their immature pods, immature seeds, and nutritious dry seeds. They are legumes and, with the help of certain soil-dwelling bacteria, can transform nitrogen from the air into nitrogen compounds that plants can absorb. A wide range of bean types and cultivars are available.

Culture

Beans thrive in most garden soils with a pH between 5.5 and 6.8 and average soil fertility; high nitrogen levels in the soil will delay maturity. Soak seed in compost tea for 25 minutes before planting to help prevent disease and speed germination. To promote nitrogen fixation, treat seed before sowing with an inoculant labeled for the type of bean you are planting. Buy fresh inoculant each year, or check the date on the package for viability.

For a healthy, trouble-free crop, plant beans after soil has warmed. Optimum soil temperature for germination is 80°F. At soil temperatures below 60°F, most bean cultivars germinate poorly and are more susceptible to pests and root rot. Choose light, well-drained soil for early plantings, if possible, and cover the seedbed with row covers or clear plastic until seedlings emerge. If you use clear plastic, be sure to remove it as soon as the seeds germinate to avoid "cooking" the seedlings. Spray young plants with seaweed extract to prevent micronutrient deficiencies and improve overall plant health.

Don't work amid bean plants when foliage is wet, to avoid spreading diseases. Compost plants after harvest. Prevent problems by not planting beans in the same location more often than every 3 years.

Whole Plant Problems

Seedlings die or fail to emerge; plant stunted. Causes: Seedcorn maggots; root rot. Look for ¼-inch-long, yellow-white maggots feeding on seeds and seedlings. Adults are small flies. Seedlings that do come up are deformed and spindly. Control the soil-dwelling pests by applying parasitic nematodes to the soil before replanting.

Root rot causes reddish black streaks on the roots; plants are stunted and yellow. Cool, wet soil encourages this fungal disease. Destroy wilted plants. Replant with fresh seed in well-drained, warm soil. Soak seed in compost tea before planting.

Plant yellow and stunted, wilts during hot days and recovers at night. Causes: Wireworms; bean leaf beetle larvae; root-knot nematodes. If you suspect any of these pests, pull up a plant and examine the roots. Wireworm larvae are up to 1½-inch-long, yellow to reddish brown, slender, tough-bodied, segmented grubs. Adults are ½-inch-long, dark-colored, elongated click beetles. Apply parasitic nematodes to the soil to control.

Slender white grubs up to ⅓ inch long feeding on roots are bean leaf beetle larvae. See "Leaves with large holes" on page 44 for more information.

Root-knot nematodes cause swollen and darkened enlargements of roots. Destroy infested plants. See "Root-Knot Nematodes" on page 340 for a photo of infected roots and control recommendations. Small, round, pinkish nodules attached to the roots are caused by nitrogen-fixing bacteria and are beneficial.

Leaf Problems

Leaves with yellow, curling margins. Causes: Potato leafhoppers; calcium deficiency; salt injury. Look for leafhoppers on plants. Adults are ⅒-inch, yellow-green, winged insects. Nymphs are smaller and wingless. Severe infestations cause plants to wilt and flowers and pods to drop. Leafhoppers can spread viruses from plant to plant, so control is important. Cover emerging seedlings with row cover if leafhoppers have been a problem. Wash nymphs from plants with stiff sprays of water, repeated frequently; attract natural enemies (predatory flies and bugs and parasitic wasps); spray with insecticidal soap. As a last resort, spray with neem. Controls are most effective on wingless nymphs, since adults fly when disturbed. Be sure to spray the undersides of leaves where nymphs congregate.

Salt injury is common in areas of the country with saline soils, because beans are very sensitive to sodium. Planting in raised beds (with lots of compost worked in) and watering thoroughly may help.

If plants are also stunted and shoot tips turn black and die, suspect calcium deficiency. Keep soil evenly moist to help prevent problems. If a soil test shows deficiency, add gypsum, or calcitic lime if pH is below 6.2.

New growth distorted and yellow. Cause: Tarnished plant bugs. Adults are oval, light green to brown, ¼-inch-long bugs. Nymphs are smaller and yellow-green. Grow groundcovers and pollen plants to attract native predators (bigeyed bugs, damsel bugs, pirate bugs); remove weeds, especially red-stemmed pigweed. Apply garlic sprays as a repellent; apply *Beaveria bassiana* to young nymphs. As a last resort, spray infested plants with insecticidal soap or pyrethrin.

Leaves yellow; growth stunted. Cause: Nitrogen deficiency. This problem is often brought on by waterlogged soil. Spray foliage and drench roots with fish emulsion or liquid kelp to alleviate symptoms. Prevent problems by adding compost to the soil and providing good drainage.

Leaves yellow and withered. Cause: Bean aphids. Adults are small, black, soft-bodied, sucking insects. For mild infestations, knock pests off plants with a blast of water. Spray persistent infestations with insecticidal soap or neem.

Leaves mottled with golden yellow, and crinkled or curled. Cause: Bean mosaic. Leaves of infected plants curl downward, and plants are stunted. Seeds are small and shriveled. Remove and destroy plants infected with this viral disease. Prevent problems by controlling aphids that spread the disease and by planting tolerant cultivars, such as 'E-Z Pick', 'Gold Mine', 'Provider', 'Rocdor', 'Roma 2', 'Royal Burgundy', 'Sungold', 'Tender-crop', and 'Venture'.

Leaves puckered and curled downward; plant dwarfed. Cause: Curly top virus. Remove and destroy infected plants. Prevent problems by controlling aphids that spread the disease and by planting resistant or tolerant cultivars, such as 'Hystyle', 'Jade', and 'Pike'.

Leaves with white growth or water-soaked spots. Causes: Downy mildew; powdery mildew; white mold; bacterial blight. Warm, damp weather encourages these diseases, the first three of which are caused by fungi. Downy mildew only infects lima beans, causing young shoots and flowers of infected plants to develop white growth; leaf veins are twisted and purplish. Powdery mildew and white mold can attack all types of beans. Leaves develop a powdery or fuzzy white coating.

To control fungal diseases, thin plants to increase air movement. Plant a cultivar—such as 'Provider'—that tolerates all three diseases. Organic fungicides, including *Bacillus subtilis,* potassium bicarbonate, or a baking-soda-and-soap spray (1 teaspoon baking soda, 1 teaspoon liquid dish soap, 1 quart water) may prevent further infection.

Water-soaked spots caused by bacterial blight turn brown with a yellow halo and then become dry and brittle. Spray plants with sulfur or biofungicide products that contain *Bacillus subtilis* to reduce the spread of the disease if plants are setting fruit. If no new pods are forming, don't bother to spray; remove and destroy infected plants.

Leaves with dark streaks; black petioles and veins on undersides of leaves. Cause: Anthracnose. Spots exude salmon-colored ooze in cool, moist weather. This disease thrives in wet, humid conditions. Prevent problems by planting tolerant cultivars, such as 'Caprice', 'Carson', 'Espada', 'Nickel', 'Rocdor', and 'Savannah'.

Leaves with numerous small, round, reddish brown blisters on undersides. Cause: Rust. As this fungal disease progresses, leaves turn yellow and drop. Spots also appear on pods and stems. Rust usually develops in late summer. Biofungicide products that contain *Bacillus subtilis* may help to control foliage symptoms of rust and to limit the spread of the disease. Plant rust-tolerant cultivars, such as 'Boone', 'Crockett', 'Jade', 'Roma II', and 'Romano Gold', to prevent problems.

Leaves pale and stippled or bronzed. Cause: Spider mites. Hot, dry weather encourages outbreaks. Look for these tiny, spiderlike creatures on the undersides of leaves, where they appear as pale or dark specks. There may be fine webbing on the undersides of leaves. To control, spray plants with water or insecticidal soap in the evening.

Leaves with wandering, white or translucent tunnels. Cause: Leafminers. Adults are tiny black-and-yellow insects. Larvae are pale green and maggotlike, and they tunnel into leaves. Remove and destroy mined leaves. Apply row cover as soon as plants emerge to prevent problems. As a last resort, spray with neem.

Leaves riddled with tiny holes. Cause: Flea beetles. These small, shiny, black beetles hop when disturbed. Prevent problems by covering young plants with row cover. See "Flea Beetles" on page 265 for more information and controls.

Leaves skeletonized. Cause: Mexican bean beetles. In severe infestations, pods are chewed as well. Adults are oval, ¼-inch-long, yellowish brown beetles with 16 black spots on the wing covers. Nymphs are yellowish orange and spined. Eggs are yellow and found in groups on the undersides of leaves; look for these and destroy any that you find. A tiny parasitic wasp, *Pediobius foveolatus,* provides effective control. Release the wasps when bean beetle larvae are present. In cold climates you must release the wasps each year, as they cannot overwinter. Spined soldier bugs are also effective predators. Spray insecticidal soap, focusing on the undersides of leaves; apply neem as a last resort.

Leaves with large holes. Causes: Bean leaf beetles; cucumber beetles; various caterpillars. Bean leaf beetles are ¼ inch long and dark yellow with 6 black dots. The larvae are white, up to ⅓ inch long, and feed on roots and underground stems. Cucumber beetles are ¼ inch long and greenish yellow with black stripes or spots. Prevent problems by covering plants with row cover. Spray kaolin clay to deter leaf feeding; reapply after rains. Apply parasitic nematodes to soil to control larvae.

Many caterpillars also feed on bean leaves. Spray plants with BTK to control.

Flower and Pod Problems

Blossoms appear but no pods form. Causes: Excessive heat; mechanical injury; zinc deficiency. Hot days (85°F or more) or mechanical damage caused by heavy rains or strong water sprays can cause flowers to drop. Wait for new blossoms.

Zinc deficiency can also cause pods to drop. Spray plants with seaweed extract to prevent deficiency problems.

Pods with dark, round, sunken spots with lighter centers. Cause: Anthracnose. Salmon pink ooze appears in wet weather. See "Leaves with

dark streaks; black petioles and veins on undersides of leaves" on page 43 for controls.

Pods with water-soaked or brown patches; seeds yellow and blotched. Cause: Bacterial blight. See "Leaves with white growth or water-soaked spots" on page 43 for controls.

Pods with white spots. Causes: Powdery mildew; white mold; downy mildew. See "Leaves with white growth or water-soaked spots" on page 43 for more information and controls. Lima bean pods infected with downy mildew shrivel and turn black.

Pods rough, mottled, and deformed. Cause: Bean mosaic. See "Leaves mottled with golden yellow, and crinkled or curled" on page 43 for controls.

Pods with wartlike pimples. Cause: Green stink bugs. Adults are large, flat, shield-shaped, green bugs. Nymphs have reddish markings. Handpick adults to control mild infestations. As a last resort, dust with pyrethrin.

Pods with chewed holes. Cause: Caterpillars. Cover plants with row cover to exclude egg-laying moths if caterpillars have caused damage in the past. Control feeding worms with BTK spray.

Pods pitted and browned. Cause: Cold injury. Most cultivars may be damaged at temperatures below 45°F. Protect late crops with row cover.

Dry beans tunneled. Cause: Bean weevils. Adults are gray or brown, ¹⁄₁₀- to ⅛-inch-long snout beetles. Larvae are small and light-colored. To control this storage pest, dry seed in a 125°F oven for 25 minutes, or store at 0°F for 3 to 4 days to kill larvae.

BEET *Beta vulgaris* Crassa group (Chenopodiaceae)

Beets are biennial vegetables grown as annuals for their firm, sweet roots and succulent greens. Cultivars with red, yellow, and red-and-white roots are available.

Culture

Beets grow best in deep, well-drained soil with a pH between 6.5 and 7.5. They are cool-season plants and will tolerate temperatures as low as 40°F. However, beets will bolt if exposed to 2 or 3 weeks of temperatures below 50°F after the first true leaves have formed. Beets grow poorly when temperatures rise above 75°F. Keep soil moist, but not soggy, since rapid, uninterrupted growth produces the best roots. Avoid planting beets in the same location more often than every 3 years.

Leaf Problems

Leaves with purplish patches. Cause: Phosphorus deficiency. This is common in cool spring soils. Plants usually outgrow the problem when soils warm. Spray leaves with seaweed extract to speed up recovery.

Leaves yellow; plant stunted. Cause: Nitrogen deficiency. This deficiency affects older leaves first. Spray foliage and drench roots with fish emulsion to alleviate symptoms.

Leaves yellow and curled; plant stunted. Cause: Aphids. Adults are soft-bodied, small, green, gray, black, or pinkish sucking insects, sometimes with a white fluffy coating. Knock aphids off the plants with a blast of water, or spray plants with insecticidal soap to control. If soap spray is not affective, apply neem as a last resort.

Leaves with brown tips. Cause: Excessive heat. Bright sun and 80°F temperatures may injure beet leaves. Plant in a partially shaded location or provide shade in climates with hot summers.

Leaves with dark-bordered tan spots. Cause: Cercospora leaf spot. Water early in the day to allow foliage to dry; avoid overhead watering as much as possible. Thin plants to promote good air circulation. Eliminate weeds that can harbor the disease. Destroy spotted leaves. Plant disease-resistant cultivars, such as 'Pacemaker III' and 'Red Ace Hybrid'.

Leaves with light-colored spots on upper leaf surfaces. Cause: Downy mildew. Leaves infected with this fungal disease have spots covered with white fuzzy growth on the undersides. See "Downy Mildew" on page 313 for controls. 'Merlin' and 'Pacemaker III' are disease-resistant cultivars.

Leaves stunted and crinkled. Cause: Curly top virus. There is no cure once plants are infected; destroy infected plants. Leafhoppers spread the virus as they feed; control them with sprays of insecticidal soap; use neem for severe infestations. Prevent problems by covering seedbed with row cover after planting.

Leaves with wandering, white or translucent tunnels. Cause: Leafminers. Pale green, maggotlike larvae feed inside leaves, leaving empty tunnels behind. Adults are tiny black-and-white insects. Once larvae have entered leaves, spraying will not control them. Destroy mined leaves and remove weeds that may serve as hosts. Prevent problems by covering plants with row cover as soon as they emerge.

Leaves riddled with small holes. Cause: Flea beetles. These small, shiny, black, brown, or bronze beetles hop when disturbed. Prevent problems by covering plants with row cover as soon as they emerge.

Leaves with large, ragged holes. Causes: Beet armyworms; garden webworms. Greenish brown, 1½-inch-long caterpillars with a light-colored stripe on each side are beet armyworms. Pale green to nearly black, 1-inch-long caterpillars with a black or light stripe down their backs and dark spots are garden webworms. Webworms roll leaf edges over. Handpick or spray actively feeding caterpillars with BTK in the evening.

Root Problems

Roots distorted, with rough, cracked skin. Cause: Downy mildew. See "Leaves with light-colored spots on upper leaf surfaces" on page 45 for controls.

Roots with raised, rough, brown spots on surface. Cause: Scab. Prevent this fungal disease by adding compost to soil; plant in raised beds to improve drainage.

Roots with black, dead, hard spots in flesh. Cause: Boron deficiency. Roots may be wrinkled or cracked. Plants can be stunted; leaf edges may be brown and lower leaf surfaces may be reddish purple. Prevent deficiency problems by spraying plants with seaweed extract as soon as the first true leaves appear, and every few weeks thereafter. Check deficiency with a soil test. Correct by adding 1 tablespoon of borax dissolved in 1 gallon of water, or 10 pounds of kelp, per 100 square feet of soil.

Roots forked. Cause: Calcium deficiency. Prevent problems by keeping soil evenly moist. If soil test shows deficiency, add gypsum, or if pH is below 6.2, calcitic lime.

Roots small and poorly developed. Causes: Nitrogen deficiency; crowded roots. If leaves are small and yellow, feed plants with fish emulsion or compost tea to boost nitrogen level. Thin plants so roots don't touch to allow further growth.

Roots covered with hairy side roots; flesh woody. Cause: Curly top virus. See "Leaves stunted and crinkled" on page 45 for controls.

Roots unusually dark-colored. Cause: Potassium deficiency. Affected roots are prone to rot. If soil test confirms deficiency, amend soil as needed.

Roots light-colored; zoned rings in flesh very evident. Causes: Excessive heat; uneven soil moisture. Prevent problems by keeping soil evenly moist and mulching with straw during hot weather.

BEGONIA Begonia

The genus *Begonia* provides many beautiful species that are well adapted to garden culture. Outdoors, the common types are the fibrous-rooted and tuberous-rooted begonias. Each type has its own habits and needs.

The fibrous-rooted wax begonia, with its prolific flowering habit, is among the most popular bedding plants. Clusters of single or double, pink, white, or reddish flowers, up to 2 inches across, appear in spring and continue until frost. Wax begonias do not always compete successfully with other annuals. Spotlight them in masses of a single color. These are good plants to line the front of a sunny or partially shady border, growing only 6 to 9 inches tall and up to 1 foot wide. In mild climates (Zone 10 and warmer) they may overwinter and live for years. They do well in window boxes and are widely grown as flowering and ornamental houseplants. Glossy wax begonia leaves are shades of green or red.

Tuberous-rooted begonias have fewer but larger and showier blooms. The single or double flowers can grow to 6 inches or more across. They bloom on upright plants, growing to 2 feet tall, in bright and pastel shades of white, pink, red, yellow, and combinations. Tuberous-rooted begonias brighten up shady beds and borders.

Because dustlike wax begonia seeds require much nurturing, many gardeners prefer to buy bedding plants in spring for direct garden placement. If you do decide to grow your own, sow the tiny seeds indoors, 5 months before the final frost. Use a mix of fine peat and sand as the medium. Fluorescent lighting helps keep the desired warm temperature. Water seedlings from the bottom. When they are large enough to handle, transfer to 3-inch pots; transplant outdoors when night temperatures remain above 50°F. Set plants 9 inches apart.

Start tuberous-rooted begonias indoors, planting tubers 8 to 10 weeks before your frost-free date in a loose growing medium. Barely cover tubers with the concave side up (it should have little pink buds coming out of the center) and moisten lightly. Give lots of water and light after the shoots emerge. Move tubers to individual 4- or 5-inch pots when shoots are 1 to 3 inches tall. After all danger of frost is past, plant in partial shade in fertile, moist but well-drained soil, with plenty of organic matter. Water liberally in warm weather. Feed every 3 weeks or so with compost tea or fish emulsion.

Begonias need rich, very well-drained, light soil. Work in generous amounts of leaf mold, dehydrated manure, humus, and bonemeal. They tolerate full sun in cool climates only; in hot climates, leaves in full sun may show dry spotting from sunscald. Heavy shade, however, results in leggy plants and fewer flowers. Partial shade is generally best. Water when the soil 1 inch below the surface is still moist but not wet. Fertilize every 3 to 4 weeks.

If you want to overwinter tuberous-rooted begonias, lift the plants (with the soil still attached) in fall when the leaves are yellow and withered. After a week or so, cut the stems to within a few inches of the tuber. Once the stem stub dries completely, shake the soil off the tubers and store in dry peat or coarse sand at 45° to 55°F. Start them again in spring.

Some gardeners dig up favored wax begonias, bring them indoors before first frost to use as houseplants, then take cuttings in spring for garden use. As houseplants, begonias may bloom most of the year. Pinch back stems by at least half to promote new growth. Keep soil damp but not wet. Mist leaves occasionally. Keep in sun or some shade. When bringing any plant indoors, consider that you also may be transferring pests and diseases indoors. These can spread rapidly to other household plants.

Problems

Leaves with powdery white patches. Cause: Powdery mildew. This fungal disease is very common on begonias. For control information, see "Powdery Mildew" on page 322.

Flower buds drop off. Causes: Excess water; high temperatures. Poor drainage and overwatering are the prime causes of early bud drop. Ease up on the watering and plant begonias in humus-rich soil with good drainage next time. Overly high temperatures also cause bud drop. In areas with unexpected hot spells, mulch roots and mist plants in late morning.

Leaves with angular brown blotches. Cause: Leaf nematodes. Microscopic, wormlike creatures, known as leaf nematodes, may be feeding on the affected leaves. They cause brown blotches that enlarge until the leaves curl up and drop off. Symptoms usually appear on lower leaves first and spread to upper leaves. Plant growth is stunted; new leaves may not appear.

Remove and destroy infected leaves and the next two leaves directly above them. Do not let affected plants touch unaffected ones. Water from below rather than above; nematodes can move from one plant to another through water. Leaf nematodes can survive 3 or more years in the soil or surrounding debris. If you have a problem, don't replant begonias in that area.

Leaves with fuzzy, brown or gray spots. Cause: Botrytis. Also called gray mold, *Botrytis* fungus tends to attack weak plants, causing fluffy, gray, white, or tan mold. Once established, the disease moves into healthy plant tissue. High humidity and cool temperatures favor the infection process, as do crowded plantings, rain, and overhead watering. Botrytis can be a year-round problem in mild winter areas. Remove and destroy infected leaves, stems, and flowers. Thin plants to encourage good air circulation. See "Botrytis Blight" on page 312 for more information.

Leaves with spots. Cause: Leaf spot. Both bacteria and fungi cause leaf spot on begonias. Bacterial leaf spot produces small blisters that are brown with yellow margins; fungi may form brown, black, or transparent spots. For control information, see "Leaves with spots" on page 99.

Leaves, stems, and buds distorted. Cause: Aphids. See "Aphids" on page 250 for controls.

Leaves yellow; plant weakened. Cause: Whiteflies. For controls, see "Whiteflies" on page 290.

Leaves and stems with white, cottony clusters. Cause: Mealybugs. See "Mealybugs" on page 273 for control information.

Stems with soft, water-soaked spots. Cause: Stem rot. Both bacterial and fungal infections can cause begonia stems to rot. If you catch the stem spots when they are small, try cutting them out with a razor blade or sharp knife. Remove and destroy seriously infected leaves, stems, and plants. These diseases can spread quickly, so wash your hands and tools after working with infected plants. Avoid overcrowding and overhead watering; pick a site with good air circulation. Keep mulch a few inches away from

the stem. Don't replant begonias in affected areas.

Leaves with reddish brown lines. Cause: Thrips. These tiny, light brown, fast-moving insects generally attack leaves, causing reddish brown lines or spots on upper leaf surfaces and silvery blotches on leaf undersides. Stems, buds, and flowers can also be affected. Remove and destroy severely infested plants.

Leaves with large, ragged holes. Cause: Slugs and snails. See "Slugs/Snails" on page 284 for controls.

BERBERIS Barberry

Barberries are spiny, deciduous or evergreen shrubs commonly used as hedges, barriers, or foundation plants. Many states prohibit growing common barberry (*Berberis vulgaris*), which is an alternate host to a rust fungus that also attacks cereal grains; it has also been designated as an invasive plant. Check with your extension agent for local restrictions.

Barberries grow in sun or partial shade and prefer well-drained soil. They require little care and tolerate even severe pruning. Set out container-grown or bareroot plants in spring or fall. Pests and diseases are seldom a problem on cultivated barberries.

Problems

Leaves and shoots blackened; leaves with moist or brown sunken spots. Cause: Anthracnose. See "Leaves and shoots blackened; leaves with moist or brown sunken spots" on page 214 for control suggestions.

Leaves wrinkled and discolored. Cause: Aphids. See "Aphids" on page 250 for control measures.

Leaves chewed; branch tips with webbing. Cause: Barberry webworms. These 1½-inch black caterpillars tie together leaves and twigs, forming a web nest in midsummer as they feed on the leaves. If not too numerous, remove nests by hand. Control large infestations with three applications of BTK made 1 week apart. Use pyrethrin as a last resort.

Leaves shrivel and turn brown. Cause: Barberry wilt. This soilborne fungus attacks water-conducting tissue, causing leaves to wilt and eventually killing the entire plant. Remove the whole affected plant and its surrounding soil; replace with fresh soil.

Leaves with notched leaf margins. Cause: Japanese weevils. The ¼-inch brown adults attack foliage, and the legless white grubs feed on roots. See "Root Weevils" on page 279 for controls.

Twigs covered in small reddish brown bumps. Cause: Barberry scale. Heavy infestations may cause yellowing foliage and stunted growth, leading to the death of the plant. See "Leaves yellow; stems and leaves covered with small bumps" on page 213 for controls.

Whole plant stunted and lacking vigor. Cause: Nematodes. See "Whole plant stunted and lacking vigor" on page 215 for more information.

BERGENIA Bergenia

Bergenias are sturdy, low-growing border plants with rose-pink flower clusters borne above the foliage in early spring. Broad, glossy leaves are 10 inches long and heart-shaped in the case of heartleaf bergenia (*Bergenia cordifolia*), oval in the case of leather bergenia (*B. crassifolia*). The foliage takes on a dark burgundy color in fall; leaves are evergreen but often damaged by cold weather. Space plants 1 to 1½ feet apart in average, well-drained soil in a partially shaded spot.

Bergenia's large, low leaves form a haven for slugs and snails. See "Slugs/Snails" on page 284 for control information.

BETULA Birch

Birches are deciduous trees with simple leaves. They are popular as single or multiple-stemmed specimen trees; attractive features include their striking trunks, peeling bark, graceful branches, and magnificent fall color.

Most birches grow best in cool climates and almost invariably perform better in the northern portions of their range. Choose a species suited to your area by consulting with your local extension service or a reputable nursery. Choose a site with light shade and moist but well-drained, acidic soil. Transplant in spring as balled-and-burlapped specimens. Don't prune in winter or early spring, when trees can "bleed" sap; late summer is a better time.

Birches are relatively short-lived, especially when stressed, and they are beset by a number of insect pests that can cause serious damage and even loss. Fortunately, you can prevent most of the common problems by planting trees in the right conditions and keeping them vigorous. Fertilize regularly, and water deeply during drought. Some species, such as river birch (*Betula nigra*), are less prone to common birch pests.

Species that are noted for their predominantly white bark develop this characteristic slowly; do not be disturbed if the young plant you have acquired is not white when you get it!

Problems

Leaves blister and turn brown. Cause: Birch leafminers. Perhaps the most serious and prevalent of all birch pests, birch leafminers produce ¼-inch white larvae that feed between the upper and lower surfaces of the leaves. Several generations occur each year; the first, usually active in May, is most destructive. White-barked birches are especially susceptible, including European white birch (*B. pendula*) and paper birch (*B. papyrifera*). Selecting appropriate species for your area is the best control. Remove infested leaves. Repeated applications of insecticidal soap will kill the small, black, sawfly-like adults, reducing future populations.

Leaves yellow; branch tips dead or dying; trunk with lumps under bark. Cause: Bronze birch borers. The adults are ½- to 1-inch blunt-headed, reddish gray beetles that feed on the foliage, and then lay their eggs in slits in the bark. The eggs hatch into light-colored grubs that tunnel through the bark into the sapwood, starting from the top of the tree and working downward. By the time you see the symptoms, it is usually too late to save the tree. If the damage is not yet severe, you could try pruning out and destroying the infested parts. The best control for borers is planting trees in the right conditions and keeping them healthy and vigorous. Avoid planting European white birch (*B. pendula*), which is very susceptible to this pest.

Leaves skeletonized. Causes: Cankerworms; birch skeletonizers; Japanese beetles. Cankerworms are ½- to 1-inch yellow, green, or brown caterpillars that feed on the foliage of birches, often defoliating the tree. To avoid this problem, apply a paper or foam tree band coated with a sticky substance, such as Tanglefoot, around the base of the tree in spring to keep females from climbing up to lay their eggs. Apply fresh coats in September and February to trap both spring and fall canker-worms. If their feeding becomes a problem, spray with BTK as soon as you notice them, and con-tinue every 2 weeks until the pests are gone.

Birch skeletonizers also feed on foliage, leaving brown leaves with visible leaf veins behind. These ¼-inch yellowish green caterpillars do the most damage in July and August. In most cases this pest is a problem only every few years, and the damage happens so late in the season that no control is necessary. If you want to protect young trees from serious damage, apply BTK or superior oil as soon as you spot pests in midsummer.

Japanese beetles are foliage feeders, too. For information on controlling them, see "Japanese Beetle" on page 269.

Plant defoliated. Cause: Gypsy moths. See "Gypsy Moth" on page 268 for control suggestions.

Trunks or branch crotches with swollen, cracked lesions. Cause: Canker. This fungal disease attacks at the forks of branches, causing swellings that crack open to expose the wood. See "Trunk or branches with oozing lesions; branch tips die back."

Leaves tunneled. Cause: Leafminers. See "Leaves tunneled" on page 213 for controls.

Leaves wilt or curl and pucker. Cause: Birch aphids. These small, pear-shaped insects attack the foliage, weakening and distorting the growth. They also produce copious quantities of honeydew, which attracts ants and encourages the growth of black-colored, sooty mold. Spray plants with a strong jet of water to knock off the pests. See "Leaves wrinkled and discolored" on page 211 for more controls.

Branches die. Cause: Dieback. This fungal disease produces symptoms very similar to those caused by bronze birch borers, except for the lumpy bark. Trees weakened by drought, low fertility, or borers are most susceptible to infection. Prevent this problem by planting trees in the right spot and watering during drought to keep them growing vigorously. If symptoms do occur, prune out and destroy or dispose of infected branches.

Leaves with powdery white coating. Cause: Powdery mildew. See "Leaves with powdery white coating" on page 213 for controls.

Leaves with spots. Cause: Leaf spot. See "Leaves with spots" on page 213 for control suggestions.

BLACKBERRY *Rubus* **spp. (Rosaceae)**

Blackberries are perennials that bear fruit on second-year canes. Some cultivars grow erect and some bear long, trailing canes. Blackberries are hardy in Zones 5–9.

Like other bramble fruits, blackberries need full sun and well-drained, moisture-retentive soil. Train plants to posts or fences. Prune annually. Pull unwanted suckers. On erect blackberries, pinch the tips of 3-foot canes to force growth of lateral shoots. During the dormant season, shorten all lateral shoots to about 1 to 1½ feet. For both types of blackberry, cut away all fruiting canes right after harvest. In winter thin canes to leave 3 or 4 canes per clump for erect types and 8 to 12 canes per clump for trailing types.

Blackberries are self-pollinating and require no cross-pollination to set fruit. Blackberries belong to the same genus as raspberries and are affected by similar pests and diseases. For more information on problems and solutions, see the "Raspberry" entry, beginning on page 179.

Problems

Flowers with reddish, twisted petals; no fruit set. Cause: Double blossom. Also known as rosette, this fungal disease causes plants to form witch's brooms—dense masses of deformed twigs with pale leaves. Remove infected canes as soon as you notice them. To help prevent the spread of the fungus, spray the whole planting with copper two or three times at 10-day intervals. If the disease is rampant, mow down the whole planting and destroy the newly cut canes. Avoid planting sites near wild brambles, which may carry the disease. Resistant cultivars include 'Apache', 'Arapaho', 'Hull', 'Humble', and 'Navaho'.

Fruit covered with light gray fuzz. Cause: Fruit rot. Especially common during wet weather, this fungal disease appears less frequently where plants have good air circulation and proper pruning. To control fruit rot, harvest berries often. Pick infected fruit and discard it far away from your blackberry patch.

Fruit fails to ripen or remains red and sour. Cause: Redberry mites. A growing-season dilution of horticultural oil applied just as fruits begin to turn pink and repeated at 2- to 3-week intervals gives good control of these microscopic mites. If infestations have been severe in past seasons, apply lime-sulfur in early spring when new shoots are 1 inch long and again when canes have about 1 foot of new growth.

Canes and leaves with purple spots. Causes: Anthracnose; leaf and cane spot disease. Controls are the same for both of these fungal diseases. Keep plantings well pruned to promote good air circulation. Remove and destroy infected canes right after harvest. Spray with lime-sulfur just as buds begin to turn green. Resistant cultivars include 'Apache', 'Arapaho', "Black Satin', 'Choctaw', 'Dirksen Thornless', and 'Navaho'.

Leaf undersides with bright orange pustules appearing in spring. Cause: Orange rust. This incurable fungal disease infects the entire plant. Plants become weak and unfruitful. Diseased plants never recover; infection spreads quickly to neighboring plants. Dig and destroy plants as soon as you notice disease symptoms. Avoid sites near wild blackberries, which may carry the disease.

Late in the season, a benign leaf rust appears on some blackberries; disregard it. The cultivars 'Cheyenne', 'Chickasaw', 'Comanche', 'Ebony King', 'Eldorado', 'Raven', and 'Shawnee' are resistant to orange rust.

Canes dying. Cause: Borers. For information on identifying and controlling borers, see "Canes dying; break off easily" and "Cane tips wilted and dying" on page 182.

Canes turn yellow and die in midsummer. Cause: Verticillium wilt. This is a common soilborne fungal disease. Typically, leaves yellow, wilt, and fall before the entire cane dies. Avoid planting blackberries in the same spot as other Verticillium-susceptible crops, such as strawberries, potatoes, tomatoes, and eggplants. Soil solarization may prevent the disease. Verticillium-resistant cultivars include 'Logan', 'Marion', and 'Olallie'.

Canes with wartlike or corky swellings; canes dying. Cause: Crown gall. Crown gall bacteria live in the soil and enter plants through wounds. For information and controls, see "Crown Gall" on page 340.

BLUEBERRY *Vaccinium* spp. (Ericaceae)

Blueberries are deciduous shrubs ranging in height from 1 foot for lowbush blueberries (*Vaccinium angustifolium*) to 6 feet for highbush blueberries (*V. corymbosum*) to over 30 feet for rabbiteye blueberries (*V. ashei*). The flowers look like dainty white bells and appear in spring on shoots that grew the previous season. Blueberries are hardy in Zones 3–9, depending on species and cultivars.

Culture

Blueberries require full sun and well-drained, moisture-retentive, acidic soil with a pH of 4.0 to 5.0. Of the three species, highbush blueberries are the most finicky about soil. Blueberries generally grow well in soil enriched with acidic organic material, such as peat moss, composted pine needles or oak leaves, or compost made from pine, oak, or hemlock bark. Fertilize with acidic fertilizers, such as cottonseed meal or soybean meal. Blueberries enjoy thick organic mulch.

Most blueberries are not wholly self-pollinating. Plant at least two different cultivars near each other for adequate cross-pollination.

Prune plants each winter, beginning when bushes are about 4 years old. On highbush and rabbiteye plants, remove drooping or very old branches and thin out branches where growth is too dense. Cut lowbush plants to the ground every third year for a harvest in 2 of every 3 years.

Flower and Fruit Problems

Berries soft and mushy. Cause: Blueberry maggots. If you find ⅜-inch white maggots inside berries, you've discovered the larvae of the blueberry maggot fly. This insect, closely related to the apple maggot fly, deposits eggs just under the skin of the fruit from late June to August. Eggs hatch into fruit-devouring maggots that later drop to the soil and pupate over the winter. To reduce the number of maggots that pupate in the soil through the next winter, harvest frequently and destroy any infested berries you find. Another control is to trap adult flies on sticky red spheres like the ones used to trap apple maggot flies. Hang one trap per highbush plant or one per several lowbush plants before the first berries turn blue. For information on making these maggot fly traps, see "Fruit dimpled; brown tunnels through flesh" on page 32.

Berries shriveled and webbed together with silk. Causes: Cherry fruitworms; cranberry fruitworms. Berries will contain sawdustlike material and either a white caterpillar (cherry fruitworm) or a yellowish green caterpillar (cranberry fruitworm). These are the larvae of two different moth species that lay eggs on berries in spring. Larvae hatching from these eggs bore into berries near the stem end and web berries together as they feed. You cannot spray anything to kill worms inside the fruit. To reduce damage from these pests without sprays, harvest berries frequently and destroy infested fruit to prevent larvae from maturing. Regularly clean up dropped and damaged berries.

Berries drop early; mature berries turn gray, shriveled, and hard. Cause: Mummy berry. This fungal disease overwinters on dried, diseased berries called mummies and spreads most rapidly in cold, wet springs. Control mummy berry by picking all mummies off the plant. In the spring, cultivate around bushes to bury dropped mummies, or add mulch to cover the remaining fungal spores. Resistant cultivars include 'Bluejay', 'Bluetta', 'Burlington', 'Collins', 'Darrow', 'Dixie', 'Jersey', and 'Rubel'.

Blossoms covered with brown splotches or brownish gray mold. Cause: Botrytis blight. This fungal disease spreads most rapidly when cool, wet weather extends throughout the bloom period. An effective control for Botrytis is to carry a paper bag into the garden and carefully pick off and discard blighted blossoms and foliage as soon as you find them. After working around infected plants, wash your hands thoroughly before working with healthy plants. Also space and prune plants to encourage good air circulation and rapid drying of plants after rain. Avoid wetting the foliage when watering and avoid excess fertilization, which brings on lush growth and increased susceptibility to this blight.

Fruit disappears. Cause: Birds. These creatures love blueberries so much that unprotected bushes are often stripped clean of berries, even before they are fully ripe! The only sure protection is a net draped over the planting and secured at ground level to prevent birds from getting underneath.

Leaf and Branch Problems

New leaves with black centers; growing tips wilted. Cause: Mummy berry. This fungal disease spreads most easily in cold, wet spring weather. For more information, see "Berries drop early; mature berries turn gray, shriveled, and hard" on this page.

Leaves or twigs covered with brownish gray mold. Cause: Botrytis blight. An effective control for this fungal disease is to remove and discard blighted foliage as soon as you see it. For more information, see "Blossoms covered with brown splotches or brownish gray mold" on this page.

New leaves yellow with green veins. Cause: Iron deficiency. The soil usually has sufficient iron but is not acidic enough to make iron available to the plant. Spray leaves with iron salts or chelates for quick relief of symptoms. A long-term solution is to reduce the soil pH by mulching with an acidic material, such as pine needles.

Cane dieback. Causes: Blueberry cane canker; Fusicoccum canker; Phomopsis twig blight. Blueberry cane canker, most prevalent in the South, shows up as reddish, conical stem swellings. The next year these swellings become blisterlike, light gray, and then black and fissured. If this disease is a problem in your area, plant rabbiteye blueberries, which are not susceptible to cane canker. Or plant a highbush cultivar resistant to cane canker, such as 'Jersey'.

Fusicoccum canker, a fungal disease more common in colder regions, begins as red stem spots that enlarge and develop a bull's-eye pattern. 'Rancocas' is a resistant cultivar; 'Bluecrop', 'Coville', and 'Rubel' are moderately resistant.

Phomopsis twig blight causes symptoms similar to those of Fusicoccum canker but without the characteristic bull's-eyes. Phomopsis infection causes berries to ripen prematurely. Resistant cultivars include 'Bluetta' and 'Elliott'.

Other blights also cause cane dieback, and the best course for all such problems is to prune away diseased branches as soon as you spot them. Prune and cultivate carefully to avoid wounds that admit fungi. To avoid spreading disease further as you prune, sterilize pruning tools between cuts in isopropyl alcohol or a 10 percent bleach solution (1 part bleach to 9 parts water).

Leaves skeletonized. Cause: Japanese beetles. Beginning in early summer, these metallic blue-green beetles with bronze wing covers like to feed on plants in the sun. In early morning, shake beetles from plants onto dropcloths, then drown them in soapy water; or shake beetles into a can of soapy water to drown. Traps baited with floral or fruit scents plus pheromones may be effective if placed at some distance from plants, but a trap placed in the middle of a planting may attract more beetles than normal to the garden. If you use traps, be sure to place them well away from the plantings you're trying to protect.

Populations of this pest naturally decline by midsummer. Where damage is severe, cover plants with floating row cover; spray plants attacked by beetles with insecticidal soap. As a last resort, spray with neem.

BRACTEANTHA Strawflower

These 1½- to 3-foot Australian natives are best known as an integral part of dried flower arrangements. If picked when partially opened, strawflow-ers hold their color well and last for several years indoors. Colors include white, yellow, salmon, red, and pink.

Sow seeds indoors 6 to 8 weeks before the last outdoor frost. Do not cover seeds; they need light during the 7- to –10-day germination period. Transplant seedlings 9 to 12 inches apart. Where summers are long, direct-sow strawflowers in late spring or early summer. Plant in full sun in well-drained, moderately fertile, slightly moist soil. They are fairly drought tolerant once established. Taller cultivars may need staking. Little fertilizer is needed; too much fertilizer results in many leaves and few flowers. Pests and diseases are rarely a problem.

BROCCOLI *Brassica oleracea* Botrytis group (Cruciferae)

Broccoli is a cool-season vegetable grown for its crisp green heads of flower buds. Broccoli and cabbage require similar culture and are attacked by the same diseases and insects: See the Cabbage entry beginning on page 56 for culture and information.

Prevent problems by planting the following improved cultivars: 'Arcadia', 'Eureka', 'Fiesta F1', and 'Greenbelt F1' are black-rot resistant; 'Fiesta F1' is resistant to Fusarium yellows; 'Arcadia', 'Diplomat', 'Gypsy F1', 'Marathon F1', and 'Windsor F1' are tolerant of downy mildew; and 'DeCicco' resists flea beetles.

In addition to the problems listed on the opposite page, transplants exposed to cool temperatures (35° to 45°F) for 10 days or more may form tiny, useless flower heads prematurely. High temperatures can cause similar tiny head formation. Broccoli grows best at temperatures between 45° and 75°F. Harvest heads when buds are still tight and dark green or dusky violet, except for 'Romanesco', which should be yellow-green.

Problems

Heads small and uneven; stems hollow.
Cause: Potassium deficiency. Prevent problems by spraying plants with seaweed extract every 2 weeks. Check soil potassium with a soil test and amend as necessary.

Heads with black or discolored centers.
Causes: Fungal rot; cold injury. Broccoli heads rot when water collects between the individual flower buds. Avoid wetting heads when watering. Cold weather can also cause black areas in the center of heads. Protect plants with row cover when temperatures below 40°F are predicted.

BROWALLIA Browallia, sapphire flower

Browallias bear profuse quantities of purple or blue, 1- to 2-inch flowers. They grow in bush form, 10 to 18 inches high, or will cascade over container edges. They bloom in summer and into fall and do well as bedding plants, hanging baskets, or houseplants.

Browallias grow easily from seed sown indoors in March. Do not cover seed; they need light to germinate. Seedlings appear in 2 weeks. Pinch when 6 inches tall for bushier plants. Transplant when night temperatures remain consistently above 50°F; space 10 inches apart.

Browallias need partial shade and moderately rich soil. Keep the soil evenly moist. Fertilize lightly but regularly. Pests and diseases seldom bother browallias. Whiteflies sometimes feed on plants; see "Whiteflies" on page 290.

BRUSSELS SPROUTS *Brassica oleracea* Gemmifera group (Cruciferae)

Brussels sprouts are a cool-season vegetable grown for their small, cabbage-shaped buds. They are one of the hardiest members of the cabbage family and can tolerate a lower soil pH (5.5 to 6.8) than any of the other brassicas. But they are less tolerant of heat. In warmer climates, grow sprouts in soil with high clay content if you have a choice, and shade the soil around roots. Harvest sprouts when they are 1 inch in diameter or smaller and still tight. Twist them off gently, starting at the base of the stem.

Brussels sprouts and cabbage require similar culture and are attacked by the same diseases and insects: See the Cabbage entry beginning on page 56 for culture and information on problems.

In addition to problems outlined in the cabbage entry, a combination of cold injury and viral disease can cause leaves with black specks. Destroy infected plants. Caterpillars will bore small holes into sprouts; see "Leaves with large, ragged holes" on page 59 for more details and controls. Plants deficient in potassium have poorly developed sprouts: Spray with seaweed extract at transplanting and repeat several times to prevent problems. Check potassium levels with a soil test, and amend as necessary.

BUDDLEIA Butterfly bush

Butterfly bush (*Buddleia davidii*) is a deciduous shrub producing long spikes of bloom in midsummer. In severe climates plants die back to the roots over winter and are grown as perennials; where this does not occur, cut them back to near ground level to promote healthy growth and flowering.

Buddleias thrive in rich, loamy soil in full sun. They are remarkably free of insect and disease problems. They have been designated as invasive plants in many states. Japanese beetles have been known to attack them, but rarely severely. Handpicking will usually suffice; stronger control methods can endanger the butterflies that these plants attract.

BULBS *See* "Flowers" on page 96

BUXUS Boxwood

Evergreen shrubs with glossy, opposite leaves, boxwoods are widely used for hedges.

Boxwoods prefer a site partially sheltered from winter winds. They will flourish in a range of conditions, from full sun to deep shade, and can adapt to almost any soil except poorly drained sites or heavy clays. Set out as balled-and-burlapped or container-grown plants in spring. Set out plants no deeper than they grew in the nursery. A thick layer of mulch will help keep roots cool and retain moisture. Clean up all fallen leaves and remove debris from branch crotches in autumn.

Problems

Leaves blistered and browned. Cause: Boxwood leafminers. The ⅛-inch orange larvae tunnel and feed within leaves. After they feed, the maggots change to the adult form and emerge as ⅛-inch orange, mosquito-like flies. Use yellow sticky traps to monitor the emergence of adults. When they begin to appear (usually late April and early May), spray plants with horticultural oil at a growing-season dilution.

Leaves curled and cupped around stem tips. Cause: Boxwood psyllids. The eggs and larvae of this tiny green insect overwinter on buds and infest new leaves in spring. At the first sign of damage, spray plants with insecticidal soap. Use pyrethrin as a last resort for serious infestations.

Leaves stippled with yellow; foliage

webbed. Cause: Spider mites. See "Mites, Spider" on page 275 for controls.

Leaves brown; twigs die back. Cause: Winter damage. Cold, dry winter winds can seriously injure tender growth. Avoid damage by spraying leaves with an antidesiccant in fall, or provide shelter for plants with burlap windbreaks. Mulch heavily in fall, and water well before the ground freezes. Fertilize plants in early spring only; summer feeding promotes easily damaged, late-season growth. Prune out affected parts.

Leaves yellow; stems and leaves covered with small bumps. Cause: Scales. See "Scales, Armored" on page 282 for control suggestions.

Leaves yellow, sparse, distorted, or with brown edges; branches die; growth stunted. Cause: Decline. For more information, see "Leaves yellow, sparse, distorted, or with brown edges; branches die; growth stunted" on page 214.

Whole plant stunted and lacking vigor. Cause: Nematodes. See "Whole plant stunted and lacking vigor" on page 215 for controls.

CABBAGE *Brassica oleracea*, Capitata group (Cruciferae)

Cabbage is a cool-season biennial vegetable grown as an annual for its crisp, dense leaf heads. There are green, red, and purple cultivars; Chinese types; and types with savoyed, or crinkled, leaves.

Culture

Plant cabbages in full sun in fertile, well-drained soil with a pH between 6.0 and 6.8. If you have a choice of sites, spring plantings do best in lighter, sandier soils, while fall plantings do better in soils that contain more clay. Plants grow best in temperatures between 40° and 75°F. Transplants exposed to cool temperatures (35° to 45°F) for 10 or more days may bolt, or go to flower, prematurely. High temperatures also cause bolting.

These plants have very shallow roots, so be sure to keep the top few inches of soil from drying out. Fluctuations in soil moisture after the heads have formed may cause them to split. Mulching helps to balance and conserve moisture. Most fungi that cause cabbage diseases spread in running water or by water droplets, so don't water with overhead sprinklers. Cabbages are heavy feeders and are susceptible to several nutrient deficiencies, including boron, calcium, phosphorus, and potassium.

To avoid diseases and pests that persist in the soil, don't plant cabbages where members of the cabbage family (broccoli, cauliflower, brussels sprouts, or kale) have grown for at least 3 years. Also, avoid areas with cabbage-family weeds, such as wild mustard. Destroy all crop residues, including roots, after harvest.

Problems

Stems of transplants shrunken and dark near soil line. Cause: Wirestem. Weak plants may wilt and die as the disease progresses; seedlings that survive yield poorly. Later in the season, the same fungal disease rots the head from the bottom up. Spray plants with copper before symptoms develop if you have had problems in the past.

Leaves of transplants purple. Cause: Phosphorus deficiency. Phosphorus is not readily available in cool spring soils. Spray plants with seaweed extract to correct.

Leaves yellow; plant stunted. Cause: Nitrogen deficiency. When this deficiency develops, older leaves turn yellow first. Spray plants and drench roots with fish emulsion to correct.

Leaves yellow; plant stunted; plant wilts on bright, hot days. Causes: Club root; root-knot nematodes; cabbage maggots. If you suspect any of these pests, pull up a plant and examine the roots. Roots that are enlarged and clublike indicate club root, a fungal disease; remove and destroy diseased plants. Prevent problems by rotating crops and improving drainage. Add lime to raise the soil pH to 7.2 or above. Cabbage can tolerate this pH, but club-root fungi will be less active.

Cabbage roots covered with irregularly shaped galls are infected with root-knot nematodes. Destroy severely infected plants. Reduce the number of nematodes in the soil by solarizing the soil, keeping the area clear of crops and weeds for a summer, or by planting a winter cover crop of wheat. Applying parasitic nematodes or chitin to the soil can also helps control pest nematodes.

Cabbage roots riddled with slimy, winding tunnels are infested with cabbage maggots. Larvae are white, $\frac{1}{4}$-inch maggots that feed on roots and transmit bacterial and fungal diseases. Adults look somewhat like houseflies and lay eggs on the soil near the base of the plant. Remove and destroy infested plants. Frequent, light cultivation when plants are young helps to decrease larval populations. Or plant each transplant through an X-shaped slit in the center of a 6- to 8-inch square of tar paper to prevent the adults from laying eggs near the stems. Solarizing the soil will help reduce maggot populations in problem areas.

Leaves yellow; plant stunted; stems twisted. Cause: Fusarium yellows. Leaves of afflicted plants drop off, starting at the bottom and working up, often leaving a bare stem. Cut stems reveal darkened vascular tissue in afflicted areas. This fungal disease usually occurs soon after transplanting. Destroy infected plants. Use at least a 5-year rotation to prevent problems, or plant resistant cultivars such as 'Blue Dynasty', 'Bravo', 'Charmant', 'Early Jersey Wakefield', 'Green Cup', 'Market Prize', 'Market Victor', 'Platinum

Dynasty', 'Red Danish', 'Stonehead', and 'Tender-sweet'.

Leaves curled and yellow; plant stunted.
Cause: Aphids. Look for small, green, pink, gray, black, or white, fluffy-coated, soft-bodied insects feeding on plants. Aphids can also transmit viral diseases. Control by knocking the pests off the plant with a blast of water, or use an insecticidal soap spray. Spray severe infestations with neem.

Leaves with yellow, V-shaped spots on margins. Cause: Black rot. As this bacterial disease progresses, yellow areas on the leaves enlarge and veins turn black. Infected leaves die and drop off. Stems have internal black streaks. Heads are dwarfed and often one-sided. Destroy infected plants. If you've had past problems with black rot, preventive sprays of copper may be helpful when wet weather favors disease development. Resistant cultivars include 'Atlantis, 'Blues F1', 'Green Cup', 'Minuet', and 'Platinum Dynasty'.

Leaves with yellow-brown, concentrically ringed spots. Cause: Alternaria blight. This fungal disease attacks lower leaves first. Spots merge and leaves die as the disease progresses. Plants eventually die. Spray plants with copper at the first sign of symptoms. Plant tolerant cultivars such as 'Hybrid H' to prevent problems.

Leaves with white and yellow blotches.
Cause: Harlequin bugs. Leaves turn brown, wilt, and die in severe infestations. Look for flat, ½-inch-long, shield-shaped stink bugs with red and black, spotted markings. Nymphs look like adults but are smaller and more round. Handpick to control mild infestations; dust with pyrethrin as a last resort. Destroy crop residues after harvest to eliminate pests.

Leaves with pale spots, white growth on undersides. Cause: Downy mildew. Infected heads have dark patches on leaves. As the disease progresses, infected areas enlarge and turn tan and papery. Control by spraying plants with potassium bicarbonate or baking-soda-and-soap spray (1 teaspoon baking soda, 1 teaspoon liquid dish soap, 1 quart water). Resistant cultivars include 'Blues F1', 'China Pride', 'Minuet', and 'Tendersweet'; 'Hybrid H' is tolerant of downy mildew.

Leaves with white-bronze spots. Cause: Thrips. Severe infestations cause leaves to wilt. These tiny insects look like grains of pepper. Trap with sticky blue traps or spray insecticidal soap, making sure to cover undersides of leaves where thrips feed. Thrips-tolerant cultivars include 'Farao F1', 'Huron', and 'Super Red 80 F1'.

Leaves with brown to gray spots; stem has sunken areas. Cause: Black leg. Leaf spots are speckled with tiny black dots. As sunken areas on the stem enlarge, they may girdle the plant and cause it to wilt and die. Dead leaves remain attached to the plant. Spray plants, especially the stems, with copper at the first sign of this fungal disease. When spraying stems, try to avoid spraying copper on the soil, because it is toxic to many soil organisms, including earthworms. Prevent black leg by using a 4-year rotation and improving soil drainage.

Leaves with brown tips. Causes: Excessive heat; calcium deficiency. Browning of the tips of outer leaves is caused by extreme heat. Cabbage is sensitive to bright sun and temperatures above 80°F. Plant cultivars that resist tipburn, such as 'Greenwich', 'Multikeeper', and 'Red Dynasty'.

Brown leaf tips inside the head are caused by calcium deficiency. Many factors contribute to poor calcium uptake. To prevent problems, keep soil moisture constant and side-dress plants with compost to provide balanced nutrition.

Leaves cracked and corky; stem water-

soaked or head hollow. Cause: Boron deficiency. Plants in the cabbage family need lots of boron. Spray plants with seaweed extract when transplanting and repeat several times until head formation to help prevent problems. Raise the boron level of the soil by adding 1 tablespoon of borax dissolved in 1 gallon of water, or 10 pounds of kelp, per 100 square feet.

Leaves riddled with small holes. Cause: Striped flea beetles. These small, shiny, black beetles hop when disturbed. They can transmit viral and bacterial diseases. Protect young plants with row cover until they have at least six leaves. 'Early Jersey Wakefield' tolerates flea beetle damage better than most cultivars.

Leaves with large, ragged holes. Cause: Caterpillars. Look for dark green excrement at the base of leaves or plant. Imported cabbageworm is a velvety green, slow-moving caterpillar up to $1\frac{1}{4}$ inch long. Adults are small white butterflies. Cabbage loopers are light green, $1\frac{1}{2}$-inch-long caterpillars with a white stripe along each side. They travel with a characteristic "looping" movement, like an inchworm. Adults are gray moths. Diamondback moth caterpillars are pale green with light brown heads, $\frac{5}{16}$ inch long, pointed at both ends, and covered with fine black hairs. Adults are slender, $\frac{1}{2}$-inch-long moths.

Apply a BTK spray as soon as active caterpillars or feeding are observed; remember to look inside heads for early signs of feeding. Pheromone traps are available for male cabbage looper moths; spray with BTK 1 to 2 weeks after the first moths are caught in the traps. Help reduce problems by planting cultivars—such as 'Danish Ballhead', 'Early Jersey Wakefield', and 'Red Ace'—that are less susceptible to cabbage looper and imported cabbageworm feeding.

These caterpillars are all parasitized by wasps, and other beneficials feed on both eggs and larvae. A native virus may also kill caterpillars later in the season. Infected caterpillars move slowly, become yellow, and die. Let nature work for you and avoid handpicking or spraying if caterpillars are infected or covered with the small, white, spindle-shaped eggs of parasitic wasps.

Heads small and soft; color poor in red cabbage. Cause: Potassium deficiency. Check with a soil test and amend as needed.

Heads split. Cause: Excessive water. Keep soil constantly moist, but not saturated, especially when heads are forming. 'Charmant', 'Farao F1', and 'Tendersweet' are among several cultivars that resist splitting.

Heads rot. Cause: Fungal diseases. A variety of fungi cause cabbage heads to rot. Destroy rotted plants. Spray plants with copper before symptoms develop if you have had problems in the past.

CALENDULA Calendula, pot marigold

Calendulas are herbs that have 1- to 3-inch, orange or yellow flowers, giving bouquets of color for borders and indoor use. Plants grow 1 to 3 feet high with a bushy habit. Calendulas blend well into bedding schemes, herb gardens, and containers.

Sow seeds outdoors in early spring, when a light frost is still possible, or in fall. Indoors, sow 6 to 8 weeks before the last spring frost date, and transplant into warm spring soil. Direct-seed in early summer in mild-summer climates for color in late summer or fall. Plant seeds $\frac{1}{4}$ inch deep; they need darkness to germinate. They should sprout in 1 to 2 weeks. Thin seedlings to 1 inch apart.

For earliest color, transplant or seed in full sun. In hot climates plants appreciate some afternoon shade. While calendulas tolerate poor soil, they prefer average soil and must have good drainage. Water regularly, keeping soil slightly moist. When first buds appear, pinch back the main stem to promote maximum flowering. In adverse conditions, such as excess heat, calendulas may still flower, but stems will be shorter.

Problems

Leaves, stems, and buds distorted. Cause: Aphids. For controls, see "Aphids" on page 250.

Leaves with large, ragged holes. Causes: Imported cabbageworms; slugs and snails. Cabbageworms are green caterpillars with a yellow back stripe and yellow side spots. Handpick cabbageworms or spray leaves with BTK when pests first appear.

Slugs and snails cause similar damage, and leave behind slimy trails of mucus. For controls, see "Cabbageworms, Imported" on page 255 and "Slugs/Snails" on page 284.

Leaves greenish yellow; growth poor. Cause: Aster yellows. For more information see "Yellows" on page 321.

CALLISTEPHUS China aster

Not true asters, China asters provide showy, single or double, daisylike blossoms from midsummer until autumn with successive plantings. There are early, mid-season, and late-flowering cultivars. A range of color choices is available, including blue, purple, pink, red, rose, yellow, or white. Individual flowers can reach 5 inches wide; petal types are quilled, spooned, or curled. Plant size varies from 9 to 24 inches high, with a possible 1½-foot spread. Low-growing cultivars make good edging plants. Taller cultivars are popular for long-lasting cut flowers. Plants will not rebloom once flowers have been cut.

Direct-sow outdoors a week or two after the last frost, barely covering the seed. Seeds germinate within 2 weeks. Or, for earlier flowers, sow seeds indoors 6 to 8 weeks before the last frost. Move seedlings to individual 3-inch pots when the first true leaves appear. Move plants outdoors when nights are consistently above 50°F. Handle carefully during transplanting to avoid damaging the roots. Space 6 to 15 inches apart. Each plant blooms for about 4 weeks. Successive plantings 2 weeks apart are the key to a long display season.

China asters tolerate light shade only. They thrive in fertile, moist but well-drained soil in full sun. China asters are shallow-rooted, so cover soil with a 1-inch mulch to retain soil moisture and keep roots cool. Pinch growing tips to promote bushiness. Water regularly so soil stays slightly moist. Uneven care that slows growth makes the plant susceptible to disease. Remove old flowers. Tall cultivars may need staking to support heavy flowers on the slim stems.

Problems

Leaves greenish yellow; growth poor. Cause: Aster yellows. See "Yellows" on page 321 for controls.

Lower leaves yellow, wilt, die. Cause: Fusarium wilt. Other symptoms of this common fungal disease include yellowing and wilting of one side of plant only; drooping flower heads; stunted mature plants; dark brown areas on stems; and partial or total root decay. Once introduced on diseased plants or transmitted by wind, water, or handling, Fusarium wilt lives on indefinitely in soil. There is no cure. Remove infected plants and dispose of them in sealed containers in household trash. Never plant China asters in the same location 2 years in a row. Wilt-resistant cultivars are available, but they are not completely immune.

Leaves, stems, and buds distorted. Cause: Aphids. For control measures, see "Aphids" on page 250.

CAMELLIA Camellia

Camellias are evergreen shrubs or small trees that bear spectacular flowers. They are popular as foundation plants or hedges in areas where they are hardy. In cold climates grow these plants in a cool greenhouse.

Camellias require a moist, peaty, acidic soil, well enriched with organic matter. Set out as bareroot or container-grown plants in partial shade. A thick layer of mulch will protect the shallow roots and help retain soil moisture.

Problems

Leaves yellow; stems and leaves covered with small bumps. Cause: Scales. See "Scales, Armored" on page 282 for control suggestions.

Flowers turn brown and fall off. Cause: Flower blight. This soilborne fungus causes small brown spots that expand to cover entire petals. See "Flower Blight of Camellia" on page 327 for controls.

Leaves with notched edges. Cause: Fuller rose beetles. The adult is a ⅓-inch, grayish brown beetle with a cream-colored stripe on each side of its body. It feeds at night on foliage. The yellowish, brown-headed larvae feed on plant roots. Handpick adults as they hide in foliage during the day. Place sticky barriers, such as Tanglefoot, around the base of plants to keep adults from climbing up to the leaves. Drench soil around the plant with a solution of parasitic nematodes to control larvae.

CAMPANULA Bellflower, harebell

The profuse, dainty, blue, purple, or white, bell-shaped flowers of *Campanula* spp. brighten gardens from spring through summer. This large genus includes annual, biennial, and perennial species that range in size from low-growing Carpathian harebells (*C. carpatica*) to 2- to 3-inch-tall, peach-leaved bellflowers (*C. persicifolia*).

Mountain natives, bellflowers prefer full sun to light shade; well-drained, organic soil; and regular watering. Siberian bellflower, *C. poscharskyana,* tolerates drought, but most other bellflowers do not. A layer of mulch helps keep the root zone cool and holds in moisture during hot summer weather; a winter mulch protects roots from heaving. Divide plants in spring every 3 to 4 years.

Problems

Leaves, stems, and buds distorted, sticky; clusters of small insects. Cause: Aphids. See "Aphids" on page 250 for controls.

Leaves with large, ragged holes. Cause: Slugs and snails. For controls, see "Slugs/Snails" on page 284.

Leaves and flowers distorted and with brown spots. Cause: Thrips. The same thrips that feed on onions feed on bellflowers. Damage to young plants is most severe. Water stress encourages thrip multiplication and damage. These ¹⁄₅₀- to ¹⁄₂₅-inch, yellow, brown, or black pests are difficult to see with the naked eye, but the streaking, spotting, and distortion caused by a heavy thrips infection is distinctive. See "Thrips" on page 287 for controls.

Leaves yellow and wilting; stems blackened at base; plant topples over. Cause: Stem, root, and crown rots. These problems are common when bellflowers are kept overly wet or are grown in poorly drained soil. The base of an infected plant may show grayish white mold; dark lesions blacken the stem from the soil up, eventually girdling the plant. Remove and destroy infected plants and surrounding soil. Let soil dry somewhat between waterings, and incorporate organic matter to improve soil drainage. Avoid overwatering and overcrowding; keep winter mulch away from the crowns to prevent excess moisture. Protect crowns from injury, especially when plants are dormant and hard to see. Wash tools after working around infected plants.

CANNA Canna

Cannas' large, paddle-shaped leaves and brightly colored red, yellow, orange, pink, white, or variegated flowers add a tropical look to summer and fall gardens. These heat-loving hybrids (*Canna × generalis*) grow 1½ to 8 feet tall with a spread of about 3 feet.

In Zones 8–10 cannas will survive winter temperatures, but in northern zones, the rhizomes are overwintered indoors. In either case, plant rhizomes 3 to 5 inches deep and 1 foot apart in average, moist but well-drained soil in full sun. Both shade and excess nitrogen fertilizer will reduce bloom. In cold-winter areas, start rhizomes indoors in pots as early as February. Move outdoors in spring. If necessary, divide roots at spring planting time. Use a sharp knife, and leave at least one good-size bud on an ample piece of rhizome. Let divisions dry overnight before planting. To overwinter, carefully dig up the rhizomes in fall after frost blackens the leaves. Allow them to dry for a few days, then store them in containers of barely moist sand or perlite in a cool place.

Cannas are vigorous plants, seldom troubled by pests. Japanese beetles along with slugs and snails can chew holes in leaves and flowers. See "Japanese Beetle" on page 269 and "Slugs/Snails" on page 284 for controls. Leafrollers roll leaves into tubes and fasten them with webbing while feeding. Handpick and destroy rolled leaves; encourage parasitic *Trichogramma* wasps. See "Leafrollers" on page 272 for more controls.

CANTALOUPE *Cucumis melo*, Reticulatus group (Cucurbitaceae)

Cantaloupe is a name commonly used for muskmelons in the United States. See the Melon entry, beginning on page 138, for culture and pest information. Harvest when fruit smells ripe and the stem separates easily (slips) from the vine.

CARPINUS Hornbeam

Hornbeams are bushy, slow-growing, alternate-leaved trees. They are occasionally used as specimen trees, but difficulty in transplanting limits their use.

Set out balled-and-burlapped or container-grown plants in early spring. Hornbeams are excellent urban trees and, while preferring full sun, will grow satisfactorily in partial shade. They are widely tolerant of various soil types.

Hornbeams are remarkably free of pest and disease problems. Maple phenacoccus scale may detract from the appearance of the plant, coating the undersides of leaves with fluffy white egg masses. See "Scales, Armored" on page 282 for controls.

CARROT *Daucus carota* var. *sativus* (Umbelliferae)

Carrots are biennial vegetables grown as annuals for their crisp, sweet roots. They are a cool-season crop, hardy enough to be undisturbed by light frosts in spring and fall.

Culture

Carrots grow best in deeply worked, loose soils with a pH between 5.5 and 6.8. No other vegetable is as sensitive to poor soil structure. Misshapen carrots are more often a result of lumpy or compacted soil than any pest problem. Carrots do well in raised beds. Work in a generous amount of compost or well-rotted manure before planting. Cultivars with short roots will tolerate shallow or poor soil better than long, thin cultivars.

Carrots grow best when temperatures are between 60° and 70°F. They grow poorly above 75°F, but will tolerate temperatures as low as 45°F. Most cultivars grow short roots at high temperatures, and longer, more pointed roots at lower temperatures.

Abundant water is necessary for good root development. It is especially important to give emerging seedlings an edge against weeds. Keep soil evenly moist, but not saturated.

To prevent problems with diseases and pests, do not plant carrots where carrots or parsley have grown for 3 years.

Carrots require moderate to high levels of potassium and phosphorus, but only moderate levels of nitrogen, so avoid high-nitrogen fertilizers. Carrots are very sensitive to salt injury and do poorly in soils with high sodium levels.

Leaf Problems

Young leaves yellow and dwarfed; growth bushy. Cause: Aster yellows. Older leaves of plants infected with this disease may be purplish. Once a plant is infected, there is no cure; destroy infected plants. The disease is spread by green or brown, wedge-shaped, $1/10$- to $1/8$-inch-long leafhoppers. Cover emerging seedlings with row cover if

leafhoppers have been a problem. Control leafhoppers by spraying plants with insecticidal soap in the evening; for severe infestations, spray with neem.

Leaves yellow and curled or distorted. Causes: Aphids; tarnished plant bugs. Aphids are small, soft-bodied, green, black, gray, pink, or white fluffy-coated insects that suck plant sap. For a mild infestation, knock pests off plants with a blast of water. Control them by spraying plants with insecticidal soap or with neem if infestation is severe.

Tarnished plant bugs are oval, light green to brown, $1/4$-inch-long bugs with a lighter triangle on each wing. Nymphs are smaller, yellow-green insects with black spots. Use row cover to protect young plants. Control them with white sticky traps and use garlic sprays to repel them from carrot foliage. Spray troublesome infestations with insecticidal soap; spray or dust plants with pyrethrin in the evening, as a last resort. Turn under crop residues after harvest to reduce future problems.

Leaves yellow; plant wilts during bright, hot days but recovers at night. Cause: Root-knot nematodes. See "Roots misshapen and covered with numerous hairlike roots" on page 64 for controls.

Older leaves yellow; plant stunted. Causes: Nitrogen deficiency; waterlogged soil. Spray foliage and drench roots with fish emulsion to alleviate symptoms. Plant carrots in well-drained soil. Keep soil evenly moist, but not saturated.

Leaves with dark, yellow-bordered spots. Causes: Cercospora leaf blight; Alternaria leaf blight; bacterial leaf blight. For the fungal blights, pick off spotted leaves and spray foliage with fish emulsion to promote vigor and encourage new growth. If disease continues to spread, spray foliage with sulfur. Plant cultivars, such as 'Bolero',

'Magnum', and 'Sugarsnax 54', that are resistant to Alternaria.

Bacterial blight also causes dark brown streaks on petioles. Destroy the whole plant. Spray plants with copper if bacterial blight has been a problem in the past.

Root Problems

Roots forked and misshapen. Cause: Lumpy or compacted soil. Prevent problems by working soil deeply and adding lots of compost. Plant shorter-rooted cultivars in rocky or clay soil.

Roots misshapen and covered with numerous hairlike roots. Causes: Root-knot nematodes; aster yellows. Root-knot nematodes cause tiny round swellings on side roots. Prevent future root-knot nematode problems by applying chitin or parasitic nematodes to the soil before planting. See "Root-Knot Nematodes" on page 340 for more control information.

Roots infected with the disease aster yellows are small, woody, hairy, and taste bitter. See "Young leaves yellow and dwarfed; growth bushy" on page 63 for controls.

Roots with green shoulders. Cause: Light exposure. Keep carrot roots covered with 2 inches of soil to prevent greening.

Roots with dark tunnels. Causes: Carrot weevils; carrot rust flies; carrot beetles. Carrot weevils usually attack the upper and outer parts of the root. Tunnels are often in a zigzag pattern. Larvae are creamy white, 1/3-inch-long grubs with brown heads. Adults are coppery brown, 1/6-inch-long snout beetles. Destroy infested roots; don't put them in compost. Control larvae by applying parasitic nematodes to the soil. Control adults, which emerge early in spring to lay eggs, by covering the seedbed with row cover.

Carrot rust fly maggots feed throughout the root, leaving randomly patterned tunnels filled with a rust-colored, sawdustlike material. Larvae are 1/3-inch-long, white maggots. Adults are small flies with yellow heads. Apply parasitic nematodes to soil to control larvae. Prevent problems by planting after June 1 to avoid the first hatching of the season. Cover seedbed with row cover to prevent adults from laying eggs on soil.

Carrot beetle larvae are 1-inch, bluish white grubs that feed on the roots. Adults are 1/2-inch, reddish brown or black beetles. Fall cultivation reduces overwintering populations; crop rotation will also help.

Roots with small, irregular holes; plant may be stunted and yellow. Causes: Wireworms. Damage usually occurs later in the season and is worse in dry years. Larvae are up to 1½-inch-long, yellow to reddish brown, slender, tough-bodied, segmented grubs with brown heads. Adults are 1/3- to 3/4-inch-long, dark-colored, elongated click beetles. Control wireworms by applying parasitic nematodes to the soil.

Roots or crowns rotted. Causes: Various fungal or bacterial diseases. Root rot is often brought on by soggy, poorly drained soil or previous insect damage to the roots. Plant carrots in loose, well-drained soil and keep soil moist, but not soggy. Use raised beds to improve drainage.

Roots with internal cavities; may split open. Cause: Cavity spot. This condition is caused by a combination of factors: calcium deficiency, high levels of potassium, and possibly various diseases. To prevent problems, keep soil moist, but not soggy. Add gypsum, or high-calcium lime if pH is below 6.2, to raise calcium level, and withhold high-potassium fertilizer.

Roots with jagged cracks. Causes: Freezing injury; uneven soil moisture; cavity spot. Temperatures below 30°F cause cracked roots with a water-soaked appearance. Protect roots with mulch before temperatures fall.

Roots can also crack if soil is wetted after being dry. Prevent problems by keeping soil evenly moist.

Severe cases of cavity spot can cause open cracks. See "Roots with internal cavities; may split open" on the opposite page for causes and controls.

Roots poorly formed or pale. Causes: Nutrient deficiency; extreme temperatures. Spindly, short roots can be caused by potassium deficiency or excessive heat. Poor color and taste are caused by magnesium deficiency, phosphorus deficiency, and low or high temperatures. Copper deficiency can also cause poor root development. Spray foliage with seaweed extract to prevent deficiencies. Do a soil test and amend soil as needed.

CAULIFLOWER *Brassica oleracea*, **Botrytis group (Cruciferae)**

Cauliflower is a cool-season crop grown for its dense, white heads of flower buds. Cultivars with purple or orange heads are also available; these do not require blanching like white types. Cauliflower and cabbage require similar culture and are attacked by many of the same diseases and pests. See the Cabbage entry, beginning on page 56, for culture and more information on problems. 'Snow Crown' is resistant to Fusarium yellows and tolerates heat and cold; 'White Rock' is tolerant of cabbage root maggots; 'Super Snowball A' tolerates flea beetles better than most cultivars.

Cauliflower is more fussy about temperatures than the other brassicas. Plants will only tolerate a low of 45°F and grow poorly above 75°F. Transplants exposed to cool temperatures (35° to 45°F) for 10 days or more may form tiny, unusable flower heads. High temperatures can cause the same problem. The optimum temperature range is 60° to 65°F.

Problems

Heads with black spots on surface. Cause: Downy mildew. Control this fungal disease by spraying plants with potassium bicarbonate or baking-soda-and-soap spray (1 teaspoon baking soda, 1 teaspoon liquid dish soap, 1 quart water) at the first sign of disease. Repeat weekly if weather is wet. 'Snow Mountain' resists downy mildew; 'Snowy White' and 'Flora 99' are downy mildew tolerant.

Heads with brown or discolored curds. Causes: Light exposure; boron deficiency; cold injury. Cauliflower heads develop green or purple pigments when exposed to sunlight. To blanch cauliflower, tie the outside leaves loosely up over developing heads so that air can move through, but water cannot drip in. Save time by growing self-blanching cultivars such as 'Fremont' and 'Amazing'.

Boron deficiency turns curds brown and makes them appear water-soaked. Prevent problems by spraying plants with seaweed extract when transplanted and every 2 weeks thereafter. Raise the boron level of the soil by adding 1 tablespoon of borax dissolved in 1 gallon of water, or 10 pounds of kelp, per 100 square feet.

Curds will also turn brown in response to cold and freezing injury. Protect cauliflower heads with row cover below 45°F.

Heads with loose or irregular flower curds. Causes: Excessive heat; molybdenum deficiency. If weather has been hot, suspect heat stress. Prevent problems by growing cauliflower as a fall crop when temperatures are cooler. Prevent molybdenum deficiency by spraying plants with seaweed extract at transplanting and every few weeks thereafter.

CEDRUS Cedar

Cedars are among the most attractive evergreen trees. They have horizontal branching habits and bear large, upright cones. All are ideal as specimen trees.

All cedars like a deep loamy soil, well-drained but enriched with organic matter. Plant them in spring as small, balled-and-burlapped or container-grown plants, setting them in a sunny location. Cedars are remarkably free of serious insect pests. Keep your trees healthy by applying compost mulch and watering thoroughly during periods of drought to minimize damage.

Problems

Leaves reddish brown; branch tips die back. Cause: Deodar weevils. This ½-inch-long, reddish brown beetle has irregular white spots on its back. It will occasionally gnaw through bark and feed on the growing tissue beneath, girdling small branches. The grubs also feed on branch tips. This pest rarely attacks healthy trees, so fertilize and water trees regularly to keep them vigorous. Drench soil around the plant with a solution of parasitic nematodes. As a last resort for severe infestations, spray leaves with pyrethrin.

Trunk or branches with oozing lesions; branch tips die back. Cause: Canker. See "Trunk or branches with oozing lesions; branch tips die back" on page 214 for more information.

Leaves yellow and wilt. Cause: Root rot. See "Leaves yellow and wilt" on page 213 for details.

Leaves yellow; stems and leaves covered with small bumps. Cause: Scales. See page 213 for controls.

CELERY *Apium graveolens* var. *dulce* (Umbelliferae)

Celery is a biennial vegetable grown for its crisp leaf stalks. It is in the same family as carrots and is troubled by many of the same pests and diseases. See the Carrot entry, beginning on page 62, for more information on culture and problems.

Celery does well if given plenty of moisture, rich soil with a pH between 6.0 and 6.8, and cool temperatures or light shade. Celery will withstand a light frost, but will bolt (flower prematurely) and produce only a few small stalks if temperatures are below 55°F for more than 10 days when plants are young. 'Conquistador' resists bolting.

Celery is a heavy feeder. Boron deficiency causes brown, mottled leaves and horizontal cracks on stalks. 'Tendercrisp' is tolerant of low boron and magnesium. Magnesium deficiency causes yellow leaves. Calcium deficiency causes the center of the plant to blacken and die. 'Utah 52-70R Improved' is tolerant of low calcium. Discolored streaks on stalks are a symptom of potassium deficiency. Phosphorus deficiency causes plants to form rosettes. Prevent problems by adding plenty of compost to the soil and by spraying plants with seaweed extract every 2 weeks. Check suspected deficiencies with soil tests and amend soil as needed.

Stalks become tough, bitter, and stringy if plants do not have enough water or nutrients, if temperatures are too high, or if they are not harvested promptly.

Problems

Leaves with dark, yellow-bordered spots. Cause: Blight diseases. Various fungal blight diseases attack celery. Stalks of afflicted plants may also develop spots or dark areas. Destroy spotted leaves. Spray plants with copper if symptoms are serious. Plant cultivars, such as 'Emerson Pascal' and 'Golden Self-Blanching', that tolerate certain blights.

Leaves yellow; plant stunted; veins in stalks reddish. Cause: Fusarium yellows. Destroy plants with this fungal disease. Prevent problems by planting tolerant cultivars, such as 'Bishop', 'Deacon', 'Starlet', 'Summit', and 'Ventura'; 'Fuerte' is resistant to Fusarium yellows.

Leaves yellow and mottled; stalks twisted; plant dwarfed. Cause: Celery mosaic. Destroy infected plants. Control aphids because they can spread viral diseases as they feed. Prevent problems by planting resistant cultivars, such as 'Florida 683', 'Tendercrisp', and 'Utah 52-70R Improved'.

Leaves and stalks with irregular tan spots. Cause: Brown spot. Control this fungal disease by spraying plants with Bordeaux mix when spots appear, to prevent further spread. Plant a tolerant cultivar, such as 'Florigreen'.

Leaves with chewed holes or rolled edges. Cause: Caterpillars. Handpick caterpillars or spray plants with BTK to control.

Stalks or crowns rotted. Cause: Bacterial and fungal diseases. Various bacteria and fungi will rot celery stalks and crowns. Destroy infected plants. Prevent problems by controlling insect pests—such as carrot rust flies—that injure roots, creating openings for disease organisms. Also, avoid handling plants while they are wet, and plant in raised beds if possible.

CELOSIA Celosia, cockscomb

Celosias form feathery plumes or velvety crests in shades of pink, red, orange, and yellow. Blossoms appear in summer through late fall; plants grow 7 to 36 inches tall. Plumed types are great in beds and borders; crested types are ideal for the cutting garden.

Give celosias a sunny, well-drained site. Plants tolerate drought and poor soils, but they bloom poorly and become leggy if shaded. Sow seeds indoors 4 weeks before last frost, or direct-seed outdoors after the soil warms up. Cover lightly so seeds receive some light but don't dry out. Tall-growing, crested types are often top-heavy and benefit from staking.

Celosias are usually trouble free. Careless transplanting can injure the terminal bud and reduce flowering. Damping-off may cause seedlings to rot at the soil line; see "Seedlings die" on page 343 for controls.

CENTAUREA Cornflowers, bachelor's-buttons, knapweeds

Usually seen in shades of blue, cornflowers—or bachelor's-buttons—are available in red, pink, white, and violet, too. These 12- to 26-inch-high garden favorites provide 1-inch flowers all spring. Seeds are favored by birds, particularly finches. Use in beds and borders or for cutting. Perennial species range from 18 inches to 5 feet and are easy-to-grow clump formers.

Direct-sow annuals outdoors in early spring where growing seasons are short, and in later summer through fall where winters are mild. Indoor seeding in April is an option, but seedlings transplant poorly. Sow perennials in pots set in a protected spot outdoors or in a cold frame. When direct-sowing, sow evenly to avoid overcrowding, which results in weak flower stalks and slow growth. Seedlings appear in 2 weeks. Thin to 6 to 9 inches apart.

For best results, give *Centaurea* spp. full sun and rich, moist, neutral soil. They will, however, tolerate average soil and drought. Always water early in the day to give the leaves a chance to dry before nightfall. Add organic matter or fertilizer to the planting site before seeding, and do not fertilize again; extra fertilizer promotes the development of leaves rather than flowers. By midsummer, annual bachelor's-buttons tend to become woody and unsightly. Picking flowers prolongs bloom until July, but plan on pulling out the spent plants and replacing them with a later-blooming annual, such as marigolds or celosias.

Annual bachelor's-buttons have very few problems or pests. They may reseed too prolifically for some gardeners, but removing spent flowers decreases this possibility. If plants look too leggy, they are not getting enough sun; plant on a sunnier site next year. Rusts may cause orange spots on leaves; see "Rust" on page 315. Aster yellows can cause plants to turn yellow; see "Yellows" on page 321.

CHAENOMELES Flowering quince

Flowering quinces are spring-blooming deciduous shrubs with alternate leaves and thorny branches. The plants are used as deciduous hedges, in foundation plantings, or in shrub borders.

Flowering quinces require full or nearly full sun. While not particular as to soils, they prefer a good, well-drained loam. Renewal pruning (removal of a few of the oldest canes each year) is recommended to keep them flowering freely.

Aphids may feed on young shoots and leaves; see "Aphids" on page 250. Scales may also be a problem; see page 213 for management information.

CHARD *Beta vulgaris,* Cicla group (Chenopodiaceae)

Chard, also known as Swiss chard, is a type of beet grown for its succulent tops. It does not form enlarged roots. Green, red, purple, yellow, and white cultivars are available.

Chard grows vigorously from late spring to fall frost. Plants prefer sandy, well-drained soil with a pH of 6.5 to 7.5. They will tolerate a wide range of temperatures and will withstand light frost. To keep leaves tender, provide chard with plenty of water and nitrogen. Compost worked into the soil at planting followed by alfalfa meal sprinkled on the soil surface after seeding usually provides chard's requirements.

Chard and beets are susceptible to the same diseases and pests. See the Beet entry, beginning on page 44, for descriptions and controls.

CHERRY *Prunus* spp. (Rosaceae)

Cherries are deciduous trees growing to 35 feet for standard-size sweet cherries (*Prunus avium*) and to 20 feet for standard-size sour cherries (*P. cerasus*). These plants are hardy in Zones 4–9.

Culture

Cherries need full sun and, especially for sweet cherries, well-drained soil. Choose a site free of late spring frosts. Train sweet cherries to a central leader form and sour cherries to an open center form. For more pruning information, see "Pruning and Training" on page 104.

Mature sweet cherries need little or no annual pruning. Sour cherries need enough pruning each winter to thin out branches and stimulate a moderate amount of growth.

To set fruit, most sweet cherries need cross-pollination from a second compatible cultivar planted nearby. Some sweet cherry cultivars need specific cultivars for cross-pollination. A few sweet cherries, such as 'Lapins', 'Stella', and 'Sweetheart' are self-pollinating. Sour cherries are self-pollinating. For more information, see "Setting Fruit" on page 103.

Fruit Problems

Fruit malformed and shrunken; drops early.
Causes: Plum curculio larvae; cherry fruit fly maggots. Check affected fruit for crescent-shaped scars and small, brown-headed grubs inside. These are larvae of plum curculio beetles common to the East. The crescent-shaped scar marks the site where these pests lay eggs. To control curculios without sprays, spread a dropcloth beneath the tree and tap the trunk and branches twice a day with a padded mallet. Collect and destroy curculios that fall onto the sheet. For more information see "Plum Curculio" on page 278.

Creamy white, ¼-inch maggots inside fruit are the larvae of cherry fruit flies. These flies, which are half the size of houseflies, emerge in late spring from pupae in the soil and lay eggs in fruit. Eggs hatch into fruit-feeding maggots that later drop to the ground to pupate until next spring. To control this pest, trap adult flies from early to late May, using traps made from dark red balls coated with a sticky coating, such as Tangle-Trap. Buy commercial traps or make your own from any apple-size red sphere. Hang one trap per dwarf tree or 4 to 8 traps per full-size tree. Hang traps at eye level, 2 to 3 feet in from branch tips, near fruit but not completely hidden by leaves. Clean traps every few days and reapply the sticky coating. Collect and destroy dropped fruit daily.

Fruit with small brown spots that enlarge and become fuzzy in humid weather. Cause: Brown rot. This fungal disease may also cause blossoms to turn brown and decay. Infected cherries may drop early, or remain on the tree as dried, shriveled fruit, known as mummies. To control brown rot, inspect trees in early spring. Remove and destroy mummified fruit and twigs with gummy-looking lesions. For further control, spray sulfur early in the season to control the disease on blossoms, then again later in the season to protect fruit. Since injured fruit is more susceptible to brown rot, control fruit-damaging insects, such as plum curculios.

Leaf and Branch Problems

New leaves twisted or curled and covered with a sticky coating. Cause: Black cherry aphids. Look on leaf undersides for clusters of these tiny black insects. The sticky coating is honeydew secreted by these pests. Leaves also may be covered with a black fungus, called sooty mold, which grows on the honeydew. Aphids leave by midsummer, so if an infestation isn't severe, just wait it out.

For heavy infestations, knock aphids off leaves with a strong spray of water. Or try insecticidal soap spray, which kills aphids on contact. Neem also kills aphids, but reserve this as a last resort since it also kills beneficial insects. Spray horticultural oil at a dormant-season dilution in the winter to suffocate aphid eggs.

Many natural predators keep aphids in check, including parasitic wasps, lady beetles, and hover flies. To attract aphid predators, grow nectar-producing flowers, such as dill and buckwheat, near your trees, or spray commercial or homemade yeast-and-sugar mixtures on your trees. Introduced lacewings often control aphids. Buy these at commercial insectaries or from organic farm supply companies. Ants often introduce an aphid infestation; trap ants with sticky barriers around the tree trunks. Avoid excessive use of high-nitrogen fertilizer, which favors aphid reproduction.

Leaves covered with lacy, brownish patches. Cause: Pear slugs. These green-black, slimy creatures are not true slugs; they're the larvae of the pear sawfly, a black-and-yellow insect slightly larger than a housefly. In the spring sawflies emerge from cocoons in the soil and lay eggs on leaves. Eggs hatch into sluglike larvae that skeletonize leaves. Remove them by handpicking or with blasts of water. For heavy infestations, use insecticidal soap, neem, or horticultural oil at a growing-season dilution; spray serious infestations with pyrethrin.

Growing shoots wilt and die. Cause: Oriental fruit moth larvae. Slit the stem below the wilted portion and look for a pinkish white, ½-inch caterpillar—the larvae of an oriental fruit moth. Larvae tunnel into shoots and remain for 2 weeks before leaving to pupate for 10 days in cocoons suspended in trees. Larvae from later generations bore into and ruin fruit. Use pheromone traps to monitor and control the pests. Mating disruption pheromones are also effective. Replace them every 90 days throughout the growing season. For heavy infestations, spray horticultural oil at a growing-season dilution in summer to kill eggs and larvae.

Leaves with purple spots. Cause: Cherry leaf spot. This fungal disease, prevalent during rainy springs in the East and Midwest, causes circular purple leaf spots that later turn brown and drop out, leaving small holes. Leaves may yellow and drop early. Infected trees decline in fruit production and winter hardiness. Since the disease overwinters in fallen leaves, control it by thoroughly removing leaves before spring growth begins. If infections have been severe in previous seasons, apply preventive sprays of sulfur starting at petal fall. Plant cultivars that tolerate or resist leaf spot, including 'Meteor' and 'Northstar' sour cherries and 'Regina' and 'WhiteGold' sweet cherries.

Leaves covered with a white powdery coating. Cause: Powdery mildew. Leaves may also be twisted or stunted and a powdery coating may cover fruit. Rainy weather does not cause this fungal disease to spread. It is most common in weather patterns featuring cool nights changing to warm days. Drought stress makes plants more susceptible to infection; keep cherries well watered during dry weather. Organic fungicides, including *Bacillus subtilis*, potassium bicarbonate, or a 0.5 percent solution of baking soda (1 teaspoon baking soda in 1 quart water) may be applied as preventives or to help to control the disease. Spray infected trees thoroughly. 'Northstar' sour cherry and 'Chelah' sweet cherry are resistant to powdery mildew.

Young twigs brown and decaying. Cause: Brown rot. With this fungal disease, limbs may develop gummy-looking lesions. For more information, see "Fruit with small brown spots that enlarge and become fuzzy in humid weather" on page 69.

Leaves wilting and dying on whole branches. Causes: Bacterial canker; Valsa canker; shothole borers. With both cankers, trees may not leaf out in spring, and branches may develop sunken, elliptical lesions that ooze a reddish gum. With bacterial canker, this gum smells sour, and leaves may have small, angular spots. For either canker, prune wilted or dying branches off below the infection point, sterilizing tools in isopropyl alcohol or a 10 percent bleach solution (1 part bleach to 9 parts water) between cuts. Valsa canker enters trees through bark injuries; prevent it with cultural practices that avoid bark injury. Cultivars resistant to bacterial canker include 'Early Burlat', 'Ebony', 'Hartland', 'Sam', 'Vandalay', and 'White-Gold' sweet cherries. For more information, see "Cytospora Canker" on page 333.

Dying branches covered with numerous small holes are the work of tiny beetles called shothole borers. Inside the sawdust-filled tunnels look for white, ⅛-inch borer larvae with reddish brown heads. Shothole borers prefer injured or diseased trees. Vigorous, healthy trees are much less susceptible to problems.

Leaves yellowing; limb dieback. Cause: San Jose scale. Colonies of these sucking insects cling to the bark and appear as small gray bumps that can easily be scraped off with a fingernail. Control San Jose scale with dormant oil spray applied in late winter or early spring just before blossoms open. For more information, see "Scales, Armored" on page 282.

Twigs and branches bearing tarry, black galls. Cause: Black knot. In fall or late winter, prune off infected limbs 6 to 12 inches below the knots; disinfect pruners in between cuts with a 10 percent bleach solution (1 part bleach to 9 parts water). Destroy the prunings. If possible, remove any wild plum or cherry trees nearby. For persistent infections, apply two sprays of lime–sulfur 7 days apart, before the buds begin to grow in spring. Spraying can help to limit the spread of this disease, but needs to be combined with conscientious removal of galls as soon as they are identified.

Whole Plant Problems

Tree lacking vigor. Cause: Peachtree borers. The larvae of a clear-winged moth, these 1-inch, white borers create holes and a gummy exudate on trunks near or just below ground level. Dig borers out, being careful to minimize tree damage, or kill them by inserting a wire into holes. Cultivate shallowly around the base of the tree to discourage these pests. Peachtree borers are attracted to weak trees. Keep trees vigorous and avoid mechanical damage.

Tree stripped of fruit. Cause: Birds. Birds especially love red sweet cherries. Yellow-fruited cultivars are somewhat less attractive to birds. Cover small trees with netting. For more information on controlling birds, see "Birds" on page 304.

CHESTNUT *Castanea* spp. (Fagaceae)

Chestnuts are deciduous trees with large, alternate leaves. The nuts are enclosed in prickly burrs, a drawback to the use of the trees for ornamental purposes.

At one time, American chestnut (*Castanea dentata*) was the dominant tree in eastern forests. It was a splendid specimen tree, highly valued for its wood and for the nuts it yielded. Unfortunately, the fungus that causes chestnut blight was introduced into the United States in the early 1900s, and virtually all American chestnuts have died back from the disease. Infected trees sometimes produce new sprouts, but they don't grow to maturity. Using these sprouts, researchers are working to develop resistant strains. Until then, blight-resistant species, such as Japanese chestnut (*C. crenata*) and Chinese chestnut (*C. mollissima*), are practical alternatives to American chestnut.

Chestnuts are not especially demanding in their soil requirements, as long as drainage is good. They are remarkably heat tolerant. Plant in a sunny location; set out in spring or fall as balled-and-burlapped plants.

Problems

Leaves skeletonized. Causes: Cankerworms; Japanese beetles. The ½- to 1-inch-long, green, yellow, or brown cankerworm caterpillars feed on foliage, often defoliating the tree. To avoid this problem, apply a band of a sticky substance, such as Tanglefoot, around the base of the tree in spring to keep females from climbing up the tree and laying their eggs. Apply fresh coats in September and February to trap both spring and fall cankerworms. If their feeding becomes a problem, spray with BTK as soon as you notice them; continue every 2 weeks until pests are gone.

Japanese beetles often feed on chestnut leaves, causing similar symptoms. See "Leaves skeletonized or plant defoliated" on page 212 for control suggestions.

Plant defoliated. Cause: Gypsy moths. See "Leaves skeletonized or plant defoliated" on page 212 for controls.

Leaves skeletonized or with large holes; branches may be webbed. Cause: Caterpillars. See "Leaves skeletonized or with large holes; branches may be webbed" on page 212 for more information.

Nuts damaged. Cause: Chestnut weevils. The larvae of this pest feed inside the nuts, and then enter the soil when the nuts fall to the ground. Pick fallen nuts from the ground daily to reduce future populations.

Trunk or branches with small holes; limbs die or break off. Cause: Borers. Several kinds of borers attack chestnuts; see "Trunk or branches with small holes; limbs die or break off" on page 214 for controls.

CHIVES *Allium* spp. (Liliaceae)

Common chives (*Allium schoenoprasum*) are a hardy (Zone 3) perennial herb grown for their mild, onion-flavored leaves and pink flowers. Garlic chives (*A. tuberosum*) are slightly less hardy

(Zone 5), and have larger, straplike leaves and white, rose-scented flowers. To grow healthy, trouble-free plants, sow seed indoors in 60° to 70°F soil mix, or outdoors after soil has warmed. Chives do best in moderately rich, moist, well-drained soil with a pH between 5.0 and 7.0. Chives need full sun.

Chives are closely related to onions and prone to the same problems, especially rust, downy mildew, and smut. See the Onion entry, beginning on page 144, for information.

CHRYSANTHEMUM Chrysanthemum, garden mum

Early wild chrysanthemums, mentioned in 5th-century BC writings, bore rather plain, yellow blossoms. Later, whites and purples were found and cultivated. Today, hundreds of cultivars in many different forms and colors are available. Although botanists have since reclassified several of these plants into separate genera—including Shasta daisy (*Leucanthemum* × *superbum*), ox-eye daisy (*L. vulgare*), painted daisy or pyrethrum (*Tanacetum coccineum*), and feverfew (*T. parthenium*)—their pests and diseases are all included here, since their symptoms are similar.

Full sun and fertile, well-drained soil promote healthy mums and daisies. Fertilize plants in spring with compost or a slow-acting, general-purpose fertilizer. Give garden mums supplemental feedings monthly during the growing season; stop fertilizing in August. Start plants from stem cuttings, divisions, or seeds. When buying mums and daisies, look for compact, bushy plants, which will flower better than larger specimens. Space 1 foot apart, avoiding areas already occupied by tree and shrub roots. When plants reach 6 to 8 inches, pinch growing tips back to stimulate branching and flower bud production. Give these shallow-rooted plants ½ to 1 inch of water weekly; water stress causes woody stems and lower leaf drop. Overwatering, particularly when combined with poor drainage, causes yellowing leaves that blacken and drop. Cut plants back to within a few inches of the ground after blooming. Protect roots with a winter mulch.

Although the list of pests and diseases that *may* attack chrysanthemums and daisies is long, these plants are relatively trouble free. Unless they are stressed by unfavorable growing conditions, few pests will seek them out; fewer still will cause significant damage.

Problems

Leaves, stems, and buds distorted, sticky; clusters of small insects. Cause: Aphids. See "Aphids" on page 250 for controls.

Leaves with yellow-brown spots or blotches; leaves die and turn brittle. Cause: Foliar nematodes. These microscopic roundworms overwinter in soil or plant debris, then travel up a plant's stem in the film of water created by spring rains. Symptoms move up the plant; foliar nematodes may even infest the petals. See "Foliar Nematodes" on page 317 for more information and controls.

Leaves with tan or brown blotches or serpentine tunnels. Cause: Leafminers. These tiny, pale green fly larvae feed between the upper and lower surfaces of leaves. Prune off and destroy infested leaves until only healthy growth remains. Remove debris in fall to destroy overwintering leafminers. Let parasitic wasps control these pests. See "Leafmining Flies" on page 271 for more on controls.

Leaves and flowers greenish yellow, distorted; new growth spindly. Cause: Viral diseases. Chrysanthemums are prone to several viruses, which are spread by sucking insects such as aphids and leafhoppers. Control such pests to limit virus problems. Remove and destroy infected plants; do not compost them. Wash tools used around infected plants. Viruses overwinter in perennials and weeds such as daisies and plantains.

CITRUS *Citrus* **spp. (Rutaceae)**

Citrus trees are evergreens that grow in flushes throughout the year. They bear fragrant flowers and fruit that hangs for months without dropping. These plants are hardy in Zones 9–10.

To flourish and bear well, citrus trees require a site with excellent drainage and full sun. Prune to remove dead wood, to keep trees in bounds, and to thin centers where growth is too dense. Citrus flowers attract bees; don't plant them in high-traffic areas. Citrus trees bear fruit without cross-pollination.

Fruit Problems

Fruit with raised, light brown, corky areas. Cause: Citrus scab. Leaves also may show scabby lesions. This fungal disease, common in Florida, attacks mainly grapefruit, 'Temple' and 'Murcott' honey oranges, lemons, sour oranges, satsumas, and some tangelos. To control citrus scab, prune and site trees so that foliage and fruit remain as dry as possible during spring growth.

Fruit with small, brown, sunken spots that turn dark and are raised. Cause: Melanose. This fungal disease usually attacks trees more than 10 years old and is worst during wet springs. As rain washes spores over fruit, a tear-streaked pattern of infection develops. Copper spray applied just once at fruit set controls this disease, but since fruit damage is only cosmetic, spraying isn't really necessary. Keep melanose in check by pruning out dead wood, which may harbor the disease.

Fruit with firm, light brown spots on the rind. Cause: Brown rot. In humid weather brown rot may appear as a white mold on the rind. Rain splashes the spores of this fungal disease from the ground onto low-hanging fruit. The simplest control is to mulch the soil around the tree and prune away low-hanging branches. Copper spray applied to the ground and low-hanging limbs also works. This disease spreads easily in stored fruit; keep infected fruit away from clean fruit.

Fruit contains webbing. Cause: Navel orangeworms. These reddish orange, brown-headed moth larvae bore into cracked fruit and spin their cocoons inside. Control pests by picking off damaged fruit. Clean up dropped fruit. Spray BTK to kill larvae before they enter fruit.

Leaf and Branch Problems

Leaves with pale yellow stipples. Cause: Citrus mites. These pests may also attack fruit, causing it to turn brown or silver and drop prematurely. Pesticides tend to kill natural mite predators, so unsprayed trees are less prone to mite infestation. You can also introduce predatory mites, such as *Amblyseius* species. The simplest mite remedy is to hose down the tree with plain water or insecticidal soap solution. For more serious infestations, spray with horticultural oil at a growing-season dilution, or sulfur as a last resort.

Leaves with oily brown spots on undersides. Cause: Greasy spot. With this fungal disease, yellowish brown blisters on leaf undersides eventually turn oily brown and coalesce. Superficial pitting may appear on fruit rind. Since the disease overwinters on leaf litter, the simplest control is to collect and destroy fallen leaves. Wet foliage encourages spread of the fungus; keep leaves as dry as possible, especially during the early summer. For recurrent greasy spot, spray with horticultural oil at a growing-season dilution, or copper as a last resort.

Trunk with brown patches exuding a thick, amber gum. Cause: Brown rot gummosis. Eventually brown patches form dark, sunken cankers. Lower branches above the canker may wither and die. This disease begins when spores of *Phytophthora* fungus splash up from the ground and enter the trunk through a bark injury. To control this disease, scrape away the canker into healthy bark, allow it to dry, and spray it with copper. To prevent this disease, keep surface water and sprinkler water away from the trunk. Plant only in well-drained soil using trees grafted onto *Phytophthora*-resistant rootstocks, such as trifoliate orange, sour orange, and 'Troyer' citrange.

Leaves with small, dark, circular depressions bearing yellow margins. Cause: Melanose. For more information, see "Fruit with small, brown, sunken spots that turn dark and are raised," on page 73.

Leaves turn pale green or yellow. Cause: Nutrient deficiency. If old leaves turn yellow and drop off, suspect nitrogen deficiency, a condition that sometimes occurs when cold soil slows root activity. If young leaves turn yellow with green veins, suspect iron deficiency, a condition common to wet or alkaline soils, even if the soil contains enough iron. To correct nitrogen deficiency, apply an organic nitrogen source directly to the soil. To correct iron deficiency, adjust the soil pH to be more acidic. You can also spray either of these nutrients directly on the leaves for immediate help.

Leaves turn yellow and fall; tree declines. Cause: Scales. Various types of scales infest citrus trees, causing decline. Trees may suffer from twig dieback and reduced vigor, and leaves may be covered with honeydew excreted by the scales as well as sooty mold, which feeds on the honeydew. Cottony cushion scale looks like white, cottony masses clustered on leaves, stems, and branches. Red, brown, or black scale may look like crusty, waxy, or smooth bumps on leaves, trunks, stems, or fruit. Many natural enemies keep scale insects in check. If scale infestation is heavy, introduce outside predators for additional control. You must choose the species of predator that feeds on your species of scale. For example, Vidalia beetles (*Rodolia cardinalis*) feed on cottony cushion scale, and the parasite wasp *Aphytis melinus* preys on California red scale. Ants protect scales by destroying their natural predators, so keep ants out of trees by placing sticky barriers around trunks. You can also control scale by spraying specially refined horticultural oil.

Leaves with white, cottony masses. Cause: Mealybugs. Leaves may also be covered with sticky honeydew excreted by mealybugs or with black sooty mold, which grows on the honeydew. Natural enemies, such as lacewings, usually keep mealybugs in check, but you can speed along the process by introducing the mealybug destroyer, an Australian predatory beetle available through commercial insectaries and organic farm suppliers. Ants protect mealybugs by destroying their natural predators. Restrict ants from trees by placing sticky barriers around trunks and removing branches that droop to the ground.

New leaves curled or twisted. Cause: Aphids. Look on leaf undersides for clusters of these tiny sucking insects. Many natural enemies keep aphids in check, including parasitic wasps and hover flies. Provide food for natural predators and parasites by growing nectar-producing flowers, such as dill and buckwheat, near your trees. Or spray commercial or homemade yeast-and-sugar mixtures on your trees to attract predators. Introduced lady beetles may not control aphids effectively, but introduced lacewings often do. Ants protect aphids by destroying their natural predators, so restrict ant movement into your trees with sticky barriers around the trunks. Excessive use of nitrogen fertilizer favors aphid reproduction.

For heavy infestations, apply a strong spray of water or insecticidal soap solution to trees, making sure you spray undersides of leaves as well. Horticultural oil sprays kill aphid eggs. Neem also controls aphids, but use it only as a last resort, since it also kills beneficial insects.

CLEMATIS Clematis

Clematis are mostly deciduous vines that climb by means of twining leaf stalks. They bear attractive flowers in a range of sizes and colors.

Clematis prefer neutral to slightly alkaline soils, well-enriched with compost. Set out small, container-grown plants in spring or fall. Provide some sort of support. Clematis perform best in full sun, but they do like to have their roots cool and shaded; a rich, deep, organic mulch is of great benefit, as is a site with the base shaded by a low wall or perennials, for example. Well-drained soil is a must. Clematis may be slow to initiate top growth; they must first establish a substantial root system. Be careful to support the top of the plant when planting, because stems are brittle and break off easily.

Problems

Vines droop and shrivel. Cause: Clematis wilt. This fungal disease is one of the most serious problems for clematis. When it strikes, prune out and destroy all affected parts. If you set the plant a few inches deeper than it was growing in the nursery at transplanting time, new vines may come up from the buried stem portion and produce new, healthy top growth. If the whole plant dies, don't try to grow another clematis on that site.

Plant stunted; top dies back. Cause: Clematis borers. These ²⁄₃-inch-long, white-bodied, brown-headed grubs feed on the roots and crowns of clematis vines. To control, cut out and destroy infested stems, and dig the larvae out of the crowns. Dig out and destroy severely infested plants.

Leaves yellow; stems and leaves covered with small bumps. Cause: Scales. See "Scales, Armored" on page 282 for control suggestions.

COLCHICUM Autumn crocus

These hardy, autumn-flowering corms are not crocuses, despite their common name. Pink, white, or purple, 2- to 4-inch-tall flowers bloom in fall and the foliage comes up in early spring and dies off by midsummer. Narrow dark green leaves grow 6 to 12 inches tall.

Plant autumn crocus corms in July and August, setting them 3 inches deep in average, well-drained soil in full sun to light shade. Lift and separate corms after foliage fades if necessary to reduce crowding or to move plantings; replant immediately.

Almost no pests or diseases bother these corms, which are quite poisonous if eaten.

COLEUS See "Solenostemon" on page 189

COLLARD Brassica oleracea, Acephala group (Cruciferae)

Collards are a cool-season vegetable grown for their leafy, cabbage-type greens. Collards can stand more heat than other members of the cabbage family. They prefer growing temperatures of 65° to 70°F and tolerate 40° to 80°F. 'Champion' and 'Vates' are cold-hardy cultivars. Soil pH should be between 5.5 and 6.8.

Collards are grown like cabbage and are attacked by the same diseases and insects. See the Cabbage entry, beginning on page 56, for culture and information on problems.

CONVALLARIA Lily-of-the-valley

Fragrant lily-of-the-valley (*Convallaria majalis*) scents springtime air with small, white, dangling bell-shaped flowers carried on stalks above 6-inch-long, pointed green leaves. Attractive but poisonous red berries follow the blossoms.

Lily-of-the-valley spreads by thick rhizomes. Purple shoots appear in April, followed by buds.

Plants multiply rapidly; in favorable conditions they can be invasive, a trait that makes lily-of-the-valley useful as a groundcover in controlled situations. Late fall division encourages bloom. Plant lily-of-the-valley about 5 inches apart in moist, well-drained, organic soil. The light shade beneath deciduous trees is fine for these woodland natives; heavy shade decreases bloom. Fertilize in fall.

Lily-of-the-valley is seldom bothered by pests or diseases. Spider mites may cause stippled, reddish to yellow leaves with fine webbing. Slugs and snails can chew large, ragged holes in foliage. See "Mites, Spider" on page 275 and "Slugs/Snails" on page 284 for controls.

COREOPSIS Coreopsis, tickseed

Golden daisylike flowers grace plantings of coreopsis from mid-June well into July. Most species of these 1- to 3-foot plants are hardy perennials, although tickseed (*Coreopsis grandiflora*) performs as a biennial north of Zone 7, and calliopsis (*C. tinctoria*) is an annual. Prolific 1- to 3-inch, single or double blooms attract beneficial syrphid flies.

Space perennial coreopsis 15 inches apart in well-drained, average to poor soil in full sun. Once established, these natives are very drought-tolerant but bloom better with regular waterings. Excess feeding encourages rank, spindly growth; a single spring application of fertilizer is sufficient. Remove spent flowers to prolong bloom and reduce the tendency to self-sow. Divide clumps every 3 to 4 years.

Problems

Leaves, stems, and buds distorted, sticky; clusters of small insects. Cause: Aphids. See "Aphids" on page 250 for controls.

Buds and leaves deformed or dwarfed. Cause: Four-lined plant bugs. For recommended controls, see "Buds and leaves deformed or dwarfed" on page 99.

Leaves stippled, distorted. Cause: Leafhoppers. See "Leafhoppers" on page 271 for control options.

CORN *Zea mays* var. *rugosa* (Gramineae)

Corn is an annual vegetable grown for its large ears of tasty kernels. Sweet corn is harvested when the ears are tender and immature. Sweet corn cultivars are classified into three groups: normal sugary (traditional corn flavor, hybrid or open-pollinated), sugar enhanced (increased tenderness and sweetness, hybrid), and supersweet (almost candy-sweet, hybrid). Be sure to plant supersweets at least 25 feet away from any other corn cultivars or cross–pollination will cause starchy, tough kernels. Be aware that whether you plant other cultivars or not,

supersweet cultivars generally suffer from more than their share of pests.

While most gardeners stick to sweet corn, other types of corn are just as easy to grow. Popcorn, ornamental corn, dent (field) corn, and flint (Indian) corn are harvested when the seeds are hard and mature and the husks are dry.

Culture

Corn does best in rich, sandy, or well-worked soil with a pH between 5.5 and 6.8. Prepare soil by working in a generous amount of compost. Side-dress plants with alfalfa meal when they are 1 foot high and again when silk first shows at the end of the ears. Periodically spraying plants with seaweed extract or compost tea also improves your harvest and prevents deficiencies.

Plant corn seed only after the soil is at least 60°F, or 75°F for supersweets. Seed planted in cooler soil is prone to many problems, including poor germination. To help speed soil warming, cover soil with clear plastic at least 2 weeks before you want to plant. After planting, use row cover for about a month to give seedlings a boost.

Corn needs at least 1 inch of water a week. Keep soil moist, but not soggy. Mulch plants to conserve moisture and cut down on weed competition.

Plant corn in blocks rather than long single rows to ensure good pollination. Do not plant corn where it has grown in the past 2 years to prevent problems. After harvest, cut or mow stalks and let them dry. Then turn them under or collect and compost them. Destroy any diseased or infested material.

Leaf and Whole Plant Problems

Seedlings cut off at ground level; leaf margins ragged. Cause: Cutworms. Young cutworms feed on leaves. Most cutworms are gray or dull brown and up to 2 inches long. Spray seedlings with BTK in the evening if cutworms are still feeding on leaves. Sprinkle moist bran mixed with BTK on the soil surface in the evening, or add parasitic nematodes to the soil to control stem-girdling cutworms. For small plantings, place cutworm collars around plants or groups of plants to prevent damage.

Seedlings fail to emerge or are stunted. Causes: Cool soil; corn rootworms; seedcorn beetles; wireworms; seedcorn maggots; white grubs. Corn seed germinates poorly in cool soil and is more prone to insect damage and rots. Plant seeds after soil is warm to prevent problems. Do not plant corn where grass grew the year before because many pests of corn live in sod.

Corn rootworms are white, slender, ½-inch-long larvae with brown heads. Adults are beetles. Western rootworm beetles are ¼ inch long and yellow with three black stripes. Northern rootworm adults are yellow to pale green, and southern rootworms (spotted cucumber beetles) are yellow-green with 11 black spots. Rootworm larvae feed on seeds, and adults feed on leaves, silks, and tassels.

Seedcorn beetle larvae are white, slender, ½-inch-long grubs; adults are ⅓-inch-long ground beetles with light brown edges. Both larvae and adults feed on seeds.

Wireworms are 1½-inch-long, yellow to reddish brown, slender, tough-bodied, segmented larvae with brown heads. Adults are dark-colored, elongated click beetles.

Seedcorn maggots are ¼ inch long, yellow-white, and spindle-shaped. Adults are small flies. White grubs have thick, soft, ¾-inch bodies and curl into a C-shape when disturbed. Adults are Japanese or June beetles. Wireworms, seedcorn maggots, and white grubs eat corn seed.

Apply parasitic nematodes to the soil before planting to control soil-dwelling pests. Prevent adults from laying eggs on or near the seedbed by covering it with a large piece of row cover after planting. Remove row cover when tassels appear.

Seedlings purplish. Cause: Phosphorus deficiency. Phosphorus is not readily available in cool soils. Spray plants with seaweed extract or compost tea to alleviate symptoms.

Plant stunted and yellow. Causes: Nitrogen deficiency; too much or too little water; nematodes. If older leaves turn yellow first, suspect nitrogen deficiency. Drench roots and spray plants with fish emulsion or compost tea to alleviate symptoms.

To avoid root damage, keep the soil evenly moist. Plant in raised beds to ensure good drainage.

If entire plant is yellow and doesn't green up when sprayed with seaweed or compost, and soil is well drained and not too dry, suspect pest nematodes. Roots may be stubby or have swellings or beadlike galls. Control by applying chitin or parasitic nematodes to soil.

Leaves yellow and curled; plant stunted. Cause: Aphids. These small, soft-bodied, green, black, gray, pink, or white fluffy-coated insects suck plant sap. For mild infestations, knock pests off plants with a blast of water. Spray infested plants with insecticidal soap; spray severe infestations with neem.

Leaves mottled yellow and green. Cause: Maize dwarf mosaic. The stem doesn't grow normally, so new leaves are very close together. Leaves may develop lengthwise stripes. There is no cure; destroy infected plants. Prevent problems by controlling aphids, which spread the virus as they feed, and perennial weeds such as Johnsongrass, which can harbor the disease. Plant tolerant cultivars such as 'Bellringer', 'Earlibelle', 'Enforcer', and 'Merit'.

Leaves with lengthwise yellow stripes; plant may wilt. Cause: Bacterial wilt, also called Stewart's wilt or disease. Leaves are dwarfed. Cut off the infected plant near the soil line and look for yellow bacterial slime oozing from the cut stem to confirm diagnosis. Destroy infected plants. Control flea beetles and cucumber beetles that spread the disease. Prevent problems by planting resistant cultivars such as 'Ambrosia', 'Bonus', 'Bravado', 'Candy Store', 'Delectable', 'Eliminator', 'Merlin', 'Merit', 'Mystique', 'Silverado', and 'Silver Queen'.

Leaves with yellow, tan, or gray spots or blotches. Causes: Northern or southern corn leaf blight; other fungal leaf spots. Spray infected plants with sulfur to prevent blight from spreading. Prevent problems by using a 3-year rotation for corn and by planting cultivars such as 'Silver Queen' and 'Sugar Buns', which are tolerant of northern leaf blight, or 'Augusta', 'Brocade', 'Delectable', and 'Seneca Dancer', which tolerate both blights.

Leaves with orange-brown raised spots. Cause: Rust. Spray infected plants with sulfur early in the day and thin plants to maintain good air circulation. If rust is a recurrent problem, try spraying plants with an antitranspirant before symptoms develop to prevent infection. (Do not spray with antitranspirant when corn is silking.) Plant rust-tolerant cultivars such as 'Earlibelle', 'Excellency', 'Prevailer', 'Sweetie', 'Miracle', 'Country Gentleman', and 'Sugar Time'.

Leaves with numerous small holes. Causes: Flea beetles; billbugs. Leaves may develop bleached-out spots or stripes. Flea beetles are tiny black insects that hop when disturbed. They can transmit disease and are likely to be more numerous after mild winters. Cover plants with row cover as soon as they come up to exclude beetles. Remove row cover when tassels form. Spray plants with neem to control severe infestations.

If holes are arranged in rows, look for billbugs. These hard-shelled, nearly black, ¼- to ½-inch snout beetles are usually seen only at night. Spray heavily infested corn plants with pyrethrin.

Leaves with large, ragged holes. Causes: Corn earworms; European corn borers; armyworms; other caterpillars. Handpick or spray plants with BTK if caterpillars are feeding. See "Ears with tunnels and chewed kernels" below for controls.

Leaves skeletonized. Cause: Japanese beetles. Silk and tassels may be chewed. Adults are ½-inch-long, metallic blue-green beetles with bronze wing covers. Handpick or trap adults. See "Japanese Beetle" on page 269 for more information and controls.

Stems girdled at base; stems and ears with tunnels. Cause: Southwestern corn borers. These white, dark-spotted, brown-headed larvae bore into stalks and ears. To reduce future damage, plant corn early and use resistant cultivars. Cut corn stalks down at the soil level and remove them right after harvest.

Ear Problems

Ears with tunnels and chewed kernels. Causes: Corn earworms; European corn borers; fall armyworms. Leaves and silk may be chewed. Stalks and tassels may be tunneled and may snap off. Corn earworm larvae are light yellow, green, pink, or brown caterpillars up to 2 inches long, with lengthwise stripes. Adults are tan moths. European corn borer larvae are beige, brown-spotted caterpillars up to 1 inch long, with brown heads. Adults are pale yellow to tan moths with wavy lines on their wings. Armyworm larvae are greenish brown caterpillars up to 1½ inch long, with a characteristic inverted Y on their heads. Adults are pale gray moths and have a 1½-inch wingspan.

Cover plants with row cover until tassels emerge to exclude the first generation of pests, especially if you have had problems in previous years. Use insect-specific pheromone traps to catch male moths of various pest species, or ask your local extension agent when moths usually appear in your area. If you are growing large quantities of corn, you may want to try using a blacklight trap to catch all types of moths; be aware that many kinds of beneficial insects are also attracted to and killed by these traps. See "Light Traps" on page 360 for more information.

Even before the tassels emerge, check the upright, topmost leaves of your plant every 2 to 3 days for signs of caterpillar feeding. Spray BTK as soon as any feeding holes are found. Make sure to spray the undersides of leaves and insides of unfolding leaves where pests feed.

Once silks appear, spray them with BTK or sprinkle a few grains of granular BTK directly on each silk. Apply a few drops of mineral oil to each silk 4 to 5 days after they wilt to discourage any resident pests, or inject a few drops of parasitic nematode suspension around the tip of the ear to kill larvae.

Kernels at tips or upper half of ears hollowed out. Cause: Sap beetles. These small black beetles with yellow spots invade ears after the silks turn brown. Handpick beetles, or spray ear tips with pyrethrin for severe infestations. Sap beetles can be trapped in containers baited with fermenting fruit.

Ears with dried tips exposed; ears stripped or missing. Causes: Birds; raccoons. Birds peck at tips of ears, exposed tips turn dry and greenish brown. Raccoons harvest ripe, juicy corn, usually the night before you would pick it yourself. Repel birds with loud noises or visual scare devices. Frustrate raccoons by surrounding your corn with a three-strand electric fence with wires 3 to 4 inches apart and off the ground. See "Birds" on page 304 for further information.

Ears misshapen or with areas of undeveloped kernels. Causes: Poor pollination; nutrient deficiency; viral diseases. Insufficient or ineffective pollination can cause undeveloped bare tips, scattered kernels, or entirely bare cobs. Plant corn in a block, rather than a long row, to ensure effective wind pollination. Insects feeding on silks before pollination occurs can prevent pollination, as can very dry conditions. Control insects that feed on silk, and keep soil moist but not wet, to ensure even pollination.

Ears with bare, undeveloped tips can also be caused by potassium deficiency. Phosphorus deficiency also causes small, irregular ears. If ears are misshapen and kernels have corky, brown bands at their bases, suspect boron deficiency. Spray young plants with seaweed extract or compost tea to help prevent deficiencies. Confirm deficiencies with a soil test and amend soil as needed.

Viral diseases such as maize dwarf mosaic can cause poor kernel formation at the base of ears or bare ears. See "Leaves mottled yellow and green" on page 78 for more symptoms.

Ears or tassels with enlarged galls. Causes: Corn smut. Young galls are firm and whitish; older ones are spongy and filled with black powder. Remove galls before they split open, and destroy infected plants. Do not compost them. Prevent problems by planting resistant cultivars such as 'Bellringer', 'Delectable', 'Gold Cup', 'Merit', and 'Sweet Sue'.

CORNUS Dogwood

Dogwoods are deciduous trees or shrubs, usually with opposite leaves. These plants provide year-round landscape interest with their showy flowers, attractive fruit, striking fall color, and interesting bark. Use dogwoods as specimen plants, in woodland plantings, or as informal barriers.

Culture

Spring is the best time to plant dogwoods, as balled-and-burlapped or container-grown plants. Most thrive in well-drained soil enriched with organic matter. The tree forms, in particular, do not tolerate drought, so water them thoroughly in dry weather. A deep organic mulch helps to conserve moisture and keep down weeds. The shrub types will grow in sun or partial shade; the trees are best in dappled shade.

Dogwoods vary widely in their susceptibility to pests and diseases. Some, such as flowering dogwood (*Cornus florida*), tend to have more problems than resilient species like kousa dogwood (*C. kousa*) and cornelian cherry dogwood (*C. mas*). To avoid problems with any dogwood, keep plants growing vigorously with regular watering and fertilization. Avoid damaging the trunk with lawn mowers, string trimmers, or pruning equipment; many dogwood problems, such as canker or borers, enter plants through wounds in the bark.

Problems

Trunks with lumpy swellings; limbs die or break off; bark falls off. Cause: Borers. Several species of borers attack dogwoods. The most common type, the dogwood borer, has white-bodied, brown-headed larvae. They hatch from eggs laid on the bark and enter the tree through wounds or scars in the bark. Dogwood borers often attack young, newly transplanted trees. See "Trunk or branches with small holes; limbs die or break off" on page 214 for more information and controls.

Leaves with small, purple-rimmed spots or large brown blotches; twigs die back. Cause: Dogwood anthracnose. This fungal disease can be a serious problem on flowering dogwood. Lower branches die back as the disease progresses; eventually the whole tree may die. The problem is most serious in woodland settings, where the dogwoods may already be weakened by lack of light and competition for food and water. Vigorously growing plants are more resistant. Keep roots covered with 3 inches of organic mulch, but keep mulch away from the base of the trunk. Water during drought, and avoid high-nitrogen fertilizer, since it encourages the rank growth that is most susceptible. If disease does strike, prune out affected parts; clean up and destroy fallen leaves in autumn. See "Anthracnose" on page 310 for more controls.

Leaves yellow, sparse, distorted, or with brown edges; branches die; growth stunted. Cause: Decline. In recent years, flowering dogwoods have been afflicted by decline. The exact cause is unknown. Trees that are stressed by insects, disease, or environmental changes are very susceptible to further pest and disease problems. Dogwood anthracnose (see above) commonly attacks already weakened trees, for example. For more information, see "Leaves yellow, sparse, distorted, or with brown edges; branches die; growth stunted" on page 214.

Twigs die back. Cause: Twig blight. Prune off affected parts back to live wood. Keep the tree growing vigorously with regular watering and fertilization.

Trunk or branches with oozing lesions; branch tips die back. Cause: Canker. See

"Trunk or branches with oozing lesions; branch tips die back" on page 214 for more information.

Twigs with clublike galls. Cause: Gall midges. The orange larvae of these small, reddish brown midges tunnel into young shoots. One-inch-long swellings form around the developing larvae on the twig; leaves on the branch may wilt or turn brown. Prune off and destroy galls as soon as you see them.

Leaves yellow; stems and leaves covered with small bumps. Cause: Scales. See "Scales, Armored" on page 282 for controls.

Leaves tunneled. Cause: Leafminers. See "Leafmining Flies" on page 271 for suggested controls.

Leaves with powdery white coating. Cause: Powdery mildew. See "Powdery Mildew" on page 322 for controls.

COSMOS Cosmos

The daisylike flowers of these fast-growing plants come in many shades of red, yellow, white, pink, lavender, and magenta. Cosmos bloom on 1½- to 4-foot, slender stems covered with finely cut foliage.

Direct-sow cosmos outdoors from March through July. Seedlings appear in 10 days. Cosmos are also easy to transplant and grow from purchased plants. Space plants 8 to 24 inches apart, depending on ultimate size. They prefer full sun and a light, average soil kept slightly on the dry side. Avoid overwatering, and do not fertilize.

Pinch back seedlings before flower buds form to encourage compact bushy plants, or buy lower-growing cultivars. Staking is necessary for large cosmos. Plant in groups or among sturdier bedding plants for extra wind protection. Plants may self-sow.

Problems

Stems break. Cause: Stalk borers. These long, thin, striped caterpillars eat their way through cosmos stalk centers. Small, round stem holes may betray their presence. Once plants are visibly affected, there is no cure. If borers are a regular problem, spray plants with BTK early in the season as borers enter plants.

Leaves, stems, and buds distorted. Cause: Aphids. See "Aphids" on page 250 for controls.

Leaves greenish yellow; growth poor. Cause: Aster yellows. For more information and control measures, see "Yellows" on page 321.

Plant wilts suddenly. Cause: Bacterial wilt. This disease causes a soft rot at the base of the stem, killing plants quickly. Remove and destroy infected plants. Do not replant cosmos in that area.

COTONEASTER Cotoneaster

Cotoneasters are alternate-leaved evergreen or deciduous shrubs with persistent red or black fruit. They are useful as groundcovers, in the rock garden, in foundation plantings, or overhanging a wall.

Plant in spring as balled-and-burlapped or container-grown plants. Although not particular as to soils, avoid poorly drained sites. Cotoneasters do best in full sun and can withstand wind, dry soil, and even salt spray.

Problems

Leaves, flowers, and branches blackened. Cause: Fire blight. This bacterial disease causes new shoots to wilt suddenly, turn dark, and die back. This disease eventually spreads, killing the whole plant. Lush new growth is particularly susceptible, so avoid overfertilizing. Prune out diseased tissue, cutting back at least 6 inches beyond the discolored area; destroy or dispose of prunings. Disinfect pruners after each cut in a 10 percent bleach solution (1 part bleach to 9 parts water) to avoid spreading the disease to healthy wood. See "Fire Blight" on page 336 for more controls.

Leaves wrinkled and discolored. Cause: Aphids. See "Aphids" on page 250 for controls.

Leaves pale and mottled. Cause: Lace bugs. See "Lace Bugs" on page 270 for controls.

Leaves yellow; stems and leaves covered with small bumps. Cause: Scales. See "Scales, Armored" on page 282 for more information.

Leaves skeletonized; branches webbed. Cause: Cotoneaster webworms. These ½-inch, yellowish green to brown caterpillars feed on leaves and spin silken webs around leaves and stems. Young plants may die; older ones can be seriously weakened. Break up and remove the webs; spray plants with BTK.

Leaves stippled with yellow; foliage webbed. Cause: Spider mites. See "Mites, Spider" on page 275 for controls.

Leaves with brownish blisters underneath. Cause: Pear leaf blister mites. These microscopic mites live and feed on tissue inside leaves. They overwinter on buds and infest new leaves in spring. Spray plants in late winter with horticultural oil at a dormant-season dilution.

Trunk or branches with small holes; limbs die or break off. Cause: Borers. See "Trunk or branches with small holes; limbs die or break off" on page 214 for controls.

CRATAEGUS Hawthorn

Hawthorns are small, thorny, deciduous trees with alternate leaves and showy, white, pink, or red flowers. Hawthorns make attractive specimen trees, barriers, or hedges.

Set out balled-and-burlapped or container-grown plants in full sun in early spring. Hawthorns are undemanding as to soil, but avoid poorly drained areas. Choose planting sites with good air circulation to minimize disease problems. To avoid rust diseases, don't plant hawthorns where Eastern red cedar (*Juniperus virginiana*) is common.

Hawthorns share many insect and disease problems with apples. For symptoms and controls, see the Apply entry, beginning on page 31.

CROCUS Crocus

Much like the first robins, dainty crocuses signal spring's arrival. These low-growing flowers bear blooms of yellow, white, pink, and purple amid dark green, grasslike foliage in late winter and early spring. Less well-known fall-blooming species include showy crocus (*Crocus speciosus*), a blue- or white-flowered plant that blooms before leaves extend fully. Most species grow only 3 to 6 inches tall.

Plant both spring- and fall-flowering species as soon as corms are available. Corms are occasionally infected with dry rot; examine them carefully when purchasing and select ones that are solid and heavy for their size. Full sun and well-drained soil are crocuses' main requirements; corms will grow and multiply undisturbed for years. Set corms 3 to 4 inches deep and 2 to 6 inches apart with pointed growing tips right-side up. Avoid cutting foliage back until it fades naturally; early removal of leaves reduces flowering in subsequent years. Divide large clumps as needed after leaves die back; replant full-size corms and cormels (small corms growing from base of parent corm) immediately.

Problems

Plant disappears; corms missing. Cause: Animal pests. Rodents such as mice, voles, squirrels, and gophers will eat crocus corms and can quickly make a planting disappear. The presence of a pet dog or cat often deters rodents; if pets aren't an option, try other techniques (see "Animal Pests" on page 304). Line planting beds with screen or hardware cloth to keep pests from burrowing around corms. Lay mesh over the top, too; crocus shoots can still squeeze through.

Leaves yellow, distorted; flowers absent; corms rotted. Cause: Bulb mites. If you suspect these pests, dig the corms, and use a magnifying glass to look for whitish, $\frac{1}{50}$- to $\frac{1}{25}$-inch mites. Bulb mites favor rotting bulbs, but will move from there to healthy bulbs, carrying harmful bacteria and fungi with them. Their feeding causes corky, brown spots that become powdery. Inspect corms carefully for damage or signs of infestation. Destroy badly infested bulbs and discard surrounding soil. Solarize the soil before planting corms in previously infested ground.

CUCUMBER *Cucumis sativus* (**Cucurbitaceae**)

Cucumbers are annual vegetables grown for their crisp and crunchy fruit, which are typically eaten fresh or pickled.

Culture

Cucumber seeds won't germinate until the soil reaches 60°F, so wait until weather is warm before planting. Make a second planting 4 to 5 weeks after the first, so that you have fruit all season. Use row cover to protect young plants from insects and late cold snaps. Remove row cover when plants begin to flower so insects can pollinate the blossoms, or you will not get any fruit.

Cucumbers do best in well-drained, loose-textured soils with lots of organic matter and a pH ranging from 5.5 to 6.8, preferably above 6.0. Evenly moist soil is necessary for healthy growth, but soggy conditions invite disease problems. Use mulch to help conserve water and, where needed, to warm the soil. If fruit rots where it touches the ground, place wood scraps, paper plates, handfuls of straw, or similar material under the developing fruits to raise them up slightly.

Rotate crops so that no member of the cucurbit family (squash, melon, and cucumber) is grown in the same place more often than every 4 years.

Caution: Cucumber leaves are easily damaged even by organically acceptable sprays, such as insecticidal soap. Use the most dilute solution recommended and use sparingly. Do not spray plants in direct sun or if temperatures are above 80°F, and don't spray drought-stressed plants.

Leaf and Vine Problems

Leaves with chewed holes. Cause: Cucumber beetles. Adults are $\frac{1}{4}$-inch-long, greenish yellow beetles with black stripes or spots. They attack young leaves and should be controlled immediately, as they can spread bacterial wilt and viruses. To deter beetle feeding, apply kaolin clay, especially to leaf undersides, and reapply after rain; handpick or vacuum beetles. As a last resort, spray infested plants with pyrethrin. Plant cultivars, such as 'Liberty' and 'Wisconsin SMR58', that are tolerant of cucumber beetles. If beetles are a perennial problem in your garden, choose cultivars with resistance to diseases spread by cucumber beetles. Clean up crop residues in fall to remove overwintering sites.

Leaves with pale green patches; afflicted leaves wilt and blacken. Cause: Squash bugs.

Adults are brownish black, ½-inch-long bugs. Immature bugs are whitish green or gray with dark heads and legs. Both emit a strong, sharp smell when crushed. Eggs are bright orange and laid on undersides of leaves. Handpick adults and eggs. Trap bugs by laying a board on the soil near plants. Squash bugs will hide underneath it and can be destroyed each morning.

Leaves with yellow patches; older leaves mottled and distorted. Cause: Mosaic. Remove and destroy diseased plants. Control aphids and cucumber beetles, which spread the virus. Choose mosaic-resistant cultivars, such as 'Eureka', 'Fancipak M', 'General Lee', 'Indy F1', 'Marketmore 76', and 'Stonewall'.

Leaves yellow, curled, and wilted. Cause: Aphids. Look for small, green, pink, gray, black, or white fluffy-coated, soft-bodied insects feeding on plants. Aphids can also transmit viruses. For mild infestations, knock pests off plants with a blast of water. Control persistent infestations with a weak insecticidal soap spray; see "Caution" on the opposite page before spraying. Reflective silver mulch confuses aphids and keeps them from finding your plants (see "Reflective Mulch" on page 357 for more information).

Leaves mottled yellow between veins; leaf undersides have purple spots. Cause: Downy mildew. As the disease progresses, older leaves turn brown and die and younger leaves become infected. Remove and destroy badly infected leaves. Downy mildew thrives during cool, moist weather. Avoid wetting foliage when watering, especially when conditions favor this fungus. Sprays of potassium bicarbonate may give some control and may reduce the spread of the disease. Plant mildew-resistant cultivars such as 'Diva F1', 'Eureka F1', 'Fancipak M', 'General Lee', and 'Marketmore 76'.

Leaves with spots, blotches, or brown areas. Causes: Powdery mildew; angular leaf spot; scab; anthracnose. Various fungal diseases affect cucumbers. Reduce problems by keeping foliage dry when watering and by not working amid wet plants. Remove and destroy infected foliage; provide good air circulation around plants; water and mulch to prevent drought stress. Powdery white spots on leaves, especially on upper surfaces, are caused by powdery mildew. Water-soaked spots that turn gray, die, and drop out leaving shotholes are caused by angular leaf spot or by scab. Angular leaf spot causes small, brown, angular spots on fruit. Scab-damaged fruit develops sunken, brown spots with sticky ooze. Scab is worse in cool, moist weather. Organic fungicides, including *Bacillus subtilis,* potassium bicarbonate, or a 0.5 percent solution of baking soda (1 teaspoon baking soda in 1 quart water) may slow the spread of an infection and give some control. Spray infected plants thoroughly. Many disease-resistant or tolerant cultivars are available, including 'Diva F1', 'Eureka F1', 'Fancipak M', 'General Lee', and 'Marketmore 76', all of which resist infection by downy mildew and scab fungi. 'Fancipak M' and 'Indy F1' resist angular leaf spot infection. Look for cultivars that resist or tolerate problems that are most prevalent in your area.

Yellow spots that turn brown are caused by anthracnose. Infected leaves eventually die. Infected fruit has circular, black, sunken cankers. Resistant cultivars include 'Fancipak M', 'Indy F1', 'Olympian', and 'Sweet Slice'.

Vines wilt suddenly. Cause: Squash vine borers. These fat, white, 1-inch-long larvae burrow into stems, leaving masses of yellow-green, saw-dustlike excrement at their entry points. Although this pest attacks all members of the cucurbit family, cucumbers typically are less affected than squash and gourds. For control information, see "Squash Vine Borer" on page 285.

Vines wilt at midday, starting with younger leaves; leaves remain green. Cause: Bacterial wilt. As the disease progresses, leaves fail to recover, and die. Cut wilted stems and press out drops of sap. If it is milky, sticky, and astringent, your plant is infected. Destroy infected plants immediately. Prevent problems by controlling cucumber beetles, since they spread the disease. Plant a resistant cultivar, such as 'Little Leaf'.

Fruit Problems

Fruit shrivels. Cause: Bacterial wilt. See "Vines wilt at midday, starting with younger leaves; leaves remain green" above for controls.

Fruit misshapen, one end not filled out. Causes: Diseases; poor pollination; nutrient deficiency. Many diseases cause misshapen fruit; use leaf symptoms to determine the disease causing the problem. If leaves are healthy, high temperatures may have damaged pollen, or bees may not have been active during bloom. Early in the season, wait for better conditions, or pollinate the flowers yourself by dusting pollen from male flowers onto female flowers. Later in the season, pull plants and wait for second planting to bear. If plants appear to be healthy and temperatures are not extreme, try spraying plants with compost tea or liquid kelp to correct possible nutrient deficiency.

Fruit with spots; flesh may rot. Causes: Angular leaf spot; Alternaria blight; black rot; scab; other fungal or bacterial diseases. See "Leaves with spots, blotches, or brown areas" on page 85 for controls.

Fruit dull bronze. Cause: Phosphorus deficiency. Spray plants with compost tea or liquid kelp to correct possible nutrient deficiency. Check with a soil test and amend soil as needed.

CURRANT *Ribes* spp. (Saxifragaceae)

Currants are upright or spreading, deciduous bushes growing 3 to 5 feet high. European black currants (*Ribes nigrum*) bear fruit mostly on the previous season's growth; red and white currants (*R. petraeum, R. rubrum,* and *R. sativum*) bear on the previous season's growth and on spurs—short branches that elongate only a fraction of an inch per year—on older stems. Currants are hardy in Zones 3–8.

Plant currants in full sun or partial shade and apply thick, organic mulch. To winter-prune red and white currants, cut all but six of the previous season's shoots to the ground. Remove all shoots more than 3 years old. To winter-prune black currants, cut two to five of the oldest branches to the ground and shorten any tall, old branches to vigorous young side shoots. Most currants are self-pollinating.

Problems

Leaves blistered or reddened. Cause: Aphids. You'll find these tiny insects clustered on leaf undersides. If damage is not severe, ignore it; otherwise, spray with insecticidal soap or neem, making sure to get the undersides of the leaves. Horticultural oil applied at a dormant-season dilution in winter helps prevent aphids.

Leaves yellow; stems die back. Cause: Currant borers. As spring growth begins, you can easily spot borer-infested canes because the leaves look weak and sickly. Currant borers spend the winter in canes, pupate in spring, and emerge as moths to reinfect currant bushes. The easiest control is to cut out and destroy infested canes as soon as you notice them.

Leaves spotted, yellow, and drop early. Causes: Septoria leaf spot; anthracnose. Since both of these fungal diseases overwinter on old leaf litter, rake up the leaves or bury them under thick mulch in autumn. If infection is severe enough to threaten plant vigor, spray with copper. Late-season defoliation rarely causes significant harm.

Leaves with rust-colored pustules on undersides. Cause: White pine blister rust. This fungal disease is passed back and forth between white pines (or other five-needled pines) and various species of currents. The disease is much more devastating to pines than to currents, so currents plantings are sometimes banned where pines are economically important. European black currants are most susceptible. Red and white currants generally are not much affected. Avoid planting susceptible currants near white pines.

Leaves with white powdery coating. Cause: Powdery mildew. Usually this fungal disease is harmless, but if it becomes severe, spray plants with potassium bicarbonate or sodium bicarbonate (baking soda). Thin plants to improve air circulation and water during dry spells to prevent moisture stress, which promotes powdery mildew infection.

Fruit colors and drops early. Cause: Currant fruit fly larvae. For more information, see "Fruit colors and drops early" on page 108.

Foliage stripped from bushes just as leaves expand. Cause: Imported currantworms. For controls, see "Foliage stripped from bushes just as leaves expand" on page 109.

DAHLIA Dahlia

Descended from species native to Central and South America, modern dahlia hybrids are most often grown as annuals in temperate climates and the roots are dug, overwintered indoors, and replanted the following spring. Thousands of culti-vars offer a huge array of flower shapes, colors, and sizes to gardeners willing to meet dahlias' rigorous growth requirements. They are thick-stemmed, rather coarse-textured plants ranging from 1 to 8 feet tall; midsummer to fall blossoms may be 1 to 15 inches in diameter.

Select a planting site in full sun and prepare the soil to a depth of 1 foot, incorporating plenty of compost or other organic matter. Dahlias require good drainage; raised beds help meet this need. Plant tuberous roots after all danger of frost has passed; place them horizontally in the soil with the buds upward and fleshy roots spread out in the planting hole, 6 to 8 inches below the soil surface. Cover the buds with about 3 inches of soil at planting, then gradually fill in as the shoots grow. All but the shortest cultivars need support for heavy flower heads. Set stakes at planting time.

Pinching shoots back during the growing season promotes bushier growth and increased flowering; removal of some buds increases the size of the remaining flowers. These heavy feeders benefit from side-dressings of compost or general-purpose fertilizer throughout summer. Avoid high-nitrogen fertilizers, which encourage weak growth and pest and disease problems. Dahlias need at least 1 inch of water weekly; soil should be neither soggy nor completely dry. Mulch to retain moisture.

Dahlias survive winter outdoors in Zones 9–10, given good drainage; otherwise they must be dug and stored. Cut plants back to about 1 foot and dig the roots in fall after the first frost. Shake away loose soil and lay roots in the sun to dry for several hours. After drying, remove the tops and store the roots in a cool, dark, dry place. Check roots at regular intervals to make sure they're not so dry that they shrivel up.

Problems

Leaves wilt; stems collapse. Cause: Borers. Both European corn borer and stalk borer caterpillars are long, thin, and striped. They tunnel within dahlia stems and flower stalks, causing collapse. Inspection of damaged plants reveals small, round holes in stems. Remove and destroy infested stems; clean up debris where pests overwinter. If borers have been a problem in past years, spray BTK weekly in early summer before borers enter stems.

Leaves mottled white or yellow. Cause: Leafhoppers. Feeding by wedge-shaped leafhoppers gives leaves a speckled appearance followed by dry, brown blotches; foliage becomes distorted and falls off. In addition to feeding injury, leafhoppers can spread aster yellows and other diseases. Encourage natural predators such as bigeyed bugs and parasitic wasps. See "Leafhoppers" on page 271 for more controls.

Leaves yellow-green or deformed; shoots spindly, stunted. Cause: Viral diseases. Several viruses infect dahlias, causing stunted growth and yellowed leaves with ring spots, mottling, and pale or dead areas. Aphids and leafhoppers spread viruses; control pests to limit infection. Dig and destroy dahlias showing symptoms.

Flowers and foliage with gray mold. Cause: Botrytis blight. During wet, cloudy weather, *Botrytis* fungi can cause flowers to turn brown and rot. Pick and destroy infected plant parts. See "Botrytis Blight" on page 326 for more controls.

DAPHNE Daphne

Daphnes are small evergreen or deciduous shrubs; most produce fragrant flowers. They are excellent foundation shrubs.

Daphnes are not the easiest plant to grow; there is considerable controversy as to their soil preferences. Furthermore, for no known reason, plants will occasionally die. Plant them in organically enriched soils in sun or light shade and be sparing with fertilizer and water. Spring planting as container-grown or balled-and-burlapped plants suits them best.

Daphnes are little troubled by insects. In warmer climates scales may be a problem; see "Scales, Armored" on page 282.

DELPHINIUM Delphinium, larkspur

Dense flower spikes of lavender, true blue, pink, and white make delphiniums summer garden showstoppers. Towering flower stalks range in height from 1½ to 8 feet, depending on the cultivar. Large, lobed, and deeply toothed leaves cluster near the ground.

Soil for delphiniums must be high in organic matter, slightly alkaline, well-drained, and moist. Select a site protected from damaging winds, and provide stakes for brittle, hollow flower stems. These plants prefer full sun, but benefit from afternoon shade where summers are long and hot. Delphiniums need cool summers and may die during extended hot, humid periods. Even under favorable conditions, most plantings lose vigor and need renovation every 3 to 5 years.

Problems

Leaves, stems, and buds distorted, sticky; clusters of small insects. Cause: Aphids. See "Aphids" on page 250 for controls.

Leaves with tan or brown blotches or serpentine tunnels. Cause: Leafminers. For recommended controls, see "Leafmining Flies" on page 271.

Leaves with large, ragged holes. Cause: Slugs and snails. See "Slugs/Snails" on page 284 for control information.

Leaves covered with white powder. Cause: Powdery mildew. See "Powdery Mildew" on page 322 for controls.

Stems exude sawdustlike material and break; leaves wilt. Cause: Borers. See "Stems exude sawdustlike material and break; leaves wilt" on page 100 for more information.

Leaves stippled, reddish to yellow, with fine webbing. Cause: Spider mites. Mites target water-stressed plants in hot, dry weather; adequate watering guards against them. Hose down infested plants; a strong stream knocks mites off plants, but may damage brittle flower stalks. See "Mites, Spider" on page 275 for more controls.

Stems blacken at base; leaves wilt; plant falls over. Cause: Crown or root rots. Both fungi and bacteria cause crown and root rot of delphiniums. Plants may wilt suddenly or turn yellow and wilt slowly. Stems and roots may turn black; mold may appear. Poorly drained, overly wet soil promotes rot; choose well-drained sites and add organic matter to improve drainage. Avoid injury to crowns when digging near plants; keep winter mulch away from crowns. Remove and destroy infected plants; wash tools used around diseased plants. Solarize the soil before replanting.

Leaves with yellow, brown, or black spots. Cause: Fungi. Several fungi cause spots on leaves. As spots enlarge, entire leaves may wither. Remove and destroy infected foliage; space plants to encourage good air circulation; avoid wetting foliage when watering. Dig and destroy seriously infected plants. Keep the garden free of debris, and cut plants to the ground at the end of the growing season. Apply preventive sulfur sprays if leaf spot is a serious problem.

DEUTZIA Deutzia

Deutzias are a group of low-growing, deciduous, spring-blooming shrubs of rounded form. They are excellent in the shrub border or massed as an informal hedge.

Deutzias tolerate virtually any soil in sun or very light shade. Set out in spring as bareroot, balled-and-burlapped, or container-grown plants. They bloom on the previous year's wood, so prune after blooming, cutting back the branches that have flowered.

While deutzias are relatively free of major insect problems, aphids may feed on the leaves. For controls, see "Aphids" on page 250. Leafminers may occasionally damage the leaves; see "Leafmining Flies" on page 271.

DIANTHUS Pink, carnation

Sprightly pinks bear fringed flowers in shades of pink, white, maroon, and red over tidy, gray-green, grasslike leaves. *Dianthus* spp. range in height from 4 to 18 inches with spreads of 1 to 2 feet; most bloom profusely from late spring through summer. Many hybrids are available, and popular species include sweet William (*D. barbatus*), a short-lived perennial often grown as an annual, and mat-forming maiden pinks (*D. deltoides*).

Well-drained, average soil with neutral to slightly alkaline pH is best for pinks. Most prefer full sun, but tolerate light shade, especially where summer temperatures are high. Pinks may decline in the heat of summer; select heat-resistant cultivars for southern gardens. Avoid overwatering but don't let plants wilt from drought stress. Cut plant back at the end of the blooming season to encourage new growth. Rejuvenate plantings by dividing them every 2 to 3 years.

Problems

Leaves stippled, reddish to yellow, with fine webbing. Cause: Spider mites. See "Mites, Spider" on page 275 for controls.

Leaves, stems, and buds distorted, sticky; clusters of small insects. Cause: Aphids. These pests damage plants by sucking sap from leaves, stems, and buds. In addition, aphids transmit viruses that can injure plants long after the pests are vanquished. Use a strong spray of water to knock aphids off plants. See "Aphids" on page 250 for more controls.

Leaves and flowers greenish yellow, distorted; new growth spindly. Cause: Viruses. Several viruses may infect pinks, stunting growth and mottling and spotting foliage. Control aphids and leafhoppers that spread viruses; there is no cure for infected plants. Remove and destroy plants with viral symptoms; don't compost diseased materials.

Leaf surfaces pale; powdery orange spots beneath. Cause: Rust. This fungus sometimes bothers sweet Williams, deforming leaves and stems and causing early leaf drop. See "Rust" on page 315 for controls.

Plant wilts; stems rot at soil level. Cause: Fungal or bacterial rots. Pinks are susceptible to various diseases that cause plants to wilt suddenly or to rot at or below the soil surface. This is especially true of plants growing in wet or poorly drained soil or in crowded conditions. Prevent problems by planting in well-drained sites, and avoid overwatering and overcrowding; keep mulch away from stem bases. Remove and destroy infected plants; do not compost diseased materials.

If the problem is serious, solarize the soil before replanting a site.

DICENTRA Bleeding heart

These graceful plants carry prolific stems of dainty, heart-shaped flowers. Common bleeding heart (*Dicentra spectabilis*) is a Japanese native with dangling, pink and white blooms in late spring to early summer; native fringed bleeding heart (*D. eximia*) has fernlike leaves and bears pink or white blossoms on 1-foot spikes throughout the summer. Plants range from 1 to 3 feet in height and spread.

Plant bleeding hearts in moist, rich, and well-drained soil in light shade. Plants tolerate full sun only where summers are cool. Avoid sites with standing water, which is an invitation to stem rot. Mark the spot where you plant bleeding heart's fleshy roots—common bleeding heart foliage typically dies back after blooming and all species disappear in winter. Plant bleeding heart roots 2 feet apart and don't disturb them; roots are brittle and do not transplant or divide easily. Few pests or diseases pose serious trouble for well-grown bleeding hearts.

Problems

Stems blacken at base; leaves wilt; plant falls over. Causes: Wilts; stem rot. Many destructive fungi live in soil and will attack plants at soil level. Plants may wilt suddenly or yellow and wilt slowly. Stems and roots may turn black; mold may appear. Discolored, water-soaked lesions girdle stems; plants gradually die. Poorly drained, overly wet soil promotes wilt and rot; choose well-drained sites and add organic matter to improve drainage. Avoid overwatering and overcrowding; keep mulch away from the base of stems. Remove and destroy infected plans; wash tools used around diseased plants.

DIGITALIS Foxglove

Common foxgloves (*Digitalis purpurea*) are actually biennials that self-sow so well that they often function as perennials. Bell-like flowers in shades of purple, pink, and white cover 2- to 5-foot spires in late spring. Large, coarse, dark green leaves cluster near the plant's base. True perennial species are available, including rusty foxglove (*D. derruginea*) and yellow foxglove (*D. grandiflora*).

Foxgloves enjoy a shady site with rich, moist, well-drained, slightly acidic soil. Plants tolerate full sun, but favor cool weather and need shade in extreme summer heat. Water regularly to maintain soil moisture. Stake tall cultivars to support flower spikes; plant in a sheltered site. Remove foxgloves after they have set seed and self-sown next year's crop. Cutting flowers before they set seed promotes second-year blooms, but flowering is reduced the second year.

Problems

Leaves and/or flowers with holes. Cause: Japanese beetles. See "Japanese Beetle" on page 269 for control information.

Leaves covered with white powder. Cause: Powdery mildew. See "Powdery Mildew" on page 322 for information on controlling this common and troublesome fungal disease.

Leaves with large, ragged holes. Cause: Slugs and snails. Slugs and snails may hide below foxgloves' low, broad foliage. Limit them by removing faded leaves and plant debris. See "Slugs/Snails" on page 284 for more control information.

Leaves, stems, and buds distorted, sticky; clusters of small insects. Cause: Foxglove aphids. These pests feed on other plants but overwinter as eggs on foxgloves. Good gardening practices will slow the spread of foxglove aphids. Remove spent plants in fall to reduce aphid activity in following years. See "Aphids" on page 250 for controls.

DILL *Anethum graveolens* (Umbelliferae)

Dill is an annual herb grown for its tangy leaves and seeds. Sow seed outdoors where the plants are to grow after the soil is warm. Dill prefers a site in full sun with rich, well-drained, moist soil and a pH between 5.0 and 8.0.

Dill is rarely troubled by pests or diseases. Virus-infected leaves are dwarfed and deformed and abnormally colored. Destroy infected plants and control leafhoppers, as they spread viruses. Leaf blight causes dark spots with yellow edges. To control this fungal disease, spray plants with fish emulsion. Bright green caterpillars with yellow and black markings dining on your dill are probably the larvae of black swallowtail butterflies; handpick them if you can't bear to share, or let them have the dill in exchange for their future, beautiful adult forms. See the Vegetables entry beginning on page 219 for other possible problems.

ECHINACEA Purple coneflower

Purple, daisylike petals surround the prickly, brown centers of purple coneflower's (*Echinacea purpurea*) 1- to 4-inch-wide blossoms. Plants grow 3 to 4 feet tall and bloom from early summer until frost. The cone-shaped centers persist throughout the winter, providing interest after the petals have fallen. Pale coneflower (*E. pallida*) has creamy white petals.

These durable prairie natives like full sun, but endure poor soils and tolerate some drought once established. Shaded sites cause tall, spindly growth, as does excess fertilization. Pinch in spring to encourage sturdy, branching growth. Coneflowers are somewhat short-lived; divide clumps every 3 years or so to rejuvenate plantings, placing divisions 20 inches apart. Plants also start easily from seeds, which need light to germinate. If you are growing improved cultivars of coneflower, be aware that self-sown seedlings will overtake hybrid clumps, so weed out or relocate seedlings when they appear.

Japanese beetles can quickly damage flowers and skeletonize the foliage of purple coneflowers. See "Japanese Beetle" on page 269 for controls.

EGGPLANT *Solanum melongena* **var.** *esculentum* (**Solanaceae**)

Eggplants are tender perennials that are grown as annuals in temperate regions for the firm-fleshed fruit. Fruit shapes range from long and thin to short and blocky and may be white, yellow, green, red, or dark purple. Harvest fruit at any size, preferably before seeds turn brown and harden.

Culture

Eggplants do best in full sun and well-drained, fertile soil with lots of organic matter and a pH of 6.0 to 6.8 (they will tolerate a pH as low as 5.5). Eggplants need a high level of nitrogen and moderate levels of phosphorus and potassium. Have the soil tested and correct any deficiencies. They grow best at temperatures between 70° and 85°F, and perform poorly when temperatures rise above 95° or fall below 65°F. Soil that is evenly and consistently moist but not soggy promotes plant health and productivity. A raised bed supplied with drip irrigation and covered by black plastic mulch to warm the soil makes an ideal site for growing eggplants.

Purchase stocky, pest- and disease-free plants, or start your own from seed indoors. Eggplant seeds germinate best between 80° and 90°F. Grow seedlings at 70°F and keep them indoors until average daily temperatures have reached 65° to 70°F. Protect transplants from wind, and water new transplants well with seaweed extract or compost tea to give them a good start. Spray plants with seaweed extract with 1 teaspoon of Epsom salts added per gallon when the first flowers open to improve fruit set.

Eggplants are susceptible to many of the same problems, pests, and diseases as tomatoes, including flower drop or misshapen fruit due to extreme temperatures, flea beetles, Colorado potato beetles, aphids, hornworms, mites, Verticillium and Fusarium wilts, tobacco mosaic virus, and anthracnose fruit rot. See the Tomato entry beginning on page 205 for symptoms, causes, and controls.

Cultivars that tolerate tobacco mosaic virus include 'Blacknite', 'Classy Chassis', 'Dusky Hybrid', and 'Epic'.

Problems

Leaves turn yellow, then brown. Cause: Lace bugs. Leaves eventually die. These flat, gray to brown, $\frac{1}{10}$-inch-long insects have lacelike wings and feed on the undersides of leaves. Spray with insecticidal soap, paying particular attention to leaf undersides; apply pyrethrin as a last resort if infestation is severe and damaging. Prevent lace bug damage by covering plants with row cover until they flower.

Leaves with large holes. Cause: Blister beetles. These $\frac{3}{4}$-inch-long, elongated beetles have yellow and black stripes. Wear gloves to handpick, since these beetles secrete a substance that may cause blisters. Blister beetle larvae help control grasshoppers, so try to avoid spraying to control them. Use row cover over plants until they bloom to keep blister beetles at bay. Spray with pyrethrin as a last resort, if damage to plants is excessive and the beetles can't be controlled by other means.

Leaves with light-centered, gray to brown spots; fruit with pale, sunken spots. Cause: Phomopsis blight. Stems may also develop dark areas. Fruit spots enlarge and run together, affected flesh is discolored and may rot and shrivel. Spray plants with copper if symptoms are present and if weather is wet or humid. Prevent problems by planting resistant cultivars like 'Florida Beauty' and 'Florida Market.'

Fruit with dry, brown chew marks. Cause: Colorado potato beetles. See "Colorado Potato Beetle" on page 259 for description and controls.

EPIMEDIUM Epimedium

These 6- to 12-inch-tall, evergreen to semi-ever-green plants bear clusters of ¾-inch, yellow, white, or pink flowers in early spring. Compound leaves consist of 2- to 3-inch-long, heart-shaped leaflets, tinged pink or red in spring and turning yellow or bronze in fall.

Epimediums are slow to establish, but can form a hardy groundcover for most partially shaded locations and will grow in sites where low soil fertility limits other perennials. They also will grow in dry shade. Cut foliage low to the ground in early spring to keep it from hiding the flowers. Epimediums are seldom bothered by pests, although slugs and snails can attack. See "Slugs/ Snails" on page 284 for controls.

EUONYMUS Euonymus, spindle tree

Euonymus are evergreen or deciduous trees, shrubs, or vines, always with opposite leaves and generally with toothed leaves. Shrubby species are good for hedges or specimen plants; vining species are great as groundcovers or on walls. A number of species have been listed as invasive; consult your local Cooperative Extension for a list of the species that are a problem in your area.

Set euonymus out in spring or fall as balled-and-burlapped or container-grown plants. The plants are tolerant of sun or shade, but heavy shade may decrease fruiting.

Problems

Leaves yellow; stems and leaves covered with small bumps. Cause: Scale insects are the most common insect pests. For control measures, see "Scales, Armored" on page 282.

Trunk or roots with swollen, wartlike growths. Cause: Crown gall. For controls, see "Trunk or roots with swollen, wartlike growths" on page 214 or 340.

Leaves wrinkled and discolored. Cause: Aphids. See "Aphids" on page 250 for controls.

Leaves and shoots blackened; leaves with moist or brown sunken spots. Cause: Anthrac-nose. See "Anthracnose" on page 310 for controls.

Leaves with powdery white coating. Cause: Powdery mildew. See "Powdery Mildew" on page 322 for controls.

EUPHORBIA Spurge

The perennial species of *Euphorbia* grown in gardens range in size from prostrate myrtle euphorbia (*E. myrsinites*) to 1- to 1½-foot, clump-forming cushion spurge (*E. epithymoides*) to 2- to 3-foot-tall Griffith's spurge (*E. griffithii*). Brightly colored flowers, which are actually showy bracts, bring shades of yellow and red-orange to the garden from early spring through summer, depending on the species. Plants remain attractive after bracts have faded; some offer red fall color. Also characteristic of this genus is milky sap that can cause skin irritation and burning; wear gloves when handling spurges and avoid contact with the sap.

Spurges prefer full sun and well-drained, moist soil but may become invasive under these ideal conditions. In southern zones, they need partial shade during the heat of summer to prevent leggy, open growth. Spurges don't mind average to poor soil and most tolerate some drought. Divide vigorously growing plants every 2 to 3 years to check their spread, being sure to leave solid roots on each division.

Problems

Plant wilting. Cause: Lettuce root aphids. Spurges are occasionally infested by tiny white to yellow insects that feed underground on its roots as well as those of lettuce. Remove weeds to prevent aphids from multiplying in early spring. Add compost to soil to encourage beneficial nematodes, ground beetles, and other soil predators. Improve watering to help plants withstand root damage. In severe cases, drench the soil around spurges with neem.

FAGUS Beech

Beeches are deciduous trees with gray bark and alternate leaves. They are one of the finest specimen trees for large landscapes. They do not, however, thrive on city conditions, and their spreading growth and extensive surface roots make it virtually impossible to grow other plants beneath them.

Set out balled-and-burlapped plants in spring in well-drained, evenly moist soil. Full sun is best but they'll tolerate part shade. Beeches are very sensitive to root zone disturbances—cuts, fills,

compaction—so keep them safe from such abuse. A thick layer of organic mulch will protect the shallow roots and help keep them cool and moist.

Problems

Leaves skeletonized. Causes: Cankerworms; other caterpillars. Cankerworms are $\frac{1}{2}$- to 1-inch, yellow, green, or brown caterpillars that feed on beech leaves, often defoliating the tree. To avoid this problem, apply a band of sticky coating, such as Tanglefoot, around the base of the tree in spring to keep females from climbing up and laying their eggs. Apply fresh coats in September and February to trap both spring and fall cankerworms. If their feeding becomes a problem, spray leaves with BTK as soon as you notice the pests; continue every 2 weeks until they are gone.

Several other caterpillars, including gypsy moths, loopers, and tent caterpillars, feed on beeches. See "Leaves skeletonized or with large holes; branches may be webbed" and "Leaves skeletonized or plant defoliated" on page 212 for more information and controls.

Trunks or branches with small holes; limbs die or break off. Cause: Borers. See "Trunk or branches with small holes; limbs die or break off" on page 214 for controls.

Leaves yellow; stems and leaves covered with small bumps. Cause: Scales. A number of scale insects attack beeches, including the white-colored beech scale. Note that beeches may be damaged by applications of horticultural oil; instead, spray lime-sulfur on the trunk and branches in late winter. For other controls, see "Leaves yellow; stems and leaves covered with small bumps" on page 213.

Trunks or branches with oozing lesions; branch tips die back. Cause: Canker. Bleeding canker is spread by the beech scale, which feeds on

FIG   95

the bark, causing wounds that permit entry of the fungus. Control the insect and you'll prevent the disease. For more on dealing with canker, see "Trunk or branches with oozing lesions; branch tips die back" on page 214.

Leaves wrinkled and discolored. Cause: Aphids. See "Aphids" on page 250 for controls.

Leaves with powdery white coating. Cause: Powdery mildew. See "Leaves with powdery white coating" on page 213 for controls.

Leaves with spots. Cause: Leaf spots. See "Leaves with spots" on page 213 for controls.

FIG *Ficus carica* (**Moraceae**)

Figs are deciduous, subtropical trees or bushes that grow 10 to 30 feet tall and bear yellow, green, or brown fruit on 1- and 2-year-old wood. They are hardy in Zones 8–10.

Fig trees need abundant sunlight but tolerate a wide range of soil types. In colder areas, plant figs against a wall or wrap them for the winter to minimize dieback from cold. Each winter, head back long branches to maintain tree shape and induce vigorous new growth. Thin out crowded, weak, diseased, or crossed branches. Cultivars such as 'Celeste' and 'Mission', which fruit best on last year's wood, should be pruned more lightly than cultivars such as 'Magnolia' and 'Kadota', which fruit heavily on new growth. Some figs need cross-pollination; others develop fruit without pollina-tion. Check pollination needs before buying plants.

Fruit Problems

Fruit soured, mushy, or smutty. Cause: Sour bugs. These small black beetles crawl into the eye of fruit and lay eggs that hatch into white grubs. The grubs carry bacteria that cause figs to turn sour, mushy, or smutty. Soured fruit may have a

drop of pink, sticky fluid at its eye and a fermented odor. Smut produces dusty black spores. To prevent sour bug damage, grow closed-eye cultivars such as 'Celeste', 'Green Ischia', 'Mission', and 'Sierra'. Clean up fallen fruit, which attracts beetles, and trap beetles in containers of fermenting fruit.

Fruit with ants inside. Cause: Insect feeding. Ants enter the fruit eye to feed on ripe fruit. To thwart ants, band stems with plastic or heavy paper coated with sticky material. Or place ant bait stations containing boric acid around trees. Wood ashes sprinkled around the base of trees also help prevent ants from climbing up to fruit.

Leaf and Branch Problems

Leaves with raised, rusty spots on undersides. Cause: Rust. Leaves may yellow and die. To control this fungal disease, rake up and destroy fallen leaves. Where the problem is severe, spray with copper.

Leaves spotted. Cause: Leaf blight. Various fungal diseases attack fig leaves and twigs. Control all these conditions by raking up and destroying fallen leaves and fruit. Prune to remove infected twigs and allow sunlight to reach inner branches.

Whole Plant Problems

Whole plant lacking vigor; bumps on twigs and leaves. Causes: Scales; nematodes. Scales look like yellow, gray, white, or reddish or purplish brown bumps that you can scrape off stems or leaves with your fingernail. Many natural enemies, including lady beetles and chalcid wasps, help keep scales in check. Prune off heavily infected branches and destroy them. For serious infestations, spray before growth begins with horticultural oil at a dormant-season dilution.

Nematodes are soil-dwelling, microscopic worms. Some nematodes perform helpful tasks, such as breaking down organic matter; others attack plant roots and cause diseaselike symptoms. Figs grown in sandy soils are especially susceptible to nematode infestation. If you have sandy soil, plant your fig tree near a building and apply a thick, organic mulch. Both of these strategies seem to deter nematodes. If nematodes are common in your area, solarize the soil for 1 or 2 months during the summer before planting figs. Buy figs grafted onto nematode-resistant rootstocks. Planting a cover crop of marigolds or adding chitin to the soil also helps control nematodes.

FILBERT *Corylus avellana, C. Americana* (Betulaceae)

Filberts grow as deciduous trees or shrubs reaching about 20 feet. They are hardy in Zones 4–8. To set nuts, most filbert cultivars need cross-pollination with a second cultivar.

Filberts blossom very early in spring, so they need a site not prone to spring frosts. Plant in full sun. Since plants blossom on last year's wood, annual pruning is needed to stimulate current season's growth, which will bear next year's nuts.

Problems

Nut kernels blackened; nut shell has small hole. Cause: Filbertworms. These are the larvae of a brown moth. The easiest control is to keep the ground beneath trees free of debris, such as leaves, fallen nuts, and shells, because the larvae pupate on the ground throughout winter.

New leaves twisted or curled and covered with a sticky coating. Cause: Aphids. Look on leaf undersides for clusters of these tiny black insects. Leaves also may be covered with a black fungus, called sooty mold, which feeds on honeydew secreted by these pests. Wash aphids from

leaves with a strong spray of water, or spray with insecticidal soap, focusing on the undersides of leaves. Use neem as a last resort for persistent infestations. Spray with a dormant-season dilution of horticultural oil in late winter to kill overwintering eggs.

Flower buds swollen. Cause: Bud mites. Infected flowers don't produce nuts. Resistant cultivars, including 'Barcelona', 'Cosford', 'Delta', and 'Epsilon', have tight bud scales that resist mite penetration. In severe cases, spray trees with superior oil, generally in May, when the mites crawl out of the swollen buds to attack healthy buds.

Branches blighted. Causes: Eastern filbert blight; western filbert blight. Eastern blight has no cure. It is present in the East and carried on American filberts. Young branches are destroyed first, then older branches and the trunk, without killing the roots. American filberts have some tolerance for the fungus, so they have been used in breeding with other filbert species in an attempt to create disease-resistant plants bearing high-quality nuts. 'Geneva' and 'Slate' are blight-resistant cultivars.

In the Pacific Northwest, blight is caused by western filbert blight, a bacterial disease. Small, angular spots appear on leaves, water-soaked at first, then turning reddish brown. Cankers form on branches, which then may die. Control this blight by preventing sunburn and winter injury, especially on young plants, which are most susceptible. On older plants, only smaller twigs die. Spray with copper and prune out infected twigs in winter.

FLOWERS Perennials, Annuals, Biennials, and Bulbs

Your approach to pests and diseases will probably vary depending on the type of flower that has been attacked. Perennials are plants you hope to have around for a long time, so eliminating hungry insects and disfiguring diseases becomes more important—especially if you are dealing with a newly transplanted specimen that is just becoming established. With few exceptions, the pests and diseases that plague perennials are best controlled through good site selection and cultural practices, as described in the individual plant entries.

Controlling pests and diseases on annual plants is largely a matter of prevention. Since annuals die naturally after one season, insect and disease control is less critical than on more permanent plants. Sometimes, though, pest problems can cut short the bloom season and your enjoyment of the flowering annuals, so you'll need to be aware of the few potential problems.

The symptoms listed below represent damage caused by pests and diseases that attack a wide variety of flowers. Controls for these problems do not vary significantly among plant species.

Leaf Problems

Leaves stippled with yellow; foliage webbed. Cause: Spider mites. See "Mites, Spider" on page 275 for controls.

Leaves yellow; plant weakened. Cause: Whiteflies. These tiny, white, mothlike flies and their flattened, scalelike larvae feed on leaves, sucking out the plant juices. The adults often fly up in a cloud when you disturb an infested plant. Whiteflies secrete a sugary substance called honeydew, which makes leaves sticky and may encourage the growth of sooty mold fungus; see "Leaves with black coating" on page 99 for more information.

Eliminating garden weeds helps keep whitefly populations down. It is also important to inspect purchased plants carefully to avoid bringing an infestation home from the garden center. See "Whiteflies" on page 290 for controls.

Leaves and/or flowers with holes. Causes: Japanese beetles; other leaf-eating beetles. Perennial beds attract a number of hungry beetles, including ¾-inch black blister beetles; ¹⁄₁₀-inch flea beetles; ⅓-inch, reddish brown rose chafers; and nocturnal, ⅓-inch, gray Fuller rose beetles. Iridescent blue-green with bronze wing covers, ½-inch Japanese beetles top this list of troublesome pests; the adults devour the leaves, stalks, and flowers of nearly 300 plant species, while the ¾-inch, C-shaped grub larvae feed on roots and are a major pest of lawn grasses.

Injury caused by adult beetles ranges from small holes in leaves to skeletonized foliage to complete defoliation. Feeding by weevils, such as long-nosed Fuller rose beetles, resembles "ticket punches" around leaf margins. Japanese beetles are fond of flowers and often do most of their damage there. Most beetles are active during the day and are large enough to be readily visible while they feed. Most weevils feed at night; use a flashlight to find them.

Handpick adult beetles into a can of soapy water or a 5 percent solution of isopropyl alcohol. Wear gloves if your pests are blister beetles; contact with crushed beetles can cause burns and blisters on skin. Shake infested plants in early morning to knock beetles onto a dropcloth, then scoop them up and destroy them. See "Japanese Beetle" on page 269 and "Root Weevils" on page 279 for more controls.

Leaves with large, ragged holes. Cause: Slugs and snails. Differing only in the presence or absence of a shell, slugs and snails range in size from ⅛ inch to 8 inches and may be gray, tan, green, black, yellow, or spotted. The cool, moist soil conditions favored by many perennials make plantings appealing to these busy mollusks. Mulch and plants with low-growing leaves provide shady hiding places from which they emerge to feed nocturnally. All species rasp large holes in leaves, stems, and bulbs; slimy trails of mucus also signal their presence. See "Slugs/Snails" on page 284 for more information and controls for these pests.

Leaves, stems, and buds distorted, sticky; clusters of small insects. Cause: Aphids. Several species of pear-shaped, $\frac{1}{32}$- to $\frac{1}{8}$-inch aphids plague perennials, clustering under leaves and on growing tips. Aphids suck plant sap, causing leaf and bud distortion and blossom and leaf drop. Their feeding

Healthy Bulb Basics

Healthy bulbs and good culture go a long way toward successful plantings of bulbs, which have a variety of underground storage organs, including corms, rhizomes, and tuberous roots. Some of these are modified stems, while others are simply enlarged roots. Although structurally different, all store food for plant growth in subsequent seasons and spread (in the case of rhizomes) or otherwise multiply asexually to increase a plant's population.

Whether they are hardy corms, such as crocuses, that bloom year after year in the same spot, or tender rhizomes, such as cannas, that must be dug up and stored over winter in cold-winter regions, bulbs generally enjoy similar growing environments and suffer similar problems. Pest and disease prevention is preferable to applying controls after trouble arises. The following bulb-buyer's guidelines will help you avoid most bulb problems.

■ Buy only dormant bulbs that show little, if any, root development and no topgrowth other than a pale, fat bud. (Lilies, however, are never completely dormant; their bulbs often have fleshy roots attached.)

■ Purchase and plant bulbs at the right time. Reputable dealers sell bulbs in defined seasons: fall for spring-flowering bulbs (daffodils, tulips), spring for summer-flowering bulbs (lilies, glads), and summer for fall-flowering species (some crocuses).

■ Look for bulbs that have their papery skins—called tunics—intact. These contain natural compounds that inhibit disease and premature sprouting.

■ Choose bulbs packaged in materials that permit air to enter. Damp bulbs in plastic bags often rot.

■ Select bulbs that are firm with few wrinkles and no soft spots. Healthy bulbs seem somewhat heavier than their size suggests. Avoid unusually lightweight bulbs and those with cuts, dark or water-soaked spots, or discolored or scabby areas.

Growing healthy, trouble-free bulbs also depends on good cultural practices. Fleshy bulbs are prone to bacterial and fungal rot organisms, most of which thrive in wet conditions. Prepare planting beds well and make sure the soil is well-drained. Handle bulbs carefully when planting, to avoid injuries that provide access to diseases. Remove problem plants quickly to keep pests and diseases from spreading. Always let bulb foliage die back naturally to allow food production for growth and flowering in subsequent years. Mark sites where bulbs are planted so you can find them after foliage has faded. Clean up flower beds in fall to remove plant debris that offers shelter to many pests and diseases.

may spread diseases such as aster yellows. As they feed, they excrete sticky honeydew on which sooty mold grows; see "Leaves with black coating" below for more information. Wash aphids from plants with a strong spray of water; repeat as needed to control infestations. See "Aphids" on page 250 for more controls.

Leaves with black coating. Cause: Sooty mold. This fungus grows on the sugary, sticky honeydew produced by aphids and other sucking pests such as scales, whiteflies, and mealybugs. The black fungal coating doesn't harm leaves directly, but it does shade the leaves and reduce growth. The best control is to deal with the pests that are producing the honeydew. Identify the pest and apply the appropriate control. (If the plant itself doesn't show signs of pest damage, the honeydew may be dripping down from an overhanging plant.) On small plants, wipe the leaves with a damp cloth to remove the honeydew and the sooty mold.

Leaves covered with white powder. Cause: Powdery mildew. Powdery white or grayish fungal patches grow on upper leaf surfaces of plants subject to poor air circulation or hot, humid weather. As the disease spreads, leaves become distorted and may drop off. The fungus feeds on plant nutrients, causing leaf yellowing. Powdery mildew is more severe when growing conditions are unsatisfactory, and fungus from one plant can spread through a crowded area within days. See "Powdery Mildew" on page 322 for controls.

Leaves greenish yellow; growth poor. Cause: Aster yellows. This is a common disease of many annuals. Leafhoppers carry the disease, spreading it through their sap-sucking feeding habits. These tiny, green or brown, wedge-shaped insects move about by running sideways or by hopping. They usually feed on the undersides of plant leaves. Affected plants branch abnormally.

Flowers are deformed or absent. Flowers, regardless of original color, turn a yellow-green. There is no cure. Remove and destroy infected plants. See "Leafhoppers" on page 271 for controls of the pests that spread this disease.

Buds and leaves deformed or dwarfed. Cause: True bugs. Several of the generally shield-shaped true bugs (order Hemiptera), including tarnished plant bugs, four-lined plant bugs, lace bugs, and lygus bugs, feed on perennials. While many species of true bugs are beneficial insects, the pests in this group pierce plant tissue to drink sap, injecting toxins that deform plant tissues. In addition to dwarfing and deforming plants, feeding by true bugs causes sunken, rounded, tan to dark brown spots on foliage. As leaves grow, the dead areas tear into small holes.

Many of these pests overwinter in garden refuse; remove weeds and debris from area in spring and fall. Plant groundcovers and pollen plants to encourage populations of predatory insects. Handpick pests and drop them into a jar of soapy water. See "Plant Bugs" on page 278 for more controls.

Leaves and stems with white, cottony clusters. Cause: Mealybugs. At first, mealybugs may be hard to see, but as the plant wilts, and mealybugs rapidly multiply, colonies become quite visible. These minute insects are covered with a fluffy white coating. They suck plant sap and cause the plant to look unhealthy. Mealybugs secrete a sugary substance called honeydew, which makes leaves sticky and may encourage the growth of sooty mold fungus; see "Leaves with black coating" on this page for more information. Control small infestations by spraying them off the plant with water. See "Mealybugs" on page 273 for more controls.

Leaves with spots. Cause: Leaf spots. A large

number of fungi and bacteria cause spots on plant leaves, in a variety of colors, shapes, and sizes. In some cases, the spots may spread to cover entire leaves, stunting plant growth.

Fortunately, the same controls are effective against many leaf spot diseases. Remove and discard infected leaves. Thin plants and avoid crowding future plantings. Wash your tools and hands after handling infected plants. Avoid overhead watering. Inspect bedding plants before purchase. Clean up plant debris to remove over-wintering sites.

Leaves rolled. Cause: Leafrollers. These ½- to 1-inch, green-bodied, brown-headed caterpillars web leaf edges together and feed on the enclosed leaves and buds. If the infestation is light, break open the "envelopes" and pick off the cater-pillars; for heavier infestations, spray the leaves with BTK.

Stems exude sawdustlike material and break; leaves wilt. Cause: Borers. A variety of borers, including striped stalk and burdock borers, make small holes in the base of perennial plants and plant stems as they enter to feed. Sawdustlike castings around the holes mark the presence of these moth larvae. Prevent borers by removing weeds and plant debris where eggs might overwin-ter; applications of BTK give control only if applied just as borers are entering plants. You can also control borers by slitting affected stalks lengthwise, removing the borers, and binding the stems together—a time-consuming task in a large planting.

Whole Plant Problems

Seedlings or young plants cut off at soil level. Cause: Cutworms. The fat, gray or dull brown, 1-inch caterpillars of 1½-inch brown or gray moths, cutworms feed on stems at night, cutting off transplants and sometimes eating entire seedlings. Missing seedlings or seedlings lying on the ground are evidence of cutworm activity. Some species climb plant stems, cutting off leaves and side shoots as they feed. Most active in May and June, cut-worms can destroy several plants each night. These caterpillars remain below the soil surface during the day.

Protect plants by placing a collar, such as a toilet paper roll or an open-ended can, around each young plant. Make each collar 2 to 3 inches tall and 1½ to 2 inches in diameter; push it into the soil so that about half the collar is below the soil surface. For more controls, see "Cutworms" on page 263.

Seedlings die. Cause: Damping-off. Damp-ing-off is caused by various soil fungi. Sometimes seedling stems rot before they even appear above the surface; in other cases, seedlings are affected after they emerge. The weak, blackened stems will collapse, resulting in seedling death.

Damaged seedlings cannot be cured. To prevent damping-off, let the soil surface dry slightly between waterings. Indoors, run a low-speed fan near your seedlings to promote good air circulation. Outdoors, thin seedlings to avoid overcrowding. Do not add nitrogen fertilizers until seedlings have produced their first true leaves.

Leaves yellow or distorted; bulbs decayed. Cause: Bulb mites. These $\frac{1}{50}$- to $\frac{1}{25}$-inch, whitish mites feed in groups on bulbs. Infested bulbs have corky, brown spots that become powdery. Bulb mites are attracted to damaged or rotting bulbs, but can move to healthy ones, carrying rot-producing fungi and bacteria as they travel. When buying bulbs, inspect them carefully for damage or signs of infection. Dip bulbs in hot (120°F) water for a few minutes to kill mites. Dig and destroy severely infested bulbs; discard the surrounding soil.

Solarize the soil before planting in previously infested ground.

FORSYTHIA Forsythia

Forsythia is the most well-known spring-flowering, deciduous shrub. It is effective as a hedge, grouped for landscape accent, or in a shrub border.

Set out bareroot, container-grown, or balled-and-burlapped plants in spring or fall. They require at least partial sun but flourish in almost any soil. Right after bloom, cut out some of the oldest canes to maintain strong flowering.

Forsythias are seldom troubled by insects. Crown gall may be a problem; see "Trunk or roots with swollen, wartlike growths" on page 214.

FRAXINUS Ash

Ashes are deciduous trees with opposite, compound leaves that turn yellow to purple in the fall. Male and female flowers may appear on the same or different trees; all-male trees are preferred for landscaping because they don't produce undesirable seedlings. Ashes are used as street trees or specimens for large properties.

Set out trees in spring or fall. Full sun is best; the soil should be deep and moist but well-drained. Although often found growing along streams, ashes tolerate dry conditions and a range of soil pH. Vigorously growing ashes are fairly trouble-free.

Problems

Leaves yellow; stems and leaves covered with small bumps. Cause: Scales. These are a serious pest of ash trees, with oystershell scale the most important, especially in the Midwest. Putnam scale, San Jose scale, and soft scale (in warmer climates) also occur. For control information, see "Leaves yellow; stems and leaves covered with small bumps" on page 213.

Trunk or branches with small holes; limbs die or break off. Cause: Borers. See "Trunk or branches with small holes; limbs die or break off" on page 214 for controls.

Leaves skeletonized or with large holes; branches may be webbed. Cause: Caterpillars. For control information, see "Leaves skeletonized or with large holes; branches may be webbed" on page 212.

Branches with small masses of galls. Cause: Ash flower gall mites. These tiny mites attack male flower clusters on white ash (*Fraxinus americana*). Infested flowers develop abnormally, producing galls that dry and remain on the tree. Spray branches and galls with horticultural oil at a dormant-season dilution in late winter for control.

Leaves with spots. Cause: Leaf spots. See "Leaves with spots" on page 213 for details.

Trunk or branches with oozing lesions; branch tips die back. Cause: Canker. See "Trunks or branches with oozing lesions; branch tips die back" on page 214 for controls.

Leaves distorted, orange-yellow spots on leaf undersides. Cause: Rust. This fungus produces orange pustules, distorting the leaves and making branch tips swell. Rust usually doesn't harm the tree much, except for detracting from the appearance. Clean up and destroy fallen leaves and branches in autumn. See "Rust" on page 315 for more controls.

Leaves skeletonized. Cause: Sawflies. See "Sawflies" on page 281 for controls.

FRITILLARIA Fritillary

Red, orange, or yellow, bell-shaped blooms hang downward in groups of 8 to 10 from crown imperial's (*Fritillaria imperialis*) 3-foot-tall flower stalks. Smaller checkered lilies (*F. meleagris*) bear individual purplish flowers, marked with a checkerboard of dark purple, on 1-foot stems. Both the bulbs and the lance-shaped, dark green foliage have a musky odor that is reputed to discourage rodents.

Plant bulbs in early autumn as soon as they are available. Handle carefully to avoid bruising, and don't let them dry out before planting. Set bulbs 6 inches deep in humus-rich, moist, very well-drained soil under partial shade. Plants bloom in early spring; choose a site that offers protection from late frosts. Water during bloom. Well-grown fritillaries are troubled by few pests or diseases.

FRUIT

Unlike vegetable crops, which share many of the same pests, fruit crops are affected by a wide variety of insects and diseases. Because fruit crops are borne on so many types of plants—including fruit trees, berry bushes, vines, and herbaceous plants such as strawberries—they have a wide range of cultural requirements as well. However, regardless of the crop you are growing, there are basic steps you can take to help prevent and control insects and diseases.

Site Selection

Full sun is a must for nearly all fruit crops: Even 1 or 2 hours of shade a day may result in smaller crops and less-flavorful fruit. Well-drained soil is also essential. In sites where drainage is a problem, plant in raised beds.

A location near the top of a gentle slope is ideal for fruit growing. A north-facing slope will help delay spring flowering, which is a plus in areas where frost damage is common. Planting about 15 feet from the north side of a building also helps delay flowering. To help protect winter-tender trees, look for a sheltered site on the south side of a building.

Avoid planting in frost pockets where late spring frosts may damage blossoms and early fall freezes may shorten the harvest season. Frost pockets develop because cold air tends to sink and collect in depressions. Frost pockets occur at the bottom of valleys and on the uphill side of woods or buildings on slopes. If your whole property is a frost pocket, try training trees taller so they can blossom above the frost pocket, and try planting hardier cultivars.

While good air circulation helps reduce disease problems, blustery winds in open areas or on hilltops can make training difficult, knock fruit off trees early, or topple trees altogether. To encourage air movement, space plants far enough apart so they won't grow into each other or nearby plants.

Fruit Selection

Fruit trees and berry bushes are a long-term investment. Before you plant, learn about the types of fruit suitable to the local climate and soil type. Look for cultivars that will tolerate local conditions. Northern gardeners should choose cultivars that will survive winter cold, blossom late enough to escape late spring frosts, yet still set and mature fruit before the end of the growing season. Southern gardeners need cultivars that will tolerate intense summer heat and humidity and don't require much of a winter chilling period. If available, disease-resistant cultivars are desirable.

It's a good idea to consult nearby nurseries, botanical gardens, and fruit hobbyists—as well as local orchardists and extension agents—for information on growing fruit in your area. The more you know about local problems affecting fruits, the better your chances for selecting the right cultivars.

Almost all fruit trees and many grapevines are grafted onto a rootstock selected for strong rooting characteristics, disease resistance, or dwarfing effect. Many nurseries only offer one or two rootstocks that grow moderately well in a wide range of conditions. Some mail-order nurseries, however, offer a selection of rootstocks for the same fruit cultivars. Once you have identified a specific rootstock that should do well in your conditions, you may want to look for a source that carries it.

Some fruit trees come grafted on rootstocks that produce dwarf, semidwarf, and standard-size trees. Most home gardeners prefer dwarf or semidwarf trees, which fruit at a younger age than standard trees and are easier to tend.

Setting Fruit

When selecting fruit trees, it's important to understand their pollination requirements. Many fruit tree cultivars will only set fruit if the flowers receive pollen from a different but compatible cultivar. For example, 'Red Delicious' apples are self-unfruitful, meaning 'Red Delicious' trees can't pollinize one another, although they are good pollinizers for other cultivars. On the other hand, 'Winesap' apples are not only self-unfruitful, they're also unable to provide pollen for other cultivars. To get fruit from a self-unfruitful plant, you need to plant another suitable cultivar for cross-pollination. 'Golden Delicious' is both self-pollinizing (self-fruitful) and a good pollinizer for other apples—including 'Winesap' and 'Red Delicious'.

Reputable nurseries will describe pollination requirements and suggest suitable pollinizers. Most apples, pears, sweet cherries, and Japanese plums require cross-pollination to set a good crop. Most peaches, apricots, sour cherries, and some Euro-pean plums are self-fruitful, although they often bear more heavily if cross-pollinated. Not all cultivars are compatible, so check with your supplier.

Note: A *pollinizer* is a plant that is a source of pollen for itself or others; a *pollinator* is the agent, such as a bee or a fly, which carries pollen from plant to plant, although the term *pollinator* is often used to describe a plant that is a compatible pollen source.

Planting

Proper planting will encourage healthy, vigorous plants that resist attack by insects and diseases. Choose your location and prepare the planting site before the plants arrive. Test the soil and amend as needed. Work lots of organic matter into the top 6 to 8 inches of soil, and remove all perennials weeds.

Most fruit plants are shipped bareroot and dormant. As soon as they arrive, inspect them for damage, such as broken roots or branches. Keep plants cool and the roots moist, but not wet, until you can plant them.

Dig a hole large enough to spread out the roots without cramping them. Cut back any damaged roots and shorten unusually long ones, if necessary. Most plants should be planted at the same level at which they were growing in the nursery. Plant grafted trees with the graft union (which looks like an angle or an enlarged section near the base of the trunk) at least 1 inch above the soil line. Exceptions to this rule may be noted in special instructions supplied with the plant.

Refill the hole with the soil you had removed, and water the plant well to give the plant a good start. Stake or trellis as needed to prevent damage, and reduce disease by encouraging good air circulation around the branches and between plants. Mulch to keep weeds under control, supply slow-release soil amendments or organic matter, and conserve soil moisture.

Protect your new trees by painting the trunks with white latex paint diluted with an equal amount of water to prevent sunscald. Frustrate gnawing rodents by placing a 1-foot-high, ¼-inch hardware cloth guard around the trunk, sunk into the soil 1 inch.

Pruning and Training

Fruit trees are pruned to develop strong branches, to remove dead or damaged growth, and to allow more air and sunlight into the center of the plant to help prevent disease and insect problems. Pruning and training also help control size and encourage sturdy, well-spaced branches with wide crotch angles.

Start training trees as soon as they are planted. Prune off any damaged branches and any that are growing at a narrow angle to the trunk. Let the rest of the branches grow for a full year before starting to select your main branches.

It's important to establish sturdy, well-placed main branches while trees are young. Training can reduce the upward growth (affecting the amount of pruning you need to do) and will stimulate early fruit bearing. Train young branches to grow at a wide angle (about 45 degrees) by clamping a clip clothespin to the trunk just above each branch while they are still green and malleable. Older branches can also be spread, but with more difficulty. Use 1- to 2-foot-long boards with a notch in each end and brace them between the trunk and the branch, or tie the branch to a weight (such as a rock) or the trunk. Gradually spread the branch during the season by moving the brace or tightening the string.

Prune apples, pears, grapes, and berries in late winter or early spring before they break dormancy. Prune peaches, plums, and cherries just after the buds burst in spring, when they are less prone to canker infection. Remove dead and diseased branches on all kinds of fruit-bearing plants if they appear during the growing season. Summer pruning is also useful for controlling the growth of overly vigorous trees, as it stimulates less regrowth than dormant pruning does. Do not prune after August; fall pruning can increase the risk of winter injury.

There are two general types of pruning cuts: heading and thinning. Cutting a branch back partway to shorten it is a heading cut. Heading back a branch tends to encourage a flush of new shoots to spout near the cut end. This is a useful technique for stimulating new branches when necessary, but too many heading cuts can cause overgrown, overly bushy trees. A thinning cut removes a branch altogether by cutting it back to a main or side branch. Thinning encourages the remaining branch to grow, and unlike a heading cut, does not stimulate new ones to sprout. For this reason, thinning cuts are the best choice for developing an open framework and a sturdy, compact tree.

Fruit trees are usually trained and pruned into one of two general shapes: central leader (which has an upright stem in the middle of the tree) or open center (no central, upright stem). Modified central leader is intermediate between the two. The individual fruit tree entries include training recommendations. Grapes are usually trained on a trellis or arbor. Berry plants are thinned out in the appropriate season. Consult with an experienced fruit grower or your Cooperative Extension agent for advice on how to prune the type of fruit crops you've planted and/or reference books or Web sites with detailed pruning instructions.

Thinning

Fruit trees often set more fruit than they can ripen. Resulting fruit will be small and the excess weight can damage branches. Crowded fruit is also more susceptible to fungal diseases. Thin early in the season when fruit is as small as possible. First, clip or twist off all insect-damaged or deformed fruit. Then, remove the smaller fruit, leaving the biggest and best.

Space fruit so it will not touch each other as it grows. If you can't reach the upper limbs, tap them with a padded pole to shake loose some of the extras.

Preventive Care

Many disease and insect problems can be controlled or greatly reduced by simple sanitation. Clean up and dispose of branches after you prune, especially when removing diseased wood. Many insects pupate in the soil or in loose bark or dead plant debris. For this reason, rake and remove fallen leaves in fall. Also remove dropped fruit during the season and dry, diseased fruit (known as mummies) clinging to the branches after harvest. Inspecting bark in the winter and removing and destroying egg masses is also effective.

It's a good idea to find out what insects and diseases may attack your plants. Inspect plants regularly and control problems before they get out of hand. When problems do arise, start with the most environmentally gentle controls, such as handpicking, pruning, attracting or releasing predatory insects, or using mating disruption. Then move on to applying products such as kaolin clay, horticultural oil, insecticidal soap, BT, or sulfur. Use botanical pesticides, such as neem or pyrethrin, or copper compounds, only as a last resort after you have tried other, less-toxic, methods.

GARLIC *Allium sativum* and *A. ophioscorodon* (Liliaceae)

Garlic is a perennial herb grown for its pungent bulbs and greens. It is easy to grow healthy, trouble-free garlic. Plant cloves in fall and cover with mulch after the weather turns cold. Garlic prefers full sun and rich, deep, moist but well-drained soil with lots of organic matter and a pH between 6.0 and 7.0. Plants need extra water during summer, while bulbs are forming. Water deeply when soil is dry. Once stalks begin to droop and brown at the end of summer, withhold water.

Garlic is closely related to onions and prone to the same problems, especially onion maggots. See the Onion entry beginning on page 144 for more information.

GERANIUM Cranesbill

The cranesbills, *Geranium* spp., are hardy, easy-to-grow perennials that are often confused with the more-tender zonal or bedding geraniums, which actually belong to the genus *Pelargonium*. Although related to the better-known zonal geranium, cranesbills (also called hardy or true geraniums) are distinctly different from their tender relatives. Most have a mounding growth habit with spread roughly equal to height. Plants range from 4 inches to 4 feet tall with lobed to deeply divided foliage. Flowers bloom in spring and early summer in shades of pink, purple, red, and blue; many blossoms feature darker contrasting veins in petals or dark eyes. Some geraniums have a spreading growth habit; these are ideal for use as groundcovers.

Grow cranesbills in full sun to partial shade. Some species will grow in heavy shade, but, in general, too much shade reduces flowering and causes leggy growth. Plants tolerate some drought, but perform best in moist, well-drained soil of average fertility. Rich, moist soils encourage invasive growth in some species. Divide every 3 to 4 years in spring or fall. Some cranesbills form taproots that resist division; increase these types through root cuttings, stem cuttings, or seeds.

Hardy and fairly pest free, cranesbills suffer few problems beyond those common to most perennials. Aphids and four-lined plant bugs may attack them; see "Aphids" on page 250 and "Plant Bugs" on page 278 for information on controls.

GLADIOLUS Gladiolus, glad

Showy, 2- to 4-foot-tall glads brighten summer with tall spikes of trumpet-shaped, often bicolored flowers. The six-petaled blooms range from 2 to 5 inches wide and open from the bottom of the spike upward. Glads are upright plants with narrow, sword-shaped, 1- to 1½-foot-long leaves. Hundreds of cultivars of common gladiolus (Gladiolus × hortulanus) offer gardeners a spectrum of flower colors and forms from which to choose.

Select and plant gladiolus corms in spring. Do not buy or use corms that are lightweight, spongy, or showing signs of decay. See "Healthy Bulb Basics" on page 98 for more on selecting healthy bulbs. Good corms are about 1½ inches wide with high tops. Large, healthy corms flower more quickly than smaller ones. Plant corms after danger of frost has passed. To create a succession of bloom, plant at 2-week intervals or plant different-size corms all at one time. Allow at least 3 months between planting and the first frost.

Prepare soil to 1 foot deep in a sunny location. Add plenty of organic matter to ensure good drainage. Plant corms from 3 to 8 inches deep—about four times their thickness; space about 6 inches apart. Make sure pointed growing tips face upward. Water regularly; glads need about 1 inch of water per week. Mulch to help retain soil moisture. Side-dress with compost or slow-release, general-purpose fertilizer when plants emerge and when flowers show color. Plan to stake the tall, flower-laden spikes; nearly all cultivars require some form of support.

In the South, gladiolus corms overwinter safely in the ground, but in most of the country they must be dug and stored indoors before hard frost. Allow leaves to die back naturally for about 6 weeks after flowering stops. After leaves and stalks turn brown, dig corms and shake off loose soil; cut away stems just above the top of the corms. Let corms dry out of the sun for a few days. Do not remove husks, as they help retain moisture. Discard withered old corms. Separate cormels, the tiny offspring surrounding a mature bulb, and store for planting—these bloom in 1 to 2 years. Check all corms for decay, spotting, or other disease symptoms. Dust with sulfur to guard against disease problems; store in a cool (40°F), dry, well-ventilated place.

Problems

Flowers deformed; leaves and petals with white flecks. Cause: Thrips. Gladiolus thrips are a very destructive, common pest. These $\frac{1}{25}$-inch, yellow to black, flying insects feed by rasping petals and leaf surfaces, leaving silvery spots and streaks. They hide under leaf sheaths and inside flowers. Other symptoms are partial bloom, failure to bloom, and shriveling. Thrips' wastes may appear as black spots on the underside of leaves. Infested corms are dark, sticky, and rough.

Cut away and destroy severely infested plant parts. Use blue sticky traps to monitor and trap pests. Encourage native predators such as pirate bugs, lacewings, and lady beetles. Insecticidal soap sprays give some control of thrip populations, but may affect beneficials as well. To limit thrips infestation, dig corms early in fall and cut off tops before thrips move down into corms. Bag and discard debris. If thrips have been a problem, dust corms with pyrethrin to control them in storage. Or soak them in a Lysol solution (1½ tablespoons in 1 gallon water) for several hours before planting.

Leaves, stems, and buds distorted, sticky; clusters of small insects. Cause: Aphids. Plants infested with aphids have growth that may be curled, puckered, or stunted. Leaves may turn yellow or brown; feeding can seriously damage flower buds or blooms. As aphids feed, they excrete sticky honeydew; black, sooty mold fungus often forms on honeydew, further disfiguring plants. Use a strong spray of water in the morning to knock aphids off glads, paying particular attention to the underside of leaves. Destroy seriously infested plants. See "Aphids" on page 250 for more controls and information.

Leaves yellow, distorted; flowers absent; corms decayed. Cause: Bulb mites. These ⅟₅₀-inch, whitish pests favor damaged, rotting corms, but travel from those to healthy ones. See "Leaves yellow or distorted; bulbs decayed" on page 100 for controls. Examine corms carefully when purchasing. For hints on choosing healthy bulbs, see "Healthy Bulb Basics" on page 98.

Leaves yellow; plant dies early. Cause: Dry rot. Other symptoms of this fungal disease include dry, brown or black, corky spots on corms and husk coverings. You may see black fungal growth spots on decayed leaf bases. Plants may turn yellow and die prematurely. Choose corms carefully to avoid infected specimens. Destroy infected plants. Do not replant in the same area. Replant only in well-drained soil.

Leaves mottled yellow and distorted; flowers small and faded. Cause: Fusarium yellows. This soilborne fungal disease is first seen as bending and curling of leaves and stems; foliage yellows and dies, starting with the oldest leaves. On corms, small reddish brown lesions enlarge and darken; entire corms may become hard, dry, and mummified. Immediately destroy infected corms. Do not replant corms in the same area. Some cultivars are more resistant than others; check with a reputable nursery or call your local extension agent for area-specific recommendations.

Leaves stippled and pale; growth poor; webbed foliage. Cause: Spider mites. Wash plants with strong sprays of water when first signs appear on foliage. Mites prefer drought-stressed, dusty plants. Remove and destroy badly infested plants. See "Mites, Spider" on page 275 for controls.

Stems eaten through at base. Cause: Wireworms. Larvae of click beetles, these are common in soils formerly covered by sod or with high organic content. The slender, hard-bodied, yellowish worms drill holes in corms as they feed, damaging them and hastening decay. See "Wireworms" on page 291 for controls.

Flowers, leaves, and stalks spotted; corms rotted. Cause: Botrytis blight. This fungal disease also causes slimy, collapsed leaves and flowers. It is most prevalent in cool, damp weather. Prevention includes planting gladiolus in areas with good air circulation. Avoid low or shaded areas. Water so leaves dry before sunset. Remove all debris at the end of the season and destroy. See "Botrytis Blight" on page 312 for more controls.

Leaves with reddish brown spots; corms with pale to brown spots. Cause: Scab. This bacterial disease also causes brown spots on blossoms; plants rot at the base and fall over. Spots on corms turn dark brown with sunken centers and scabby margins. Dig and destroy infested plants; do not replant corms in infested soil.

GLEDITSIA Honey locust

Honey locusts are deciduous trees with alternate, fine-textured leaves. They cast dappled shade and, except for their thorniness and messy pods, are excellent as specimen or street trees. Thornless, nonfruiting cultivars are preferable. *Gleditsia triacanthos* var. *inermis* is thornless honey locust, from which most cultivars have been selected for landscape use.

Set out in spring or fall as bareroot or balled-and-burlapped plants. Honey locusts are undemanding and are well suited to city conditions. While they prefer moist, fertile, slightly alkaline soil, they tolerate drought and salt.

Problems

Leaves skeletonized or with large holes; branches may be webbed. Cause: Caterpillars. Webworms can be a serious problem on honey locust. Some cultivars, such as 'Moraine', show some resistance to webworm damage. For other control information, see "Leaves skeletonized or with large holes; branches may be webbed" on page 212. Gypsy moths also feed on leaves, but they don't form webs. See "Leaves skeletonized or plant defoliated" on page 212 for controls.

Plant defoliated; branches bear cocoonlike bags. Cause: Bagworms. See "Plant defoliated; branches bear cocoonlike bags" on page 212 for control suggestions.

Trunk or branches with small holes; limbs die or break off. Cause: Borers. See "Trunk or branches with small holes; limbs die or break off" on page 214 for controls.

Trunk or branches with oozing lesions; branch tips die back. Cause: Canker. For details, see "Trunk or branches with oozing lesions; branch tips die back" on page 214.

GOOSEBERRY *Ribes hirtellum, R. uva-crispa* (Saxifragaceae)

Gooseberries are thorny bushes with arched branches growing 3 to 5 feet. The inconspicuous flowers are borne laterally on 1-year-old wood and on short spurs—short branches that elongate only a fraction of an inch per year—on older wood. Gooseberries are hardy in Zones 3–8.

In cool climates plant gooseberries in full sun. Choose partial shade in hot climates. Maintain thick, organic mulch beneath plants to keep soil cool and moist. Prune mature plants every winter, cutting away all but six of the shoots that grew the previous season at ground level. Also remove all wood more than 3 years old. Gooseberries are self-pollinating.

Fruit Problems

Fruit with powdery white or gray coating. Cause: American gooseberry mildew. This fungal disease spreads most rapidly during periods of warm days followed by cool nights. Under these conditions the crop can be ruined overnight. For more information, see "Leaves with powdery white patches; leaves stunted and deformed" on the opposite page.

Fruit with holes when nearly ripe; fruit and leaves covered with webs. Cause: Gooseberry fruitworms. These are the yellow-green larvae of a moth that infests both gooseberries and currants. Damaged fruit may be hollowed out and may change color prematurely. Clean up and destroy damaged fruit to reduce future populations. Spray BTK at the first sign of webbing to control caterpillars before they enter fruit.

Fruit colors and drops early. Cause: Currant fruit fly larvae. The currant fruit fly lays eggs on gooseberries and currants in spring. The larvae that hatch from these eggs feed on berries and cause them to drop. Infested berries have a dark spot surrounded by a red halo. Early-bearing cultivars, such as 'Oregon Champion" and 'Welcome', may escape damage. Control this pest by destroying all infested berries as soon as you find them.

Leaf Problems

Leaves with powdery white patches; leaves stunted and deformed. Cause: American gooseberry mildew. To prevent this fungal disease, avoid overfertilizing plants. Lush, sappy growth is more susceptible to infection. Plants well supplied with potassium are best able to resist mildew. Organic fungicides, including *Bacillus subtilis*, potassium bicarbonate, or a 0.5 percent solution of baking soda (1 teaspoon baking soda in 1 quart water) may be applied as preventives or to help to control the disease. Spray infected plants thoroughly. Mildew-resistant cultivars include 'Captivator', 'Glendale', 'Hinnonmaki Yellow', 'Lepaa Red', 'Poorman', and 'Welcome'.

Leaves with spots; leaves yellow and drop. Causes: Septoria leaf spot; anthracnose. Since both these fungal diseases overwinter on leaf litter, rake up leaves or bury them under thick mulch. Copper sprays also control both diseases. If defoliation occurs late in the season, it does little harm.

Foliage stripped from bushes just as leaves expand. Cause: Imported currantworms. These are the larvae of a sawfly that lays eggs on gooseberry bushes. The larvae devour the leaves, then drop to the ground to pupate. Control with sprays of insecticidal soap, neem, or horticultural oil at a growing-season dilution. Spray serious infestations with pyrethrin. Make sure to spray

into the center of the bush. Controlling the first brood may eliminate the need for additional sprays.

Leaves blistered and reddened. Cause: Aphids. These tiny insects cluster on leaf undersides. Use a strong spray of water to knock them from the foliage. If damage is severe, spray with insecticidal soap or neem, making sure to coat the undersides of the leaves.

GRAPE *Vitis* spp. and hybrids (Vitaceae)

Grapes, one of the most ancient cultivated crops, are perennial woody vines that cling to a support by means of tendrils. Under ideal conditions vines may live for more than 100 years. Fruit is produced on shoots that grow off 1-year-old wood.

There are four main types of grapes grown in North America: European, or wine grapes (*Vitis vinifera*); American (*V. labrusca*), such as 'Concord'; hybrids between European and American; and muscadine (*V. rotundifolia*). European grapes generally are most susceptible to diseases. American grapes are the most cold-hardy. Their hardiness (Zones 4–10) depends on the species and cultivar.

Culture

Plant in a sunny site with deep, well-drained, moderately fertile soil and good air circulation to promote disease resistance. Train vines to a fence or trellis. Prune in late winter to keep the fruit within reach, to increase cluster size, and to allow air and sunlight to penetrate the branches. Enclose fruit clusters in paper bags to keep birds away from berries and to control some insects and diseases. Many muscadines need cross-pollination, but the other types are self-pollinating.

Fruit Problems

Young fruit covered with a white coating; fruit ripens unevenly or covered with blotches. Causes: Powdery mildew; downy mildew. Early in the season, fruit infected with powdery mildew has a white, dustlike coating on the berries. Infected plants may set few berries. Later on, the infection can halt the growth of the berry skins, causing them to split while green. Ripened clusters have blotchy, poor-tasting fruit, but have no white growth.

Ripening fruit clusters infected with downy mildew may have a mix of hard, reddish green, infected berries and soft, juicy, healthy berries. The fuzzy coating on fruit apparent early in the season may not be present. For information on control of these diseases, see "Leaves with a white, powdery coating on the upper surfaces" on the opposite page for powdery mildew symptoms; for downy mildew, see "Leaves with white, cottony growth on undersides" on the opposite page.

Fruit with light brown spots that enlarge and darken. Cause: Black rot. Common east of the Rockies, especially in hot, humid weather, black rot causes fruit to shrivel into hard, black berries (known as mummies) that remain on the cluster. Overwintering mummies and infected canes or shoots carry the disease from one growing season to the next. For control, remove and destroy all mummies. For persistent infection, apply copper sprays. Cultivars moderately resistant to black rot include 'Cascade', 'Chancellor', 'Cayuga White', 'De Chaunac', 'Delaware', 'Elvira', 'Fredonia', 'Hunt', 'Ives', 'Mars', 'Scuppernong', 'Vidal Blanc', and 'Vignoles'.

Fruit with small, dark-ringed, sunken spots with light centers. Cause: Anthracnose.

For more information on this disease, also called bird's-eye rot, see "Leaves with dark-ringed, sunken spots with light centers" on the opposite page.

Fruit clusters enveloped with a fluffy, gray-brown coating. Cause: Botrytis bunch rot. This fungal disease appears in tight fruit clusters and in vines with poor air circulation, or in clusters where western grapeleaf skeletonizers are feeding. Thin out some berries within clusters and remove some leaves around fruit. Clean up prunings, cluster stems, and mummified fruit by early spring. Plant resistant cultivars, including 'Baco No. 1', 'Cascade', 'Catawba', 'Concord', 'Delaware', 'De Chaunac', 'Fredonia', 'Himrod', 'Ives', and 'Niagara'. Check for skeletonizers; if found, take steps to prevent them next season (see "Leaves papery or skeletonized" on page 112).

When the timing of this infection is perfect, it imparts a special flavor to European wine grapes. In this case it is called "noble rot," for the flavor it gives to wine made from those grapes.

Fruit webbed together with holes chewed from one berry to another. Cause: Grape berry moths. This pest, common east of the Rockies, is a green or brown, $\frac{7}{16}$-inch caterpillar that moves from fruit to fruit, feeding on pulp and seeds. Pick and destroy infested berries, which shrivel and color prematurely. Larvae also feed on flowers and newly set fruit. Larvae cut flaps in the edges of leaves and roll them over with webbing to pupate. At the end of the season, collect and destroy or bury fallen leaves, which may harbor overwintering pupae. For heavy infestations, spray BTK to kill the caterpillars.

Fruit covered with a sticky coating and black mold. Causes: Grape whiteflies; grape mealybugs. Whiteflies and mealybugs secrete a sticky coating, called honeydew; sooty mold, a black superficial fungus, feeds on the honeydew. Both whiteflies and mealybugs are serious grape pests in California.

To control whiteflies, remove nearby buck-thorns (*Rhamnus* spp.), where the pest overwinters. Or spray nearby buckthorns in winter with dormant oil spray.

Natural enemies usually keep mealybugs in check, but for heavy infestations, introduce mealybug destroyers (*Cryptolaemus* spp.), also called Australian lady beetles. Buy these natural predators from commercial insectaries or natural farm and garden suppliers. In contrast, ants protect mealy-bugs from predators and feed on their honeydew. To make mealybugs more susceptible to predators, control ants by placing bait stations containing boric acid on the ground around vines.

Fruit with holes. Cause: Birds. Birds peck holes in ripening berries and are especially fond of red or blue cultivars. Damaged fruit attracts bees and wasps for further feeding. Drape a net over the whole vine or bag fruit clusters in paper bags.

Leaf and Branch Problems

Leaves with a white, powdery coating on the upper surfaces. Cause: Powdery mildew. Infected leaves eventually become distorted, turn brown, and fall. Dark patches appear on canes. This fungal disease weakens vines and diminishes yield. More common in the West, it spreads fastest when days are dry and warm and nights are cool. Organic fungicides, including *Bacillus subtilis,* potassium bicarbonate, a 0.5 percent solution of baking soda (1 teaspoon baking soda in 1 quart water) or plant-oil-based fungicides may be applied as preventives or to help to control the disease. In highly suscep-tible plantings, apply sulfur spray in spring. Plant resistant cultivars, including 'Canadice', 'Cayuga White', 'Ives', and 'Steuben'.

Leaves with white, cottony growth on undersides. Cause: Downy mildew. Other symptoms of this fungal disease include small yellow leaf spots, distorted or brown leaves, and early leaf drop. Older leaves are affected first, but the disease also attacks shoots and tendrils. Remove and destroy badly infected leaves. Sprays of potassium bicarbonate may give some control as well as reduce the spread of the disease. To limit future outbreaks of downy mildew, remove and destroy all diseased leaves and tendrils in fall. Where this disease is a perennial problem, you may have to spray vines with copper several times throughout the growing season to control the disease. Do not spray copper during flowering. Plant resistant cultivars, including 'Aurora', 'Baco No. 1', 'Cascade', 'Concord', 'Foch', 'Himrod', 'Mars', and 'Steuben'.

Leaves with dark-ringed, sunken spots with light centers. Cause: Anthracnose. Also called bird's-eye rot, this fungal disease weakens but usually doesn't kill vines. For control, remove and destroy diseased portions, including infected berries, and spray in spring with lime-sulfur. Muscadine grapes and the American cultivars 'Concord', 'Delaware', 'Moore's Early', and 'Niagara' are anthracnose resistant.

Leaves with reddish brown spots with black specks. Cause: Black rot. Leaves may wilt and shoots may show large, black, elliptical lesions. For more information, see "Fruit with light brown spots that enlarge and darken" on the opposite page.

Leaves or leaf petioles with reddish swellings. Cause: Grapevine tomato gall. The ½-inch swellings are galls made by a very small fly called a midge. If you slit one of the galls open, you may find small pinkish orange maggots inside. These galls are harmless. Just prune them off.

Leaves with green, pealike swellings on undersides. Cause: Grape phylloxeras. Phylloxeras are aphidlike insects that make leaf galls to hold eggs and young. Inside one gall, you may find hundreds of yellowish nymphs. Grape phylloxeras are native to the United States and are tolerated by American grapes, but they're serious pests of European grapes. In fact, when phylloxeras were accidentally transported to France in the late 1800s, they spread rapidly through vineyards and killed almost a third of the grapevines there. To avoid problems with phylloxeras, plant American or French hybrid grapes, both of which are resistant to this pest. Phylloxeras also attack roots of susceptible species, causing death of the whole vine.

Leaves with pale stipples along leaf veins. Cause: Leafhoppers. These green or brown, $1/10$- to $1/2$-inch insects suck juices from leaf undersides, causing foliage to be stippled with tiny white spots. Heavily infested leaves may turn yellow or brown and drop from the vine. Though they are quite common, leafhoppers rarely cause serious damage to backyard grapes. Many natural enemies keep them in check. Where further control is needed, spray leaves with insecticidal soap.

Leaves skeletonized. Cause: Japanese beetles. These $1/2$-inch, metallic blue-green insects with bronze wing covers feed on leaves in early summer. For light infestation, visit plants in the morning while beetles are sluggish and knock them off leaves into jars filled with soapy water. For more information, see "Japanese Beetle" on page 269.

Leaves papery or skeletonized. Cause: Western grapeleaf skeletonizers. These small caterpillars feed on the undersides of grape leaves. Young larvae are cream colored; older larvae are yellow with purple and black stripes. Older larvae skeletonize the leaves. Control by handpicking or by spraying young larvae with spinosad or BTK.

Canes or shoots break easily. Cause: Grape cane girdlers. This $1/8$-inch beetle punctures a cane, lays a single egg inside, and then encircles the cane with 2 rows of punctures. Damaged canes or shoots then break off easily. Damage is usually minor, but to control this pest, remove and destroy the injured cane a few inches below the area with punctures marks.

Canes or shoots with reddish or green swellings above nodes. Cause: Grape cane gallmakers. This $1/8$-inch beetle deposits a single egg in a cane and then makes additional punctures in a vertical row above the original egg-laying site. The area where the egg is deposited enlarges to a red or green gall about twice the diameter of the cane. Larvae tunnel in canes, and canes often break off at the galls. Damage is usually minor, but to control this pest, remove and destroy the injured cane a few inches below the gall.

Whole Plant Problems

Vines stunted, unproductive, eventually dying. Causes: Grape phylloxeras; grape scale; Pierce's disease. Grape phylloxeras are aphids that infest both leaves and roots. Leaf infestation causes harmless, pealike leaf galls. Root infestation causes knotlike root galls that prevent nutrient uptake and cause stunting and death of the vine.

Phylloxeras are difficult to eradicate. Where they are a problem, plant American grapes or Euorpean grapes grafted onto American grape rootstock, both of which are resistant to this pest. For more information on grape phylloxeras, see "Leaves with green, pealike swellings on under-sides" on page 111.

Grape scales are tiny, round, immobile insects resembling light gray bumps. Scales usually hide under the loose bark of older canes or trunks, where they suck sap and cause the vine to slowly decline. For control, spray with a dormant-season dilution of horticultural oil in late winter and prune old growth severely.

Pierce's disease, a bacterial disease common in the South, is spread by leafhoppers. Infected vines typically show scorched, dried leaves in midsummer, wilted dried fruit, and eventual death of the vine. There is no cure for this disease. Dig up infected plants and replant with disease-free stock. Most muscadine grapes are resistant to Pierce's disease, as are some American grape cultivars, including 'Champanel', 'Herbemont', and 'Lenoir'.

GYPSOPHILA Baby's-breath, gypsophila

The delicate white or pink flower sprays of baby's-breath (*Gypsophila paniculata*) are a mainstay of floral arrangements. Sprays may have more than 1,000 single or double flowers, each just ⅙ inch wide. This mounding plant is equally delightful in the garden, where it grows 2 to 3 feet tall and 2 feet wide, bearing copious blooms over slender, gray-green leaves. Creeping baby's-breath (*G. repens*) forms a blossom-covered mat only 4 to 8 inches tall and is useful for edging or rock gardens.

Plant baby's-breath in sites where it won't be disturbed or moved; its large fleshy roots do not transplant well. Given full sun, alkaline soil, and good drainage, plants thrive with little care. Remove spent flowers to prolong bloom. Protect plants with winter mulch; don't cover crowns until after the ground is frozen to avoid rotting.

Problems

Leaves stippled; growth poor. Cause: Leafhoppers. Slender, wedge-shaped, greenish yellow pests only ⅛ inch long, aster leafhoppers suck sap from the underside of leaves as they feed, discoloring and distorting the foliage. Damaged leaves

shrivel and drop. See "Leafhoppers" on page 271 for controls.

Leaves and flowers greenish yellow, distorted; new growth spindly. Cause: Aster yellows. Feeding leafhoppers may transmit this disease. There is no control for aster yellows. Remove and destroy infected plants; do not compost them. Prevent the disease spread by controlling sucking pests such as leafhoppers and aphids.

HAMAMELIS Witch hazel

Witch hazels are alternate-leaved shrubs with narrow-petaled, twisted, yellow or coppery flowers appearing either in late fall or late winter. They flourish in well-drained but moisture-retentive soils, enriched with lots of organic matter.

Witch hazels are relatively free of serious insect pests. Caterpillars and Japanese beetles may cause some damage; see "Leaves skeletonized or with large holes; branches may be webbed" and "Leaves skeletonized" on page 212 for controls. Witch hazel cone gall, which appears as a conical gall on the upper leaf surfaces, is caused by a kind of aphid, as are elliptical galls on the flower buds. Neither is usually a major problem; control both by repeated applications of insecticidal soap in late spring, early summer, and autumn.

HEDERA Ivy

Ivies are vigorous evergreen vines, climbing by means of rootlike appendages. Although widely planted as groundcovers and as vines on walls, they are quite invasive and easily escape areas where they are planted, smothering nearby planted areas and woodlands. Before you plant, check local invasive plant lists and with your local extension service to determine if ivy is a problem in your area. Ivies also are grown as houseplants.

If you do plant, select a site where ivy will be naturally contained, such as one bounded on all sides by walkways. Set out bareroot plants in spring or fall. Almost any moisture-retentive soil will suit ivy. In the North, strong winter sun can scorch leaves; it's best to choose a site where some shade is available. Cut back in late winter to promote denser growth.

Problems

Leaves wrinkled and discolored. Cause: Aphids. For controls, see "Aphids" on page 250.

Leaves yellow; stems and leaves covered with small bumps. Cause: Scales. See "Scales" on page 282 for control information.

Leaves stippled with yellow; foliage webbed. Cause: Spider mites. See "Mites, Spider" on page 275 for controls.

Leaves with circular brown spots. Cause: Bacterial leaf spot. This bacteria can cause water-soaked spots on lower leaves. These spots turn brownish black and may spread to form large patches of dead tissue. To prevent the spread of this disease, avoid working around wet plants. Remove and destroy affected parts.

Stems or branches with oozing lesions; tips die back. Cause: Canker. See "Trunk or branches with oozing lesions; branch tips die back" on page 214 for controls.

Leaves with powdery white coating. Cause: Powdery mildew. For controls, see "Powdery Mildew" on page 322.

HELIANTHUS Sunflower

Rapid growth, showy flowers, and tasty seeds make annual sunflowers fun to grow as well as nutritious. The plants can grow up to 10 feet tall. Individual flowers may reach 14 inches across, with golden petals and a brown center that becomes a mass of seeds by late summer. Perennial species are robust, tall specimens with showy flowers suitable for the back of perennial borders and in wild areas.

Annual sunflowers need warmth to germinate. Direct-sow seeds ½ inch deep in average soil in early May. They will germinate within 10 days. Space tall-growing cultivars 2 feet apart, or they will crowd each other. All sunflowers perform well in average soil and full sun, although they will tolerate light shade. Apply a general-purpose fertilizer once, about midway through the growing season.

Problems

Leaves, stems, and buds distorted. Cause: Aphids. For control measures, see "Aphids" on page 250.

Leaves with ragged holes. Cause: Caterpillars. Caterpillars of all kind find large sunflower leaves a tasty food supply. A healthy plant can generally withstand an attack. Handpick pests, or spray leaves with BTK.

Leaves wilt. Causes: Lack of water; fungal wilt. If a good soaking does not perk up your plant by the next day, suspect a fungal wilt. These fungi live in the soil and move upward through the plant. Leaves may be mottled with green and yellow, and dark brown areas may appear on and within sunflower stems. There is no control; remove and destroy infected plants. Avoid replanting sunflowers in that area.

Leaves with powdery white patches. Cause: Powdery mildew. For controls, see "Powdery Mildew" on page 322.

HELLEBORUS Hellebore

Hellebores flower in winter and early spring, earn-ing names such as Christmas rose (*Helleborus niger*) or Lenten rose (*H. × hybridus*). Most have green, creamy white, rose, or dull purple to black blooms, carried over low evergreen foliage.

Plant in partial shade, such as that found under deciduous trees, in moist, well-drained, neutral soil rich in organic matter. Maintain even soil moisture with a summer mulch. Established plants tolerate dry shade. A suitable site with well-drained soil eliminates most problems with these tough perennials. The brittle rhizomes make this plant difficult to divide. If you must transplant, do so with care.

HEMEROCALLIS Daylily

Daylilies are easy-to-grow, nearly problem-free plants that perform best in full sun. Most also toler-ate partial shade; in fact, plants may grow better in part shade in southern zones. There are thousands of hybrids from which to choose. Plants range in height from 1½ feet to 3 feet and offer blossoms in every color but true white and blue. A mature planting provides hundreds of 2- to 6-inch, trum-pet-shaped flowers and graceful, swordlike, bright green leaves. Each flower lasts a day, then closes at night, but numerous buds provide extended peri-ods of bloom.

Plant these tough perennials in well-drained, average soil and water regularly to get the plants established. After that, limited water is fine, but don't let them dry out while blooming. Excess fertility encourages lush foliage and fewer flowers. Plants grow vigorously if undisturbed; clumps expand over time but are usually not invasive. Remove spent flower stalks to prolong bloom. In

fall, cut all stems to the ground and remove dead foliage. Divide large clumps every 3 to 5 years. Roots are tough, heavy, and tuberous, so this is not an easy job. Leave one to several crowns and several solid roots on each division.

Daylilies are seldom troubled by pests. Flower thrips can cause buds to die and corky lesions to form on leaves or stems. Infested plants have distorted blooms, and in severe cases, flower stalks fail to develop. See "Thrips" on page 287 for controls. If spider mites cause stippled leaves or webby foliage, see "Mites, Spider" on page 275 for controls.

HERBS

Herbs are grown for their savory, aromatic, or medicinal parts. They include annuals, biennials, and perennials. In general, herbs are little troubled by pests and diseases if given good growing conditions.

To grow healthy, trouble-free plants, choose a well-drained site with as much sun as possible. Most do not need rich soil, and some actually prefer dry, poor soil; check individual entries for specific preferences. For solutions to problems that affect a wide range of garden plants, see the Vegetables entry, starting on page 219.

HEUCHERA Alumroot, coral bells

Two types of heucheras grace gardens: coral bells (*Heuchera sanguinea*) is grown for its erect stems of dainty bell-shaped flowers. Foliage heucheras are grown for their low-growing clumps of rounded, lobed, heart-shaped, or maplelike foliage. These include cultivars of American alumroot (*H. ameri-cana*) and small-flowered alumroot (*H. micrantha*), both grown more for foliage than flowers; they offer leaves in shades of purple, green, and silver.

Plant alumroots in well-drained, richly organic

soil in a sunny or lightly shaded spot. Partial shade is best for foliage and for plants in the South. Shallow, fleshy roots need regular watering and benefit from summer mulching; however, excess moisture, combined with poor drainage, promotes rot.

Problems

Leaves covered with white powder. Cause: Powdery mildew. Powdery mildew may mar foliage and is best limited through sanitation and air circulation. See "Powdery Mildew" on page 322 for controls.

Crowns blacken and die; leaves notched. Cause: Strawberry root weevils. The grubs of ¼-inch, black snout beetles feed on alumroots' crowns starting in early spring. Adults feed at night on foliage. Remove and destroy infested plants; clean up debris where pests overwinter. Drench soil around roots with parasitic nematodes. See "Root Weevils" on page 279 for more information and controls.

HIBISCUS Hibiscus, rose-of-Sharon

These old-time favorites have bushy but upright habits and bloom in mid- to late summer. They are easy to grow, even withstanding seashore conditions. Avoid unwanted volunteer seedlings by planting sterile cultivars.

Set out in spring or fall as bareroot or container-grown plants. They prefer full sun and average soil with added organic matter. Hibiscus are fairly problem free. Aphids or Japanese beetles may feed on foliage; see "Aphids" on page 250 and "Japanese Beetle" on page 269 for controls.

HOSTA Hosta, plantain lily

Grown primarily for their attractive, 5- to 10-inch, broadly lance-shaped leaves and durability as groundcovers, hostas are unparalleled perennials for shady areas. Handsome ribbed leaves may be short and narrow or broad and up to 1½ feet long; leaf colors range from light to dark green or blue-green and may be variegated with yellow, light green, cream, or white. Spikes of tubular, 2-inch, white to purple flowers show nicely above foliage from mid- to late summer.

Hostas look their best in light to deep shade. Sunny sites encourage flowering but also cause foliage color to bleach and brown and sunburned spots to appear on leaves. Set plants 1 to 3 feet apart, depending on leaf size, in moist but well-drained, organic soil. Give plants ½ to 1 inch of water weekly; mulch to avoid splattering water onto leaves.

Hostas may be increased by division, although plantings will prosper undisturbed for many years. If desired, divide plants every 5 years or so. Remove faded flower stalks to improve appearance, and cut back foliage at the end of the growing season.

All hostas go dormant in winter. New leaves emerge in spring.

Problems

Leaves small, light brown, papery, scorched, or bleached. Causes: Lack of water; too much sun. An easy way to ruin hostas is to let them dry out, even for a little while. Even if they continue to grow, plants will be stunted. Sunburned edges or spots reduce a hosta's ornamental value significantly and are best avoided through proper selection of planting site.

Leaves with large, ragged holes. Cause: Slugs and snails. Hostas' broad, low-growing foliage welcomes these slimy pests. See "Slugs/Snails" on page 284 for controls.

Stems blacken at base; leaves yellow and wilt; plant collapses. Cause: Crown rot. Hostas are susceptible to fungal and bacterial attack when grown in poorly drained soil. Crown injury and excess moisture during dormancy also increase the chances of infection. Choose well-drained sites; add organic matter to improve soil drainage; keep mulch from touching crowns. Remove and discard infected plants and the surrounding soil.

HYACINTHUS Hyacinth

Cultivars of *Hyacinthus orientalis,* the only species in this genus, are prized for the heady aroma they bring to the spring garden. Tubular or bell-shaped blossoms cover dense, blunt, 10- to 12-inch-tall, upright spikes; each bulb produces one spike of white, pink, blue, or yellow flowers. Narrow, strap-like leaves surround the base of the stalk.

Plant bulbs in fall at least 1 month before the ground freezes. Select a site in full sun with humus-rich, well-drained soil; sheltering from wind reduces injury to rigid flower stalks. Set bulbs 4 to 5 inches deep with pointed growing tips facing upward. Hyacinths multiply less freely than other bulbs and flowering tends to diminish with age. Plant new bulbs every 2 to 3 years for optimal floral display. Remove spent flowers to prevent seed formation; let foliage die back naturally.

Problems

Leaves yellow or distorted; bulbs decayed. Cause: Bulb mites. Like most bulbs, hyacinths may be infested by bulb mites. See "Leaves yellow or distorted; bulbs decayed" on page 100 for controls.

Leaves and stems with spots, gray mold, or yellow slime; bulbs decayed; growth poor. Cause: Bacterial and fungal rots. Hyacinths are subject to a number of rot diseases. Rots are prevalent in poorly drained soil; control through careful bulb selection and culture. For tips on buying healthy bulbs, see "Healthy Bulb Basics" on page 98.

Leaves with swollen spots; plant fails to grow. Cause: Bulb and stem nematodes. Tiny roundworms feed on bulbs; plants fail to grow in spring or fail to bloom. Swollen, yellow-green spots appear on leaves; an infested bulb, cut in half, reveals dark blotches or rings. Wet soil encourages nematodes. Dig and destroy infested bulbs; check new bulbs carefully for pests. Plant in well-drained soil.

HYDRANGEA Hydrangea

Hydrangeas are opposite-leaved, deciduous shrubs and vines. The flowers are small but borne in large clusters. Hydrangeas are ideal for shrub borders or grouped for landscape interest.

Hydrangeas are among the few flowering shrubs that bloom well under shaded conditions, although they flourish in full sun in cooler climates. They prefer acid soils. Set out in spring or fall as balled-and-burlapped or container-grown plants.

Problems

Leaves wrinkled and discolored. Cause: Aphids. For control information, see "Aphids" on page 250.

Leaves tied together over flower buds. Cause: Hydrangea leaftiers. The ½-inch, green-bodied, brown-headed caterpillar causes the foliage to become ragged, turn brown, and die. If the infestation is light, break open the "envelopes" and pick off the caterpillars; for heavier infestations, spray plants with BTK.

Leaves deformed; shoot tips blackened. Cause: Tarnished plant bugs. This pest is an active, ¼-inch, light green to brown bug mottled with white, yellow, red, and black. When it feeds on the leaves, it produces a toxin that deforms the leaves and blackens the terminal shoots and flowers. See "Plant Bugs" on page 278 for controls.

Leaves with powdery white coating. Cause: Powdery mildew. See "Powdery Mildew" on page 322 for controls.

Flowers rot. Cause: Botrytis blight. In wet seasons, *Botrytis* fungi can cause a blight on hydrangeas that will spoil the flowers. Pick off and destroy affected blooms.

Leaves stippled with yellow; foliage webbed. Cause: Spider mites. See "Mites, Spider" on page 275 for suggested controls.

Leaves and flowers skeletonized. Cause: Rose chafers. This $\frac{1}{3}$-inch, reddish brown beetle with thick, yellowish hairs on its wing covers appears in late spring and damages both leaves and flowers. Handpicking is the best control. See "Rose Chafer" on page 280 for more controls.

Leaves and flowers browned and wilted. Cause: Bacterial wilt. This disease can spread quickly, killing the plant in hot weather. Remove infected parts as soon as you seen them; destroy seriously infected plants.

IBERIS Candytuft

These very hardy evergreen border plants brighten spring with clusters of tiny blossoms of pure or pink-tinged white. Evergreen candytuft (*Iberis sempervirens*) grows to about 1 foot tall with a spread of $1\frac{1}{2}$ to 2 feet, while rock candytuft (*I. saxatilis*) is even more compact, reaching heights of 3 to 6 inches. The $1\frac{1}{2}$- to 2-inch inflorescences last several weeks.

Plant candytufts in full sun in well-drained soil. Plants tolerate light shade, but it reduces flowering, as does drought. Cut plants back after flowering to encourage compact growth. Foliage may brown in cold, windy conditions; mulch lightly to reduce injury. Few pests or diseases trouble candytufts.

ILEX Holly

Hollies are deciduous or evergreen trees or shrubs with alternate leaves. The male and female flowers are borne on different plants; female plants produce striking red or black fruit. Hollies are useful as foundation shrubs, accent plants, informal hedges, and specimen plants.

Hollies prefer a moist, acid soil, well-enriched with organic matter. Plant in sun or shade. Set out as balled-and-burlapped or container-grown plants in spring or fall; make sure that the top of the root ball is at the same level at which the plant grew in the nursery. Hollies' roots grow close to the surface, so don't cultivate around them; a deep organic mulch will keep down weeds and provide a cool, moist root zone.

Protect evergreen hollies from winter sun and drying winds with a burlap screen or an anti-transpirant spray. Remember to plant both male and female plants so you'll get the pollination necessary for berries.

Problems

Leaves tunneled. Cause: Leafminers. This tiny insect is by far the most serious pest of hollies. For control information, see "Leaves tunneled" on page 213.

Leaves webbed together. Cause: Bud moths. These $\frac{3}{8}$-inch, greenish white caterpillars web together and feed on the tips of new holly shoots in May. Fully grown larvae usually drop to the ground and overwinter in plant debris. Remove fallen leaves around plants. Destroy webs and handpick caterpillars. Spray leaves with BTK in April and May.

Leaves yellow; stems and leaves covered with small bumps. Cause: Scales. See "Leaves yellow; stems and leaves covered with small bumps" on page 213 for control information.

Leaves stippled with yellow; foliage webbed. Cause: Spider mites. For controls, see "Leaves stippled with yellow; foliage webbed" on page 212.

Leaves with notched margins. Cause: Japanese weevils. The ¼-inch brown adults attack foliage, and the legless white grubs feed on roots. See "Root Weevils" on page 279 for more controls.

Leaves yellowed. Cause: Nitrogen deficiency. This is usually most noticeable on older leaves. Regular fertilization helps keep hollies green and vigorous. Apply cottonseed meal or a generous mulch of compost in early spring.

Leaves and shoots blackened; leaves with moist or brown sunken spots. Cause: Anthracnose. See "Leaves and shoots blackened; leaves with moist or brown sunken spots" on page 214 for more details.

Leaves with spots. Cause: Leaf spots. See "Leaves with spots" on page 213 for controls.

Leaves with powdery white coating. Cause: Powdery mildew. For control information, see "Leaves with powdery white coating" on page 213.

Trunk or branches with oozing lesions; branch tips die back. Cause: Canker. See "Trunk or branches with oozing lesions; branch tips die back" on page 214.

Leaves mottled yellow. Cause: Whiteflies. These tiny, white, mothlike insects and their even smaller larvae feed on the undersides of leaves,

weakening the plant. See "Whiteflies" on page 290 for controls.

IMPATIENS Impatiens, balsam

In American gardens, the two most widely grown species of the genus *Impatiens* are garden balsam (*I. balsamina*) and impatiens (*I. wallerana*). Garden balsam grows upright to 2 feet with a 1½-foot spread. The clustered flowers resemble small double camellias. Impatiens reach 6 to 24 inches high and about 1 foot wide, with open, single flowers. Flower colors include white, red, rose, and orange.

While many gardeners prefer to buy nursery-grown plants, the best color choices usually come in seed packets. Sow seed indoors 8 weeks before the last frost. Do not cover the small seeds with soil; they need light to germinate. Germination time is 5 days for balsam, 2 weeks for impatiens. Transplant outdoors 2 weeks after last frost.

Balsam can grow in full sun, while impatiens prefer some shade, especially in warm weather. These otherwise rather carefree plants do not tolerate cold, wet weather. They do require slightly moist soil with lots of organic matter. Water regularly to keep the soil moist but not soggy. Feed balsam once a month to maintain the dark green leaf color. Impatiens don't need extra feeding; too much fertilizer gives ample foliage but few flowers. Pinch back young plants for denser growth. Plants often self-seed.

Fortunately, these popular annuals are seldom troubled by pests. If aphids cause distorted leaves, stems, or buds, or slugs and snails chew large, ragged holes in leaves, see "Aphids" on page 250 and "Slugs/Snails" on page 284 for controls. Impatiens can also die because of damping-off. See "Seedlings die" on page 344 for controls.

IPOMOEA Morning glory

These quick-growing tropical vines have white, pink, red, or blue, trumpet-shaped flowers that may reach 3 inches wide. Older types close by midday, but new cultivars stay open longer. Vines may reach 10 feet high within 2 months of seeding and flower profusely from July until November. Use morning glories to beautify a fence or wall, or as a temporary groundcover.

Direct-seed outdoors in early April. Soak the hard-coated seed in tepid water for 8 hours, or notch them with a file to speed germination. Place in loose, well-prepared, average soil. Or start seeds indoors in 4-inch pots and transplant outdoors after frost.

Full sun is best. Plants require little water or fertilizer once established. Insects and diseases rarely attack plants.

IRIS Iris, flag

Irises offer a huge range of colors and patterns, heights, and bloom times, with variations on a common flower shape and plant form. The basic iris flower consists of three inner (often erect) petals, called standards, surrounded by three outer petals (usually arching out), called falls. Long, flat leaves resemble swords or grass; they grow in rather open to quite dense upright or arching clumps from bulbs or creeping rhizomes.

By far the most popular group is the large collection of hybrids termed the bearded irises, named for the hairy, caterpillar-like feature creeping out of the center of each fall. Flowers range from 2 to 7 inches wide in one of the widest color ranges of any plant group, lacking only pure red. They bloom in early summer, ranging from 2 inches to nearly 5 feet tall above stiff, swordlike leaves.

In place of a beard, "beardless" irises flaunt a colorful spot, called a signal, or an intricate pattern of lines. Blooms on Siberian iris (*Iris sibirica*) rarely exceed 3 inches wide; they occur in shades of white, red-violet, blue, and purple (occasionally pinks and yellows) in upright, grassy clumps averaging 3 feet tall. They bloom as bearded irises stop flowering. Japanese irises (*I. ensata,* formerly *I. kaempferi*) bear 4- to 10-inch flattish or double flowers in shades of white, pinkish lavender, red-violet, blue, and violet, often edged, lined, or speckled. Most grow to about 3 feet and bloom a few weeks later than Siberian irises.

Very early spring-blooming, bulbous reticulated iris (*I. reticulata*) hybrids have fragrant, narrow-petaled, 3-inch blooms, mostly in blues and purples with orange or yellow signals, amid sparse, four-sided leaves that grow to 1½ feet after bloom.

Most bearded irises are easy to grow, but they do have specialized needs. Plant and divide (every 3 to 4 years) in summer or early fall, splitting them into individual "fans" with the rhizome attached, or into divisions with a few fans. Trim leaves back before planting to make up for root loss. Plant in full sun or very light shade and average to rich, well-drained soil. Barely cover the rhizome and point the leafy end in the direction you want it to grow.

Bearded irises tolerate drought very well when dormant (usually beginning about 6 weeks after bloom), but water them well until dormancy sets in and after division. Fertilize routinely in spring and early fall, keep weeds and other plants away from rhizomes, mulch loosely the first winter after division, and plan to stake tall-growing cultivars when in bloom.

Siberian irises enjoy conditions similar to those favored by bearded irises, but tolerate wetter soil and need less-frequent division in spring or fall. Replant as soon as possible after dividing.

Grow Japanese irises in much the same way, providing shade from the hottest sun. Water well before and during bloom. They need acid soil and benefit from a few inches of mulch in summer.

Plant reticulated irises in fall, about 3 inches deep and a few inches apart in average to more fertile, very well-drained soil. Grow with annuals and perennials to fill gaps left by their leaves, which wither by summer.

Problems

Leaves with irregular tunnels; rhizomes damaged or rotted. Cause: Iris borers. The most destructive pest of irises, these moth larvae favor bearded irises, but may feed on all species. They seldom bother Siberian irises. Borer eggs overwinter in foliage and hatch in spring, producing up to 2-inch-long, fat, pinkish larvae. The larvae enter a fan at the top and tunnel down toward the rhizome, where they may eat the whole interior without being noticed. Borers often introduce soft rot bacteria into rhizomes as they feed.

In fall, remove dead, dry leaves, which often carry borer eggs, and destroy badly infested fans in spring. You can also crush borders in the leaves by pinching toward the base of the telltale ragged-edged leaves or by running your thumb between the leaves and squashing any borers you find. Check rhizomes when you divide the clumps for this pest. If you find a few borers, try cutting them out; destroy badly infested rhizomes.

Leaves with large, ragged holes. Cause: Slugs and snails. These slimy pests live and feed amid dense iris foliage. See "Slugs/Snails" on page 284 for controls.

Flower buds die; petals distorted; growth stunted. Cause: Thrips. Several species of tiny thrips infest irises; Japanese irises are especially susceptible. Thrips feed on inner folds of leaves, causing stunted growth and russet or sooty areas on leaves. Tops of plants eventually turn brown and die. Flowers may appear discolored, flecked with white, or deformed. These pests are difficult to control, for they burrow into plant tissue. Don't buy sickly looking irises that may be infested. Remove and destroy severely infested plant parts. See "Thrips" on page 287 for controls.

Leaves with yellow, brown, or black spots. Cause: Leaf spots. Irises may develop leaf spot, caused by several different species of fungi, especially in wet weather. Remove infected plant parts; clean up debris in fall to remove disease spores.

Leaves with water-soaked spots; rhizomes rotted and soft. Cause: Bacterial soft rot. Soft rot attacks during wet seasons in poorly drained soil, entering through wounds in the rhizome made by premature leaf removal or cultivation, or carried on the bodies of iris borers. Crowded plants in shady locations are more susceptible to this disease. Infected rhizomes are dry on the outside, but wet, smelly, and slimy inside. This rot may start in the leaves following borer attack. Water-soaked streaks appear on leaves, which then turn yellow and wilt, starting from the tips. Eventually the entire leaf cluster may fall to the ground. Bulbous irises are not infected by this particular rot.

Control borers to reduce soft rot infection; see "Leaves with irregular tunnels; rhizomes damaged or rotted" on this page. Remove and destroy rotting rhizomes. Wash tools when cultivating or dividing irises to avoid transmitting the infection. Choose rhizomes carefully, inspecting them for signs of infestation; plant in well-drained soil with adequate sunlight.

Leaves mottled or streaked. Cause: Mosaic

virus. Bulbous irises that are stunted and streaked with yellow may carry this virus. Flowers may be mottled and smaller than normal. There is no cure for infected plants; remove and destroy irises showing symptoms. Mosaic virus is spread by sucking insects such as aphids and leafhoppers. Control pests to reduce risk of infection. See "Aphids" on page 250 and "Leafhoppers" on page 271 for controls.

Stems rot at base. Cause: Crown rot. Crowded plants are most susceptible to this fungal disease. Leaves and stems turn brown at the base, foliage turns yellow, and black spores may appear on stems. White or brown mold may be present. Rhizomes may also rot. Dig and divide bearded iris clumps every few years to avoid overcrowding. Plant in well-drained soil. Avoid damaging crowns when cultivating; keep winter mulch away from crowns.

JUNIPERUS Juniper, red cedar

Junipers are a large group of evergreen trees and shrubs. Foliage in young plants is awl-shaped, in mature plants, flat and scalelike. Plants are either male or female; the females bear small, berrylike cones. Many species and cultivars are valuable in the landscape. Depending upon their form, junipers are valuable for foundation plantings, as groundcovers, or even as specimen trees. Because they respond well to pruning for shape, they also make effective evergreen hedges.

Junipers tolerate all but poorly drained soils. They withstand drought and grow in low-fertility soils—even seaside conditions. Set them out as balled-and-burlapped or container-grown plants in spring or fall. Full sun suits them best; grown in too much shade, they become spindly and unattractive.

Problems

Branches with large galls. Cause: Rust. Cedar-apple rust, cedar-hawthorn rust, and cedar-quince rust are fungal diseases that spend part of their life cycles on junipers, the rest on alternative hosts, such as apples and crabapples. Large galls form and eventually swell to release the spores, especially in warm, moist weather.

Other than producing the galls, rust does little harm to junipers. Cut off and destroy or dispose of galls before early spring. Avoid planting Eastern red cedar (*Juniperus virginiana*) and its cultivars, which are very susceptible to rusts. See "Leaves with pale yellow spots that enlarge and turn orange" on page 34 for information about this disease on apples.

Plant defoliated; branches bear cocoonlike bags. Cause: Bagworms. See "Plant defoliated; branches bear cocoonlike bags" on page 212 for control measures.

Leaves wrinkled and discolored. Cause: Aphids. Several kinds of aphids feed on junipers. For control information, see "Aphids" on page 250.

Leaves yellow; stems and leaves covered with small bumps. Cause: Scales. For control measures, see "Leaves yellow; stems and leaves covered with small bumps" on page 213.

Leaves yellow; whole plant weakened. Cause: Juniper mealybugs. The tiny, powdery white adults generally congregate on the trunks and interior branches, making them difficult to see until the plant starts to weaken. Control by spraying the plant (especially the bark) with horticultural oil at a growing-season dilution or repeated applications of insecticidal soap.

Leaves stippled with yellow; foliage webbed. Cause: Spider mites. For control measures, see "Leaves stippled with yellow; foliage webbed" on page 212.

Branch tips webbed together. Cause: Juniper webworms. The larvae of this ½-inch pest web together small juniper twigs and feed inside the webs. If left unchecked, this can kill the twigs. Remove and destroy the nests, and spray with BTK or pyrethrin as a last resort.

Needle bases blistered; shoot tips die. Cause: Juniper midges. The tiny yellow larvae of this pest feed on the bases of needles, damaging shoot tips. Prune off infested parts, then spray the whole plant with insecticidal soap. Clean up debris around the base of the tree to reduce the pest population.

Branch tips browned. Causes: Twig blights; cedar bark beetles. Fungal blights may attack junipers in spring or summer. These diseases spread progressively, killing branches or entire plants. Control by pruning and destroying affected branches on a dry day. Avoid by planting resistant cultivars, such as *J. chinensis* var. *sargentii* 'Glauca'; ask your local nursery owner or extension agent for others recommended for your area.

Cedar bark beetles can cause similar symptoms on recently transplanted junipers or those weakened by drought or infestations by other insects. The white larvae of this tiny black beetle tunnel under the bark, sometimes killing weakened trees. The adult beetles chew holes in twig crotches, often causing shoot tips to dangle from the branch. Prevent by keeping trees healthy: water during dry spells and fertilize regularly. If damage occurs, prune off damaged tips. As a last resort, spray with pyrethrin, making two applications 3 to 4 days apart.

KALE *Brassica oleracea,* **Acephala group (Cruciferae)**

Kale is a cool-season vegetable grown for its crinkly, blue-green leaves. It is a very hardy member of the cabbage family, tolerating temperatures below 40°F. In fact, frost improves its taste. It is less tolerant of heat than other members of the cabbage family. In warmer climates, grow kale in soil with high clay content if you have a choice, and shade soil around roots.

Grow kale as you would cabbage. It is occasionally bothered by the same diseases and insects as cabbage. See the Cabbage entry, beginning on page 56, for culture and information on problems.

KALMIA Mountain laurel

Mountain laurels are broad-leaved evergreen shrubs with clusters of white, pink, or red flowers in spring. They are splendid for woodland plantings, shrub borders, or foundation plantings.

In spring, set out balled-and-burlapped or container-grown plants. Select a partially shaded location (the farther south, the more shade) with moist but well-drained acid soil rich in organic matter. Don't cultivate around these shallow-rooted plants; instead, use a deep organic mulch, which will keep weeds down and provide the cool, moist root zone the plants need.

For information on pests and diseases, see the Rhododendron entry, beginning on page 182.

KIWI *Actinidia arguta, A. deliciosa,* **and** A. *kolomikta* (**Actinidiaceae**)

Kiwis are vigorous, twining vines. Fruit is borne toward the base of new shoots that grow off last year's canes. The kiwi found in produce markets, *Actinidia deliciosa,* grows in Zones 7–9. *A. arguta* is hardy in Zones 4–7; *A. kolomikta* is hardy in Zones 3–7.

Grow kiwis in full sun or partial shade in perfectly drained soil. Allow about 200 square feet of trellis or arbor for each plant. Male and female flowers appear on separate plants; therefore, a plant of each sex is required for fruit set. A few cultivars are self-pollinating. Check before you buy.

Problems

Leaves skeletonized. Cause: Japanese beetles. These ½-inch, metallic blue-green insects with bronze wing covers like to feed in the sun. Check plants early in the morning while beetles are sluggish and knock them into jars filled with soapy water. Scent-baited traps may be effective if placed at some distance from plants. Populations of this pest naturally decline by midsummer, but for very heavy infestations, spray with neem. For more information, see "Japanese Beetle" on page 269.

Vines chewed, bedraggled. Cause: Cats. Strange as it may seem, cats like kiwis as much as they like catnip. Protect plants with chicken wire, if necessary.

Plant stunted; leaves yellow. Cause: Crown rot. Kiwis require perfectly drained soil to avoid crown rot. Avoid planting in poorly drained sites and modify soil before planting to assure good drainage.

KOHLRABI *Brassica oleracea,* **Gongylodes group (Cruciferae)**

Kohlrabi is a cool-season vegetable grown for its crisp, bulbous, green or purple stems. It looks like an aboveground turnip. Kohlrabi can tolerate temperatures below 40°F and a soil pH between 5.5 and 6.8.

The trick to growing tender kohlrabi is encouraging rapid growth. Keep young plants well watered. Harvest bulbs when they are 2 to 3 inches in diameter; they may become fibrous and bitter if allowed to grow larger.

Kohlrabi and cabbage require similar culture and are attacked by the same diseases and insects. See the Cabbage entry, beginning on page 56, for culture and information on problems.

LAGERSTROEMIA Lagerstroemia, crape myrtle

Lagerstroemias, also known as crape myrtles, are popular summer-flowering shrubs and small trees grown throughout the warmer portions of the United States.

They require full sun and moist but well-drained soil enriched with organic matter. Since they produce flowers on the current season's wood, they withstand severe pruning in early spring and still bloom.

Powdery mildew can be a serious problem; choose resistant cultivars. For more information, see "Leaves with powdery white coating" on page 213. Aphids may feed on leaves; see "Leaves wrinkled and discolored" on page 211 for controls.

LANTANA Lantana, shrub verbena

Lantana brings masses of color to containers, rock gardens, and hanging baskets. The quick-growing plants can grow to 4 feet high by 8 feet wide. They are covered with 1- to 2-inch clusters of small flowers in shades of pink, yellow, orange, red, and bicolors. The plants are frost-sensitive, although they may bloom throughout the year in mild areas. Birds, bees, and butterflies find the plants quite attractive.

Take softwood cuttings from existing plants, or start seeds indoors in midwinter (they germinate in about 8 weeks). In warm climates direct-sowing is effective. Lantanas need full sun and average, well-drained soil. Plant 1½ feet apart. Water deeply but let soil dry out between waterings. Fertilize lightly; over-fertilization or excess water decreases bloom.

Problems

Leaves yellow; plant weakened. Cause: Whiteflies. See "Whiteflies" on page 290 for controls.

Leaves and stems with white, cottony clusters. Cause: Mealybugs. See "Mealybugs" on page 273 for control measures.

Leaves mottled, with shiny black flecks underneath. Cause: Lace bugs. See "Lace Bugs" on page 270 for controls.

LARIX Larch

Larches comprise a unique genus—a group of deciduous, needle-leaved conifers. They are trees for cold climates.

Set out in spring or fall as balled-and-burlapped plants. Plant in full sun in moist, acid soil. Larches do not tolerate shade, dry soils, or urban conditions.

Problems

Leaves mined, yellowed, and shriveled. Cause: Larch casebearers. The tiny reddish brown larvae of this moth feed and overwinter inside the leaves. Adult moths emerge in May or June. Natural parasites usually keep this pest under control. For severe infestations, apply a dormant spray of lime-sulfur to branches.

Branches defoliated. Cause: Larch sawflies. The small, wasplike adults lay eggs in the side of larch shoots in spring, causing shoots to twist. These ½- to 1-inch, grayish green, caterpillar-like larvae emerge about a week later, feeding on needles, starting with lower branches. See "Sawflies" on page 281 for controls.

Trunks or branches with oozing lesions. Cause: Larch branch canker. This fungus produces sunken areas on the bark that are surrounded with drops of resin. Cut out and destroy affected parts as soon as detected; once established, there is no control. European larch (*Larix deciduas*) is prone to serious infections; Japanese larch (*L. kaempferi*) is less susceptible to the disease.

LATHYRUS Sweet pea

These fragrant, climbing annuals make excellent cut flowers. Clusters of lavender, pink, or white blossoms appear in spring. Plants can grow 1 to 6 feet tall. Hot weather kills cultivars that aren't heat-resistant.

Soak seeds for 24 hours in warm water to speed germination. Direct-sow in early spring as soon as soil can be worked. Indoors, start in individual peat pots about 7 weeks before last frost. Seeds germinate in 2 weeks.

Plant sweet peas in full sun in a deeply worked bed amended with lots of organic matter. Water deeply and frequently. Remove spent flowers to prolong blooming.

Powdery mildew can occur if air circulation is poor; see "Powdery Mildew" on page 322. If aphids are a problem, see "Aphids" on page 250.

LAWNS

Good organic lawn maintenance is the secret to having an attractive lawn without using synthetic chemicals. If you select the right mix of grass species for your area and maintain soil organic matter content, pH, and fertility, you'll have few problems with insects and diseases.

If your lawn is out of condition, or if you've been relying on synthetic fertilizers and pesticides to keep it growing, here are some steps you may need to take to develop a lush, organic lawn.

■ Mow high—3 or 4 inches is best for most types of grass. Mowing high promotes drought tolerance and suppresses weed growth. Keep mower blades sharp.

■ Leave the clippings on the lawn. Grass clippings are one of the best organic fertilizers for lawns.

■ Check soil pH, and adjust if necessary. Most grasses do best at a pH of 6.5 to 7.0. If you need to add lime to raise pH, also test for the calcium and magnesium content of your soil. If calcium level is low, use calcitic lime. If magnesium is low, use dolomitic lime. Apply lime in fall or early spring.

■ Revive the living organisms in your soil by drenching it with compost tea. See "Compost Tea" on page 6. You can use a backpack sprayer to apply compost tea to a small lawn, or hire an organic lawn care company to apply it to a large lawn.

■ Top-dress your lawn with a ¼- to ⅜-inch layer of finished compost. Aerate the lawn first, cut it to 2 inches tall, then rake the compost over the soil.

■ Fertilize once a year—in late summer to early fall for northern lawns, in spring or summer for southern lawns.

■ Water deeply and infrequently to encourage grasses to develop deep roots so they'll be more drought tolerant.

■ If your lawn gets lots of foot or vehicle traffic or is growing in heavy soil, aerate the soil to loosen it and encourage deeper root growth. You can rent a motorized or power-driven aerator, or aerate manually with a spading fork. At 1-foot intervals all over your lawn, insert a spading fork into the turf at a 45-degree angle. Push the tines in to a depth of 4 inches. Press down slightly on the fork handle to loosen the soil, and then pull out the fork.

■ If your lawn has a buildup of thatch—undecomposed plant debris at the soil surface—thin it out by raking the lawn with a special thatching rake, available from nursery suppliers and mail-order tool companies. For very large lawns, you will need to rent a machine called a dethatcher.

■ If your lawn is in bad condition, or suffering from severe insect or disease problems, you may decide to start from scratch. If so, be sure to choose the best grass or mixture of grasses for your area. Cool-season grasses, which grow the most in spring and fall and are dormant in midsummer, are best for the northern half of the country. Warm-season grasses, which are dormant in winter and begin growing in early summer, are best for the desert southwest and the Sun Belt. There are many disease- and insect-resistant cultivars available. One group, the endophyte-containing grasses, hosts fungi that produce a substance that deters feeding by some insect pests and is actually toxic to other pests. Check with your local extension office or garden center for the best new cultivars for your areas. You can replace your entire lawn or add new grass by a technique called overseeding: Cut the grass very short, rake out thatch and rough up the soil, then spread the new seed. Cover the newly sown seed with sand or topsoil and keep it moist until new seedlings are established.

Problems

Turf has bare or ragged patches. Cause: Army-worms. These greenish brown caterpillars with white stripes and black heads chew grass blades down to the crowns, leaving bare areas or ragged patches of grass. They are a common pest on ber-mudagrass during cool, wet periods. In the South, as many as six generations may occur in 1 year. Spray affected areas with parasitic nematodes while larvae are still feeding. Spray young larvae with BTK or insecticidal soap. Remove dead areas of turf. Reseed and overseed with resistant grasses such as the endophyte-containing cultivars.

Grass blades yellowed; thinned, brown turf. Cause: Mites. These tiny, eight-legged creatures suck sap from grass blades, causing them to turn yellow or straw-colored. Heavy infestations can kill plants, leaving turf looking brown and sparse. Mites thrive on poorly fed lawns and during dry conditions. Improve fertility and keep lawns well-watered during dry spells. For serious infesta-tions, spray with insecticidal soap.

Turf with yellow or brown patches. Cause: Billbugs. Billbug larvae are white grubs with yellow-brown heads that feed on grass stems, causing shoots to turn brown and die. In warm weather the grubs tunnel into the soil and feed on roots and rhizomes. Billbugs are brown or nearly black, $\frac{1}{4}$- to $\frac{1}{2}$-inch weevils. Apply a mix of *Steinernema* and *Heterorhabditis* nematodes to prevent or control billbugs. Prevent future problems by aerating the lawn, watering deeply, removing thatch, and adding organic matter. Reseed or overseed with endophytic cultivars.

Yellowed round patches on lawn. Cause: Chinch bugs. These bugs suck plant sap, causing grass to turn yellow and die off in patches. To check for chinch bugs: Remove both ends from a large coffee can. Push one end 2 inches into the sod, using a knife to cut the ground so the can inserts easily or a board to hammer it in place. Fill the can with water. Chinch bugs will float to the surface within 10 minutes. If there are 20 or more bugs in the can, monitor the population weekly, and take steps to control, if necessary. Drive out chinch bugs by keeping the soil very moist. Wet it to a depth of 6 inches, and maintain the moist condition for 3 to 4 weeks. See "Chinch Bug" on page 257 for controls.

Turf has irregular streaks of brown grass. Cause: Mole crickets. These $1\frac{1}{2}$-inch, light brown insects have short forelegs and shovel-like feet. They are serious lawn pests in the South. See "Mole Crickets" on page 275 for controls.

Small, irregular dead spots on lawn. Cause: Sod webworms. Webworms sever grass blades just above the thatch line and pull the blades into a silken tunnel in the ground to eat. They are most often a problem on bluegrass, hybrid bermu-dagrasses, and bentgrasses in the South. Hot, dry conditions and thatch buildup encourage the pests. See "Webworms, Sod" on page 289.

Turf thins, turns yellow, and dies. Cause: White grubs. Damaged turf can be easily lifted from the lawn. Ten or more grubs per square foot is a serious infestation. See "White Grubs" on page 290 for controls.

Turf has brown circular patches. Cause: Brown patch. This fungus causes circular areas of grass up to 2 feet in diameter to turn brown and die. It tends to attack St. Augustine grass, bent-grass, bermudagrass, zoysia grass, tall fescues, and ryegrasses, especially during hot, humid weather. Close cutting, poor drainage, overwatering, excessive nitrogen, and low pH all contribute to brown patch. Control the disease by reducing nitrogen fertilization, mowing less frequently, aerating, and dethatching. Top-dress with humus-building material. Water less frequently and only during the day so grass dries off quickly. Rake out dead grass and replant bare spots with resistant grasses.

Tan or straw-colored spots on lawn. Cause: Dollar spot. This fungus causes tan or straw-colored spots the size of silver dollars to appear on the lawn. The fungus occurs widely on golf greens, but may also be a severe problem on low-nitrogen, poorly drained lawns. Aerate the soil and improve drainage by top-dressing with finished compost. In the meantime, keep soil well watered. Apply a nitrogen fertilizer; applying seaweed extract is also helpful. Mow less frequently, if possible. Overseed in fall with resistant cultivars.

Green spots outlined with brown on lawn. Cause: Fairy ring. A lawn with bright green circular areas that seem to grow more rapidly than the rest of the lawn is probably infected by fairy ring fungus. A ring of grass around the green spots turns brown; the green areas eventually will brown out also. A circle of mushrooms usually develops around the edge of the infested area. Rake and discard the mushrooms as they appear. Spike the area with a spading fork every day. Water well. Encourage beneficial soil microbes by top-dressing with finished compost or an organic lawn fertilizer. Eradicate the fungus by digging out the soil in the area of the ring. Dig down 2 feet and extend the hole outward at least 1 foot from the ring. Remove the soil carefully, being sure not to spill any infected soil on the healthy lawn. Fill in the hole with humusy topsoil and finished compost, and reseed.

Reddish brown, tan, or yellow patches develop on lawn. Cause: Fusarium blight. This disease is common on Kentucky bluegrass during periods of hot, humid weather. Infected lawns develop spots of reddish brown grass 2 to 6 inches in diameter. The spots later turn tan and finally yellow. Roots will rot and may be covered with pink mold. Dethatch and aerate the lawn. Apply 1 to 2 inches of water each week. Raise the mowing height in summer. Don't fertilize in late spring or early summer. Rake out dead grass and replant with Fusarium-resistant cultivars.

Grass blades have dark spots. Causes: Leaf spots; leaf blights. Several fungi cause grass to develop reddish brown to black spots on the leaf blades. Grass shrivels and roots rot. Hot, humid conditions favor fungal growth. Fight leaf spots and blights by building soil fertility. Set mowing height as high as recommended for your grass mix. Don't mow during disease outbreaks, to avoid spreading the fungi. Keep soil evenly moist. Restore diseased areas by raking out diseased grass and top-dressing with finished compost. Reseed or overseed with resistant cultivars.

Grass water-soaked, blackened. Cause: Cottony blight. Infection by *Pythium* fungi causes patches of grass to turn black and look water-soaked. In humid conditions a cottony mold may appear. The disease usually occurs in wet, poorly drained areas that have been overfertilized. It spreads rapidly once established. Alkaline soils and calcium deficiency encourage the disease. Aerate and dethatch lawn. Have the soil tested and correct calcium deficiency, if necessary. Reduce nitrogen fertilization, particularly in fall. Keep soil evenly moist. Maintain slightly acid soil. In severely infected areas enrich soil with organic matter to improve drainage, and replant.

Circular, scorched patches or pink, gelatinous masses on lawn. Causes: Red thread; pink patch. Lawns infected by red thread fungus have circular patches of dried grass that have red or rusty threads on the blades. Lawns suffering from pink patch will develop pink, gelatinous masses on leaf blades. These related fungal diseases are common on bentgrass, bluegrass, fescue, and ryegrass, especially in cool, humid regions. Apply an organic fertilizer with nitrogen in readily available form, such as seaweed extract. Mow regularly to remove infested leaf tips. Water regularly and thoroughly.

Grass blades develop yellow to red, powdery blisters. Cause: Rust. Infection by this fungus causes yellow to rusty red, powdery spore blisters to appear on leaf blades. Seriously infected lawns turn yellow and wither. Rust typically occurs in late summer on dry lawns lacking nitrogen. To avoid problems, water the lawn well in the early morning, so the grass can dry off quickly. Fertilize using seaweed extract or other nitrogen-rich fertilizer. Mow regularly. Rake out dead grass and overseed with resistant cultivars.

LETTUCE *Lactuca sativa* (**Compositae**)

Lettuce is a hardy annual grown for its tender leaves. The three most common types of lettuce are leaf or bunching, head (including butterhead and crisphead), and cos or romaine.

Culture

Lettuce grows best in rich, loose soil with a pH between 6.0 and 6.8. It likes full sun, but in hot weather does better with light shade in the heat of the day. Lettuce needs to grow rapidly and without interruption. Provide plenty of nitrogen in both quicker-release forms, such as blood meal or soybean meal, and slower-release forms, such as compost or alfalfa meal. Spray the plants with seaweed extract every other week to give them an extra boost.

Lettuce grows best at temperatures between 60°

and 65°F. Most cultivars grow poorly above 75°F, but will tolerate temperatures as low as 45°F. Plants exposed to high temperatures will bolt. Prevent bolting by providing plants with partial shade in the heat of the summer, harvesting promptly, and planting bolt-resistant cultivars.

To grow tender, trouble-free lettuce, keep the soil moist, but not soggy. Unlike most vegetables, lettuce responds well to having its foliage sprinkled with water. Avoid planting lettuce in soil where it has been grown within the last 3 years.

Lettuce seeds will not germinate if soil temperatures are above 80°F. In the heat of the summer, start seedlings in a cool, shaded location and then transplant them into the garden.

Various nutrient deficiencies can affect lettuce. Boron or phosphorus deficiency causes malformed plants. Calcium deficiency causes browning of young leaves. Poor heart formation is a symptom of molybdenum deficiency. Copper deficiency prevents heads from forming. Spray seedlings with seaweed extract to help prevent nutrient deficiencies. Continue to spray plants with seaweed extract every 2 weeks to boost plant health. Do a soil test to confirm a deficiency, and amend soil accordingly.

Problems

Seedlings rot near soil line and fall over; seeds do not germinate. Cause: Damping-off. Keep soil moist, but not soggy. Thin seedlings and spray with compost tea as soon as first true leaves open to help prevent problems.

Seedlings clipped off at soil line. Cause: Cutworms. Once a seedling is clipped off, there is nothing to do but protect the remaining seedlings from nocturnal cutworm attacks. Check for fat, 1- to 2-inch-long, brown or gray caterpillars in the soil near the base of plants. Place cutworm collars around transplants, sprinkle moist bran mixed with BTK on the soil surface in the evening, or add parasitic nematodes to the soil at least 1 week before planting to control them. See "Cutworm Collars" on page 354.

Leaves yellow. Causes: Excessive heat; nitrogen deficiency; waterlogged soil. Plants are stunted and leaves are tough and bitter. Temperatures above 80°F will produce these symptoms. Prevent problems by planting heat-tolerant cultivars and providing partial shade for plants in the heat of summer.

If weather is not extremely hot, the problem is probably nitrogen deficiency. Spray plants and drench roots with fish emulsion or seaweed extract to alleviate symptoms. Waterlogged soil produces the same symptoms by damaging roots. Grow lettuce in raised beds if drainage is a problem.

Plant yellow and stunted; plant wilts during bright, hot days and recovers at night. Causes: Wireworms; nematodes. Wireworms are yellow to reddish brown, slender, tough-bodied, segmented worms up to 1½ inches long, with brown heads. Adults are dark-colored, elongated click beetles. Apply parasitic nematodes to the soil to control them, and avoid planting where sod was the previous year.

Root-knot nematodes cause enlargements or galls on roots. Control pest nematodes by applying chitin or parasitic nematodes to the soil.

Young leaves yellow and distorted. Causes: Tarnished plant bugs; aphids; big vein. Tarnished plant bugs are oval, light green to brown, ¼-inch-long insects with triangles on their backs. Nymphs are smaller and yellow-green. When they feed, they inject a toxin into plants that causes distorted growth. Trap them with white sticky traps. Grow groundcovers and pollen plants to attract native predators (bigeyed bugs, damsel bugs, pirate bugs);

remove nearby weeds, especially red-stemmed pigweed. Till soil after harvest to reduce overwintering pests.

Aphids are soft-bodied, small, green, black, gray, pink, or white fluffy-coated, sucking insects that can spread diseases. For light infestations, knock pests off plants with a blast of water. Spray plants with insecticidal soap to control; apply neem as a last resort. Cover plants with row cover when they emerge to prevent problems.

Big vein is a viral disease that causes light green or yellow, crinkled leaves with lighter, enlarged veins. Infected plants are stunted and head formation is impaired. Destroy infected plants. Prevent problems by not planting in cold, wet soils or where big vein has been a problem in the past.

Leaves pale; plant stunted. Cause: Leafhoppers. Leaves may appear stippled. These green or brown, wedge-shaped, ⅒- to ½-inch-long insects feed on plant sap and can spread diseases. Protect newly emerged seedlings and young transplants with row cover. Use a strong spray of water to knock nymphs from plants. Treat infested plants with insecticidal soap in the evening.

Leaves dull gray-green or silvery. Cause: Thrips. Leaves may turn brown and papery. These tiny, winged insects can barely be seen with the naked eye. To check for thrips, tap a leaf over a white paper and look for moving specks. Trap thrips with sticky traps, or spray plants with insecticidal soap to control them. Try blue, yellow, and white sticky traps placed just above plant height to see which color works best.

Young leaves are dwarfed, curled, or twisted. Cause: Aster yellows. There is no cure for infected plants; destroy them. Control leafhoppers because they spread this disease. See "Leaves pale; plant stunted" above for leafhopper controls.

Leaves mottled and ruffled. Cause: Mosaic

virus. Plants are stunted. Destroy infected plants as soon as possible. Control aphids that spread the disease. See "Young leaves yellow and distorted" on the opposite page for controls. Prevent problems by planting resistant or tolerant cultivars such as 'Eruption', 'Fallgreen', 'Magenta', 'Nancy', 'Nevada', and 'Parris Island'.

Leaves covered with white powdery coating. Cause: Powdery mildew. Older leaves are usually affected by this fungal disease. Infected leaves curl, turn yellow, and eventually turn brown and die. Remove affected leaves. Spray plants with potassium bicarbonate or a baking soda solution (1 teaspoon per quart of water), as soon as disease appears, to prevent further infection. Thin plants to increase air movement.

Leaves with yellow or light green spots. Cause: Downy mildew. Undersides of spots develop a fluffy white growth. Affected areas eventually turn brown. In severe cases plants become brown and stunted. Downy mildew is a fungal disease common in warm, damp, foggy weather. To prevent problems, plant cultivars such as 'Black-Seeded Simpson', 'Magenta', 'Nancy', 'Nevada', 'Optima', and 'New Red Fire', which are tolerant of downy mildew.

Leaves with dark or water-soaked spots. Cause: Various bacterial or fungal leaf spot diseases. Destroy badly spotted plants or leaves. Thin plants to increase air movement, and avoid wetting leaves when watering. Prevent problems by maintaining plant vigor with sprays of seaweed extract.

Leaf margins brown and dried. Causes: Tipburn; freezing injury. Tipburn also causes dark spots on veins. This condition is prevalent in hot weather and is related to uneven soil moisture and a shortage of calcium in the leaves. To prevent problems, keep the soil moist, but not soggy. Plant cultivars that resist tipburn, such as 'Grand Rapids',

'Green Star', 'Harmony', 'Parris Island', 'Rex', 'Slobolt', 'Summer Time', 'Tropicana', 'Vulcan', and 'Waldmann's Dark Green'.

Temperatures below 35°F cause outer leaf margins to turn tan and leaves to blister. Protect plants with row cover if low temperatures are predicted.

Leaves with discolored midribs. Cause: Excessive heat. Midribs remain firm. Temperatures above 80°F can cause midrib discoloration. Cover plants with shade cloth when temperatures soar, or plant in partial shade. Certain cultivars, such as 'Ithaca', are less susceptible to this condition.

Whole plant collapses or rots. Causes: Bottom rot; lettuce drop; gray mold. Bottom rot first infects the lower leaves that touch the ground. Dark, sunken spots develop on midribs, then entire leaves turn brown and slimy. Entire plant may be affected in severe cases. The same fungus causes diseases on many different vegetables, so preventive rotation is difficult. Prevent bottom rot by planting resistant cultivars such as 'Cherokee', 'Magenta', and 'Nevada'.

Lettuce drop fungus causes plants to wilt and collapse; outer leaves are affected first. Gray mold fungus also starts at the bottom of the plant and turns it into a slimy, brown mess. The center stem and heart may rot out before the outer leaves are affected.

Destroy infected plants or leaves and thin remaining plants to increase air movement. Prevent problems by working lots of compost into the soil before planting; plant lettuce in raised beds to improve soil drainage.

Leaves with wandering, white or translucent tunnels. Cause: Leafminers. Larvae are white and maggotlike and burrow through leaves, leaving empty tunnels. Adults are tiny, black-and-yellow insects. Cover seedlings with floating row cover; pick and destroy mined leaves and remove egg clusters; remove nearby dock or lamb's-quarters, which are hosts for beet leafminers. Once larvae are inside leaves, spraying is generally useless.

Leaves with small holes. Cause: Flea beetles. These small, shiny, black beetles hop when disturbed. Protect plants with row cover as soon as they germinate. Flea beetles are most problematic during droughts; watering the garden can sometimes reduce outbreaks.

Leaves with large holes. Causes: Caterpillars; slugs or snails. If there are green droppings on leaves and below plants, look for caterpillars feeding on leaves. Spray plants with BTK to control them.

If there are shiny slime trails on the remaining leaves, slugs and snails are at work. Sprinkle wood ashes or diatomaceous earth around plants, or trap the pests in shallow pans filled with stale beer and empty traps daily. For more slug control tips, see "Slugs/Snails" on page 284.

Leaves cut back or missing. Cause: Animal pests. Lettuce is a favorite snack for rabbits and groundhogs. See "Groundhogs" on page 306 and "Rabbits" on page 308 for control methods.

LIATRIS Gayfeather, blazing-star

These striking upright plants provide bottle-brush-type flower spikes of pink to purple as well as white with stemless, grasslike leaves that become smaller as they progress up the spikes. Gayfeathers range in height from 3 to 6 feet; flowers open from the tops of spikes downward and bloom in summer and into fall.

Plant in full sun. These tough natives of the Great Plains tolerate poor to average soils, heat,

cold, and some drought, but are at their best in moist, well-drained soil. Gayfeathers may self-sow under optimum conditions but are rarely invasive. Cut spent spikes back by a third, leaving the rest to produce food for continued growth. Tall species and cultivars may need staking. Divide every 4 years if plants seem crowded.

Gayfeathers have no significant pests or disease, but in some states the southern root-knot nematode is a problem, causing plants that fail to thrive. See "Root-Knot Nematodes" on page 340 for controls.

LIGUSTRUM Privet

Privets are opposite-leaved, deciduous or evergreen shrubs. They are easy to grow and readily lend themselves to pruning, which helps explain their popularity for hedges. Many species have become invasive, however, so check with your local Cooperative Extension office to see if they are a problem in your area.

Privets will grow in full sun or partial shade and tolerate almost all soils except poorly drained ones. Set out in spring or fall. They benefit from a deep organic mulch.

Problems

Leaves wrinkled and discolored. Cause: Aphids. For control measures, see "Leaves wrinkled and discolored" on page 211.

Leaves tunneled. Cause: Leafminers. See "Leaves tunneled" on page 213 for controls.

Leaves yellow; stems and leaves covered with small bumps. Cause: Scales. For controls, see "Leaves yellow; stems and leaves covered with small bumps" on page 213.

Leaves with notched margins. Cause: Japanese weevils. The ¼-inch, brown adults attack foliage, and the legless white grubs feed on roots. See "Root Weevils" on page 279 for controls.

Leaves stippled with yellow; foliage webbed. Cause: Spider mites. See "Leaves stippled with yellow; foliage webbed" on page 212 for suggested controls.

Leaves and shoots blackened; leaves with moist or brown sunken spots. Cause: Anthracnose. See "Leaves and shoots blackened; leaves with moist or brown sunken spots" on page 214 for controls.

Leaves with powdery white coating. Cause: Powdery mildew. See "Leaves with powdery white coating" on page 213 for controls.

LILIUM Lily

Hybridizers have created a glorious mix of lilies with 3- to 12-inch flowers in a variety of distinctive shapes, resembling peaked caps, turbans, bowls, trumpets, or broad, curly stars. They bloom in shades and combinations of white, pink, red, yellow, orange, lilac, and green, many dotted in maroon or near-black. Plants bear a few to two dozen or more flowers atop 2- to 7-foot, upright stems clothed in narrow leaves. Most lilies are hardy in Zones 3–8, with protection in the North, especially during the first winter.

Lilies thrive in sun or part shade in deep, fertile, moist but well-drained, humus-rich soil out of strong winds. Unlike the hard, dense bulbs of tulips and daffodils, a lily bulb is a fragile package of individual scales joined together rather loosely, making it quite prone to damage and drying out. Also, lilies never go completely dormant; plant them carefully, as soon as possible after you receive them. It is preferable to plant them in fall, although spring planting is quite common. Many specialists prepare the soil to 1½ feet deep on a warm fall day and mulch the site heavily to keep the soil unfrozen and ready for planting in very late fall, which is when many dealers ship lilies. Most lilies produce roots along the length of their belowground stems, which help to feed and support the large plants. Therefore, even tiny lily bulbs should have no less than 6 inches of soil above the top of the bulb.

Mark the planting sites to help avoid injuring the newly emerging shoots. When they appear in spring (sometimes surprisingly late), carefully cultivate and scratch in the first of two organic fertilizer meals for the season. Fertilize again before bloom; avoid excessive nitrogen applications. Mulch with several inches of compost or finely shredded bark to keep the soil cool. Water during dry spells. Stake tall lilies and deadhead after bloom. After the tops die, cut the stems down to a few inches to mark the spot for next year. Clear away faded foliage and plant debris to remove overwintering pests and diseases.

Move or divide lilies only when overcrowding makes it absolutely necessary; their fragile bulbs and fleshy roots resent any disturbance. Dig bulbs after stalks die back; replant immediately or wrap them in a plastic bag of barely moist perlite to keep the roots from drying out, and store in a cool place. Discard any bulbs that appear diseased or damaged. Expect minimal growth the first year after transplant. Small bulbils or bulblets may form in leaf axils or near the base of stalks; harvest and plant these at the end of the growing season to produce new plants.

Problems

Leaves yellow; plant wilts; bulbs decay. Cause: Bacterial or fungal rots. Control these rots with proper culture: Plant lilies in well-drained soil; select a site with good air circulation; avoid excess water in the soil or on foliage; dig and cultivate with care to prevent injury to bulbs.

Leaves yellow or distorted; bulbs decayed. Cause: Bulb mites. These mites are especially problematic when bulbs are injured by careless digging or cultivation. See "Leaves yellow or distorted; bulbs decayed" on page 100 for controls.

Leaves, stems, and buds distorted, sticky; clusters of small insects. Cause: Aphids. See "Aphids" on page 250 for controls.

Leaves with orange or reddish brown spots; buds rotted. Cause: Botrytis blight. This most common disease of lilies progresses from leaf spots to limp, blackened foliage starting with the lower leaves and moving up. Distorted flowers may have brown flecks. Some lily species and cultivars are more resistant to Botrytis than others. Choose resistant lilies, if identified, when buying bulbs; otherwise rely on good culture and healthy plants to limit disease. For tips on buying healthy bulbs, see "Healthy Bulb Basics" on page 98. See "Botrytis Blight" on page 326 for more information and controls.

Leaves mottled; plant stunted. Cause: Viral diseases. A variety of viruses cause yellowed, mottled, or streaked leaves and stunted stems on lilies. Flowers may be discolored. Aphids and other sucking insects carry viruses from infected lilies or from carrier plants that show no disease symptoms. Tulips and cucurbits also carry viruses that affect lilies. Infected plants eventually wilt and die.

There is no cure for viral diseases. Remove and destroy infected plants immediately. Wash tools and hands after working around diseased plants. To limit the spread of viruses, routinely check lilies for aphids, and control the pests if necessary; see "Aphids" on page 250 for control measures. Buy bulbs and plants from reputable sources—some will certify stock as "virus free." Do not plant lilies in sites where diseases have occurred on bulbous plants. Separate lilies from tulips, cucurbits, and wild lilies.

Leaves pale above with dusty blisters on undersides. Cause: Rust. See "Rust" on page 315 for controls.

Leaves chewed; black debris on plants. Cause: Lily leaf beetle. Lily leaf beetle larvae feed on leaves and buds and pile their black frass on their backs. Plants may be defoliated. Handpicking the adults and larvae can be difficult (wear gloves to handpick larvae). Experimental releases of natural enemies of this imported pest are ongoing and may provide control in the future. If the beetle is a continuing problem on your lilies, spraying larvae with neem or spinosad may help; thorough coverage is important.

Shoots disappear or do not emerge. Cause: Animal pests. Deer and groundhogs relish lily shoots; rodents enjoy the bulbs. Plant lilies where regular human activity will discourage wildlife; pet cats or dogs also deter animal pests. Line planting beds with hardware cloth to exclude burrowing rodents; cover beds with screen wire in winter. Experiment with repellents such as dried blood, human hair, or garlic sprays. Some gardeners use a few musky-smelling fritillary bulbs planted among the lilies to repel animal pests. Keep flower beds free of brush and plant debris, which offer shelter to hungry wildlife.

LIQUIDAMBAR Sweetgum

Sweetgums are native deciduous trees bearing alternate, star-shaped leaves that turn brilliant scarlet in autumn. While a handsome tree for the large lawn, sweetgum is intolerant of air pollution and is a poor choice for urban sites.

Set out in spring as balled-and-burlapped plants, in full sun. A deep, slightly acid, moist soil of average fertility is best. Allow plenty of room for the tree's extensive root system. The plants are slow to establish; a thick layer of mulch and regular watering for the first few years will promote root development. Once they settle in, sweetgums are fairly problem free.

Problems

Leaves skeletonized or with large holes; branches may be webbed. Cause: Caterpillars. See "Leaves skeletonized or with large holes; branches may be webbed" on page 212 for controls.

Leaves yellow; stems and leaves covered with small bumps. Cause: Scales. For controls, see "Leaves yellow; stems and leaves covered with small bumps" on page 213.

Trunk or branches with sunken, oozing areas. Cause: Bleeding necrosis. It is natural for the tree to exude some sticky "gum" from the trunk as it grows. However, excessive amounts of sap from dark, sunken areas in the bark may indicate a disease problem; left unchecked, it can quickly kill the tree. Cut out diseased areas as soon as you find them.

Plant defoliated; branches bear cocoonlike bags. Cause: Bagworms. See "Plant defoliated; branches bear cocoonlike bags" on page 212 for control measures.

LIRIODENDRON Tulip tree, yellow poplar

Tulip trees are tall trees with alternate, three-lobed leaves. Yellow flowers appear near the top of the tree in late spring or early summer. Tulip tree makes a fine specimen tree for large properties.

Set out in spring as a balled-and-burlapped plant. Full sun and slightly acid, deep, well-drained but moisture-retentive soil suits it best.

Problems

Leaves wrinkled and discolored. Cause: Aphids. The small green tuliptree aphid can be abundant on the undersides of leaves, secreting copious amounts of honeydew. For control information, see "Leaves wrinkled and discolored" on page 211.

Leaves yellow and drop early. Cause: Lack of water. Leaf yellowing is a common problem on newly planted trees as well as established ones that don't get enough water. Avoid by watering during dry periods and using a thick layer of organic mulch.

Leaves yellow; stems and leaves covered with small bumps. Cause: Scales. See "Leaves yellow; stems and leaves covered with small bumps" on page 213 for controls.

Leaves with spots. Cause: Tuliptree spot gall. Circular brown or purple spots surrounded by a circle of yellow on the leaves reveals the presence of tuliptree spot gall, caused by a kind of midge. Damaged leaves may fall early. While unsightly, the problem is not serious and is best countered by raking up and destroying all affected fallen leaves.

Leaves with powdery white coating. Cause: Powdery mildew. See "Leaves with powdery white coating" on page 213 for controls.

LOBELIA Lobelia

Lobelia's numerous species of annual and perennial flowers offer gardeners a broad array of plant heights and flower types. Annual edging lobelia (*Lobelia erinus*) bears blue, purple, pink, or white flowers on mounding to trailing 4- to 9-inch plants. Perennial cardinal flower (*L. cardinalis*) features spikes of brilliant red, three-lobed flowers that hummingbirds find irresistible. Other perennial species bear star-shaped blooms in shades of blue and lavender; lobelias with red or bronze foliage are also available. Perennials grow 2 to 5 feet tall with a spread of about 2 feet.

Lobelias prefer shady sites where the soil is consistently moist but well-drained. Plants tolerate full sun in cool climates if ample moisture is provided, but generally need at least partial shade to thrive. Summer mulch helps retain much-needed soil moisture; a light winter mulch helps protect crowns. Perennial species are short-lived plants; renovate plantings by division or reseeding every 2 to 3 years. Cover seeds lightly to keep them from drying out.

A number of pests may feed on lobelias, but damage is rarely significant enough to require treatment. Clusters of aphids can cause distorted leaves, stems, and buds. See "Aphids" on page 250 for control information. A variety of fungi cause leaves with spots or rotted patches that are best treated culturally. Remove infected plants and plant parts; keep gardens free of plant debris and weeds where diseases can overwinter; space plantings to permit good air circulation.

LOBULARIA Sweet alyssum

Alyssums are popular, mound-forming plants that bloom from spring until frost. Plant size is 3 to 8 inches high and to 10 inches wide. Flowers are pink, purple, or white and appear in multiple ¾-inch clusters. When planted in masses, the sweet honey smell of alyssum reminds some gardeners of fresh-mowed hay. Bees like the aroma, too; use alyssum near fruit trees that need pollinating. Alyssum is ideal for borders or as groundcovers for small areas.

Alyssum likes full sun and well-drained average soil. Direct-sow in loose soil 5 weeks before last frost. Do not cover seeds; they require light to germinate. Seedlings appear within 2 weeks. Thin to 5 inches apart; cut, rather than pull out, to avoid damage to intertwined roots of other seedlings. Plants may flower within 6 weeks of seeding.

Water regularly for best growth, even though alyssum can tolerate temporary drought. Use a general-purpose fertilizer once, in spring. Excess fertilizing gives ample foliage but few flowers. Flowering mounds tend to become sparse and rangy toward midsummer; shear the plants back and they will resume blossoming.

Fungi cause the biggest problems for sweet alyssums: damping-off can kill seedlings and fungal wilt can cause stems and roots to rot. See "Damping-Off" on page 344 for more on damping-off. If rotted lower leaves and stems indicate fungal wilt, discard plants. Plants growing in well-drained soil are less susceptible. To avoid transferring the fungus to healthy plants, wash your hands and gardening tools after handling infected plants.

LONICERA Honeysuckle

Honeysuckles are alternate-leaved shrubs and vines. Many species bear fragrant flowers. Flowers are followed by colorful fruit. Some species, including Japanese honeysuckle (*Lonicera japonica*), are extremely invasive. Check with your local extension service office for a list of problem species in your area.

Plant honeysuckles in spring or fall in sun or partial shade. They can tolerate a range of soil conditions, but moist, well-drained sites suit them best.

Problems

Leaves wrinkled and discolored. Cause: Aphids. See "Leaves wrinkled and discolored" on page 211 for control measures.

Leaves with powdery white coating. Cause: Powdery mildew. For controls, see "Leaves with powdery white coating" on page 213.

Leaves yellow; stems and leaves covered with small bumps. Cause: Scales. See "Leaves yellow; stems and leaves covered with small bumps" on page 213 for controls.

Leaves rolled and chewed. Cause: Leafrollers. These ½-inch, green-bodied, brown-headed caterpillars form small webs on shoot tips and feed on leaves and buds inside. Break open webs and handpick larvae; spray BTK at the first sign of damage.

Leaves with sunken, discolored spots. Cause: Four-lined plant bugs. See "Plant Bugs" on page 278 for controls.

Trunks or branches with oozing lesions; branch tips die back. Cause: Canker. See "Trunk or branches with oozing lesions; branch tips die back" on page 214 for controls.

Plant defoliated. Cause: Honeysuckle sawflies. The 1-inch, gray-and-yellow, caterpillar-like larvae feed ravenously on foliage. See "Sawflies" on page 281 for controls.

LUPINUS Lupine

Two-foot-long stalks, thick with blue, yellow, rose, cream, or bicolored, ½- to 1-inch, pealike flowers make lupine plantings early summer showpieces. Bright or grayish green, palmlike, compound leaves add a tropical effect. Several species occur worldwide, but cultivars, especially the Russell hybrids, are favored for the array of colors and color combinations they offer. Plants range from 1½ to 3 feet tall and form 2-foot-wide clumps.

Lupines are best adapted to areas where summers are cool and not too dry. They suffer in heat, but serve well as annuals where conditions are not optimal. Full sun and moist, well-drained, neutral to acidic soil promote healthy growth. Water and mulch to keep soil moist. Lupines are short-lived plants, but can be perpetuated through division. Self-sowing also occurs, but seedlings often have different colors from the parent plants.

Lupines attract their share of pests and diseases, although most problems stem from unfavorable growing conditions. Aphids and powdery mildew may appear; see "Aphids" on page 250 and "Powdery Mildew" on page 322 for controls.

MAGNOLIA Magnolia

Magnolias are alternate-leaved, deciduous or evergreen trees with bold leaves; conspicuous, cup-shaped flowers; and interesting bright red fruit. They make beautiful specimen or accent plants.

Set out in spring as balled-and-burlapped or container-grown plants. Magnolias grow well in full sun or light shade. They prefer moist soil enriched with organic matter.

Problems

Leaves yellow; stems and leaves covered with small bumps. Cause: Scales. For control measures, see "Leaves yellow; stems and leaves covered with small bumps" on page 213.

Blossoms brown and limp. Cause: Frost damage. The flowers of early-blooming magnolias are often subject to frost damage. Avoid planting sites with southern exposures, which can encourage buds to open while there is still danger of frost. Or plant later-blooming species or cultivars.

Leaves discolored, wilted, or dropping; lacking vigor. Cause: Mealybugs. The tiny, powdery white adults generally congregate on the trunks and interior branches, making them difficult to see until the plant starts to weaken. See "Mealybugs" on page 273 for controls.

Leaves stippled with yellow; foliage webbed. Cause: Spider mites. See "Leaves stippled with yellow; foliage webbed" on page 212.

Trunk or branches with oozing lesions; branch tips die back. Cause: Canker. For more details, see "Trunk or branches with oozing lesions; branch tips die back" on page 214.

Leaves with spots. Cause: Leaf spots. See "Leaves with spots" on page 213 for controls.

MAHONIA Mahonia, holly grape

Mahonias are broad-leaved, evergreen shrubs. They are used for hedges, foundation plantings, and shrub borders.

Set out in spring as balled-and-burlapped or container-grown plants. Choose a partially shaded location to avoid winter leaf burn. Almost any good, well-drained garden soil will suit them; moist, acid soil is ideal.

Problems of mahonias are few and relatively unimportant. Barberry aphid, a small yellowish green insect, can be abundant on the West Coast; see "Leaves wrinkled and discolored" on page 211 for controls. Scale insects can attack twigs and sometimes foliage; for control information, see "Leaves yellow; stems and leaves covered with small bumps" on page 213.

MALUS Apple, crabapple

Apples and crabapples are trees with alternate, deciduous leaves. They produce beautiful spring flowers and attractive red or yellow fruit. Crabapples are valued as specimen trees; smaller species can be used in shrub borders. Birds are fond of crabapple fruit.

Plant in spring in moist but well-drained soil in full sun. They adapt well to a range of soil conditions. To avoid removing the following year's flower buds, it is best to prune soon after flowering. Keeping the center of the plant open to light and air will help reduce disease problems. Crabapples commonly produce suckers from the roots; cut these shoots down to the ground as soon as you see them.

Crabapples and apples share many of the same problems, including fire blight, cedar-apple rust, powdery mildew, and apple scab. Fortunately, disease-resistant cultivars are available, and many crabapples are resistant to several different diseases. Check with your local nursery owner or extension agent to learn about the best ones for your area. Be aware that even resistant cultivars may have problems if the conditions promoting disease are very favorable. Planting trees on sites with good air circulation and keeping trees growing vigorously are easy ways to avoid problems. For more information on crabapple pests and diseases, see the Apple entry, beginning on page 31.

MELON Cucumis melo and other genera (Cucurbitaceae)

Melons can be challenging to grow, especially in cooler climates. But if you have the patience, there is nothing more satisfying than a fragrant, sun-ripened melon.

Culture

Melon seeds need 60°F soil to germinate. In northern areas start plants indoors 2 to 3 weeks before the last frost date and transplant outside once temperatures are reliably warm. Melons need lots of sunlight and warm temperatures—90°F is ideal. Melons are especially vulnerable to pests and cool temperatures when plants are young. Plants exposed to temperatures below 50°F can be permanently injured and fail to set fruit. Cover plants with floating row cover or clear plastic tunnels as soon as they are set out. If temperatures exceed 90°F inside the tunnels, vent them by making a 6-inch cut in the plastic directly over each plant. Remove row cover when melons begin to flower so insects can pollinate the blossoms, or you will not get any fruit. In fall, temperatures below 50°F cause cold stress and rapid wilting. Cover plants on cool nights.

Melons do best in well-drained, loose-textured soils with lots of organic matter. They prefer a pH between 6.0 and 6.8, but can tolerate a pH as high as 7.6. Melons are shallow-rooted and may wilt on hot, dry days even when they are healthy. Keep them well watered, but do not let the soil become saturated. Wet soil can cause stems to rot at soil level. Overwatering, or uneven watering, can cause fruit to split. Potassium deficiency can also cause split fruit.

Prevent disease problems by keeping the leaves dry. Water carefully or use drip irrigation. Mulch melons to help conserve water: Black plastic is a good choice for central and northern areas, but in extremely warm areas it can heat the soil too much. Organic mulches are good, but also provide shelter for pests like squash bugs.

Rotate crops so that no member of the cucurbit family (squash, cucumbers, or melons) is grown in the same place more often than every 4 years.

Caution: Melon leaves are easily damaged by even organically acceptable sprays, such as insecticidal soap. Use the most dilute solution recommended and use sparingly. Do not spray plants in direct sun or if temperatures are above 80°F, and don't spray drought-stressed plants.

Leaf and Vine Problems

Leaves with chewed holes. Cause: Cucumber beetles. Adults are ¼-inch-long, greenish yellow beetles with black stripes or spots. They attack young leaves and should be controlled immediately, as they spread bacterial wilt and viruses. To deter beetle feeding, apply kaolin clay, especially to leaf undersides, and reapply after rain; handpick or vacuum beetles. As a last resort, spray infested plants with pyrethrin. Clean up crop residues in fall to remove overwintering sites.

Leaves with pale green patches; afflicted leaves wilt and blacken. Cause: Squash bugs. Adults are brownish black, ½-inch-long bugs. Immature bugs are whitish green with dark heads and legs. Both emit a strong, sharp smell when crushed. Eggs are bright orange and are laid on the undersides of leaves. Handpick adults and eggs. Trap bugs by placing a board on the ground near plants. Lift it each morning and destroy the squash bugs hiding underneath.

Leaves with yellow patches; older leaves mottled and distorted. Cause: Mosaic. Afflicted plants are unproductive and fruit is bitter. Remove and destroy diseased plants. Control aphids and cucumber beetles, because they spread the virus.

Leaves yellow, curled, and wilted. Cause: Aphids. Look for small, green, pink, gray, black, or white fluffy-coated, soft-bodied insects feeding on plants. Aphids can also transmit viral diseases. Control them by knocking them off the plant with a blast of water, or use a weak insecticidal soap spray; see the caution above before spraying. Use foil mulch to keep aphids from finding plants.

Leaves yellow and puckered, becoming bronzed. Cause: Mites. These tiny, red, yellow, or green, spiderlike creatures are more abundant in dry, hot weather. In severe cases leaves dry out and drop off. There may be fine webbing on the undersides of leaves. Spray plants with a weak insecticidal soap spray to control; see the caution on page 139 before spraying.

Leaves mottled yellow between veins; leaf undersides have purple spots. Cause: Downy mildew. As the disease progresses, older leaves turn brown and die, and younger leaves become infected. Remove and destroy badly infected leaves. Downy mildew thrives during cool, moist weather. Avoid wetting foliage when watering, especially when conditions favor this fungus. Sprays of potassium bicarbonate may give some control as well as reduce the spread of the disease. Prevent problems by planting resistant cultivars such as 'Cream de Menthe', 'Honey Brew', and 'Primo'.

Leaves with powdery white spots, especially on upper surfaces. Cause: Powdery mildew. As the disease progresses, leaves turn brown and dry, and plants may die. Organic fungicides, including *Bacillus subtilis,* potassium bicarbonate, or a 0.5 percent solution of baking soda (1 teaspoon baking soda in 1 quart water) may slow the spread of an infection and give some control. Prevent problems by planting resistant cultivars such as 'Athena, 'Earli-Dew F1', and 'Eclipse F1'.

Leaves with spots, blotches, or brown areas. Causes: Alternaria leaf blight; anthracnose; angular leaf spot; scab; gummy stem blight; other fungal and bacterial diseases. Various diseases attack melons. Reduce problems by keeping the foliage dry when watering and by not working amid wet plants. When available,

choose cultivars that resist or tolerate the most prevalent diseases in your area. Dilute sprays of copper may help prevent foliar infections from spreading to developing fruits but run the risk of injuring tender foliage and should only be used as a last resort.

Dark brown spots with concentric rings, usually appearing on older leaves first, are caused by Alternaria leaf blight. As the disease progresses, leaves curl down and eventually drop off. Fruit infected with this disease has brown, concentrically ringed, sunken spots. Prevent problems by planting a resistant cultivar, such as 'Earligold', 'Pulsar', and 'Saticoy F1'.

Yellow spots that turn brown are caused by anthracnose. Infected leaves eventually die. This disease causes fruit with circular black cankers. Prevent problems by planting anthracnose-resistant muskmelon cultivars, such as 'Passport', and resistant watermelon cultivars, such as 'All Sweet', 'Crimson Sweet', and 'Sweet Favorite'.

Water-soaked spots that turn gray, die, and drop out leaving shotholes are caused by angular leaf spot or scab. Fruit infected with angular leaf spot has small, cracked, white spots. Scab causes fruit with sunken, brown spots with gummy ooze; damage is worse in cool, moist weather. Pale, round leaf spots with dark margins are caused by Cercospora leaf spot.

Brown to gray spots on leaves and stems, and dark, gummy stems are caused by gummy stem blight. Infected leaves turn yellow and die. Disease begins as spots on stems, which become streaks; stems then turn dark and gummy. When it attacks fruit, the disease is called black rot; infected fruit has round, black spots and the fruit flesh collapses.

Vines wilt suddenly. Cause: Squash vine borers. Check for fat, white, 1-inch-long larvae burrowing into stems, and masses of yellow-green, sawdustlike excrement. Slit stems lengthwise above injury with a sharp knife and kill larvae. Cover cut stems with moist soil so they will form new roots. Injecting stems with BTK or parasitic nematodes may also control borers. Spraying stem bases with BTK once a week in late spring and early summer may prevent damage.

Vines wilt at midday; leaf margins brown. Cause: Fusarium wilt. As the disease progresses, vines fail to recover, and die. Destroy infected plants. Prevent problems by planting resistant muskmelon cultivars, such as 'Athena', 'Eclipse F1', 'Saticoy F1', and 'Starship', and resistant watermelon cultivars, such as 'Crimson Sweet', 'Millenium', and 'Sweet Favorite'.

Vines wilt at midday, starting with younger leaves; leaves remain green. Cause: Bacterial wilt. As the disease progresses, leaves fail to recover, and die. Cut a wilted stem and touch the tip of your knife to the sap. If it is milky, sticky, and astringent, your plant is infected. Destroy infected plants immediately. Prevent problems by controlling cucumber beetles, since they spread the disease.

Fruit Problems

Fruit with spots; flesh may rot. Causes: Angular leaf spot; Alternaria blight; scab; black rot; anthracnose. Several fungal and bacterial diseases cause these symptoms on melon fruit. For complete symptoms, controls, and resistant cultivars, if available, see "Leaves with spots, blotches, or brown areas" on the opposite page.

Fruit flesh not sweet. Causes: Premature harvest; overwatering; nitrogen deficiency. Harvest muskmelons and honeydews when they smell ripe and the stem separates easily (slips) from the vine when the fruit is gently lifted. Harvest watermel-ons when the bottom of the fruit turns from pale yellow to golden yellow. Excess rain or irrigation while fruit is swelling can dilute sugars. Keep soil evenly moist throughout the season. If leaves are small and yellow, and growth is stunted, plants are nitrogen starved. Spray foliage and drench roots with fish emulsion.

Fruit rots on underside. Cause: Damp soil or mulch. To prevent rot, raise fruit off the ground on scraps of wood or other low supports.

MERTENSIA Bluebells

Native Virginia bluebells (*Mertensia virginica*) seem to materialize from the floors of eastern forests in early spring. Clusters of pink buds that open to tubular blue flowers are carried on graceful stems over rounded, medium green foliage. Plants grow 1 to 2 feet tall and spread to about 1 foot wide.

Rich, moist, well-drained soil and partial shade are bluebells' requirements. Plantings increase slowly but steadily in sites that resemble their woodland habitat. Leaves yellow and die back in summer; plants disappear by July. Do not cut back fading foliage; allow it to die back naturally. Root rot may damage bluebells in poorly drained soil; they are otherwise trouble free.

MINT *Mentha* spp. (Labiatae)

Mints are hardy (Zone 5) perennial herbs grown for their fragrant leaves. They are usually grown from cuttings. Plant in rich, moist, well-drained soil with a pH between 5.0 and 7.5, in full sun or part shade.

Mints are vigorous, trouble-free plants. They can be quite invasive once established. Let them take over a wild area or plant them in containers or in bottomless buckets sunk into the garden to limit their spread.

Fungi can cause dark, sunken spots on leaves. Spray foliage with fish emulsion. Tan to red blisters on leaves are caused by rust. Avoid wetting leaves to prevent its spread. Pale, stippled or bronzed leaves are caused by mites—tiny, spiderlike creatures that thrive in hot, dry weather. Rinse plants with water to disrupt mite activity or control with insecticidal soap. See the Vegetables entry beginning on page 219 for other possible problems.

MONARDA Bee balm

Brightly colored, spidery flower heads and dense, dark green, aromatic foliage attract gardeners to these native plants. Hummingbirds, bees, and butterflies are also drawn to bee balms' blossoms, especially the red ones. Plants form dense clumps, 2 to 5 feet tall and 3 feet wide; the mintlike foliage remains attractive after flowers fade.

Found in the wild along shady stream banks, bee balms favor similar sites in the garden— consistently moist, well-drained soil and light shade. Giving such favorable surroundings, however, encourages bee balms' invasive nature; plantings can spread out rapidly. Planted in full sun, bee balms still grow nicely but are more easily controlled. Water and mulch in summer to prevent water stress, which quickly disfigures plantings. Clumps tend to die out in the center; divide every 3 years to keep growth compact. Remove spent flower heads to prolong bloom.

Leaves covered with white powder indicate powdery mildew, a fungal disease almost guaranteed to appear on bee balm foliage. Resistant cultivars are available. See "Powdery Mildew" for controls and more information on page 322.

NARCISSUS Daffodil, narcissus

Daffodils are welcome harbingers of spring. Hundreds of cultivars, classified by flower type and bloom time, bloom in shades of yellow, orange, white, and pink; many are bicolored. Each flower has a trumpet or cup-shaped center, surrounded by six petal-like structures; many are fragrant. Bluish green leaves are straplike and upright, 1 to 1½ feet long and ¾ inches wide. Plants grow from 6 inches to 1½ feet tall, depending on the cultivar.

Buy daffodils from a reputable source or ensure that you get healthy, pest-free bulbs. Look for double- or triple-nosed bulbs, so named because of their multiple growing points that produce more flowers than single-nosed bulbs. Plant bulbs in fall, at least 1 month before the ground freezes. Select a site in full sun or in shade under deciduous trees with humus-rich, well-drained soil. Set bulbs 4 to 8 inches deep—roughly 1½ times bulb height. A location behind annuals or perennials helps hide the yellowing foliage that remains after flowering ends. Remove spent flowers, but allow leaves to die back naturally; this lets bulbs store food for next year's floral display. Tying, cutting, or covering the leaves reduces the amount of light they receive and jeopardizes flowering in subsequent years.

Daffodil bulbs multiply gradually to form clumps. While plants will grow undisturbed for years, overcrowding eventually reduces flower size. Dig bulbs after foliage fades and shake away loose soil. Place them out of the sun to dry for a few days, then gently separate offsets from parent bulbs and replant. Small offsets may take a couple of years to bloom.

The animal pests that eat most other bulbs turn up their noses at daffodils, so bulbs, flowers, and foliage remain undisturbed. See "Healthy Bulb

Basics" on page 98 for information on buying healthy bulbs.

Problems

Flowers and leaves with silvery flecks. Cause: Thrips. See "Thrips" on page 287 for controls.

Leaves with white or brown streaks; foliage wilted. Cause: Viral decline. Plants suffering from viral decline develop white or brown streaks on the leaves late in their growing season. Foliage may wilt and topple over. There is no cure for decline. Remove diseased plants. Control aphids, which spread decline and other viral diseases; for control techniques, see "Aphids" on page 250.

Plant fails to appear; bulbs soft. Cause: Bulb flies. Narcissus bulb flies resemble small bumblebees; lesser bulb flies are ⅓-inch-long, blackish green flies. Both lay their eggs at the base of bulb leaves; larvae hatch and bore into bulbs to feed—usually one maggot per bulb in the case of narcissus bulb flies and several per bulb in the case of lesser bulb flies. Their holes admit rot organisms into bulbs. Discard infested bulbs. If bulb flies are a problem in your area, try covering plants with floating row cover during the egg-laying period (late spring). Treat plants weekly with a commercial pyrethrin dust if pests have been a problem in past years.

Plants stunted; flowers deformed. Cause: Basal rot. Infection by Fusarium basal rot causes the base of the bulb to turn soft and brown. The rot spreads up through the bulb. Infected plants are stunted and have few flowers. Dig and destroy bulbs that show signs of disease. Avoid injuring bulbs during planting or cultivation; fungi most often infect bulbs through wounds.

Plant fails to grow and/or flower; leaves with swollen spots. Cause: Bulb and stem nematodes. Feeding by microscopic roundworms causes deformed leaves with yellow-green spots and small, swollen areas. Bulbs develop dark internal circles or blotches and may fail to grow or bloom in spring. Dig and destroy severely infected bulbs and foliage. Soak mildly infested bulbs in hot (110°F) water for 3 hours, then plunge them immediately into cold water. Let them dry; then store in a cool, dark place until fall, when they can be replanted. Solarize infected soil or treat with a chitin source.

NICOTIANA Flowering tobacco

These handsome annuals bring clusters of starlike, tubular flowers to the summer garden in shades of red, pink, lime, lavender, or white. Many are fragrant. Group these 1- to 5-foot-tall plants together for best showing. Older kinds bloom in evening only, but new offerings bloom in daylight. Night-blooming whites are most fragrant; day-blooming cultivars of flowering tobaccos (*Nicotiana alata*) are often not fragrant. New blossoms open each day to replace spent ones.

Sow seed indoors in April; bottom heat will speed germination. Or direct-seed outdoors in late spring. Do not cover very small seeds, which need light to germinate. Seedlings appear within 3 weeks and grow rapidly. Thin or transplant to 9 inches apart. Nicotiana grows best in average soil in full sun or partial shade. Water well during hot, dry weather. Give less fertilizer and water in late summer to keep plants blooming longer. Nicotianas self-sow but may not come true to color.

Do not grow nicotianas in dusty areas; the sticky, fuzzy leaves attract and hold dirt. Also, do not plant near tomatoes. Nicotianas may attract insect pests and diseases that will quickly move on to any nearby tomatoes.

Nicotianas are seldom troubled by pests or diseases. Aphids cause distorted leaves, stems, and buds, while whiteflies lead to yellow leaves and weakened plants. See "Aphids" on page 250 and "Whiteflies" on page 290 for more information and controls. Cutworms can also cut off seedlings or young plants at the soil level. See "Cutworms" on page 263.

OKRA *Abelmoschus esculentus* (**Malvaceae**)

Okra is an annual vegetable grown for its fleshy seedpods. Okra does best in loose, well-worked soil with a pH between 6.0 and 7.0, and full sun. It needs lots of phosphorus, so work in plenty of bonemeal and compost before planting.

Okra grows best at temperatures between 70° and 85°F and does not tolerate temperatures below 60°F.

Warm soil at planting time is very important. Wait until the soil is at least 60°F before planting. Okra does not germinate well and is more susceptible to pests in cooler soil. If you have cool soils with high clay content, cover the planting area with clear plastic to warm up the soil at least 2 weeks before you want to plant. Cover planted seeds with clear plastic or row cover for a few weeks to give them a good start. Remove the clear plastic as soon as seeds germinate. Soil-warming black plastic mulch also benefits okra.

Okra is susceptible to several common vegetable crop problems, including damping-off, aphids, fungal wilts, leafminers, and mites. See the Vegetables entry, beginning on page 219, for symptoms and controls.

Problems

Leaves turn yellow, wilt, and fall off; stem rotted at soil line. Cause: Southern blight. White to pink fungal growth may spread over the soil around the base of infected plants. Severely infected plants die. Destroy infected plants and dig out and dispose of the top few inches of soil within 6 inches of the stem. Adding lots of compost to the soil helps prevent this disease.

Plant yellow and stunted, wilts during bright, hot days; roots have swollen galls. Cause: Root-knot nematodes. Galls may be up to 1 inch in diameter. Destroy infected plants. Control pest nematodes by adding chitin and parasitic nematodes to the soil.

Buds, flowers, and seedpods malformed and drop prematurely. Cause: Stink bugs. Seedpods may have hard, callused bumps. Adults are flat, shield-shaped, green, tan, brown, or gray insects that emit a sharp odor when crushed. Handpick these pests to control mild infestations. Dust plants with pyrethrin if injury is serious.

Flowers turn brown; seedpods rot. Causes: Choanephora blight; gray mold. Infected parts may be covered with white or gray growth. Spray plants with compost tea as soon as plants start to bloom and repeat every few weeks to help prevent these fungal diseases. Remove and destroy infected plant parts; thin to improve air circulation around plants. Spray with sulfur to keep infections from spreading.

Seedpods with chewed holes. Cause: Caterpillars. Leaves may also have holes. Handpick or spray plants with BTK if you see caterpillars.

Seedpods pitted, discolored, or with water-soaked areas. Cause: Cold injury. Prevent damage by protecting plants with row cover when cold nights are expected.

ONION *Allium cepa* and other species (**Liliaceae**)

Onions are biennial vegetables grown for their sweet to pungent bulbs and greens. Dried or fresh, raw or cooked, onions are indispensable ingredients in cuisines from around the world.

Culture

Onions grow best in full sun and deep, fertile, well-drained soil with lots of organic matter. Work in a generous amount of compost before planting. Onions need high levels of nitrogen and potassium and moderate to high levels of phosphorus, so do a soil test and amend soil as needed before planting. Onions grow well in raised beds or ridges, especially if soil is clayey.

Onions grow best between 55° and 75°F, and will tolerate temperatures as low as 45° and as high as 85°F. They prefer cool temperatures early in their growth and warm temperatures near maturity.

Keep the soil moist, since onions have shallow roots, but don't allow soil to become saturated because onions are susceptible to several root rot diseases. Mulching onions with composted leaves or straw helps to maintain soil organic content, prevent disease, and suppress weeds. Wait until soil warms to apply mulch. Avoid planting onions where onion family members have been grown during the previous 3 years. In general, white onions are more prone to problems than yellow or red ones.

You can grow onions from seeds, transplants, or sets. Soak sets, roots, or seeds in compost tea for 15 minutes before planting to help prevent disease. Onion bulb formation is controlled by day length, so selecting suitable cultivars for your area is crucial. In the North choose "long-day" cultivars, and in the South choose "short-day" cultivars.

Allow tops to fall over naturally, then pull bulbs and let them air-cure for 2 weeks. After curing, sort out damaged bulbs and those with thick necks and put aside for immediate use. Store others at temperatures just above 32°F.

Plant and Leaf Problems

Seedlings fall over. Cause: Damping-off. Prevent problems by planting in raised beds and presoaking seeds in compost tea.

Plant wilts rapidly. Cause: Cutworms. Check for a hole in the stem at or just below the soil line and fat, 1- to 2-inch-long, dull brown or gray caterpillars in the soil near the base of plants. Sprinkle moist bran mixed with BTK on the soil surface in the evening, or add parasitic nematodes to the soil at least a week before planting to control them.

Plant stunted; leaves may be yellow. Causes: Nitrogen deficiency; waterlogged soil; aphids; pink root. Onions need ample nitrogen; deficient plants are pale and grow slowly. Waterlogged soil damages roots and produces the same symptoms. Spray plants and drench roots with fish emulsion or kelp extract to alleviate symptoms. Plant in raised beds to improve drainage and add compost before planting to prevent problems.

Aphids are soft-bodied, pale green, black, gray, pink, or white fluffy-coated, sucking insects. Check for them on young leaves. For mild infestations, knock the pests off the plants with a blast of water. Spray plants with insecticidal soap to control them; use neem spray if infestation is severe.

If roots and bulb are pinkish, the plant has pink root. Roots infected with this fungal disease shrivel and die. Destroy infected plants. Prevent problems by ensuring good drainage and adding ample organic matter to the soil. Plant resistant cultivars such as 'Early White Supreme', 'Gunnison', 'Super Star', 'Tokyo Long White', and 'Yellow Granex'.

Plant yellow and wilted. Causes: Fusarium bulb rot; onion maggots; lesser bulb flies;

wireworms. Onions infected with Fusarium bulb rot have soft necks, and entire bulbs may be soft and brown. Destroy infected plants. Prevent problems by planting cultivars—such as 'Cortland', 'Early Yellow Globe', 'Green Banner', 'Long White Summer Bunching', 'Pulsar', and 'Southport Red Globe'—that are somewhat resistant.

Onion maggots feed on roots, killing seedlings and older plants. They also burrow into bulbs, making them unfit for use. Onion maggots are ¼-inch-long, white, and taper to a point at the head. Adults are small gray flies that lay eggs early in the spring. Destroy infested plants. Do not compost them; Onion maggots thrive in compost piles. To prevent problems, apply parasitic nematodes to the soil before planting and cover plants with row cover as soon as they come up to prevent flies from laying eggs. Trap maggots by planting a few onions at scattered points around the garden a few weeks before the main planting date. These larger plants will attract egg-laying adults; remove and destroy them when infested. 'Egyptian Tree' onions are tolerant of onion maggots. In general, white cultivars are more susceptible to maggot attack than are yellow or red cultivars.

Lesser bulb fly larvae are ½ inch long, wrinkled, and yellow-gray. They cause injury similar to onion maggots and are controlled the same way.

Yellow to reddish brown, slender, tough-bodied, segmented worms up to 1½ inches long feeding on roots and bulbs are wireworms. Adults are dark-colored, elongated click beetles. Apply parasitic nematodes to the soil before planting to control them.

Leaves with white streaks or blotches. Causes: Precipitation damage; thrips. Excessive rain or hail can spot onion leaves. Spots are various sizes, and damage doesn't spread. Maintain good air circulation and make sure soil is well-drained to minimize problems.

If leaf tips are distorted or brown, and leaves are stippled with white, look for onion thrips. Heavy infestations cause plants to wither and turn brown. Adults are tiny, slender, yellow to brown, rapidly moving, winged insects. The larvae can barely be seen with the naked eye. Thrips thrive in hot, dry weather. Trap them with sticky traps hung just above plant level. Try blue, yellow, and white traps to see which work best. Spray plants with insecticidal soap; dust with pyrethrin to control severe infestations.

Leaves with water-soaked or papery white spots with vertical splits. Cause: Onion leaf blight. Leaf tips turn yellow, then brown. Spray plants with sulfur as soon as you see symptoms if weather is cool and humid. Prevent problems by planting tolerant cultivars such as 'Highlander' and 'Tokyo Long White'.

Leaves with pale green to brown spots. Causes: Downy mildew; ozone injury. Downy mildew thrives in cool, humid weather and tends to stop spreading when the weather is warm and dry. Leaf tips turn yellow, then brown, and may be covered with a fuzzy mold. As the disease progresses, spots turn black with a purple, fuzzy mold, and leaves yellow and die. Sprays of potassium bicarbonate may give some control as well as reduce the spread of the disease. Don't handle plants when wet to avoid spreading the disease.

Irregular areas with tiny brown flecks are caused by high levels of ozone in the air. Spray plants with seaweed extract and fish emulsion to encourage new growth.

Leaves with sunken, light-colored spots with concentrically ringed, purple centers. Cause: Purple blotch. Spots enlarge and girdle leaves, which wither and fall over. Spray plants with sulfur if disease is present to keep it from spreading. Cool soil makes plants more prone to this fungal disease. Warm soil by covering it with clear plastic for a few weeks before you plant.

Leaves with small, reddish orange blisters. Cause: Rust. Leaves infected with this fungal disease may turn yellow and die. Bulbs are small. Clean up and dispose of tops to eliminate overwintering spores. One type of rust infects both onions and asparagus, so keep the two crops apart to prevent problems.

Leaves with black streaks filled with dark brown powder. Cause: Smut. Young plants are usually affected. Cool soil makes plants more prone to this fungal disease. Warm soil by covering it with clear plastic for a few weeks before you plant. Prevent problems by planting tolerant cultivars such as 'Evergreen Hardy White' and 'Tokyo Long White'.

Bulb Problems

Bulbs small and soft; roots pinkish or shriveled. Cause: Pink root. See "Plant stunted; leaves may be yellow" on page 145 for controls.

Bulbs rot in the ground. Cause: White rot. Bulbs may be covered with a white fluffy growth. Destroy infected plants; don't compost them. Prevent problems by providing good drainage and presoaking seeds in compost tea.

Bulbs with gray, water-soaked outer layers. Cause: Heat or cold injury. If temperatures are above 85°F, protect plants with thick straw mulch and keep soil moist. Protect overwintering onions with mulch, or dig and store just above freezing temperature.

Bulbs with bleached, soft patches. Cause: Sunscald. Protect onions from direct sun while curing, especially in hot weather. White cultivars are especially sensitive to sunscald.

Bulbs with thick necks that do not cure well. Causes: Potassium deficiency; seed stalk formation. Confirm deficiency with soil test and amend soil as needed before planting. Use bulbs with thick necks first.

Onions form seed stalks after any dormant period. Improperly stored sets or cultivars not suited to the day length in your area may go to seed before forming bulbs. Fluctuating temperatures or drying and wetting of soil may cause seed stalk formation. Harvest and use bulbs as soon as possible.

Bulbs with dark green or black, concentrically ringed spots. Cause: Onion smudge. The fungus that causes anthracnose in many garden crops also causes onion smudge, which usually appears near harvest or in storage. Destroy infected bulbs. All white onion cultivars are susceptible to smudge; choose yellow or red globe onions to avoid problems with this disease.

Bulbs with sunken, dry, brown to black areas around neck. Cause: Neck rot. Necks of bulbs rot and gray mold develops inside bulbs. This fungal disease usually appears near harvest or in storage. Destroy infected bulbs. To prevent problems, cut back on watering as onions begin to mature, especially near harvest. Be careful not to injure bulbs while weeding or harvesting. Cure bulbs properly before storing them in a cool place.

OREGANO *Origanum heracleoticum* (Labiatae)

Oregano is a hardy (Zone 5) perennial herb grown for its aromatic leaves. Start oregano from cuttings or plants rather than from seed. Seedlings are quite variable and may have very little flavor. Oregano does best in average, well-drained soil with a pH between 5.0 and 8.0, and at least 4 hours of sun per day. Oregano needs little added fertilizer or water, but does like a layer of mulch to protect its shallow roots.

Oregano is usually quite trouble free. Pale, stippled, or bronzed leaves are caused by mites—tiny, spiderlike creatures that thrive in hot, dry weather. Rinse plants with water to disrupt mite activity or control with insecticidal soap. See the Vegetables entry, beginning on page 219, for other possible problems.

PACHYSANDRA Pachysandra, spurge

Low-growing pachysandras top the list of durable, shade-tolerant groundcovers. Japanese pachysandra (*Pachysandra terminalis*) has glossy evergreen foliage. Native pachysandra (*P. procumbens*) has mottled foliage and is semi-evergreen. Both are 8 to 12 inches tall and spread quickly, providing excellent cover below trees and on slopes. Clusters of tiny, tubular, white flowers appear in late spring.

Plant in partial to deep shade in slightly acid, moist but well-drained soil rich in organic matter. Mature plants endure drought but do best with about 1 inch of water per week. Pachysandras compete well with taller plants and prosper in shady sites where few other plants will grow. Cut Japanese pachysandra back by about one-quarter in spring to promote compact growth.

Most problems arise when plantings are stressed by drought, poorly drained soil, or overcrowding. Fungal diseases favor damp, crowded conditions; thin to improve air circulation and remove infected plants. Scale insects also prefer tightly spaced plantings, where their populations swell rapidly if undeterred. Spider mites infest drought-stressed plants when weather is hot and dry; water adequately and use a strong stream of water to knock pests off.

PAEONIA Peony

These attractive, long-lived, bushy plants bear numerous 3- to 8-inch blossoms in early summer, in shades of pink, red, white, and yellow amid glossy, lobed, green foliage; plants form neatly rounded clumps roughly 3 to 4 feet tall.

Peonies prefer full sun and moist, well-drained soil rich in organic matter, although they tolerate light shade, which may prolong bloom in the South. A protected site limits wind damage to blossoms. Most are hardy to Zone 5 and do best in cold-winter climates.

Easy to care for in most respects, peonies are finicky about planting. Set rootstocks so that the reddish buds or "eyes" are no more than 1 to 2 inches below the soil surface. Mulch after the ground freezes the first winter after planting to prevent heaving. Divide roots in fall, if necessary, leaving at least three buds on each section. Cut stems back to below ground level in fall.

Problems

Flower buds absent. Causes: Improper planting; excess shade; immature plant; large, old crown; excess nitrogen; disturbed roots. Choose planting sites carefully; set roots at the proper depth; be patient with new plants. Do not apply high-nitrogen fertilizers. If mature peonies stop blooming, rule out other possible problems and divide if needed—division and other root disturbances also reduce bud formation.

Flower buds don't open. Causes: Late spring frost; drought; high temperatures; low soil fertility. Weather extremes notwithstanding, water adequately and feed peonies with compost or a slow-acting, general-purpose fertilizer in spring. If summer heat is the problem, plant early-flowering cultivars.

Flower buds die or petals distorted. Cause: Flower thrips. These ⅟₂₅-inch insects feed on buds, stem tips, and flowers, causing distortion or white, brown, or red flecks. See "Thrips" on page 287 for controls.

Stems with sunken lesions. Cause: Anthracnose. Sunken lesions with pink blisters appear on stems. Plants may die. Cultural controls such as regular fall cleanup and thinning stems to improve air circulation are effective. See "Anthracnose" on page 310 for more controls.

Shoots wilt, collapse; crowns with gray mold. Cause: Fungal diseases. Several fungi cause blights or stem and crown rots in peonies. Botrytis blight causes shoots to wilt suddenly and fall over. Stem bases blacken and rot; gray mold may appear near soil; buds may wither and blacken. Flowers and leaves may turn brown and develop mold. Remove and destroy infected plant parts. Don't put manure near plant crowns; clear mulch from crowns in spring to let soil dry. Avoid overwatering and wet, poorly drained soil. If problems persist, scrape away the top 2 inches of soil around plants and replace with clean sand. To save a plant of extraordinary value, as a last resort spray shoots in spring with Bordeaux mix.

Plant stunted; leaves yellow, spotted; roots with tiny galls. Cause: Root-knot nematodes. See "Root-Knot Nematodes" on page 340 for controls.

PAPAVER Poppy

Poppies bring brightly colored blooms with crinkled petals to the garden in spring and early summer. The diminutive alpine poppy (*Papaver alpinum*) offers 1-inch blooms and 8- to 10-inch height, while Iceland poppy (*P. croceum*) is 1 foot tall with 3-inch blooms, and Oriental poppy (*P. orientale*) is 1½ to 3 feet tall with 4- to 7-inch flowers. Deeply divided, hairy, gray-green foliage surrounds leafless flower stems.

Most poppies are very hardy and perform best in cool summers followed by cold winters; grow them as annuals or biennials in warmer climates. (A few species are true annuals.) Full sun to light shade and well-drained soil satisfy poppies' needs; established plants tolerate some drought, but soggy soil guarantees rotting of fleshy roots. Oriental poppy foliage dies back after flowering ends, and plants disappear by late summer. Mark the spot to avoid digging injury to roots. New leaves appear in fall. Divide every 5 years, in late summer, to maintain vigor. Poppies self-sow if allowed to set seed; seedlings do not come true to parents.

Problems

Leaves, stems, and buds distorted, sticky; clusters of small insects. Cause: Aphids. See "Aphids" on page 250 for controls.

Leaves with water-soaked spots; foliage and flowers blacken. Cause: Bacterial blight. Infected plants turn brown and lose leaves; girdled stems die. Dig and destroy infected plants and surrounding soil. Solarize soil before replanting with disease-free seed; water early in the day so leaves dry quickly.

PARSLEY *Petroselinum crispum* (**Umbelliferae**)

Parsley is a biennial herb grown as an annual for its leaves. Sow seed outdoors once the soil has reached 50°F; seeds may take up to 3 weeks to germinate. Plant in cool, moist, well-drained soil in a site that receives at least 3 hours of full sun daily.

Parsley has few problems. Handpick leaf-eating caterpillars or spray plants with BTK.

Parsleyworms, the 2-inch-long green, yellow, and black caterpillars that occasionally feed on parsley, are the larvae of black swallowtail butterflies; if you don't mind sharing your parsley you can enjoy the caterpillar's elegant adult form within a few weeks.

Dwarfed or abnormally crinkled leaves can be caused by viruses. Destroy infected plants, and control aphids and other sucking insects that spread viral diseases. Dark, yellow-bordered spots are leaf blight caused by fungi. Pick off infected foliage and spray with fish emulsion. Carrot weevils eat parsley roots and make leaves yellow; for controls, see "Carrot Weevil" on page 257. See the Vegetables entry, beginning on page 219, for other possible problems.

PARSNIP *Pastinaca sativa* (**Umbelliferae**)

Parsnips are biennial vegetables grown as annuals for their long, white, sweet-flavored roots. Culture is much like that of carrots, except that parsnips require less fertilizer and prefer a pH between 6.0 and 6.8. They grow best at cool temperatures, poorly above 75°F, and tolerate temperatures as low as 40°F. Parsnip seed can take up to 3 weeks to germinate. Soak seed overnight before planting, keep seedbed moist, and always use fresh seed to prevent germination problems.

Parsnips are in the same family as carrots and are troubled by many of the same pests and diseases. See the Carrot entry beginning on page 62 for culture and information on problems.

Problems

Roots with dark cankers; leaves with water-soaked or dark spots. Cause: Brown fungal canker. Interior of root may be discolored; other diseases may enter root through cankers and cause

rotting. Destroy severely infected plants. Prevent problems by not planting parsnips where susceptible crops (beets, carrots, parsnips) have been grown for 3 years. Vigorous parsnips, growing in well-drained soil, are less prone to canker infection. Control pests, such as carrot rust fly, that can weaken plants; keep soil over shoulders of roots, and plant resistant cultivars such as 'Andover', 'Cobham Improved Marrow', and 'Javelin'.

PARTHENOCISSUS Boston ivy, Virginia creeper, woodbine

These are deciduous, alternate-leaved vines that climb by means of rootlike holdfasts.

Plant container-grown creepers in spring. A moist, loamy soil is best, in sun or shade. These plants are very adaptable to difficult conditions.

Boston ivy is a tough, fairly trouble-free plant. Although Japanese beetles, scales, powdery mildew, and leaf spots can attack it, they seldom pose serious problems. See the Trees, Shrubs, and Vines entry on page 210 for symptoms and solutions.

PEA *Pisum sativum* (**Leguminosae**)

Peas are annual vegetables grown for their tasty seeds and, in some cases, seedpods. Fresh peas are a special treat you have to grow yourself to enjoy.

Culture

Peas grow well in almost any soil, but do best in soil with lots of organic matter and a pH between 5.5 and 6.8. A 1-inch layer of compost worked well into the soil before planting will provide sufficient nutrients for a good crop.

Peas are a cool-season, moisture-loving crop. They grow best between 60° and 75°F, poorly at temperatures above 75°F, but will tolerate temperatures as low as 45°F. Pea foliage can withstand a light frost, but pods and flowers will be damaged unless they are covered.

Most disease problems in peas can be avoided with proper culture. Do not plant in wet soils. Plant in raised beds and add plenty of compost to loosen the soil. Rapid germination is essential to avoid root rot problems. Choose lighter soils for earlier plantings if you have a choice, and keep soil moist, but not wet. Avoid working amid wet plants. Dispose of vines after harvest and till soil to reduce future problems. Plant peas where no peas or beans have grown for at least 3 years.

Soak seed in compost tea for 15 minutes or as long as overnight to help prevent disease and speed germination. Treat seed with an inoculant labeled for garden peas before planting to promote nitrogen fixation. Buy fresh inoculant each year, or check the date on the package for viability.

Peas are susceptible to certain micronutrient deficiencies. Spray young plants with seaweed extract every 2 weeks to maintain vigor and boost productivity.

Leaf and Whole Plant Problems

Seeds do not germinate; seedlings stunted or dying. Causes: Seedcorn maggots; damping-off; root rot. Seedcorn maggots are ¼-inch-long, yellow-white, spindle-shaped seed eaters. Adults are small flies. Seedlings that do come up are deformed and spindly. Remove damaged seedlings and plant fresh seed about a week after applying parasitic nematodes to the soil to control maggots. Seedcorn maggots thrive in cool, wet soil; wait until soil is warm before planting to avoid this pest problem.

Damping-off is caused by soil-dwelling fungi that thrive in cool, wet conditions. Keep soil moist but not soggy, thin seedlings to improve air circulation, and spray them with compost tea as

soon as the first true leaves open to prevent problems.

Pea root rot can kill seedlings. Older infected plants are stunted and have shrunken, discolored roots and stems near the soil line. Prevent problems by planting in well-drained soil with lots of organic matter. Beans are susceptible to the same fungus, so keep the two crops apart. Prevent problems by planting a cultivar, such as 'Bolero', that is somewhat tolerant to pea root rot.

Seedlings clipped off at soil line. Cause: Cutworms. Check for fat, 1- to 2-inch-long, dull brown or gray caterpillars in the soil near the base of plants. Sprinkle moist bran mixed with BTK on the soil surface in the evening, or apply parasitic nematodes to the soil at least a week before planting to control them.

Leaves yellow; growth slow. Causes: Nitrogen deficiency; waterlogged soil. Drench soil and spray foliage with compost tea or fish emulsion, or side-dress plants with compost to alleviate deficiency symptoms. Waterlogged soil damages roots and prevents them from using nutrients available in the soil. Prevent problems by choosing well-drained sites, adding organic matter to the soil to improve drainage, and planting in raised beds.

Leaves yellow and distorted. Causes: Tarnished plant bugs; pea aphids; potato leafhoppers. Tarnished plant bugs are oval, light green or brown, ¼-inch-long bugs that inject a plant-deforming toxin as they feed on young leaves. Trap them with white sticky traps or spray with insecticidal soap in the evening. Spray pyrethrin to control severe infestations.

Pea aphids are soft-bodied, small, light to dark green, sucking insects usually found on new growth. Infested leaves are thickened and curled and may be covered with sticky honeydew excreted by the aphids. Knock pests off plants with a blast of water. Spray plants with insecticidal soap in the evening if further control is needed. Repel aphids with reflective mulch or by planting cultivars with silvery leaves. As a last resort, spray severe infestations with neem.

Potato leafhoppers are green or brown, spindle-shaped, $\frac{1}{10}$- to $\frac{1}{2}$-inch-long, winged insects. Nymphs are smaller and wingless. Infested leaves have curled margins; flowers or pods may fall off. Trap leafhoppers with yellow sticky traps or spray as for pea aphids above. Cover seedlings with row cover if leafhoppers have been a problem in the past.

Leaves yellow; plant wilting and stunted. Cause: Fusarium wilt. Stem near soil line is yellow-orange to black when cut open. If pods form, they contain few seeds. Destroy plants infected with this fungal disease. To prevent problems, plant resistant cultivars such as 'Dakota', 'Daybreak', 'Green Arrow', 'Knight', 'Maestro', 'Oregon Sugar Pod II', 'Snowflake', and 'Sparkle'.

Leaves mottled, yellow, rolled and/or distorted. Causes: Mosaic viruses; pea leaf roll virus. Infected plants are stunted and weak; destroy them. Control aphids and cucumber beetles that spread viruses, and leguminous weeds, such as vetch, that can harbor viruses. Prevent problems by planting cultivars such as 'Knight', 'Maestro', 'Oregon Giant', 'Oregon Sugar Pod II', and 'Sugar Sprint' that resist mosaic viruses. 'Snow Green', 'Sugar Daddy', 'Sugar Star', and 'Super Snap' are resistant to pea leaf roll virus.

Leaves stippled with white. Cause: Mites. Leaves become bronzed when severely infested. These tiny, spiderlike pests thrive in hot, dry weather. Look for tiny moving specks on the undersides of leaves. Rinse plants with water to suppress mite activity; spray with insecticidal soap

in the evening to control mites. Use neem as a last resort on severe infestations.

Leaves with water-soaked or white spots. Causes: Downy mildew; powdery mildew. Downy mildew is common in damp weather. Leaves and pods are covered with a thick, white growth that turns violet-black. Powdery mildew is more common in dry weather. The whole plant may be covered with white powdery growth. Organic fungicides, including *Bacillus subtilis,* potassium bicarbonate, or a 0.5 percent solution of baking soda (1 teaspoon baking soda in 1 quart water) may be applied as preventives or to help to control mildew. Prevent problems by planting cultivars resistant to downy mildew, such as 'Green Arrow' and 'Knight', or to powdery mildew, such as 'Cascadia', 'Dakota', 'Knight', 'Maestro', 'Oregon Sugar Pod II', and 'Snowflake'.

Leaves with light brown to purple spots. Cause: Blight. Stems and pods are also spotted. Leaves may turn yellow and plants may die. Various fungi and bacteria can cause these disease symptoms. Remove severely infected plants. Presoak seed in compost tea and don't touch plants when they are wet to help prevent problems.

Leaves with wandering, white or translucent tunnels. Cause: Leafminers. Larvae are white maggots that tunnel through leaves. Adults are tiny black-and-yellow insects. Once tunnels appear, the larvae are inside leaves and spraying will not kill them. Destroy infected leaves. Trap future generations of adults with yellow sticky traps; spray plants with neem if large numbers of adults are trapped. Prevent problems by protecting plants with row cover as soon as they come up to exclude egg-laying adults.

Leaves with small holes. Cause: Cucumber beetles. Damage usually occurs on young plants. Beetles are yellow or greenish, $\frac{1}{4}$ inch long, with spots or stripes. Spray foliage with kaolin clay to deter feeding; use pyrethrin as a last resort if damage is severe. Cover emerging seedlings with row cover to prevent problems.

Leaves with large holes. Cause: Caterpillars. Many caterpillars feed on leaves and pods. Handpick, or spray plants with BTK if worms are feeding.

Pod Problems

Blossoms drop; no pods form. Causes: Weather extremes; nutrient imbalances. Excessive heat or rain can cause blossoms to drop. Wait for new blossoms to form. Copper and/or molybdenum deficiency cause the same symptoms. Spray plants with seaweed extract to help prevent deficiencies. If plants are very dark green and no blossoms form, suspect too much nitrogen. Wait for blossoms to form. Avoid high-nitrogen fertilizers.

Young pods distorted and withered; older pods with water-soaked or purplish spots. Cause: Blight. See "Leaves with light brown to purple spots" on the opposite page for controls.

Pods mottled, deformed, and rough. Cause: Mosaic viruses. See "Leaves mottled, yellow, rolled and/or distorted" on the opposite page for controls.

Pods with white spots. Causes: Downy mildew; powdery mildew. See "Leaves with water-soaked or white spots" on the opposite page for controls.

Pods with chewed holes. Cause: Caterpillars. Various caterpillars eat pea pods. Handpick, or spray plants with BTK if caterpillars are feeding. Cover young plants with row cover to prevent moths from laying eggs.

Seeds with brown spots or cavities. Cause: Manganese deficiency. Spray plants with seaweed extract every 2 weeks to prevent deficiencies.

Seeds with small, round holes. Cause: Pea weevils. Seeds may be hollow. Fat, white, $\frac{1}{3}$-inch-long larvae feed on seeds. Adults are $\frac{1}{5}$-inch-long, dark beetles with light markings that may feed on pea flowers. Discard infested seeds; do not compost them. Cover seeded areas with row cover to prevent adults from laying eggs. Spray plants with pyrethrin if adults are present.

PEACH *Prunus persica* (**Rosaceae**)

Peaches are deciduous trees growing from 4 to 20 feet, depending on soil, rootstock, and cultivar. In very early spring, pink blossoms appear on last year's shoots. Nectarines belong to the same species as peaches and have the same cultural requirements as well as the same diseases and pests. Both are hardy in Zones 5–9.

Culture

Plant in full sunlight in an area with well-drained soil and no late spring frosts. Prune each winter to stimulate growth, to thin next year's fruit, and to allow sunlight to penetrate the tree. Train trees to a framework of well-spaced, wide-angled branches. Prune bearing trees each winter to admit light into the tree and encourage good air circulation. As you prune, remove diseased and spindly wood and crossed branches. Where growth is too dense, remove extra shoots at their bases. To develop growth on spindly shoots, prune off the end of the shoot just above an outward-facing bud. For more pruning information, see "Pruning and Training" on page 104. Thin fruit each spring so it has room to develop.

Peach trees need a period of cold-weather rest or dormancy. The number of hours of cold between 32° and 45°F each cultivar needs before it breaks dormancy is referred to as chill hours. (Cold below 32°F doesn't count toward meeting the dormancy requirement.) Once the number is reached, the tree assumes winter is over and resumes growing the next warm day. Peaches bloom rapidly once their requirement has been met, which makes them more prone to frost damage than other fruit trees that are slower to burst into bloom. Call your local extension service to find out how many chill hours your area receives and what cultivars match that requirement. If you choose a cultivar that needs fewer chill hours than you normally receive, an unseasonable winter thaw in your area may bring the tree into flower weeks before spring actually arrives. But if you choose one that needs more chill hours than your climate supplies, the tree won't get enough chilling to stimulate normal bloom.

Most peaches are self-pollinating, but a few cultivars require cross-pollination. For more information on setting fruit, see "Setting Fruit" on page 103.

Fruit Problems

Young fruit with crescent-shaped scars. Cause: Plum curculios. These beetles, common east of the Rockies, leave characteristic scars as they lay eggs in fruit. Damaged fruit often drops. For control, spread a dropcloth under the tree and jar the trunk and branches with a padded mallet. Collect and destroy beetles that fall onto the sheet. For best results, do this twice a day, beginning when you see the first scarred fruit. Also, to prevent curculio eggs from hatching, collect and discard dropped fruit. For more information, see "Plum Curculio" on page 278.

Fruit with small brown spots that enlarge and grow fuzzy in humid weather. Cause: Brown rot. This fungus may also cause blossoms to wither and die. Fruit is most prone to infection 3 weeks before ripening. Infected fruit may drop

early or turn soft and brown, then wither into hard, black, shriveled fruit (known as mummies) that remains on the tree. For control, inspect trees before growth begins in spring. Remove and destroy both mummies and twigs or branches with gummy lesions. If more control is needed, spray sulfur early to protect blooms, then again later to protect fruit. Since damaged fruit is more prone to infection, control insects such as plum curculios, which puncture fruit and allow infection to enter. In general, nectarines are more susceptible to brown rot than peaches. Peach cultivars with some resistance to brown rot include 'Babygold No. 5', 'Elberta', and 'Glohaven'.

Fruit with olive green spots mostly near stems. Cause: Peach scab. Spots first appear on immature fruit and then turn brown and velvety. Fruit skin cracks; fruit is distorted or dwarfed. Infection arises from twig lesions, but damp weather spreads the fungus throughout leaves, fruit, and twigs. Infection is worst in warm climates and in late-fruiting cultivars. To control scab, remove infected fruit and clean up fallen leaves and fruit. For persistent infection spray sulfur or lime-sulfur every 10 to 21 days throughout the growing season. If spring weather is unusually warm and wet, spray sulfur weekly from the time flower buds first show green until blossoms begin to open.

Fruit with small, dark, sunken spots or cracks on skin. Cause: Bacterial leaf spot. This disease, common east of the Rockies, spreads in spring from oozing cankers. Twig cankers appear water-soaked. Leaves turn yellow and drop. Infection weakens trees, makes them prone to winter injury, and reduces fruit quality and yields. Preventive sprays of *Bacillus subtilis* may be practical where bacterial spot has been a problem in previous seasons; you can also protect susceptible trees with copper sprays. Resistant cultivars include 'Belle of Georgia', 'Candor', 'Dixiered', 'Early-Red-Free', 'Encore', 'Harbelle', 'Harbrite', 'Harken', 'Loring', 'Madison', 'Red Haven', 'Redskin', and 'Mericrest' and 'Westbrook' nectarines.

Fruit with sunken, corky lesions. Cause: Tarnished plant bugs. Bugs hibernate in nearby weeds and move into trees in spring. For control, remove weeds and plant debris. For persistent infestation, hang white sticky traps in lower tree branches.

Fruit with pinkish worms. Cause: Oriental fruit moth larvae. For more information, see "Growing shoots wilted or dying" below.

Leaf and Branch Problems

Growing shoots wilted or dying. Causes: Oriental fruit moth larvae; peach twig borers. Both pests tunnel into growing shoots and cause wilting. With oriental fruit moths, the tree may look unusually bushy from growth of new lateral shoots below wilted parts. To find oriental fruit moth larvae, slit stems below the wilted sections and look for a pinkish white caterpillar, up to ½ inch long. Later, a second larval generation bores into and ruins fruit. Where possible, plant early-bearing cultivars that are harvested before midsummer; to destroy overwintering larvae, cultivate soil 4 inches deep around trees in early spring. Controls that help keep this pest in check include repeated, timely sprays of BTK. Use pheromone traps to monitor and control the pests. Disrupt mating by applying pheromone patches to lower limbs of trees (one patch per four trees); spray horticultural oil at a growing-season dilution in summer to kill eggs and larvae.

Wilting plus gummy exudates from twigs may indicate peach twig borers. This pest also damages fruit. The second generation of these brown, ½-inch caterpillars tunnels into fruit, usually near the stem. For control, find borer entry holes and cut off wilted branches just below the hole. Destroy infested prunings. For large branches, slide a wire into the hole to kill the borer. Peach twig borers prefer weak trees; keep trees strong through proper fertilization, pruning, and irrigation.

Growing shoots covered with a white powdery coating. Cause: Powdery mildew. This disease also causes new growth to be stunted and distorted. Rainy weather does not cause the disease fungus to spread. In fact, it is most common in weather patterns featuring cool nights changing to warm days. Sprays of *Bacillus subtilis,* potassium bicarbonate, or a 0.5 percent solution of baking soda (1 teaspoon baking soda in 1 quart water) may be applied as preventives or to help control powdery mildew.

Young twigs and leaves wilted, brown, or dying back. Cause: Brown rot. Shoots and leaves may turn brown and decay. Gummy branch or twig lesions may also form. For more information, see "Fruit with small brown spots that enlarge and grow fuzzy in humid weather" on the opposite page.

Leaves puckered and reddish. Cause: Peach leaf curl. Later in the season, infected leaves may yellow, shrivel, and drop. New growth is stunted and swollen and often dies. Fruit often drops prematurely and may have a reddish, irregular, rough surface. You can't cure this fungal disease during the current season, but sprays of lime-sulfur, sulfur, or Bordeaux mixture in fall and in early spring before buds swell can help prevent new infection. Cultivars showing some resistance include 'Blood Free', 'Candor', 'Clayton', 'Com-Pact Red Haven', 'Five Star Curlless', 'Frost', and 'Red Haven'.

Leaves with dark, angular spots; some spots with holes. Cause: Bacterial leaf spot. Eventually, infected leaves may yellow and drop.

For more information, see "Fruit with small, dark, sunken spots or cracks on skin" on page 154.

Leaves with small purple spots, some spots with centers missing. Cause: Shothole disease. Spots also appear on fruit and then turn scabby. Centers of leaf spots often enlarge to about ¼ inch then fall out. You can't cure this fungus once symptoms appear, but if infection has been damaging in previous seasons, apply preventive sprays of sulfur starting at petal fall. Clean up leaves in fall to remove source of re-infection next spring. Dormant-season pruning of infected buds and twigs, which have a varnished appearance, helps prevent the disease next year.

Leaves stippled yellow. Cause: European red mites. These extremely tiny spider mites suck juices from leaves, causing yellow speckles on foliage. For light infestations, knock mites off leaves with a strong spray of water; for heavy infestations, spray with insecticidal soap. To kill overwintering mite eggs, apply horticultural oil at growing-season dilution in spring, when leaf buds are about ½ inch long.

Branches wilting and dying, fail to leaf out in spring. Causes: Bacterial canker; Valsa canker. Look on the branches for sunken, elliptical lesions, often oozing a reddish gum. With bacterial canker, this gum smells sour, and leaves may have small, angular spots. For both cankers, prune wilted or dying branches off below the infected area. Sterilize pruning tools in isopropyl alcohol or a 10 percent bleach solution (1 part bleach to 9 parts water) between cuts. On large limbs, cut out the canker into healthy wood, which has a lighter color. Copper sprays help control bacterial canker.

Valsa canker is a fungal disease that enters through injured bark. To prevent bark damage, make sure trees harden off in fall by avoiding late-season fertilization or pruning. Paint trunks with white latex paint diluted with an equal amount of water to reduce bark-damaging temperature fluctuations. Prune during bloom time, when wounds heal fastest. Cultivars adapted to cold climates or that drop leaves early are most resistant to Valsa canker.

Whole Plant Problems

Leaves yellow; dieback of whole limbs. Cause: Scales. Colonies of these sucking insects cling to the bark and appear as small bumps that can be easily scraped off with a fingernail. Control scale by spraying trees with a dormant-season dilution of horticultural oil in winter. Also control ants, which encourage scale insects, by wrapping a band of paper or plastic around the trunk and covering it with a commercial sticky coating such as Tangletrap.

Tree declines; gummy exudates mixed with sawdustlike material on trunk near ground. Cause: Peachtree borers. Inspect the trunk near or just below the ground; you may find holes and gummy exudates made by peachtree borers, which are the larvae of a clear-winged moth that bore into the inner bark. Dig borers out, being careful to minimize tree damage, or kill them by inserting a wire into holes. Cultivating shallowly around the base of the tree discourages these pests. Peachtree borers are attracted to weak trees. Keep trees vigorous and avoid mechanical damage; resistance to borer damage is largely a function of plant health.

Leaves unusually small; leaves yellow or oddly shaped. Cause: Viral infection. A few viral diseases cause leaf anomalies in peach trees. Peach rosette causes trees to produce shoots that have abnormally short distances between the leaf nodes. Avoid viruses by starting with clean stock. Avoid planting near possible virus carriers, such as old peach trees or wild chokecherries (*Prunus virginiana*). Remove and destroy infected trees.

PEAR *Pyrus communis* and hybrids (Rosaceae)

Pears are deciduous trees ranging in size from about 8 feet to more than 30 feet, depending on the cultivar and rootstock. The white blossoms appear in spring, mostly on spurs—short growths that elongate less than an inch each year. Fruit ripens from late summer into autumn. Most gardeners are familiar with European pears, including the familiar 'Bartlett' and 'Bosc' cultivars. However, Asian pears, which have crisp, juicy, almost-round fruit, will also grow well in most parts of the United States and Canada. Pears are hardy in Zones 4–9.

Culture

Pears require full sun. They grow best in well-drained, moderately fertile soil, but tolerate heavy or poorly drained soils more easily than most other fruits. Since pears flower later than most other common fruits, they do not require a site completely free of spring frost. Train European pears to a central leader system and Asian pears to an open center system. Prune bearing trees enough to allow light into the tree and to stimulate new growth to replace old spurs or branches that have been removed. For more pruning information, see "Pruning and Training" on page 104. To set fruit, most pear cultivars require cross-pollination from a second compatible cultivar planted nearby. For more information, see "Setting Fruit" on page 103.

Fruit Problems

Fruit with olive-brown, corky spots that turn dark brown. Cause: Pear scab. This fungal disease may also cause malformed fruit. It overwinters on fallen litter and infected twigs and spreads to the tree in spring, when warm air currents and splashing rain move fungal spores from the ground into the tree. To control pear scab, remove old leaves from beneath trees and compost or bury them. Prune out infected twigs, which bear small, blister-like pustules. Do both of these chores in late winter or early spring before growth begins. Regular sprays of sulfur or lime-sulfur applied early in the growing season help prevent the spread of scab to new foliage and fruit. Scabby fruit may be unattractive, but it is still edible once diseased portions are cut away. Some pear cultivars resist scab infection, but even these may develop symptoms when conditions favor the disease. Scab rarely infects Asian pears.

Fruit with holes surrounded by brown, crumbly excrement. Cause: Codling moth larvae. Fat, white or pinkish, $\frac{7}{8}$-inch caterpillars tunnel through fruit and may have departed by the time you discover their holes, which may be filled with what looks like moist sawdust. Infested fruit may drop prematurely. To control this pest, start in early spring by getting rid of loose bark to remove overwintering cocoons. Spray trees with horticultural oil at a dormant-season dilution. Hang one codling moth trap per dwarf tree (up to four traps per large tree) and maintain it according to manufacturer instructions; apply kaolin clay to deter egg laying and prevent larvae from entering young fruits, or cover fruits with nylon barriers before they reach 1 inch diameter; check trees weekly and remove and destroy any infested fruit; trap larvae in tree bands, destroy daily. For more information, see "Codling Moth" on page 259.

Fruit covered with a shiny, sticky coating that turns black. Cause: Pear psyllas. These $\frac{1}{10}$-inch, red to green, winged insects resemble cicadas. They overwinter in tree crevices and ground litter and emerge in early spring to lay eggs in trees. Newly hatched psylla nymphs pierce and suck juices from both foliage and fruit. Most regions support at least four generations of this pest per year, allowing plenty of opportunity for infestation throughout the growing season.

The sticky coating on fruit is honeydew excreted by the psyllas, and the black blotches are sooty mold that grows on the honeydew. Frequently, yellow jackets congregate around honeydew-coated leaves. You can clean the honeydew or mold off the fruit before eating it. Excessive psylla feeding will weaken the tree. To control psyllas, spray horticultural oil at a growing-season dilution in spring; spray kaolin clay in spring and throughout the growing season to deter feeding. As a last resort, spray infested trees with insecticidal soap.

Leaf Problems

Leaves suddenly blacken, with tips of growing shoots bent over. Cause: Fire blight. Don't confuse this bacterial disease with sooty mold, a black fungus that rubs off easily. Fire blight bacteria enter the tree at the growing tips and may travel down toward the roots and kill the whole tree.

Fire blight most readily affects very succulent growth; to make trees a little more blight-resistant, avoid heavy pruning or nitrogen fertilizer, both of which induce vigorous growth. When pruning, thin out whole branches rather than heading them back. This reduces the total number of cuts and avoids stimulating the growth of soft, blight-susceptible side shoots.

Prune off infected branches, including 6 to 12 inches of healthy tissue below injured areas. Between cuts, dip pruning shears into isopropyl alcohol or a 10 percent bleach solution (1 part bleach to 9 parts water) to prevent spreading the disease as you prune. As the growing season

progresses, fire blight bacteria advance from blighted shoots down branches and toward the roots. In fall, the bacteria form sunken, dark cankers in which to overwinter. During winter, inspect branches for these cankers and prune off damaged branches at least 6 inches below the cankers.

One way to prevent fire blight from killing an entire tree is to purchase trees in which a blight-susceptible cultivar has been grafted onto blight-resistant stock. Good rootstocks include the 'Old Home' ✕ 'Farmingdale' series, *Pyrus betulifolia*, and *P. calleryana*.

Sprays of products containing *Bacillus subtilis* may also protect against fire blight. If infections have appeared in previous seasons, apply Bordeaux mix during dormancy to help prevent recurrence. Copper sprays applied in spring may also reduce the incidence of fire blight, but spraying alone will not control the disease. Cultivars with good resistance to fire blight include 'Ayers', 'Blake's Pride', 'Magness', 'Maxine', 'Moonglow', 'Orient', 'Potomac', 'Seckel', 'Shenandoah', 'Shinseiki', 'Twentieth Century', and 'Warren'.

Leaves suddenly blacken in autumn. Cause: Pseudomonas blight. You might mistake this disease for fire blight, but fire blight symptoms appear in warm spring weather, and its cankers ooze in spring. Pseudomonas blight first appears during cool fall weather and its cankers do not ooze in spring. Control it by pruning, as for fire blight (see "Leaves suddenly blacken, with tips of growing shoots bent over" on this page).

Leaves with small, round, dark spots having purple margins. Cause: Fabraea leaf spot. This disease, most common east of the Mississippi River, may cause leaves to turn yellow and drop, weakening the tree; fruit may also develop spots. Since the disease overwinters in twig cankers as well as fallen leaves, garden sanitation does little to control the disease. Where foliar infection has been extensive in past years, sprays of sulfur, lime-sulfur, or copper, applied when leaves are half out and at 2-week intervals until midsummer, will reduce further injury and help prevent infection of developing fruit.

Leaves with dark, velvety patches. Cause: Pear scab. The spots are mostly on leaf undersides; the infected leaves often pucker and drop. For more information, see "Fruit with olive-brown, corky spots that turn dark brown" on page 157.

Leaves covered with lacy brown patches. Cause: Pear slugs. These green-black, slimy creatures are not true slugs; they're the larvae of the pear sawfly, a black-and-yellow insect slightly larger than a housefly. In spring, sawflies emerge from soilborne cocoons and lay eggs on leaves. Eggs hatch into sluglike larvae that skeletonize leaves. Remove them by handpicking or knock them down with blasts of water. If more control is needed, spray insecticidal soap, neem, or horticultural oil at a growing-season dilution; spray serious infestations with pyrethrin.

Leaves with small brown blisters on undersides. Cause: Pear leaf blister mites. Inside these blisters are small, enlongated, white mites that you need a magnifying glass to see. Damage usually is cosmetic and can be ignored, but if control is necessary, spray lime-sulfur before buds open or horticultural oil at a growing-season dilution as buds swell. Apply oil thoroughly to kill adults hiding in bud scales.

Leaves turn yellow; limbs die back. Cause: San Jose scale. If limb dieback is preceded by extensive leaf yellowing, look for the small gray bumps of San Jose scale clinging to the bark. Colonies of these nearly immobile insects cling to bark and weaken trees by sucking sap. Control scale with a dormant-season dilution of horticultural oil applied in late winter.

PECAN *Carya illinoinensis* (**Juglandaceae**)

Pecans are large, deciduous trees with separate male and female flowers borne on the same plant. They are hardy in Zones 6–9. Trees grown at the northern edge of their hardiness limit may not have a long enough season to ripen nuts.

Plant pecans in deep, well-drained soil in full sun. Trees need almost no pruning. Since male and female flowers on a given tree often mature at different times, plant two different cultivars to ensure pollination.

Problems

Nuts contain insect larvae. Causes: Pecan weevil grubs; hickory shuckworms; pecan nut casebearer larvae. Pecan weevils, snouted beetles similar to plum curculios, lay eggs within newly formed nut kernels; larvae that hatch from these eggs feed on the nut and emerge several weeks later through tiny holes in the shell and husk. Infested nuts are worthless and generally cling to the tree instead of splitting normally from the hulls. To control this pest, place dropcloths beneath the tree and jar the limbs with padded poles. Collect and destroy the fallen adult beetles. Do this every 2 weeks beginning in midsummer until weevils no longer drop.

Cream-colored, $\frac{3}{8}$-inch hickory shuckworms eat the kernels of immature nuts that drop early as a result of the infestation. These pests are the larvae of gray moths; the final larval generation overwinters on the ground in dropped shucks. To control shuckworms, keep dropped hulls picked up or bury them at the end of the season.

Pecan nut casebearers, the $\frac{1}{2}$-inch, green larvae

of a gray moth, spin webs around nuts and then enter to feed. Infested nuts may drop prematurely. Overwintering larvae leave cocoons in early spring and bore into growing shoots, causing wilting. Damage is worst early in the season. To help control casebearers, pick up and destroy all dropped infested nuts. The parasitic wasp *Trichogramma minutum* attacks and parasitizes casebearer eggs. For heavy infestations of casebearers, release 5,000 of these wasps per infested tree.

Leaves with olive-brown spots on undersides; shucks with small, velvety, olive-brown spots. Cause: Pecan scab. Leaf spots may enlarge to large black areas. The spots on the shucks may spread into large, sunken, black lesions. Nuts may drop prematurely. This fungal disease is worst in humid areas and overwinters on infected twigs, shucks, and leaves. To reduce infection the following season, clean up plant debris in autumn and knock off old leaf stems and shucks before trees leaf out in spring. Cultivars that have shown good resistance to scab include 'Carter', 'Elliott', 'Gafford', 'Jenkins', 'Kanza', 'McMillan', and 'Sumner'.

Tree declines; leaves yellow, die, but remain on tree. Cause: Cotton root rot. Roots of infected trees are brownish, rotted, and soft. Cotton root rot fungus lives in the soil for 5 years or more, thriving especially in areas with heavy, moist, alkaline soil. Prevent problems by planting pecans in well-drained, neutral to slightly acidic soil. Remove dying trees; do not replant with pecans.

PELARGONIUM Pelargonium, geranium

Pelargoniums, commonly known as geraniums, are popular, easy-to-grow plants most often grown for their clusters of red, pink, lilac, salmon, or white flowers that appear all season over 1- to 3-foot plants. Other geraniums are grown primarily for their fragrant leaves, which release powerful scents when brushed. Geraniums can also have attractively shaped and variegated foliage, with up to four colors in just one leaf. In mild climates geraniums persist throughout the year. They are delightful in beds, borders, pots, and hanging baskets.

Buy new nursery-grown plants each year, or start your own from seed or cuttings. Sow seeds indoors in late winter or early spring. Good window or artificial light is needed indoors. Cover seeds lightly. Germination is erratic, within 3 to 8 weeks. When seedlings have two or three true leaves, transplant them to individual 3-inch pots. After the last frost, plant outdoors 10 inches apart.

Geraniums usually need full sun. In the Deep South, give them light shade, or plants may burn. Soil should be well-drained, medium rich, and slightly acid to neutral. Water regularly, letting the soil dry out slightly between waterings. Fertilize regularly but lightly; overfeeding results in large leaves and fewer flowers. Remove spent flower heads to prolong blooming. Pinching back growing tips in early stages promotes fullness. Cut plants back if they become leggy.

Problems

Leaves yellow; plant weakened. Cause: Whiteflies. For controls, see "Whiteflies" on page 290.

Leaves stippled with yellow; foliage webbed. Cause: Spider mites. For control measures, see "Mites, Spider" on page 275.

Leaves, stems, and buds distorted. Cause: Aphids. See "Aphids" on page 250 for controls.

Stems with rotted sections; leaves wilt. Cause: Stem rot. This fungal disease starts at the base of plants and works upward. It commonly affects cuttings, but can also injure full-grown plants. Stems often turn black. Take cuttings only from healthy plants, and stick them in a sterile medium. Remove and destroy affected parts or plants.

Leaves with spots. Cause: Leaf spots. See "Leaves with spots" on page 99 for control information.

Leaves with large, ragged holes. Cause: Slugs and snails. See "Slugs/Snails" on page 284 for controls.

PEPPER *Capsicum annuum* var. *annuum* (Solanaceae)

Peppers are tender perennials that are grown as annuals in temperate climates for their sweet to fiery hot fruit. Pick peppers when they are unripe and green (or sometimes yellow or purple-black) or after they ripen to red, orange, yellow, or brown, depending on the cultivar. In general, ripe peppers are sweeter or less hot than unripe ones of the same cultivar.

Culture

Peppers require deeply worked, well-drained soil with lots of organic matter and a pH between 6.0 and 6.8 (they tolerate pH as low as 5.5). Peppers require a moderate to high level of nitrogen and moderate levels of phosphorus, potassium, and calcium. Have the soil tested and amend as needed before planting. Peppers grow best between 65° and 80°F. Temperatures above 85° or below 60°F can cause blossoms to drop without setting fruit.

Peppers tolerate drought, but do best in soil that is evenly moist, but not soggy. Stake peppers to keep fruit from touching the ground and use mulch to control weeds and prevent soilborne diseases from splashing up on the fruit.

Do not plant peppers where tomatoes, potatoes, eggplants, or peppers have been planted within the

past 3 to 5 years, and try to separate these crops in the garden. Compost or till under all plant residues at the end of the season, and cultivate to reduce overwintering pests.

Purchase sturdy, insect- and disease-free plants, or start your own from seed indoors. Pepper seeds germinate best above 80°F. Once seedlings are up, they grow best at 70°F during the day and 60°F during the night. Wait until soil temperatures reach 65°F before setting out transplants. Spray transplants with an antitranspirant to help reduce disease problems, and water them with seaweed extract or compost tea to give them a good start. To improve fruit set, spray plants with 1 teaspoon of Epsom salts added to 1 gallon of seaweed extract when the first flowers open.

Leaf and Whole Plant Problems

Seedlings fall over; stems girdled or rotted at soil line. Cause: Damping-off. Disinfect reused pots and flats by dipping them in a 10 percent bleach solution and letting them air dry before filling them with fresh seed-starting mix. Sow seeds thinly to allow for air movement around seedlings. Cover seed with a thin layer of soilless mix or vermiculite. Water only enough to keep soil moist, not soggy. Thin seedlings and spray with compost tea as soon as first true leaves open to help prevent the problem.

Seedlings clipped off at soil line. Cause: Cutworms. Check for fat, 1- to 2-inch-long, dull brown or gray caterpillars in the soil near the base of plants. Once they chew off a seedling, there is nothing you can do except protect the remaining seedlings from nocturnal cutworm attacks. Place cutworm collars around transplants, sprinkle moist bran mixed with BTK on the soil surface in the evening, or add parasitic nematodes to the soil at least a week before planting to control cutworms.

Leaves pale green and small. Cause: Nitrogen deficiency. Spray plants and drench roots with fish emulsion to alleviate symptoms, and side-dress with compost.

Leaves yellow, distorted, and sticky. Cause: Aphids. These small green, pink, black, gray, or white fluffy-coated insects suck plant sap. For mild infestations, knock pests off plants with a blast of water. Spray plants with insecticidal soap in the evening to control; spray with neem if infestation is severe.

Leaves mottled with yellow; young growth malformed. Causes: Tobacco mosaic virus; other viral diseases. Destroy diseased plants. Choose resistant cultivars to prevent problems. Wash hands after handling tobacco and before touching peppers to prevent tobacco mosaic virus. Control aphids, because they spread viral diseases as they feed. Resistant cultivars are widely available and are the best way to prevent problems; look for seeds or plants labeled to indicate resistance to major viruses that affect peppers: CMV (cucumber mosaic virus), PMV (pepper mosaic virus), PVY (potato virus Y), TEV (tobacco etch virus), and TMV (tobacco mosaic virus).

Leaves yellow; plant stunted and wilts in hot weather. Cause: Nematodes. Plants eventually die. Roots may have swollen galls. Destroy infested plants; do not compost them. To control these pests, apply parasitic nematodes to the soil.

Older leaves yellow; shoots or whole plant wilts. Cause: Fusarium or Verticillium wilt. Fusarium wilt and Verticillium wilt are both fungal diseases and are difficult to tell apart. Both Fusarium and Verticillium wilt begin with yellowing and wilting of the lower leaves. Plants are stunted and do not recover when watered. Cut open a stem near the soil line and look for internal discoloration. Verticillium fungi are active between 68° and 75°F, while Fusarium is active between 80° and 90°F. Destroy infected plants. Pepper Fusarium infects only peppers, while Verticillium infects a wide range of plant species, making effective rotation control difficult. Control pest nematodes to help reduce wilt problems. Few wilt-resistant cultivars are available.

Leaves stippled yellow, or bronzed. Cause: Mites. Leaves turn dry and papery. These tiny, spiderlike insects thrive in hot, dry weather. Rinse plants with water to disrupt mite activity; spray with insecticidal soap if infestation is severe.

Leaves with small, sunken, yellow-green spots. Cause: Bacterial spot. Spots eventually turn brown with lighter centers. Clean up debris where bacteria overwinter; remove and destroy severely infected plants. Preventive sprays of biofungicide products that contain *Bacillus subtilis* may be practical where bacterial spot has been a problem in previous seasons. Cultivars with resistance to various races of this disease are available, including 'Alliance', 'Declaration', 'Early Sunsation', 'Hot Spot X3R', 'Naples', 'Patriot', 'Red Knight X3R', and 'Snapper'.

Leaves with gray-brown spots. Cause: Cercospora leaf spot. This fungal disease only occurs in very warm climates. Spots develop a "frog-eye" appearance with light centers and dark edges. Infected leaves may drop; infection on fruit stems may cause deformed or dropped peppers. Clean up or deeply bury plant residues at the end of the season. Where this disease is common and damaging, spray plants with copper as soon as symptoms appear to prevent further symptom development.

Leaves with wandering, white or translucent tunnels. Cause: Leafminers. White, maggot-like larvae feed inside leaves, leaving empty tunnels behind them. Once larvae have entered leaves, spraying will not control them. Destroy mined leaves and remove nearby dock and lamb's quarters, which are also hosts. Cover plants with row cover until flowers open to prevent adults from laying eggs on plants. As a last resort, spray with neem.

Leaves with small holes. Cause: Flea beetles. Young transplants are the most susceptible. These tiny, black, brown, or bronze insects hop when disturbed. Protect transplants with row cover until they start to flower. Apply garlic spray or kaolin clay to repel pests, repeating as needed. Flea beetles are most problematic during droughts; watering the garden can sometimes reduce outbreaks.

Leaves with large holes. Causes: Hornworms; other caterpillars. Hornworms are 3- to 4½-inch caterpillars with white diagonal stripes. The tobacco hornworm has a red horn projecting from the rear, while the tomato hornworm has a black horn. Handpick or spray plants with BTK to control them. Do not spray caterpillars that are covered with small white cocoons; these cases contain the larvae of parasitic wasps that are natural hornworm predators.

Other caterpillars such as European corn borers and corn earworms sometimes feed on pepper leaves and fruit. Handpick, or spray plants with BTK if many caterpillars are feeding.

Flower and Fruit Problems

Few flowers form; flowers may drop without setting fruit. Causes: Excess nitrogen; extreme temperatures; pepper weevils. Plants with excess nitrogen are dark green and vigorous, but produce few flowers. Wait for flowers to form. Prevent problems by avoiding high-nitrogen soil amendments.

Temperatures over 85° or below 60°F can damage flowers and cause them to fall without

setting fruit. Wait for new flowers to form. Protect plants with row cover until night temperatures remain above 60°F.

Check flowers for pepper weevils, which are ⅛-inch, reddish brown to black insects. These pests may also cause misshapen and discolored fruit. Destroy infested fruit; spray with insecticidal soap; use neem as a last resort.

Fruit misshapen. Causes: Extreme temperatures; pepper maggots; viral diseases. Temperatures over 85° or below 60°F can damage flowers and prevent complete pollination. Resulting fruit is lopsided and deformed, but ripens evenly.

Pepper maggots are white with pale heads and grow up to ¼ inch long. Adults are small yellow-and-brown flies. Ripening fruit is blotchy. Destroy infested fruit. When plants begin to set fruit, spray with kaolin clay to deter egg-laying adults; repeat as needed. If maggot damage has been severe in past years, dust or spray with pyrethrin.

If ripening fruit is blotchy but no maggot feeding is found, the plants may have a virus. See "Leaves mottled with yellow; young growth malformed" on the opposite page for controls.

Fruit with green to dark brown, raised, wartlike spots. Cause: Bacterial spot. Spots can provide entry for more destructive rot fungi in wet weather. Spotted fruit is edible if not rotted. See "Leaves with small, sunken, yellow-green spots" on the opposite page for controls.

Fruit with small, rotten spots or shallow depressions. Cause: Pepper maggots. See "Fruit misshapen" above for description and controls.

Fruit with faded or gray-white, sunken patches or pits. Causes: Sunscald; cold injury. Green or ripe fruit can be sunscalded. Damage shows up as a large, sunken patch on the exposed side. Patches turn dry and may develop black mold. Control leaf diseases to prevent defoliation, so fruit will be shaded and protected from direct sun. Stake plants.

Pepper fruits are damaged by temperatures below 37°F and develop small, sunken pits or large, discolored areas. Cover plants with row cover if temperatures near freezing are predicted.

Fruit with water-soaked, sunken areas at the blossom end. Cause: Blossom end rot. Seen on green or ripe fruit. Affected area becomes dark and shriveled. This condition is caused by calcium deficiency in the fruit. It is aggravated by drought or uneven soil moisture, root damage, high salt levels in the soil, and excess nitrogen. If a soil test indicates deficiency, add high-calcium lime to the soil. Prevent problems by keeping soil evenly moist and by spraying plants with seaweed extract when the first flowers open and again when green fruit is visible.

Fruit with water-soaked areas near stem; entire fruit collapses into a slimy mess. Cause: Bacterial soft rot. Pick fruit as soon as water-soaked areas appear, and discard soft portions. Destroy rotted fruit. Prevent problems by controlling insect damage, staking and spacing plants so they dry out rapidly, and mulching to prevent soilborne bacteria from splashing up on plants during watering. Spray fruiting plants with copper if the weather is wet and you have had severe problems in the past.

Fruit with concentrically ringed, sunken spots. Cause: Anthracnose. Spots appear on green or ripe fruit. Plant in well-drained soil (use raised beds if necessary); avoid working amid wet plants. Destroy infected fruit.

Fruit colors prematurely; small holes and sawdustlike material visible near stems. Causes: European corn borers; corn earworms. Once caterpillars are feeding in fruit, it is too late to control them by spraying. Pick fruit and cut out damage or destroy infested fruit. Both of these

pests feed on leaves for a few days before they enter fruit, so reduce damage by spraying plants with BTK if caterpillars are feeding on leaves. Prevent adults from laying eggs on plants by covering them with row cover.

PERENNIALS *See* "Flowers" on page 96

PETUNIA Petunia

Showy petunias are popular everywhere for their single or double, plain or ruffled, trumpet-shaped flowers, produced all summer on 8- to 18-inch plants. Flower colors include lavender, yellow, red, pink, purple, and white, in both solid and bicolors. Plant in masses for eye-catching effect in beds, borders, containers, or hanging baskets.

Sow seed indoors 9 weeks before the last frost. Do not cover the extremely tiny seeds. Transplant carefully outdoors when frost danger passes. Many gardeners prefer to buy bedding plants. Get sturdy young plants, not leggy ones, which won't grow well.

Single-flowered cultivars do well in average soil and are hardier in general; fancy ruffled types grow best in richer soil. Petunias need sunshine at least half the day, and prefer more. Water frequently during hot weather. Monthly light feedings encourage bigger and better flowers; overfertilization gives stem and leaf growth rather than blooms. In midsummer plants may begin looking straggly. Cut stems back to 6 inches, fertilize, and give a good soaking to revitalize.

Problems

Flowers with gray or brown spots; leaves with brown spots. Cause: Botrytis blight. This fungus, a real problem in humid climates, produces spots that may become fuzzy with mold. The initial attack is on weak plants but spreads to healthy ones on contact, or by wind, rain, or handling. See "Botrytis Blight" on page 326 for more controls.

Leaves mottled and crinkled. Cause: Viral diseases. Several viruses can attack petunias. They are spread by contact or by insects, such as aphids and leafhoppers. Remove and destroy infected plants. Wash your gardening tools and hands after touching infected plants. Also, don't smoke in the garden, to avoid introducing viruses from the tobacco.

Leaves and/or flowers with round or irregular holes. Causes: Caterpillars; beetles; slugs and snails. Both moth and butterfly caterpillars feed on petunia leaves and buds. Handpick, or spray with BTK on appearance. Many types of beetles, including flea beetles, Japanese beetles, Colorado potato beetles, and cucumber beetles feed on petunias. Handpick larger beetles. Spray plants attacked by beetles with insecticidal soap. As a last resort, spray with neem. Slugs and snails like petunias, too. For control information, see "Slugs/Snails" on page 284.

PHILADELPHUS Mock orange

Mock oranges are deciduous shrubs, grown primarily for their white, late-spring flowers. They are useful in shrub borders.

Set out in fall or spring in full sun or light shade. While they can adapt to varying soil conditions, mock oranges prefer a moist but well-drained site rich in organic matter.

Mock oranges are remarkably free of serious problems. Aphids sometimes infest the leaves; see "Leaves wrinkled and discolored" on page 211 for controls. Leafminer larvae make curved mines in

the leaves; see "Leaves tunneled" on page 213. Plants crowded together are susceptible to powdery mildew; for controls, see "Leaves with powdery white coating" on page 213.

PHLOX Phlox

Showy, long-flowering plants that produce clusters of trumpet-shaped blooms in many colors, phlox range from tall, upright plants to low, trailing ones. Bountiful flowers of white, purple, pink, and blue—often with contrasting centers—cover the various species. Garden phlox (*Phlox paniculata*) grows 3 to 4 feet tall and blooms in mid- to late summer; creeping phlox (*P. stolonifera*) is a 9- to 12-inch spring bloomer; 5- to 6-inch-tall moss pink (*P. subulata*) flowers in early spring. Lance-shaped, 3-inch-long, light green leaves are typical of most phlox, although moss pink's fine, semi-evergreen foliage is needlelike.

In general, plant upright phlox and moss pink in full sun, and give trailing species partial shade. Garden phlox tolerates light shade, but weaker plants result. Moist, well-drained, and richly organic soils are favored by all phlox; add compost to soil at planting. Choose sites with good air movement to limit diseases; taller phlox need shelter from wind and may require staking. Phlox do not endure drought well; give ½ to 1 inch of water weekly, applying it at soil level to avoid wetting leaves. Mulch to retain moisture in summer.

Remove spent flowers to prolong blooming and reduce seed set. Seedlings gradually take over garden phlox plantings if plants are allowed to self-sow; flower color and plant size may change dramatically over time, as seedlings are not true to parents. Shear low-growing moss pink back by half to encourage bushy growth. Divide as necessary to improve air circulation and reduce clumps.

The severity of pest and disease attacks varies among phlox species; most are durable plants that easily withstand problems. Garden phlox, however, is injured by a number of pest and disease organisms, as described below.

Problems

Buds and leaves deformed and dwarfed. Cause: Phlox plant bugs. See "Plant Bugs" on page 278.

Leaves covered with white powder. Cause: Powdery mildew. See "Powdery Mildew" on page 322 for controls.

Leaves deformed; stems swollen or deformed; plant stunted. Cause: Bulb and stem nematodes. Plants infested with these tiny roundworms have crinkled, thin, or threadlike leaves, distorted shoot tips, and swollen stems. Stunted plants fail to flower and may die. Nematodes travel over wet plants on a film of water or on garden tools and gardeners moving among plants. There is no cure for infested plants; remove and destroy them. Do not grow phlox in sites where nematodes are present. Remove debris from gardens in fall to control pest populations.

Leaves stippled, reddish to yellow, with fine webbing. Cause: Spider mites. See "Mites, Spider" on page 275 for controls.

Leaves with brown spots. Cause: Fungal diseases. Several fungi cause leaf spots that enlarge, run together, and form blotches. Don't overcrowd plants; avoid working with phlox when leaves are wet; remove and destroy infected plant parts and severely infected plants. If leaf spots are a regular problem, and other controls don't work, spray with sulfur or Bordeaux mix as a last resort.

PICEA Spruce

Spruces are evergreen, needle-leaved, cone-bearing trees. In general, they grow as rigidly upright, pyramidal trees, reaching more than 100 feet in height. They make impressive specimen trees on large properties. Their large size, formal habit, and tendency to lose their lower branches make spruces less desirable for the average home landscape. There are many dwarf and compact cultivars available.

Before you plant a spruce, be sure you have enough room to let the tree reach its normal size; check the size at maturity on the plant label. Set out in spring as balled-and-burlapped or container-grown plants on a sunny or lightly shaded site. Spruces need a moist but well-drained, slightly acid soil with lots of organic matter. They grow best in cool, northern climates.

Caution: When controlling pests, be aware that horticultural oil sprays will remove the blue color from the foliage of blue spruces until new normal foliage is produced. Other spruce species may also be sensitive to oil sprays; read the product label, apply at a reduced rate if recommended, and test spray on a branch before treating the whole plant.

Problems

Branches with brown tips. Cause: Spruce budworms. This pest is widely distributed over the northern United States. The brown, 1-inch caterpillars have two rows of white dots along their backs; they tunnel into opening buds, destroying the terminals and gradually migrating to the younger foliage, leaving the tree looking as if it had been swept by fire.

Handpicking works if only a few caterpillars are present; usually, however, they are so numerous as to require an application of BTK. Remember to reapply after rain.

Leaves light gray or bronze. Cause: Spruce spider mites. These tiny, spiderlike pests damage needles as they feed; the injury weakens the plant and can kill young trees. Mites start feeding on lower, older needles and progress upward and outward; tiny webs may be visible on needles. See "Leaves stippled with yellow; foliage webbed" on page 212 for controls.

Shoot tips with conelike swellings. Cause: Spruce gall adelgids. The pests themselves are seldom seen; in the spring the young insects feed on the new needles, causing the spruce to produce galls that enclose the pests. See "Adelgids" on page 249 for more information and controls.

Leaves discolored; branch tips webbed. Cause: Spruce needleminers. The ½-inch, greenish caterpillars feed at the base of needles, mining as they go, and sometimes web together the needles at the tips of twigs. Control by spraying the plant with a strong blast of water in fall or late winter to knock the webs and loosen needles from the tree; then clean up all fallen debris.

Plant defoliated; branches bear cocoonlike bags. Cause: Bagworms. For controls, see "Plant defoliated; branches bear cocoonlike bags" on page 212.

Plant defoliated. Causes: Gypsy moths; sawflies. See "Leaves skeletonized or plant defoliated" on page 212 for controls.

Terminal shoot curled and brown. Cause: White pine weevils. For more information, see "Terminal shoot curled and brown" on page 168.

Trunk or branches with small holes; limbs die or break off. Cause: Borers. For controls, see "Trunk or branches with small holes; limbs die or break off" on page 214.

Leaves yellow; stems and leaves covered with small bumps. Cause: Scales. See "Leaves yellow; stems and leaves covered with small bumps" on page 213 for controls.

Trunk or branches with oozing lesions; branch tips die back. Cause: Canker. For more information, see "Trunk or branches with oozing lesions; branch tips die back" on page 214.

Branch tips die back. Cause: Blight. This fungal disease attacks mostly during cool, wet weather. Good air circulation discourages its onset. Leaves of infected plants shrivel and twigs die back. Cut off and destroy dead or diseased wood. As a last resort in a very cool, wet spring, spray with Bordeaux mix, starting when new growth appears on the trees and repeating at 2-week intervals until the weather gets warmer and drier.

Leaves yellow and drop. Cause: Rust. Whitish blisters on the undersides of the leaves followed by yellowing and leaf drop indicates rust. Prune out and destroy infected branch tips. See "Rust" on page 315 for more controls.

PIERIS Pieris

Pieris are broad-leaved, evergreen shrubs. The waxy, white flowers are borne in terminal clusters and open in early spring. Pieris are used in foundation plantings and are ideal for woodland gardens.

Set out in spring as balled-and-burlapped or container-grown plants. Moist, rich but well-drained, acid soils suit them best. Apply an organic mulch to keep down weeds and maintain a cool, moist root zone. Pieris thrive in sun or partial shade; plants survive in dense shade, but flower less.

Pieris are subject to some of the insects and diseases that attack rhododendrons; see the Rhododendron entry, beginning on page 182, for symptoms and controls.

PINUS Pine

Pines are needle-leaved, cone-bearing evergreens important both for their wood and ornamental value. In the landscape, some are useful as informal screens, others as hedges and foundation plants, and the more picturesque ones as specimens in the lawn or rock garden.

Set out in spring as balled-and-burlapped plants. A well-drained, somewhat acid soil enriched with organic matter suits them best. Pines prefer full sun, but will grow, although with a somewhat more open habit, in partial shade.

Problems

Branches dead; bark with yellow-orange blisters. Cause: White pine blister rust. This fungal disease needs two kinds of plants to complete its life cycle: a pine and a currant or gooseberry plant. While it does little damage to currants or gooseberries, this disease can quickly kill infected pines. It enters through the needles and grows into the bark, where it causes cankers that can girdle stems and branches. These cankers develop orange-yellow blisters that release spores.

Avoid planting white or other five-needled pines within 200 feet of currants or gooseberries. For other control measures, see "Trunk or branches with oozing lesions; branch tips die back" on the opposite page.

Leaves brown at base; shoots ooze resin. Cause: Tip blight. This fungal disease causes needles to brown in early and midsummer, when they are about half their normal size. Entire shoot tips may be killed, most commonly on lower branches. Resin oozing from infected tips is another common symptom.

Tip blight most commonly attacks old or stressed trees. To avoid problems, keep plants growing vigorously with proper pruning, mulching, and watering (during drought). Remove the source of infection by pruning out dead branches during dry autumn weather. (Sterilize pruners between cuts in a solution of one part bleach to nine parts water.) Also clean up fallen cones and other debris around the base of the tree. If the infested pine tree is a valuable one, as a last resort spray with Bordeaux mix the following spring, when the new shoots start to grow; repeat the treatment when the shoots are half grown and again 2 weeks later.

Branches with brown tips. Causes: Pine tip and pine shoot moths; spruce budworms. The larvae of these pests all cause similar damage, boring into the bases of needles and tunneling into shoot tips all over the plant. Their damage differs from that of white pine weevils in that the weevils only attack the top shoot (leader) of a plant. Handpicking works if only a few caterpillars are present. Pruning off and destroying infested tips in winter is a very effective control. Spraying with BTK before the caterpillars enter the shoots may be effective.

Terminal shoot curled and brown. Cause: White pine weevils. The ⅓-inch, pale yellow larvae bore into the terminal shoot, distorting and eventually killing it. The ¼-inch, mottled brown adult weevils emerge in late summer to feed on buds and bark. Early in the season, cut off damaged shoots several inches below the affected area. To replace the damaged leader, select a horizontal branch right below the cut and fasten it to a stake in an upright position. If damage is severe, reduce populations of adult weevils by spraying weekly with pyrethrin in spring or in fall when adults emerge. Do not apply pyrethrin if adults are not visible.

Bark damaged; leaves yellowish. Causes:

Beetles; weevils; pine bark adelgids. A wide variety of pests attack the bark of pines. Beetles and weevils make small holes in the trunk where they bore through the bark and tunnel underneath. Pine bark adelgids are small, cottony, white insects that congregate on the bark of the trunk and limbs.

Beetles and weevils most commonly attack already stressed trees, so the best control for these pests is prevention. Keep trees growing vigorously by watering during dry spells; fertilize if plants are injured or stressed. See "Adelgids" on page 249 for information on controlling these pests.

Leaves light gray or bronze. Cause: Spruce spider mites. For control measures, see "Leaves stippled with yellow; foliage webbed" on page 212 for controls.

Leaves discolored and drop. Cause: Needle-casts. Several kinds of fungi attack pine foliage, causing spots or bands or total browning of the needles. These symptoms usually appear in early spring the year after the needles are infected. Planting trees where they will have good air circulation is the best way to avoid problems. Cleaning up fallen needles and pruning out damaged tips will help reduce the source of infection. To avoid symptoms, as a last resort, spray the following year with Bordeaux mix when the new shoots are half grown; repeat 2 weeks later.

Trunk or branches with oozing lesions; branch tips die back. Cause: Canker. Several kinds of fungi cause cankers on pines. For more information, see "Trunk or branches with oozing lesions; branch tips die back" on page 214.

Leaves partially eaten; plant or branches defoliated; branches may be webbed. Cause: Caterpillars. See "Leaves skeletonized or with large holes; branches may be webbed" and "Leaves skeletonized or plant defoliated" on page 212.

Plant defoliated. Cause: Sawflies. Several species of sawflies cause similar damage in mid-summer or early fall. Natural parasites usually keep them in check. See "Sawflies" on page 281 for more controls.

Leaves yellow; stems and leaves covered with small bumps. Cause: Scales. See "Leaves yellow; stems and leaves covered with small bumps" on page 213.

Plant defoliated; branches bear cocoonlike bags. Cause: Bagworms. See "Plant defoliated; branches bear cocoonlike bags" on page 212.

Trunk or branches with small holes; limbs die or break off. Cause: Borers. For more information, see "Trunk or branches with small holes; limbs die or break off" on page 214.

Leaves tunneled. Cause: Leafminers. The brown larvae of the pine leafminers enter the needles and excavate them. Injured tips turn yellow and dry up. See "Leaves tunneled" on page 213 for control measures.

Branches with knotlike swellings. Cause: Gall rusts. Large galls, up to several inches in diameter, form on branches and eventually release yellowish spores. Pine-gall rusts produce spores that only infect pines; pine-oak gall rusts also attack oak trees, causing galls on their leaves. Control both kinds by pruning the galls from pine trees as soon as you spot them.

Leaves yellow and wilt. Cause: Root rot. For more information, see "Leaves yellow and wilt" on page 213.

PLATANUS Sycamore, planetree

Sycamores are deciduous, alternate-leaved trees with colorful, exfoliating bark and ball-shaped fruit. They are widely used as street trees since they withstand urban conditions.

Set out sycamores in spring or fall, planting in

full sun or very light shade. They are remarkably tolerant of a range of soil conditions.

Problems

Leaves and shoots blackened; leaves with moist or brown sunken spots. Cause: Anthracnose. This fungal disease is very common on American planetree (*Platanus occidentalis*); London planetree (*P.* × *acerifolia*) is generally more resistant. For control information, see "Leaves and shoots blackened; leaves with moist or brown sunken spots" on page 214.

Trunk and branches with elongated, sunken, cracked areas; leaves yellow or sparse. Cause: Canker stain. This is a serious disease that can spread quickly, girdling and killing branches or the whole tree. Remove and destroy seriously affected trees. Prevention is the best control; avoid creating any wounds that allow the disease to enter the tree. Summer pruning, for example, often encourages canker stain on the branches; winter pruning is best. Also, be careful when using lawnmowers or other equipment around the tree to avoid damage to the trunk.

Leaves stippled with red or yellow spots. Cause: Sycamore lace bugs. This widespread and serious pest feeds on the undersides of planetree foliage. As the $\frac{1}{10}$-inch, silvery white lace bugs feed, they puncture the leaves and then exude a toxin that turns the area around these punctures red or yellow. Spraying leaves with insecticidal soap just after the leaves unfold should control this pest.

Leaves with powdery white coating. Cause: Powdery mildew. See "Leaves with powdery white coating" on page 213.

Trunk or branches with oozing lesions; branch tips die back. Cause: Canker. See "Trunk or branches with oozing lesions; branch tips die back" on page 214.

Leaves with spots. Cause: Leaf spots. See "Leaves with spots" on page 213.

Leaves yellow; stems and leaves covered with small bumps. Cause: Scales. Heavy infestations can seriously weaken sycamores; see "Leaves yellow; stems and leaves covered with small bumps" on page 213 for controls.

Trunk with shelflike growths. Cause: Wood rots. A number of fungus-caused wood rots can occur; see "Trunk with shelflike growths" on page 214.

PLUM *Prunus* spp. (Rosaceae)

Plums are deciduous trees that grow from 5 to 20 feet, depending on soil, rootstock, and cultivar. Japanese plums (*Prunus salicina*) bear fruit on spurs—short branches that elongate only a fraction of an inch per year—that are 1 year old or older. European (*P. domestica*) and hybrid plums bear fruit on spurs 2 years old or older. Plums are hardy in Zones 4–10, depending on species and cultivar.

Plant plums in a well-drained, sunny site free from late spring frosts. Prune European plums to a central leader and Japanese plums to a modified central leader. For more pruning information, see "Pruning and Training" on page 104. Some plums need cross-pollination; for more information, see "Setting Fruit" on page 103.

Fruit Problems

Young fruit with crescent-shaped scars. Cause: Plum curculios. These snouted beetles appear around bloom time and leave a characteristic scar as they lay eggs in fruit. Infested fruit usually drops. Egg-laying ceases by early summer, but insects return later in the season to feed.

To control this pest, spread a dropcloth beneath the tree and tap the tree with a padded mallet. Collect and destroy curculios that fall onto the cloth. For best results, tap the tree twice a day, beginning as soon as you see the first scarred fruit. In addition, collect and discard dropped fruit to prevent newly laid eggs from hatching. A traditional control is to keep chickens beneath the trees to consume adult curculios and grubs from fallen fruit. To deter egg-laying curculios, spray trees with kaolin clay beginning at petal fall and continuing weekly for up to 8 weeks. In areas where severe infestations occur, check developing fruit for egg scars twice a week; when the first fruit scars appear, apply pyrethrin and repeat in 7 to 10 days. Do not spray before petals drop—it may kill beneficial pollinators.

Fruit with small brown spots that enlarge and grow fuzzy in humid weather. Cause: Brown rot. This fungus may also cause blossoms to wither and die. Fruit is most prone to infection 3 weeks before ripening. Infected fruit may drop early or turn soft and brown, then wither into hard, black, shriveled mummies that remain on the tree. For control, inspect trees before growth begins in spring. Remove and destroy mummies and twigs or branches with gummy lesions. If more control is needed, spray sulfur early to protect blooms, then again later to protect fruit. Since damaged fruit is more prone to infection, control insects such as plum curculios, which puncture fruit and allow infection to enter. The cultivars 'AU-Rosa' and 'Crimson' resist this fungus.

Fruit with brown, sunken spots on the surface. Cause: Bacterial leaf spot. Brown or black angular leaf spots may also appear. Preventive sprays of biofungicides that contain *Bacillus subtilis* may be practical where bacterial spot has been a problem in previous seasons. Resistant cultivars include 'AU-Amber', 'AU-Producer', 'AU-Rosa', 'AU-Rubrum', 'Bruce', and 'Crimson'.

Fruit spongy, bladderlike, large, and misshapen. Cause: Plum pocket. A fungal disease related to peach leaf curl, plum pocket starts as small white blisters that spread to cover entire fruit. Shoots and leaves may be curled, thickened, and distorted. Sprays of lime-sulfur, sulfur, or Bordeaux mixture in fall and in early spring before buds swell help prevent new infection.

Leaf and Branch Problems

New leaves twisted or curled and covered with a sticky coating. Cause: Aphids. For heavy infestations, apply a strong spray of water or insecticidal soap solution to trees. For more control information, see "Aphids" on page 250.

Twigs and branches bearing tarry, black galls. Cause: Black knot. To control this fungal gall, prune out branches to a few inches below galls. Spray infected trees with lime-sulfur in early spring before bud swell. Resistant cultivars include 'AU-Cherry', 'AU-Producer', 'AU-Rosa', 'AU-Rubrum', and 'Crimson'.

Branches wilting and dying, fail to leaf out in spring. Causes: Bacterial canker; Valsa canker. Look on the branches for sunken, elliptical lesions, often oozing a reddish gum. For more information and controls for these diseases, see "Cytospora Canker" on page 333. The cultivars 'AU-Amber', 'AU-Cherry', 'AU-Rosa', 'AU-Rubrum', 'Crimson', and 'Homeside' are resistant. 'Myrobalan' rootstock confers some resistance.

Tree stunted or dying. Cause: Plum leaf scald. This disease is common in the Southeast. There is no cure. Dig up infected plants and replant with a resistant cultivar such as 'AU-Amber', 'AU-Cherry', 'AU-Producer', 'AU-Rosa', 'AU-Rubrum', 'Explorer', 'Homeside', or 'Morris'.

POPULUS Poplar

Poplars are deciduous trees, generally fast-growing and weak-wooded. Male and female flowers appear on different plants. Females produce cottony seeds, so choose male cultivars to minimize the mess.

Easy to grow, poplars need full sun but can adapt to a range of soil conditions. They have spreading roots that can invade drains and water pipes; make sure you site plants away from these features. The extensive root system makes poplars tolerant of drought. These trees are naturally short lived and are prone to many pest problems.

Problems

Trunk or branches with oozing lesions; branch tips die back. Cause: Canker. This is a widespread and serious problem on poplars. See "Trunk or branches with oozing lesions; branch tips die back" on page 214 for controls.

Trunk or branches with small holes; limbs die or break off. Cause: Borers. See "Trunk or branches with small holes; limbs die or break off" on page 214 for controls.

Leaves skeletonized or with large holes; foliage may be webbed. Cause: Caterpillars. For control information, see "Leaves skeletonized or with large holes; branches may be webbed" on page 212.

Leaves with powdery white coating. Cause: Powdery mildew. See "Leaves with powdery white coating" on page 213.

Leaves yellow; stems and leaves covered with small bumps. Cause: Scales. For controls, see "Leaves yellow; stems and leaves covered with small bumps" on page 213.

Leaves wrinkled and discolored. Cause: Aphids. See "Leaves wrinkled and discolored" on page 211 for controls.

PORTULACA Moss rose, garden portulaca

These bright-flowered, mat-forming annuals come in several colors, including red, purple, pink, white, and yellow. The ruffled flowers are 1 inch wide. Plants grow 4 to 8 inches high and can spread to 1½ feet. Flowers open in sunlight and close with dark or cloudy skies.

Sow seed indoors 7 weeks before the last frost date. Set plants out in late spring when the soil is warm. Direct-seed outdoors in warm soil and full sun after the last frost. Mix the tiny seed with sand to get an even distribution. Press seeds down firmly, but don't bury them. Water gently, keeping the soil moist until seedlings appear (about 10 days).

Drought-tolerant moss rose thrives in rocky soil and sand. It enjoys full sun, high temperatures, and good drainage. Pests and diseases are seldom a problem.

POTATO *Solanum tuberosum* (Solanaceae)

Potatoes are annual vegetables grown for their nutritious, starchy tubers. They are commonly known as white potatoes, but different cultivars have white, yellow, pink, or even bluish flesh, and yellow, brown, red, or purple skin.

Culture

Potatoes require deeply worked, well-drained soil with lots of organic matter, and a pH between 5.0 and 6.8. Potatoes require moderate to high levels of nitrogen, phosphorus, potassium, calcium, and sulfur. Have the soil tested and amend as needed before planting. Gypsum is a good source of calcium and sulfur for potatoes.

Keep soil moist, but not soggy, and do not allow it to dry out. Alternating dry and wet soil can cause cracked or knobby tubers. Once tops begin to yellow near harvest, you can let the soil dry out without damaging tubers.

Do not plant potatoes where tomatoes, potatoes, eggplants, peppers, strawberries, or brambles have been planted within the past 4 to 5 years. Also, try to separate these crops in the garden. Don't plant potatoes where sod or small grains were grown the previous year: Wireworms, a common sod pest, also feed on potato tubers. Compost or till under all plant residues at the end of the season. Tilling the soil helps prevent pests from overwintering.

Potatoes are usually grown from seed potatoes (tubers) or "buds" (tiny tissue-cultured tubers), but a few cultivars, such as 'Catalina', are grown from true seeds. Prevent problems by planting only certified disease-free tubers. Planting true seeds or buds also helps avoid many tuber-borne diseases.

Pre-condition tubers by storing them between 65° and 70°F for 2 weeks before planting to encourage rapid growth. Soak pieces in compost tea for several hours before planting to help prevent disease problems. Plant them out when soil is at least 40°F.

Leaf and Whole Plant Problems

Sprouts fail to emerge; seed pieces rot. Cause: Various fungal and bacterial rots. Soak seed pieces in compost tea before planting to help suppress diseases. Plant in warm, well-drained soil and cover lightly to encourage rapid sprouting. Cold, wet soil encourages rot.

Leaves discolored and puckered or curled. Causes: Leafhoppers; aphids; viral diseases; bacterial ring rot. If leaves have yellow patches and brown edges, look for leafhoppers—tiny green or brown insects that suck plant sap and hop, scuttle sideways, or fly when disturbed. Wash nymphs

from plants with a strong spray of water. Spray with insecticidal soap. Prevent infestations by covering plants with row cover when they come up.

If leaves are stippled yellow and stunted, look for aphids. Potato aphids are tiny pink insects and are often found on young leaves. Knock pests off plants with a blast of water. Spray plants with insecticidal soap in the evening to control. Prevent infestations by covering plants with row cover when they come up.

If leaf edges roll upward and are yellow-green, the plants may have leafroll virus. Other viral diseases cause dark green or yellow-mottled foliage. Potato virus Y (PVY) causes necrotic spots on leaves and, later, in tubers. Destroy infected plants. Prevent problems by controlling aphids, which spread viruses as they feed, or by planting resistant cultivars. 'Katahdin' and 'Yukon Gold' resist leafroll virus; 'Eva', 'Dark Red Norland', 'Belrus', 'Kennebec', and 'Sebago' are resistant to PVY.

If leaves turn yellow between the veins and curl upward, the plant is probably suffering from bacterial ring rot. Shoots are stunted at the tip and may wilt. Wilted stems cut near the soil exude whitish ooze. Destroy infected plants. Prevent problems by planting certified disease-free tubers and by washing your knife after each tuber while cutting seed pieces.

Leaves yellow; plant stunted and may be wilted. Causes: White grubs; tuberworms; wireworms; black leg; root-knot nematodes; Verticillium wilt. If plants wilt suddenly, look for fat white grubs with brown heads, pinkish white larvae, or yellow to reddish brown, hard, segmented larvae chewing on roots or tubers. See "Potatoes riddled with tunnels" on page 176 for descriptions and controls.

If the stem is black and shrunken for a few inches above the soil line, the plant has black leg, a bacterial disease. Destroy diseased plants. To avoid black leg, plant potatoes in well-drained soil and don't overwater. Cultivars such as 'Green Mountain', 'Kennebec', and 'Russet Burbank' are resistant.

Stunted roots with swollen galls and tubers with warty skin are symptoms of root-knot nematode infestation. Tubers are edible if peeled. Destroy infested plants; do not compost them. To control these pests, apply chitin or parasitic nematodes to the soil.

If roots and stem are undamaged, the plants may have Verticillium wilt. Stems cut near the soil line are discolored inside. This fungal disease usually appears when the plants flower. Destroy infected plants. Prevent problems by planting tolerant cultivars such as 'Atlantic', 'Belrus', and 'Green Mountain'.

Leaves with gray-brown, concentrically ringed spots. Cause: Early blight. Spots may merge and cover entire leaf, which then yellows and falls off. This fungal disease is active during warm, rainy weather. Where available, biofungicide products containing *Trichoderma harzianum* or *Bacillus subtilis* may be applied to soil or to transplants' roots as a preventive. Preventive copper-based fungicide sprays may help reduce the spread of early blight. Remove and destroy severely infected plants. Prevent problems by spraying plants with an antitranspirant before symptoms appear if you have had problems in the past, or by planting resistant cultivars such as 'Centennial', 'LaRouge', 'Sangre', and 'Sebago'.

Leaves with olive green to brown spots. Cause: Late blight. Spots expand rapidly and sometimes develop a light yellow halo. A white, velvety growth appears on the undersides of spots in wet weather. Stems are also infected and become brown or black and water-soaked. This fungal disease is active during moderately warm, rainy weather. Once infected, symptoms can quickly worsen. Monitor plants carefully, and uproot plants that develop symptoms, but only when conditions are dry. Bury them deeply away from the garden or discard them in sealed bags with your household trash. For future crops, choose tolerant cultivars such as 'Atlantic', 'Butte', 'Chieftain', 'Kennebec', 'Krantz', 'Onoway', and 'Sebago'. Apply *Bacillus subtilis* products to help prevent the disease. Remove volunteer plants and space plants to allow good air movement; avoid wetting foliage unnecessarily. Spraying plants with compost tea when they come up and every 2 weeks throughout the season may also help prevent the disease. See "Late Blight" on page 314 for more control information.

Leaves with small holes. Cause: Flea beetles. These tiny black, brown, or bronze insects hop when disturbed. Prevent problems by covering newly planted potatoes with row cover until they are large enough to tolerate insect damage. Use garlic spray or kaolin clay to repel pests. Apply parasitic nematodes to the soil to help control overwintering flea beetle larvae in the soil; for serious infestations, apply *Beauveria bassiana* or spinosad (repeat sprays may be needed).

Leaves with large, ragged holes or leaves missing. Causes: Colorado potato beetles; blister beetles. Colorado potato beetles are oval, yellowish orange, hard-shelled, $\frac{1}{3}$-inch-long beetles with black stripes. Larvae are soft-bodied, humpbacked, dark orange grubs with two rows of black spots down each side of their body. Eggs are orange and are laid in rows on undersides of leaves. Overwintering adults appear on young plants in spring; handpick beetles zealously to reduce subsequent generations. Squash any eggs you see as well. Prevent problems by covering plants with row cover before beetles appear. A thick mulch of loose straw around the plants may help prevent Colorado potato beetle damage. See "Colorado Potato Beetle" on page 259 for more controls.

Blister beetles are ¾-inch-long, elongated and thin, metallic, black, blue, purple, or brown insects. Wear gloves to handpick, since these beetles secrete a substance that may cause blisters. Blister beetle larvae help control grasshoppers, so think twice before spraying to control them if grasshoppers are a problem in your area.

Tuber Problems

Potatoes small. Cause: Poor growing conditions; calcium deficiency. See "Culture" on page 172 for growing guidelines. If soil test indicates calcium deficiency, amend soil as needed.

Potatoes with green patches on skin. Cause: Exposure to light. Tubers exposed to light often turn green and develop a toxic substance known as solanine. Peel off green tissue before eating. Prevent greening by hilling plants with soil or mulch and renewing it as necessary. Store potatoes in the dark.

Potatoes with brown or black spots or patches on skin. Cause: Scurf. Peel off spots before using tubers. Soak seed pieces in compost tea before planting to help suppress fungal diseases. Do not plant spotted tubers: The resulting plants will produce only small tubers, many of which will rot. Resistant cultivars include 'Chieftain' and 'Goldrush'.

Potatoes with rough, corky spots on skin. Cause: Scab. Trim out spots before using tubers. Prevent this fungal disease by keeping soil pH below 5.5 and planting resistant cultivars such as 'Atlantic', 'Chieftain', 'Goldrush', 'LaRouge', 'Norland', 'Russet Norkotah', 'Russian Banana', and 'Superior'.

Potatoes with wartlike bumps. Cause:

Root-knot nematodes. See "Leaves yellow; plant stunted and may be wilted" on page 173 for controls.

Potatoes knobby. Cause: Uneven soil moisture. If tuber growth is interrupted because of lack of soil moisture, tubers are often deformed. Keep soil moist, but not soggy, and never let it dry out.

Potatoes with a black, rotted ring at stem ends. Cause: Bacterial ring rot. Tubers have a soft, light brown ring in the flesh near the skin. See "Leaves discolored and puckered or curled" on page 173 for controls.

Potatoes with dark blotches on skin; flesh with dark, corky areas. Causes: Early blight; late blight. Trim out corky areas before using; discard severely affected tubers. See "Leaves with gray-brown, concentrically ringed spots" and "Leaves with water-soaked brown spots" on the opposite page for controls.

Potatoes with gray to black areas in flesh; centers may be hollow. Causes: Waterlogged soil; extreme temperatures; potassium or phosphorus deficiency; mechanical injury; viral disease. Potatoes grown in wet, poorly drained soil often grow too fast and may develop a discolored and/or hollow area in the center. Prevent problems by keeping soil moist, but not soggy.

Extremely hot weather or cold snaps before potatoes are harvested can cause similar symptoms. Keep tubers well covered with hilled-up soil or mulch.

Phosphorus or potassium deficiency can cause spots or patches of dark flesh. Oversize tubers with hollow centers may also indicate potassium deficiency. If deficiencies are suspected, have soil tested and amend as needed. If plants show symptoms of phosphorus deficiency, raise soil pH to 6.0 so the mineral will be more available to the plants.

Rough handling can cause mechanical injury, such as bruising, that appears as discolored areas on the flesh. Viral infections may cause deformed or discolored tubers. See "Leaves discolored and puckered or curled" on page 173 for controls.

Potatoes riddled with tunnels. Causes: Tuberworms; wireworms. If tubers have browned, silk-lined tunnels, look for tuberworms. These pinkish white larvae are ½ inch long and feed in tubers, stems, and leaves. Destroy infested tubers and plants. Keep tubers hilled with soil as they grow, and remove the dead vines before digging tubers. Cover plants with row cover to prevent adult moths from laying eggs.

Wireworms are yellow to reddish brown, hard, segmented larvae up to 1½ inches long that tunnel into tubers and chew on roots. Adults are dark-colored, elongated click beetles. Apply parasitic nematodes to the soil before planting to control them. Avoid planting potatoes where sod or grain grew the previous season, because wireworms are often numerous there.

Potatoes spoil in storage. Cause: Bacterial or fungal rots. Poor growing conditions or improper curing or storage may encourage various rot diseases. See "Culture" on page 172 for growing guidelines.

Let vines yellow and dry before carefully digging tubers. Sort out any bruised, cut, cold-injured, or diseased potatoes and keep them cool (around 40°F) until they can be used. Cure healthy tubers by storing them between 50° and 60°F for 2 to 3 weeks, then store them between 35° and 45°F in a humid place.

PRIMULA Primrose

This large genus includes more than 400 species of mostly low-growing plants noted for numerous brightly colored and often fragrant blossoms. The many species, hybrids, and cultivars range from 5 inches to over 2 feet tall. Spring flowers bloom in a wide range of colors. Primrose foliage is coarse and crinkled; large, bright green leaves form a rosette below the flowers.

Primroses are hardy (some to Zone 3), but prefer humid regions without extreme heat or cold. Moisture is critical for primroses; few tolerate any drought. Plant in partial shade in well-drained, rich, organic soil. Healthy primroses have few pest problems. Low leaves and moist soil attract slugs; see "Slugs/Snails" on page 284 for controls.

PYRACANTHA Firethorn

Firethorns are thorny, evergreen plants grown for their handsome glossy foliage and the persistent red, orange, or yellow fruit. Firethorns adapt well to foundation plantings; upright cultivars are excellent for hedges.

Set out in spring as balled-and-burlapped or container-grown plants in full sun or light shade. Avoid alkaline soils and locations subject to strong winter winds. When possible, choose disease-resistant cultivars like 'Apache', 'Mohave', or 'Teton'.

Problems

Leaves, flowers, and branches blackened. Cause: Fire blight. This bacterial disease causes new shoots to wilt suddenly, turn dark, and die back, eventually killing the whole plant. See "Fire Blight" on page 336 for controls.

Leaves and berries with black, scabby areas. Cause: Scab. Infected leaves eventually turn yellow and brown before falling off the plant. Damaged fruit is unsightly. Scab is most problematic in cool, moist weather. Clean up fallen leaves and berries and destroy them or discard them in the trash. Plant scab-resistant cultivars. As a last resort, spray plants the following year with Bordeaux mix, once when buds break in spring and again when flower petals fall.

Leaves skeletonized; branches webbed. Cause: Webworms. These 1-inch, pale green to nearly black caterpillars have a dark or light stripe down the back and three dark spots on the side of each segment. They feed on leaves and spin silken webs around leaves and stems. Young plants may die; older ones can be seriously weakened. Break up and remove the webs; spray leaves with BTK.

Leaves wrinkled and discolored. Cause: Aphids. See "Leaves wrinkled and discolored" on page 211 for controls.

Leaves pale and mottled. Cause: Lace bugs. See "Lace Bugs" on page 270 for controls.

Leaves yellow; stems and leaves covered with small bumps. Cause: Scales. See "Leaves yellow, stems and leaves covered with small bumps" on page 213 for more information.

Leaves stippled with yellow; foliage webbed. Cause: Spider mites. See "Leaves stippled with yellow; foliage webbed" on page 212 for controls.

QUERCUS Oak

Valued both for their ornamental effect and for their wood, oaks are trees that typically have large, lobed leaves and rough bark. Most oaks are slow-growing and long-lived. Those suitable for northern planting are deciduous; there are a number of evergreen oaks grown in the South. The larger species are primarily used as ornamentals on large properties; some of the shorter-growing ones are valued as street trees and for smaller gardens.

Set out in spring as balled-and-burlapped plants. Full sun and deep, fertile, well-drained, somewhat acid soils suit them best. Oaks vary in their moisture requirements; ask your local nursery owner or extension agent about the needs of your oak trees.

Problems

Plants defoliated. Cause: Gypsy moths. The larvae of the gypsy moth are particularly fond of oaks and can easily defoliate a tree. For control measures, see "Leaves skeletonized or plant defoliated" on page 212.

Leaves skeletonized or with large holes; branches may be webbed. Cause: Caterpillars. Many caterpillars feed on oak foliage. See "Leaves skeletonized or with large holes; branches may be webbed" on page 212.

Leaves or stems with brown, white, or green swellings. Cause: Galls. A number of tiny mites and insects feed on oaks, causing swellings on leaves and twigs. Damage is rarely serious. Prune off and destroy affected leaves and twigs.

Leaves with roundish, puckered areas. Cause: Leaf blister. This fungal disease causes yellowish white blisters, up to ½ inch in diameter, on oak foliage. Although symptoms may appear serious, little actual harm is done to the tree, so control isn't necessary.

Leaves with powdery white coating. Cause: Powdery mildew. See "Leaves with powdery white coating" on page 213 for controls.

Leaves and shoots blackened; leaves with moist or brown sunken spots. Cause: Anthracnose. For controls, see "Leaves and shoots blackened; leaves with moist or brown sunken spots" on page 214.

Leaves yellow; stems and leaves covered with small bumps. Cause: Scales. See "Leaves yellow; stems and leaves covered with small bumps" on page 213.

Trunk or branches with oozing lesions; branch tips die back. Cause: Canker. For more information, see "Trunk or branches with oozing lesions; branch tips die back" on page 214.

Leaf edges browning; leaves wilt and drop early. Cause: Oak wilt. Symptoms of this fungal disease usually show up first on the top of the tree, eventually spreading to the lower branches. Infected trees die quickly, often within 1 year of infection. There is no cure; remove and destroy infected trees.

Leaves stippled with white. Cause: Oak lace bugs. Adult lace bugs are $\frac{1}{10}$-inch, flattened, dark insects with lacy-patterned, silvery white wings. Both the adults and the tiny nymphs feed on the undersides of leaves, sucking the sap and producing a gray, splotched, or stippled appearance to the upper sides of the foliage. Leaves may curl, turn brown, and drop early. See "Lace Bugs" on page 270 for controls.

Leaves rolled and chewed. Cause: Leafrollers. These $\frac{1}{2}$-inch, green caterpillars form small webs on shoot tips and feed on leaves and buds inside. Break open webs and handpick larvae; spray BTK at first sign of damage.

Leaves with spots. Cause: Leaf spots. For controls, see "Leaves with spots" on page 213.

Leaves tunneled. Cause: Leafminers. See "Leaves tunneled" on page 213 for controls.

Leaves stippled with yellow; foliage webbed. Cause: Spider mites. For controls, see "Leaves stippled with yellow; foliage webbed" on page 212.

RADISH *Raphanus sativus* (Cruciferae)

Radishes are annual and biennial vegetables grown for their crisp, peppery roots. Certain cultivars do not have fleshy roots, but are grown for their crunchy seedpods.

Most radishes do best in cool, moist conditions. They need a pH between 5.5 and 6.8 and light, relatively rich soil. Plant radishes as soon as soil can be worked in spring. Make small plantings weekly until early summer for a continuous supply of radishes. Temperatures between 50° and 65°F produce the best radishes; growth above 75°F is poor. Some cultivars of Daikon radishes are designed for summer planting and will flower without forming large roots if planted too early.

The secret to mild, tender radishes is rapid growth. Water heavily the first 2 weeks after seedlings sprout if soil is dry. A light application of compost is usually enough for a good radish crop. Radishes will not tolerate soils high in salt.

Radishes are related to cabbage and suffer from many of the same problems. Since leaves are not harvested, more insect damage can be tolerated than in cabbage plants. See the Cabbage entry, beginning on page 56, for descriptions and controls. Prevent problems with Fusarium yellows by planting resistant cultivars such as 'Altabelle', 'Altaglobe', 'Cabernet', 'Fuego', 'Minowase Summer Cross', 'Mister Red', and 'Scarlet Knight'.

Root Problems

Roots enlarged and clublike. Cause: Club root. Destroy plants suffering from this fungal disease. Prevent the problem by rotating crops and providing good drainage. 'Cabernet' is a tolerant cultivar.

Roots riddled with slimy, winding tunnels. Cause: Cabbage maggots. Maggots are white and $\frac{1}{4}$ inch long. Adults look somewhat like houseflies and lay eggs on the soil near the base of the plants. Frequent, light cultivation when plants are young helps to decrease maggot populations. Remove and destroy infested plants.

Roots small and imperfect. Causes: Nitrogen deficiency; phosphorus deficiency; lack of water; excessive heat; wrong season for cultivar. Yellow or pale leaves suggest nitrogen deficiency. Purple leaves suggest phosphorus deficiency. Spray leaves with fish emulsion or side-dress with compost to correct either deficiency. If soil was dry, water subsequent plantings well. Do not try to grow most radishes in the hottest summer months; wait until cooler fall weather. Planting radishes in the shade of other plants may extend the spring season somewhat. Check proper planting season before planting Daikon cultivars.

Roots tough and dry; flesh pithy with white spots. Cause: Excessive heat. Few radishes tolerate high summer temperatures. Select heat-tolerant cultivars such as 'Cherry Bomb II Hybrid', 'Minowase Summer Cross', 'Sora', 'Szechuan Red', and 'Tama Cross', or plant earlier or later.

Roots with rough, dark spots on skin. Cause: Scab. This fungal disease is a problem in dry soil when pH is high and magnesium is low. Keep soil moist and maintain a pH below 6.5. Spray foliage with Epsom salts (1 tablespoon per gallon of water) or side-dress with compost to add magnesium.

Roots cracked; skin and flesh normal. Causes: Overmaturity; uneven soil moisture. Radishes are at their best for only a few days. If left unharvested, they quickly develop harsh flavor and often crack open. Make small plantings every week until early summer for a continuous supply, and pull them as soon as ready. Keep soil evenly moist.

Roots cracked; skin rough; flesh dark. Causes: Downy mildew; black root. Prevent these fungal disease problems by providing well-drained soil and by using a 4-year rotation. 'Fuego' is resistant to black root; 'Altabelle', 'Altaglobe', and 'Tae Black' resist downy mildew.

Roots soft and shriveled. Cause: Cold injury. Protect roots with mulch below 32°F.

RASPBERRY *Rubus* spp. (Rosaceae)

Raspberries are perennials that usually bear fruit on second-year canes. Canes of black (*Rubus occidentalis*), purple (*R.* ✕ *neglectus*), and summer-bearing red (*R. idaeus*) raspberries bear fruit in their second season of growth. Everbearing red raspberries bear in late summer on new canes and again the next summer farther down the same canes. Red raspberries spread by underground runners. Black and purple raspberries spread by taking root where cane tips touch the ground. Raspberries are hardy in Zones 3–9, depending on species and cultivar.

Culture

Plant in a sunny site with good air circulation and well-drained soil. Start with disease-free stock. Plant in hills or rows well away from wild or abandoned raspberries, which may carry diseases. Provide posts or a wire fence to support the canes.

For black, purple, and summer-bearing red raspberries, cut off all fruit-bearing canes at ground level as soon as harvest is over, or when growth begins in spring. In late winter or early spring thin out new canes that emerged the previous season; save the sturdiest ones and leave six canes per hill or 6 inches between row-planted canes. Shorten lanky canes to 4 or 5 feet. Since black and purple raspberries fruit most heavily on side branches, induce side branching during the summer by pinching the growing tips of canes when they reach 2½ feet. The following late winter or early spring, shorten the side branches to about 1 foot.

For everbearing red raspberries, remove fruiting canes each summer as soon as the second fruiting is complete. Or sacrifice the second berry crop (which may be light anyway) and cut the entire planting to the ground as soon as leaves drop in fall. Although this approach yields only one crop instead of two, it has several advantages. Pruning all canes to the ground eliminates winter injury to canes, results in vigorous new canes for next fall's crop, and cuts down on overwintering pests that will appear next spring.

Raspberries are self-pollinating. A well-maintained planting may fruit heavily for many years, but disease often appears as plants age. Plan on establishing a new raspberry bed every 10 years (less if plants begin to decline).

Fruit Problems

Fruit covered with light gray fuzz. Cause: Fruit rot. Especially common during wet weather, this fungal disease appears less frequently where plants have good air circulation and proper pruning. To control fruit rot, harvest berries often. Pick and discard infected fruit far away from plants.

Fruit covered with a powdery white coating. Cause: Powdery mildew. This fungal disease, most common on red raspberries, makes fruit inedible and may weaken or kill whole canes. Pruning out old canes to provide good air circulation aids control. Apply *Bacillus subtilis,* potassium bicarbonate, or a 0.5 percent solution of baking soda (1 teaspoon baking soda in 1 quart water) as preventives or to help to control the disease. Spray infected plants thoroughly. Resistant cultivars include 'Meeker', 'Sumner', and 'Willamette'.

Fruit of red raspberries small and crumbly. Cause: Crumbly berry virus. This disease is incurable. Dig out and destroy infected plants and replant at a new site with virus-free (also called virus-indexed) plants.

Fruit small, tasteless, and dry. Cause:

Verticillium wilt. For more information, see "New canes die in midsummer" on page 182. Drought can also cause these symptoms.

Fruit infested with slender white grubs. Cause: Raspberry fruitworms. These ¼-inch larvae feed in ripening fruit and may cause berries to drop prematurely. Adults are ⅛-inch, brown beetles that feed on flowers and leaves before laying eggs on fruit. Handpick adult beetles; collect and destroy worm-infested fruit to prevent larvae from dropping to the ground and overwintering. Cultivate the soil beneath raspberries in early fall to expose pupae to predators. Spray plants with pyrethrin as blossom buds appear, and again when flowers open, if you have had problems in the past.

Leaf and Branch Problems

Canes with dark blotches; side shoots may wilt and canes may die. Causes: Spur blight; cane blight; anthracnose. Spur blight causes reddish brown blotches around leaf bases. This fungal disease appears mostly in midsummer on new canes of red raspberries. The following spring, blotches will be gray and leaf buds of affected cane areas will be dead. Side shoots may wilt and entire canes may die. For prevention, plant resistant cultivars, including 'Brandywine', 'Festival', 'Haida', 'Hilton', 'Latham', and 'Newburgh'.

Cane blight causes canes with large, brownish purple areas extending over several buds. This fungal disease, most common on black raspberries, usually enters through a wound. Side shoots may wilt and entire canes may die.

Anthracnose causes canes and leaves with gray spots surrounded by red or purple margins. Infected leaves have small yellowish white spots, the centers of which may dry and fall out. Side shoots may wilt and entire canes may die. To help prevent this fungal disease, plant anthracnose-resistant cultivars, including 'Black Hawk', 'Jewel', and 'Newburgh'.

Good cultural habits can help to prevent all three of these diseases. Maintain good air circulation by selecting a sunny, well-drained site. Each fall, remove diseased or crowded canes at ground level. Prune when plants are dry and rain is not expected for the next 3 days. For persistent fungal infections, apply lime-sulfur spray just as leaf buds break in the spring.

Leaves lightly stippled, curled, and dry. Cause: Mites. Tap a leaf over a sheet of white paper. Mites will appear on the paper as moving red, green, or yellow specks. Mites are most prevalent under dusty conditions and on water-stressed plants. For prevention, keep plants mulched and well watered. For light infestation, spray plants with water; for heavy infestations, spray with insecticidal soap. Lime-sulfur spray applied early in the growing season also aids control. Mites often are controlled by natural enemies, including predatory mites; keep in mind that sprays to kill the pest mites will also kill the predators.

Leaves and growing tips of canes covered with powdery white coating. Cause: Powdery mildew. For more information, see "Fruit covered with a powdery white coating" on the opposite page.

Leaves with greenish black spots that later turn gray. Cause: Raspberry leaf spot. Leaf spots may become holes; leaves may drop early. Good air circulation aids prevention of this fungal disease. Choose a sunny, well-drained planting site and thin plantings each fall or winter to prevent overcrowding of canes. For persistent infection, apply lime-sulfur spray just as leaf buds begin to green in spring.

Leaf undersides with bright orange pustules. Cause: Orange rust. This incurable fungal disease appears only on black or purple raspberries, and blackberries. Diseased plants never recover; infection spreads quickly to neighboring plants. Dig up and destroy plants as soon as you notice disease symptoms. Install new plantings well away from wild brambles, which are a source of infection.

Leaves skeletonized. Causes: Raspberry sawfly larvae; Japanese beetles; raspberry fruitworm beetles. The prickly, pale green, ½-inch larvae of raspberry sawflies usually cluster on leaf undersides. They feed on leaves for up to 2 weeks before descending to the ground, where they pupate and emerge the following spring as adult sawflies. Blast larvae from branches with a strong stream of water; handpick larvae and drop in soapy water. Spray insecticidal soap when larvae are still small, focusing on undersides of leaves.

Japanese beetles are ½-inch, metallic blue-green insects with bronze wing covers. For light infestations, check plants in the morning while beetles are sluggish and knock them off leaves into jars filled with soapy water. Traps baited with floral or fruit scents may reduce damage if placed at some distance from plants. Place traps well away from plantings you wish to protect. Japanese beetle populations naturally decline by midsummer, but for heavy infestations, spray with insecticidal soap; as a last resort, spray with neem.

If Japanese beetles are a consistent problem in your area, avoid planting raspberry cultivars particularly attractive to these pests. Cultivars *to avoid* include 'Fall Gold', 'Festival', 'Heritage', 'Latham', 'Newburgh', 'Reveille', 'Ruby', and 'Skeena'.

Raspberry fruitworm beetles also chew leaves into a lacy pattern. For more information, see "Fruit infested with slender white grubs" on the opposite page.

Whole Plant Problems

New canes die in midsummer. Cause: Verticillium wilt. Typically leaves yellow, wilt, and fall before the entire cane dies. There is no cure for this soilborne fungal disease, which may be carried by other host plants such as tomatoes, potatoes, peppers, or eggplants. Avoid planting raspberries where other Verticillium host plants formerly grew. Red raspberries are generally more resistant to Verticillium wilt than black raspberries. For extra precaution, solarize the soil to kill the fungus before planting (see "Soil Solarization" on page 20).

Canes with wartlike or corky swellings; canes dying. Cause: Crown gall. Look for irregular corky swellings on the roots and crown area as well as the canes. Crown gall bacteria live in the soil and enter plants through wounds, so avoid injury to roots or crowns of plants. When working with infected plants, use isopropyl alcohol or a 10 percent bleach solution (1 part bleach to 9 parts water) to disinfect shovels and other tools before you move from one plant to the next.

Avoid introducing the infection into your soil by planting only healthy stock from a reputable grower. Many different types of plants are susceptible to crown gall, including roses, melons, and chrysanthemums. If your soil is infected, don't plant susceptible plants on that site for at least 3 years. If you must plant raspberries in soil with a history of crown gall, pretreat plants with a *Trichoderma* biocontrol agent. 'Boyne' and 'Willamette' have some tolerance to crown gall.

Canes dying; break off easily. Cause: Raspberry crown borers. The adult form of this insect, a clear-winged moth, lays eggs on leaf undersides. Eggs hatch into white, ½-inch grubs that feed on crowns, roots, and cane bases. Heavily infested canes may be hollowed out entirely. Dig out and destroy infested crowns. Vigorous canes are less likely to be attacked.

Cane tips wilted and dying. Causes: Rednecked cane borers; raspberry cane borers; raspberry horntails. All of these insects lay eggs near cane tops, causing tips to wilt and die. Gall-like, cigar-shaped swellings on canes indicate rednecked cane borers. Canes girdled with spiral-shaped galls have been attacked by horntails. In all three cases, the adult insect lays eggs in the canes. Eggs hatch into grubs that feed and overwinter inside canes. For control, prune out and destroy infested canes as soon as you notice the injury. For heavy infestations, apply pyrethrin just before plants come into bloom.

Leaves mottled with irregular yellow spots. Cause: Mosaic virus. This disease is transmitted by aphids and appears only on black or purple raspberries. Red raspberries may carry the virus but will show no symptoms. Infected purple or black raspberries eventually become stunted and develop small, misshapen leaves with green blisters. The only control is to dig up infected plants and replant with virus-free (virus-indexed) stock. Avoid planting raspberries in sites near wild or abandoned raspberries. Since red raspberries may carry the disease, separate plantings of black and purple raspberries from red raspberries. 'Royalty' purple raspberry is less susceptible to mosaic than other purple raspberries because it is seldom infested with the species of aphid that transmits the disease.

RHODODENDRON Rhododendron, azalea

Rhododendrons and azaleas, both members of the genus *Rhododendron,* are deciduous, semi-evergreen, or evergreen, broad-leaved shrubs. Rhododendron leaves are usually large and evergreen, while azalea leaves are generally small and deciduous. Gardeners prize both plants for the colorful flowers. Best adapted to cool, moist climates, they are commonly used in foundation and woodland plantings.

Set out in spring as balled-and-burlapped or container-grown plants. Sun or partial shade suits them well; the further south, the more shade they need. Rhododendrons and azaleas require cool, moist, highly organic, acid soil. Choose a site where they receive shade during the hottest part of the day in warm climates and won't be exposed to drying winter winds. Their feeding roots are close to the surface, so be sure to set out plants at the same level at which they were growing in the nursery.

Cultivation can damage the shallow roots, so apply a thick layer of organic mulch to help keep down weeds and maintain a cool, moist root zone. Rhododendrons and azaleas don't tolerate drought, so take care to water them thoroughly during dry spells. Some azaleas may be damaged by insecticidal soap sprays, so test the product on a few leaves before spraying the whole plant.

Problems

Leaves mottled, with shiny, black flecks underneath. Cause: Lace bugs. These pests are most common on plants growing in full sun. Both adults and the tiny nymphs feed on the undersides of leaves, sucking the sap and producing a gray, splotched or stippled appearance to the upper sides of the foliage. See "Lace Bugs" on page 270 for controls.

Leaves with notched edges. Cause: Black vine weevils. See "Root Weevils" on page 279 for controls.

Leaves yellow and wilt; branches break off. Cause: Rhododendron borers. These small, clear-winged, wasplike moths lay eggs on leaves,

twigs, and bark. The eggs hatch into ½-inch, whitish larvae that burrow into weakened stems and branches. See "Clearwing Borers" on page 258 for controls.

Leaves with spots. Cause: Leaf spots. Several kinds of fungi cause spots on azalea and rhododendron leaves. For control measures, see "Leaves with spots" on page 213.

Petals with pinhead-size spots; blooms rot. Cause: Flower petal blight. Remove and destroy infected flowers and branch tips. Rake debris from around the base of the plant and replace with fresh mulch.

Stem tips die; leaves brown and wilt. Cause: Dieback. Besides causing leaves to brown, roll, and wilt, dieback may kill stem tips and cause cankers to form on stems. Avoid dieback by keeping plants healthy, with regular watering and good winter protection. Prune out diseased tips several inches below the damaged areas. As a last resort, spray the plant with Bordeaux mix after the plant blooms, and again 10 days later.

Leaves yellow; stems and leaves covered with small bumps. Cause: Scales. For controls, see "Leaves yellow; stems and leaves covered with small bumps" on page 213.

Leaves yellowed. Cause: High soil pH. Chlorosis (yellowed leaves) is most common on azaleas and rhododendrons used in foundation plantings. Lime leaches from the foundation of the house, making the soil too alkaline. Restore soil acidity by applying 2 to 3 pounds of sulfur per 100 square feet of growing area; scratch it lightly into the soil. Mulching with evergreen needles or chopped leaves will help maintain the proper pH.

Leaves mottled yellow. Cause: Whiteflies. See "Whiteflies" on page 290 for controls.

Leaves tunneled. Cause: Leafminers. See "Leaves tunneled" on page 213 for controls.

Leaves with green, white, or brown galls.
Cause: Azalea leaf gall. This fungal leaf gall attacks both azaleas and rhododendrons. Pick off and destroy infected leaves as soon as you spot the galls.

RHUBARB *Rheum rhabarbarum* (Polygonaceae)

Rhubarb is a hardy perennial grown for its red and green leaf stalks that are sweetened and used in pies, or stewed. Rhubarb leaves contain toxic quantities of oxalic acid. Don't eat them: Trim them off harvested stalks and compost them.

Culture

Rhubarb grows best in areas with cool, moist summers and requires a winter cold enough to freeze the top few inches of soil and induce a dormancy period. Choose a weed-free location with deep, sandy (if you have it), well-drained soil, with lots of organic matter. Rhubarb grows best with a pH between 6.0 and 6.8. It is a heavy feeder and will not produce large stalks if underfertilized. Work in plenty of compost before planting and mulch with several inches of high-nitrogen compost each spring. Mix compost with a high-nitrogen supplement such as blood meal or soybean meal to boost its nitrogen content.

Most disease problems can be avoided with proper culture. Do not plant in wet or clayey soils. Use disease-free crowns and soak them in compost tea for 5 minutes before planting. Dispose of dead leaves in the fall to prevent pests and diseases from overwintering.

Do not harvest new plantings for at least 2 years. When you do start to harvest, choose only thick stalks and let the thin stalks feed the roots for the following year. Harvest for only 5 to 7 weeks, then stop, so that plants can store energy for next season. Cut out seed stalks as soon as they form to prevent them from using the plant's energy.

Problems

Stalks thin and small; leaves yellow; crown rotted. Causes: Young plants; overharvested plants; nutrient deficiency; overcrowding; crown or foot rot; waterlogged soil. Spray young plants with fish emulsion or liquid kelp to promote strong early growth. Follow the information under "Culture" on this page to prevent overharvesting or nutrient deficiency.

Rhubarb roots spread vigorously and need to be divided every 5 years or so. As plants become crowded, they produce thinner and thinner stalks.

If the roots or crown are also soft and rotted, the plant is suffering from crown or foot rot. Destroy plants infected with these fungal diseases. Prevent both diseases by planting in raised beds or hills.

Waterlogged soil will produce the same symptoms. Do not let soil get saturated; plant in raised beds.

Leaves yellow; stalks collapse. Causes: Verticillium wilt; crown or foot rot. Destroy dying leaves and plants suffering from these fungal diseases. Do not plant rhubarb where any Verticillium-susceptible crops have grown within the last 3 to 5 years. Prevent fungal disease problems by planting in raised beds.

Leaves yellow with curled margins; plant wilted. Cause: Leafhoppers. These green or brown, spindle-shaped, $\frac{1}{10}$- to $\frac{1}{2}$-inch-long insects suck plant sap. Spray plants with insecticidal soap in the evening to control mild infestations; spray neem as a last resort.

Leaves with small, round, brown spots. Cause: Leaf spots. Fungal leaf spots rarely reduce yields. Destroy diseased leaves after harvest.

Stalks with soft, watery areas. Cause: Anthracnose. Leaves wilt and die. Destroy diseased stalks. Follow recommendations under "Culture" on the opposite page to prevent this fungal disease.

Stalks with small, dark spots or bored holes. Cause: Rhubarb curculios. These yellowish gray, powder-covered, ½- to ¾-inch snout beetles damage stalks by boring holes in which to lay eggs. Handpick adults. Eliminate dock plants from weedy areas; curculios feed on it.

Stalks with brown, sunken spots at base. Cause: Crown or foot rot. Destroy plants infected with these fungal diseases. Prevent both by planting in raised beds or hills.

Stalks and/or leaves with chewed holes. Cause: Caterpillars; Japanese beetles. Ignore damage unless it is severe. Handpick insects. Spray plants with BTK if caterpillars are feeding. Protect plants with row cover early in the spring if caterpillars or beetles have been a problem in the past.

ROSA Rose

Roses are flowering shrubs with compound leaves, usually thorny stems, and flowers in a wide range of forms, colors, and fragrances. Most species are deciduous; there are a few evergreen or semi-evergreen species. In many instances their attractive fruit offers fall and winter interest.

Use roses in shrub borders, in small groups for landscape emphasis, or as single specimens. Climbers can be grown against walls, on trellises and arbors, on fences, or even trained up small trees. Hybrid teas, floribundas, and grandifloras, because they are so demanding in the care they require, are generally grown in beds devoted to roses alone. For low-maintenance roses, stick to the many new disease-resistant landscape roses, such as the Knockout series roses.

Culture

Set out roses in late winter or spring as bare-root or container-grown plants. They grow best in full sun (at least 6 hours per day) and a deep, rich, well-drained soil high in organic matter. Roses tend to do better in loamy or clayey, rather than sandy, soils. Allow plenty of room between plants for good air circulation.

In planting the modern hybrids, pay particular attention to the bud union (the knob where the graft is made). In severe climates, set the bud union 2 inches below the soil surface; in moderate climates, set it even with the soil surface; and in frost-free or nearly frost-free areas, set the bud union 2 inches above the soil surface. Roses are heavy feeders, so fertilize liberally. Don't feed after midsummer, though, or the plant may produce soft growth that will be subject to winter damage.

Problems

Leaves wrinkled and discolored. Cause: Aphids. See "Leaves wrinkled and discolored" on page 250 for controls.

Leaves skeletonized; buds and flowers damaged. Causes: Japanese beetles; sawflies; bristly rose slugs. For controls, see "Leaves skeletonized or plant defoliated." on page 212. Rose sawfly, curled rose sawfly, and, most important, bristly rose slug, have sluglike larvae that skeletonize foliage. They are especially destructive early in the growing season. Handpicking is effective, but be sure to wear gloves; handling these pests can severely irritate your skin. Or spray leaves with insecticidal soap. As a last resort, dust with pyrethrin to control severe infestations.

Leaves skeletonized; flowers eaten. Cause: Rose chafers. Rose chafers, also known as rose bugs, skeletonize foliage and damage flowers. See "Rose Chafer" on page 280 for controls.

Leaves and stems with black spots. Cause: Black spot. Hybrid tea, floribunda, and grandiflora roses are most susceptible to black spot, but hybridizers have introduced many resistant cultivars. Species and shrub roses are little troubled by this disease. To some extent, mulch will prevent the spores from splashing up from the ground onto the leaves during rains; pick off and destroy all diseased leaves and clean up all fallen ones. See "Black Spot" on page 311 for more controls.

Leaves with powdery white coating. Cause: Powdery mildew. The grayish white powdery deposits of this disease form first on young leaves, then spread to older ones and to buds. See "Powdery Mildew" on page 322 for controls.

Flower buds fail to open. Cause: Thrips. These pests cause flower buds with brown edges that fail to open and also cause spots or streaks on open blooms. See "Thrips" on page 287 for controls.

Leaves stippled with yellow; foliage webbed. Cause: Spider mites. For control measures, see "Leaves stippled with yellow; foliage webbed" on page 212.

Canes with discolored or dead areas. Cause: Cankers. A number of fungal cankers attack roses. Pruning off and destroying diseased canes is the best approach to this problem.

Leaf undersides with powdery orange pustules. Cause: Rust. In the western United States, rust causes reddish orange bubbles to appear on the undersides of the leaves. Later, they spread to the upper surfaces. Pick off and destroy infected leaves. See "Rust" on page 315 for more controls.

Leaves with yellow-green mottling. Cause: Viral diseases. Besides discoloring leaves, viruses may also stunt the plant's growth. A number of insects spread viruses as they feed, so keeping insect pests under control will reduce the chances of viral problems. Destroy infected plants immediately.

Flowers fail to open; petals with holes. Cause: Beetles. Rose curculios are $\frac{1}{4}$-inch, bright red, black-beaked insects. Rose leaf beetles are $\frac{1}{8}$-inch, shiny, blue or green pests. Both of these insects bore into flower buds, preventing them from opening. If there are only a few pests, handpicking is the best control. Remove and destroy infested buds. As a last resort for severe infestations, spray leaves and buds with pyrethrin.

Flower buds and new shoots deformed or dead. Cause: Rose midges. The white larvae of this tiny yellow-brown insect feed on flower buds and tender shoot growth, causing the injured parts to turn brown and die. Cut off and destroy all infested buds to reduce future damage.

Shoot tips wilted; leaves with large holes. Cause: Leafcutter bees. Cleanly cut holes in the leaves, either round or oval, suggest the activity of leafcutter bees. After damaging the leaves, these pests bore into canes to lay their eggs, causing the shoots to wilt. Control by pruning out the injured tips several inches below the damaged area. Seal the cut end of the cane with grafting wax or putty.

Shoot tips die back; canes swollen or with small holes. Cause: Stem girdlers and borers. Rose stem girdler causes spiral swellings in the bark; raspberry cane borer causes the tips to die back; and rednecked cane borer and flatheaded appletree borer burrow inside the canes. Cut off and destroy all dead and dying wood.

Leaves stippled with white. Cause: Leafhoppers. See "Leafhoppers" on page 271 for controls.

Leaves yellow; stems and leaves covered with small bumps. Cause: Scales. For controls, see "Leaves yellow; stems and leaves covered with small bumps" on page 213.

Buds fail to open, turn brown. Cause: Botrytis blight. Should the buds on your roses turn brown and decay instead of opening normally, it may indicate a fungal blight. Pick off and destroy diseased blooms; spray plants weekly with sulfur.

Leaves skeletonized or with large holes; branches may be webbed. Cause: Caterpillars. See "Leaves skeletonized or with large holes; branches may be webbed" on page 212 for controls.

Trunk or roots with swollen, wartlike growths. Cause: Crown gall. For more information, see "Trunk or roots with swollen, wartlike growths" on page 214.

ROSEMARY *Rosmarinus officinalis* (Labiatae)

Rosemary is a half-hardy (Zone 8) perennial commonly grown for its aromatic, needlelike leaves. This herb also bears attractive white, pink, or pale or dark blue flowers. In the South, rosemary is an evergreen shrub that can grow 3 inches to 6 feet tall. In the North, grow it in pots and move it indoors during the winter. Start rosemary from cuttings or purchase plants. Seedlings grow very slowly. Rosemary does best in full sun with very well-drained soil and a pH between 6.0 and 8.2. Keep the soil evenly moist.

Rosemary has very few problems except root rot and powdery mildew. Avoid root rot by being careful not to overwater. When planting in containers, choose a very porous potting mix. Powdery mildew can cause fuzzy white growth on leaves and stems. Spray affected plants with potassium bicarbonate or a 0.5 percent solution of baking soda (1 teaspoon baking soda in 1 quart water) for control and to prevent further infection.

RUDBECKIA Coneflower, black-eyed Susan

Cheery, daisylike coneflowers provide masses of warm yellow, gold, or orange blossoms from summer until frost. A dozen or so slightly droopy petals—actually ray florets—surround the rounded, raised, dark brown or greenish center that gives black-eyed Susan (*Rudbeckia hirta*) its name. Plants range from 1½ feet to 6 feet tall with rather coarse, toothed, dark green foliage.

Plant coneflowers in full sun to partial shade in average, well-drained soil. Plants are hardy and moderately tolerant of drought; excess moisture promotes fungal diseases. Coneflowers self-sow but are not invasive. Divide clumps every 4 to 5 years to maintain vigorous, trouble-free plantings.

SAGE *Salvia officinalis* (Labiatae)

Sage is a hardy (Zone 5) perennial herb grown for its pleasantly bitter-tasting leaves. Start sage from cuttings or purchased plants, as seedlings are quite variable. It does best in moderately rich, well-drained soil with a pH between 5.0 and 8.0, and at least 4 hours of sun per day.

Sage is normally quite trouble free. Aster yellows can cause dwarfed, abnormally colored leaves and bushy growth. Destroy infected plants, and control leafhoppers and other sucking insects that spread diseases. Tan or red blisters on leaves are caused by rust. Destroy infected leaves and avoid wetting leaves to prevent its spread. See the Vegetables entry, beginning on page 219, for other possible problems.

SALIX Willow

Willows are deciduous trees and shrubs with simple, alternate leaves. The tree-forming species are principally valued for their graceful, pendulous form; among the shrubs, the immature catkins are valued for cutting and forcing.

Willows love moisture and have questing roots that can invade drains and water pipes. Take care not to locate willows near such structures. Set willows out in spring or fall, in moist (even swampy) soil with sun or light shade.

Problems

Leaves skeletonized or with large holes; branches may be webbed. Cause: Caterpillars. For controls, see "Leaves skeletonized or with large holes; branches may be webbed" and "Leaves skeletonized or plant defoliated" on page 212.

Leaves skeletonized. Causes: Japanese beetles; imported willow leaf beetles. For Japanese beetle controls, see "Leaves skeletonized or plant defoliated," on page 212. Adult imported willow leaf beetles are ¼ inch long, with shiny, blue-black wings. Their ¼-inch larvae, which also feed on leaves, are black and sluglike. Attract beneficial insects to your garden to help control leaf beetles. As a last resort, dust small plants with pyrethrin.

Trunk or branches with small holes; limbs die or break off. Cause: Borers. See "Trunk or branches with small holes; limbs die or break off" on page 214 for controls.

Leaves with brown blotches or tiny holes; shoot tips damaged. Cause: Willow flea weevils. The tiny black adult weevils overwinter in debris on the ground, feed on shoot tips in late spring, and lay eggs on leaves. The larvae emerge in early summer and feed by tunneling within the leaves. The pests come out of the leaves as adults and chew small holes in leaves until winter. On small plants if infestations are severe, control willow flea weevils in the adult stage (spring or fall) by spraying or dusting leaves with pyrethrin.

Leaves wrinkled and discolored. Causes: Aphids; willow lace bugs. See "Leaves wrinkled and discolored" on page 211 for more information on aphids. Willow lace bug adults and larvae also feed on willow leaves, causing severe discoloration. See "Lace Bugs" on page 270 for controls.

Leaves wilted and discolored; branches die back. Cause: Blight. Both a bacterial and a fungal blight attack willows, causing similar symptoms. Prune out and destroy infected branches during the dormant season. Disinfect pruners after each cut in a 10 percent bleach solution (1 part bleach to 9 parts water). As a last resort, spray twice in spring with Bordeaux mix at 10-day intervals, starting when the leaves first unfold.

Trunk or roots with swollen, wartlike growths. Cause: Crown gall. For more information, see "Trunk or roots with swollen, wartlike growths" on page 214.

Trunk or branches with oozing lesions; branch tips die back. Cause: Canker. See "Trunk or branches with oozing lesions; branch tips die back" on page 214 for details.

Leaves yellow; stems and leaves covered with small bumps. Cause: Scales. See "Leaves yellow; stems and leaves covered with small bumps" on page 213.

SALVIA Sage, salvia

This genus of the mint family contains hundreds of perennial and annual species grown for flowers, foliage, and herbal uses. Tubular flowers are carried on upright spikes over bushy, smooth to densely hairy, and often fragrant foliage. Red-flowered plants, such as scarlet sage (*Salvia splendens*), are often annuals or tender perennials, while most perennial species, including garden sage (*S. officinalis*), flower in shades of blue or purple. Silver sage

(*S. argentea*) bears unimpressive white flowers that pale next to the large, crinkly, woolly leaves. Plants grow from 1 to 4 feet tall with similar spread.

Grow sages in full sun or light shade in average, well-drained soil. Some species tolerate heat and drought, but most flower more freely if kept evenly watered. Very hot weather may interrupt blooming, even if plants are well tended. A summer mulch helps retain moisture in the soil and keeps roots cool. In areas where temperatures fall below 0°F, protect perennial species by applying a winter mulch after the soil freezes. Remove faded flower spikes to encourage branching. Few pests or diseases cause significant damage to sages.

SEDUM Sedum, stonecrop

Hundreds of species of durable, succulent plants make up this genus. Some are low-growing creepers that spread vigorously, even in the poorest of soils, while others form 2-foot-tall, upright clumps. Light green, fleshy leaves, tinged with white, red, or bronze in some species, may upstage the blooms. However, showy yellow, pink, or red flowers are the hallmark of sedums such as showy stonecrop (*Sedum spectabile*) and hybrid 'Autumn Joy', which bear profuse, flattened clusters of blooms. Flowering occurs from spring through summer, depending on the species.

Favored as rock garden plants, sedums perform well in most well-drained soils. They endure poor, dry soil. Full sun is best; sedums tolerate some shade, but resulting stems will be weaker. Although drought tolerant, sedums bloom better if watered regularly. Excess moisture encourages rots, especially in winter. Sedum stems and leaves form roots readily.

Sedums are relatively untroubled by pests and

diseases. Aphids are occasionally troublesome; see "Aphids" on page 250 for control information.

SENECIO Dusty miller

Although they sometimes bear 1-inch, yellow flowers, dusty millers are generally grown for their foliage. The lacy leaves of the plant are covered with white hairs, giving the foliage a silvery appearance. Plants grow 1½ to 2 feet tall. Dusty millers are ideal annuals for edging beds and borders, or in window boxes.

Sow seeds indoors in late winter. Don't cover seeds; they need light to germinate. Seedlings appear in 10 days. Because seedlings develop slowly, most gardeners prefer to start with nursery-grown plants. Set out after the last frost, 8 to 10 inches apart.

Dusty millers grow best in full sun with average to fertile, well-drained soil. Pinch off flower heads as they appear. Few pests or diseases bother dusty millers.

SOLENOSTEMON Coleus

Brilliant red, maroon, cream, and green leaves make coleus a colorful addition to the shady garden. They can grow to 3 feet but are usually smaller. The flowers are insignificant, so pinch them off to promote leaf growth.

Sow seeds indoors 10 weeks before the last spring frost. Seeds need light to germinate, so don't cover them. After the last frost, transplant outdoors into rich, well-drained soil and moderate shade. Or, propagate coleus by cuttings, and use cuttings to overwinter colorful forms of this popular annual, which is actually a tender perennial.

Too much sun fades leaves and causes leaves to droop, although new 'Sun Coleus' hybrids withstand full sun. Feed with a balanced fertilizer to encourage vigorous growth and good leaf development.

Coleus are usually trouble free. Mealybugs may feed on plants; see "Mealybugs" on page 273 for controls.

SORBUS Mountain ash

Mountain ashes are fast-growing, alternate-leaved, deciduous trees grown principally for the profuse clusters of white flowers that are followed by brightly colored fruit in autumn. Although rather weak-wooded and very subject to pests and diseases, they are popular as ornamental specimen trees.

Set out in spring as balled-and-burlapped plants. Mountain ashes need sun and a slightly acidic, well-drained location. They are rather intolerant of the air pollution common to cities. Mountain ashes are best adapted to northern gardens; high summer temperatures stress the plant and make it more susceptible to problems.

Problems

Leaves, flowers, and branches blackened. Cause: Fire blight. See "Fire Blight" on page 336 for controls.

Leaves skeletonized. Causes: Japanese beetles; sawflies. For controls, see "Leaves skeletonized or plant defoliated" on page 212.

Trunk or branches with oozing lesions; branch tips die back. Cause: Canker. See "Trunk or branches with oozing lesions; branch tips die back" on page 214 for details.

Leaves distorted, orange-yellow spots on leaf undersides. Cause: Rust. See "Rust" on page 315.

Leaves and berries with black, scabby areas. Cause: Scab. Infected leaves eventually turn yellow and brown before falling off the plant. Damaged fruit is unsightly. Clean up fallen leaves and berries. As a last resort, spray plants the following year with Bordeaux mix, once when buds break in spring and again when flower petals fall.

Leaves wrinkled and discolored. Cause: Aphids. See "Leaves wrinkled and discolored" on page 250 for controls.

Trunk or roots with swollen, wartlike growths. Cause: Crown gall. See "Trunk or roots with swollen, wartlike growths" on page 214 for more information.

Leaves with brownish blisters underneath. Cause: Pear leaf blister mites. These microscopic mites live and feed on tissue inside leaves. They overwinter on buds and infest new leaves in spring. Spray plants in late winter with horticultural oil at a dormant-season dilution or as a last resort with lime-sulfur.

Trunk or branches with small holes; limbs die or break off. Cause: Borers. See "Trunk or branches with small holes; limbs die or break off" on page 214 for controls.

Leaves yellow; stems and leaves covered with small bumps. Cause: Scales. See "Leaves yellow; stems and leaves covered with small bumps" on page 213 for more information.

SPINACH *Spinacia oleracea* (Chenopodiaceae)

Spinach is a cool-season annual vegetable grown for its tender green leaves. It can be grown in spring or fall, and may even survive over winter. Cultivars have smooth or savoyed (crinkled) leaves.

Culture

Grow spinach in well-drained soil with lots of organic matter and a pH between 6.0 and 7.0.

Spinach seed germinates best at soil temperatures between 45° and 75°F, but will germinate as low as 35°F. Mature spinach can survive temperatures of 20°F if gradually hardened. However, prolonged exposure of young plants to temperatures below 45°F will cause bolting—production of a flower stalk—and plants will produce few, low-quality leaves. Temperatures above 75°F and long days also cause bolting. In warmer climates, plant spinach in filtered shade to extend its productivity into the warmer months.

Keep soil moist, but not soggy. Do not allow it to dry out, or plants may bolt. Spread a thin layer of mulch around plants to conserve moisture, suppress weeds, and keep soil cool.

Soak seed in compost tea for 30 minutes before planting to speed germination and help suppress soilborne diseases.

Spinach requires moderate levels of potassium and phosphorus and high levels of nitrogen. It is also sensitive to low levels of calcium and boron. Have the soil tested and amend as necessary. Fast-acting sources of nitrogen, such as blood meal and soybean meal, are good fertilizers for spinach.

Problems

Plant sends up a flower stalk. Causes: Extreme temperatures; long days. Prolonged exposure of young plants to temperatures below 45°F causes plants to bolt, or send up a flower stalk at the expense of succulent leaves. Temperatures above 75°F and long days also cause bolting. Discard bolted plants. Prevent problems by covering early spring plantings with row cover until temperatures are stable and by planting bolt-resistant cultivars. Try planting New Zealand spinach (*Tetragonia tetragonioides*) in summer. Its flavor is similar to that of regular spinach, and it thrives in hot weather.

Leaves yellow; plant stunted and may be wilted. Causes: Nitrogen deficiency; waterlogged soil; Fusarium wilt. If leaves are pale or yellowish, and plants are stunted but not wilted, they may be suffering from nitrogen deficiency or waterlogged soil. Spray plants and drench roots with fish emulsion or liquid kelp to encourage the production of dark green leaves. Prevent problems by choosing well-drained sites, adding organic matter to the soil to increase fertility and improve drainage, and planting in a raised bed.

Wilted plants that are not drought stressed have Fusarium wilt. Destroy infected plants. This fungal disease thrives in warm (70° to 80°F) soil, so avoid problems by raising spinach while the soil is cool in spring or fall.

Leaves yellow and deformed. Causes: Aphids; curly top virus; mosaic virus. Yellow curled leaves and stunted growth can be caused by aphids. Check for these green, pink, black, gray, or white fluffy-coated, soft-bodied, small insects on the undersides of lower leaves, often near the leaf midrib. Spray plants, especially the undersides of the leaves, with water to discourage aphids, or with insecticidal soap if infestation is severe.

If young leaves are yellow, deformed, and stunted, the plant has curly top virus. Deformed leaves may die. If older leaves are also mottled, the plant is suffering from mosaic virus, also called blight or yellows. Destroy infected plants. Control aphids, which spread mosaic as they feed, and beet leafhoppers, which transmit curly top. Prevent some problems by planting mosaic-tolerant cultivars such as 'Melody', 'Renegade', 'Tyee', and 'Winter Bloomsdale'.

Leaves with pale yellow patches on upper surfaces. Causes: Downy mildew; white rust. If spots develop a grayish mold on the undersides of the leaves, they are suffering from downy mildew, a fungal disease. Destroy infected leaves or plants. Prevent problems by thinning plants to increase air circulation and by planting resistant or tolerant cultivars such as 'Lombardia', 'Melody', 'Olympia', 'Samish', 'Space', and 'Tyee'.

If spots develop white blisters on the undersides of the leaves, they have white rust, another fungal disease. Destroy infected leaves or plants. Prevent problems by thinning plants to increase air circulation and by planting tolerant cultivars such as 'Early Prolific' and 'Samish'.

Leaves with water-soaked or brown spots. Causes: Anthracnose; other fungal leaf spots. Spots may enlarge rapidly, especially in wet weather. Destroy infected leaves or plants. Prevent problems by thinning plants to provide good air movement; avoid working amid wet plants.

Leaves with light-colored tunnels or blotches. Cause: Leafminers. Larvae are creamy white, ⅛-inch-long maggots that feed on leaf tissue. Destroy mined leaves. Prevent problems by tilling soil after harvest. Remove weeds that serve as hosts.

Leaves with small holes. Cause: Flea beetles. These tiny, black, brown, or bronze beetles hop when disturbed. Larvae are ¾-inch white grubs with brown heads that feed on roots in the soil. Prevent problems by covering young plants with row cover, which can be left on until harvest as long as temperatures are moderate. Flea beetles can also be discouraged by planting in partial shade.

Leaves with large, ragged holes. Cause: Caterpillars. Various caterpillars will feed on spinach. Handpick, or spray plants with BTK if caterpillars are feeding, or protect plants with row cover.

SPIRAEA Spirea

Spireas are alternate-leaved, deciduous shrubs that flower in late spring. They are best in shrub borders or masses on banks.

Set out in spring or fall in full sun or light shade. A pH below 6.5 suits spireas best, and ample organic matter will ensure the moisture they require. Make sure they are well-mulched and well-watered going into winter.

Problems

Leaves wrinkled and discolored. Cause: Aphids. For control measures, see "Leaves wrinkled and discolored" on page 211.

Leaves rolled and chewed. Cause: Leafrollers. These ½-inch, green caterpillars with brown heads form small webs on shoot tips and feed on leaves and buds inside. See "Leafrollers" on page 272 for controls.

Leaves skeletonized or with large holes; branches may be webbed. Cause: Caterpillars. For controls, see "Leaves skeletonized or with large holes; branches may be webbed" on page 212.

Leaves yellow; stems and leaves covered with small bumps. Cause: Scales. See "Leaves yellow; stems and leaves covered with small bumps" on page 213 for controls.

Leaves, flowers, and branches blackened. Cause: Fire blight. See "Fire Blight" on page 336 for controls.

Whole plant stunted and lacking vigor. Cause: Nematodes. See "Whole plant stunted and lacking vigor" on page 215 for controls.

Leaves with powdery white coating. Cause: Powdery mildew. For controls, see "Leaves with powdery white coating" on page 213.

SQUASH *Cucurbita* spp. (Cucurbitaceae)

Squash are frost-tender annuals grown for their fleshy fruit. Summer squash, such as zucchini, are eaten before the seeds and rinds harden. Winter squash are harvested after the fruit is mature. The name pumpkin is used for some winter squash. Species include: *Cucurbita maxima, C. mixta, C. moschata,* and *C. pepo.*

Culture

Squash seeds need 60°F soil to germinate, so wait until warm weather to plant. Cover plants with floating row cover to protect them from insects and late cold snaps. Remove row cover when plants begin to flower so insects can pollinate the blossoms, or you will not get any fruit.

Squash do best in well-drained, loose-textured soils with a pH between 5.5 and 6.8, but prefer a pH above 6.0. Although squash need lots of water, don't let soil become saturated. Prevent disease problems by keeping the leaves dry. Mulch squash to help conserve water. Black plastic is a good choice for northern areas, but in extremely warm areas it can warm the soil too much. Organic mulches are good, but may provide shelter for pests like squash bugs. Foil mulches help prevent aphid problems. To prevent rot, raise fruit off the soil on scraps of wood.

Rotate crops so that no member of the cucurbit family (cucumbers, melons, and squash) is grown in the same place more often than every 4 years.

Caution: Squash leaves are easily damaged by even organically acceptable sprays such as insecticidal soap. Use the most dilute spray recommended and use sparingly. Do not spray plants in direct sun or if temperatures are above 80°F, and don't spray drought-stressed plants.

Leaf and Vine Problems

Leaves with chewed holes. Cause: Cucumber beetles. Adults are ¼-inch-long, greenish yellow beetles with black stripes or spots. Larvae chew on roots. They attack young leaves and should be controlled immediately, as they can spread bacterial wilt or viral diseases. To deter beetle feeding, apply kaolin clay, especially to leaf undersides, and reapply after rain; handpick or vacuum beetles. As a last resort, spray infested plants with pyrethrin. Reduce problems by planting cultivars, such as 'Baby Pam', 'Bennings Green Tint', 'Blue Hubbard', 'Early Butternut Hybrid', 'Seneca', and 'Table Ace', that tolerate beetles.

Leaves with pale green patches; afflicted leaves wilt and blacken. Cause: Squash bugs. Adults are brownish black, ½-inch-long bugs. Immature bugs are whitish green with dark heads and legs. Eggs are bright orange and laid on undersides of leaves. Handpick adults and eggs. Trap bugs by laying a board near plants. Squash bugs will hide underneath it and can be destroyed each morning. To reduce problems, plant cultivars that tolerate squash bugs, such as 'Early Prolific', 'Early Summer', 'Royal Acorn', 'Sweet Cheese', and 'Table Queen'.

Leaves with yellow patches; older leaves mottled and distorted. Cause: Mosaic. Several types of mosaic viruses are found on squash. Besides affecting leaves, mosaics may also cause deformed fruit that is mottled with yellow and green. Remove and destroy diseased plants. Control aphids and cucumber beetles; they spread the disease. Reduce problems by planting cultivars, such as 'Bobcat', 'Lioness', 'Lynx', 'Multipik', 'Plato', 'Superpik', 'Superset', and 'Tigress', that tolerate mosaic.

Leaves yellow, curled, and wilted. Cause:

Aphids. Look for small, green, pink, gray, black, or white fluffy-coated, soft-bodied insects feeding on plants. Aphids can also transmit viral diseases. Control aphids by knocking them off the plants with a strong blast of water. Or spray with weak insecticidal soap; read the caution on page 193 before spraying. Prevent problems by using a reflective silver mulch or by planting silver-leaved cultivars, such as 'Cocozelle', that confuse or don't attract aphids.

Leaves yellow and puckered, becoming bronzed. Cause: Mites. These tiny, red, yellow, or green, spiderlike pests are worst in dry, hot weather. In severe cases leaves dry out and drop off. There may be fine webbing on the undersides of leaves. Spray plants with a weak insecticidal soap spray to control; see the caution on page 193 before spraying.

Leaves mottled yellow between veins; purple spots on leaf undersides. Cause: Downy mildew. As the disease progresses, spots enlarge, older leaves turn brown and die, and younger leaves become infected. Remove and destroy badly infected leaves. Downy mildew thrives during cool, moist weather. Avoid wetting foliage when watering, especially when conditions favor this fungus. Sprays of potassium bicarbonate may give some control as well as reduce the spread of the disease. Prevent problems by planting tolerant cultivars such as 'Sunray'.

Leaves with spots, blotches, or brown areas. Causes: Powdery mildew; angular leaf spot; scab; Alternaria leaf blight; other fungal and bacterial diseases. Various diseases attack squash. Reduce problems by keeping foliage dry when watering and by not working amid wet plants. Remove and destroy infected foliage; provide good air circulation around plants; water and mulch to prevent drought stress. Organic fungicides, including *Bacillus subtilis,* potassium bicarbonate, or

a 0.5 percent solution of baking soda (1 teaspoon baking soda in 1 quart water) may slow the spread of an infection and give some control. Spray infected plants thoroughly.

Powdery white spots, especially on upper leaf surfaces, are caused by powdery mildew. As the disease progresses, leaves turn brown and dry, and plants may die. Prevent problems by planting resistant cultivars such as 'Anton', 'Bush Delicata', 'Lynx', 'Metro PMR', 'Soleil', 'Sunray', and 'Tiptop PMR'.

Water-soaked spots that turn gray, die, and drop out leaving shotholes are caused by angular leaf spot. Fruit infected with angular leaf spot has small, cracked, white spots. Water-soaked spots can also be caused by scab. Scab causes sunken brown spots with gummy ooze on fruit; damage is worst in cool, moist weather.

Dark brown spots with concentric rings, usually appearing on older leaves first, are caused by Alternaria leaf blight. As the disease progresses, spots enlarge and merge, and leaves curl down and eventually drop off. Infected fruit has dark, concentrically ringed, sunken spots.

Vines wilt suddenly. Cause: Squash vine borers. These fat, white, 1-inch-long larvae burrow into the stems and exude masses of yellow-green, sawdustlike excrement. Slit stems lengthwise above injury with a sharp knife and kill larvae. Cover cut stems with moist soil so they will form new roots. Injecting stems with BTK or parasitic nematodes may also control borers. To reduce problems, plant the cultivar 'Sweet Mama Hybrid', which is resistant to vine borers. Or spray base of stems with BTK once a week in late spring and early summer.

Vines wilt at midday, starting with younger leaves; leaves remain green. Cause: Bacterial wilt. As the disease progresses, leaves fail to recover, and die. Cut wilted stems and press out drops of sap. If it is milky, sticky, and astringent, your plant is infected. Destroy infected plants immediately. Control cucumber beetles, since they spread the disease.

Fruit Problems

Flowers appear but no fruit develops. Cause: Male flower; lack of pollination. Male flowers open a week or more before female flowers and don't form fruit. If female flowers fail to set fruit, or if small fruit turns black and rots starting at blossom end, they haven't been pollinated. Pollinate open female flowers by hand.

Fruit misshapen. Causes: Diseases; poor pollination. Many diseases cause misshapen fruit; use leaf symptoms (if any) to diagnose the problem (see "Leaf and Vine Problems" on page 193). If leaves are healthy, high temperatures may have damaged pollen, or bees may not have been active.

Fruit with spots; flesh may rot. Causes: Angular leaf spot; Alternaria blight; scab. Several fungal and bacterial diseases cause these symptoms on squash fruit. For complete controls, see "Leaves with spots, blotches, or brown areas" on the opposite page.

Fruit tunneled. Cause: Pickleworms. Larvae are pale green with black, and up to ¾ inch long. Keep fruit off ground or mulch, since worms feed at soil level.

STRAWBERRY *Fragaria × ananassa* (**Rosaceae**)

Strawberries are herbaceous perennials growing from crowns that send forth whorls of leaves, flowers, and surface runners with new daughter plants at their nodes. June-bearing strawberries bloom in spring for a single crop. Everbearing strawberries bloom and fruit in spring and again in fall. Day-neutral strawberries are unaffected by day length

and bear heavily from June through frost in northern areas; January through August in milder climates. Day-neutrals are somewhat more difficult to grow than the other types; they are fragile and sensitive to heat, drought, and weed competition.

Culture

Plant strawberries in well-drained soil rich in organic matter. The ideal location is in full sun on high or sloping ground. Avoid frost-prone, low-lying areas.

To prevent diseases associated with overcrowding, allow a square foot of space for each plant. Choose one of three different planting systems: hill, matted row, or spaced runner. For a hill system, space plants 1 foot apart each way in double rows, with 2 to 3 feet between each double row. Remove every runner so plants channel their energy into producing large berries. Since plants are well spaced, the hill system minimizes diseases associated with crowding. For a matted-row system, space plants 1½ to 2 feet apart in rows 4 feet apart. Allow the runners and daughter plants to grow in all directions to form a wide, solid row. For the spaced-runner system, set plants closer than the matted row; remove all but a few runners. Pin down runner tips so daughter plants are about 8 inches apart in every direction.

Even well-managed strawberries will decline after a few seasons. Start a fresh bed in a new site with new plants every few years. Renovate June-bearers each year right after harvest. Cut off and rake away leaves; dig out old, woody plants; and thin out remaining plants. Then fertilize and water.

Flower and Fruit Problems

Fruit deeply furrowed or gnarled (cat-faced). Causes: Tarnished plant bugs; frost damage. Tarnished plant bugs can damage strawberries by injecting a toxin into fruit while sucking fluids from stem tips, buds, and fruit. Since they overwinter in dead garden refuse, the simplest control is to clean out dead plant tops at the end of the season. A floating row cover applied during the growing season also helps minimize damage. As a last resort, apply pyrethrin to flowering plants.

Flowers damaged by frost will produce deformed, cat-faced fruit. If spring frost threatens, cover beds overnight.

Fruit with holes. Causes: Slugs and snails; earwigs; birds. Silvery trails near holes indicate slugs or snails. Keep these pests out with barriers of copper flashing, dry ashes, or diatomaceous earth. After rain, renew ashes or diatomaceous earth. Or trap slugs under boards, in overturned clay pots, or in saucers of beer.

Earwigs, leathery brown insects with pincers at their abdomen tips, nibble holes in fruit. Since they hide in dark places, trap them in short lengths of hose or rolled-up newspaper. Check traps and destroy captured earwigs daily.

The best defense against birds is a net, well secured at the edges. See "Birds" on page 304 for controls.

Fruit rotted. Causes: Gray mold; leather mold. Both diseases strike during rainy weather. Fruit that rots rapidly and then turns into fuzzy balls is infected with gray mold. Blossoms infected with gray mold turn brown and die.

Leather mold causes fruit to turn dark and leathery. Infected fruit is bitter tasting. To minimize fungal diseases, thin plants to reduce overcrowding and mulch beds to keep fruit off the soil. Pick and dispose of infected fruits as soon as you notice them. Annual bed renovation helps control gray mold.

Leaf Problems

Leaves with spots. Causes: Leaf spot; leaf blight; leaf scorch. Leaf spot causes small purple spots that develop tan centers on foliage. Leaf blight is characterized by oval or V-shaped spots with purple centers and tan borders. Irregular, purplish blotches are symptoms of leaf scorch. When severe, these diseases kill leaves, weakening plants. Berries are spotted as well. You can control all three fungal diseases by annual bed renovation. Cultivars resistant to leaf blight and leaf spot include 'Albritton', 'Apollo', 'Atlas', 'Earlibelle', 'Sentinel', 'Sumner', and 'Surecrop'. 'Cardinal', 'Delite', 'Guardian', 'Jewel', 'Lateglow', 'Primetime', 'Redchief', 'Surecrop', and 'Winona' are resistant to leaf spot and leaf scorch.

Leaves with a white powdery coating. Cause: Powdery mildew. The powdery coating may be less apparent on strawberries than with other mildew-afflicted plants. The undersides of infected leaves turn reddish and the edges roll up. Infected fruit is stunted, rotted, or fails to ripen. Keeping plants adequately spaced and cleaning up dead plant debris help minimize this fungal disease. Water and mulch to prevent drought stress. Apply *Bacillus subtilis,* potassium bicarbonate, or a 0.5 percent solution of baking soda (1 teaspoon baking soda in 1 quart water) as preventives or to help to control the disease. Mildew-resistant cultivars include 'Albritton', 'Catskill', 'Earlibelle', 'Sparkle', 'Sunrise', or 'Surecrop'.

Leaves rolled up. Cause: Strawberry leafrollers. These green or brown, ½-inch caterpillars mine leaves in early spring and later form webs and roll leaves as they feed. Leaves may brown and die; fruit is deformed. For light infestations, pick and destroy rolled leaves along with the caterpillars inside. Treat heavy infestations with BTK.

Leaves surrounded by frothy white mass.
Cause: Spittlebugs. These tiny tan, brown, or black insects, which hide inside the frothy masses of bubbles they produce, suck sap from leaves, stems, and flowers. Spittlebugs rarely cause significant damage. Wash them off plants with a strong spray of water.

Leaves with brown, dry undersides and fine webbing. Cause: Spider mites. Heavy pesticide use often kills naturally occurring mite predators, resulting in an abundance of spider mites. Spider mites also multiply in dry, dusty conditions. Repeated sprays with plain or soapy water usually control mites. For heavy mite infestation, purchase and release predatory mites (*Phytoseiulus persimilis* or similar species). As a last resort, spray with insecticidal soap or neem.

Whole Plant Problems

Whole plant wilted or collapsed. Causes: Black root rot; red stele disease; Verticillium wilt; strawberry crown moth larvae; strawberry crown borers. To discover which cause applies, remove a plant from the soil and examine its roots.

Rotting black roots indicate black root rot; plants are stunted, produce few fruits, and may die at fruiting time. If roots have few or no side roots and are red inside when slit lengthwise, red stele is the problem. Both fungal diseases survive in soils for up to 10 years without a host plant; the only control is to plant new plants in well-drained soil at a new site. Cultivars resistant to some strains of red stele include 'Allstar', 'Cavendish', 'Delmarvel', 'Earliglow', 'Guardian', 'Redchief', 'Sparkle', 'Tribute', 'Tristar', and 'Winona'.

Wilted plants with no root damage may have Verticillium wilt. Verticillium-infected plants look stunted and may collapse during their first summer in the ground; inner leaves may remain green until the plant dies. There is no cure for Verticillium wilt. You must plant a new bed where you haven't grown strawberries or other Verticillium-susceptible plants, such as tomatoes, peppers, potatoes, or eggplants, for the past few years. Verticillium-resistant cultivars include 'Catskill', 'Guardian', 'Lateglow', 'Robinson', 'Sunrise', 'Surecrop', and 'Tristar'.

Wilted plants with healthy roots may be infested with strawberry crown moth larvae or strawberry crown borer larvae. Crown borers are ¼-inch snout beetles and crown moths are large, clear-winged moths. Both pests lay eggs on strawberries. The resulting grublike larvae burrow into plant crowns and cause wilting and death. Cut crowns of wilted plants in half. If you find a large tunnel, your plants are infected with one of these pests. The only cure is to dig up and destroy these plants immediately. Crown borers don't fly and can't crawl more than 300 feet, so starting with clean plants planted far from old infested beds keeps this pest in check.

Whole plant stunted; roots and crown chewed. Cause: Strawberry root weevils. The brown-headed, white larvae feed on plant crowns and roots; the black, ¼-inch adult weevils may feed on leaves. Apply parasitic nematodes to the soil to control larvae. Shake weevils off plants at night onto a dropcloth and destroy them.

SWEET POTATO *Ipomoea batatas* (**Convolvulaceae**)

Sweet potatoes are perennial vegetables grown as annuals in temperate regions for their tuberous roots. While they are tropical natives, you can grow them if you get at least 100 frost-free days. Cultivars have light yellow to purplish red skin, and white to deep orange flesh.

Culture

Sweet potatoes prefer loose, well-drained soil with a pH between 6.0 and 6.5. They require moderate amounts of nitrogen and boron, moderate to high levels of phosphorus, and high levels of potassium. Have the soil tested and amend as necessary before planting. Sweet potatoes do well in raised beds. Work in lots of organic matter before planting. Avoid top-dressing after early summer, or root formation may be interrupted.

Keep soil moist, but not soggy, until the vines begin to spread. After that, water only if vines wilt. When the roots begin to enlarge in late summer, keep the soil moist again until harvest. Mulch plants to suppress weeds and conserve moisture. Black plastic mulch will also warm the soil.

Plant sweet potatoes where they have not been grown for at least 2 years. After harvest, cut vines and let dry, then compost or till under to reduce disease buildup.

Purchase disease-free plants, or start your own from healthy, overwintered roots. Plant out when nights stay above 60°F. Soak plant roots in compost tea for 5 minutes before planting to help reduce disease problems. Water in with fish emulsion or liquid kelp after planting to give the plants a good start.

Dig potatoes gently before the first frost, after foliage starts to yellow. Dry them for 2 to 3 hours in the garden. Sort out any damaged or diseased potatoes to use as soon as possible. Cure healthy potatoes for 10 days in an 80° to 85°F humid area. Gradually reduce temperature and store them in a 55° to 60°F humid room.

Leaf and Whole Plant Problems

Leaves yellow between veins. Causes: Stem rot; Fusarium wilt. Symptoms of stem rot, also known as bacterial soft rot, usually appear when temperatures are above 90°F. Leaves turn yellow, vines wilt, and stems are black and shiny at the base. Destroy diseased plants. Roots may already be rotted or will rot in storage, so use any healthy potatoes as soon as possible. Prevent problems by planting disease-free plants or tolerant cultivars such as 'Earlysweet', 'Eureka', 'Excel', and 'Redgold'.

If young leaves are yellow and wilted, and older leaves drop, the plant is suffering from Fusarium wilt. The stems may have a faint purple coloration just below the soil line. Destroy plants infected with this fungal disease. Prevent problems by planting disease-free plants or resistant cultivars such as 'Allgold', 'Beauregard', 'Carolina Ruby', 'Carver', 'Excel', 'Jewel', 'Hernandez', 'Patriot', and 'White Regal'.

Leaves with purple-bordered yellow spots. Cause: Internal cork. Destroy infected plants. See "Potatoes with hard, dark, corky spots in the center of flesh" on the opposite page for controls.

Leaves yellow with dead, brown spots; plant stunted. Cause: Nematodes. See "Potatoes with rough, rotted pits" on the opposite page for controls.

Leaves thin and pale, plant stunted. Cause: Pox. See "Potatoes with rough, rotted pits" on the opposite page for controls.

Leaves riddled with small holes. Cause: Flea beetles. These tiny, black, brown, or bronze insects hop like fleas when disturbed. Adults can transmit disease when feeding, and larvae damage roots. Control flea beetle adults by covering plants with row cover as soon as they are planted out. Use garlic spray or kaolin clay to deter feeding on leaves. Apply parasitic nematodes to the soil to help control larvae. Reduce problems by planting tolerant cultivars such as 'Carolina Ruby', 'Centennial', 'Jewel', and 'Patriot'.

Leaves with large, round holes. Causes: Tortoise beetles; caterpillars. Tortoise beetles are ¼-inch-long, oval, flattened beetles with varying colors and patterns on their wing covers. Larvae are ½ inch long and have flattened bodies with spiny margins and a forked horn at the tail end. Both adults and larvae damage young plants. Handpick to control mild infestations, or spray plants with insecticidal soap; use pyrethrin if damage is severe.

Caterpillars sometimes feed on sweet potato leaves. Spray plants with BTK if caterpillars are feeding.

Root Problems

Potatoes long and spindly. Causes: Potassium deficiency; growing season too short. Check for deficiency with a soil test and amend soil as necessary. Sweet potatoes need a long growing season. Prevent problems by planting cultivars suited to your region.

Potatoes cracked. Cause: Uneven soil moisture. If soil is alternately dry then wet, roots may split their skins. Prevent problems by keeping soil evenly moist and storage humidity constant. Some cultivars, such as 'Covington' and 'Sunnyside', are somewhat resistant to cracking.

Potatoes with dark discolored patches on skin. Cause: Scurf. Symptoms often appear in storage. Initial damage is only skin deep, but subsequently, skin may split open, causing the flesh to shrivel up. Prevent this fungal disease by planting disease-free plants and by keeping storage temperatures above 50°F.

Potatoes with black, circular, corky depressions. Cause: Black rot. Symptoms of this fungal disease may develop in the garden or in storage. Flesh under spots is brown to green and has a bitter taste, so trim well before using. Pre-vent problems by starting with disease-free plants, controlling root-feeding insects, and by planting resistant cultivars such as 'Allgold', 'Apache', 'Hernandez', 'Nugget', 'Redgold', and 'Sunnyside'.

Potatoes with hard, dark, corky spots in the center of flesh. Cause: Internal cork. This condition develops if storage conditions are too warm and may be caused by a viral disease. Store potatoes between 55° and 60°F to reduce problems. Prevent problems by planting tolerant cultivars such as 'Allgold', 'Centennial', 'Eureka', 'Excel', 'Jewel', 'Redgold', and 'White Regal'.

Potatoes with rough, rotted pits. Causes: Pox; nematodes. Plants with pox, a bacterial disease, may be pale and stunted, and roots often resemble a string of irregular beads. Destroy infected plants; use any healthy roots as soon as possible. Prevent problems by planting disease-free plants. Adjust the soil pH to below 5.2 by adding sulfur if pox has been a major problem in the past. While this is below the optimal pH range for sweet potatoes, they will tolerate it and the bacteria will be inactive.

Root-knot and other pest nematodes cause poorly colored, deformed potatoes with rotted areas under the skin, surface blemishes, and surface cracks. Control pest nematodes by applying chitin or parasitic nematodes to the soil. Prevent problems by planting nematode-resistant cultivars such as 'Apache', 'Carver', 'Excel', 'Jewel', 'Hernandez', 'Nemagold', 'Nugget', 'Patriot', 'Ruddy', and 'White Regal'.

Potatoes with small holes, tunnels, or shallow splits. Causes: Flea beetle larvae; sweet potato weevils; wireworms. Sweet potato flea beetle larvae tunnel just under the skin. As the roots grow, the skin over the tunnels splits open, leaving shallow scars. Larvae are 3/16-inch, slender, and white. Striped flea beetle larvae are white and up to ¾ inch long; they tunnel into the center of roots leaving wandering, branched tunnels. See "Leaves riddled with small holes" on page 198 for controls.

Sweet potato weevil adults are small, reddish, antlike insects. Larvae are white with pale brown heads and grow up to ⅜ inch long. Larvae tunnel into potatoes in the field or in storage. Weevils do not hibernate and must have food to survive. Destroy all plant residue and weeds after harvest to control them. Apply parasitic nematodes to the soil if weevils have been a problem in the past.

Wireworm larvae are yellow to reddish brown, slender, tough-bodied, segmented worms with brown heads and grow up to 1½ inches long. Adults are dark-colored, elongated click beetles. To prevent problems, don't plant sweet potatoes in soil where grass or grain grew the previous season. Apply parasitic nematodes to the soil before planting, and plant tolerant cultivars such as 'Allgold', 'Nugget', 'Patriot', and 'Ruddy'.

Potatoes with large, shallow feeding scars or hollow cavities. Causes: White grubs; cutworms; cucumber beetles. White grubs are fat, whitish larvae that tend to feed over the whole surface of the potato. Adults are Japanese or June beetles. Apply parasitic nematodes to the soil before planting to control.

Cutworms are grayish or dull brown caterpillars that curl up when disturbed and are active at night. Cutworms tend to feed near the ends of potatoes. Sprinkle moist bran mixed with BTK on the soil surface in the evening, or add parasitic nematodes to the soil before planting to control cutworms.

Spotted cucumber beetle larvae (also called southern corn rootworms) are white with brown heads and grow up to ½ inch long. Adults are ¼-inch, greenish yellow beetles with black spots. Handpick or vacuum adult beetles; spray kaolin clay to discourage leaf feeding. Prevent problems by covering plants with row cover. Spray infested plants with pyrethrin if the damage is severe.

Potatoes turn spongy in storage. Cause: Cold injury. Cool temperatures can damage sweet potatoes. Harvest when air is above 50°F and store above 50°F to prevent injury.

Potatoes rot in storage. Cause: Various bacterial and fungal diseases. Prevent problems by planting disease-free plants and curing and storing potatoes at the recommended temperatures and humidity levels; see "Culture" on page 198 for instructions.

SYRINGA Lilac

Lilacs are among the most popular of deciduous flowering shrubs. They bloom in late spring in shades of white, purple, lavender, and pink; borne in large clusters, the flowers are exquisitely fragrant. Lilacs are plants of cool weather; with few exceptions, they do not flourish south of Zone 7. Lilacs are best used in the mixed shrub border, grouped for emphasis in the landscape, or planted for screening.

Plant in spring or fall in full sun with neutral or slightly alkaline soil enriched with ample organic matter. Prune and deadhead them immediately after blooming. Lilacs are available either on their own roots or grafted onto privet roots; the former are much preferred. Cut back to the ground any suckers that form.

Problems

Leaves with powdery white coating. Cause: Powdery mildew. For more on this very common problem, see "Leaves with powdery white coating" on page 213 for controls.

Leaves tunneled. Cause: Leafminers. For controls, see "Leaves tunneled" on page 213.

Leaves yellow; stems and leaves covered with small bumps. Cause: Scales. See "Leaves yellow, stems and leaves covered with small bumps" on page 213 for control measures.

Trunk or branches with small holes; limbs die or break off. Cause: Borers. For details, see "Trunk or branches with small holes; limbs die or break off" on page 214.

Leaves wilted and discolored; branches die back. Cause: Blight. Both a bacterial and a fungal blight attack lilacs, causing similar symptoms. Prune out and destroy infected branches during the dormant season. Disinfect pruners after each cut in a 10 percent bleach solution (1 part bleach to 9 parts water). As a last resort, in spring, spray twice with Bordeaux mix at 10-day intervals, starting when the leaves first unfold.

Leaves with spots. Cause: Leaf spots. See "Leaves with spots" on page 213 for controls.

Leaves pale and drop early; branches wilt and die. Cause: Wilt. Prune off dead and diseased branches. Feeding with a high-nitrogen fertilizer may help plants recover. Remove and destroy badly infected shrubs, and don't plant lilacs in the same soil.

Leaves skeletonized or with large holes; branches may be webbed. Cause: Caterpillars. For control measures, see "Leaves skeletonized or with large holes; branches may be webbed" on page 212.

Shoots clustered tightly, with small leaves. Cause: Witch's broom. This problem is usually not serious; merely prune out and destroy the dense, bushy growth.

TAGETES Marigold

Hearty marigolds are a mainstay of the early summer to late fall garden. Flower colors range from palest yellow and near white to red, orange, and mahogany; many are bicolored. Single or double blooms may be 1 to 6 inches wide. The 6- to 36-inch plants are covered with finely cut leaves. Marigolds may have a strong odor; if you dislike the scent, look for an odorless cultivar. Marigolds are good bedding plants, container plants, and cut flowers.

It's easy to raise marigolds by sowing the seed directly into the garden 2 to 3 weeks before the last frost. For best results, hold the white tuft of each seed and place the long dark section into the ground at an angle. Indoors, seeds sown in flats germinate within 2 weeks at about 70°F. Move outdoors only after all frost danger has passed. Thin or plant 8 to 18 inches apart.

Marigolds thrive in full sun, except in southern and southwestern areas, where afternoon shade prolongs bloom. They demand regular watering and well-drained, average soil. Pick off old flower heads. Taller cultivars need staking. Avoid overhead watering, as even the small blossoms hold water like cups, and the weight may cause the brittle stems to snap. If you work compost into the soil at planting time, no extra fertilizer is necessary.

Problems

Leaves skeletonized; flowers eaten. Cause: Japanese beetles. See "Japanese Beetle" on page 269 for controls.

Leaves stippled with yellow; foliage webbed. Cause: Spider mites. For control measures, see "Mites, Spider" on page 275.

Flowers covered with gray mold. Cause:

Botrytis blight. See "Botrytis Blight" on page 326 for controls.

Stems turn black at base; plant wilts. Cause: Stem rot. Caused by either bacteria or fungi, stem rot starts at the soil level and works upward. Remove and destroy infected plants. Don't replant marigolds in that area unless you first solarize the soil.

Leaves greenish yellow; growth poor. Cause: Aster yellows. For more information, see "Yellows" on page 321.

TAXUS Yew

Yews are evergreen shrubs and trees with needle-shaped leaves arranged densely and spirally on the branches. The male and female flowers are separate on the plants, with the females producing fleshy red berries, each surrounding a toxic seed. Yews can be used as foundation plants, hedges, and even specimens.

Set out in spring as balled-and-burlapped or container-grown plants. Yews prefer a well-drained but moisture-retentive soil and grow well in full sun or partial shade.

Problems

Leaves with notched edges. Cause: Black vine weevils. See "Root Weevils" on page 279 for controls.

Leaves stippled with yellow; foliage webbed. Cause: Spider mites. See "Leaves stippled with yellow; foliage webbed" on page 212 for controls.

Leaves discolored, wilted, or dropping; plant lacking vigor. Causes: Mealybugs; blights. The tiny, powdery-looking, white adult mealybugs generally congregate on the trunks and interior branches, making them difficult to see until the plant starts to weaken. See "Mealybugs" on page 273 for controls.

Various blights can cause similar symptoms on yews. If you don't see the fluffy white masses that are a sign of mealybugs, suspect blight. Cutting off the affected portion of the plant is the best way to deal with this disease.

Leaves yellow; stems and leaves covered with small bumps. Cause: Scales. See "Leaves yellow; stems and leaves covered with small bumps" on page 213 for controls.

Leaves yellow. Causes: Low pH; waterlogged soil. Yews prefer soils with a neutral or slightly acid pH (around 6.5). They do not grow well in highly acid soils, so avoid interplanting them with rhododendrons or other acid-loving plants. Raise the soil pH around your yews by adding 3 pounds of ground limestone per 100 square feet of soil area.

Too much water around plant roots causes similar symptoms. Avoid overwatering and planting in poorly drained areas. Improving the drainage around plants will help them recover.

THALICTRUM Meadow rue

Tall plants with blue-green, fernlike foliage and loosely fluffy clusters of lavender or yellow flowers, meadow rues range from 1 foot to over 5 feet tall. Columbine meadow rue (*Thalictrum aquilegifolium*) has leaves resembling columbine foliage; other species' leaves look like those of maidenhair ferns.

Grow meadow rues in moist, well-drained, richly organic soil and partial shade. Tall flower stems need shelter from strong winds and may require staking. Water regularly to maintain soil moisture. Divide every 4 to 5 years to reduce crowding.

Meadow rues have few insect pests. Fungal

diseases such as powdery mildew may damage foliage and are best controlled with cultural practices. See "Powdery Mildew" on page 322 for controls.

THUJA Arborvitae

Arborvitaes are evergreen trees and shrubs with flat sprays of scalelike leaves. They are excellent in foundation plantings and used as hedges; upright cultivars make strong specimen plants.

Set out in spring or fall as container-grown or balled-and-burlapped plants. Arborvitaes thrive in deep, moist, well-drained soil in full sun. If possible, choose a site protected from strong winter winds to avoid damage.

Problems

Plant defoliated; branches bear cocoonlike bags. Cause: Bagworms. These pests are one of the most common problems on arborvitae. For control measures, see "Plant defoliated; branches bear cocoonlike bags" on page 212.

Leaves yellow; stems and leaves covered with small bumps. Cause: Scales. For controls, see "Leaves yellow; stems and leaves covered with small bumps" on page 213.

Leaves stippled with yellow; foliage webbed. Cause: Spider mites. See "Leaves stippled with yellow; foliage webbed" on page 212.

Plant defoliated. Cause: Hemlock loopers. The 1-inch-long, greenish yellow, black-spotted caterpillars usually appear in June. They feed on the needles, starting from the branch tips and working toward the center of the plant. Hand-pick small populations; control large infestations with BTK.

Leaves tunneled. Cause: Leafminers. See "Leaves tunneled" on page 213 for controls.

Trunk or branches with small holes; limbs die or break off. Cause: Borers. For more information, see "Trunk or branches with small holes; limbs die or break off" on page 214.

Leaves with spots. Cause: Leaf spots. See "Leaves with spots" on page 213 for controls.

Branch tips die back. Causes: Blight; winter injury; sun scorch; drought stress. Blight, a fungal disease, attacks mostly during cool, wet weather. See "Branch tips die back" on page 167 for more information and controls.

If you see the same symptoms in very early spring or during hot, dry weather, your arborvitae may be suffering from winter injury, sun scorch, or drought stress. Minimize damage by watering deeply and regularly during dry periods. A thick mulch may also help by retaining moisture and keeping roots cool.

THUNBERGIA Thunbergia

Thunbergias are showy, twining climbers ranging from 10 to 20 feet high. The 1½- to 3-inch flowers may be orange with dark brown centers, white with red centers, pure orange, or purple-blue. All need some type of support unless used in hanging baskets.

Sow seeds indoors 6 weeks before the last frost. Germination takes 2 to 3 weeks. Seedlings grow slowly. Place outdoors when night temperatures are above 50°F. Thunbergias have little cold tolerance, even as mature plants.

Grow plants in full sun to light shade with fertile, well-drained soil. Avoid sites with reflected light, which can cause leaf sunburn. If spider mites attack leaves, see "Mites, Spider" on page 275. Powdery mildew can also be a problem; see "Powdery Mildew" on page 322 for controls.

THYME *Thymus vulgaris* and other species (Labiatae)

Thyme is a hardy (Zone 5) perennial herb grown for its tiny, aromatic leaves. It does best in light, dry, well-drained soil with a pH between 5.0 and 8.0. Thyme needs at least 4 hours of full sun per day. Start pinches of seed indoors in 70°F planting mix, purchase plants, or grow them from cuttings.

Thyme is normally quite problem free. Dark spots on leaves are caused by fungal leaf spot. Spray foliage with fish emulsion to prevent the spread of mild infections. Tan or red blisters on leaves are caused by rust, a fungal disease. Destroy infected leaves and avoid wetting leaves to prevent its spread. See the Vegetables entry, beginning on page 219, for other possible problems.

TILIA Linden

Lindens are deciduous shade trees, principally valued for their foliage. Their summer flowers are fragrant and attractive to bees. Lindens are widely used as street trees and, because they adapt well to pruning, for tall hedges.

Set out in spring or fall in full sun. Lindens tolerate drought and a wide range of soil conditions, although they perform best in deep moist soils.

Problems

Leaves wrinkled and discolored. Cause: Aphids. These pests, and the black, sooty mold that grows on the sticky honeydew they produce, are a common problem on lindens. For control measures, see "Leaves wrinkled and discolored" on page 211.

Leaves skeletonized. Causes: Japanese beetles; sawflies. See "Leaves skeletonized or plant defoliated" on page 212 for controls.

Plant defoliated; branches bear cocoonlike bags. Cause: Bagworms. For controls, see "Plant defoliated; branches bear cocoonlike bags" on page 212.

Leaves skeletonized or with large holes; branches may be webbed. Cause: Caterpillars. Numerous caterpillars feed on foliage to varying degrees. See "Leaves skeletonized or with large holes; branches may be webbed" on page 212 for suggested controls.

Leaves yellow; stems and leaves covered with small bumps. Cause: Scales. See "Leaves yellow; stems and leaves covered with small bumps" on page 213 for control measures.

Trunk or branches with small holes; limbs die or break off. Causes: Borers. See "Trunk or branches with small holes; limbs die or break off" on page 214 for controls.

Leaves and shoots blackened; leaves with moist or brown sunken spots. Cause: Anthracnose. See "Leaves and shoots blackened; leaves with moist or brown sunken spots" on page 214 for control measures.

Leaves with powdery white coating. Cause: Powdery mildew. See "Leaves with powdery white coating" on page 213 for controls.

Leaves tunneled. Cause: Leafminers. See "Leaves tunneled" on page 213 for controls.

Trunk or branches with oozing lesions; branch tips die back. Cause: Canker. For more information, see "Trunk or branches with oozing lesions; branch tips die back" on page 214.

Leaves pale and drop early; branches wilt and die. Cause: Wilt. Prune off dead and diseased branches. Feeding with a high-nitrogen fertilizer may help plants recover. Remove and destroy badly infected trees, and don't plant new trees in the same area; they may also be attacked.

TOMATO *Lycopersicon esculentum* (Solanaceae)

Tomatoes are tender perennials that are grown as annuals in temperate climates. Their fruits can be pale greenish white, yellow, orange, pink, purple-black, or red, and anywhere from currant size to well over a pound apiece. There are two main types: Determinant cultivars grow to a certain height and stop, putting all their energy into producing fruit heavily over a 4- to 6-week period; indeterminant cultivars grow and produce fruiting clusters until frost.

Culture

Tomatoes require full sun and deep soil with a pH between 6.0 and 6.8. Work in plenty of compost before planting to add organic matter. Tomatoes require moderate levels of nitrogen and phosphorus, and moderate to high levels of potassium and calcium. Tomatoes grow best between 75° and 90°F. Temperatures over 100° can kill blossoms, while temperatures below 50°F can cause chilling injury.

Keep soil moist, but not soggy, and do not allow it to dry out. Avoid wetting leaves when watering to help prevent diseases. Tomatoes do well in raised beds with drip irrigation and mulch. Black plastic is a good mulch in cool areas because it helps warm the soil and it suppresses weeds and conserves water. Organic mulch helps keep the soil cooler in very warm areas while adding organic matter. Mulch also helps avoid disease by preventing the fruit from touching the ground and by preventing disease organisms from splashing onto plants during rains.

Choose cultivars that are adapted to local growing conditions. Many are resistant to one or more problems. Resistant cultivars are usually denoted in seed catalogs as follows: F = Fusarium resistant, V = Verticillium resistant, T = Tobacco mosaic virus resistant, N = Nematode resistant, TSWV = Tomato spotted wilt virus resistant.

Do not plant tomatoes where tomatoes, potatoes, eggplants, or peppers have been planted within the past 3 to 5 years. Also, try to separate these crops in the garden. Compost or till under all plant residues at the end of the season to reduce overwintering pests. After tilling, spread 2 to 4 pounds of blood meal or soybean meal per 100 square feet to encourage rapid breakdown of plant material.

Purchase stocky, insect- and disease-free plants, or start your own from seed indoors. Tomato seeds germinate best between 75° and 90°F. Once seedlings are up, they grow best between 60° and 70°F. Water transplants thoroughly with fish emulsion or compost tea to give them a good start. Spray young plants with seaweed extract to help prevent transplant shock and nutrient deficiencies.

Leaf and Whole Plant Problems

Seedlings fall over; stems girdled or rotted at soil line. Cause: Damping-off. Disinfect reused pots and flats by dipping them in a 10 percent bleach solution and letting them air dry before filling them with fresh seed-starting mix. Sow seed thinly to allow air movement around seedlings. Cover seed with a thin layer of soilless mix or vermiculite. Water only enough to keep soil moist, not soggy. Thin seedlings and spray with compost tea as soon as first true leaves open to help prevent the problem.

Seedlings clipped off at soil line. Cause: Cutworms. Check for fat, 1- to 2-inch-long, dull brown or gray caterpillars in the soil near the base of plants. Once they chew off a seedling, there is nothing you can do except protect the remaining seedlings from nocturnal cutworm attacks. To prevent cutworm damage, place cutworm collars around transplants, sprinkle moist bran mixed with BTK on the soil surface in the evening, or add parasitic nematodes to the soil at least a week before planting.

Leaves yellow or pale. Cause: Nutrient deficiency. Spray young plants with seaweed extract to help prevent deficiencies, and add compost to the soil. Have the soil tested and amend as necessary.

If young leaves are yellow with green veins, suspect iron deficiency. Reduce soil pH to help make iron more available. If dark spots develop in the yellow areas, and leaves are small and narrow, the problem may be zinc deficiency. If older leaves are yellow with green veins, and then become bronzed, suspect potassium deficiency.

If young leaves are pale and growing tips die, the problem may be calcium deficiency. Add high-calcium lime, dolomitic lime if magnesium is also low, wood ashes, or gypsum to the soil.

Plants that are stunted and have yellow or pale older leaves may be nitrogen deficient.

Leaves yellow, distorted, and sticky. Cause: Aphids. Leaves may develop brown spots. These small green, black, gray, pink, or white fluffy-coated insects suck plant sap. For mild infestations, knock pests off plants with a blast of water. Spray plants with insecticidal soap in the evening to control, or with neem if infestation is severe.

Leaves of young plant purple. Causes: Phosphorus deficiency; lack of dark period. Phosphorus is unavailable in cool soil; symptoms usually fade as soil warms. Spray plants with seaweed extract to alleviate symptoms.

Seedlings grown under lights may be purple if the lights are left on continuously. Give seedlings 8 hours of darkness each night to reverse or prevent purpling.

Leaves stippled or bronzed. Cause: Mites. Fine webbing may be present below or between leaves. Infested leaves dry out and fall off. These tiny, spiderlike insects feed on plant sap and thrive in hot, dry weather. Disrupt mite activity by spraying plants with water; control damaging infestations with insecticidal soap sprays.

Leaves mottled with yellow; young growth narrow and twisted. Cause: Tobacco mosaic virus. Destroy diseased plants. Choose resistant cultivars to prevent problems. Wash hands after handling tobacco and before touching tomatoes to prevent TMV, and control aphids, which spread viruses as they feed.

Leaves yellow; plant stunted and wilts in hot weather. Cause: Root-knot nematodes. Plants eventually die. Check roots for swollen sections or galls up to 1 inch in diameter. Destroy infested plants; do not compost them. Apply chitin or parasitic nematodes to the soil to control the pests. Choose nematode-resistant cultivars to avoid problems.

Older leaves yellow; shoots or whole plant wilts. Cause: Walnut, Fusarium, or Verticillium wilt. Walnut wilt occurs in soil containing black walnut roots, which secrete a substance that is toxic to many kinds of plants. Tomatoes within 50 feet of black walnut trees or stumps wilt and die suddenly. The toxic compound remains in the soil for some years after trees are cut down. Plant your tomatoes at least 50 feet from walnut trees. If this is impossible, grow tomatoes in containers in a good organic potting mix.

Fusarium wilt and Verticillium wilt are both fungal diseases and are difficult to tell apart. Both Fusarium and Verticillium wilts begin as a yellowing and wilting of the lower leaves. Plants are stunted and do not recover when watered. Cut open a stem near the soil line and look for internal discoloration. Verticillium wilt usually affects the whole plant while Fusarium may infect individual shoots before the whole plant is affected. Fusarium thrives in warmer temperatures (80° to 90°F) than Verticillium does (68° to 75°F). Destroy infected plants. Tomato Fusarium infects only tomatoes; Verticillium infects a wide range of plant species, making effective rotation control difficult. Prevent problems by planting resistant cultivars. Control pest nematodes to help reduce wilt problems.

Whole plant wilts; leaves remain green. Cause: Southern bacterial wilt. Plants do not recover when watered. This disease is most damaging in the Deep South. Destroy infected plants. Prevent problems by planting tolerant cultivars such as 'Saturn' and 'Venus'.

Leaves with small dark spots. Causes: Bacterial speck; bacterial spot. Centers of spots may dry and fall out. Leaves may turn yellow, then brown, and fall off. Buy certified disease-free seed or transplants from a reputable source. Practice crop rotation and clean up debris and weeds that may harbor disease spores. Preventive copper sprays may give some protection if applied until developing fruits reach about one-third of their mature size, but should only be used as a last resort if bacterial speck has been a problem in previous seasons and when cool, moist weather conditions favor this disease. Warm, humid weather favors the development of bacterial spot; be on the lookout for symptoms when conditions are favorable and avoid working amid plants when they are wet. Use mulch to keep bacteria from splashing from soil onto plants. Remove and destroy severely infected plants.

Leaves with dark, water-soaked patches. Causes: Late blight; Septoria leaf spot. Water-soaked patches that turn brown, dry, and papery are symptoms of late blight. In wet weather the patches may develop a ring of white mold. Stems may have blackened areas. Infected fruit have large, irregular, firm, greasy-looking brown spots. This fungal disease often occurs during periods of humid weather with cool nights (below 60°F) and warm days (70° to 85°F), and it can spread rapidly. Monitor plants carefully, and uproot plants that develop symptoms. Bury them deeply away from the garden or discard them in sealed bags with your household trash. At the end of the season, compost or destroy plant debris and culled tomatoes. To prevent future problems, remove volunteer plants and space plants to allow good air movement; avoid wetting foliage unnecessarily. Preventive applications of *Bacillus subtilis* products or copper sprays may help reduce the spread.

If the patches develop into circular, dark spots with light centers peppered with dark specks, suspect Septoria leaf spot, another fungal disease. Older leaves are affected first. Remove and destroy infected leaves. Spraying transplants with an antitranspirant may help prevent Septoria. Don't apply antitranspirant when tomatoes are blooming.

Leaves with dark, concentrically ringed spots. Cause: Early blight. Lower leaves and stems are affected first. Disease occurs when plants are loaded with fruit and during humid, warm (75° to 85°F) weather. Where available, biofungicides containing *Trichoderma harzianum* or *Bacillus subtilis* may be applied to soil or to transplants' roots as a preventive. Preventive copper-based fungicide sprays may help reduce the spread of early blight. Remove and destroy severely infected plants. Prevent problems by planting resistant cultivars such as 'Manalucie FST', 'Mt. Fresh Plus', 'Old Brook', 'Plum Dandy', and 'Tommy Toe'. Spraying transplants with an antitranspirant may help to prevent this disease; do not apply when plants are blooming.

Leaves with dark brown ringspots; dark brown streaks on stems and petioles; stunted growing tips; one-sided growth. Cause: Tomato spotted wilt virus. Immature tomato fruits show light green rings with raised centers; ripening fruits are mottled orange and red, eventually developing blackened areas. Tomato spotted wilt virus is spread almost entirely by thrips; control them (see "Thrips" on page 287) to limit the spread of the virus. Clean up weedy areas in and around your gardens; several common weeds, including chickweed, lamb's-quarters, morning glory (bindweed), and sowthistle, serve as alternate hosts for the virus. Remove and destroy infected plants. Because this virus is widespread among many greenhouse crops, growing your own plants from seed is a way to avoid introducing it into your garden. Where this disease is prevalent, choose resistant cultivars such as 'Amelia VR', 'BHN-444', 'Bolseno', 'Crista', 'Cupid', 'Muriel', and 'Sweet Cluster'.

Leaves with brown edges. Cause: Bacterial canker. Lower leaves wilt and curl up; stems develop light-colored streaks and are brown and mealy inside. Destroy infected plants. To prevent problems, avoid wounding plants; don't work amid wet plants.

Leaves with small holes. Cause: Flea beetles. Young transplants are the most susceptible. These tiny black, brown, or bronze insects hop when disturbed. Spray garlic solution or kaolin clay to deter feeding. Protect transplants with row cover until they start to flower.

Leaves with large, ragged holes or leaves missing. Causes: Colorado potato beetles; hornworms; other caterpillars. Colorado potato beetles are yellowish orange, oval, hard-shelled, $\frac{1}{3}$-inch-long beetles with black stripes. Larvae are soft-bodied, humpbacked, dark orange grubs with a row of black spots down each side of their bodies. Eggs are orange and laid in rows on undersides of leaves. Severe infestations can defoliate plants. Handpick insects or spray plants with BTSD if young larvae are feeding.

Hornworms are 3- to 4½-inch caterpillars with white diagonal stripes. The tobacco hornworm has a red horn projecting from the rear, while the tomato hornworm has a black horn. Handpick, or spray plants with BTK to control them. Do not spray if caterpillars are covered with small, white, cigar-shaped projections, which are actually parasitic wasp cocoons.

Other caterpillars, such as cabbage loopers and beet armyworms, sometimes feed on tomato leaves. Handpick or spray plants with BTK if many caterpillars are feeding.

Flower and Fruit Problems

Few flowers form; flowers may drop without setting fruit. Causes: Excess nitrogen; shading; extreme temperatures; drought stress. Excess nitrogen causes plants that are dark green and vigorous, but produce few flowers. Wait for flowers to form. Prevent problems by avoiding high-nitrogen soil amendments.

Tomatoes need at least 6 hours of sun a day to produce flowers; prevent problems by not planting them in shaded areas.

Temperatures over 100° or below 55°F can damage flowers and cause them to fall without setting fruit. Wait for new flowers to form. Protect plants with row cover until night temperatures remain above 55°F.

Dry soil may also cause blossom drop. Keep soil evenly moist, but not soggy.

Fruit with large, faded or gray-white, sunken patches. Cause: Sunscald. Green or ripe fruit can be affected. Control leaf diseases to prevent defoliation, so fruit will be shaded and protected from direct sun by the plant's leaves.

Fruit gnarled and malformed with dry scars near the blossom end. Cause: Cold injury. Cat-facing, as this symptom is also called, is caused by prolonged cool weather during blossoming. Poor pollination may be partially responsible. Protect plants with row cover until nights remain above 55°F.

Fruit ripens unevenly and has grayish yellow blotches. Cause: Graywall. Green fruit has grayish skin blotches and interior is discolored. Ripe fruit has green or brown areas in interior. This condition can be caused by dense shade from crowded plants, cool temperatures (below 60°F) during ripening, wet or compacted soil, excess nitrogen, potassium deficiency, or various diseases, including tobacco mosaic virus. Prevent problems by providing good growing conditions.

Fruit with green, water-soaked spots. Cause: Late blight. Spots expand into large, greasy-looking, brown areas but remain firm. See "Leaves with dark, water-soaked patches" on page 207 for controls.

Fruit with pale yellow spots just under the skin; spots may have a central puncture. Cause: Stink bugs. Flesh under spots is white and spongy. These brown, tan, gray, or green, ½-inch-long, shield-shaped bugs inject a toxin when they feed on green fruit. Many species of weeds are also host plants. Keep garden well weeded to prevent problems.

Fruit with small, raised spots. Causes: Bacterial canker; bacterial spot; bacterial speck. If spots are tan with white margins and look like "bird's eyes," the plants are suffering from bacterial canker. See "Leaves with brown edges" on the opposite page for controls.

If spots are brown, scabby, and rough with sunken centers, the plants have bacterial spot. If spots are tiny, dark brown, and surrounded with white borders, the plants have bacterial speck. See "Leaves with small dark spots" on page 207 for controls.

Fruit with concentrically ringed, sunken spots. Causes: Anthracnose; early blight. If these spots appear on ripe fruit, and fruit eventually rots, the problem is probably anthracnose. Keep plants dry when watering to prevent spread. Pick fruit promptly, as overripe fruit is more susceptible. Sprays of organic fungicides such as sulfur and copper may provide some protection but are rarely effective once symptoms appear on fruits. Use them as a last resort only where previous years' anthracnose infections have been severe.

Spots that appear near the stem while fruit is green are symptoms of early blight. See "Leaves with dark, concentrically ringed spots" on page 207 for controls.

Fruit with black, sunken area at blossom end. Cause: Blossom end rot. Seen on green or ripe fruit. First fruit to ripen is more likely to be affected than fruit that ripens later. This condition is due to calcium deficiency in the fruit. It is aggravated by drought or uneven soil moisture, root damage, high salt levels in the soil, and excess nitrogen. If soil test indicates deficiency, add high-calcium lime to the soil. Prevent problems by keeping soil evenly moist and by spraying plants with seaweed extract when the first flowers open and again when green fruit is visible.

Fruit with cracks around the stems; shoulders may be green or yellow. Cause: Uneven irrigation. Cracks start at the stem and extend out, or are semi-circular splits on the shoulders of the fruit. Rots may invade fruit through cracks. Prevent problems by keeping soil evenly moist throughout the season and by planting crack-resistant cultivars such as 'Abe Lincoln', 'Beefmaster', 'Cupid', 'Juliet', 'Mt. Spring', 'Park's Whopper', 'Supersonic', and 'Sweet Million'.

Ripe fruit rots. Cause: Various fungal and bacterial diseases. Remove infected fruit from plants. Stake plants to keep them off the ground and mulch to prevent soil from splashing up on fruit. Keep plants dry when watering and avoid touching them when wet. Grow crack-resistant cultivars and harvest ripe fruit promptly.

Fruit with narrow, black tunnels through flesh and small holes near stem. Cause: Tomato pinworms. Larvae are small and gray and may have reddish markings. Destroy infested fruit. Till soil after harvest to prevent pests from over-wintering.

Fruit with small holes on surface; interior rotted and hollow. Cause: Tomato fruitworms. Fruit appears to collapse like a deflated balloon. Larvae of tomato fruitworm, also called corn earworm, are light yellow, green, pink, or brown and grow up to 2 inches long with spines and lengthwise stripes. Once larvae are inside fruit, there is nothing to do but destroy the infested fruit. If you see larvae feeding on leaves before attacking fruit, spray plants with BTK to control. Prevent eggs from being laid on plants by covering them with row cover until they flower.

Green fruit with large, chewed holes. Causes: Hornworms; Colorado potato beetles; other caterpillars. Ripe fruit may have brown, calloused pits. See "Leaves with large, ragged holes or leaves missing" on page 208 for descriptions and controls.

Ripe fruit with large, chewed holes. Causes: Slugs and snails; various animal pests. Slugs and snails can eat into a tomato quite rapidly. They often leave a shiny slime trail on the plant or ground marking their passage. Slugs hide under

objects during the day. Place inverted flowerpots around the garden, check them daily, and destroy slugs hiding under them.

Various feathered and furry pests like tomatoes, too. See "Animal Pests" on page 304 for controls.

TREES, SHRUBS, AND VINES

Controlling pests and diseases on landscape plants is largely a matter of common sense and simple preventive measures. Choosing the right plants and supplying their simple needs will help make pest control a minimal part of your gardening chores.

Searching Out Stress

When your plants are showing signs of insect damage or disease, the first step to controlling the situation is to figure out what caused the problem in the first place. Plants that are stressed by any of several causes—such as drought, extreme cold, or soil compaction—are the most susceptible to insects and disease.

The solutions to these problems often depends on your identifying the stress that is weakening the plant. Once you know the source of the stress, you can take steps to remedy it. Sometime it's easy to determine what's causing the problem. During dry spells, for instance, lack of water is an obvious possibility. Other noticeable stresses include wounds caused by equipment or root damage from construction activity.

In other cases, the initial problem may be more subtle. Plants growing near streets and walkways are often damaged in winter by the deicing salts that are washed into the soil, although symptoms may not appear until spring. Keep your eyes open for potential problems, and you may be able to minimize the damage to your plants before pests or disease attack.

Getting a Good Start

When you are buying new plants, you can avoid a lot of future problems by choosing locally adapted plants or resistant cultivars. Plants that are native to an area are often less prone to problems because they are growing in the environment to which they are best adapted. Read about the plants you intend to buy, and avoid very pest-prone species. If you have your heart set on a plant that is especially vulnerable to some problem, consider buying a resistant cultivar if one is available. Look for this information on the Internet or in catalogs, or ask your local nursery owner or extension agent for more information on the plants best adapted to your area.

Once you get your plant home, some basic care will help it get established quickly. Good soil preparation will provide the ideal conditions for strong root development. Providing ample water for the first few years after planting also encourages vigorous growth. A 2- to 3-inch-thick layer of organic mulch helps keep the soil moist and weeds down; just be sure to keep the mulch a few inches away from the trunk or main stem to discourage animal and insect pests from attacking the base of the plant. Do any necessary pruning or staking carefully, and avoid making wounds in the stems with lawn mowers or string trimmers.

Choosing a Control

If a problem does require control, try the least drastic solution, like handpicking insects or pruning off diseased parts. Observing your plants often will help you catch problems before they require more severe controls.

When dealing with large plants like trees, realize that controlling insect and disease problems may be impractical. If the tree is otherwise healthy, most disorders will not cause permanent damage. To deal with serious infestations or infections on large plants, consider getting the advice of your local extension agent or a qualified tree-care professional; this is especially true before attempting a drastic control, like removing the plant.

Following is a discussion of some of the most common insect and disease problems in trees, shrubs, and vines.

Leaf Problems

Leaves wrinkled and discolored. Cause: Aphids. These $\frac{1}{32}$- to $\frac{1}{8}$-inch, pear-shaped, green,

Proper Planting

Use the following planting techniques to ensure that trees, shrubs, and vines get off to a good start.

■ Dig a wide planting hole no deeper than the height of the root ball. Ideally, newly planted trees should sit on undisturbed soil. The top of the root ball should be at the same level it was growing in the nursery.

■ Rough up the sides of the hole to encourage roots to penetrate the soil and grow outward.

■ Do not amend the soil with compost, peat moss, or other materials.

■ Fill in the hole, water thoroughly, then add a 2- to 3-inch layer of mulch. Keep mulch an inch or two away from the main trunk or stems.

pink, black, dusty gray, or white fluffy-coated insects cluster on leaves, buds, and young stems. As they feed, they drop sticky honeydew on lower leaves. Sooty mold fungi often grow on the honeydew on aphid-infested foliage—as well as on the plants growing beneath them; see "Leaves with black coating" on the opposite page for more information. Heavy infestations may result in summer leaf drop. Avoid overfeeding, which promotes succulent growth attractive to aphids. Spray plants vigorously with water several times a day for 2 to 3 days to knock off the pests. See "Aphids" on page 250 for more controls.

Leaves stippled with yellow; foliage webbed. Cause: Spider mites. These tiny, spider-like pests generally feed on the undersides of plant leaves. They suck sap from plant leaves, initially causing a yellow flecking on the upper leaf surfaces. Severe infestations can cause leaves to turn yellow or white; damaged leaves will eventually turn brown and drop. Tiny webs may be evident on leaves and stem tips. The leaf damage these pests cause may stunt the growth of the plant. Control spider mites by spraying plants thoroughly with water (especially the undersides of the leaves) 2 to 3 times a day for several days. Spraying a tree or shrub with horticultural oil at a dormant-season dilution in winter before growth starts is also effective. For more controls, see "Mites, Spider" on page 275.

Leaves skeletonized or with large holes; branches may be webbed. Cause: Caterpillars. Several kinds feed on foliage, including tent caterpillars and webworms. Attract birds and other natural insect predators to your yard to help with control. Control all of these pests by manually destroying their nests or egg cases, or by spraying leaves with BTK at the first sign of damage. As a last resort, use pyrethrin spray.

Leaves skeletonized or plant defoliated. Causes: Japanese beetles; sawflies; gypsy moths. Japanese beetles have metallic blue-green bodies with bronze wing covers. Besides feeding on leaves, the adult beetles often chew on buds and flowers. See "Japanese Beetle" on page 269 for controls.

Sawflies, related to bees and wasps, may also cause similar damage. The larval stage is the most destructive stage; sawfly larvae feed on and skeletonize plant leaves or completely defoliate the plant. They range in size from $\frac{1}{5}$ to $1\frac{1}{2}$ inches and often closely resemble caterpillars, although sawfly larvae have more than five pairs of "legs." Damage may occur throughout the summer because different species feed at different times. Control larvae as soon as you spot them by blasting colonies with a strong spray of water from the hose. See "Sawflies" on page 281 for more information.

Gypsy moth larvae are up to $2\frac{1}{2}$-inch-long, gray-brown, hairy caterpillars with red and blue spots on their backs. Unlike tent caterpillars and webworms, gypsy moth larvae do not make webs. These caterpillars feed mainly at night and crawl down the trunk every morning. To trap them on their way back up the tree, wrap a wide piece of burlap around the trunk, tie string around its center, and fold down the top half. Check the band every afternoon, and collect and destroy the larvae that are trapped there. From late April through mid-June, spray leaves with BTK every 10 to 14 days and after each rain to provide more widespread control. See "Gypsy Moth" on page 268 for more information and controls.

Plant defoliated; branches bear cocoonlike bags. Cause: Bagworms. These pests are actually $\frac{3}{4}$- to 1-inch, brown caterpillars, although you'll seldom see them. They feed from inside bags they create out of silk and the leaves of whatever plant they're feeding on. That's why the bags look different on maples, for example, than they do on pine or spruce trees. On some needle-leaved evergreens, you might even mistake the bags for cones at first glance. Handpick and destroy the bags as soon as you notice them. See "Bagworm" on page 253 for more controls.

Leaves tunneled. Cause: Leafminers. The larvae of some flies, moths, sawflies, and beetles feed in between upper and lower leaf surfaces; these pests are collectively known as leafminers. They may cause narrow, curved tunnels in the leaves or large, silvery brown blotches. Severe infestations can cause leaves to brown and wilt or drop. The most effective control is handpicking and destroying infested leaves. See "Leafmining Flies" on page 271 and "Leafmining, Sawflies" entries on page 272.

Leaves with black coating. Cause: Sooty mold. This fungus grows on the sugary, sticky honeydew produced by aphids, scales, whiteflies, and mealybugs. The black fungal coating doesn't harm leaves directly, but it does shade the leaves and reduce growth. The best control is to deal with the pests that are producing the honeydew. Determine what pests your plant has and apply the appropriate control. (If the plant itself doesn't show signs of pest damage, the honeydew may be dripping down from an overhanging plant.) On small plants, you can wipe the leaves with a damp cloth to remove the honeydew and the mold.

Leaves with spots. Cause: Leaf spots. A large number of fungi and bacteria cause spots on plant leaves, in a variety of colors, shapes, and sizes. In some cases the spots may spread to cover entire leaves, stunting plant growth. Other leaf spots have centers that die and fall out of the leaf, giving a "shothole" effect. To prevent leaf spot diseases from

worsening, pick off infected leaves. Rake up and destroy fallen leaves and branches in autumn to eliminate overwintering spores.

Leaves with powdery white coating. Cause: Powdery mildew. Commonly attacking the foliage of many kinds of plants, powdery mildew may also appear on buds and shoot tips. Although it is unsightly, this fungal disease seldom causes serious damage, especially if it occurs late in the season. Reduce the chances of disease by leaving plenty of room around plants for good air circulation. Clean up and destroy or dispose of infected leaves.

Leaves yellow and wilt. Cause: Root rot. Caused by various species of fungi, root rot leads to reduced growth, branch dieback, and the ultimate death of the plant. At the soil level, the stem wood may be discolored; stringlike fungal structures may be present. Yellow-orange mushrooms sometimes appear at the base of dying trees. Remove infected trees as soon as possible to reduce the spread of the fungus to other trees.

Leaves yellow; stems and leaves covered with small bumps. Cause: Scales. As they feed, these tiny pests cover themselves with $\frac{1}{10}$-inch-long shells in a range of shapes and colors. Some scales have hard, shiny shells, while others form cottony, white coatings. These insects often feed on the undersides of the leaves, causing a generally unhealthy plant appearance and yellowish blotches on the upper leaf surfaces. Other types of scales feed on twigs and branches. Sooty mold fungi often grow on the honeydew on scale-infested foliage, as well as on the plants growing beneath them; see "Leaves with black coating" above for more information.

Prune out badly infested growth, or use a soft brush and soapy water to gently scrub the scales off the stems (if the plant isn't too bushy or spiny).

Apply a horticultural oil spray at a dormant-season dilution to the trunk and branches before growth starts in spring, or horticultural oil at a growing-season dilution during the growing season.

Trunk and Branch Problems

Trunk or branches with small holes; limbs die or break off. Cause: Borers. Numerous borers attack woody plants, mining the inner bark and wood of branches and trunk. To make plants less susceptible to attack, keep them healthy with proper pruning, mulching, and watering (during drought). Although tree wraps have long been recommended to protect trees, especially dogwoods, from borers, research has shown that these guards are not a good idea. They tend to keep bark soft and moist, actually protecting borer larvae. If you want to use a tree wrap to protect plants from winter deer damage, remove the guard during the growing season.

Avoid wounding bark unnecessarily. Be especially careful when using a lawn mower or string trimmer around trunks of woody plants. Prune off borer-infested branches. If you see borer holes in your trees, probe into them with a flexible wire or inject a solution of parasitic nematodes; after treatment, seal holes with putty. Remove and destroy seriously infected trees.

Trunk or branches with oozing lesions; branch tips die back. Cause: Canker. Several kinds of fungi cause cankers on twigs, trunk, and branches. As they spread, these sunken areas can girdle stems, killing the branch tips and stunting growth.

Mildly affected plants may recover from an attack of this fungus. Remove and destroy affected branches. If possible, cut away and destroy the cankered area, along with 2 inches of healthy bark around the edge of the damaged area. Heavily

diseased plants cannot be cured; remove and destroy them. The best prevention is to provide good growing conditions; healthy plants resist attack. Avoid damaging plants with lawn mowers, string trimmers, or pruning tools; wounds are a common place for cankers to start.

Trunk or roots with swollen, wartlike growths. Cause: Crown gall. This bacterial disease causes wartlike swellings on plant roots, stems, or branches. It can enter the plant through wounds caused by lawn-maintenance equipment or chewing insects. See "Crown Gall" on page 340 for controls.

Trunk with shelflike growths. Cause: Wood rots. Wood rots near the base of the tree, caused by various species of fungus, are indicated by the appearance of shelflike growths. Prevent the disease by maintaining general health and treating injuries to the tree. Once established over a large area of the trunk, there is little that can be done; remove the tree.

Whole Plant Problems

Leaves and shoots blackened; leaves with moist or brown sunken spots. Cause: Anthracnose. This fungal disease is particularly a problem in cool, wet springs. In severe cases, twigs die back and defoliation can occur. Gather and dispose of fallen diseased leaves, and cut off affected branches several inches below the damaged area. No control is needed on larger trees; they'll produce new healthy leaves when the weather becomes warmer and drier. See "Anthracnose" on page 310 for more controls.

Leaves yellow, sparse, distorted, or with brown edges; branches die; growth stunted. Cause: Decline. Decline does not refer to a particular pest or disease organism; rather, it relates to a general loss of plant vigor that is not due to a specific cause. It is usually a result of a number of stresses acting on a tree over a period of years. Plants mismatched to their sites, soil compaction, root damage, trunk injuries, repeated attack by insects or disease, and improper pruning are among the factors that can stress plants and lead to decline.

If you can identify and eliminate the sources of the problem, you may be able to restore the plant's health. A seriously weakened plant may be too far gone for recovery, and you'll need to remove it. If you have identified the source of the original problem and have taken steps to resolve it but to no avail, consider replanting with a suitable species.

Whole plant stunted and lacking vigor. Cause: Nematodes. Parasitic species of these microscopic, wormlike creatures attack the roots and make plants look sickly and stunted. If you dig up the plant, you may find knotlike galls on the roots. The best control measures are preventive: Mulch regularly with compost or other organic mulch to ensure that soil organic matter levels remain high. For more controls, see "Root-Knot Nematodes" on page 340.

Whole tree falls over. Cause: Windthrow. If an otherwise healthy tree suddenly falls over, roots and all, the problem may be due to improper planting. The roots of trees planted in small holes and backfilled with heavily amended soils may not extend out of the planting area in search of nutrients. The small root system that develops may not be enough to anchor the tree if a sudden strong wind gust comes along.

To avoid damage, follow the guidelines given in "Proper Planting" on page 211. If windthrow does happen to a young tree, you may be able to save the plant. While the roots are exposed, use your fingers or a tool to gently loosen the congested root mass. Loosen the soil to a depth of about 8 inches, in a circle a few feet out from the trunk. Then carefully pull the tree upright, and stake it on several sides to hold it upright. Water the tree thoroughly, and mulch well with compost to promote new root growth.

Leaves yellow; growth stunted; top of plant breaks off from roots. Cause: Graft incompatibility. This problem occurs when the root system and the top of a grafted plant do not join properly. This lack of connection interferes with the flow of water and nutrients, and the top of the plant may die and break off at a graft union. This problem most commonly occurs within a few months of grafting, but it can also happen after several years of apparently healthy growth. Fortunately, this problem does not happen often. If your plant is damaged, remove it; there is no cure.

TROPAEOLUM Nasturtium

Available in shades of red, yellow, orange, and white, these easy-to-grow plants thrive in warm, sunny weather. Flowers are 2 inches wide and borne singly. Some cultivars have a bushy habit. Others climb quickly if given any type of support; otherwise, they sprawl along the ground, spreading by as much as 6 feet.

Direct-sow nasturtium seeds in late spring; they germinate in 1 to 2 weeks. Plants prefer sun, but some afternoon shade is beneficial in very hot areas. They are not fussy about the soil conditions, but too much fertilizer encourages excessive foliage growth and fewer flowers. Space plants 8 inches apart. Water only as needed to prevent wilting.

Problems

Leaves, stems, and buds distorted. Cause: Aphids. For controls, see "Aphids" on page 250.

Leaves with tan or brown blotches or

serpentine tunnels. Cause: Leafminers. See "Leafmining Flies" on page 271 for controls.

Plant yellows, wilts, and dies. Cause: Bacterial wilt. The stems have black streaks, and roots will rot. There is no cure. Avoid planting nasturtiums near other susceptible crops, such as eggplants, tomatoes, or peppers. Solarize the soil before replanting with susceptible plants.

Leaves with many tiny holes. Cause: Flea beetles. See "Flea Beetles" on page 265 for controls.

TSUGA Hemlock

Hemlocks are narrow-leaved, evergreen, cone-bearing trees. Often used as attractive hedges, they can be allowed to grow naturally or be sheared to any height and width.

Hemlocks are best adapted to moist, cool climates. They are shallow-rooted and easily transplanted; set out in spring as balled-and-burlapped plants. Hemlocks prefer moist, acid soil rich in organic matter. They flourish in shade and partial shade; if planted in sun, make sure to water during drought.

Problems

Leaves drop; plant weak or dead. Cause: Hemlock woolly adelgids. These pests appear as woolly colonies near the base of the needles. See "Adelgids" on page 249 for controls.

Leaves yellow; stems and leaves covered with small bumps. Cause: Scales. See "Leaves yellow; stems and leaves covered with small bumps" on page 213.

Branches with brown tips. Cause: Spruce budworms. For more information, see "Branches with brown tips" on page 166.

Plant defoliated. Causes: Hemlock loopers;

gypsy moths. The 1-inch-long, greenish yellow, black-spotted hemlock loopers usually appear in June. They feed on the needles, starting from the branch tips and working toward the center of the plant. Handpick small populations; control large infestations with BTK. Gypsy moths cause similar damage; for a description and control measures, see "Leaves skeletonized or plant defoliated" on page 212.

Plant defoliated; branches bear cocoonlike bags. Cause: Bagworms. See "Plant defoliated; branches bear cocoonlike bags" on page 212.

Leaves light gray or bronze. Cause: Spruce spider mites. See "Leaves light gray or bronze" on page 167 for controls.

Trunk or branches with small holes; limbs die or break off. Cause: Borers. See "Trunk or branches with small holes; limbs die or break off" on page 214 for details.

Branch tips die back. Causes: Blight, sun scorch; drought stress. Blight, a fungal disease, attacks mostly during cool, wet weather. See "Branch tips die back" on page 167 for more information and controls.

If you see the same symptoms during hot, dry weather, your hemlock may be suffering from sun scorch or drought stress. Minimize damage by watering deeply and regularly during dry periods. A thick mulch may also help by retaining moisture and keeping roots cool.

Leaves yellow and drop. Cause: Rust. Whitish blisters on the undersides of the leaves followed by yellowing and leaf drop indicate rust. Prune out and destroy infected branch tips. See "Rust" on page 315 for more controls.

Trunk or branches with oozing lesions; branch tips die back. Cause: Canker. See "Trunk or branches with oozing lesions; branch tips die back" on page 214 for details.

TULIPA Tulip

Perhaps the best loved of the spring-flowering bulbs, tulips have been admired and prized for centuries. Plant breeders have developed thousands of hybrids and cultivars from the more than 100 species in this genus. Tulips are grouped into 15 divisions, based on bloom time, flower form, and parentage. They bear cup-shaped blossoms on 6- to 24-inch-tall flower stalks. Flowers come in all colors except true blue; bicolors are common. Thick, 6- to 8-inch-long, straplike leaves surround flower stems.

Hardy bulbs, tulips require winter chilling to bloom. Where temperatures don't fall low enough, several weeks in a refrigerator at 40°F provides the necessary cold period. In cold-winter climates, plant tulips in fall, at least 1 month before the ground freezes. Keep bulbs cool until planting; exposure to temperatures above 70°F reduces flower size. Plant 6 to 10 inches deep in full sun and well-drained soil. Poor drainage promotes bulb rot. Mulch lightly in winter. Top-dress with compost and bonemeal in spring, about 1 month before bloom. Remove spent flowers to promote bulb growth. As clumps enlarge, flower size may decline. Dig crowded clumps after foliage fades, shake off loose soil, and air-dry bulbs in shade for a few days. Divide offsets and parent bulbs and replant.

Problems

Leaves with large, ragged holes. Cause: Slugs and snails. See "Slugs/Snails" on page 284 for controls.

Leaves yellow or distorted; bulbs decayed. Cause: Bulb mites. These mites may arrive on new bulbs. See "Leaves yellow or distorted; bulbs decayed" on page 100 for controls.

Plant fails to appear in spring; bulb missing. Cause: Animal pests. Rodents like to feed on tulip bulbs; droppings or disturbed soil may appear in flower beds. Plant bulbs where human activity will discourage wildlife; pet cats or dogs also deter animal pests. Line planting beds with hardware cloth to exclude burrowing rodents; cover beds with screen wire in winter. Try repellents such as dried blood, human hair, or garlic sprays. Keep flower beds free of debris where pests may hide.

Leaves yellow; plant stunted. Cause: Tulip bulb aphids. These aphids infest both the bulbs and aboveground portions of the plant. They suck sap from leaves, stems, and flowers, causing foliage to curl, pucker, and yellow. Flower buds may be stunted. Inspect bulbs carefully before you buy; look for clusters of gray, waxy aphids under the bulb coat. Spray infected plants with insecticidal soap or as a last resort try dusting them with pyrethrin. Destroy seriously infested bulbs.

Leaves streaked or spotted; flowers rotted. Cause: Botrytis blight. Also known as tulip fire, this fungus causes red-brown leaf spots that later turn gray. Plants may be stunted or pale yellow-green with deformed flowers and rotting stems. Dark spots form on bulbs; gray mold may be present. Dig and destroy infected plants. Limit disease spread by watering early in the day so leaves have time to dry before evening. Trim off leaves as soon as they turn yellow; remove spent flowers. In severe cases, and as a last resort, apply Bordeaux mix when shoots appear in spring; repeat 1 week later.

Leaves and flowers streaked or mottled; foliage spindly or deformed. Cause: Viral diseases. Several viruses infect tulips. Some bicolor tulip cultivars get their flower colors from viral infections; the resulting blooms are said to be "broken." Aphids and leafhoppers may spread the virus from broken tulips to solid-colored ones and also to lilies. Viruses weaken tulips without killing them; remove infected plants to halt disease spread to healthy tulips. Wash tools used around infected plants; control sucking insects; see "Aphids" on page 250 for information on controlling aphids.

TURNIP *Brassica rapa,* **Rapifera group** **(Cruciferae)**

Turnips are a cool-season vegetable grown for their crisp roots and tasty greens. They require cool, moist, rich soil with a pH between 5.5 and 6.8. Plant seed directly in the garden. Turnips grow best between 60° and 65°F. They grow poorly above 75°F, but will tolerate temperatures as low as 40°F. Harvest greens and roots when they are small and tender.

Turnips are in the same family as cabbage and are troubled by many of the same pests and diseases. See the Cabbage entry, beginning on page 56, for descriptions and controls.

Root Problems

Roots are riddled with slimy, winding tunnels. Cause: Cabbage maggots. Maggots are white and ¼ inch long. See "Cabbage Maggot" on page 255 for description and controls.

Root flesh black but firm; skin rough and cracked. Cause: Downy mildew. Symptoms of this fungal disease may appear as bright yellow spots on leaves long before root infection is evident. Remove and destroy badly infected leaves. Sprays of potassium bicarbonate or baking-soda-and-soap spray (1 teaspoon baking soda, 1 teaspoon liquid dish soap, 1 quart water) may give some control as well as reduce the spread of the disease.

Prevent problems by planting tolerant cultivars such as 'Scarlet Queen Hybrid', 'Topper', 'Tornado', 'White Count', and 'White Knight'.

Roots black and rotted. Cause: Black rot. Leaves have yellow, V-shaped spots on margins. Destroy infected plants.

Roots with dry, sunken spots. Cause: Anthracnose. Avoid this fungal disease by planting in cool soil (early spring or fall).

Roots with small, water-soaked spots or pits on surface. Cause: Cold injury. Protect plants with mulch if temperatures are below 30°F.

ULMUS Elm

Elms are alternate-leaved, deciduous trees valued for their ornamental use as specimen or street trees. There was a time when virtually every town and city in the northeastern United States was dominated by the majestic, vase-shaped American elm (*Ulmus americana*); unfortunately, with the appearance and spread of Dutch elm disease (DED), most have died. Research continues on identifying resistant American elms; resistant cultivars are available, and new ones are being released.

Elms are susceptible to many insects and diseases. If you do decide to plant one, consider planting lacebark elm (*U. parvifolia*), which is more resistant to Dutch elm disease and elm leaf beetles. Plant elms in spring or fall as bare-root or balled-and-burlapped trees. Full sun and well-drained soils are best.

Problems

Leaves with rectangular holes or skeletonized. Cause: Elm leaf beetles. This is a ¼-inch, yellow-green beetle with a dark line on the outer edge of each wing cover. It lays its eggs in spring on the undersides of leaves; these eggs hatch in June. One to several generations may occur each year.

Both the adults and the ½-inch, black-spotted, yellow larvae feed on the leaves, eating everything but the veins. Trees are often defoliated and so weakened that they are susceptible to other insect and disease problems. Control beetles by spraying leaves with BTSD, particularly in June.

Leaves wilted and yellow or brown, drop early; branches show symptoms one at a time. Cause: Dutch elm disease. Caused by a fungus, Dutch elm disease is spread by the feeding of elm bark beetles, and by natural root grafts between elm trees growing in the same area. Keep trees healthy with proper pruning, mulching, and watering (during drought). Quickly repair all wounds to help prevent insect attacks and subsequent infection. Once the disease is established, there is no effective remedy. Remove and immediately destroy all diseased or dying elms. Remove the stump if possible, or peel the bark off to below the soil line to deter elm bark beetles from feeding there.

Bark tunneled. Cause: Elm bark beetles. These ¹⁄₁₀-inch, dark reddish brown beetles attack weakened elm trees and serve as vectors of Dutch elm disease. See "Bark Beetles" on page 253 for more information and controls.

Leaves skeletonized. Cause: Cankerworms. Both spring and fall cankerworms are ½- to 1-inch, yellow or greenish caterpillars that feed on foliage, often defoliating the tree. For control measures, see "Leaves skeletonized" on page 50.

Japanese beetles also skeletonize elm leaves. See "Leaves skeletonized or plant defoliated" on page 212 for controls.

Leaves wilted and yellow or brown, drop early; entire crown of tree affected. Cause: Phloem necrosis. In later stages, the inner bark (phloem) is discolored and smells faintly of wintergreen. This disease, also known as elm yellows, kills plants quickly, often in a single growing season. It is spread from tree to tree by leafhoppers.

Controlling leafhoppers may reduce the spread of phloem necrosis. (See "Leafhoppers" on page 271 for controls.) If trees are close together, however, the disease can also spread underground by means of natural root grafts. Once plants are infected, there is no control; remove and destroy infected trees.

Leaves wrinkled and discolored. Cause: Aphids. See "Leaves wrinkled and discolored" on page 211 for controls.

Leaves tunneled. Cause: Leafminers. For more information and controls, see "Leaves tunneled" on page 213.

Leaves yellow; stems and leaves covered with small bumps. Cause: Scales. See "Leaves yellow; stems and leaves covered with small bumps" on page 213 for controls.

Trunk or branches with small holes; limbs die or break off. Cause: Borers. For more information, see "Trunk or branches with small holes; limbs die or break off" on page 214.

Trunk or branches with oozing lesions; branch tips die back. Cause: Canker. For more information, see "Trunk or branches with oozing lesions; branch tips die back" on page 214.

Leaves with spots. Cause: Leaf spots. See "Leaves with spots" on page 214 for controls.

Leaves with powdery white coating. Cause: Powdery mildew. For controls, see "Leaves with powdery white coating" on page 213.

VEGETABLES

Vegetables (including herbs) are plants grown for their edible roots, stems, leaves, seeds, fruit, and other plant parts. Most vegetables are annuals; a few are biennials or perennials grown as annuals; and some are hardy perennials. Vegetables grow best in deeply worked, well-drained soil with lots of organic matter. Most require full sun to produce well. See individual vegetable entries for specific cultural requirements and problems. The following problems affect many vegetables and herbs.

Problems

Seedlings fall over; stem girdled or rotted at soil line. Cause: Damping-off. Disinfect reused pots and flats by dipping them in a 10 percent bleach solution (1 part bleach to 9 parts water) and letting them air dry before filling them with fresh seed-starting mix. Sow seed thinly to allow for air movement around seedlings. Cover seed with a thin layer of soilless mix or vermiculite. Water only enough to keep soil moist, not soggy. Thin seedlings and spray with compost tea as soon as first true leaves open to help prevent the problem.

Seedlings clipped off at soil line. Cause: Cutworms. Check for fat, 1-inch-long, brown or gray caterpillars in the soil near the base of plants. Once they chew off a seedling, there is nothing you can do except protect remaining seedlings from nocturnal cutworm attacks. To prevent damage, place cutworm collars around transplants, sprinkle moist bran mixed with BTK on the soil surface in the evening, or add parasitic nematodes to the soil at least a week before planting.

Leaves turn yellow beginning at base of plant; plant stunted. Causes: Nitrogen deficiency; waterlogged soil. Spray foliage with compost tea or fish emulsion, or side-dress plants with compost. Waterlogged soil damages roots and prevents them from using nutrients available in the soil. Prevent problems by choosing well-drained

sites, adding organic matter to the soil to improve drainage, and by planting in raised beds.

Leaves yellow and curled; new growth distorted. Cause: Aphids. These small, soft-bodied, green, black, or pinkish insects suck plant juices. They may spread various diseases or leave sticky honeydew on leaves and fruit that in turn supports the growth of black, sooty mold. For mild infestations, knock pests off plants with a blast of water. Spray plants with insecticidal soap to control aphids, or with neem if infestation is severe.

Leaves yellow; plant wilts; stems, crowns, or roots water-soaked and rotted. Cause: Fungal or bacterial rots. Various fungi and bacteria cause stem, root, or crown rot. Poor drainage or overwatering encourages the development of these diseases. Destroy infected plants or plant parts. Thin plants to increase air movement and reduce moisture around plants. Plant in well-drained soil or in raised beds to prevent problems.

Texas root rot occurs in warm climates and is favored by high temperatures and a pH above 7.0. If pH is high, add sulfur to the soil to lower it. Use a 3-year rotation to starve the fungus out of the soil.

Plant yellow and stunted, wilts during bright, hot days; roots may have swollen galls. Cause: Root-knot and other pest nematodes. These microscopic, wormlike creatures invade and feed on plant roots. Pull and destroy infected plants. Control pest nematodes by adding chitin or parasitic nematodes to the soil. Solarize infested areas to reduce future problems.

Leaves yellow; plant wilts gradually. Causes: Verticillium wilt; Fusarium wilt. Leaves may roll up as the disease progresses. Stems that are cut open are discolored. Severely infected plants eventually die. There is no cure for these fungal diseases. Destroy infected plants. There are many species of Fusarium, each of which infects only one plant or plant family. One species of Verticillium wilt, however, can infect over 300 species of cultivated plants including eggplants, tomatoes, peppers, potatoes, brambles, fruits, and ornamentals; so preventive rotation is difficult. Avoid planting wilt-susceptible plants where any wilt symptoms have developed within the last 3 years.

Leaves with dark, yellow-bordered spots. Cause: Leaf blight. This disease is caused by various fungi. Leaves may turn yellow or drop off as the disease progresses. Spray foliage with fish emulsion or with sulfur to prevent the spread of mild infections.

Leaves or other plant parts covered with tan to gray, fuzzy growth. Cause: Gray mold. This fungal disease attacks a wide range of edible and ornamental plants. Pick off and destroy moldy parts. Thin plants to increase air movement and reduce moisture around leaves, since the mold thrives in damp conditions. Remove faded flowers promptly. Spray foliage with compost tea to control mold. Spray plants with sulfur to prevent further symptom development if the weather is wet and cool and the disease is severe.

Leaves with powdery white growth on upper surfaces. Cause: Powdery mildew. This symptom is caused by a number of fungi, each of which attacks only specific plants. Thin plants to increase air movement and reduce moisture around leaves. Maintain even soil moisture to prevent drought stress, which makes plants more susceptible to infection. Organic fungicides, including *Bacillus subtilis,* potassium bicarbonate, or a 0.5 percent solution of baking soda (1 teaspoon baking soda in 1 quart water) may be applied as preventives or to help to control the disease.

Leaves with wandering, white or translucent tunnels. Cause: Leafminers. Larvae are tiny white maggots that feed on leaf tissue. Adults are tiny black-and-yellow insects. Once maggots enter leaves, no spray will control them. Destroy mined leaves. Apply row cover as soon as plants emerge or are set out to prevent problems. As a last resort, spray with neem.

Leaves pale and stippled. Cause: Mites. Leaves may become bronzed. These tiny, spiderlike insects thrive in hot, dry weather and feed on the undersides of leaves. Rinse plants with water to disrupt mite activity. Spray plants with insecticidal soap in the evening to control them; spray neem as a last resort.

Leaves riddled with small holes. Cause: Flea beetles. These small, shiny, black beetles hop when disturbed. They can transmit viral and bacterial diseases. Deter leaf feeding with garlic sprays or kaolin clay. Flea beetles are most problematic during droughts; watering the garden can sometimes reduce outbreaks. Prevent problems by protecting young plants with row cover.

Leaves with large, ragged holes. Causes: Caterpillars; snails and slugs; various animal pests. Many different caterpillars feed on vegetables. Look for dark green excrement at the base of leaves or plants. Handpick, or spray plants with BTK as soon as active caterpillars or feeding are observed. Let nature work for you and avoid handpicking or spraying if caterpillars are sluggish and yellowish (infected with a fatal virus) or covered with the small, white, cigar-shaped cocoons of parasitic wasps.

Slugs and snails eat leaves and fruit, often leaving shiny slime trails on the plants or ground marking their passage. Slugs hide under objects during the day. Place inverted flowerpots around the garden, check them daily, and destroy slugs hiding under them. If slug problems are severe, use a copper strip edging around beds to exclude them.

Various furry and feathered pests eat vegetables; see "Animal Pests" on page 304 for control ideas.

VERBENA Verbena, vervain

Verbenas' hardiness and long growing season make them favorites of beginners as well as long-time gardeners. Compact flower clusters range from white to deep purples and reds; they bloom from summer through autumn. Plants grow 6 to 10 inches tall with a spread of 1 to 2 feet. Use verbenas to edge beds and borders, or in containers and window boxes.

Where summers are short, start seeds indoors 3 months before the last frost. Ample light and 70°F soil for 4 weeks are needed for germination. Move outdoors when night temperatures are above 50°F. Space plants 1 foot apart. Or direct-seed outdoors as soon as the weather warms up, although germination may be poor. Many gardeners prefer to buy nursery-grown plants.

Verbenas need full sun, average water, and fertile, well-drained soil. In very hot climates give light shade to prevent drought stress, which reduces flowering.

Problems

Leaves with powdery white patches. Cause: Powdery mildew. See "Powdery Mildew" on page 322 for controls.

Leaves stippled with yellow; foliage webbed. Cause: Spider mites. For control information, see "Mites, Spider" on page 275.

Branch tips wilt. Cause: Budworms. These ½-inch, greenish yellow caterpillars feed on new shoots. Prune and destroy infested tips.

Leaves, stems, and buds distorted. Cause: Aphids. See "Aphids" on page 250 for controls.

Leaves with tan or brown blotches or serpentine tunnels. Cause: Leafminers. See "Leafminers" on page 271 for controls.

VERONICA Speedwell, brooklime

Ranging from prostrate to strongly upright in habit, and from 3 to 48 inches in height, speedwells form a varied genus of mostly blue-flowered, summer-blooming plants. Leaves are lance-shaped and green to gray-green; numerous small blossoms cover tall spikes that arise from the plant tops or from the leaf axils. Woolly speedwell (*Veronica incana*) is grown for its 1- to 3-inch, silvery white, fuzzy leaves as well as its blue blossoms.

Planting requirements vary somewhat among species but, in general, speedwells require average, very well drained soil and full sun. Plants tolerate some shade, but most do not appreciate drought, extreme heat, or humidity. Speedwell plantings enlarge via new shoots appearing at edges, but are not invasive. Divide every 4 years to reduce crowding. Remove spent flowers to prolong bloom.

Few insect pests attack speedwells, but fungal diseases are likely, especially when the plants' rather strict moisture requirements are not met. Prevent problems with good drainage, garden sanitation, and air circulation. Various fungi cause brown, black, or yellow leaf spots that may enlarge and kill entire leaves. Downy mildew causes white or gray powdery patches on upper and lower leaf surfaces, along with distorted stems and flowers that fail to open. For both problems, remove severely infected plants and plant parts. Avoid wetting leaves when watering. As a last resort, apply sulfur sprays when symptoms appear, to avoid further damage.

VIBURNUM Viburnum

Viburnums are opposite-leaved shrubs or small trees valued for their flowers, fruit, foliage, and growth habit. Most are deciduous; some are semi-evergreen or evergreen. They are excellent in shrub borders and woodland plantings.

Set out in fall or spring in well-drained soil amply enriched with organic matter. Viburnums grow well in sun or partial shade. Be aware that sulfur-containing fungicides may harm the foliage of some viburnums. Test the spray on a few leaves before treating the whole plant.

Problems

Leaves wrinkled and discolored. Cause: Aphids. For control measures, see "Leaves wrinkled and discolored" on page 211.

Leaves with spots. Cause: Leaf spots. See "Leaves with spots" on page 213 for controls.

Leaves with powdery white coating. Cause: Powdery mildew. For controls, see "Leaves with powdery white coating" on page 213.

Leaves and shoots blackened; leaves with moist or brown sunken spots. Cause: Anthracnose. See "Leaves and shoots blackened; leaves with moist or brown sunken spots" on page 214 for controls.

Leaves skeletonized or plant defoliated. Cause: Japanese beetles. For suggested controls, see "Leaves skeletonized or plant defoliated" on page 212.

Trunk or roots with swollen, wartlike growths. Cause: Crown gall. See "Trunk or roots with swollen, wartlike growths" on page 214 for controls.

Leaves yellow; stems and leaves covered with small bumps. Cause: Scales. See "Leaves yellow; stems and leaves covered with small bumps" on page 213 for controls.

VINCA Periwinkle, vinca, myrtle

Two species of ground-covering vines represent *Vinca* in the United States: greater periwinkle (*V. major*) and common periwinkle (*V. minor*). Both feature glossy, dark green, opposite leaves and blue, funnel-shaped flowers in spring. Greater periwinkle has larger leaves and is hardy to Zone 7; common periwinkle's foliage is smaller and plants are hardy to Zone 5, making it the more widely used landscape plant. Stems bearing flowers stick up 6 to 8 inches aboveground; the vines are otherwise prostrate. White-flowered and variegated cultivars are available.

Periwinkles grow rapidly in moist, sunny to lightly shaded spots; roots form along stems touching the ground. They have been listed as invasive in many states and easily escape to woodlands and wild areas. It is best to avoid planting them unless you have a site where they will be well contained. Average, well-drained soil is fine. Plants tolerate light foot traffic.

In the landscape, periwinkles have few severe insect problems, although several pests trouble greater periwinkles in greenhouse or subtropical conditions. Wet soil causes most problems by encouraging fungal diseases; prevent problems by selecting a site with good soil drainage, keeping the garden clean, and thinning plantings to promote air circulation.

VIOLA Pansy

Colorful pansies help to brighten up the spring garden. The 6-inch-tall plants bear cheerful blossoms in a wide color range. They bloom from spring to early summer, providing a perfect complement to spring bulbs.

For very early bloom, sow pansy seeds in August and overwinter plants in a cold frame. From Zone 7 south, plants can be set out in fall to bloom in late winter. Otherwise, sow seeds indoors in winter. Make sure seeds are covered; they need darkness to germinate. Seeds sprout in 14 days. After hardening the plants off, set them out into the garden about a month before the last frost. Pansies like cool weather; rich, loose soil; and filtered sun. Mulching keeps roots cool. Water plants regularly, and apply diluted liquid fertilizer every 4 weeks. Remove spent flowers to encourage more blooms. Cut plants back hard in midsummer and they may rebloom in fall.

Pansies are troubled by few pests. Slugs and snails can chew holes in leaves and flowers.For controls, see "Slugs/Snails" on page 284. Aphids, which cause distorted leaves, stems, and buds, along with spider mites, which cause leaves that are webbed and stippled with yellow, sometimes attack. See "Aphids" on page 250 and "Mites, Spider" on page 275 for control information. Cutworms can also cut off seedlings or young plants at the soil level. See "Cutworms" on page 263.

WALNUT *Juglans* spp. (Juglandaceae)

Walnuts are large, deciduous trees bearing separate male and female flowers on the same plant. To increase nut production, plant two different cultivars for cross-pollination. The most commonly grown types are black walnut (*Juglans nigra*) and English walnut (*J. regia*). Walnuts are hardy in Zones 4–8.

Walnuts need a site free of late spring frost; they prefer deep, well-drained soil. Prune lightly in winter to allow sunlight into the tree and to remove dead, diseased, or crossing branches.

Problems

Immature nuts dry up and drop early. Cause: Codling moth larvae. These fat, white or pinkish, $7/8$-inch caterpillars tunnel into nuts and may have departed by the time you discover the damage. Nuts may have a hole filled with what looks like moist sawdust. Late-blooming cultivars, such as 'Hartley' and 'Vina', are less susceptible to codling moths. For control information, see "Codling Moth" on page 259.

Husks have soft, black, smooth spots and maggots inside. Cause: Walnut husk fly maggots. Adult walnut husk flies lay eggs in nut husks; these hatch into small, cream-colored maggots. Although the larvae never eat the shells, larval feeding in the husk causes shells to blacken or shrivel. Since nuts themselves are unaffected, you can usually just ignore this pest. To control the flies, collect and dispose of infected husks. Deter egg laying by adults by spraying with kaolin clay; apply spinosad to control this pest. For severe infestations, capture adult flies with apple maggot fly traps (four to six traps per tree). For information on apple maggot fly traps, see "Fruit dimpled; brown tunnels through flesh" on page 32. Resistant cultivars include 'Howard' and 'Payne'.

Husks blacken; nuts blacken, shrivel, and drop prematurely. Cause: Walnut blight. Leaves may also bear angular brown spots, and dead, sunken lesions may appear on shoots. This bacterial disease overwinters in attached nuts, diseased buds, and twig lesions; prune out and destroy infected parts. To control blight, keep the canopy dry by pruning to allow good air circulation at the centers of the trees. Avoid overhead irrigation. For severe infection, use copper spray. Resistant cultivars include 'Hartley' and 'Howard'.

Leaves twisted or curled and covered with a sticky coating. Cause: Aphids. The shiny coating is honeydew, a substance excreted by feeding aphids. Black sooty mold fungus that feeds on honeydew may coat leaf surfaces. Sprays of water or insecticidal soap solution help control aphids. Spray with neem as a last resort.

Leaves with circular brown spots. Cause: Anthracnose. This fungal disease, common in wet, humid summers, may weaken trees and cause nuts to shrivel and drop early. To control anthracnose, keep trees well-nourished with nitrogen and clean up fallen leaves. 'Myers', 'Sauber 1', and 'Sparrow' are resistant cultivars.

Tree stunted and bears yellow leaves. Causes: Crown rot; blackline. If the trunk near the soil line is discolored or oozing sap, suspect crown rot, a disease caused by too much water and poor soil drainage. Improved drainage may help. If you find small holes or cracks at the graft union, remove some bark around the area and look for a black line. Blackline virus infects English walnuts grafted onto *J. hindsii* rootstocks. There is no cure.

WATERMELON Citrullus lanatus (Cucurbitaceae)

Watermelons belong to the same family as muskmelons and honeydews. See the Melon entry, beginning on page 138, for culture and pest information. Harvest watermelons when the bottom of the fruit turns from pale yellow to golden yellow.

WEIGELA Weigela

Weigelas are opposite-leaved, deciduous shrubs grown for their bright flowers, which appear in late spring and early summer. Because they lack interesting fruit and autumn color, weigelas are best used in the mixed shrub border.

Set out in spring or fall in full sun or light shade (the further south, the more shade). They prefer a well-drained soil, but one that does not dry out; a summer mulch is beneficial.

Weigelas are remarkably free of serious problems. Powdery mildew will coat the leaves with its typical white powder, more unsightly than threatening; see "Leaves with powdery white coating" on page 213 for controls.

WISTERIA Wisteria

Wisterias are vigorous vines with alternate, compound leaves. Chinese and Japanese wisteria (*Wisteria sinensis* and *W. floribunda*) are invasive plants in the Southeast. Instead, plant native American wisteria (*W. frutescens*). Because of their ultimate size, wisterias require strong supports. Their long flower clusters, often fragrant, appear in late spring, and a plant in full bloom is a delightful sight in the landscape.

Wisterias grow best in full sun but tolerate some shade. Set out in spring or fall in deeply prepared, moisture-retentive soil. Wisterias are often reluctant to bloom, sometimes taking many years. They seem to grow and flower best when given ample water; reluctant plants can sometimes be induced to bloom by severe root pruning, combined with pruning off some of the most vigorous shoots.

In warmer areas, where wisterias grow with amazing vigor, they are sometimes allowed to climb up dead trees; be sure not to train them on a live one—it will quickly be strangled.

Few pests trouble wisterias. Caterpillars can skeletonize leaves or chew large holes in them. See

"Leaves skeletonized or with large holes; branches may be webbed" on page 212. Black vine weevils can also chew notches in leaf edges. See "Root Weevils" on page 279 for controls.

YUCCA Yucca, Adam's needle

Clumps of stiff, sword-shaped, light green leaves arising from the ground give yuccas a strong presence in any landscape. Native in the southwestern United States and Mexico, where many species assume treelike form and heights up to 30 feet, only a few yuccas are hardy north of Zone 7. Adam's-needle (*Yucca filamentosa*) is a popular 3-foot plant, hardy to Zone 4, with evergreen, 1½-inch-wide leaves and tall spikes of midsummer white flowers. Variegated cultivars are available.

Succulent yuccas grow well in conditions resembling the semidesert of the Southwest: full sun and well-drained, sandy soil. Excess moisture, especially in winter, encourages rots. Insect pests such as yucca plant bugs and scales are more prevalent and likely to cause damage where yuccas are native. Aphids may infest Adam's needle; see "Aphids" on page 250 for controls. Fungal leaf spots may appear and are best controlled with cultural practices: Limit excess water on foliage and remove severely infected plant parts.

ZINNIA Zinnia

These annuals grow from 6 to 36 inches, with button-size to dinner-plate-size flowers that are single or double, smooth or ruffled, solid, multicolored, or striped. Just about every color is represented except blue. Flowering is possible from spring until frost.

Zinnias are easy to raise from seed and can bloom within 2 months. Sow successive crops every few weeks to give continuous flowering. Indoors, sow seeds in individual pots 8 weeks before the last frost. Move seedlings outdoors very carefully when soil is consistently warm. Zinnias resent transplanting, so direct-sowing is preferred. In fact, some double-flowered cultivars revert to single on transplanting. Direct-sow in spring and early summer when night temperatures stay above 50°F. Cover lightly and press soil down firmly. Germination takes 6 days. When seedlings are 3 inches tall, thin to allow 4 to 12 inches between plants, depending on final size.

If you purchase seedlings or potted zinnias, look for those that have not begun flowering or setting buds. Expect slow growth initially after transplanting. Make certain roots don't dry out in the process, water immediately, and give temporary shade in hot weather while plants adjust.

Zinnias need sun, ample water, good drainage, fertile soil, regular fertilizer, and good air circulation. They grow poorly in cool weather. Pinch initial buds to encourage side growth and flower formation. Remove spent flowers to prolong the blooming period. Water only from below; overhead watering weighs down the already heavy flowers, causing stems to snap. Overhead watering also burns foliage and encourages mildew. Feed monthly with a complete fertilizer.

Problems

Leaves with powdery white patches. Cause: Powdery mildew. Zinnias are extremely prone to mildew if not given excellent air circulation. For more information on controlling powdery mildew, see "Powdery Mildew" on page 322.

Plant wilts; leaves ragged. Cause: Stalk borers. Borers are long, thin, striped caterpillars that may have purple stripes. These larvae feed on leaves and within the wide zinnia stems. A small hole in the stalk marks their initial entrance. Stalk feeding can kill the plant.

Cut affected stems below the borer's hole; some plants may develop sideshoots that later flower. To save prized zinnias, try slitting affected stems and removing the borer, then binding stems together with green twine and keeping plants particularly well watered. Or inject BTK or parasitic nematodes into the stem with a syringe. A foliar application of BTK may be effective if borers feed on the leaves. Keep the garden weed free to eliminate overwintering sites.

Leaves stippled with yellow; foliage webbed. Cause: Spider mites. For controls, see "Mites, Spider" on page 275.

Seedlings or young plants cut off at soil level. Cause: Cutworms. See "Cutworms" on page 263 for controls.

Blossoms and foliage disappear. Cause: Blister beetles. These metallic, dark-colored, ¾-inch beetles begin chewing on flowers and leaves in early summer. See "Blister Beetles" on page 254 for controls.

Seedlings die. Cause: Damping-off. See "Damping-Off" on page 344 for controls.

PART 3

IDENTIFYING PESTS AND DISEASES

The pests that eat our treasured ornamentals and rob a share of our home garden harvest are only a tiny fraction of the total insect and mite populations around us. The overwhelming majority of insects and mites are harmless members of the natural community. Many are directly beneficial in their role as crop pollinators, natural enemies of pests, and decomposers of plant material. They can be as common as houseflies, distributed globally, or as rare as the flea that lives on the skin of certain sea mammals or the midge that lives in the tiny pool of water in a pitcher plant.

Unlike insect pests, which are usually easy to spot, most organisms that cause disease are too small to see without a magnifying glass or microscope. Disease symptoms can be variable and subtle, so they're tricky to diagnose and sometimes easy to miss until the problem is quite severe. Bacteria, fungi, nematodes, and viruses can all cause plant disease, but as with insects, the beneficial species of most types of microorganisms outnumber the harmful ones.

Understanding Insects, Mites, and Diseases

It's important to keep the broader picture of the good side of insects, mites, nematodes, and micro-organisms in mind when dealing with garden problems. Some control products, especially some organic sprays and dusts, kill helpful organisms as readily as they kill pests. The goal for the organic gardener is to assume that any insect or mite is a good one until proven otherwise, and to work with nature as much as possible to let populations of pests and beneficial organisms balance one another.

WHAT ARE INSECTS?

Insects are animals in the class Insecta, which is part of the large group of animals known as arthropods, meaning creatures with jointed legs. Arthropods are cold-blooded animals that wear their skeletons on the outside like armor.

Mites, spiders, millipedes, crabs, and lobsters are also arthropods. Insects differ from these creatures because they have wings and only six legs. Their bodies are divided into three sections: the head; the thorax or midsection, where legs and wings are attached if they have them; and the abdomen or tail section, where the digestive and reproductive organs are located. On their heads, insects have a pair of antennae or "feelers," which are complex sensory organs. Insects also have at least one pair of eyes and often extra rudimentary eyes (called ocelli) as well. They breathe through a system of small, round openings, or spiracles, along the sides of their bodies. These open into small, branching tubes, known as trachea, that carry oxygen through their tissues.

Insect Life Cycles

Although there are insects with weird quirks in their life cycles that seem like something out of science fiction, the development of most insects follows one of two basic patterns of metamorphosis, or change of form.

Complete Metamorphosis

This pattern has an immobile stage, called a pupa, between the immature and adult forms of the insect. During the pupal stage, the tissues of the immature insect transform into an adult with an entirely different appearance. Butterflies, moths, wasps, beetles, and flies exhibit this type of metamorphosis.

The cycle begins with an egg, which hatches into a tiny, immature insect called a larva. All young insects are larvae, but we often use the terms *caterpillar* for moth or butterfly larvae, *grub* for beetle or wasp larvae, and *maggot* for fly larvae. As a larva grows, it periodically molts its skin to accommodate its enlarging body.

When the larva reaches maximum size, usually after a number of molts, it contracts into a shorter, legless pupa. The pupa has a hardened skin that protects the developing adult inside. Some larvae spin a silken outer cocoon or chrysalis before pupating, for protection during the resting state. When the adult is ready to emerge, it splits open the pupal case and crawls out, still damp and soft. It slowly expands its wings. After its outer skeleton darkens and hardens, it is ready to fly away.

Larvae that undergo complete metamorphosis usually eat different food and live in different habitats from the adults of the species. This is important to remember if you want to attract helpful insects to your garden. Generally, the adult form of beneficial species is the winged form that can migrate to your garden. These adults feed on pollen and nectar flowers. Be sure to provide a food source for them in order to reap the benefits of having their predatory offspring living among your plants.

Incomplete Metamorphosis

Insects that develop gradually from immature stages to adults without pupating follow a pattern of incomplete metamorphosis. True bugs, including pests such as tarnished plant bugs and box-elder bugs, as well as praying mantids, aphids, and whiteflies, exhibit incomplete metamorphosis.

The cycle starts with an egg, which hatches into a larva, usually called a nymph, that looks like a miniature, wingless version of the adult insect. The resemblance of nymphs to adults increases with each molt. They grow larger, their bodies lengthen, and small wing buds appear. With the final molt, they become adults with fully formed wings and reproductive organs. Adults and nymphs of species with this pattern usually eat the same kind of food.

Feeding Habits

Insects eat an incredible variety of foods: leaves, roots, plant sap, wood, other insects, other arthropods, blood of birds and mammals, decaying plant material, pollen, nectar, dung, particles of algae, and even fungi. Some, like cockroaches, can digest nearly anything they can get their mandibles (jaws) on, while others must find a particular species of plant to eat or they will die. The disappearance of many butterfly species is due to the loss of their particular host plants when wild areas are cultivated or paved.

PLANT EATERS. Plant-eating insects usually are no friend to gardeners. They are adapted to chewing, sucking, or boring into leaves, stems, or roots. However, some species that eat weeds are beneficial. Plant-eating insects usually must consume a large volume of plant material relative to their size to obtain enough nutrients to continue their development and reproduction.

CARNIVORES. Most of us are familiar with carnivorous insects such as mosquitoes, deer flies, and biting midges. These pests land on mammals or birds, suck blood for a short period of time, and then fly away. Others that feed on blood, such as lice and fleas, live on the skin of animals, hidden in their fur. Gardeners should also get to know the large group of carnivorous insects that feed on insects or other arthropods. These are divided into two main groups—predators and parasites.

Predatory insects such as lady beetles or ground beetles eat many other insects during their life cycles. Some have restricted tastes; for example, aphid midges feed only on aphids. Others, like praying mantids or assassin bugs, may be able to eat almost any species of insect they catch. These general predators often eat pollen and may also suck plant juices when food is scarce or they need water.

Insects that parasitize other insects are called parasitoids or parasites. They lay eggs singly or in groups near, on, or inside the bodies of other insects. The parasitoid larvae develop as internal parasites. Parasitoids eventually kill the host, then pupate inside or crawl outside and pupate near the dead husk.

SCAVENGERS. Dung beetles, carrion beetles, housefly larvae, and other insect species feed on decaying plant or animal material. These creatures perform a valuable task by breaking down these materials and hastening decomposition.

OMNIVORES. The ultimate survival strategy is to be able to eat nearly anything—a strategy favored by cockroaches, earwigs, and other pests. These species feed on all kinds of animal and vegetable materials, including soap, starch, or glue.

FUNGUS FEEDERS. Fungus gnat larvae, many kinds of soil-dwelling insects and mites, and a few species of lady beetle larvae actually eat fungi.

WHAT ARE MITES?

Mites are more closely related to spiders than insects. Like spiders, mites have eight legs and hard bodies. A few types are well-known garden pests, including spider mites and rust mites. These tiny plant-feeding mites suck juice from plant cells or burrow into tissue on leaf undersides. Their feeding results in damage symptoms on leaves or flowers; plants are weakened, causing leaves to drop and fruit to be stunted. Some mite species have a short life cycle; eggs can hatch in as little as 1 day, and nymphs develop to adults in 5 to 10 days.

Predatory mites are extremely small. Native species of mites found in trees, shrubs, and surface litter are very valuable natural enemies of plant pests. Phytoseiid mites control many kinds of plant-feeding mites, such as spider mites and rust mites. Some also prey on thrips and other small pests. Many types of soil-dwelling mites eat nematodes, insect eggs, fungus gnat larvae, or decaying organic matter.

WHAT IS DISEASE?

What do we mean when we say a plant is diseased? If you accidentally skin the bark off the base of a tree with your lawn mower, is that tree diseased? If spring frosts slightly burn the leaves on broccoli transplants, are those plants diseased? Are pea plants infected with beneficial root-nodule bacteria diseased?

Even plant pathologists—scientists who study plant diseases—don't agree on a single definition of *disease*. A working definition accepted by most is that disease is an irritation that disturbs a plant's normal functions (such as water uptake or cell division). Some scientists further restrict the above definition to conditions or organisms that cause continuous irritation, making the above-mentioned "lawn mower blight" not a disease.

In this chapter, we'll divide plant diseases into two broad categories. Infectious diseases are those diseases that can be transmitted from one plant to another. Noninfectious diseases—which we call plant disorders—are problems that cannot be transmitted between plants.

How Diseases Affect Plants

The effect of a disease or disorder on a plant can range from a hardly noticeable decrease in yield to sudden wilting and death. All diseases interfere with normal plant growth, but the ways in which different diseases cause damage vary. Diseases caused by fungi and bacteria often weaken plants by literally eating food the plant has made for itself. Disease-causing organisms also harm plants by injecting them with toxins and by plugging up water and nutrient-conducting vessels. A disease can alter the hormone balance within a plant, resulting in galls that upset movement of food and water within a plant. Disorders such as nutrient deficiencies can slow growth and prevent proper development of flowers or fruit.

However, not all conditions that meet the

technical definition of *disease* are detrimental to plants. Nodules on the roots of peas and beans caused by bacteria, for example, are beneficial because these special bacteria take nitrogen from the air and convert it into a form that plants can use. Similarly, the roots of almost all plants are infected with mycorrhizal fungi. These beneficial fungi send a huge network of threadlike mycelia through the soil to garner nutrients, which they then share with their host plants.

When we talk about diseases in relation to animals or humans, we talk about their being spread by germs. Germs are the tiny organisms such as viruses and bacteria that can cause disease. These types of organisms also cause plant diseases.

A more scientific term for disease-causing organisms is the word *pathogen*. In addition to fungi and bacteria, viruses, nematodes, and parasitic plants are plant pathogens. These organisms run the spectrum in food preferences. Some are nourished mostly from dead organic materials, and occasionally a living plant. Others can grow and multiply only when they have infected a living plant. Plant pathogens do not attack humans or other animals. An exception is certain viruses that multiply within the insects that carry them.

Various environmental and cultural problems can upset a plant's normal function in ways that are similar to diseases caused by pathogens. Since they can't be transmitted from plant to plant like diseases can, these problems are termed disorders. Fortunately, disorders are often easy to avoid and to remedy with good garden management. It's important to be aware of the various factors that affect plant growth, so you can try to keep them balanced. It's also important to recognize the symptoms of disorders so you can treat them effectively, instead of mistaking them for an infectious disease.

How Infectious Disease Develops

If you place a Colorado potato beetle on a potato leaf, and the beetle doesn't eat anything, you don't have a pest problem. Similarly, if you put rust fungus particles on a snapdragon leaf, and they don't infect the leaf, you don't have a disease problem. Disease only occurs when the proper environmental conditions exist that allow the pathogen to penetrate and grow in the host plant. Before any disease symptoms show up on your plant, the following three conditions must be met:

1. **THE PATHOGEN MUST BE PRESENT.** The stage of the pathogen that can infect a plant is called the inoculum. An inoculum may be a virus particle, a bacterial cell, a fungal spore or hypha, a nematode, or a seed or piece of a parasitic plant.

2. **THERE MUST BE A SUSCEPTIBLE HOST PLANT.** For example, a tomato plant is susceptible to damping-off disease when it is a small seedling, but is resistant to this disease when it is growing luxuriantly in midsummer. Club root fungi in the soil can attack cabbage roots, but cannot infect tomato roots.

3. **ENVIRONMENTAL CONDITIONS MUST BE FAVORABLE.** The most important environmental factors affecting disease development are moisture, temperature, light, and soil fertility. In the case of many diseases, a susceptible plant and the inoculum are present throughout the growing season. Daily changes in the environment are what determine the extent of disease. A summer thundershower or a gusty, drying wind can change conditions almost within minutes, perhaps providing the right environment for disease to develop.

The Disease Cycle

The steps that a disease goes through over time are known as the disease cycle. The survival and spread of a disease depend on its success in completing all stages of its cycle.

INOCULATION. This first step occurs when the inoculum comes into contact with the plant. Inocula can be spread by wind, rain, insect feeding, contaminated tools, and in infected seeds or transplants.

PENETRATION AND INFECTION. If the environment is right, infection begins soon after inoculation. Bacteria, viruses, and mycoplasmas can infect plants only through wounds or natural openings. Wounds are holes in the plant caused by pruning, animal feeding, storm damage, or rough handling by the gardener. Natural openings include leaf pores, called stomates. The scar that remains when a leaf falls may also provide entry for disease. Flowers provide natural openings for pathogen entry, and insects seeking nectar sometimes carry pathogens to flowers. The bark and branches of woody plants are pocked with small pores (called lenticels) developed for gas exchange; these pores also provide entry for pathogens.

Fungi, nematodes, and parasitic plants may enter host plants either through natural openings or directly through intact surfaces. As spores of fungi and seeds of parasitic plants germinate, they develop small shoots and thin, elongating strands that can push right into the plant. Then, as they grow, the fungi secrete enzymes or toxins that dissolve or kill plant cells in their path. Parasitic plants send tentacle-like structures into the stem of the host plant. Nematodes penetrate cells with their sharply pointed mouthparts.

Just because a pathogen penetrates a host does not mean that the host will become diseased.

Sometimes pathogens enter hosts that are not susceptible to the disease; in this case, the pathogen will die and no disease symptoms develop. However, once the pathogen successfully penetrates a susceptible host, the pathogen can establish contact with a cell and begin getting nourishment from the host plant. This is known as infection.

INCUBATION AND INVASION. The time between infection and the appearance of visible symptoms is called the incubation period, and it may last days, months, or even years (in the case of some viral diseases). During this time, the pathogen will be growing, multiplying, and spreading, even though no symptoms are evident.

Disease organisms may infect only a part of the plant, or may spread through the entire plant. Viruses and bacteria are systemic, living within the cells. In contrast, the fungus that causes sooty mold never penetrates the plant at all. (This fungus feeds on insect honeydew dripped on the surfaces of leaves and fruit.) Powdery mildew fungi grow mostly on the outside of the plant, except for small structures called penetration pegs that grow into the plant to extract food. In a disease such as apple scab, the fungus grows just beneath the outer layer of plant cells. The fungus that causes peach leaf curl lives within the plant but between plant cells, while club root fungus invades plant cells.

REPRODUCTION AND SPREAD. As disease organisms spread through a host and obtain nutrients, they increase in size, number, or both. Fungi produce spores, bacteria split apart, viruses are replicated by the cells they infect, nematodes lay eggs, and parasitic plants produce seeds.

Wind or water can spread inocula over great distances. Inocula may also hitchhike on insects. Many viruses, for example, are carried from one plant to the next on the mouthparts of aphids. Birds and animals may carry inocula on their feet.

Humans can spread inocula as they work in the garden, touching plants with their hands and tools. A soilborne fungus such as Fusarium may be carried from infected soil to healthy soil on a trowel. Nematodes also transmit viruses as they feed and can carry bacteria and fungal spores as they move from plant to plant.

Plant Defenses against Disease

Considering the many methods pathogens have evolved to ensure their survival, you may wonder how you can have any healthy plants at all in your garden! Fortunately, plants are by no means passive players in the disease process.

STRUCTURAL DEFENSES. Plants have natural features that help ward off attack by a pathogen. A thick, waxy layer on the leaf surface can stop penetration by fungi; an impenetrable cell wall may impede progress of a fungus within a plant. A plant may be resistant to bacterial attack because it has small pores that bacteria cannot get through easily. Similarly, hairs on the leaves or fruit of many plants may shed water, increasing resistance to diseases that can develop only in a film of water.

PHYSIOLOGICAL DEFENSES. Plant cells commonly release various substances, some of which may be toxic to nearby fungi or bacteria. For example, the roots of wilt-resistant pea cultivars exude a substance that is toxic to wilt-producing fungi. Plant cells may also contain protective substances that can slow or stop the growth of a fungus or bacterium once it penetrates the plant. Part of the Verticillium resistance of potatoes is due to such protective biochemicals within the cells of resistant cultivars.

Other protective substances are produced only after a plant has been attacked by a disease-causing organism. For example, one way fungi advance into plant tissue is by secreting enzymes that dissolve cell walls. If a particular plant can produce a substance that inactivates the enzyme, the attack will be stopped.

In other cases, a plant might produce substances directly toxic to the attacking pathogen. And some plants, such as tomato cultivars resistant to Fusarium wilt, can transform a toxin produced by a pathogen into a nontoxic substance.

Fungi

The disease problems you'll deal with most frequently are caused by fungi. All plants are susceptible to attack by some type of fungus. There are more than 100,000 species of fungi, about 8,000 of which cause plant diseases, including powdery mildew, damping-off, late blight, apple scab, and corn smut.

What They Are

From the gardener's perspective, fungi are generally beneficial. Fungi decompose dead plants and animals, recycling nutrients back into the soil. Fungi also help aggregate soil particles into clumps, creating pore spaces that allow the soil to hold both air and water. Many beneficial fungi suppress the development of other fungi that cause plant diseases.

If you examine the roots of almost any plant, you'll find that they are infected with a beneficial type of fungus called mycorrhizal fungus. Infection actually helps the plants by improving the uptake of nutrients, especially phosphorus. The fungi also influence a plant's ability to tolerate drought and to ward off microorganisms that attack roots. Sterilizing soil and applying pesticides to soil discourages mycorrhizal associations.

Fungi can often be seen with the naked eye. Fungi are multicelled and have threadlike bodies called hyphae that spread over plants. The hyphae may grow mostly on plant surfaces but sometimes penetrate plant cells to send in feeding pegs, or secrete enzymes that dissolve cell walls as they proceed.

Fungi also form spores, which are tiny, seedlike structures ranging from 1 micron (0.001 millimeter) to 1 millimeter in size. Spores are more tolerant of unfavorable conditions, such as winter

Significant Symptoms

Infectious diseases are often classified by the type of symptom they cause. If you can identify the symptoms, you may be able to successfully control the disease, even if you don't know the specific pathogen causing the infection. If any of the symptoms described below seem to match those on your plants, turn to "Guide to Disease Symptoms" on page 309, where you'll find additional descriptions and photographs of particular diseases as well as information on how to prevent and control them.

BLIGHTS. Leaves or branches suddenly wither, stop growing, and die. Later, plant parts may rot. Common blights include fire blight, Alternaria blight, and bacterial blights.

CANKERS. Cankers usually form on woody stems and may be cracks, sunken areas, or raised areas of dead or abnormal tissue. Sometimes cankers ooze conspicuously. Cankers can girdle shoots or trunks, causing everything above the canker to wilt and die.

GALLS. These swollen masses of abnormal tissue can be caused by fungi, bacteria, insects, or mites. If you cut open a gall and there is no sign of an insect inside, suspect disease.

LEAF BLISTERS AND CURLS. Blisters are yellow bumps on the upper surfaces of leaves, with gray depressions on the lower surfaces. On plants suffering from leaf curl diseases, the new leaves are pale or reddish and the midrib doesn't grow properly. The leaves become puckered and curled as they expand.

MILDEWS. There are two common types of mildew: downy mildew and powdery mildew. The primary symptom of downy mildew is a white to purple, downy growth, usually on the undersides of leaves and along stems, which turns black with age. Powdery mildew first appears as a white to grayish powdery growth, usually on the upper surfaces of leaves.

ROTS. Rots are diseases that decay roots, stems, wood, flowers, and fruit. Some diseases cause leaves to rot, but those symptoms tend to be described as leaf spots and blights. Rots can be soft and squishy or hard and dry.

RUSTS. Typical rust symptoms include a powdery tan to rust-colored coating or soft tentacle-like growths. Rusts such as cedar-apple rust and white pine blister rust are caused by fungi. Many types of rust fungi require two different plant species as hosts to complete their life cycles.

WILTS. Plants wilt when they don't get enough water. When fungi or bacteria attack or clog a plant's water-conducting system, they can cause permanent wilting, often followed by the death of all or part of the plant. Wilt symptoms may resemble those of blights. Wilting may also be from a cultural problem, such as improper watering.

cold or summer heat, than actively growing hyphae, so spores are the overwintering form of most fungi.

Most fungi produce two or three different types of spores during their life cycles; fungi that cause rust diseases may produce five types. Spores may be produced on fruiting bodies that range in size from microscopic to the size of a basketball. Mushrooms and truffles are also fruiting bodies.

What You See

Fungal diseases result in a spectrum of plant symptoms on roots, stems, leaves, and flowers. Fungal diseases fall into one of two general categories: those from fungi that live in the soil, attacking roots or crowns of plants; and those from fungi whose spores are dispersed in the air, attacking aboveground parts of plants.

The list below identifies some of the most common symptoms caused by fungal diseases.

- **Damping-off** can kill seedlings before they even break through the soil, but it also strikes seedlings just an inch or so tall. The fungi rot the stem right at the soil line and, overnight, infected seedlings topple over.

- **Root rots** generally attack older plants, killing the tiny rootlets and appearing aboveground as stunting and wilting.

- **Fungal wilts** damage a wide range of plants, plugging up the plant's water-conducting vessels and causing leaves to wilt and die.

- **Club root** commonly infects cabbage family plants, causing large swellings on roots and stunted or dead plants.

- **Blights** include early and late blight, which attack tomatoes and their relatives. The fungi can damage or kill leaves and cause rot in the fruit or tubers. Other fungal blights, such as juniper blight, attack woody plants.

- **Mildews** include downy and powdery mildew. Infection results in spots or white patches on leaves, shoots, and other plant parts. Downy mildew can kill plants rapidly; powdery mildew commonly causes poor growth and lower yield, but seldom kills the plant.

- **Rusts** produce orange or white spots, usually on leaves and stems, weakening plants and reducing crop yields.

- **Leaf spot** symptoms are caused by a wide range of fungi, including Alternaria, Septoria, and anthracnose.

Other fungal diseases cause swelling on plant parts, such as black knot of plum and cherry, or sunken areas in stems, as with Cytospora canker. On fruit, fungi can cause hard, black patches (scab), soft spots (rot), or fuzzy gray mold (Botrytis rot).

How They Spread

Fungal spores are easily picked up and carried by water or animals—including gardeners! Spores are light enough to waft up into plants from the ground, as apple scab spores do when they drift from dead leaves lying on the ground up into apple trees in spring. Spores of a fungus such as cedar-apple rust can travel miles from cedars to infect apples, and spores of a disease such as wheat rust can hitchhike hundreds of miles on the atmospheric jet stream.

Bacteria

Bacteria are found almost everywhere on Earth, even in such inhospitable habitats as deserts and hot springs. These single-celled organisms are an

Name That Disease

Scientists classify living organisms by genus and species. Usually, these names are derived from Latin words. In most cases gardeners don't use scientific names when describing diseases. However, in some cases knowing the scientific name of a disease can be helpful.

For example, both apples and cucumbers can suffer from powdery mildew. *Podosphaera leucotricha* is the organism that causes powdery mildew on apples, while *Sphaerotheca fuliginea* is the one that causes powdery mildew on cucumbers. Knowing that these diseases have different scientific names, you can conclude that the fungus that causes powdery mildew on apples is different from the one that causes powdery mildew on cucumbers. Thus, you need not worry about mildew spreading from your apple tree to your cucumber plants, or vice versa.

A virus usually has a common name that includes the plant it was first identified on, along with the symptom produced. Thus, cucumber mosaic virus was first identified on cucumbers, and it produces a patchy yellow mottling of the leaves. But cucumber mosaic virus also attacks many other plants, including beans, celery, petunias, and delphiniums, and it doesn't always produce the distinctive mosaic symptom. Scientists are working on a more precise classification system for viruses, based on their chemical makeup, their shape, and their mode of transmission.

essential part of the decay process in soils and compost piles, but they can cause many serious plant diseases, including soft rot, crown gall, fire blight, and bacterial wilt.

What They Are

Bacterial cells are large enough to be visible through the common light microscope; still, 25,000 cells laid end-to-end would make up only 1 inch. The cells are of various shapes, including spheres, rods, spirals, and filaments. Those that cause plant diseases are mostly rod-shaped.

Bacterial cells divide by fission: Each cell pinches itself in half, then the halves separate, resulting in two cells. Under ideal conditions, a single cell can divide every 30 minutes. If the resulting cells from each division keep on dividing, this would result in 8,388,608 bacterial cells in only 12 hours! We are not knee-deep in bacteria because conditions are rarely ideal for their continued growth. As bacterial populations grow, they become overcrowded, use up their food supply, and wallow in their own waste products. Growth then stops or slows dramatically. Bacteria also are susceptible to infection by viral diseases.

Most bacteria are beneficial, increasing the fertility of the soil as they take nitrogen from the air and make it available to plants, and recycling nutrients in dead plants and animals. A single teaspoon of good garden soil is teeming with millions of bacteria. Friendly bacteria inhabit the digestive tracts of animals (including humans), aiding digestion, and are used in making yogurt and cheese. Special strains of bacteria even have been used to help clean up oil spills.

About 200 different bacteria are responsible for

plant diseases. Warmth and moisture are most conducive to bacterial growth, so bacterial diseases generally are worse in warm, humid climates.

What You See

One distinctive symptom of some bacterial diseases is sticky, gummy material, which is secreted by the bacterial cells. If the leaves on your cucumber plant are wilting and you suspect bacterial wilt disease, cut the stem or leaf stalk with a sharp knife. If you see threads of slime when you pull the stem or stalk apart, this confirms bacterial wilt disease. Active fire blight cankers are covered with a similar bacterial slime. In many cases the bacterial slime has an unpleasant odor.

The following list explains some other common bacterial disease symptoms.

- **Wilts** grow within a plant, causing bacteria to clog the plant's water-conducting vessels and the leaves to droop. If your cucumbers have ever been infected with bacterial wilt, you have seen a dramatic demonstration of this symptom— plants collapse almost overnight.

- **Leaf spots** can appear on leaves when bacteria kill cells within the leaves.

- **Soft rot** develops when bacteria infect fleshy fruit, tubers, or roots, secreting enzymes and perhaps toxins that break down the cells. These infections begin as small, water-soaked spots that turn mushy and smelly.

- **Galls** form when plants respond to bacterial attack by growing an excess of new cells. Crown gall, for example, produces swollen knots or plant tissue on roots and stems.

- **Cankers** are sunken areas produced by dead plant cells. Cankers often ooze a slimy or gummy substance.

How They Spread

Bacterial cells are spread by splashing rainwater, running water, insects, and animals, or on tools and diseased plants that you move from one place to another. Once bacterial cells are close to a susceptible plant, they can enter through wounds or natural openings. Insects such as cucumber beetles transmit bacterial wilt as they feed; nematodes help spread bacterial wilt of tomato. Wounds from hail damage also provide easy entry for bacteria.

Viruses

Among plant pathogens causing infectious diseases, the smallest are viruses and related viruslike organisms. Viruses attack every form of life on Earth, including humans (causing such diseases as smallpox, measles, and mumps) and other animals, trees, herbaceous plants, algae, fungi, and bacteria.

What They Are

Virus particles are only about 0.1 to 0.01 micron in size (1 micron = 0.001 millimeter). They can only be seen with the aid of an electron microscope. The typical virus can hardly be considered alive, consisting not of a cell but merely of nucleic acid (RNA or DNA) surrounded by a protein sheath. Viroids are even simpler—each is just a strand of RNA.

Viruses and viroids are inactive outside of living cells. Once inside a live cell, though, these pathogens use the cell's "machinery" to multiply themselves, upsetting the cell's metabolism and causing disease. A single infected plant cell may become home to over a million virus particles.

While they generally are considered a problem, viruses can sometimes give a plant desirable properties. For example, solid-color tulips, when infected with certain viruses, become mottled with bold blotches of color (these types are sold as

Rembrandt tulips). Another virus infects an apple cultivar known as 'Malling 9', which is used as a rootstock to produce dwarf apple trees.

What You See

Of all potential problems you encounter in your garden, viral diseases may be the most difficult to identify. Symptoms of a specific viral disease can vary from one plant to the next, and also may vary depending on plant age or growing conditions. A plant can harbor a virus but not show any symptoms, or show symptoms only when cool weather slows growth. Virus symptoms may be hardly noticeable, causing a slight reduction in yields or growth, or may slowly become more pronounced, causing a gradual decline and ending in death of the plant.

You may be able to identify a viral disease that produces characteristic symptoms and is common in your area. Green and yellow mottling on cucumber leaves, for example, very likely indicates cucumber mosaic. Some general types of symptoms that characterize viral diseases include:

- **Mosaic** causes normally green leaves or fruit to become mottled with patches of light green, yellow, or white areas. On flowers, mosaics can result in color breaks, and the flowers may be disfigured as well.

- **Rosetting** is the term used to describe the short, bushy growth caused by some viruses. Peach rosette is an example of a virus that causes stunting by scaling down the distance from one leaf to the next along the stem. Leaves or side branches are so close together that they grow in a rosette.

- **Ring spot viruses,** including those that cause

peony or dahlia ring spot disease, show up as pale, yellow spots on the leaves.

- **Leaf curling** or deformed leaves is another common virus-produced symptom.

How They Spread

Viral diseases are not spread by wind or water. The virus particles must be brought in contact with plants and then either rubbed against or injected into the plant so they enter the sap.

Many insects, including aphids, leafhoppers, and whiteflies, carry viral diseases from infected to healthy plants. Mites, nematodes, and fungi also transmit viral diseases, as do parasitic plants. Any of these organisms cause plant damage by themselves, but they pose an even greater threat when carrying a virus. Plants tolerate a certain amount of aphid feeding, for example, with no apparent harm. However, if those aphids inject a virus into one of your plants, the plant becomes permanently diseased.

People can also unknowingly spread viral diseases to plants. Smokers are likely to pick up tobacco mosaic virus on their fingers, and from there, transmit it to other susceptible plants. The virus can infect hundreds of different plants, including tomatoes, peppers, eggplants, petunias, apples, and grapes, and can survive for decades in dried tobacco leaves.

It's also possible to transmit viruses while propagating plants. If you graft part of a virus-infected plant—even a single bud—onto a healthy tree, viruses from that grafted plant tissue may infect the whole tree. Other methods of vegetative propagation, such as division or cuttings, may also produce infected plants if the parent plant was carrying a virus. Occasionally, viruses move from one plant to another by naturally occurring bark or root grafts. Viruses are only rarely carried in seeds or pollen.

Nematodes

While most of the thousands of species of nematodes on Earth are not harmful, some nematodes parasitize and cause diseases in humans and other animals. Also, unfortunately, there are many that attack and feed on living plants.

What They Are

Often described as wormlike, nematodes are not closely related to true worms. They are multicellular animals with smooth, unsegmented bodies. The nematode species that feed on plants are so tiny that you need a microscope to see them. They are often long and slender, although some species appear pear-shaped.

Some nematodes feed on the outside surfaces of a plant, while others burrow into plant tissue. While soil-dwelling nematodes are the most common culprits, some species damage stems, foliage, and flowers.

No matter where they feed, these tiny creatures can seriously damage plants with sharply pointed mouthparts that they use to puncture cell walls. The real damage occurs when a nematode injects saliva into a cell through its mouthparts, and then sucks out the cell contents. The plant responds with swellings, distorted growth, and dead areas. Nematodes can also carry viruses and inject them into plants. The feeding wounds they make also provide an easy entrance point for bacteria and fungi.

Beneficial nematodes that live in the soil may feed on decaying material, insects, or other nematodes. For more information on these beneficial nematodes, see page 242.

What You See

Unlike most other disease-causing organisms, plant-parasitic nematodes seldom produce any characteristic symptoms. Most of the symptoms that do appear are vague and often resemble those caused by other factors, such as viruses, nutrient deficiencies, or air pollution. Nematodes feeding aboveground may cause leaves, stems, and flowers to be twisted and distorted.

If nematodes are feeding on roots, a plant may be yellowed, wilted, or stunted; infected food crops will usually yield poorly. If you suspect nematode injury to roots, carefully lift one of the infected plants and wash off the roots for easier inspection. If nematodes are causing damage, you may see small galls or lesions, injured root tips, root rot, or excessive root branching. For a positive diagnosis,

Nematodes as Pests

While most nematodes are beneficial (see "Beneficial Nematodes" on page 242 for more on their role in the garden), a few species of these translucent, unsegmented worms are plant parasites. Pest species are only about $\frac{1}{50}$ inch long and cause root knots or galls, injured root tips, excessive root branching, leaf galls, lesions or dying tissue, and twisted, distorted leaves. Plants most commonly attacked at the roots include tomatoes, potatoes, peppers, lettuce, corn, carrots, and other vegetables. Plants that sustain leaf and stem injury include chrysanthemums, onions, rye, and alfalfa. For more on root-knot nematodes (*Meloidogyne* spp.), see page 340.

Beneficial Nematodes

Slender, translucent, unsegmented worms, beneficial species of nematodes are $\frac{1}{25}$ inch to several inches long. Their roles in the garden vary. Some are soil dwellers that break down organic matter and are common in compost heaps. These decomposers are easily visible; they are about $\frac{1}{4}$ inch long.

Other nematodes (families Steinernematidae and Heterorhabditidae) attack and kill insects either by injecting bacteria (*Xenorhabdus* sp.) that kill the host within 24 to 48 hours or by entering the host, parasitizing, and feeding on it.

Beneficial nematodes are effective against a variety of pests, including weevils, clearwing borers, cutworms, sod webworms, chinch bugs, and white grubs. When purchasing and applying them, it is very important to select the right species of nematode, because different species are effective against different pests. In addition, nematodes require moist, humid conditions, and fairly warm soil to be most effective. Water application sites before and after spreading nematodes. When purchasing them, follow application directions carefully.

contact your local extension office for information on where you can have your soil tested.

How They Spread

Whether they feed above- or belowground, most nematodes spend at least part of their life cycle in the soil. While they can't move very far under their own power, they can swim freely in water, and they move more quickly in moist soil. They are also spread by anything that can carry particles of infested soil, including tools, boots, animals, and infected plants.

Parasitic Plants

Parasitic plants are not a common problem. The two most common parasitic plants are mistletoe and dodder. These plants seldom produce their own food through photosynthesis. Instead, they attach themselves to host plants and withdraw water and nutrients from their hosts.

What You See

Plants attacked by parasitic plants show a variety of symptoms and signs. Here are some common characteristics.

- **Dwarf mistletoes** generally produce small tufts of short yellowish or greenish stems. They attack many kinds of conifers, such as pines, causing cankers or swellings on stems. The plants may be stunted, deformed, or killed; branches often break off at the cankers.

- **True mistletoes** are leafy. They primarily attack deciduous trees. The clusters of green stems and leaves are most obvious in winter, when the host plant's leaves have dropped.

- **Dodder** is a twining plant that has a threadlike, leafless, orange or yellow stem. Weakened by the parasite, infested plantings are quickly smothered by the rampantly growing vines.

How They Spread

Mistletoes produce sticky berries, which are either carried by birds or dropped from the mistletoe plant. Dodder spreads by seeds, which can be brought in with crop seeds or spread by animals or equipment.

Environmental Problems

Environmental problems are caused by a lack or excess of something that a plant needs to grow. If, for example, you try to grow a plant that likes cool temperatures, shade, and moist soil on a hot, dry site, you will probably end up with a plant that looks sick. It's simple logic that choosing the right site for a plant will go a long way in preventing environmental problems.

What They Are

Some of the factors that affect plant health are water, nutrients, temperature, light, oxygen, and air pollution. An imbalance in any of these factors can interfere with normal plant growth.

What You See

Sometimes it's easy to diagnose environmental problems. If the soil is dry, your wilted tomato plant is most likely suffering from drought, not from Verticillium wilt. Other problems, though, produce much more subtle symptoms. For example, continual exposure to even low levels of air pollution can reduce yields and plant vigor, making plants more susceptible to attack by pests or pathogens. Here are some common environmental problems and their associated symptoms.

- **Excessive water** often causes greenish yellow leaves, or plant wilting due to root rot. Some plants develop a condition called edema, in which tiny white or brown blisters appear on stems or lower leaf surfaces.

- **Drought,** or too little water, can cause wilting, in addition to leaf scorch (browned leaf edges), early fruit or leaf drop, stem dieback, and plant death.

- **Irregular watering** or a sudden change in water status, such as a heavy soaking after a dry period, can cause fruit and root crops to crack and lower leaves to yellow and drop.

- **Nutrient deficiency,** if minor, may have barely noticeable symptoms. As a deficiency becomes more severe, the crop yield may decrease and the plant may show other symptoms. Symptoms common to several kinds of deficiencies include abnormal leaf color, curled leaves, dead growing tips, or smaller-than-normal leaves.

- **Nutrient excess** of some nutrients can cause symptoms similar to those of nutrient deficiencies. In other cases, the effects of a nutrient excess are indirect. Too much nitrogen, for example, will produce lush, healthy-looking plants that produce hardly any fruit.

- **Cold temperatures** can kill tender buds, growing tips, leaves, stems, flowers, or fruit. Roots may die, and trunks often crack or form cankers.

- **Excessively high temperatures,** usually coupled with strong, direct sunlight, cause browned and blistered stems, leaves, or fruit. Young plants may die.

- **Too much light** or strong sunlight may burn the leaves of shade-loving plants, causing brown patches or dead leaves. Heavy pruning may expose previously shaded tree limbs to the bright sun, producing brown patches on trunks and branches. Plants with purplish or yellow leaves often fade or burn in direct sunlight.

■ **Lack of light** or too much shade may cause pale leaves, spindly yellow stems, or death of plants. Leaves of variegated plants may turn evenly green if they don't get enough sun.

■ **Lack of oxygen** usually occurs from overwatering. Water fills up the soil pores that normally hold air, so no oxygen is available to the roots. This causes roots to die, reduciing the root area available for water uptake and causing the plant to wilt.

■ **Ozone pollution** causes mottling or yellowing of leaves, especially on the upper leaf surfaces.

■ **Peroxyacetyl nitrate (PAN) pollution** is common in urban areas. Damage due to exposure to PAN appears as silvery white or brown spots on the undersides of leaves.

■ **Sulfur dioxide pollution** may cause leaves to yellow or brown in between the veins. Sulfur dioxide also combines with moisture in the air to form acid rain. While the exact effect of acid rain on plants isn't known, it can lower the soil pH and cause nutrient imbalance symptoms.

Cultural Problems

Cultural problems are caused by the things people and other animals do that injure plants. With a little care and common sense on your part, most of the problems are easy to avoid.

What They Are

People can damage plants in a variety of ways. Some insect controls, such as soaps and oil sprays, can damage plants if you apply them at the wrong time. Other types of damage include the infamous "lawn-moweritis" and string-trimmer injury.

When these machines strike a tree, they cause unsightly wounds that are perfect entrance points for disease organisms and boring insects. Trees on construction sites are highly likely to be hit by equipment or to suffer root damage due to soil compaction. Tight plant labels and staking wires may cut into the bark of your tree and interrupt the flow of water and nutrients.

Poor cultural practices can make plants more susceptible to environmental problems. Fertilizing at the wrong time of year, for example, can encourage plants to produce tender growth that is easily damaged by cold temperatures. Cultivating too close to plants may damage their root systems, reducing their water uptake.

Animals also cause their share of plant damage. Birds such as sapsuckers can peck holes into bark, creating entry sites for diseases and insects. Tender plant crowns, roots, and bark make tasty winter fare for hungry deer, mice, and rabbits.

What You See

Cultural problems produce a wide range of symptoms, so it may be difficult to determine the exact cause of injury. Observe the plant closely, though, and the problem may become apparent. Look for wounds in the stems, stakes or plant labels that are too tight, or teeth marks caused by animals.

Keeping complete garden records may also help you make a diagnosis. If a plant's leaves suddenly become distorted or damaged, looking at your records may help you realize that you applied some form of pest control under the wrong conditions. For example, you might have applied Bordeaux mix when the weather was too cool and damp, which would account for the discolored patches on your apples.

PINPOINTING PROBLEMS

One of the most enjoyable parts of a gardener's routine is simply observing plants. It's so satisfying to see the results of your gardening efforts, be they a lush shrub border, a beautiful perennial border, or a productive food garden. Making regular observations is also critical for keeping a healthy garden, as explained on page 22. During your regular garden rounds, if you do come across a problem on some of your plants, what should you do? Nothing—until you determine what is *causing* the problem.

To pinpoint the cause, you need to look closely at the plant for more information. While some diseases may only cause a single symptom, such as leaf spots, many produce more than one indication of their presence. Finding these other clues can help you identify the problem quickly and accurately. And by being aware of common symptoms and signs of disease, you'll be able to spot problems early on, before they get out of hand.

Pest Patrol Checklist

Follow this set of steps while you're out on your garden observation rounds to make sure you don't miss any potential problems.

1. **EXAMINE THE ENTIRE AFFLICTED PLANT** and note the range of abnormal symptoms. Is the entire plant affected or just a part of it? If a part is affected, what part? Do you see symptoms only on the new growth, on old growth, or on a single branch? Is just one plant affected, or do you see symptoms along an entire row? If plants are affected randomly within a row or bed, and the symptoms do not spread to the other plants, the problem is probably not an infectious disease. Clusters of plants showing symptoms may indicate disease, or just a pocket of poor soil.

2. **EXAMINE BOTH THE AFFECTED AREAS AND HEALTHY PORTIONS** of the plant with a magnifying glass. Inspect the leaves, especially on the

Plant Detective Kit

To diagnose a plant problem effectively, it's helpful to assemble as much information as you can. When you go out to the garden, keep handy a small magnifying glass and small bags or vials for specimens. Also carry a notebook to record what symptoms occur and when. These notes may help in the diagnosis of the problem at hand and also serve as a quick reference in the future.

A rain gauge and a thermom-eter that registers minimum and maximum temperatures can also provide helpful data. Position the rain gauge and thermometer at a site similar to that experienced by your plants. To get the most accurate temperature reading, shield the thermometer from the direct rays of the sun; the north side of a post is a good location.

General weather conditions can play a major role in determining which diseases affect your plants. Prolonged rainy, cool weather, for example, promotes late blight of potatoes. Powdery mildew, on the other hand, is favored by dry weather, especially when days are hot and nights are cool. Remember that weather not only influences the development of infectious diseases, but can itself lead to disease conditions. Cold injury, for example, causes water-soaked splotches on leaves or cracks in stems.

undersides; stems; flowers; and roots, if possible. Look for signs of hidden damage, such as borer holes in stems or fine webbing on the undersides of leaves. To avoid damaging roots when you observe them, dig the plants rather than pull them from the ground. Carefully wash soil off the roots for easier inspection.

3. **CHECK THE CONDITION OF THE SOIL.** Is it poorly aerated, encouraging root rots or at least poor root function? Or is the soil droughty, so plants wilt from lack of water? If soil conditions are poor, root systems may not be able to spread in search of nutrients, and plants in that area may suffer from nutrient deficiencies.

4. **COLLECT ANY INSECTS ASSOCIATED WITH THE AILING PLANT,** or take samples of damaged leaves. Choose representative diseased samples to send out for testing: Don't send leaves that have been dead for a long time or those that are so affected that they are unrecognizable. Seal samples in pill bottles or clear plastic bags.

Putting Together a Diagnosis

Diagnosing a pest problem on a plant is easiest if you catch the culprit in the act; then it's just a matter of identifying the pest. But reaching a diagnosis often takes patience and careful observation, because the insect that caused the damage may only feed at night or underground. In addition, insect damage often resembles infections from fungi or viruses; nutrient deficiencies might look like a viral disease or vice versa. Use a systematic approach to get good results.

1. **Identify the plant first.** If you use reference books to identify symptoms and signs, you may be on a wild goose chase if you haven't first figured out what kind of plant is affected. Also, some control products, such as horticultural oil, can injure the foliage of certain plant species. If you haven't identified the plant, you won't know whether you're using the appropriate control.

2. **Observe the symptoms and signs.** When making a diagnosis, don't be too quick to assume the problem is a disease just because you can't find a pest on the plants. For example, if your geranium leaves are covered with yellow spots, they may be suffering from a bacterial or fungal disease. But if you observe the leaves closely and find webbing and tiny black specks on the leaves as well, the plants are infested with spider mites. "Pest Patrol Checklist," on page 245, provides a detailed rundown of how to examine your plants.

3. **Compare findings with common problems.** Chances are that the problem you've spotted is one that's common in your area, so start by comparing your findings with the symptoms and signs of those common problems. For example, you may live in an area where powdery mildew on lilacs, apple maggots on apples, black spot on roses, and leaf spot on tomatoes generally appear every year. Other problems may appear only sporadically in your area.

4. **Expand your research if needed.** If you don't find a match with common problems, you'll have to do some research. Start with this book. Refer to the A-to-Z listing of plants in Part 2, which includes summaries of the damage symptoms caused by the most common pests. Or if you have a sample of the pest or diseased plant tissue in hand, you can compare it to the photos in Part 3 to make an

identification, or browse through the chart of common insect damage symptoms on page 393. You may also want to refer to other insect, disease, and horticulture handbooks and Web sites (see page 397 for suggestions). Keep in mind that environmental conditions and pests and diseases can interact, or one condition might predispose the plants to another. For example, root maggots tunneling in roots directly damage them, but the reason the plants may subsequently die is because rot organisms invade the damaged areas and then spread through the entire root system.

5. **Try some TLC.** If you are still stumped, review everything you know about the conditions preferred by the plant, correct any environmental or nutritional deficiencies, and give the plants the best care you can. Many unexplained afflictions are physiological in origin and plants often grow out of them when conditions improve. Bear in mind that nutrient problems will take weeks or even months to correct. If more plants in the row become affected, as might happen if disease is spreading, pull and discard the damaged plants to reduce the source of disease.

6. **When necessary, consult with experts.** If you have a serious pest or disease problem in your garden that you cannot diagnose, you may want to turn to the Cooperative Extension Service or a private consultant for help. Your local extension agent may immediately recognize the problem. If not, he or she can serve as a contact with specialists from your state university. You also may be asked to send a sample of the diseased plant or plant part to the specialist. Succulent plant parts such as leaves or young shoots shipped in sealed plastic bags tend to rot. Instead, wrap them in several layers of newspaper, which also will prevent crushing. Dry or woody plant material ships well in plastic bags. If possible, send the entire plant, and also

Misleading Symptoms

In some cases, disease symptoms can change as a disease progresses, and secondary symptoms can develop that mask the original problem. Primary symptoms are those symptoms produced at the point where infection occurred. These are usually the most obvious clues for identifying a disease. Secondary symptoms are produced elsewhere on the plant, away from the original infection site. Tomatoes, for instance, commonly suffer from leaf spot disease. The spotted leaves are the primary symptom of disease, but as the disease progresses, the leaves may yellow and drop, exposing the fruit to intense sunlight. The resulting sunscald on the fruit is a secondary symptom.

With most root diseases, you probably will notice secondary symptoms first. If some of your cabbage plants are wilting (a secondary symptom), dig one up and inspect its roots. Are the roots white and well formed, or are they a gnarled mass (the primary symptom), indicating club root disease? Wilting strawberry plants may have damaged roots, caused by black root rot (producing darkened roots) or red stele (with no side roots and a red core evident when a root is slit lengthwise).

include a specimen of a healthy plant or part of a plant of the same species and cultivar. Pack specimens for shipping in a sturdy container, such as a cardboard box or mailing tube, to prevent crushing in the mail.

Once you're familiar with the symptoms caused by certain pest and disease organisms, you may not need to make a pinpoint diagnosis every time in order to know what to do. For example, if you see that plants in one part of a perennial bed are dying off and have blackened, soggy roots, you won't need to identify the specific organism causing the problem. You'll know that you should improve drainage in that part of the bed to make the environment less favorable for fungi and bacteria that cause root rot.

Guide to Garden Pests and Their Natural Enemies

Many of the pests that damage garden plants are widespread in the United States and Canada. Some are very damaging only in a particular region. This guide provides information on the appearance, range, host plants, damage, life cycle, and management strategies for more than 80 types of common garden pests.

Following the section on garden pests are descriptions of more than 80 types of their natural enemies, including information on the range, life cycle, and helpful effects of these beneficials, and suggestions on how to attract them to your garden.

You'll also find a special section on animal pests (which have the potential to cause more damage in a single day than other pests will all season) along with a rundown of suggested deterrents.

GARDEN PESTS

From adelgids to yellowjackets, the text that follows will help you identify pests correctly and decide on the best avenue for dealing with them. Each entry includes a section that summarizes the control options, starting with the least harmful. For in-depth information on control strategies and products, refer to Part 4.

Adelgids Family Adelgidae

DESCRIPTION: Adults: tiny ($\frac{1}{16}$ to $\frac{1}{32}$ inch), aphidlike insects, with or without wings. Nymphs: similar to adults. Hemlock woolly adelgids protect themselves and their eggs with a white waxy woolly covering. Adults and nymphs feed in colonies along the base of the needles. These nonnative pests are found in the Pacific Northwest, but are not a major problem there. On the eastern seaboard, spreading west and south, they are serious pests of native hemlocks (*Tsuga* spp.). Spruce gall adelgids cause swollen conelike growths to form on shoots and shoot tips.

DAMAGE: Adelgids suck sap with piercing/sucking mouthparts. Hemlock woolly adelgids cause stunted twigs and buds and needles that dry out, turn gray-green, and eventually drop. Limbs begin to die back within 2 to 4 years of infestation. Infested trees, which eventually die, also are more susceptible to attack by borers and other pests. On spruces (*Picea* spp.), spruce gall aphids cause stunted growth and swollen, pineapple-shaped conelike galls, which turn brown in midsummer. Infested stem tips die, disfiguring and weakening trees.

LIFE CYCLE: Adelgids spread by eggs and "crawlers." They are distributed by birds, wind, animals, and people. Hemlock woolly adelgid produces two generations, one that is not problematic. The other hatches in late spring, is wingless, and survives for about 9 months. The pests, dormant in summer, feed primarily in fall and early spring when temperatures are mild. Egg laying begins in spring. Spruce gall adelgids have complex life cycles with multiple generations. They begin laying eggs in spring. Feeding causes plant tissues to form a cell around each adelgid, and groups of cells

Hemlock woolly adelgid

merge to form ½- to 3-inch-long galls at the base or tip of the stem. Adelgids emerge in midsummer and the galls turn brown. They overwinter as unprotected nymphs. Cooley spruce gall adelgids infest Douglas fir (*Pseudotsuga menziesii*) as an alternate host, where the pests cause yellowing needles and produce white woolly protective coverings.

CONTROL: Keep hemlock trees healthy by providing good site selection and care. Apply insecticidal soap or horticultural oil. For winter applications use horticultural oil at a dormant-season dilution; in summer use a growing-season dilution. For spruce gall adelgids, prune out the conelike galls in spring and early summer while they are still green and discard them. Spray horticultural oil at a dormant-season dilution in mid-spring, before buds break; apply insecticidal soap or horticultural oil at a growing-season dilution in early fall, when insects are emerging and the galls are still green. See page 384 for guidelines on using horticultural oil on spruces and other conifers.

Aphids Family Aphididae

DESCRIPTION: Adults: pear-shaped, ⅟₃₂- to ⅛-inch insects with two short tubes projecting backward from the abdomen; long antennae; green, pink, black, dusty gray, or white with fluffy coating; with or without wings. Nymphs: similar to adults. Colonies develop quickly; winged forms appear when they become crowded. Common throughout North America.

DAMAGE: Nymphs and adults suck plant sap from most small fruits, vegetables, ornamentals,

Ants as Pests

While some ants that invade homes and other areas where humans do not want them are simply annoying, others far exceed the classification of nuisance pests. Imported red fire ants (*Solenopsis* spp.), which have spread throughout the American South and Southwest, certainly qualify as full-fledged pests. They build large mounds that can damage agricultural equipment, and sting anything that comes within striking distance—from pest insects to humans. They are omnivorous and feed on everything from plants and seedlings to insects, honeydew, and more.

Some ants tend aphids and collect their honeydew, and large tended aphid colonies can cause leaves to curl or become distorted. For the most part, however, ants are beneficial and very important to soil health. (*See* "Ants as Beneficials" on page 294 for more information.)

One old-fashioned cure that works to eliminate unwanted ant colonies is to slowly pour boiling water over their nests. Be sure to give the water time to percolate down into tunnels. When treating fire ant colonies, use at least 3 gallons and be prepared to re-treat until the colony is eliminated. Be careful when handling and pouring water to avoid serious burns.

Coat trunks and shrub stems with Tanglefoot or talcum powder to prevent ants from climbing to tend aphid colonies. (*See* above for information on controlling aphids.)

Encouraging populations of native ants as well as other insect predators is also helpful in keeping pest ants under control. A variety of nematodes, parasitic fungi, and other biological controls for controlling fire ants are available, and scientists continue to look for new controls.

Woolly aphid

Winged form of green peach aphid

Wingless aphids

and fruit and shade trees. Their feeding causes leaf, bud, and flower distortions; severely infested leaves and flowers drop. Fruit that forms on infested branches are misshapen and stunted. Aphids secrete sticky honeydew that supports growth of sooty mold on leaves and fruit. Feeding can spread viral diseases.

LIFE CYCLE: Eggs overwinter on woody stems, hatching in spring into stem females, which can give birth continuously to live nymphs without having to mate. Nymphs mature in 1 to 2 weeks. In fall, males and normal females are born; these mate to produce overwintering eggs. In greenhouses, some females continue to bear nymphs throughout the year. Some species feed on cereal crops or weeds for part of the year and on fruit trees at other times.

CONTROL: For vegetable crops and small ornamentals, spray plants frequently with a strong stream of water to knock aphids off; attract native predators and parasites by planting pollen and nectar plants; for large-scale plantings, try releasing lacewings or parasitic wasps; use homemade garlic or tomato-leaf sprays; spray insecticidal soap; as a last resort, spray infested plants with neem. For fruit or shade trees, spray horticultural oil in winter or very early spring at a dormant-season dilution before or just as buds swell to kill overwintering eggs, and plant flowering groundcovers in home orchards to attract predators and parasites.

Apple Maggot

Rhagoletis pomonella

DESCRIPTION: Adults: ¼-inch flies with yellow legs and transparent wings patterned with dark, crosswise bands. Larvae: white, ¼-inch maggots. Found in eastern United States and Canada, also northern California.

DAMAGE: Maggots tunnel through apples, blueberries, and plums. Fruit drops prematurely; early cultivars are most affected.

LIFE CYCLE: Adults emerge from overwintering pupae from early to midsummer and lay eggs in punctures in fruit skin; eggs hatch in 5 to 7 days; larvae tunnel in fruit until it drops, then leave to pupate in soil for winter. One generation per year. Some pupae remain dormant for several years.

CONTROL: Collect and destroy dropped fruit daily until fall, twice a month in fall; cover young fruits with nylon barriers; hang apple maggot traps in trees from early summer until harvest (one per dwarf tree, six per full-size tree); plant clover groundcover to attract beetles that prey on pupae; grow late-maturing cultivars.

Apple maggot fly

Apple maggot damage

Armyworms

Family Noctuidae

DESCRIPTION: Adults: pale, gray-brown moths with a white dot in center of forewing (1½- to 2-inch wingspan); active only at night. Larvae: early stages smooth, pale green; older larvae reach 1½ inches; greenish brown with white stripes on sides, dark or light stripes along backs. Eggs: greenish white, in masses on lower leaves. Found east of the Rockies and in southeastern Canada, also in New Mexico, Arizona, and California. Beet armyworm is common in southern United States.

DAMAGE: Larvae feed on corn, field crops, and garden plants at night, hiding during the day in the center of corn plants or under stones or leaf litter. When food supply is depleted, they move *en masse* to a new location. Larvae can consume whole plants in one night. First-generation larvae (early summer) usually cause the most damage.

Beet armyworm

LIFE CYCLE: Larvae (sometimes pupae) overwinter in soil or litter around roots, resume feeding in spring, then pupate for 2 weeks. Two to three generations per year.

CONTROL: Attract native parasitic wasps and flies; spray BTK to kill larvae; spray horticultural oil at a growing-season dilution in midsummer to kill eggs of second generation.

Asparagus Beetle

Crioceris asparagi

DESCRIPTION: Adults: shiny, elongate, bluish black, ¼-inch beetles with reddish brown thoraxes, four cream-colored spots and red borders on wing covers. Larvae: ⅓ inch, plump, wrinkled, and gray with dark heads and legs. Eggs: shiny, black, glued on end to stems and young spears. Common throughout North America. The

Asparagus beetle

Asparagus beetle larva

spotted asparagus beetle (*Crioceris duodecimpunctata*) causes similar damage, but is generally found east of the Mississippi River. Beetles are red-orange with twelve black spots on wing covers; larvae are orange.

DAMAGE: Adults and larvae chew on green asparagus shoots, blemishing spears; also attack older stems and leaves.

LIFE CYCLE: Hibernating adults emerge when first asparagus spears are ready to be cut; they feed and lay eggs on spears. Eggs hatch in 1 week, larvae feed for 2 weeks, then burrow into the soil to pupate. Adults emerge in 10 days. Two or three generations per year.

CONTROL: In fall, remove and destroy old fronds and garden trash where beetles overwinter, or put it in sealed containers for disposal with household trash; in spring, cover spears with floating row cover until end of harvest; handpick beetles; as a last resort, spray pyrethrin.

Bagworm

Thyridopteryx ephemeraeformis

DESCRIPTION: Adults: males are black, clear-winged moths (1-inch wingspan); females are wingless. Larvae: dark brown, ¾- to 1-inch caterpillars with white or yellow heads; feed inside 1- to 2-inch, conelike cocoons covered with debris from host plant. Eggs: light tan eggs laid inside bags. Found east of the Rocky Mountains.

DAMAGE: Larvae eat foliage of many trees and shrubs, defoliating and marring plant appearance. Severe infestations cause death.

LIFE CYCLE: Eggs hatch inside bags in spring. Larvae emerge in late spring or early summer and begin feeding on leaves. They build new bags constructed of silk and foliage of the host plant, enlarging the bags as they grow.

Bagworm damage

Bagworm larva inside bag

Larvae pupate in late summer and winged males emerge in early to mid-fall to mate with wingless females in bags. Female moths lay eggs and die; eggs overwinter in bags.

CONTROL: Handpick and destroy bags. Use a knife to cut the silk from the twig; if you tear the bag away, you'll leave a coil of tightly wound silk ready to girdle the twig. Spray with BTK in early spring; set out pheromone traps in late summer to catch males.

Bark Beetles

Family: Scolytidae, Cerambycidae

DESCRIPTION: Adults: brown or black beetles. Shothole borer (*Scolytus rugulosus*) is ¹⁄₁₀ inch with red-tipped wing covers. European shothole borer (*Xyleborus dispar)* is dark brown with yellowish hairs and is ⅛ inch. Asian longhorned beetle (*Anoplophora glabripennis*) is a glossy black, ¾- to 1⅓-inch beetle with white or yellow spots

Ips beetle damage

on wing covers and black-and-white banded antennae that curve backward and are longer than the insect's body. Ips bark beetles (*Ips* spp.) are tiny, orange-brown, ⅕-inch-long insects that attack pines. Larvae: all produce white grubs with reddish brown heads. Shothole borers and elm bark beetles are found throughout North America. Ips beetles are primarily problematic in southern and eastern North America. Asian longhorned beetle was first found in New York and Illinois.

DAMAGE: Adults and larvae bore and tunnel under the bark of many trees. Shothole borer

Shothole borer

primarily attacks peach, plum, cherry, apple, and pear, while Asian longhorned attacks many different species of shade trees, especially maples, poplars, and willows. Ips bark beetles bore through wood on both newly cut and standing timber. They carry a fungus that disrupts water flow in living trees, ultimately killing them. All bark beetles primarily attack unhealthy trees. Sap may flow from entrance holes or shothole borer holes, and piles of sawdust may appear around infested trees.

LIFE CYCLE: Bark beetle adults bore through bark and deposit eggs in galleries. Larvae tunnel under the bark, disrupting the flow of water and nutrients, then pupate there. Emerging adults bore new escape holes through bark. One to three generations per year.

CONTROL: Maintain healthy trees; destroy (burn) all infested branches or trees in winter when larvae are still in wood. Larvae can be transported in firewood and lumber, so do not move wood from infected areas. For shothole borers, destroy borers by inserting a flexible wire into burrows and protect young trees with a whitewash or latex paint diluted with an equal amount of water.

Blister Beetles
Family Meloidae

DESCRIPTION: Adults: metallic black, blue, purple, or brown, ¾-inch-long beetles with soft, elongated bodies, narrow "necks," and long legs; beetles cling to plants when disturbed. Larvae: youngest are tiny, narrow, elongated grubs with large heads; later stages are progressively fatter with smaller heads; last stage is nearly legless. Found throughout North America.

DAMAGE: Large numbers of adults feeding on flowers and foliage of many types of flowers, shrubs, and vegetables rapidly defoliate plants. Larvae of most species are beneficial because they prey on grasshopper eggs.

LIFE CYCLE: Overwintering larvae pupate in spring, adults emerge and lay eggs in midsummer in grasshopper egg burrows; larvae feed on eggs for a month, then overwinter in the burrows for up to 2 years. Most

Margined blister beetle

Blister beetle damage

species have one generation per year, coinciding with grasshopper life cycles.

CONTROL: Except in areas where large adult populations do severe damage, tolerate adults to reap the beneficial effects of larvae. To kill adults, knock them from plants into a pail of soapy water (wear gloves to avoid contact with crushed beetles, which cause skin burns); protect plants with floating row covers or screens in midsummer. Spraying with pyrethrin will kill the beetles, but keep in mind that infestation occurs rapidly and then the beetles disperse; usually the damage is done before you would have time to spray.

Cabbage Looper
Trichoplusia ni

DESCRIPTION: Adults: gray moths with a silver spot in the middle of each forewing (1½- to 2-inch wingspan). Larvae: green, 1½-inch caterpillars with two white lines down their backs, one along each side; they move

Cabbage looper and damage

by looping their bodies. Eggs: light green, dome-shaped, on undersides of leaves. Common throughout most of United States and southern Canada.

DAMAGE: Larvae chew large holes in leaves of cabbage family plants and many other vegetable crops. May damage whole plants.

LIFE CYCLE: Moths emerge from overwintering pupae in mid-spring and lay eggs on leaves; larvae feed 2 to 4 weeks, then pupate 10 days in cocoons attached to stems or leaves. Three to four generations per year.

CONTROL: Scout for and destroy eggs on undersides of leaves. Handpick adults several times

Cabbage looper moth

weekly; attract native parasitic wasps by planting pollen and nectar plants; till in crop residues before adults emerge in spring; spray larvae with BTK or garlic oil. As a last resort for severe infestations, spray with pyrethrin.

Cabbage Maggot

Delia radicum (= Hylemya brassicae)

DESCRIPTION: Adults: gray, ¼-inch flies with long legs. Larvae: white, tapering, ¼-inch maggots in roots. Found throughout North America; rarely a problem in the southern half of the United States.

DAMAGE: Maggots boring into roots of cabbage family plants ruin root crops and stunt or kill plants. Wounds allow disease organisms to enter roots. First sign of injury is usually wilting in midday.

LIFE CYCLE: Adults emerge from overwintering pupae from early spring onward. Females lay eggs in soil beside roots; larvae tunnel into roots 3 to 4 weeks, then

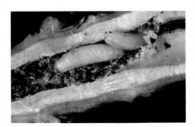

Cabbage maggots

pupate in soil for 2 to 3 weeks. Two to four generations per year.

CONTROL: Cover seedlings with floating row cover, burying edges in soil; set out transplants through slits in barriers (see page 353) to prevent the females from laying eggs; uproot and deeply bury or destroy roots of cabbage family plants after harvesting tops; apply parasitic nematodes to soil around roots. If populations are moderate, repel females by mounding wood ashes, diatomaceous earth, or hot pepper around base of stems.

Cabbageworms, Imported

Artogeia (= Pieris) rapae

DESCRIPTION: Adults: common white butterflies; forewings with black tips and two or three spots (1½- to 2-inch wingspan). Larvae: up to 1¼-inch, velvety green caterpillars with a fine yellow stripe down the back. Eggs: yellow cones laid on undersides of leaves. Found throughout North America.

Imported cabbageworm

Leaf damaged by imported cabbageworms

Fall cankerworm

Cankerworm damage

DAMAGE: Larvae eat large, ragged holes in leaves and heads of cabbage family plants, soiling leaves with dark green droppings.

LIFE CYCLE: Adults emerge from overwintering pupae in early spring to lay eggs. Larvae feed for 2 to 3 weeks, then pupate in debris on soil surface; adults emerge in 1 to 2 weeks. Three to five overlapping generations per year; all ages of larvae present all season.

CONTROL: Scout for and destroy eggs. Encourage parasitic wasps by planting small-flowered annuals in and near your garden. Cover plants with floating row cover; handpick larvae in light infestations. Apply garlic or hot pepper spray weekly, starting when butterflies appear. As a last resort, spray with BTK or spinosad when you find small cabbageworms on foliage.

Cankerworms
Family Geometridae

DESCRIPTION: Adults: males are light gray moths (more than 1-inch wingspan); females are wingless with fuzzy, ½-inch bodies. Larvae: slender, light green, yellow, or brown, ½- to 1-inch caterpillars with white stripes; they loop their bodies as they crawl. Eggs: gray-brown, round; laid in compact masses on plants. Found from Nova Scotia to North Carolina, west to Missouri, Montana, and Manitoba. Also found in Colorado, Utah, and California.

DAMAGE: Larvae chew on young leaves and buds of apple trees and many deciduous shade trees and ornamental shrubs. They also feed on larger leaves, leaving only midribs and large veins. Heavily damaged trees look scorched.

LIFE CYCLE: Adults emerge in late fall to early winter and lay eggs on twigs and branches; eggs hatch in spring as first leaves open on trees. Larvae feed for 3 to 4 weeks, then pupate in soil until early winter. One generation per year.

CONTROL: Trap females in sticky tree bands as they climb trees to lay eggs; handpick and destroy egg masses on branches; spray with horticultural oil at a dormant-season dilution to kill eggs in winter or very early spring before or just as buds swell; spray BTK to kill larvae.

Carrot Beetle See White Grubs

Carrot Rust Fly *Psila rosae*

DESCRIPTION: Adults: shiny, metallic greenish black, ¼-inch flies with yellow legs and head. Larvae: white, tapering, ⅓-inch maggots. Found throughout North America.

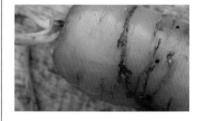

Carrot rust fly damage

DAMAGE: Maggots eat root hairs and tunnel through roots of carrot family plants, stunting or killing plants, ruining root crops, and allowing disease organisms to enter. Maggots also feed on roots in storage.

LIFE CYCLE: Adults emerge in early to mid-spring, laying eggs in soil near plants. Larvae burrow into roots for 3 to 4 weeks, then pupate. Two to three generations per year.

CONTROL: Cover seedbeds with floating row cover, burying edges in soil, before seedlings emerge. Leave plants covered until harvest; apply parasitic nematodes to soil.

Carrot Weevil

Listronotus oregonensis

DESCRIPTION: Adults: coppery brown, hard-shelled, $\frac{1}{6}$-inch weevils. Larvae: white, legless, C-shaped, $\frac{1}{3}$-inch grubs with brown heads. Found in New England and eastern United States.

DAMAGE: Larvae tunnel through stems and roots of carrot family

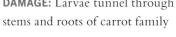

Carrot weevil damage

plants, stunting or killing plants. Infested carrot roots and celery stalks may be unfit to harvest.

LIFE CYCLE: Overwintering adults emerge from grass or garden litter in mid- to late spring, lay eggs on plant stems; larvae bore into stems and downward into roots, then pupate in soil by late spring, early summer. Second-generation adults emerge in midsummer.

CONTROL: Weevils do not fly, so plant susceptible crops in uninfested areas and for additional protection, cover the seedbeds with floating row cover. Drench infested soil with parasitic nematodes.

Chinch Bug *Blissus leucopterus*

DESCRIPTION: Adults: $\frac{1}{6}$-inch bugs that have white forewings with a black triangular spot near margin. Nymphs: $\frac{1}{8}$-inch insects; youngest are bright red with a white stripe across the back; older nymphs are dark with white spots on the middle. Most common in eastern half of United States and Canada.

DAMAGE: Adults and nymphs suck sap from roots and stems of lawn grasses, corn, and cereal grain crops. Infested grass turns yellow, and patches may die off. Large infestations can devastate a grain crop or lawn. These pests

Chinch bug damage

Chinch bug

usually congregate in open, sunny parts of the lawn. They also smell bad, especially when crushed, and you may be able to detect the odor when you walk across a severely infested lawn.

LIFE CYCLE: Adults emerge from overwintering sites in sod along fence rows and hedges. Females lay eggs on grass roots, eggs hatch in 1 to 3 weeks, and nymphs chew on roots until molting to adults in early to midsummer. Two generations per year, three in southern areas.

CONTROL: Avoid chinch bug problems by planting endophyte-containing grass cultivars. In small lawns, soak sod with soapy water (1 ounce liquid dish soap to 2 gallons water), then lay a flannel sheet over the grass to snare the bugs as they are driven out by the soapy solution; kill the bugs by washing them off the sheet in a bucket of soapy water. Encourage native predators—bigeyed bugs, minute pirate bugs, lacewings, lady beetles, and birds; chinch bugs avoid shade, so shade base of crop plants by interplanting soybeans with corn or clover with grains. Apply *Beauveria bassiana*.

Clearwing Borers

Family Sesiidae

DESCRIPTION: Adults: wasplike moths have clear wings with darker markings and black or black-and-yellow striped, 1-inch bodies. Peachtree borers (*Synanthedon* spp.) are blue-black, 1¼-inch moths with yellow or orange bands across the body and narrow translucent wings; adults resemble wasps, and, unlike most moths, are active during the day. Larvae: pale yellow or white with dark heads, ⅛ to 1 inch long, depending on age, boring into

Currant borer larva

Peachtree borer moth

canes or crowns, or under bark. Found throughout North America. *See also* Squash Vine Borer, a related pest.

DAMAGE: Fruit and cane borer larvae tunnel into stems of grape, raspberry, strawberry, currants, gooseberries, and rhododendrons. There are species of clearwing borers that attack lilacs, dogwoods, and many other shade trees. Their tunneling can weaken canes or branches, causing them to break easily, or can kill entire canes. Larvae boring into crowns girdle canes and destroy new shoots. Peachtree borers tunnel beneath bark of peach trees at the base as well as into main roots near the surface. Also may attack plum, prune, cherry, apricot, and nectarine trees. Trees are often girdled. Burrow entrance holes exude gum mixed with sawdustlike material. Young or weak trees may be seriously damaged or killed; older trees are less affected.

LIFE CYCLE: Larvae overwinter in canes or branches and pupate in early May; adults emerge in 2 weeks. Eggs are laid on canes and hatch in 10 days; larvae tunnel in canes all summer, remaining in canes for winter. Rhododendron borer larvae spend the winter in crowns of plants and work their way up into canes by July, pupating under the bark, several inches above the soil line; adults emerge in a month. Peachtree borer larvae overwinter in tree trunk burrows; in spring they spin brown silken cocoons at the surface of the burrow or in soil; cocoons may be covered with dirt and gum from the tree; first adult moths emerge in July, and adult emergence continues into early fall; in late summer females begin laying eggs on tree trunks or in cracks in soil within a few inches of trunks; eggs hatch in 10 days, and new larvae burrow into tree trunks to feed and overwinter until next year. One generation per year; some with 2-year life cycle.

CONTROL: Prune and burn all affected canes, remove infested plants; smash old stubs of plants with a mallet to kill pupae and larvae; try spraying horticultural oil in late spring at a growing-season dilution to kill eggs. For peachtree borers and other wood-boring species, since adult borer moths are attracted to injured or diseased trees, maintain vigorous trees and avoid mechanical injury to trunks; beginning in late summer and into fall, inspect tree trunks from a foot or so above ground level to a few inches below ground level, digging away soil to expose the trunk area below the ground surface; kill borers in exposed burrows by inserting a fine, flexible wire; in fall and spring cultivate soil around the base of the trunk to expose and destroy larvae and pupae; attract native parasitic wasps and predators.

Codling Moth

Cydia pomonella

DESCRIPTION: Adults: gray-brown moths; forewings with fine, white lines and brown tips, hindwings brown with pale fringes (¾-inch wingspan). Larvae: pink or creamy white,

Codling moth larva and damage

⅞-inch caterpillars with brown heads. Eggs: flattened, white. Found throughout North America.

DAMAGE: Larvae tunnel through apple, apricot, cherry, peach, pear, and plum fruit to center, ruining the fruit.

Codling moth

LIFE CYCLE: Overwintering larvae pupate in spring; adults emerge when apple trees bloom. Females lay eggs on fruit, leaves, or twigs; larvae burrow into fruit core, usually from blossom end, for 3 to 5 weeks, then leave fruit to pupate under tree bark or in ground litter. Two to three generations per year, 5 to 8 weeks apart.

CONTROL: In early spring, scrape off areas of loose bark to remove overwintering cocoons and spray horticultural oil at a dormant-season dilution; grow cover crops to attract native parasites and predators, especially ground beetles that eat pupae; hang one codling moth trap per dwarf tree (up to four traps per large tree)

and maintain it according to manufacturer's instructions; apply kaolin clay to deter egg-laying and prevent larvae from entering young fruits; cover fruits with nylon barriers before they reach 1 inch diameter; check trees weekly and remove and destroy any infested fruit; trap larvae in tree bands and destroy daily. If you've had past severe problems with codling moth, apply spinosad two or three times, 10 to 14 days apart beginning when the first codling moth eggs hatch. For subsequent generations, apply a single spray at the beginning of each new egg hatch. In large orchards, use monitoring traps to determine main flight period for moths, then release parasitic *Trichogramma* wasps to attack eggs.

Colorado Potato Beetle

Leptinotarsa decemlineata

DESCRIPTION: Adults: yellowish orange, ⅓-inch beetles with ten lengthwise, black stripes on wing covers, black spots on thoraxes. Larvae: dark orange, humpbacked, ¹⁄₁₆- to ½-inch grubs with a row of black spots along each side. Eggs: bright yellow ovals, standing on end in clusters of about two dozen on undersides of leaves. Found in most parts of North America.

DAMAGE: Both adults and larvae

Colorado potato beetle adult, larva, and eggs

Colorado potato beetles and larvae on damaged leaf

chew leaves of potatoes, tomatoes, eggplants, and related plants, including petunias. Feeding can kill small plants and reduce yields of mature plants.

LIFE CYCLE: Overwintering adults emerge from soil in spring to feed on young plants; after feeding, females lay up to 1,000 eggs during their lifespan of several months. Eggs hatch in 4 to 9 days; larvae feed 2 to 3 weeks, then pupate in soil. Adults emerge in 5 to 10 days. Two generations in most areas, three generations in southern states.

CONTROL: When overwintering adults begin to emerge, shake adults from plants onto a dropcloth in the early morning. Dump beetles into soapy water.

Pick off adults and larvae. Scout for eggs on undersides of leaves and destroy. (Note that the orange-yellow eggs resemble lady beetle eggs.) Attract native predators and parasites with pollen and nectar flowers; mulch plants with a layer of straw at least 4 inches deep; cover plants with floating row cover until harvest, or at least until midseason; for large plantings, release two to five spined solider bugs per square yard of plants; apply parasitic nematodes to soil to attack larvae as they prepare to pupate; apply *Beauveria bassiana* or spinosad to kill larvae; as a last resort, spray infested plants with neem.

Corn Borer, European

Ostrinia nubilalis

DESCRIPTION: Adults: females pale yellowish brown with darker zigzag patterns across wings (1-inch wingspan); males darker-colored. Larvae: beige with small brown spots, up to 1

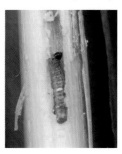

European corn borer larva

inch. Eggs: white, overlapping, laid in masses of 15 to 20 on undersides of leaves. Found throughout northern and central United States and central and eastern Canada.

DAMAGE: Young larvae feed on corn leaves and tassels and beneath husks. Older larvae burrow into corn stalks and ears; damaged stalks may break. Larvae also tunnel in stems or pods of beans, onions, peppers, potatoes, tomatoes, and other crops.

LIFE CYCLE: Larvae overwinter in plant residue and pupate in early spring. Adults emerge in June; lay eggs late June to mid-July. Eggs hatch after 1 week; larvae feed for 3 to 4 weeks. One to three generations per year.

CONTROL: Plant resistant corn cultivars; remove tassels from two-thirds of corn plants before they begin to shed pollen; spray BTK on leaf undersides and into tips of ears; apply granular BTK or mineral oil in tips of ears; rotate crops; release *Trichogramma* wasps for control in large fields; attract native parasites by allowing flowering weeds to grow between rows; pull out and destroy all infested crop residue immediately after harvest. For severe infestations, spray pyrethrin when larvae begin feeding on leaves, tassels, or ears.

Corn Earworm/Tomato Fruitworm

Helicoverpa (= Heliothis) zea

DESCRIPTION: Adults: tan moths (1½- to 2-inch wingspan). Larvae: 1 to 2 inches long, light yellow, green, pink, or brown; white and dark stripes along sides; yellow head and black legs. Eggs: white, ribbed, and round. Found throughout North America; cannot overwinter in Canada, but migrates from United States in spring.

DAMAGE: Larvae burrow into ripe tomatoes, eat buds, and chew large holes in leaves. In corn, larvae feed on fresh silks, then move down ears eating kernels, leaving trails of

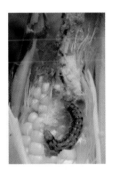

Corn earworm and damage

Corn earworm moth

excrement. Early and late corn cultivars most affected. Larvae will also feed on a broad range of vegetable crops, fruits, and flowers.

LIFE CYCLE: Adults emerge in early spring, migrating long distances to find food, if necessary. Females lay eggs on leaves or on tips of corn ears. Eggs hatch in 3 days; larvae feed 2 to 4 weeks, then pupate in soil. Adults emerge in 10 to 25 days. One to four generations per year.

CONTROL: Plant corn cultivars with tight husks to prevent larvae from entering. Attract native parasitic wasps and predatory bugs. After corn silks start to dry, apply five drops of vegetable oil to the silk of every ear. Squirt parasitic nematodes into tips of corn ears; open corn husks and dig out larvae in tip before they damage main ear; use pheromone traps to monitor appearance of moths; spray BTK or spinosad on leaves and fruit of plants where fruitworms are feeding; in case of severe infestation, spray with neem. In large plantings, release lacewings or minute pirate bugs.

Corn Rootworms

Diabrotica spp.

DESCRIPTION: Adults: ¼-inch beetles. Larvae: slender,

Western corn rootworm adults feeding on corn

wrinkled, white, ½-inch grubs with light brown heads. Eggs: laid on soil near corn roots. Western corn rootworm (*Diabrotica virgifera*) adults are gold with a black head and three black stripes on the back; in males, the black stripes merge to form a single black blotch. They are commonly mistaken for the striped cucumber beetle. Northern corn rootworm (*Diabrotica longicornis*) adults are pale yellowish green to green. Found throughout the United States. *See* Cucumber Beetle on page 262 for southern corn rootworm information.

DAMAGE: Larvae severely damage corn roots; adults feed on pollen and corn silk, damaging ears and interfering with pollination; larvae also spread bacterial wilt.

LIFE CYCLE: Females lay eggs around corn roots in late summer and fall; eggs hatch the following spring; larvae migrate to newly growing corn roots and feed until early summer, then pupate in a soilborne cell. Adults emerge in mid- to late summer. One generation per year in most areas.

CONTROL: Since larvae cannot move far through soil, rotate crops to prevent pest buildup. Populations of Western corn rootworm were discovered in Illinois that migrate from corn to soybean fields to lay eggs. These populations have spread because larvae feed on corn that is often planted following soybeans in rotation. (Adults also lay eggs in alfalfa, oat, and wheat stubble, also often followed by corn.) Avoid these rotations. Also encourage predatory ground and rove beetles by creating some permanent beds or mulched pathways where the soil will remain undisturbed; cultivate corn patches well after harvest and before seeding to kill eggs and larvae.

Cucumber Beetle, Spotted/Southern Corn Rootworm

Diabrotica undecimpunctata howardi

DESCRIPTION: Adults: greenish yellow, ¼-inch beetles with 11 black spots on wing covers. Larvae: white, ½-inch grubs with brown heads and brown patches on first and last segments. Found throughout the United States and southern

Spotted cucumber beetle

Canada, east of the Rocky Mountains. Northern populations migrate north and south as seasons change, traveling up to 500 miles in a few days.

DAMAGE: Larvae feed on roots of corn, often killing young plants; older plants are weakened and may topple easily. Adults feed on leaves and sometimes petals of squash family plants, other vegetable crops, and flowers. Both larvae and adults can transmit cucumber mosaic virus and bacterial wilt.

LIFE CYCLE: Overwintering adults emerge from under crop residues in spring, lay eggs in soil close to plants. Eggs hatch and larvae feed on roots and crown of plants for 2 to 4 weeks, then pupate. One or two generations in northern areas, three in southern areas.

CONTROL: Remove and destroy

crop residues where adults overwinter; rotate garden crops with cover crops such as alfalfa; cover seedlings or plants with floating row cover, hand-pollinating covered squash family plants; for uncovered plants, apply kaolin clay, especially to leaf undersides, and reapply after rain; handpick or vacuum beetles; apply parasitic nematodes to soil weekly to control larvae; as a last resort, spray infested plants with pyrethrin.

Cucumber Beetle, Striped

Acalymma vittatum

DESCRIPTION: Adults: yellow, elongate, ¼-inch beetles with black heads and three wide black stripes on wing covers. Larvae: slender, white grubs. Found in United States west to Colorado and New Mexico; in Canada, west to Saskatchewan.

DAMAGE: Adults feed on squash family plants, beans, corn, peas, and blossoms of many garden plants. The beetles swarm on seedlings, feeding on leaves and young shoots, often killing plants; they also attack stems and flowers of older plants and eat holes in fruit. Feeding can transmit wilt and mosaic viruses. Larvae feed on roots of squash family plants only, killing or stunting plants.

Striped cucumber beetles feeding
in squash flower

Striped cucumber beetle damage
to pumpkin leaf

LIFE CYCLE: Adults overwinter in dense grass or under leaves, emerging in early spring to early summer. They eat weed pollen for 2 weeks, then move to crop plants, laying eggs in soil at base of plants. Eggs hatch in 10 days; larvae burrow into soil, feed on roots for 2 to 6 weeks, pupate in mid- to late summer. Adults emerge in 2 weeks to feed on blossoms and maturing fruit. One to two generations per year.
CONTROL: Remove and destroy crop residues where adults overwinter; cover seedlings or plants with floating row cover, and hand-pollinate covered squash family plants; pile deep straw mulch around plants to discourage beetles from moving between plants; for uncovered plants, apply kaolin clay, especially to leaf undersides, and reapply after rain; handpick or vacuum beetles; apply parasitic nematodes to soil to control larvae; as a last resort, spray with pyrethrin when adults are seen feeding on pollen in flowers.

Cutworms Family Noctuidae

DESCRIPTION: Adults: brown or gray moths (1½-inch wingspan). Larvae: fat, greasy-looking, gray or dull brown, 1- to 2-inch caterpillars with shiny heads. Found throughout North America.
DAMAGE: At night, caterpillars feed on stems of vegetable and flower seedlings and transplants near the soil line, severing them or completely consuming small seedlings. During the day they rest below soil surface, curled beside plant stems.
LIFE CYCLE: Some species overwinter as pupae; adults emerge and lay eggs on grass or soil surface from mid-spring to

Cutworm damage to pea plant

Common cutworm on stem

early summer. Eggs hatch in 5 to 7 days, larvae feed on grass and other plants for 3 to 5 weeks, then pupate in soil. Adults emerge late summer to early fall. Other species overwinter as eggs that hatch during first warm days and feed on early seedlings. One generation per year; a late second generation may damage crops in warm fall weather.
CONTROL: Put collars made of paper, cardboard, or plastic around transplant stems at planting. Collars should be 3 or 4 inches tall; push collars into soil until about half of the collar is below soil level. One week before setting out plants, scatter moist bran mixed with BTK and molasses over surface of beds; apply parasitic nematodes to soil; dig around base of damaged transplants in the morning and destroy larvae hiding below soil surface; set out transplants later in the season to avoid damage.

Diamondback Moth

Plutella xyllostella

DESCRIPTION: Adults: ½-inch moths with light diamond

pattern visible on the back when wings are folded; wing tips flare upward. Larvae: $\frac{5}{16}$ inch and pale green with light brown heads. Found throughout North America.

DAMAGE: Youngest larvae mine tunnels in leaves of cabbage family plants and weeds. Older larvae chew small, irregular holes in leaves, bore into cabbage heads, and chew curds of cauliflower and broccoli.

LIFE CYCLE: Adults overwinter in mild climates. In spring, females lay eggs on leaves; eggs hatch in a few days; larvae feed for 2 weeks, then pupate. Adults emerge in 7 to 10 days. Three to six generations per year.

CONTROL: Cover crops with floating row cover; attract and conserve native parasites and predators, including birds; handpick and destroy larvae and adults; crush small larvae inside the leaves; spray BTK to kill larvae (in some areas, this pest has developed resistance to BTK).

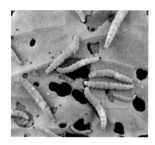

Diamondback moth larvae feeding on cabbage

Earwigs Family Dermaptera

DESCRIPTION: Glossy, flattened, $\frac{1}{2}$- to 1-inch-long, brown to black insects with a pair of curved pinchers or forceps emerging from the tip of the abdomen. Adults are wingless or have wings, but rarely fly; they also rarely pinch. Larvae resemble adults. Found throughout North America. European earwig (*Forficula auricularia*) is most problematic in northern areas; ringlegged earwig (*Euborellia annulipes*) in the South.

Earwig

DAMAGE: Earwigs are omnivorous and primarily feed on decaying organic matter as well as some pest insects, including aphids and other insect larvae. They are beneficial in compost piles and as pest predators, but are a nuisance because they are attracted to moist areas around and inside homes. They become pests when they come indoors and when outdoor populations get out of control. In gardens and greenhouses, they chew irregularly shaped holes in plant leaves and flower petals; tunnel into flower buds, and also consume seedlings.

LIFE CYCLE: Overwintering adults lay clusters of round, white eggs in the soil in late winter; larvae, which resemble adults, hatch in spring. Adults overwinter under garden debris, stones, and boards as well as in soil.

CONTROL: Clean up garden debris and organic mulches, especially around foundations, since moist areas serve as daytime hiding spots for earwigs. Spread dry gravel as mulch next to foundations. Earwigs are attracted to lights, so eliminate or reduce lighting around foundations. To trap earwigs, set out crumpled, damp newspaper, lengths of old hose, or boxes with small holes cut in the sides and baited with oatmeal; collect and dump trapped pests in soapy water. Spread diatomaceous earth in limited areas where earwigs commonly travel, and repeat applications after rains; encourage tachinid flies, which are natural predators; apply the nematode *Steinernema carpocapsae*.

Fall Webworm *See* Webworm, Fall

Flatheaded Borers/Metallic Wood Borers Family Buprestidae

DESCRIPTION: Many species are pests. Flatheaded appletree borer (*Chrysobothris femorata*) adults: flat, dark bronze, ½-inch beetles. Bronze birch borer (*Agrilus anxius*) adults: slender, dark olive bronze, ½-inch beetles. Emerald ash borer (*Agrilus planipennis*) adults: slender, ½-inch, dark metallic green beetles. Larvae: white, legless grubs with brown, retracted heads; up to 1¼ inch. Various species attack apples, honeylocust, oak, birch, ash, roses, brambles (*Rubus* spp.), and many other species. Found throughout North America. Emerald ash borer was first found in Michigan and has spread from there to southern Canada, the Midwest, and some states in the Mid Atlantic and the South.

DAMAGE: Adults feed on leaves of most fruit and shade trees, and larvae tunnel into sapwood of young trees and under bark of

Flatheaded appletree borer larva and damage

Tunnels caused by emerald ash borer

Emerald ash borer

older trees, forming galleries filled with castings. Attacked bark exudes gummy sap, turns dark, and dies; whole trees may be killed. Young trees or those in poor condition most susceptible. Bronze birch borers are especially problematic on white-barked birches.

LIFE CYCLE: Grubs overwinter in chambers in wood, pupate in spring. Adults emerge May to July and lay eggs in cracks in bark. When eggs hatch, grubs tunnel under bark for rest of summer but are usually unable to complete development on vigorous trees. May take 2 years to complete life cycle.

CONTROL: Maintain healthy, vigorous trees; select suitable sites and species (for birches, shady cool, moist sites; plant resistant species such as river birch, *Betula nigra*); avoid injury to bark, such as with lawn mowers; mulch around plants and water as necessary to provide adequate moisture to the roots. To prevent the spread of emerald ash borer, do not move firewood or lumber from infested areas.

Flea Beetles

Family Chrysomelidae

DESCRIPTION: Adults: black, brown, or bronze, $\frac{1}{10}$-inch beetles with well-developed hind legs; jump like fleas when disturbed. Larvae: thin, white, legless grubs with brown heads, up to ¾ inch, living in soil. Found throughout North America.

DAMAGE: Adults chew numerous small, round holes in leaves of most vegetable crops as well as

Flea beetle damage to eggplant

Adult flea beetle

many flowers and weeds. They are most damaging in early spring. Seedlings may be killed; larger plants usually survive. Larvae feed on plant roots. Adults may spread viral diseases as they feed.

LIFE CYCLE: Overwintering adults emerge from soil in spring; they feed and lay eggs on plant roots, then die by early July. Eggs hatch in 1 week, larvae feed 2 to 3 weeks, then pupate in soil; adults emerge in 2 to 3 weeks. One to four generations per year.

CONTROL: Delay planting to avoid peak populations; cover seedlings with row cover until adults die off. Flea beetles prefer full sun, so interplant crops to provide shade for susceptible plants; apply garlic spray or kaolin clay to plants to repel the beetles; drench roots with insect parasitic nematodes to control larvae; for serious infestations, apply *Beauveria bassiana* or spinosad (repeat sprays may be needed). Flea beetles are most problematic during droughts; watering the garden can sometimes reduce outbreaks.

Fleahopper, Garden
Halticus bractatus

DESCRIPTION: Adults: shiny, black, 1⁄16-inch plant bugs with long antennae. They suck sap

Garden fleahopper

and resemble aphids, but jump when disturbed, like flea beetles. Some forms resemble tiny tarnished plant bugs. Larvae: nymphs resemble adults but are pale green, turning darker green as they age. Found in eastern and southern United States as well as Canada

DAMAGE: Feeding with piercing-sucking mouthparts causes pale white or yellow stippling on leaves of most vegetable crops as well as herbs, annuals, and other flowers; heavily infested leaves may die. Fleahoppers are especially attracted to legumes such as clover, alfalfa, and soybeans.

LIFE CYCLE: Fleahoppers overwinter as eggs. Nymphs hatch in spring and molt through five instars before adulthood. Adults and larvae primarily feed on the undersides of leaves. Females lay eggs inside plant leaves and stems; five generations per year.

CONTROL: Pick off and destroy infested leaves; clean up the garden, especially after infestations, since eggs overwinter on plant debris;

encourage and attract native populations of parasitic wasps; monitor populations in nearby weedy patches and destroy infested plants if necessary; protect plants by spraying with kaolin clay or garlic sprays; as a last resort, spray pyrethrin.

Fruit Flies Family Tephritidae

DESCRIPTION: Adults: 1⁄4-inch flies with yellow or white markings on their bodies, and transparent wings patterned with dark, crosswise bands. Larvae: white, 1⁄4-inch maggots feeding in fruit. Found throughout North America.

DAMAGE: Larvae tunnel extensively through fruit of blueberry, currant, plum, cherry, and peach. Certain species also

Mediterranean fruit fly

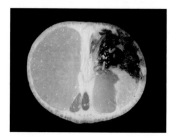
Fruit fly damage to citrus

feed on walnut, citrus, and coffee. Infested fruit shrivels or drops early; earliest cultivars suffer the most damage. In walnut, main injury is shell staining. *See also* Apple Maggot, also in this family.

LIFE CYCLE: Adult flies emerge from pupae in early summer and lay eggs in punctures in fruit skin or around stems. Eggs hatch within 1 week, larvae tunnel in fruit until it drops, then leave fruit to pupate and overwinter in the soil. Most species have one generation per year; in very warm regions generations may continue all year.

CONTROL: Pick up fallen fruit and destroy daily during summer, weekly in fall; hang yellow sticky traps baited with vials of 1 part ammonia and 1 part water or commercial fruit fly attractants in trees (one to two traps per tree); encourage ground beetles and rove beetles, which feed on fly pupae, by planting groundcovers in orchards.

Gall Wasps Family Cynipidae

DESCRIPTION: Adults: brown or reddish, tiny wasps, rarely seen. Larvae: legless white grubs. Most common in western United States and Canada; some occur in the East.

DAMAGE: Larvae feed on oaks,

Galls on oak leaf

roses, thistles, and other plants. Plants respond by producing galls—enlarged masses of cells—of various shapes, attached to stems or leaves.

LIFE CYCLE: Overwintering adults emerge from winter galls, usually on roots or fallen leaves; females lay eggs on host plants in early spring; feeding larvae stimulate gall formation, which serves as food and protects larvae. Adults emerge in summer and lay eggs that form over-wintering galls.

CONTROL: Usually not necessary; prune galls from roses or shrubs and destroy.
See also Mites, Gall; Adelgids

Grasshoppers
Family Acrididae

DESCRIPTION: Adults: brown, yellow, or green, 1- to 2-inch insects with leathery forewings and enlarged hind legs; may have brightly colored underwings. Nymphs: similar to adults, but

smaller. Found throughout North America.

DAMAGE: Adults eat any kind of vegetation. In most areas of North America, economic damage occurs only in fields of grass or cereal crops. Little damage occurs to home gardens; on rare occasions swarms of grasshoppers devastate agricultural crops over large areas.

LIFE CYCLE: In late summer females deposit elongate masses of eggs in soil; eggs hatch in spring; nymphs develop for 40 to 60 days until molting to adults. Adults feed until killed by cold weather. Swarms appear as a result of interaction of weather and biological influences.

CONTROL: Usually controlled by natural enemies (blister beetle larvae, ground beetles, predatory flies, birds, parasitic nematodes, fungal diseases); cultivate fields in fall to kill overwintering eggs; aerial sprays of commercial

Slant-faced grasshopper

protozoan disease (*Nosema locustae*) may be effective over large areas but are not useful on a home-garden scale.

Gypsy Moth *Lymantria dispar*

DESCRIPTION: Adults: females nearly white, 1-inch moths with heavy bodies, unable to fly; males are smaller, darker, strong fliers. Larvae: up to 2½-inch, gray-brown caterpillars with five pairs of blue dots and six pairs of red dots on back, long hairs in tufts on body. Eggs: in masses under fuzzy yellow covering.

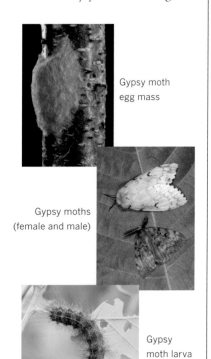

Gypsy moth egg mass

Gypsy moths (female and male)

Gypsy moth larva

Found in eastern and central United States and eastern Canada; isolated outbreaks in California and other western areas. Dispersal depends on human activity (trucking, camping, etc.) to move eggs, larvae, pupae to new areas.

DAMAGE: Larvae feed on leaves of many trees and shrubs, including conifers; heavy infestations can defoliate trees. Repeated defoliations eventually kill deciduous trees; a single defoliation kills conifers.

LIFE CYCLE: Overwintering eggs on tree trunks hatch in May, larvae feed in trees until mid-July, then pupate for several weeks. Adults emerge late July to early August. Females crawl up nearby trees or other objects to deposit egg masses that overwinter.

CONTROL: Attract predators and parasites (especially tachinid flies, ground beetles, and parasitic wasps); remove egg masses from tree trunks and branches and destroy; prevent movement of pest by checking trailers, boats, camping gear, and so on for egg masses or larvae before leaving an infested region; use pheromone traps to catch males for monitoring or to prevent mating; spray BTK to kill larvae; wrap burlap tree bands around fruit and shade

trees, check daily and destroy hiding larvae. A naturally occurring fungus, *Entomophaga maimaiga,* helps keep populations in check and reduces severity of outbreaks.

Hornworms Family Sphingidae

DESCRIPTION: Two species are common pests: tomato hornworm (*Manduca quinquemaculata*) and tobacco hornworm (*Manduca sexta*). Adult: both are large, gray or brownish moths (4- to 5-inch wingspan) with mottled wings and a dark body marked with yellow spots. Larvae: green caterpillars up to 4½ inches long with a horn on the tail. Tomato hornworms have seven yellowish, V-shaped marks along the sides with a black horn; tobacco hornworms have seven white diagonal lines with a red horn. Note that this family contains many interesting and handsome moths, commonly called hawk moths, sphinx moths, and hummingbird moths.

DAMAGE: Larvae of both species consume leaves, stems, and fruit of nightshade family plants. Feeding can kill young plants.

LIFE CYCLE: In June and July, moths emerge from soilborne pupae; adults lay eggs on

Tomato hornworm

Tobacco hornworm moth

undersides of leaves; eggs hatch in a week; larvae feed for a month, then pupate in soil until the following summer.

CONTROL: Handpick caterpillars from foliage; pick off and destroy eggs; attract native parasitic wasps; spray BTK while caterpillars are still small. Do not destroy hornworms that have white, ricelike pupae attached to their backs, as these indicate the worm has been parasitized by wasps.

Iris Borer *Macronoctua onusta*

DESCRIPTION: Adults: moths with dark brown forewings, yellowish hind wings (2-inch wingspan). Larvae: fat, pinkish borers with brown heads and a light stripe down the back, rows of black dots on sides; up to 2 inches long. Found in eastern United States and west to Iowa, and in Quebec and eastern Ontario.

DAMAGE: Young larvae tunnel within leaves, leaf sheaths, and buds of iris, moving down into crowns and rhizomes as they develop. Soft rots usually follow larval damage.

Iris borer damage

LIFE CYCLE: Eggs overwintering on old leaves hatch in early to mid-spring. Larvae enter leaves, feed for several weeks, then pupate in soil near rhizomes; adults emerge in late summer and lay eggs.

CONTROL: Remove and destroy dead iris leaves and stems in late fall to eliminate overwintering eggs; dig infested rhizomes, remove larvae and pupae, dip in or dust with sulfur fungicide before replanting if soft rot present.

Japanese Beetle

Popillia japonica

DESCRIPTION: Adults: chunky, metallic blue-green, ½-inch beetles with bronze wing covers, long legs, and fine hairs covering body. Larvae: fat, dirty white grubs with brown heads; up to ¾ inch; found in sod. Found in all states east of the Mississippi River. Many other species produce C-shaped white larval grubs; *see also* White Grubs.

DAMAGE: Adults eat flowers and skeletonize leaves of a broad range of plants; plants may be completely defoliated. Adults feed on fruit, such as raspberries and plums, opening a site for disease infection. Larvae feed on roots of lawn grasses and garden plants.

LIFE CYCLE: Overwintering larvae deep in the soil move toward the surface in spring to feed on roots, pupating in early summer. Adults emerge, feed on plants, and lay eggs in late summer; eggs hatch into larvae that overwinter in soil. One

Japanese beetle and damage

generation occurs every 1 to 2 years.

CONTROL: In early morning, shake beetles from plants onto dropcloths, then drown them in soapy water; or shake beetles into a can of soapy water to drown. Cover plants with floating row cover; apply *Heterorhabditis* nematodes or milky spore to sod to kill larvae; attract native species of parasitic wasps and flies; organize a community-wide trapping program to reduce adult beetle population; spray plants attacked by beetles with insecticidal soap. As a last resort, spray with neem.

Lace Bugs Family Tingidae

DESCRIPTION: Adults: oval or rectangular, ⅛-inch bugs with lacy patterns and wide, flattened extensions on thoraxes. Nymphs: smaller, darker, covered with spines. Eggs: inserted on undersides of leaves along midribs with conelike caps projecting from leaves. Found throughout North America.

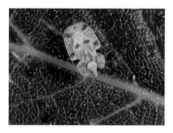

Oak lace bug

Foliage damage due to lace bug feeding

DAMAGE: Adults and nymphs suck juices from undersides of leaves of flowers, trees, and vegetable plants, especially evergreens, spotting leaves with excrement and leaving speckled white or gray, blotchy appearance on leaf surfaces.

LIFE CYCLE: Most species overwinter in egg stage, some as adults under bark of trees. Eggs hatch into nymphs that feed for several weeks until molting to adults. Three or more generations per year.

CONTROL: Spray horticultural oil at a growing-season dilution as soon as nymphs or adults are evident (not on chrysanthemum flowers); or spray with insecticidal soap. Use pyrethrin as a last resort. Proper site selection can help prevent problems, since plants growing in full sun and in dry soil are most susceptible.

Leaf Beetles

Family Chrysomelidae

DESCRIPTION: Adults: Beetles with two hard wing covers. Lily

Lily leaf beetle laying eggs

Viburnum leaf beetle larvae and damage

leaf beetles are ¼ to ½ inch long, bright scarlet red with black heads, antennae, legs, and undersides. Viburnum leaf beetles are about ¼ inch long and brown. Larvae: Sluglike grubs. Lily leaf beetle larvae are yellowish, brownish, or greenish, and cover themselves with excrement. Viburnum leaf beetles are greenish yellow. Eggs: Lily leaf beetle lay round, yellow-orange eggs in irregular rows on the undersides of lily leaves. Viburnum leaf beetles bore holes in new stems, lay eggs in neat rows, and seal them in with a mix of sawdust and excrement. Both species are introduced pests found in New England. For more on other leaf-feeding beetles, *see also* Colorado Potato Beetle, Cucumber

Beetles, Flea Beetles, Japanese Beetle, Mexican Bean Beetle, and Rose Chafer.

DAMAGE: Grubs feed on the undersides of leaves; older grubs of lily leaf beetles move to upper leaf surfaces and buds. Adults feed on leaves and flowers of lilies (*Lilium* spp.) and fritillarias (*Fritillaria* spp.) as well as nightshade family plants such as potatoes. Viburnum leaf beetle grubs feed along leaf veins, eventually skeletonizing leaves; adults chew large holes in leaves.

LIFE CYCLE: Lily leaf beetles overwinter as adults and lay eggs in mid- to late spring. Larvae feed into early summer, pupate in the soil, then emerge as adults. Viburnum leaf beetles overwinter as eggs that hatch in spring. Larvae feed, pupate in the soil, then emerge as adults. The adults feed for the rest of the season. One generation per year.

CONTROL: Monitor plants for eggs and destroy them. From fall through winter, prune out and destroy viburnum twigs with evidence of egg-laying. Handpick eggs that appear on lily leaves in spring. Handpick and destroy larvae and adults. Carefully inspect new plants to avoid introducing these pests to your garden. As a last resort, spray neem when grubs are still small; repeat weekly to eliminate populations.

Leafhoppers
Family Cicadellidae

DESCRIPTION: Adults: wedge-shaped, slender, green or brown, $\frac{1}{10}$- to $\frac{1}{2}$-inch insects; a forward point above the head is very pronounced in some species. Some have brightly colored bands on wings; all jump rapidly into flight when disturbed. Nymphs: pale, wingless, similar to adults; hop rapidly when disturbed. Found throughout North America.

DAMAGE: Adults and nymphs suck juices from stems and undersides of leaves of most fruit and vegetable crops, also some flowers and weeds. Their toxic saliva distorts and stunts plants and causes tipburn and yellowed, curled leaves with white spots on undersides. Fruit may be spotted with drops of excrement and honeydew. Leafhoppers can spread aster yellows and other diseases as they feed.

LIFE CYCLE: Overwintering adults start laying eggs in spring when leaves begin to appear on trees. Some species do not survive winter in northern United States and in Canada; they migrate from the South every summer. Females lay eggs in leaves and stems; eggs hatch in 10 to 14 days, nymphs develop for several weeks. Most species have two to five generations per year, over-

Potato leafhopper damage

Red-banded leafhopper

wintering as adults or eggs.

CONTROL: Wash nymphs from plants with stiff sprays of water, repeated frequently; attract natural enemies (predatory flies and bugs and parasitic wasps); spray with insecticidal soap. As a last resort, spray with neem.

Leafmining Flies
Family Agromyzidae

DESCRIPTION: Adults: black or black-and-yellow, $\frac{1}{10}$-inch flies; rarely seen. Larvae: pale green, stubby, translucent, $\frac{1}{8}$-inch maggots, found in tunnels in leaves. Eggs: white, cylindrical, laid in clusters on undersides of leaves. Several species found throughout North America.

Leafminer damage to columbine

DAMAGE: Larvae tunnel within leaves of many vegetable crops and ornamentals such as holly (*Ilex* spp.) and columbine (*Aquilegia* spp.). They feed on leaf tissue and make round or winding, hollow mines, often destroying seedlings. On larger vegetables, more of a nuisance than serious problem; damaging on ornamentals because mines are unsightly.

LIFE CYCLE: Adults emerge from overwintering cocoons in early spring and lay eggs on leaves. Larvae mine leaves for 1 to 3 weeks, then drop to soil to pupate 2 to 4 weeks. Two to three generations per year, more in greenhouses.

CONTROL: Cover seedlings with floating row cover; pick and destroy mined leaves and remove egg clusters; remove nearby dock or lamb's-quarters, which are hosts for beet leaf-miners; attract native parasitic wasps by planting nectar plants; as a last resort, spray with neem.

Leafmining Sawflies *Fenusa* spp.

DESCRIPTION: Adults: black, stout-bodied, ⅕-inch insects with transparent wings. Larvae: flattened, white, legless maggots with brown heads. Found in northern and eastern United States, west to Great Lakes states. Related species in Canada.

DAMAGE: Larvae mine leaves of elm, birch, or alder, feeding between upper and lower leaf surfaces and leaving brownish, wrinkled blisters or blotches in leaves; damaged trees are weakened and may be attacked by borers and other pests.

LIFE CYCLE: Larvae overwinter in cocoons in the soil, pupating in spring; adults emerge in mid-May and lay eggs in leaves; larvae feed in leaves until ready to pupate. Up to four generations per year.

Birch leafminer fly

Birch leafminer damage

CONTROL: Maintain healthy, vigorous trees.

Leafrollers

Family Tortricidae

DESCRIPTION: A huge family of moths with caterpillars that spin webs at branch tips, then feed on enclosed buds, leaves, and developing fruit. Adults are generally brown, mottled moths (¾-inch wingspan). Larvae: green caterpillars with brown or black heads. Eggs: light yellowish brown with brown coating. Found throughout North America.

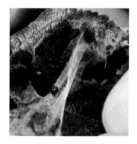

Strawberry leafroller larva and webbing

DAMAGE: Larvae spin webs at branch tips of roses and most fruit and ornamental trees and feed on enclosed buds, leaves, and developing fruit. Omniverous leafroller larvae fasten two unrolled leaves together. Larvae of oblique-banded leafroller emerge in spring and young larvae mine in leaves of apples, strawberries, roses, and other ornamentals, then move to branch tips.

LIFE CYCLE: Eggs hatch in spring to summer, depending on species. Larvae feed for 1 month, spin webs, and pupate within rolled leaves (flattened for omnivorous leafroller) or in cocoons on bark. Adults emerge early to midsummer and lay overwintering eggs on bark. One or more generations per season.

CONTROL: Scrape egg masses from branches in winter; apply horticultural oil at a dormant-season dilution to kill eggs in winter or very early spring before or just as buds swell; handpick caterpillars or webbed leaves from young trees weekly; attract native parasitic wasps; apply BTK to larvae before they spin webs; spray serious infestations with pyrethrin, again before they spin webs.

Lygus Bugs *See* Plant Bugs

Mealybugs
Family Pseudococcidae

DESCRIPTION: Adults: females are soft, oval, $\frac{1}{10}$-inch insects with distinctly segmented, pinkish bodies covered with white waxy fluff; males are tiny, two-winged insects; rarely seen. Nymphs: similar to adults, but smaller. Most species found in southern United States; long-

tailed mealybug throughout North America; all species found in greenhouses.

DAMAGE: Adults and nymphs suck plant juices from many types of fruit crops, avocadoes, potatoes, ornamentals, and tropical foliage plants. They feed on all parts of a plant, particularly new growth, causing leaves to wither and yellow and fruit to drop prematurely. Honeydew excreted on leaves supports the growth of sooty mold fungus.

LIFE CYCLE: Females lay eggs in a fluffy white mass; eggs hatch in 10 days and crawlers wander away to find feeding sites, where they develop for 1 to 2 months or longer. Several generations per year.

CONTROL: Rinse plants with stiff streams of water to dislodge mealybugs; spray with insecticidal soap; release mealybug destroyers (*Cryptolaemus montrouzieri*) in citrus or grape plantings or on indoor plants; for citrus mealybugs release parasitic wasp *Leptomastix dactylopii;* attract

Mealybug infestation on hibiscus

native parasitic wasps, which usually keep populations in check outdoors.

Mexican Bean Beetle
Epilachna varivestis

DESCRIPTION: Adults: oval, yellowish brown, $\frac{1}{4}$-inch beetles with 16 black spots on wing covers. (They are related to lady beetles.) Larvae: fat, yellowish orange, $\frac{5}{16}$-inch grubs with long, branching spines. Eggs: yellow ovals laid on end on undersides of leaves. Found in most states east of the Mississippi River; also Texas, Arizona, Utah, Colorado, and Nebraska.

DAMAGE: Both larvae and adults skeletonize leaves of

Mexican bean beetle larva and adult

Mexican bean beetle damage

cowpeas, lima beans, snap beans, and soybeans. They feed from the undersides of leaves, leaving characteristic lacy damage; severely defoliated plants may be killed. Beetles are most abundant in weedless fields.

LIFE CYCLE: Adults overwinter in leaf litter in nearby fields; in spring, females lay eggs on beans. Eggs hatch in 5 to 14 days, larvae feed 2 to 4 weeks, then pupate on leaves. One to three generations per year.

CONTROL: Plant early-season bush beans to avoid main beetle generations; plant soybeans as trap crops, destroy them when infested with larvae; handpick larvae and adults daily in small bean patches; scout for and destroy eggs; cover plants with floating row cover until plants are large enough to withstand damage; attract native predators and parasites by leaving flowering weeds between rows or by interplanting flowers and herbs; dig in crop residues as soon as plants are harvested; release spined soldier bugs (*Podisus maculiventris*) to control early generation; release parasitic wasps *Pediobius foveolatus* as soon as possible after egg clusters appear on your plants; apply insecticidal soap, especially to leaf undersides; as a last resort, spray with neem.

Millipedes

DESCRIPTION: Brownish, slow-moving, segmented arthropods with a rounded wormlike body and numerous short legs, generally with two per body segment. Common garden species range from ½ to 1½ inches. Some millipedes curl up when disturbed. (Centipedes have longer legs and move more quickly.) *See also* Centipedes, which are also largely beneficial.

DAMAGE: Generally beneficial in the garden, feeding on rotting leaves and other decaying plant tissue. They are beneficial in compost piles because they help break down organic matter. They become pests if populations get out of hand or in greenhouses, and feed on plant roots, germinating seeds, seedlings, and fruit in contact with the ground.

LIFE CYCLE: Adults lay eggs in soil. Eggs hatch into nymphs, which are similar to adults, but shorter, with fewer segments.

CONTROL: Usually not needed;

Millipede

sprinkle wood ashes or diatomaceous earth near rows of germinating seeds. Remove rotting leaves and other debris to discourage them. Keep susceptible fruit, such as strawberries, off the ground.

Mites, Gall

Family Eriophyidae

DESCRIPTION: Adults: nearly invisible, elongate, cylindrical, pale yellow or tan mites with two pairs of legs at the front end. Nymphs: similar to adults, but smaller. Found throughout North America.

American elm leaf galls

DAMAGE: Mites burrow from undersides into leaf tissue of pears, currants, and many ornamentals. Leaves react by forming raised blisters, puckers, or galls along leaf margins. Some blisters, especially on maples, are bright red, others are yellow or brown.

LIFE CYCLE: Numerous overlapping generations all season. Mites overwinter in crevices in bark, crawling onto new growth in spring.

CONTROL: Galls are unsightly, but do not cause serious injury, and control is seldom warranted. If galls have been a serious problem in your garden, spray susceptible plants while dormant with horticultural oil (dormant-season dilution) or lime-sulfur in winter or very early spring before or just as buds swell.

Mites, Rust

Family Eriophyidae

DESCRIPTION: Adults: nearly invisible, elongate, cylindrical, pale yellow or tan mites, with two pairs of legs at the head end. Nymphs: similar to adults, but smaller. Found throughout North America.

DAMAGE: Mites burrow from undersides into leaf tissue of apples, pears, tomatoes, and ornamental trees and shrubs. Infested leaves and fruit have russeted appearance.

LIFE CYCLE: Mites overwinter at base of buds or in cracks of bark, moving to developing flowers in spring. Numerous overlapping generations all season;

Rust mite damage to apple

populations usually decline in hot weather. By late summer, most species move to over-wintering sites.

CONTROL: Whenever possible, allow natural predators to keep rust mite populations in balance. If problems have been severe, spray horticultural oil (dormant-season dilution) combined with lime-sulfur on dormant trees in winter or very early spring before or just as buds swell; spray foliage with sulfur fungicide.

Mites, Spider

Family Tetranychidae

DESCRIPTION: Adults: minute, eight-legged, $\frac{1}{50}$-inch mites with fine hairs on body; reddish, pale green or yellow; most, but not all, species spin fine webs. Nymphs: similar to adults, but smaller; early stages with six legs. Found throughout North America. Cyclamen mites are similar pests.

DAMAGE: Adults and nymphs suck juice from cells on undersides of leaves of many food crops, ornamentals, and fruit trees. Plants are weakened, leaves may drop, and fruit may be stunted. Early damage to leaves appears as yellow-specked areas, with or without webbing, or leaves turn yellow or white with brown edges; webs may cover leaves and growing tips.

Spider mite webbing

LIFE CYCLE: Eggs or adults overwinter in bark crevices or garden debris, emerging in early spring. Eggs hatch in 2 to 3 days, nymphs develop to adults in 7 to 10 days. Many overlapping generations every season; reproduction continues all year in greenhouses.

CONTROL: Spray fruit trees in late winter or early spring before or just as buds swell with horticultural oil (dormant-season dilution) to kill overwintering eggs; in garden or greenhouse rinse plants with water and mist daily to suppress reproduction of mites; release predatory mites *Metaseiulus occidentalis* on fruit trees, *Phytoseiulus persimilis* or similar species in large-scale plantings of vegetables, strawberries, and flowers; as a last resort, spray insecticidal soap or neem.

Mole Crickets

Scapteriscus spp.

DESCRIPTION: Adults: light brown to tan crickets, $\frac{7}{8}$ to $1\frac{1}{8}$ inch long with enlarged forelegs. Nymphs: similar to adults, but

Northern mole cricket

Mole cricket damage

lack wings. Eggs: Gray to brownish and bean shaped; laid in clusters of 25 to 60 in burrows 2 to 10 inches belowground. Found in the southeastern United States.

DAMAGE: Adults and nymphs tunnel within 2 inches of the soil surface, deeper during dry weather. They damage roots, tubers, and stems of grass as well as vegetables and ornamentals, especially seedlings. They also feed aboveground after dark on foliage and stems, consuming seedlings, girdling seedlings and young plants, and pulling young plants below ground into burrows. Mole crickets are omnivorous and also consume insects and other soil dwellers.

LIFE CYCLE: Eggs are laid in spring and nymphs feed through summer. Nymphs become adults the following spring and lay eggs. One generation per year; two generations in South Florida.

CONTROL: Encourage local predators such as toads. Release the parasitic nematode, *Steinernema scapterisci*, if available. A parasitic fly, *Ormia depleta,* has also been released and is proving to be an effective control.

Onion Maggot *Delia antique*

DESCRIPTION: Adults: gray, bristly, humpbacked, ¼-inch flies with large wings; about half the size of houseflies. Larvae: white, blunt-ended, ¼-inch maggots. Eggs: laid in soil near plants. Found throughout the northern half of the United States as well as Canada.

DAMAGE: Maggots burrow into developing onions or leeks, killing young plants and hollowing out or stunting older plants; rot diseases enter bulbs injured by maggot feeding; one maggot can kill over a dozen seedlings during its development. This pest rarely infests onions in the South. In the North,

Onion maggot damage

infestations are worst in cool, wet weather, sometimes killing up to 80 percent of a spring crop.

LIFE CYCLE: Flies overwinter as brown pupae, resembling grains of wheat, in soil or garden trash; adult flies emerge from pupae from mid-May to the end of June and lay eggs at the bases of onion or leek plants; eggs hatch in a week; maggots burrow into onions and feed 2 to 3 weeks, then pupate in soil nearby; adults emerge in 1 to 2 weeks. Commonly two generations per growing season; a third generation may attack onions just before harvest and cause storage rot.

CONTROL: Cover seedlings with floating row cover; sprinkle rows liberally with ground cayenne pepper or chili powder; plant cull onions around the borders and down the rows of seedling onions to act as a trap crop; pull and destroy cull trap crops 2 weeks after they sprout; bury, burn, or destroy all unwanted onions at the end of harvest; plant onion sets late to avoid the first generation of flies.

Oriental Fruit Moth

Grapholitha molesta

DESCRIPTION: Adults: small, dark gray moths with dark brown mottled forewings (½-inch wingspan). Larvae: white to

Damage to peach caused by Oriental fruit moth

Oriental fruit moth larva

pinkish gray; ½-inch caterpillars with brown heads. Eggs: flat, white, laid in twigs or leaf undersides. Found in eastern states, Pacific Northwest, and Ontario.

DAMAGE: In spring, young larvae bore into green twigs of peach, almond, cherry, apple, pear, or other fruit trees, causing twig wilting and dieback; second-generation larvae bore into developing fruit, leaving masses of gummy castings; later generations enter the stem end of maturing fruit, leaving no external signs of damage; perfect-looking fruit injured through stem entry will usually break down in storage.

LIFE CYCLE: Larvae overwinter in silken cocoons on bark or weeds or in soil around trees, pupating in early spring; adults

emerge from late spring to early summer; females lay eggs, which hatch in 10 to 14 days; first-generation larvae bore into tender stems and twigs, feed for 2 to 3 weeks, then pupate. Second-generation adults appear in midsummer; second-generation larvae bore into young fruit and don't feed on twigs; a third generation of larvae arrive by the end of summer in northern United States; these bore into the stem ends of mature fruits and feed on the pits. Three to four generations in the North; six to seven in southern states.

CONTROL: Where possible, plant early-bearing peach and apricot cultivars that are harvested before midsummer; to destroy overwintering larvae, cultivate soil 4 inches deep around trees in early spring; attract native parasitic wasps and flies with flowering cover crops planted around trees; disrupt mating with pheromone patches applied to lower limbs of trees (one patch per four trees); spray horticultural oil at a growing-season dilution in summer to kill eggs and larvae.

Pear Psylla

Cacopsylla pyricola

DESCRIPTION: Adults: red to green, ¹⁄₁₀-inch-long insects,

Pear psylla adult

Pear psylla damage

resembling tiny cicadas with wings folded rooflike over the back. Nymphs: oval, green to brown, wingless, ¹⁄₈₀-inch insects. Found in eastern United States and Canada, Pacific Northwest, and California.

DAMAGE: A major pest of pears and quinces, psylla suck plant juices, causing leaves to yellow from the toxic saliva; honeydew secretions support growth of sooty mold. Feeding spreads pear decline virus.

LIFE CYCLE: Overwintering adults emerge in spring from bark and leaf litter to lay eggs on fruit spurs and buds. Nymphs spend early stages protected by honeydew; later stages are more active. Three to five generations per year.

CONTROL: Spray trees with kaolin clay in spring and repeat applications throughout the season if possible; spray horticultural oil at a growing-season dilution in spring; plant cover crops to attract native predatory insects; as a last resort, spray infested trees with insecticidal soap.

Plant Bugs Family Miridae

DESCRIPTION: Adults: oval, mottled, ¼-inch bugs; light green, yellowish, or red-brown to brown. A number of plant bug species damage garden plants. Tarnished plant bugs have a black-tipped yellow triangle on each forewing. Two similar species of lygus bugs (*L. hesperus* and *L. elisus*) have a yellow triangle just below the head. Four-lined plant bugs have four black stripes on a yellow body,

Catfacing of strawberries caused by plant bug feeding

Tarnished plant bug

with a black triangle at the base of the wings. Nymphs: generally yellow-green, wingless; similar to adults. Four-lined plant bug larvae are red with black wing pads, then change to yellow with black wing pads with a yellow stripe on each. Found throughout North America.

DAMAGE: Adults and nymphs suck plant juices of most flowers, fruits, and vegetables, causing shoot and fruit distortion, bud drop, wilting, stunting, and dieback. Feeding also causes irregularly shaped or "cat-faced" fruit on strawberries and malformed leaves on leafy vegetables.

LIFE CYCLE: Some species overwinter as adults under bark and leaf litter, then emerge in early spring to lay eggs in leaf tissue; eggs hatch in 10 days; nymphs feed 3 to 4 weeks, then molt to adult. Other species overwinter as eggs, which are laid in clusters and hatch in spring. Up to five generations per year.

CONTROL: Cover plants with floating row cover; attract native predators (bigeyed bugs, damsel bugs, pirate bugs) with groundcovers and pollen plants; remove weeds early, especially red-stemmed pigweed; apply garlic sprays to susceptible plants as a repellent; apply *Beauveria bassiana* to young nymphs; spray

infested plants with insecticidal soap or pyrethrin as a last resort.

Plum Curculio

Conotrachelus nenuphar

DESCRIPTION: Adults: dark, brownish gray, ¼-inch beetles with warty, hard wing covers, prominent snout, and white hairs on body. Larvae: plump, white, ⅓-inch grubs with brown heads. Eggs: round, white, laid individually under a crescent-shaped cut in the fruit skin. Found in eastern North America.

DAMAGE: A major plum and apple pest in many areas, adult curculios feed on petals, buds, and young fruit; females deposit a single egg just under fruit skin, leaving a crescent-shaped scar at

Plum curculio

Plum curculio damage

each egg-laying site; larvae feed inside the fruit, causing it to drop, rot, or develop deformed growth. Other susceptible fruits include pears, peaches, cherries, and apricots.

LIFE CYCLE: Adult beetles overwinter under fallen leaves, stones, logs, or other garden debris, flying to trees just as blossoms open; adults feed and lay eggs, which hatch in 5 to 10 days; larvae feed in fruit 2 to 3 weeks; when fruit drops, they exit and pupate in the soil. Second generation adults emerge from midsummer to mid-fall, feed on ripe or fallen fruit during fall, then move to shelter to hibernate. Up to two generations per year.

CONTROL: Knock beetles out of trees onto a dropcloth by sharply tapping branches with a padded stick; gather and destroy beetles; for this control to be effective, you must do it twice a day throughout the growing season. Every other day pick up and destroy all fallen fruit, especially early drops; keep chickens around fruit trees to feed on dropped fruit. To deter egg-laying adults, spray trees with kaolin clay beginning at petal fall and continuing weekly for up to 8 weeks. In areas where severe infestations occur, check developing fruit for egg scars twice a week; when first fruit scars appear, apply pyrethrin and repeat in 7 to 10 days. Do not spray before petals drop—it may kill beneficial pollinators.

Psyllid, Potato/Tomato

Paratrioza cockerelli

DESCRIPTION: Adults: tiny, ⅛-inch insects that somewhat resemble cicadas, with clear wings and alternating dark and light stripes. Nymphs: flat and scalelike with short legs; yellowish at first, turning green as they mature. Eggs: Tiny, ¹⁄₃₂-inch, orange-yellow eggs on short stalks, around edges of leaves or lower leaf surfaces. (Eggs of green lacewing, a beneficial insect, are also on stalks, but are larger and white.) Found in western United States.

DAMAGE: Adults and nymphs inject toxic saliva into foliage, causing leaves at the tops of the plants to turn yellow or purple along the midribs and curl upward. Severely infested tomatoes, as well as peppers and

Damage to potato caused by psyllid feeding

eggplant, either do not set fruit or set abundant, small, poor-quality fruit. If potatoes are infested before tubers form, they produce numerous tubers per stolon; plants infested after tubers form produce small, irregularly shaped potatoes that tend to sprout during storage.

LIFE CYCLE. Psyllids overwinter in warm southwestern states, and winged adults migrate north during summer months. They attack transplants and early potatoes primarily at first, and move to new plants as available, with populations building on tomatoes late in the season. Larvae feed on leaf undersides and on shaded upper surfaces. Four to seven generations per year.

CONTROL: In warm climates, at the end of the season remove and compost or discard susceptible plants to prevent adults from overwintering. Cover transplants with floating row cover; monitor populations with yellow sticky cards; spray infested plants promptly with insecticidal soap, horticultural oil at a growing-season dilution, or spinosad.

Root Weevils

Family Curculionidae

DESCRIPTION: Adults: oblong, brownish black to black, ¼- to

Black vine weevil

Rhododendron damaged by
black vine weevil

⅓-inch weevils. Larvae: white grubs with yellowish heads; up to ½ inch. Eggs: tiny white eggs laid in soil. Found throughout North America.

DAMAGE: Larvae feed on roots; adults feed on leaves, primarily chewing notches in leaf edges. They feed on many types of broad- and narrow-leaved evergreen trees and shrubs, strawberries, and bramble fruits. Strawberry root weevil larvae bore into crowns and roots of strawberries and many other plants.

LIFE CYCLE: Larvae overwinter in soil, pupating in spring; some adults overwinter in garden leaf litter. Adults emerge in spring. After 2 to 3 weeks, they lay eggs near the crowns of plants. Eggs

hatch in 10 days; larvae burrow into soil and feed on roots or crowns. One generation per year.

CONTROL: Shake weevils off plants at night onto a dropcloth and destroy them. Apply parasitic nematodes (*Heterorhabditis* spp.) to soil.

Rose Chafer

Macrodactylus subspinosus

DESCRIPTION: Adults: reddish brown, ⅓-inch beetles with black undersides and wing covers cloaked in thick, yellowish hairs. Larvae: small white grubs. Found throughout North America.

Rose chafer

DAMAGE: Larvae feed on roots of grass and weeds; adults chew on the flowers, leaves, and fruit of grapes, roses, tree fruits, brambles, strawberries, peonies, irises, dahlias, hollyhocks, and vegetables. Serious damage only with heavy infestation. *See also* White Grubs.

LIFE CYCLE: Larvae overwinter in soil, pupate in spring, and emerge as adults in late spring to

early summer; adults lay eggs in soil until midsummer; eggs hatch in about 2 weeks; grubs feed on roots until fall.

CONTROL: Handpick if needed; for severe infestations, spray with pyrethrin.

Rose Midge

Dasineura rhodophaga

DESCRIPTION: Adults: tiny, ¹⁄₁₆- to ¹⁄₃₂-inch mosquito-like insects with clear wings and long legs. Larvae: tiny white grubs.

DAMAGE: Larvae burrow in stem tips and buds causing them to wither and blacken.

LIFE CYCLE: Adults emerge from the soil in early spring and lay eggs in leaf tips and under flower sepals on new buds. Larvae tunnel into stems and buds, then drop to the soil to pupate. Several generations per year.

CONTROL: Handpick or prune out and destroy infested stem tips; spread parasitic nematodes (*Steinernema* spp.); spray stem tips and buds with spinosad

Damage caused by rose midges

biweekly; as a last resort, spray stem tips and buds with neem.

Roundheaded Borers/ Longhorned Beetles

Family Cerambycidae

DESCRIPTION: Adults: yellow, reddish brown, brown, or black beetles; many species are about 1 inch long, with antennae that are as long as, or longer than, the body; variously marked with striking white or black stripes and/or patches. Larvae: creamy white, dark-headed grubs. Found throughout North America.

DAMAGE: Larvae bore into trunks of many species of trees, including fruit trees and hardwood and softwood ornamental species, near ground level, girdling the tree or penetrating into heartwood. Infested trees may have discolored or wilting leaves, piled sawdust around the base of the trunk, and/or exit holes in trunk or branches.

LIFE CYCLE: Adults emerge in spring and lay eggs in bark just above soil line or in cracks in bark; larvae burrow into sapwood and eventually tunnel into heartwood. Larvae pupate in tunnels and eventually emerge as adults; they may take several weeks to several years to mature into adults. From one to three

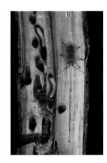

Poplar borer adult, larvae, and damage

Asian longhorned beetle

generations per year or one generation in several years.

CONTROL: Keep trees healthy and vigorous, since weakened trees are most susceptible. Avoid damaging bark with mowers and trimmers. Remove and destroy (burn or chip) infested trees to prevent spread of borers; native predators and woodpeckers also may help control borers; impale larvae in holes using flexible wire; inject parasitic nematodes in borer holes.

Sawflies

Families Tenthredinidae, Diprionidae

See also Leafmining Sawflies; Slug Sawflies.

DESCRIPTION: Adults: ¼- to ¾-inch insects with membranous

wings; rarely seen. Larvae: similar to caterpillars or sluglike, often gray, green, or greenish yellow with stripes or darker spots. Found throughout North America.

DAMAGE: Larvae strip needles or leaves from the upper branches of pines, spruces, hemlocks, birch, ash, willow, and other deciduous plants. Newly hatched larvae skeletonize leaves or scrape outer layer of needles, causing browning. Most larvae

Redheaded pine sawfly larvae on pine

Dogwood sawfly larvae

Blackheaded pine sawfly

feed as a group; when needles or leaves from a single branch are consumed, they move to another branch. Repeated infestations kill trees.

LIFE CYCLE: Most species overwinter as pupae in the ground, emerge in early summer as adults, and lay eggs on host plant. Eggs hatch and larvae molt several times before pupating in ground litter. Adults of some species emerge in fall and lay eggs, which overwinter. One to several generations per year.

CONTROL: Shrews, viral diseases, predators, and parasites generally suppress populations. Careful plant selection, proper site selection, and other measures to keep trees healthy are the best way to prevent problems. Inspect trees regularly to spot infestations early; blast larvae from branches with a strong stream of water; handpick larvae and drop in soapy water; spread dropcloths and shake branches to dislodge larvae; spray insecticidal soap when larvae are still small; direct sprays at groups of larvae, not the entire tree.

Scales, Armored

Family Diaspididae

DESCRIPTION: Adults: circular or oval, hard bumps less than $\frac{1}{10}$ inch in diameter and sometimes bearing a dimple in

California red scale on lemon

the center. Colors vary, including gray, yellow, white, and reddish or purplish brown. All secrete an armor of wax in an oyster-shell or circular pattern. Nymphs: early stages are mobile crawlers; later stages are legless and sedentary. Most species are found in southern United States, some in northern United States and southern Canada.

DAMAGE: Scales weaken plants by sucking plant juices. In the South they attack citrus, roses, palms, and tropical ornamentals; northern species attack fruit trees, shade trees, grapes, currants, raspberries, and shrubs. Scales also cause injury by injecting toxic saliva into plant tissues. Some species secrete honeydew, which attracts ants and encourages the growth of sooty mold, a fungus that feeds on the honeydew. Severe infestations may kill trees.

LIFE CYCLE: Females lay eggs or give birth to live nymphs; these wander for a few hours or days, then settle and molt to an immobile adult form, a process

that takes a month or more. Most scales overwinter as nymphs or eggs hidden in tree bark. One to two generations in northern regions; in southern regions, up to six generations per year.

CONTROL: Difficult to control with sprays because they are protected by a waxy covering. Horticultural oil is effective: Use a dormant-season dilution for good control to smother overwintering eggs in winter or very early spring before or just as buds swell, and a growing-season dilution other times of year to kill eggs and nymphs. Repeat growing-season applications every 7 to 10 days for effective control, since adults are difficult to kill once protected by waxy armor. (Note that some scales remain on the tree even though the insect is dead.) For large-scale plantings, release predatory beetles *Chilocorus nigritus* or *Lindorus lophanthae*. Release parasitic wasps *Aphytis melinus* against California red scale and oleander scale.

Scales, Soft

Family Coccidae, Eriococcidae

DESCRIPTION: Adults: females are oval or round, soft, legless bumps, $\frac{1}{10}$ to $\frac{1}{5}$ inch in diameter and without wings or appendages; males are minute, yellow-winged insects. Larvae:

Cotton cushiony scale on citrus

Brown soft scale

mobile crawlers resembling tiny mealybugs. Found throughout North America.

DAMAGE: All stages suck plant sap, weakening plants, especially citrus, fruit trees, ornamental shrubs, trees, and houseplants. In severe infestations, leaves yellow and drop and the plant dies. Most scales secrete large quantities of honeydew onto foliage and fruit. Sooty mold, a black fungus, feeds on the honeydew.

LIFE CYCLE: Females of some species lay as many as 2,000 eggs; others give birth to several nymphs per day. Mobile nymphs move around for a short time, then settle at one spot. Females molt to a legless, immobile form. Males molt to tiny, flylike insects. One or two generations per year outdoors; up to six generations on indoor plants.

CONTROL: Prune and dispose of infested branches and twigs. Attract native predatory beetles, such as soldier beetles and lady beetles as well as parasitic wasps. Remove scales from twigs with a soft brush or your fingernail, or from leaves with a soft cloth and soapy water; rinse well. For large-scale plantings, release predatory beetles *Chilocorus nigritus* or *Lindorus lophanthae*. Release parasitic wasp *Metaphycus helvolus* to control soft brown scale. Spray horticultural oil: Use a dormant-season dilution on fruit and ornamental trees in winter or very early spring before or just as buds swell; use a growing-season dilution at other times. (Do not spray citrus after July.) Repeat growing-season applications every 7 to 10 days for effective control, since adults are difficult to kill once protected by waxy armor. (Note that some scales remain on the tree even though the insect is dead.) As a last resort, spray with pyrethrin.

Slug Sawflies

Family Tenthredinidae

DESCRIPTION: Adults: small, ⅕- to ½-inch wasp relatives that resemble houseflies. Larvae: Pear sawfly or pear slug are ½ inch long, brownish or olive green, and sluglike; larger at the head end. Rose slugs and other species

Pear slug (pear sawfly larva)

of slug sawflies resemble pale green or green and brown caterpillars, some with bristly hairs. Found throughout North America.

DAMAGE: Larvae skeletonize upper or lower leaf surfaces of pears, cherries, plums, cotoneasters, roses, oaks, and other ornamentals, leaving scorched areas. Some species chew holes through leaves. Young trees may be defoliated and eventually killed. Second-generation larvae cause the most damage.

LIFE CYCLE: Larvae overwinter in cocoons in soil and pupate in spring; adults emerge in late spring; eggs hatch in a week; larvae feed 3 to 4 weeks, then pupate in soil. Second-generation adults appear in midsummer, with larvae hatching in late summer.

CONTROL: Spray trees with strong streams of water to remove larvae; spray insecticidal soap, spinosad, or horticultural oil at a growing-season dilution; spray serious infestations with pyrethrin. Note: BT is not effective against slug sawflies.

Slugs/Snails

DESCRIPTION: Adults: soft-bodied, gray, tan, green, black, yellow, or spotted, wormlike animals that are members of the same zoological group as clams, mussels, and scallops. Slugs have no shells, while snails have coiled shells. Measuring ⅛ to 8 inches, both slugs and snails leave characteristic trails of mucus wherever they crawl. Eggs: clear, oval or round, laid in jellylike masses under stone or debris. Garden slugs and snails occur throughout North America.
DAMAGE: Both slugs and snails

Common snails feeding on hosta

Slug feeding on pea

rasp large holes in foliage, stems, and bulbs. They feast on any tender plant or shrub and may demolish seedlings. Most damaging in wet years or regions.
LIFE CYCLE: Adults lay eggs in moist soil or under rocks. Eggs hatch in 2 to 4 weeks and young grow for 5 months to 2 years before reaching maturity.
CONTROL: Wrap copper strips around trunks of trees or shrubs, or use copper flashing as edging for garden beds. Trap under flowerpots or boards. Attract with pieces of raw potato or cabbage leaves set out in the garden; collect and destroy every morning. Handpick and drop slugs in a jar of soapy water. Trap in shallow pans of beer buried with the container lip flush to soil surface. Encourage predators, including birds, frogs, toads, and snakes. Encourage predatory beetles by maintaining permanent walkways of clover, sod, or stone mulch. Protect seedlings with wide bands of coffee grounds, wood ashes, or diatomaceous earth, renewed frequently. Put out iron phosphate baits, which are nontoxic to people and pets, but toxic to slugs and snails.

Sod Webworm *See* Webworm, Sod

Sowbugs/Pillbugs

DESCRIPTION: Adults: slate gray or brown, ¼- to ⅝-inch crustaceans with jointed armor and seven pairs of tiny legs; some curl up in a ball when disturbed. They are not insects, but are related to crayfish. Nymphs: same as adults, but smaller. Found throughout North America.

Pillbugs

DAMAGE: Usually none to established plants; however, in high numbers damage to seedlings can be severe. Feed on decaying organic material and young seedlings.
LIFE CYCLE: Eggs are laid in damp locations; young are similar to adults.
CONTROL: Drain wet areas to eliminate the moist, damp environments they prefer; sprinkle diatomaceous earth around foundations where bugs congregate (repeat application after rain); trap under stones or boards, then destroy; make paper traps painted with a sticky coating, such as Tanglefoot, then

folded tentlike, with sticky side down.

Spittlebug/Froghopper
Philaenus spumarius

DESCRIPTION: Adults: oval, frog-faced, ¼- to ½-inch insects; tan, brown, or black. Nymphs: yellow to yellowish green, similar to adults, but wingless; inside a foamy mass of "spittle." Eggs: white to beige, laid in rows. Found throughout North America.

Spittlebug nymphs and mass of spittle

DAMAGE: Adults and nymphs suck plant juices of strawberries, legumes, forage crops, and nursery plants, causing stunted, dwarfed, weakened plants with reduced yields. Adults migrate from hayfields to nearby crops when hay is cut.
LIFE CYCLE: Overwintering eggs hatch in mid-spring; nymphs develop in spittle masses for 6 to 7 weeks. Adults feed over summer, laying eggs in field stubble by fall.
CONTROL: Not usually a serious

problem in home gardens; if many nymphs apparent in summer, then turn in stubble of susceptible crops in fall to kill eggs.

Squash Bug *Anasa tristis*

DESCRIPTION: Adults: brownish black, flat-backed, ½-inch bugs covered with fine, dark hairs. They give off an unpleasant smell in defense. Nymphs: whitish green or gray young, similar in shape to adults, with darker thorax and abdomen as they mature; usually covered with a grainy white powder. Eggs: shiny yellow to brown ellipses, in groups on undersides of leaves. Found throughout North America.
DAMAGE: Both adults and nymphs suck plant juices of all cucurbit crops, especially squash

Squash bug nymphs on pumpkin

Squash bug adult

or pumpkins, causing leaves and shoots to blacken and die back; attacked plants fail to produce fruit. Winter squash are most severely affected.
LIFE CYCLE: Unmated adult insects overwinter under garden litter, vines, or boards, then emerge, mate, and lay eggs in spring; nymphs take all summer to develop, molting five times before maturity.
CONTROL: Maintain vigorous plant growth; handpick all stages of squash bugs from undersides of leaves; scout for and destroy reddish to brown eggs; support vines off the ground on trellises; attract native parasitic flies with pollen and nectar plants; cover plants with floating row cover (you'll need to hand-pollinate flowers).

Squash Vine Borer
Melittia cucurbitae

DESCRIPTION: Adults: narrow-winged, olive-brown, 1- to 1½-inch moths, with fringed hind legs, clear hind wings, and red abdomens with black rings. Larvae: white with brown heads. Found throughout the United States and Canada east of the Rocky Mountains and south to Mexico.
DAMAGE: Larvae bore into vines of squash, pumpkins, cucumbers, melons, and gourds. They chew

Squash vine borer moth

Squash vine borer larva

the inner tissue near the base, causing vines to wilt suddenly; girdled vines rot and die.

LIFE CYCLE: Larvae or pupae overwinter in the soil. Adults emerge in spring and lay eggs on stems and leaf stalks near the base of the plant. Newly hatched larvae bore into vine stems, causing sudden wilting and death of stems. Larvae feed for up to 6 weeks, then pupate in the soil. One to two generations per season.

CONTROL: Early in the growing season, cover vines with floating row cover; uncover later for pollinators or hand-pollinate. At times when moths are active, check stem bases and destroy any egg clusters that you find. To save attacked vines, slit infested stems and remove borers, or inject vines with BTK; after treating the vines, heap soil over the treated areas to induce rooting.

Stink Bugs, Pest

Family Pentatomidae

DESCRIPTION: Adults: shield-shaped, green, tan, brown, or gray, ½-inch bugs; most species smooth, but a few spiny or rough-textured. Nymphs: oval-shaped, wingless; similar to adults. Eggs: barrel-shaped, often with a fringe of spines at one end, laid in clusters. Found throughout North America. *See also* Stink Bugs, Predatory.

Harlequin bug

Harlequin bug egg cluster

DAMAGE: Adults and nymphs suck plant sap from leaves, flowers, buds, fruit, and seeds of cabbage family crops, squash, beans, peas, corn, tomatoes, and peaches. Feeding punctures in fruit cause scarring and dimpling known as cat-facing. The harlequin bug, a species with bright red and black markings, is the most important pest of cabbage family crops in the South.

LIFE CYCLE: Adults overwinter in weeds in waste areas; females lay 300 to 500 eggs each when weather warms; eggs hatch in a week, and nymphs develop to adults in about 5 weeks. Two or more generations per year.

CONTROL: Control weeds near susceptible crops; remove or mow weedy areas adjacent to garden beds; attract native parasitic wasps and flies by planting small-flowering plants. As a last resort, dust with pyrethrin.

Tarnished Plant Bug

See Plant Bugs

Tent Caterpillars *Malacosoma* spp.

DESCRIPTION: Adults: yellowish tan to brown moths with two narrow, diagonal stripes across wings (1- to 1½-inch wingspan). Larvae: black, hairy, 2- to 2½-inch caterpillars with a white stripe or rows of dots along the back and irregular, brownish blue or red marks along sides; most spin large "tents" of silk webbing in branch crotches of trees. Eggs: laid on twigs in masses, covered

Eastern tent caterpillar webbing
and larvae

Eastern tent caterpillar moth

with hardened foamy layer. Eggs resemble a dark, shiny belt encircling a twig. Found throughout North America.

DAMAGE: Larvae feed on leaves of most deciduous trees and shrubs, especially apples, aspens, and wild cherries. Trees may be fully defoliated in years of high caterpillar populations. Trees usually leaf out again later in summer but growth may be stunted for several years. Tent caterpillars spin thick webs in the crotches of trees, while closely related forest tent caterpillars spin mats of silk on tree branches and trunk.

LIFE CYCLE: Moths lay eggs on twigs in midsummer; eggs overwinter and hatch in early spring; caterpillars move to nearest branch crotch and spin a silk tent for protection during rain or at night, and leave it to feed during the day. After feeding 5 to 8 weeks, they pupate in white cocoons attached to tree trunks or leaf litter; adult moths emerge in 10 days. One generation per year.

CONTROL: In early morning or in the evening when most caterpillars are in the nest, prune infested branches and burn or crush the nests or put them deeply inside a hot compost pile. Another way to remove tents filled with caterpillars from branches is by winding them onto a broomstick with nails projecting from it. In winter, remove egg masses from bare branches; attract native parasitic flies and wasps by growing small-flowered herbs, such as catnip, and wildflowers, such as Queen-Anne's lace. Do not destroy wandering caterpillars with white eggs or cocoons attached to their backs; they are hosts for native parasites. Spray BTK weekly while larvae are small.

Thrips Family Thripidae

DESCRIPTION: Adults: slender, $\frac{1}{50}$- to $\frac{1}{25}$-inch-long insects; colors range from yellowish to brown or black; these fast-moving insects leap or fly away on narrow, fringed wings when disturbed; individual insects difficult to see without a magnifying glass. Nymphs: similar to small adults; light green or yellow, some with red eyes. Found throughout North America.

DAMAGE: Adults and nymphs suck contents of plant cells from a variety of garden plants, flowers, fruits, and shade trees. Their feeding leaves silvery speckling or streaks on leaves; severe infestations stunt plants and damage flowers and developing fruit; some species spread tomato spotted wilt virus.

LIFE CYCLE: Adults overwinter in sod, plant debris, or cracks in bark, becoming active in early spring. Eggs are laid in plant

Thrips damage to gladiola

Western flower thrips feeding on rose

tissue and hatch in 3 to 5 days; nymphs feed for 1 to 3 weeks, then rest in soil or on leaves until they molt to adult form in 1 to 2 weeks. Up to 15 generations per year outdoors; may breed continuously in greenhouses.

CONTROL: Spray horticultural oil at a dormant-season dilution on fruit trees in winter or very early spring before or just as buds break; encourage native predators, such as pirate bugs, lacewings, and lady beetles; for onion or western flower thrips, release the predatory mite *Amblyseius cucumeris* or minute pirate bugs (*Orius tristicolor*); hang blue or yellow sticky traps to catch adults and monitor populations. For onions, spray plants with kaolin clay to deter thrips from feeding and laying eggs. Apply *Beauveria bassiana* or spinosad; spray insecticidal soap. As a last resort, dust undersides of leaves with diatomaceous earth, or spray affected plants with neem.

Tobacco Budworm

Heliothis virescens

DESCRIPTION: Adults: Light brown, 1- to 1⅓-inch moths with darker stripes on upper wings. Larvae: 1-inch-long caterpillars; usually yellowish or yellow-green, but pinkish and

Tobacco budworm

maroon forms occur; darker bands running lengthwise; small spines; brown head. Resemble corn earworms. Eggs: white, ribbed, and round. Found throughout North America.

DAMAGE: Larvae bore into the buds of many different flowers, including geraniums, petunias, marigolds, zinnias, and nicotianas, as well as many crops such as alfalfa, cotton, tobacco, and soybeans. When flower buds are not present, they eat leafy shoot tips.

LIFE CYCLE: Moths emerge from early to late spring in the South to lay eggs on buds and shoot tips; larvae emerge to feed for about a month, then pupate. Subsequent generations migrate north, but individuals only overwinter in warm climates or warm pockets in the soil near buildings or containers of tender perennials overwintered indoors. Four to five generations per year.

CONTROL: Attract native predators and parasites; handpick larvae; spray BTK on plants with small flowers where larvae eat

most of the bloom (if they bore into buds, they tend not to consume enough BTK); spray spinosad.

Tussock Moth *Orgyia* spp.

DESCRIPTION: Adults: males are ash gray moths (1½-inch wingspan); flightless females have stubby wings. Larvae: pale yellow caterpillars with red heads; bodies covered with tufts of light and dark hairs. Eggs: covered in white, stiff lather. Found throughout eastern United States and Canada, west to Colorado and British Columbia.

DAMAGE: Larvae feed on leaves of deciduous trees and shrubs, but cause little permanent damage unless numerous.

LIFE CYCLE: Overwintering eggs hatch in spring; larvae develop for 4 to 6 weeks, then pupate in cocoons on nearby trees; adults emerge in 2 weeks, mate, and lay eggs on old cocoons. Up to three generations per year.

CONTROL: Scrape egg masses

Whitemarked tussock moth caterpillar

from tree trunks or branches; spray BTK to control larvae; attract birds and parasitic and predatory insects.

Vinegar Fly/Small Fruit Fly

Drosophila melanogaster

DESCRIPTION: Adults: yellowish, clear-winged, $\frac{1}{10}$-inch flies, also called fruit flies. Larvae: small white maggots. Found throughout North America.

Vinegar fly

DAMAGE: Flies are a nuisance around commercial canning and packing houses, also in kitchens; maggots feed on microorganisms in decaying fruit or plants.

LIFE CYCLE: Females lay up to 2,000 eggs each in overripe or fermenting fruit; maggots feed for several days, then pupate for several days. Life cycle takes 10 days.

CONTROL: The best control is sanitation, removing garbage and fermenting fruit; grow crack-resistant tomato cultivars to prevent fruit from being infested in the field.

Webworm, Fall

Hyphantria cunea

DESCRIPTION: Adults: satiny white moths with black dots on forewings ($1\frac{1}{2}$-inch wingspan). Larvae: beige caterpillars covered with dense yellow to brown hairs and long white hairs on sides. Found throughout United States and in southern Canada.

DAMAGE: Larvae chew leaves and spin large, conspicuous webs over ends of branches of many deciduous trees and shrubs.

LIFE CYCLE: Adults emerge from overwintering pupae in late spring and lay eggs; groups of larvae cover foliage with webbing and feed inside it

Fall webworm tent

Fall webworm caterpillar

through midsummer; larvae leave webs to pupate in soil debris. Up to two generations per year.

CONTROL: Prune and destroy branches with webs, ideally when first observed; spray BTK on leaves around web when larvae are small or when last-stage larvae wander outside the web; attract native parasitic wasps.

Webworm, Sod *Crambus* and *Pediasia* spp.

DESCRIPTION: Adults: tan, gray, or whitish moths, often with stripes or other markings; narrow with a snoutlike projection from the head; $\frac{3}{4}$- to 1-inch wingspan. Fly in a zig-zag pattern over lawn areas at dusk. Larvae: pinkish, light brown, to greenish, $\frac{3}{4}$-inch caterpillar with dark spots.

DAMAGE: Larvae chew off grass blades just above the crowns, feeding at night and hiding underground or in lawn thatch during the day. Feeding creates small brown patches in the lawn that gradually enlarge and eventually coalesce. Damage is especially severe in midsummer. Close examination of the brown patches reveals silken tunnels and brown fecal pellets.

LIFE CYCLE: Larvae overwinter in silk-lined tunnels underground or

Sod webworm damage

Sod webworm

in thatch; emerge in spring and pupate in late spring; adults emerge in 10 to 14 days and lay eggs. Multiple generations occur through mid-fall.

CONTROL: Plant endophyte-enhanced turfgrass; spread parasitic nematodes (*Steinernema* spp.). To detect webworms, mix one ounce of dish soap with 1 gallon of water and pour over the edge of a brown patch; webworm caterpillars will surface within a few minutes. Spray BTK; promote a healthy, vigorous lawn by not cutting it too short and keeping grass well watered; encourage populations of native predators.

Whiteflies Family Aleyrodidae

DESCRIPTION: Adults: minute sucking insects with powdery white wings; whiteflies rest in huge numbers on leaf undersides and fly out in clouds when disturbed. Larvae: flattened, legless, translucent, $\frac{1}{30}$-inch scales on leaf undersides. Eggs: gray or yellow cones the size of a pinpoint. Commonly found in greenhouses throughout North America; also found outdoors in warm regions of California, Florida, and Gulf states, and areas on the West Coast.

Greenhouse whiteflies on tomato

DAMAGE: Nymphs and adults suck plant juices from citrus, greenhouse foliage plants, ornamentals, and vegetables. Their feeding weakens plants; they also secrete a sticky, sugary substance called honeydew. Sooty mold, a black fungus, grows on the honeydew-coated leaves and fruit. Whitefly feeding can also spread viral diseases.

LIFE CYCLE: Females lay eggs on undersides of leaves; these hatch in 2 days into tiny, mobile scales; while continuing to feed on plant juices, scales molt to a legless stage in a few days. After several growth stages, nymphs rest in a sort of pupal stage before emerging as adults. Most whitefly species require 20 to 30 days for a complete life cycle at room temperature, fewer in summer. Numerous overlapping generations per year, continuing all winter in greenhouses and warm climates. In cold-winter areas, whiteflies may infest plants outdoors during warm summer weather; cold weather will kill them off.

CONTROL: Catch adults on yellow sticky traps; vacuum adults from leaves; remove infested leaves; indoors, release *Encarsia formosa* parasitic wasps to control greenhouse whitefly; outdoors, attract native parasitic wasps and predatory beetles; spray with insecticidal soap or garlic oil; as a last resort, spray with pyrethrin.

White Grubs
Family Scarabaeidae

DESCRIPTION: Adults: shiny, reddish brown or black, $\frac{1}{3}$- to $\frac{3}{4}$-inch beetles; some with rows of fine punctures on wing covers or stripes on back or fine hairs on body. Larvae: fat, white to bluish white, C-shaped, $\frac{3}{4}$- to 1-inch grubs with brown heads. Found throughout North America.

DAMAGE: Larvae feed on roots of lawn grass, corn, potatoes,

June beetle larvae

Oriental beetle

grasses, vegetable transplants, strawberries. Adults feed on many species of vegetables, flowers, trees, and shrubs, chewing irregular holes in leaves and flowers. Adults of carrot beetle feed on roots of carrot family crops, beets, corn, potatoes, sweet potatoes, and dahlias, and damage from this pest is worst in soils with high organic matter content.

LIFE CYCLE: Varies by species, but female May/June beetles lay eggs in soil; eggs hatch in 2 to 3 weeks. Grubs feed on decaying vegetation the first summer, hibernate in the soil and feed on plant roots the second summer. After hibernating again, they feed until early summer the third year, then pupate. Adults remain in pupal cells in the soil until spring of the fourth year, when they emerge to feed and lay eggs.

Largest broods appear in 3-year cycles; some species with 1- or 4-year cycles. Carrot beetle adults overwinter in soil, emerging in spring to lay eggs in soil beside host plants. Eggs hatch in 1 to 3 weeks; larvae feed on roots until they pupate in late summer. One generation per year.

CONTROL: Populations of most white grubs usually suppressed by native predators and parasites; where infestations are severe, apply parasitic nematodes to the soil to control grubs. Clean up garden debris in fall. For carrot beetles, cultivate in fall to reduce overwintering populations; rotate crops. *See also* Japanese Beetle.

Wireworms *Limonius* spp.

DESCRIPTION: Adults: hard-shelled, elongate, dark-colored, ⅓- to ¾-inch beetles with lengthwise grooves on wing covers; often called click beetles, they make a clicking sound as they flip from their backs onto their feet. Larvae: yellow to reddish brown, jointed, worm- or wirelike creatures, 1 to 1½ inches long. Found throughout North America.

DAMAGE: Larvae bore into newly planted seeds or into plant roots, tubers, and bulbs, preventing germination or stunting and

killing plants. Plants attacked include gladiolus and other flower corms, small grains, and most vegetable crops. Wireworms are most common in soil recently in sod. Adult beetles feed on leaves and flowers, but cause little damage.

LIFE CYCLE: Adults lay eggs on roots in early spring; larvae hatch in 3 to 10 days; larvae spend 2 to 6 years feeding on surface roots in spring and fall and move deeper into the soil to overwinter. Mature larvae pupate in late summer and overwinter as adults. One generation in 2 to 6 years.

Wireworms

CONTROL: Cultivate thoroughly every week for 4 to 6 weeks in fall to expose and destroy larvae; delay planting tubers and corms until soil is very warm, and keep soil bare until planting; allow chickens to run on infested ground to eat larvae; bury raw potato pieces 4 to 6 inches deep to attract larvae, check every 1 to 2 days and destroy wireworms; apply parasitic nematodes to soil.

Woollybears

Family Arctiidae

DESCRIPTION: Adults: white or yellowish moths with a small dark spot on each wing (1½-inch wingspan). Larvae: densely hairy, 1- to 2-inch caterpillars; hair may be yellow, brown, or black at either end of caterpillar and rust brown around the middle. Often seen in fall; rolls into a ball when touched. Found throughout North America.

DAMAGE: Caterpillars feed on tender stems, leaves, or flowers of garden plants and ornamentals, chewing ragged holes. Populations usually not seriously damaging.

Saltmarsh caterpillar on potato

LIFE CYCLE: Pupae overwinter in woolly cocoons among leaves, trash, or clods of soil. Moths emerge to lay eggs in spring. Two or more generations per year.

CONTROL: Control usually not necessary. Spray BTK when caterpillars are feeding on plants.

Yellowjackets and Hornets

Family Vespidae

DESCRIPTION: Adults: ½- to ¾-inch wasps commonly with a yellow-and-black, striped abdomen and two pairs of membranous wings; some species, including bald-faced hornets, which are yellowjackets, not true hornets, are black and white. Larvae: white grubs that develop inside cells in paper nests. Found throughout North America.

DAMAGE: Adults are effective predators of many pest species (*see* Paper Wasps, Yellowjackets, and Hornets on page 298), but also feed on ripe, damaged, or injured fruit, especially in late summer and during dry weather. Workers sting to defend nest sites, and when feeding they can be a hazard to anyone picking fruit.

LIFE CYCLE: Queen wasps overwinter under bark or in protected burrows, emerging in spring to build a small nucleus of paper cells, commonly in the ground, an old log, or other concealed spot. Bald-faced hornets build paper nests in exposed locations such as trees. Queens lay eggs and capture prey for the first brood of larvae, which hatch into workers; the feeding task is then taken over by succeeding broods of worker wasps. In addition to eating insects, workers scavenge garbage and carrion for food. The colony expands until late summer; then worker wasps die off before winter, and a few young, newly mated females leave the nest to overwinter in protected spots as next year's queens. The original nest is deserted. In very warm climates, colonies may overwinter.

Eastern yellowjacket

CONTROL: Pick ripe and damaged fruit promptly and clean up fallen fruit. Keep sweet drinks and other food away from areas where fruit is being picked. Remove nests from areas frequented by people; it is not necessary to remove nests located out of harm's way.

NATURAL ENEMIES AND OTHER BENEFICIALS

It's a good idea to become familiar with the appearance of all of the helpful insects listed on the following pages. They include some of the most common home garden predators and parasites of garden pests, as well as all-important pollinating insects.

Assassin Bugs

Family Reduviidae

DESCRIPTION: Adults: flattened, ¾-inch bugs with long, narrow heads and stout, curving beaks, some with flared or sculptured thoraxes; may bite when handled; some species squeak. Nymphs: smaller, similar to adults, wingless, some brightly colored, others disguised by coating of dust or debris. Found throughout North America.

BENEFICIAL EFFECT: General predators that help suppress populations of many insects, including flies and caterpillars.

LIFE CYCLE: Adults lay eggs in crevices; nymphs develop until last molt and hibernate in a pre-adult stage, then develop into adults the following June.

HOW TO ATTRACT: Naturally present in most gardens. Avoid pesticide use.

Bigeyed Bugs *Geocoris* spp.

DESCRIPTION: Adults: fast-moving, ⅛- to ¼-inch bugs with large eyes, minute black spots on heads and thoraxes. Nymphs: similar to adults, but wingless. May be mistaken for tarnished plant bugs. Common in western North America.

BENEFICIAL EFFECT: Valuable predators of aphids, leafhoppers, plant bugs, spider mites, and small caterpillars in field crops and orchards.

LIFE CYCLE: Females lay eggs on stems and leaf undersides; eggs hatch in 2 weeks; nymphs develop for 4 to 6 weeks and then molt. Adults overwinter in garden trash.

HOW TO ATTRACT: Soybeans, alfalfa, cosmos, pigweed, and goldenrod (*Solidago* spp.) are favored sites for the bugs to lay eggs. Interplant crops with soybeans; leave weedy pigweed in nearby uncultivated areas; add cosmos and goldenrods to borders.

Centipedes

DESCRIPTION: Adults: slender, 1- to 5-inch, segmented creatures with one set of legs per segment. Legs are longer than millipedes, and centipedes move more quickly. See also Millipedes, which are largely beneficial as well.

Centipede

BENEFICIAL EFFECT: Centipedes generally feed on soil-dwelling mites, insects, and insect larvae.

Assassin bug preying on deer fly

Bigeyed bug

DAMAGE: Centipedes occasionally feed on plants and earthworms.

LIFE CYCLE: Adults lay eggs in soil. Eggs hatch into nymphs, which are similar to adults, but shorter, with fewer segments.

HOW TO ATTRACT: Naturally present in most gardens. Avoid pesticide use.

CONTROL: Usually not needed; sprinkle wood ashes, diatomaceous earth, or cinders near rows of germinating seeds.

Damsel Bugs Family Nabidae

DESCRIPTION: Adults: elongate, gray or brown, fast-moving, ⅜- to ½-inch bugs. Nymphs: slender, wingless, smaller than adults. Found throughout North America.

BENEFICIAL EFFECT: Important native predators of aphids, leafhoppers, plant bugs, thrips, and small caterpillars. Commonly found in unsprayed alfalfa fields.

LIFE CYCLE: Females lay eggs in plant tissue, eggs hatch in 1 week; nymphs immediately begin feeding, often on prey larger than themselves. Nymphs develop for 3 to 4 weeks, then molt to adults. Adults overwinter. Two or more generations per season.

Damsel bug

HOW TO ATTRACT: You can collect damsel bugs in alfalfa fields using a sweep net, and release them around the garden.

Ground Beetles

Family Carabidae

DESCRIPTION: Adults: blue-black or brown, ¾- to 1-inch beetles, usually iridescent; thorax well-defined, usually narrower than abdomen. Beetles hide under stones or other cover during the day. Larvae: dark brown or black grubs with 10 segments, tapering markedly toward the rear. Common throughout North America.

BENEFICIAL EFFECT: There are more than 2,500 species of ground beetles. They prey on slugs, snails, cutworms, cabbage root maggots, and many other pests that have a soil-dwelling stage. Some species also pursue prey that live on plants and trees, such as Colorado potato beetle larvae, gypsy moths, and tent caterpillars. A single larva can eat more than 50 caterpillars; adults may live as long as 2 to 3 years and are fiercely voracious.

Ants as Beneficials

Ants commonly get a bad rap from gardeners. While it's true that they invade homes and worse (see "Ants as Pests" on page 250 for more on the negative aspects of these abundant, communal insects), for the most part ants are beneficial insects. They are as important as earthworms when it comes to moving soil. As they tunnel through the soil, they aerate it and increase water and air movement. They also carry organic matter and pieces of insects and other animals down into the soil to feed their young, enriching soil in the process. In addition, they clear away dead insects and help with the decomposition of plant and animal residue in the garden. Finally, ants are important predators of many pest insects.

LIFE CYCLE: Overwintering adults emerge from pupal cell and lay eggs in soil. Larvae feed on insects and slugs for 2 to 4 weeks, then pupate in soil. Adults remain in soil for winter, emerging in spring.

Black ground beetle

Ground beetle larva

HOW TO ATTRACT: Provide permanent beds and perennial plantings in garden to protect populations; plant white clover groundcover in orchards; make permanent stone, sod, or clover pathways throughout garden to provide refuge.

Hover Flies/Flower Flies

Family Syrphidae

DESCRIPTION: Adults: yellow- or white-and-black striped, ½- to ⅝-inch flies, often seen hovering like hummingbirds over flowers.

Hover fly

Larvae: gray or greenish, somewhat translucent, sluglike maggots. Eggs: white cylinders laid singly or in small groups near aphids. Various species common throughout North America.

BENEFICIAL EFFECT: Larvae feed on many species of aphids. Common native predators in orchards. They also are natural pollinators.

LIFE CYCLE: Females lay eggs among aphids; eggs hatch in 2 to 3 days; larvae feed on aphids for 3 to 4 weeks, then drop to the soil to pupate. Adults emerge after 2 weeks. Two to four generations per year.

HOW TO ATTRACT: Plant pollen and nectar flowers; allow flowering weeds such as wild carrot and yarrow to grow in nearby uncultivated areas.

Lacewings

Families Chrysopidae, Hemerobiidae

DESCRIPTION: Adults: fragile, green or brown, ½- to ¾-inch insects with small heads, large eyes, and netted, transparent wings. Larvae: spindle-shaped, mottled yellow or brown. Eggs: green lacewing eggs are laid on tips of fine stalks; brown lacewing eggs are glued onto buds or twigs. Found throughout North America; sold commercially.

BENEFICIAL EFFECT: Common general predators in gardens and orchards, feeding on aphids, mites, thrips, soft scales, and other pests.

Green lacewing feeding on aphids

Green lacewing larva feeding on aphids

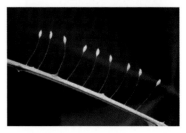

Lacewing eggs

LIFE CYCLE: Adults or pupae overwinter; adults emerge in spring to lay eggs. Eggs hatch in 4 to 7 days; larvae feed for about 3 weeks, then pupate for 5 to 7 days. One to five generations per year.

HOW TO ATTRACT: Plant pollen and nectar flowers; allow some flowering weeds to grow between rows; provide water source; scatter purchased eggs widely throughout garden.

Lady Beetles

Family Coccinellidae

DESCRIPTION: Adults: shiny, round, $\frac{1}{16}$- to $\frac{3}{8}$-inch beetles with short legs and antennae.

Pink spotted lady beetle adult and eggs

Seven-spotted lady beetle larva feeding on black bean aphids

Mealybug destroyer adult and larva

Common species are pale yellow to dark reddish orange with or without black spots; some species solid black or black with red spots. (Mealybug destroyer is black with a coral-colored head and abdomen tip.) Larvae: spindle-shaped, alligator-like, usually with short spines or knoblike projections on body. Eggs: white or yellow ovals, usually deposited in upright clusters. Numerous species common throughout North America; convergent lady beetle (*Hippodamia convergens*) sold commercially.

BENEFICIAL EFFECT: Adults and larvae of many species feed on aphids and soft-bodied pests; some species prefer mealybugs, spider mites, or soft scales. Mealybug destroyer adults and larvae prey on aboveground species of mealybugs on citrus, grapes, and ornamentals. Native lady beetles are important biological controls for aphids in gardens and orchards. In western regions, *Stethorus* spp. provide excellent control of spider mites in raspberries and other crops. *Chilocorus* spp. are voracious predators of soft scales. A few species, such as Mexican bean beetles, are plant pests.

LIFE CYCLE: In spring, overwintering adults seek food, then lay eggs among aphids or other prey. Eggs hatch in 3 to 5

days; larvae feed 2 to 3 weeks, then pupate. Adults emerge in 7 to 10 days. In fall, local species overwinter as adults in leaf litter; *H. convergens* migrates to Sierra Nevada Mountains to overwinter in large groups.

HOW TO ATTRACT: Plant pollen and nectar flowers; conserve native populations by avoiding pesticides; leave weeds such as dandelions, wild carrot, and yarrow in nearby uncultivated areas; purchased *H. convergens* is effective in greenhouses with screened vents but is not advisable for release in gardens, because they will fly away.

Mantids *Mantis* spp.

DESCRIPTION: Adults: large, elongate, green or brown insects with prominent eyes; up to 4 inches long. Nymphs: similar to adults, but smaller and without wings. Eggs: laid in a grayish frothy case of 50 to 400 eggs glued to stems or twigs. Found in southern and eastern United States, north into Ontario. (Species include European or praying mantid; Chinese mantid, which is sold commercially; and

Chinese mantid

Insect Impostors

Hold your horses! Before you squash that bug or turn on that sprayer, take a close look. There are several species of common beneficial insects that are look-alikes of equally common pest species, or that have funny-looking larval stages that one easily might mistake for a pest. Here are some that might stump you. (Hint: The good guys are always on the left.)

Before you stomp on that earwig, make sure it's not a **rove beetle**, which preys on many common garden pests.

Earwig

Rove beetle

A **lady beetle** should be one of your best friends in the garden. But its cousin, the Mexican bean beetle, can be one of your worst enemies. (P.S. The funny-looking creature next to the lady beetle is a lady beetle larva.)

Lady beetle and larva

Mexican bean beetle

Many kinds of plant bugs are pests, but **spined soldier bugs** are voracious predators of a variety of caterpillars and grubs.

Spined soldier bug

Squash bug

It's easy to confuse mealybugs with the beneficial creatures that eat them—**mealybug destroyer larvae.**

Mealybugs   Mealybug destroyer larva

Look for the big eyes! **Bigeyed bugs** are your friends, unlike chinch bugs, which munch on the roots of your lawn or corn crop.

Bigeyed bug   Chinch bug

Hover flies look like wasps that could inflict a painful sting, but the only creatures that need fear a hover fly are the aphids in your garden.

Hover fly   Yellow jacket

various native species such as Carolina and California mantids.)

BENEFICIAL EFFECT: Mantids catch and devour both pests and beneficial species. They eat virtually any insects they catch including each other.

LIFE CYCLE: Eggs are glued in a gray or tan, frothy, sticky mass to plants, where they harden and remain for winter; adults hatch in spring; one generation per year.

HOW TO ATTRACT: To protect native species, don't release purchased mantids, and avoid pesticides; provide sites for over-wintering eggs by keeping perma-nent plantings around the garden.

Minute Pirate Bug

Orius tristicolor

DESCRIPTION: Adults: quick-moving, black-and-white patterned, ¼-inch bugs. Nymphs: shiny, wingless, changing from yellow through orange to mahogany brown as they grow. Found throughout North America; sold commercially.

BENEFICIAL EFFECT: Voracious predators of thrips, spider mites, small caterpillars, leafhopper

Minute pirate bug feed on white fly nymphs

nymphs, other small insects, and insect eggs.

LIFE CYCLE: Females lay eggs in plant stems or leaves; eggs hatch in 3 to 5 days and nymphs feed on insects in flowers and undersides of leaves for 2 to 3 weeks. Adult females overwinter in crevices of bark, weeds, and plant residues. Two to four generations per year.

HOW TO ATTRACT: Plant pollen and nectar plants, especially goldenrod, daisies, yarrow, alfalfa, and stinging nettle; in green-houses, release at the rate of one pirate bug per one to five plants.

Mites, Predatory

Family Phytoseiidae

DESCRIPTION: Adults: minute, beige to reddish tan, fast-moving mites. Nymphs: similar to adults, but smaller. Found throughout North America; several species sold commercially.

BENEFICIAL EFFECT: These attack spider mites, especially European red mites and citrus red mites; some feed on pollen, thrips, or other types of mites.

LIFE CYCLE: Overwintering females emerge from crevices in bark or soil litter and lay eggs on leaves among prey; nymphs hatch in 3 to 4 days, molting several times until they reach the adult stage in 5 to 10 days. Numerous overlapping generations.

Predatory mite attacking prey mite

HOW TO ATTRACT: Avoid pesti-cide use; sustain native species by sprinkling pollen (especially from ice plants, cattails, or dan-delions) on plants. For apples and strawberries, release *Metaseiulus occidentalis* to control European red mite and other spider mites; in greenhouses, consult a benefi-cial insect distributor to identify the best species to release for control of spider mites; and release *Amblyseius cucumeris* to control small thrips on peppers and cucumbers.

Paper Wasps, Yellowjackets, and Hornets Family Vespidae

DESCRIPTION: Adults: ½- to ¾-inch yellow-and-black, black-and-white, or red-and-black wasps with two pairs of membranous wings. Larvae: white grubs that develop inside cells in paper nests either above or below the ground. Found throughout North America.

BENEFICIAL EFFECT: Good general predators of flies, caterpillars, and other pests. Adult wasps generally feed on

Bald-faced hornet feeding on nectar

Cicada killer wasp

sugary solutions, such as flower nectar or juices or ripe fruits. Can be pests at picnics. *See also* Yellowjackets and Hornets on page 292.

LIFE CYCLE: Queen wasps overwinter under bark or in protected burrows, emerging in spring to build a small nucleus of paper cells underground or in an old log or other concealed spot, or aboveground attached to a tree or building. Queens lay eggs and capture prey for the first brood of larvae, which hatch into workers; the feeding task is then taken over by succeeding broods of worker wasps. The colony expands until late summer, then worker wasps die off before winter, and a few young, newly mated females leave the nest to overwinter in protected spots as next year's

queens. The original nest is deserted. Nests may overwinter in very warm climates.

HOW TO ATTRACT: Not usually necessary to attract them or to control them. Since some species do sting when disturbed, remove nests from areas frequented by people; it is not necessary to remove nests located farther away.

Parasitic Wasps

DESCRIPTION: Adults: slender, black or brown wasps with threadlike waists. Wasps from several families parasitize insect pests. Slender-bodied ichneumon wasps, from ⅛ to 1½ inches, parasitize cutworms, corn earworms, white grubs, and caterpillars. Some ichneumon wasps have threadlike ovipositors, as much as 3 inches

Braconid wasp laying eggs
in paralyzed caterpillar

Tomato hornworm covered with braconid wasp pupae

long (sometimes mistaken for stingers). Braconid wasps have thicker bodies and range from ⅟₁₆– to ⁵⁄₁₆ inch; target pests include aphids, garden webworms, tomato hornworms, armyworms, strawberry leaf rollers, and tent caterpillars. Trichogramma wasps are chalcid wasps (family Chalcididae) and range from ⅟₆₄ to ⁵⁄₁₆ inch in length. Trichogramma wasps parasitize moth and butterfly caterpillars, including cabbageworms, tomato hornworms, corn earworms, codling moths, cutworms, armyworms, webworms, cabbage loopers, and corn borers. Other chalcid wasps attack aphids, strawberry leaf rollers, caterpillars, and other pests. Larvae: tiny cream-colored grubs that feed in or on other insects. Found throughout North America; some available commercially.

BENEFICIAL EFFECT: Important native parasites of many pests, including various caterpillars, beetles, sawflies, aphids, flies, and other insects. Larvae develop as parasites; females also kill hosts by stinging them and feeding on body fluids.

LIFE CYCLE: Females lay eggs inside host eggs or larvae; wasp larvae develop inside hosts, eventually killing hosts and pupating in or on them. Many species overwinter as mature larvae in cocoons; in some species adult females overwinter. One to three generations per year are usual; some with up to 10 generations.

HOW TO ATTRACT: Plant pollen and nectar flowers in gardens; grow flowering cover crops in orchards to attract females. Include herbs such as dill and parsley, plus daisy-family plants such as yarrow, asters, coneflowers, and daisies. Although some species are available by mail order, the best course for the homeowner is to attract native populations. They are effective when released in greenhouses.

Rove Beetles

Family Staphylinidae

DESCRIPTION: Adults: brown or black, slender, $\frac{1}{10}$- to 1-inch-long beetles with stubby wings covering only part of the body. Larvae: resemble adults, but wingless. Over 3,100 species native to North America.

BENEFICIAL EFFECT: Valuable for controlling aphids, springtails, mites, nematodes, flies, and cabbage maggots. Also help decompose organic matter.

LIFE CYCLE: Most species over-winter as adults, becoming active in spring and laying eggs in the soil; larvae molt three times as they feed, then pupate in soil.

HOW TO ATTRACT: Maintain

Rove beetle

permanent beds and plantings in garden to protect overwintering adults; interplant with cover crops or mulch planting beds; make stone or plank walks in garden to provide shelter.

Soldier Beetles

Family Cantharidae

DESCRIPTION: Adults: elongate, slender, nearly flat, $\frac{1}{3}$- to $\frac{1}{2}$-inch beetles, often with downy, leathery wing covers. Larvae: flattened, elongate, covered with hairs, and usually dark-colored. Found throughout North America.

BENEFICIAL EFFECT: Both larvae and adults prey on cucumber beetles, corn rootworms, aphids, grasshopper eggs, caterpillars, and beetle larvae.

Soldier beetle preying on
black bean aphids

LIFE CYCLE: Females lay eggs in soil; newly hatched larvae remain inactive for a short period before developing; larvae overwinter in soil and pupate in spring. Up to two generations per year.

HOW TO ATTRACT: To attract adult soldier beetles, plant goldenrod, milkweed, hydrangeas, or catnip. To protect pupating beetles, maintain some permanent plantings where soil is not disturbed.

Spiders

DESCRIPTION: Adults: eight-legged arachnids that lack wings and antennae, with bodies divided into two parts: cephalothorax and abdomen. Nymphs: also called spiderlings; resemble adults.

BENEFICIAL EFFECT: All spiders are predators, consuming large quantities of insects, insect larvae, and other invertebrates. Some spin webs to catch insects that fly or wander onto the sticky silk. Others jump or run after prey. Experts estimate spiders consume approximately 88 pounds of insects per acre per year.

LIFE CYCLE: Females lay eggs, usually inside a silken cocoon; some species attach the cocoon near a web or burrow and abandon it; others defend their eggs and/or carry the cocoon

Common garden spider

with them. Some species care for hatched young. Newly hatched spiders are immobile larvae, then molt and develop into tiny spiderlings. They can spread by "ballooning," meaning they produce silk threads that act like a parachute and then travel on the wind.

HOW TO ATTRACT: Maintain permanent beds of perennials and shrubs to provide shelter. Provide areas where the ground is not disturbed.

Stink Bugs, Predatory

Family Pentatomidae

See also Stink Bugs, Pest.

DESCRIPTION: Adults: shield-shaped, green, yellowish, tan, brown, or gray, ½-inch bugs. Nymphs: similar to adults, but wingless. Native to North America.

BENEFICIAL EFFECT: Adults and nymphs prey on larvae of many other insects including armyworms, cabbage loopers, Colorado potato beetles, and Mexican bean beetles. Spined

soldier bug (*Podisus maculiventris*) is the best-known predatory stink bug.

LIFE CYCLE: Overwintering adults emerge in spring; females lay eggs on leaves; nymphs drink water or plant juices for a short period, then become predators; nymphs develop into adults in 6 to 8 weeks; adults live 5 to 8 weeks. One to two generations per year.

HOW TO ATTRACT: Maintain permanent beds of perennials to provide shelter.

Spined soldier bug feeding on caterpillar

Tachinid Flies

Family Tachinidae

DESCRIPTION: Adults: robust, gray, brown, or black, ⅓- to ½-inch insects resembling overgrown, bristly houseflies; some with mottled bodies but without bright colors. Larvae: maggots that feed inside host insects. Found throughout North America.

BENEFICIAL EFFECT: Excellent predators of many caterpillar pests, including cutworms, armyworms, tent caterpillars,

Tachinid fly

cabbage loopers, and gypsy moth larvae; some also attack sawflies, squash bugs, and stink bugs.

LIFE CYCLE: Females lay eggs on newly hatched larvae or on leaves on which caterpillars are feeding; caterpillars then ingest eggs and larvae hatch inside the host; larvae feed and devour the host from within; in some cases females place live young on a caterpillar's skin and the maggots burrow into the host. As maggots develop inside, they kill the host, then pupate inside or in soil nearby. Up to two generations per year.

HOW TO ATTRACT: Adult flies feed on the nectar of flowers of dill, parsley, sweet clover, and other herbs, so allow them to flower throughout the garden; don't destroy caterpillars with white eggs stuck to their back—these will develop into more tachinid flies.

Yellowjackets *See* Paper Wasps, Yellowjackets, *and* Hornets, page 298

Garden Pollinators

Crucial to the success of both garden and orchard, pollinators are neither pest, parasite, nor predator. Encourage pollinators to visit your garden, and keep in mind that many types of organic sprays and dusts can be harmful to pollinators—another reason to reserve them as the strategy of last resort when dealing with pest and disease problems.

Honey Bee *Apis mellifera*

Description: Adults: gold-and-black striped, ¾-inch bees with translucent wings. Larvae: white grubs in wax combs in hives. Found throughout North America.

Beneficial Effect: Extremely important pollinators of fruit, vegetables, and agricultural crops.

Life Cycle: Bees live in social colonies numbering up to 20,000. Queen bees lay eggs in wax cells in hives; workers feed and care for larvae, feeding those destined to become new queens a special diet of royal jelly. Males mate with new queens, who leave with swarms to start new colonies. Bees overwinter clustered in hives, living on stored honey.

How to Attract: Plant pollen and nectar plants; provide a water source in dry weather; avoid spraying fruit trees when flowers are in bloom; if you must apply insecticides, spray in evenings after bees return to hive.

Bumble bee

Important wild pollinators; commercially reared colonies used as pollinators in greenhouses.

Life Cycle: Overwintering queen bee emerges from soil or leaf litter in late spring to early summer and makes nest on or below the ground. The queen lays eggs in individual cells made of pollen; feeds developing larvae pollen and honey until they mature in 3 to 4 weeks to become workers. Workers collect pollen and nectar and rear subsequent

Honey bee

Bumble Bees *Bombus* spp.

Description: Adults: plump, black-and-yellow, fuzzy, ½- to 1-inch bees; active even in cold weather. Larvae: fat, white grubs. Common throughout North America.

Beneficial Effect:

two or three broods. In the fall, young queens develop and fly away to mate, and the colony breaks up.

How to Attract: Common in most gardens. Protect bees by minimizing pesticide usage; if necessary, apply in evening when bees are not active.

Leafcutter Bees, Mason Bees, *and* Allies

Family Megachilidae

Description: Adults: dark, $3/4$-inch bees with light bands on the abdomen; resemble honey bees. Larvae: whitish grubs in cylindrical nests, often with several cylinders stacked together. Adults sting only when handled and have a less painful sting than honey bees. Common throughout North America.

Beneficial Effect: Important wild native pollinators; some species are commercially reared for pollinating agricultural crops.

Damage: Females cut semicircular pieces from the edges of leaves, primarily in

early summer. Tunneling in pithy canes and rotted wood seldom does damage, despite the appearance of sawdust piles, since the bees generally bore through pith rather than live wood.

Life Cycle: Queens lay eggs in nests constructed in holes in the ground, rotted wood, or thick, pithy plant canes. The queen does all the nest construction and rearing; these bees are not colonial. Leafcutter bees cut pieces of leaves from various plants and use them to construct

the nests, which are provisioned with pollen and nectar. Mason bees do not cut leaves. One generation per year.

How to Attract: Provide suitable nest sites by growing plants with pithy canes such as brambles, elderberries, sumac, and roses. To make a simple nest, drill 6-inch-deep holes into blocks of wood ($3/16$ to $1/4$ inch in diameter), at a slightly oblique angle and hang in trees or other sites throughout the garden.

Leafcutter bee cutting segment of rose leaf

ANIMAL PESTS

No matter where you garden—in a bustling city, near open farmland, or someplace in between—you may find that animals and birds cause you more headaches than insect pests do. The trickiest part of coping with animal pests can be identifying the pest. Since many animals feed at dawn or dusk, you may need to rely upon such signs as feeding patterns, tracks, tunnels, or excrement to figure out what culprit is invading your garden. For example, damaged strawberries may be the work of birds, mice, or slugs. Controls that work for one pest may do nothing to stop another, so it's important to determine exactly what pest is to blame before you act.

Preventing Animal Damage

Most animal deterrents fall into one of four categories.

FENCES AND BARRIERS. These usually work best in vegetable gardens where fencing and netting are unlikely to spoil the view. To be successful, barriers must block an animal's access to your plants without inter-fering with your ability to tend them.

REPELLENTS. Sprays or scent dispensers that hang in or near affected plants, these products typically must be refreshed after rain to keep them at their peak potency. Repellents that make your plants taste bad require that animal pests take a bite of your garden before they learn their lesson. Repellents can be a good choice for protecting orna-mentals that you don't want to fence, but keep in mind that when food is scarce, hungry animals will ignore bad flavors and smells in order to get the food they need to survive.

SCARE TACTICS. Gadgets such as inflatable owls, plastic snakes, hawk-shaped kites, and elaborate scarecrows have limited effectiveness. Moving them frequently from one spot to another can help. Scare devices that move in the wind—kites, balloons, and dangling CDs or pie tins—work better than stationary items, but their ability to scare still fades the longer they dangle in the same place.

TRAPS. Live-trapping animal pests may seem like a humane solution, but it rarely is. Animals trapped and released in another location rarely adapt successfully. Plus, there are regulations governing the transport and release of wild animals. Snap traps (which capture and kill the animal) can be effective for small pests such as mice and voles. Protecting your garden from hungry wildlife requires a thoughtful approach that considers an animal's behavior, its place in the local environment, and your garden's place in *its* environment. A successful strategy may involve a combination of deterrent methods—netting and scare devices over the berry patch, for example. Or you may need to replace a plant that deer find particularly tasty with something less appealing. With patience and perseverance, you can usually find a way to enjoy your garden and to peacefully coexist with your wild neighbors.

Common Animal Pests

You'll soon discover whether animal pests are a problem in your garden, and it's wise to ask neighboring gardeners what types of animal pests to prepare for. The following descriptions of damage and deterrents will help you decide which animals are raiding your garden and how to prevent further damage.

Birds

Crows are fond of garden seedlings, while fruit-eating

birds such as robins and waxwings will gladly harvest your berries and cherries. Doves and pigeons are among the species that will dine upon newly sown seeds.

DAMAGE: Birds are both the gardener's friend and foe. While they eat insect pests, they also consume entire fruits or vegetables or will pick at your produce until it is damaged enough to be unappealing.

DETERRENTS: Most bird controls involve making the area you wish to protect either less appealing to birds or less accessible. The most effective control to protect bush and vine fruits and small fruit trees is to cover them with lightweight plastic netting; cover row crops with floating row cover. You can also use a variety of commercial or homemade devices to frighten birds away from your crops. Tactics that keep birds guessing include moving a scarecrow to a different spot every few days and tying pie pans, pinwheels, or strips of plastic or foil to its arms. Other bird-scaring devices include plastic snakes, bird-scaring balloons, and inflatable owls and hawks. These are most effective when mounted on a fence at the garden's edge and relocated every few days. Bear in mind that wild birds, with the exception of European starlings, pigeons, and house sparrows, are protected; it is illegal to harm them in your efforts to keep them from eating your fruits and vegetables.

Cats and Dogs

Familiar family pets or feral wanderers, cats and dogs are mostly helpful to gardeners, chasing away or eliminating many animal pests. But an exuberant dog can cause a great deal of damage, too, by digging or simply frolicking. And cats often seek the soft soil of a new seedbed to use as their toilet.

DAMAGE: Dog-related damage tends to be the result of digging—uprooted plants and scattered seedbeds—or breakage caused by rolling or romping. Cats are inclined to leave unpleasant "surprises" buried in newly turned soil, risking the introduction of disease organisms into your vegetable garden.

DETERRENTS: Sturdy fencing and good training are the best bets for keeping dogs from wreaking havoc in your gardens. Fencing is usually a deterrent to cats, too; where that fails or is impractical, covering your seedbed with poultry netting or a similar deterrent to digging will usually keep kitties at bay.

Chipmunks and Squirrels

Ground squirrels (a.k.a. chipmunks) and their bushy-tailed tree-dwelling cousins are a common and mostly benign sight in the landscape. Most gardeners enjoy their antics without concern.

DAMAGE: Squirrels and chipmunks eat seeds, berries, bark, and flowers. A typical landscape offers enough food sources to keep them from becoming pests in the garden. Conflicts with these rodents arise when they dig up bulbs, eat the blossoms from tulips, uproot container plants, or raid your crops of berries or nuts. When water is scarce, thirsty squirrels will also "drink" from developing tomatoes and melons in your garden.

DETERRENTS: When possible, use netting to exclude squirrels from nuts and berries. Top bulb plantings with a piece of poultry netting on the soil surface to deter digging. Repellent sprays for deer and rabbits may also be useful against squirrels. Drench the soil of container plants with castor oil repellent (sold for mole control) to discourage squirrels; regular applications are necessary for best results.

Deer

Deer are typically active from dusk until early morning. Signs of deer damage include hoof prints, droppings, and raggedly torn stems, branch tips, and foliage at "deer level"—up to about 6 feet off the ground.

DAMAGE: In home gardens and orchards, deer browse a wide range of vegetable, fruit, and ornamental plants. Because deer lack upper front teeth, they leave ragged edges when they feed and often break stems and branches as they pull at the plants they're eating. Deer tend to eat tender, new growth, which may be an entire row of seedlings in your vegetable garden or twig tips and buds from your apple trees. They may also cause damage by trampling plants while feeding.

DETERRENTS: An electric fence, and not necessarily a high one, is the most effective way to keep deer out. One design suitable for small areas uses two fences, an inner chicken-wire fence 4 feet high and a single-wire electric fence only 2½ feet off the ground and located 3 feet outside the chicken wire. Deer find it hard to jump the chicken-wire fence with the electrified wire in the way. If you prefer a conventional woven-wire fence instead of going electric, choose one at least 8 feet high. A second inner fence about 3 feet high increases the effectiveness of a nonelectric fence because double obstacles confuse deer. If deer are nibbling just a few shrubs, consider enclosing these in woven-wire cages. For a slight deer problem, this is an inexpensive, effective solution.

Repellents deter deer as long as the pressures of starvation or overpopulation don't force them to eat anything in sight. Buy soap bars in bulk and hang them from strings in trees. Or nail each bar to a 4-foot stake and drive the stakes at 15-foot intervals around your property. Soap fragrance is more pervasive when the soap is wet, so a good strategy is to mist soap bars with water early in the evening just before deer begin to feed. Some gardeners report that human hair hung in mesh bags or old stockings is an effective repellent. You can probably collect all the hair you need from a barber.

One repellent that seems to work is made from eggs and water. Mix one egg per quart of water, multiplying the recipe as many times as you need to get the right amount of spray. With rainfall or heavy dew, some repellent will wash away. You can prolong the time it remains on plants by mixing it with a small amount of antidesiccant. Other homemade repellents include water solutions of blood meal, hot sauce, or garlic oil. Many commercial repellents are available, including formulas based on eggs, hot peppers, soaps, and even urine from predators such as wolves or coyotes.

Deer dining preferences vary from one region to the next and from season to season, depending on the availability of food in general. Consult local nurseries or your Cooperative Extension service to learn which landscape plants are least likely to be eaten by deer in your area, bearing in mind that even these may suffer damage in harsh winters when preferred foods are scarce.

Groundhogs

These sturdy brown rodents (also called woodchucks) feast throughout the growing season so they can hibernate through the winter months. Like rabbits, they leave a clean cut on plants when they take a bite.

DAMAGE: Green vegetation of all sorts is on the groundhog menu. Especially in early spring, when other foods are still in short supply, a hungry groundhog may demolish crops of peas, lettuce, spinach, and other early vegetables.

DETERRENTS: Excluding groundhogs from your garden is the best way to keep them from turning it into their personal salad bar. A fence of poultry netting works well and need not be especially high or sturdy, as long as it angles outward from the garden for 6 to 12 inches below the soil surface and is 18 to 24 inches tall. Groundhogs will burrow under a fence but are stopped by a belowground barrier. Support the aboveground portion of the fence with stakes but leave it on the floppy side to discourage critters that would climb over it. Deer repellents may be effective against groundhogs, but are impractical for protecting green, leafy crops intended for your own salads.

Mice, Pocket Gophers, and Voles

Mice and voles look similar but are only distantly related. Also called meadow mice, voles are larger (5 to 8 inches long, tail included) and bulkier than mice; their fur is longer and coarser than the short, almost velvety fur of mice and moles. Mice and voles make shallow burrows in mulch and vegetation on the soil surface. Pocket gophers resemble voles but burrow below the ground, like moles.

DAMAGE: All of these rodents feed on seeds, bulbs, roots, and bark. They are active year round but tend to be most damaging to gardens during the winter, when other food becomes scarce. Nesting beneath the snow at the base of fruit trees, mice and voles may spend the winter months gnawing away at the bark and fine roots until the tree is girdled or robbed of its support system. Often the first sign the gardener sees is a dead tree in the spring. Newly planted bulbs are another favorite target, since the freshly dug soil makes them easier to reach. If your lilies or tulips fail to appear in the spring after planting, suspect foul play.

DETERRENTS: Surround the trunks of fruit trees with cylinders of wire mesh (holes no larger than ¼ inch). The cylinder should be about 24 inches high; make sure that the barrier extends several inches into the soil and fits closely, to keep pests from creeping under it. Plant bulbs in baskets of poultry netting or include a layer of coarse gravel in the soil that covers them. Planting tasty tulips amid daffodils can also help to hide the desirable bulbs from hungry rodents (daffodils are toxic). Clear brush and tall vegetation away from the base of fruit trees and bushes to remove nesting and burrowing sites. Put snap traps baited with peanut butter or nutmeats along surface tunnels. Repellents used for deer and rabbits may also be effective in deterring mice and voles; reapply as needed after rains.

Moles

Moles use their powerful front claws to tunnel through the soil in search of food. The eastern mole has a bare pink snout, while the star-nosed mole's pink snout has 22 short tentacle-like structures radiating from it. Eastern moles make shallow, raised tunnels; star-nosed mole tunnels may be 1 to 2 feet below the surface and feature substantial mounds of soil at the openings.

DAMAGE: Moles eat grubs and earthworms, not plants. Nevertheless, their extensive tunnels ruin lawns and provide easy entry for mice and voles, which do dine on plant roots and bulbs. If your yard is full of mole runs, chances are your soil is full of beetle grubs, the favorite food for foraging moles. The most humane way to discourage moles is to eliminate soil grubs by applying milky disease spores (see more information about this control on page 373). When the grubs die, the moles will move on to better feeding grounds. But this approach requires patience; it may take several years after initial application of milky disease spores for the grubs to disappear.

DETERRENTS: If you'd like to dispatch an active mole immediately, you must locate a permanent tunnel leading from the underground nest. Find a long, straight tunnel and press it down in a few places. If you find the tunnel reopened the next day, you've found a permanent passage. You can try flooding the mole out by filling this passage with water, but you must be prepared to kill it as soon as it comes to the surface in order for the method to be effective. You can also place any of the various commercial mole traps along a permanent passage and eventually eradicate your pest. Deciding whether getting rid of mole tunneling warrants killing these animals is a matter of personal choice. Repellent sprays containing castor oil are also available for ridding your lawn of moles, but these products must be applied and refreshed on a regular basis to have the desired effect. Other repellent products (fumigant cartridges) and home remedies (chewing gum, mothballs) offer limited effectiveness, at best, and may pose risks to children, pets, and other wildlife. Natural predators include owls, hawks, and foxes; cats and dogs will also hunt for moles, but dogs especially may cause further damage by digging in pursuit of their prey.

Rabbits

Rabbits have prominent front incisors that leave a characteristically clean cut—damaged plants look as if they've been cut off with a sharp knife. Trees damaged by rabbits will have teeth marks in the bark just above ground/snow level to about 12 inches up the trunk. Accumulations of small, round rabbit droppings are another indication of the presence of rabbits.

DAMAGE: Rabbit damage may occur year-round. Through the growing season, rabbits are likely culprits whenever beans, peas, beet tops, carrots, or lettuce go missing; in winter they are among the varmints that feed on the bark of such trees as apple, crabapple, and poplar. In addition to these thin-barked trees, most saplings are at risk. Damage to the bark may be significant enough to girdle young trees; where snow levels permit, rabbits will also feed on buds and branch tips.

DETERRENTS: The best way to keep rabbits out of a garden is to erect a chicken-wire fence with mesh no larger than 1 inch. If you have existing picket or woven-wire fence, simply attach a 2-foot-wide strip of chicken wire to the bottom of the fence. Rabbits also sometimes burrow under a fence, so you may need to dig a 6-inch-deep trench and sink the chicken wire down into the soil to completely keep them out. If your soil is rocky, pile a 1-foot-wide border of small stones around the periphery of your fence to discourage burrowing.

To protect young trees and shrubs from rabbits gnawing bark in the winter, erect cylinders made of ¼-inch hardware cloth; the cages should be 1½ to 2 feet high (higher if you live in an area with deep snowfall) and should be sunk 2 to 3 inches below the soil surface. This method is also effective in protecting trees from bark-feeding by mice and voles.

Most deer repellents are also effective against rabbits. Some gardeners report that used cat box filler sprinkled on the lawn around ornamentals deters rabbits. Since effectiveness wears off after about a week, you'll need to reapply repellents often, especially after rain.

Guide to Disease Symptoms

Dealing with plant disease can be one of the most challenging aspects of gardening. Unlike garden pests, which are usually easy to spot, most organisms that cause disease are too small to see without a magnifying glass or a microscope. Disease symptoms can be variable and subtle, so they're tricky to diagnose and sometimes easy to miss until a problem is quite severe.

UNDERSTANDING SYMPTOMS AND SIGNS

Scientists who study plant disease separate the visible characteristics of disease into two categories: symptoms and signs. A *symptom* is a plant's response to a disease-causing organism or condition. Two common disease symptoms are changes wilting and in plant color. Disease symptoms usually result from death of cells, inhibited cell development, or overstimulated cell development.

A *sign* of an infectious disease is the disease-causing organism itself or its products (such as spores). Examples of signs produced by fungi include the white powdery spores of mildew, the black film of fungal strands on leaves with sooty mold, and the galls on cedar trees produced by cedar-apple rust. One common sign of bacteria is slimy ooze that often has a foul odor.

Diseased plants may show both symptoms and signs. Lilacs infected with powdery mildew may have curled leaves (a symptom), but even more obvious is the powdery white coating of fungal spores (a sign).

While it's not critical for you to know the technical difference between a symptom and a sign, it is helpful to know the terms used to describe common symptoms and signs of disease. If you suspect your plant is diseased, study its symptoms and signs, and then review the descriptions listed on the following pages.

Once you match your plant's signs and symptoms to one of the descriptions and/or photographs, read the corresponding discussion to learn more about the disease, including the type of problem, other common symptoms, plants affected, and prevention and control measures.

The disease guide includes photographs and discussions of common plant diseases and disorders. They are organized by plant parts affected: leaves; flowers and fruit; stems and roots; or whole plants. See the categories and where to find the disease descriptions at right.

LEAF SYMPTOMS

Leaves with spots. Pages 310–316

Leaves yellow or discolored. Pages 316–322

Leaves with white, gray, or black coating or patches. Pages 322–323

Leaves curled or distorted. Pages 323–324

Leaves wilted. Pages 324–326

FLOWER AND FRUIT SYMPTOMS

Flowers discolored. Pages 326–327

Fruit with spots. Pages 328–330

Fruit with off-color patches. Pages 330–331

Fruit rotted or deformed. Pages 331–332

STEM AND ROOT SYMPTOMS

Stems with cracks, holes, or discolored areas. Pages 333–335

Stem tips stunted or die back. Page 335–338

Stems with parasitic plants. Pages 338–339

Stems with swollen growths. Pages 339–340

Roots with swollen growths. Pages 340–341

Roots die back. Pages 341–342

Tubers discolored or rotted. Pages 342–343

WHOLE PLANT SYMPTOMS

Seedlings die or plants are stunted or die back. Pages 343–344

Leaf Symptoms
Leaves with Spots

The death of leaf cells can result in well-defined, circular spots. Spots can be of various colors and may change colors as symptoms progress. In some cases, as in cherry leaf spot, the dead cells eventually fall out, leaving holes.

Anthracnose

TYPE OF PROBLEM: Fungal
SYMPTOMS: On leaves, anthracnose diseases generally appear first as small, irregular yellow or brown spots that darken as they age. These spots may also expand and join to cover the leaves. On vegetables, anthracnose diseases can affect any part of the plant. See "Anthracnose" on page 328 for a discussion of anthracnose symptoms on fruit. On trees, infection can begin before the leaves appear, killing the tips of young twigs. Dead leaves that persist through winter and early spring may harbor the disease and allow it to spread down branches, where it forms cankers. Twig dieback may diminish production of new leaves in spring.

More often, anthracnose fungi affect young leaves, producing brown spots and patches. Defoliation may occur, forcing the tree to produce a new set of leaves in summer.

Combined with other stresses, anthracnose can cause trees to decline gradually but steadily over a few years' time.

PLANTS AFFECTED: Many kinds of woody and herbaceous plants. Vegetables such as beans, cucumbers, melons, peppers, and tomatoes are particularly susceptible. Anthracnose-prone trees include dogwoods, maples, and sycamores.

PREVENTION AND CONTROL: Avoid anthracnose on vegetables by selecting resistant cultivars, buying healthy transplants, planting in well-drained soil, and not working among plants when they're wet. Remove and destroy infected plants.

Where anthracnose is common, choose resistant tree

Dogwood anthracnose

species and cultivars. Prune out dead twigs and branch tips and new growth arising from the trunk (called water sprouts). Avoid drought stress by watering trees during dry spells and keeping the root zone mulched. Gather up and destroy infected leaves. Sprays of organic fungicides such as Bordeaux mix, just as leaves begin to open, may limit the spread of anthracnose onto new growth, but achieving adequate coverage of mature landscape trees can be difficult, and this method should be considered only as a last resort for high-value specimens.

Apple Scab

TYPE OF PROBLEM: Fungal
SYMPTOMS: Apple scab symptoms first appear on leaves as olive green spots that gradually turn black. These spots may expand and run together, forming large blotches. Leaves may drop prematurely. The leaves may be deformed or smaller than normal. Brown or black spots may also appear on the fruit; for more details, see "Apple Scab" on page 328.
PLANTS AFFECTED: Apples and crabapples
PREVENTION AND CONTROL: Plant resistant cultivars. Rake up and dispose of fallen leaves,

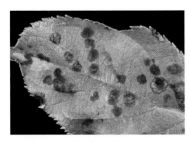

Apple scab

which carry overwintering spores. Apple scab is most prevalent in areas with cool, moist summers because the spores spread rapidly in wet weather. In such areas, regular sulfur or lime-sulfur sprays may prevent apple scab fungi from infecting young leaves and fruits, reducing damage and the chance of apple scab recurring later in the season.

Bacterial Spot

TYPE OF PROBLEM: Bacterial
SYMPTOMS: Depending on the plant they attack, these bacteria will produce round, angular, or elongated discolorations on leaves. The spots are tiny at first but may spread and join to cover whole leaves. The spots are usually brown and are sometimes surrounded with a yellow ring referred to as a halo. The damaged tissue often drops out of the leaves, leaving small holes. Severely infected leaves may fall early. The bacteria can also attack fruit, causing sunken

spots; raised, scabby spots; or cracking.
PLANTS AFFECTED: Many kinds of woody and herbaceous plants
PREVENTION AND CONTROL: Bacterial spot pathogens overwinter in infected plant parts and seeds, in the soil, or on contaminated tools and pots. Reduce the chances of disease by using clean seeds, rotating crops, and practicing good garden and greenhouse sanitation. Plant resistant cultivars. If possible, remove and destroy severely infected plants. Preventive use of biofungicide products that contain *Bacillus subtilis* may be practical where bacterial spot has been a problem in previous seasons.

Bacterial spot on tomato

Black Spot

TYPE OF PROBLEM: Fungal
SYMPTOMS: This disease appears as circular black spots on infected leaves. The spots usually have fringed or indistinct margins and are often

surrounded by a ring of yellow tissue. Severely infected leaves may fall early. Black spot fungus can also infect stems, causing purplish or black blisters on young canes.

Black spot

PLANTS AFFECTED: Roses
PREVENTION AND CONTROL: Plant resistant species or cultivars. Black spot fungus thrives in moist conditions. Avoid wetting plant leaves when watering. Prune plants to increase air circulation. If you expect black spot to be a problem based on past infections, spray plants weekly with baking soda, potassium bicarbonate, or fungicidal soap. Once symptoms appear, black spot is very difficult to control. Remove and destroy infected leaves and canes. Potassium bicarbonate sprays or a 0.5 percent solution of baking soda (1 teaspoon baking soda in 1 quart water, plus a small amount of liquid dish soap) may help to control the disease. Spray infected plants thoroughly.

Botrytis Blight

TYPE OF PROBLEM: Fungal
SYMPTOMS: Besides affecting fruit and flowers, Botrytis fungi can also damage leaves: Infected leaves develop water-soaked spots that later turn brown or dry. For information about Botrytis on flowers, see "Botrytis Blight" on page 326; for Botrytis on fruit, see "Botrytis Fruit Rot" on page 331.
PLANTS AFFECTED: A wide range of woody and herbaceous plants, including cabbage, onions, peonies, and strawberries
PREVENTION AND CONTROL: After they die down, cut or pull off and destroy the tops of herbaceous plants to remove a potential source of inoculum for the following season. Provide good air circulation through pruning and site selection. Remove and destroy infected parts. Where Botrytis has been a problem in the past, apply preventive sprays of Fungastop, a mint oil and citric acid product. Biofungicide products that contain *Bacillus subtilis* may help to control foliage symptoms of

Botrytis blight on peony

Botrytis and to limit the spread of the disease.

Cedar-Apple Rust

TYPE OF PROBLEM: Fungal
SYMPTOMS: On apples, rust symptoms commonly appear in spring. Tiny yellow spots, which later expand and turn orange, form on upper leaf surfaces and on fruit. Brown spots may appear on the undersides of leaves. For details on how cedar-apple rust affects cedar trees, see "Cedar-Apple Rust" on page 312.
PLANTS AFFECTED: Apples and crabapples. Similar rust diseases affect hawthorns (cedar-hawthorn rust) and quinces (cedar-quince rust).
PREVENTION AND CONTROL: Cedar-apple rust completes its life cycle only if fungal spores can travel between red cedars (*Juniperus* spp.) and apple trees. Fungi growing in cedars send spores to infect apple trees. However, infections on the apple tree do not spread within the tree; the fungus can only send spores back to infect cedar. Prevention is the best control. Rust fungi need moisture, so promote drying through pruning and site selection to limit disease problems. Plant apple trees only if cedars are at least 4 miles away;

Cedar-apple rust on crabapple

this will reduce the chances of the disease spreading. If you want to grow both cedars and apple trees, plant rust-resistant species or cultivars of these plants. Many fungicides (including sulfur and lime-sulfur) that are effective against other fungal diseases are not very effective against rust diseases. Biofungicide products that contain *Bacillus subtilis* may help to control foliage symptoms of rust and to limit the spread of the disease. Preventive sprays of copper-based fungicides may provide some protection, but should be used only as a last resort.

Cherry Leaf Spot

TYPE OF PROBLEM: Fungal
SYMPTOMS: The first noticeable symptoms are tiny purple spots on the upper leaf surfaces. Corresponding whitish spots on the undersides of leaves may appear. The centers of these spots often dry and fall out, giving the leaves a shothole appearance.

Cherry leaf spot

Entire leaves may turn yellow and drop early. Fruit, as well as leaf and fruit stems, can also show symptoms.

PLANTS AFFECTED: Cherries and, less often, plums

PREVENTION AND CONTROL: Plant resistant cultivars. Clean up fallen leaves in autumn to remove overwintering fungi. If your trees have had past serious infections, try preventive sulfur sprays to help reduce disease severity.

Downy Mildew

TYPE OF PROBLEM: Fungal

SYMPTOMS: Downy mildew infections begin as angular yellow spots on the upper leaf surfaces; these spots eventually turn brown. Corresponding white, tan, or gray, cottony spots form on the undersides of the leaves. Downy mildew can also attack young shoots and fruit, forming a white coating.

PLANTS AFFECTED: A wide range of woody and herbaceous plants. This disease is a serious problem on cucurbits, especially cucumbers, and grapes.

PREVENTION AND CONTROL: Downy mildew thrives during cool, moist weather. Control downy mildew on your plants by promoting drying (through pruning and site selection) and growing resistant cultivars. Plant disease-free seeds and bulbs. Remove and destroy badly infected leaves. Sprays of potassium bicarbonate may give some control as well as reduce the spread of the disease. For woody plants, Bordeaux mix or other copper-based fungicides can be used as a last resort.

Downy mildew on cucumber

Early Blight

TYPE OF PROBLEM: Fungal

SYMPTOMS: Early blight symptoms appear first on lower leaves as brown spots with concentric rings; these spots eventually spread to cover the leaves. Affected leaves drop early, exposing fruit to sunscald. Spots and cankers may also appear on stems.

PLANTS AFFECTED: Tomatoes and potatoes

PREVENTION AND CONTROL: Clean up plant debris to remove overwintering sites. Use disease-free seeds and seed potatoes. Rotate crops and plant resistant cultivars. Use stakes or cages to keep foliage and fruit off the ground; disinfect cages and stakes each season before using by cleaning them with a 10 percent bleach solution (1 part bleach to 9 parts water). Where available, biofungicide products containing *Trichoderma harzianum* may be applied to soil or to transplants' roots as a preventive. Preventive copper-based

Early blight lesions on tomato

Early blight on potato

fungicide sprays may help reduce the spread of early blight. Remove and destroy severely infected plants.

Late Blight

TYPE OF PROBLEM: Fungal
SYMPTOMS: On leaves, late blight begins as tiny brown spots, which develop into greenish gray or brown areas that can expand to cover whole leaves. These spots may be surrounded by a ring of yellow tissue on the upper surfaces of leaves and a ring of whitish fungal growth on the leaf undersides. Brownish black areas may form on stems. Fruit rots and shrivels quickly; tubers may show a reddish brown dry rot.
PLANTS AFFECTED: Potatoes and tomatoes
PREVENTION AND CONTROL: The fungus that causes potato late blight overwinters on diseased tubers. Harvesting all tubers and disposing of those that are infected limits the

Late blight on potato

disease the following season. At season's end, destroy plant debris (or hot-compost infected plants), including culled tomatoes and potatoes. Remove volunteer plants and space plants to allow good air movement; avoid wetting foliage unnecessarily. Rotate crops and select resistant cultivars. Plant only certified disease-free seed potatoes. Apply *Bacillus subtilis* products or copper sprays to help prevent the disease. Once infected, symptoms can quickly worsen. Monitor plants carefully, and uproot plants that develop symptoms. Bury them deeply away from the garden or discard them in sealed bags with your household trash.

Leaf Blister

TYPE OF PROBLEM: Fungal
SYMPTOMS: Swollen, yellow or brownish blisters appear on upper surfaces as leaves develop in spring. The spots may expand and run together to cover leaves; seriously damaged leaves may fall early.
PLANTS AFFECTED: Oaks
PREVENTION AND CONTROL: Mild, moist weather conditions promote the development of the disease. Oak leaf blister usually only attacks young, developing leaves in spring; older leaves, later in the season, are not

Oak leaf blister

affected. Control is usually not necessary. If you have young trees that were severely infected the preceding season, apply a dormant-season spray of lime-sulfur or Bordeaux mix before the buds open in spring.

Needlecast

TYPE OF PROBLEM: Fungal
SYMPTOMS: The symptoms of this disease appear on developing needles. Mottled yellow spots appear first, changing to reddish or orangish brown. Severely damaged needles may fall by midsummer.

Needlecast on Douglas fir

PLANTS AFFECTED: Many kinds of needle-leaved plants
PREVENTION AND CONTROL: Site plants where they will get good air circulation. Clean up fallen needles; prune off damaged tips. If plants have been seriously infected in previous seasons, spray with Bordeaux mix when new shoots are half grown; repeat 2 weeks later.

Rust

TYPE OF PROBLEM: Fungal
SYMPTOMS: Yellow or white spots form on upper leaf surfaces. Orange or yellow spots or streaks appear on the undersides of leaves. Spots are fungal structures that release spores.
PLANTS AFFECTED: A wide range of woody and herbaceous plants
PREVENTION AND CONTROL: Provide good air circulation and avoid wetting leaves when

Rust symptoms

watering. Remove and destroy seriously affected parts. Biofungicide products that contain *Bacillus subtilis* may help to control foliage symptoms of rust and to limit the spread of the disease. For bramble fruits, immediately destroy any infected plants and replant resistant cultivars. Dusting plants with sulfur, starting early in the season, will prevent infection or keep mild infections from spreading, but be sure to weigh the risks of using sulfur against the benefits before you decide to follow this course of action.

Salt Injury

TYPE OF PROBLEM: Environmental
SYMPTOMS: Plants respond to excess soil salt just as they would to drought: stunting, wilting, drying out of leaves, even death. White, crusty material—salt—may build up on leaves of outdoor plants exposed to salt spray or road deicing salts. A white crust on the surface of the potting mix in which you grow houseplants can indicate salt buildup due to poor drainage or overfertilization.
PLANTS AFFECTED: A wide range of woody and herbaceous plants
PREVENTION AND CONTROL: How you prevent salt damage

Salt injury to yews

depends on how salt gets to the plants. In the North, this salt may come from sodium chloride used for road deicing. Plants in coastal areas are often exposed to blowing sea spray. Some soils of the West are naturally high in salts, as are some irrigation waters in that region. Soluble salts from animal urine can also damage plant roots. Excess fertilizer, even manure, can cause salt buildup wherever drainage is poor or rainfall is insufficient to leach excess salt out of the soil.

Remove excess salts from soils by watering heavily. Use sand or sawdust rather than deicing salts to improve traction on icy sidewalks. Improve soil drainage, if necessary, by digging open trenches or burying perforated plastic drainage pipe within the soil to carry away excess water. In areas of the West where drainage is poor due to excess sodium in the soil, apply gypsum to loosen the soil structure. Choose salt-tolerant plant species and cultivars.

Septoria leaf spot on rhododendron

Septoria Leaf Spot

TYPE OF PROBLEM: Fungal
SYMPTOMS: Leaf damage starts as small yellow spots that gradually turn brown; spots are often surrounded by a ring of yellow or brownish black tissue. Whole leaves may turn yellow and drop, exposing fruit to sun, which may result in sunscald. This disease usually starts on lower leaves and progresses upward.
PLANTS AFFECTED: A wide range of herbaceous plants
PREVENTION AND CONTROL: Remove and destroy infected leaves. Clean up plant debris in fall. Use disease-free seed. Crop rotation and the use of resistant cultivars will reduce the chances of Septoria leaf spot.

Tomato Spotted Wilt Virus

TYPE OF PROBLEM: Viral
SYMPTOMS: Leaf symptoms vary widely among host plants but may include dark ring spots or streaks or general yellowing and browning of foliage. Dark brown or blackened areas may be visible on stems. Immature tomato fruits show light green rings with raised centers; ripening fruits are mottled orange and red, eventually developing blackened areas.
PLANTS AFFECTED: A wide range of herbaceous plants. Tomatoes, peppers, and impatiens have been particularly hard-hit by this virus.
PREVENTION AND CONTROL: Tomato spotted wilt virus is spread almost entirely by thrips; control them (see page 287) to limit the spread of the virus. Clean up weedy areas in and around your gardens; several common weeds,

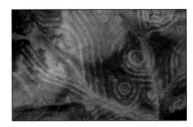

Tomato spotted wilt virus on cyclamen

including chickweed, lamb's-quarters, morning glory (bindweed), and sowthistle, serve as alternate hosts for the virus. Remove and destroy infected plants. Because this virus is widespread among many greenhouse crops, growing your own plants from seed is a way to avoid introducing it into your garden.

Leaf Symptoms

Leaves Yellow or Discolored

Leaf discoloration can be from cell death, or it can be from an interruption of plant biochemical processes as a result of nutrient deficiencies or environmental pollutants.

Allelopathy

TYPE OF PROBLEM: Environmental
SYMPTOMS: Yellowing leaves (chlorosis), wilting leaves, and plants that grow poorly and decline for no obvious reason may be suffering from the interplant competition known as allelopathy, in which some plants produce chemicals that adversely affect adjacent plants. Black walnut is perhaps the most notorious but there are numerous other examples. Sunflower seed hulls, such as may be abundant beneath a bird feeder, also can cause allelopathic injury to nearby plants.
PLANTS AFFECTED: A wide range of herbaceous and woody plants. Tomatoes and related crops are particularly sensitive to juglone, the allelopathic compound in all parts of black walnuts.

PREVENTION AND CONTROL:
Maintain a distance of at least
1½ times a walnut tree's height
between it and susceptible plants.
Clean up sunflower hulls or use
hull-less seed mixes in feeders
located in lawns or garden beds.

Foliar Nematodes

TYPE OF PROBLEM: Nematodes
SYMPTOMS: Leaves show yellow
patches (often angular or wedge-
shaped) that later turn brown or
black; these blotches may enlarge
to cover whole leaves, causing
early leaf drop. Symptoms start
near the bottom of plants and
work upward. Infected shoots
are stunted, and flowers may be
deformed.
PLANTS AFFECTED: A wide
range of herbaceous plants.
Plants that are particularly
susceptible include
chrysanthemums, asters, hostas,
dahlias, phlox, primroses,
azaleas, ferns, and strawberries.
PREVENTION AND CONTROL:
Avoid planting susceptible
species. Foliar nematodes move
up stems in a film of water.
Choose a site with good air
circulation, and thin stems for
quick drying. Clean up debris to
eliminate overwintering sites.
Destroy infected plant parts.
Heat treatment by dunking
infected plants into 120°F water
for 10 minutes may control foliar

Foliar
nematode
symptoms
on heuchera

nematodes without harming
plants if done just as plants are
breaking dormancy. Plunge into
cold tap water after heat
treatment. Sprays of insecticidal
soap may also help control
infections.

Iron Deficiency or Overly High pH

TYPE OF PROBLEM:
Environmental
SYMPTOMS: The youngest
leaves, those near the tops of
shoots, turn yellow except for
the veins, which remain green.
PLANTS AFFECTED: Acid-loving
plants, including blueberries,
oaks, hollies, azaleas, and
rhododendrons are most
susceptible but many plants
display symptoms in high pH
soils.
PREVENTION AND CONTROL:
Symptoms of iron deficiency
appear when the soil is not
sufficiently acidic. Symptoms
often occur on susceptible plants
growing near buildings because
lime that leaches out of concrete
foundations raises soil pH. In

most cases, iron is present
in the soil in adequate amounts,
but the high pH binds the iron
in a form that plants cannot
absorb. The long-term solution
to this problem is to plant in
acidic soil or to make the soil
more acidic. Planting in raised
beds amended with compost can
also provide good growing
conditions for acid-loving
plants. Mulch acid-loving plants
with evergreen needles. To save
an ailing plant quickly, spray a
commercial chelated iron
product on its leaves. Check
product labels; many chelated
products use synthetic
"carriers," but a few are
available that use lignins
(natural plant materials) as the
carriers. Spraying leaves
with seaweed extract will also
help to provide the necessary
nutrients.

Iron-deficient rhododendron

Leaf Scorch

TYPE OF PROBLEM:
Environmental
SYMPTOMS: Leaf scorch appears as yellowing and browning of leaves beginning along the margins and tips. Associated symptoms may include wilting, rolling of leaves, stunted growth, and death of the plant.
PLANTS AFFECTED: A wide range of woody and herbaceous plants
PREVENTION AND CONTROL:
The two major causes of leaf scorch are drought and reflected heat, although nutrient deficiencies and bacterial/fungal infections may also cause scorchlike symptoms. Avoid drought injury to plants with timely watering. On average, most garden plants need the equivalent of about 1 inch (2 gallons per square foot) of water per week for every foot of root depth. Avoid frequent, light watering, which promotes shallow rooting. Reflected heat from surrounding pavement is mostly a problem for street trees; there is no control. Avoid planting highly susceptible trees, such as horse chestnuts and maples, in these sites.

Mosaic

TYPE OF PROBLEM: Viral
SYMPTOMS: Mosaic-infected leaves are mottled with yellow, white, and light and dark green spots or streaks. Fruit may show similar symptoms. Plants are often stunted (see page 344).
PLANTS AFFECTED: A wide range of woody and herbaceous plants
PREVENTION AND CONTROL:
Plant resistant cultivars when available. Mosaic viruses are mostly spread by insect pests, especially aphids and leaf-hoppers. If possible, deny these carriers access to your crop by covering the plants with floating row cover. For more information on preventing and controlling aphids and leafhoppers, see pages 250 and 271. Once plants are infected, there are no controls; remove and destroy infected plants.

Nitrogen Deficiency

TYPE OF PROBLEM:
Environmental
SYMPTOMS: Nitrogen deficiency appears as a uniform yellowing of the oldest leaves (those nearest the base of the stem). A less obvious symptom is stunted and spindly growth.
PLANTS AFFECTED: All plants
PREVENTION AND CONTROL:
Yearly applications of supplemental nitrogen are most important in the vegetable garden. Other plantings can get the nitrogen they need from regular applications of compost or aged manure. Organic nitrogen sources include alfalfa and soybean meals, dried blood, composted manure, and compost. In the vegetable garden, you can provide nitrogen by growing a leguminous cover crop every

Leaf scorch symptoms

Cucumber mosaic on squash

Nitrogen-deficiency symptoms

other season. Treat ornamental plants that show deficiency symptoms with foliar sprays of fish emulsion.

Ozone Damage

TYPE OF PROBLEM: Environmental

SYMPTOMS: Ozone damage appears as white or tan stippling or flecking on leaves. High concentrations of ozone in the atmosphere may cause early fall color and leaf drop. This damage can be difficult to diagnose because symptoms mimic many other disease conditions. Check for similar damage on other ozone-susceptible plants growing in the same area.

PLANTS AFFECTED: A wide range of woody and ornamental plants. Plants such as bean, spinach, tomatoes, blackberries, sweet gums, pines, and tulip poplars are particularly sensitive to ozone.

PREVENTION AND CONTROL: Ozone levels in the air may reach damaging levels during the hot, calm days of mid- to late summer. Automobile exhaust is the major source of ozone pollution. There is no cure for ozone damage. Avoid placing sensitive plants where they will be exposed to high levels of engine exhaust.

PAN Damage

TYPE OF PROBLEM: Environmental

SYMPTOMS: Exposure to PAN (peroxyacyl nitrate) causes a silvery glaze on the lower surfaces of leaves, resembling damage due to frost, sunscald, mites, thrips, or leafhoppers. Young, rapidly growing tissue is most sensitive to PAN injury.

PLANTS AFFECTED: A wide range of woody and herbaceous plants. Plants that are particularly susceptible include petunias, beans, lettuce, peppers, and tomatoes.

PREVENTION AND CONTROL: PAN is a major component of engine exhaust and is a problem in smoggy areas. If you live where PAN damage is a recurring problem, grow plants that tolerate these pollutants, such as sugar maples, arborvitae, winged euonymus, English ivy, snapdragons, cabbage, cucumbers, and squash.

Phosphorus Deficiency

TYPE OF PROBLEM: Environmental

SYMPTOMS: A bluish or purplish cast to leaves or stems is the most common symptom of phosphorus deficiency; some plants develop purple spots. Phosphorus-deficient plants also do not flower and fruit as well as healthy plants do.

PLANTS AFFECTED: All plants

PREVENTION AND CONTROL: Phosphorus deficiency symptoms develop fairly frequently in transplants set out in early spring. Unlike some other nutrients, phosphorus does not move through the soil; roots must grow to reach it. Until the

Ozone damage symptoms

Pan damage on potato

Phosphorus-deficient corn seedling

soil warms sufficiently to stimulate root growth, plants may not be able to take up enough phosphorus.

Organic matter contains both phosphorus and potassium, so enrich your soil with plenty of compost, leaf mold, and other organic materials. Other sources of phosphorus include bonemeal and rock phosphate.

Potassium Deficiency

TYPE OF PROBLEM: Environmental

SYMPTOMS: Symptoms usually appear on older leaves first as yellowing and browning of the leaf margins. Dead areas on edges may drop, giving the leaves a ragged appearance. If deficiency is severe, young leaves will show symptoms as well; consider having leaf tissue analyzed to confirm.

PLANTS AFFECTED: All plants

PREVENTION AND CONTROL: Soil tests can alert you to deficiency problems before they become serious. Regular

Potassium deficiency symptoms

applications of compost or other organic fertilizers will help to maintain an even potassium supply. Sources of potassium include kelp meal, granite dust, greensand, and wood ashes. Use wood ashes sparingly, because they can raise soil pH to undesirable levels.

Sulfur Dioxide Injury

TYPE OF PROBLEM: Environmental

SYMPTOMS: Mild cases of sulfur dioxide damage show up as general leaf yellowing. More severe damage involves yellowing or browning of the tissues between leaf veins.

PLANTS AFFECTED: A wide range of woody and herbaceous plants

PREVENTION AND CONTROL: Sulfur dioxide is an air pollutant, primarily a result of industrial processes. Where these pollutants are a problem, grow

Sulfur dioxide damage on blackberry

tolerant trees such as ginkgoes, junipers, sycamores, and arborvitae. Vegetables that tolerate sulfur dioxide include cucumbers, corn, and onions.

Verticillium Wilt

TYPE OF PROBLEM: Fungal

SYMPTOMS: Infection by wilt fungi causes leaves to yellow and leaf stems to droop, giving plants a wilted appearance. The yellow leaf patches turn brown and may spread to cover whole leaves. Leaves often fall early, and plants will die. Symptoms usually first appear on the lower or outer parts of plants. The interior of the stem near the base may be discolored.

PLANTS AFFECTED: A wide range of woody and herbaceous plants. Some particularly suscep-tible plants include tomatoes, peppers, melons, asters, chrysan-themums, peaches, cherries, strawberries, and maples.

PREVENTION AND CONTROL: Verticillium and Fusarium wilt fungi cause similar symptoms. Verticillium wilt is more common in cool weather in temperate areas of the country. There is no cure for Verticillium wilt. The most effective preventive measure is the use of wilt-resistant cultivars, when available. Crop rotation is not very effective because so many species are susceptible to Verticillium wilt. Adding compost to soil may help by boosting populations of beneficial fungi.

If you've had problems with

Verticillium wilt on potato

Verticillium wilt in the past, try soil solarization to prevent recurrence. If plants become infected, bury the infected residues deeply or dispose of them in household trash.

Winter Injury

TYPE OF PROBLEM: Environmental

SYMPTOMS: Symptoms of cold injury can be similar to sunscald

SYMPTOMS: blotchy, water-soaked areas on leaves of broad-leaved plants; yellowing or browning of needles on conifers. Shoot tips often die back (see stem damage photograph on page 337).

Winter injury on pine

PLANTS AFFECTED: A wide range of woody and herbaceous plants

PREVENTION AND CONTROL: In winter, evergreens can suffer from drying when their roots cannot get sufficient water from frozen ground. Water plants thoroughly in late fall. Spray leaves with an antitranspirant to reduce water loss. If winter damage has been a problem in the past, move plants to a more sheltered spot or erect a barrier (such as a piece of burlap) to protect the plants from drying winds. Prune out damaged wood in spring.

Cold, or in some cases cool, temperatures also damage herbaceous plants. If you plant corn or beans too early, these heat-loving plants suffer during extended cool weather, even though the temperature never dips below freezing. Subfreezing weather in the spring can damage tender seedlings as well as new shoots and flowers of woody plants. Acclimate indoor seedlings to outdoor temperatures gradually to help the plants adapt to the cold. Protect garden seedlings and transplants with cloches or row cover.

Yellows

Some virus symptoms (e.g., leaf twisting, yellowing, rosetting), as well as phyllody (reversion of flowers to a leaflike form), are symptoms of phytoplasma infection. Vectors of phytoplasmas are usually leafhoppers. Some planthoppers and psyllids are also vectors.

TYPE OF PROBLEM: Phytoplasmal

SYMPTOMS: This disease produces a gradual yellowing of leaves that typically begins with loss of green pigment in the veins. Plant parts, including roots and flowers, may be stunted and deformed. Flowers may be green, leaflike, and distorted, a condition known as phyllody. The roots of infected carrots are covered with "hairy" roots; potatoes may produce tubers on their stems. On trees, leaves turn yellow, then brown, and may drop early. Symptoms appear over the whole crown of the tree. Plants may die in a single growing season.

PLANTS AFFECTED: A wide range of woody and herbaceous

Aster yellows on lettuce

plants. Aster yellows affects many plants, including carrots, lettuce, onions, potatoes, tomatoes, China asters, echinacea, gladiolus, marigolds, and petunias. Elm yellows (also know as elm phloem necrosis) attacks several species of elms.

PREVENTION AND CONTROL: Yellows diseases are commonly transmitted by leafhoppers, so controlling the pests will reduce the chances of disease (see page 271 for controls). Remove weeds that provide overwintering sites for the pathogen, including thistles, Queen-Anne's lace, dandelions, plantain, and wild chicory. Remove and destroy infected plants.

Leaf Symptoms

Leaves with White, Gray, or Black Coating or Patches

Discolored patches on leaves may be *signs* of the pathogen. For example, the white powdery covering of powdery mildew is actually the fungus spreading across leaf surfaces.

Powdery Mildew

TYPE OF PROBLEM: Fungal.
SYMPTOMS: Plants suffering from powdery mildew look as if they have been dusted with flour. Powdery mildew fungi mostly attack new leaves, causing distorted growth. The fungi also can affect fruit; see "Powdery Mildew" on pages 322 and 330.
PLANTS AFFECTED: A wide range of woody and herbaceous plants. Some plants that are particularly susceptible include lilacs, phlox, bee balm, squash, roses, and zinnias.
PREVENTION AND CONTROL: Powdery mildew thrives in hot weather, especially with cool nights. Drought-stressed plants

Powdery mildew symptoms

are more susceptible to powdery mildew infection; unlike most fungal diseases, it is actually less of a problem in rainy weather. Control by providing good air circulation, by watering and mulching to prevent drought stress, and by growing resistant cultivars. Organic fungicides, including *Bacillus subtilis*, potassium bicarbonate, or a 0.5 percent solution of baking soda (1 teaspoon baking soda in 1 quart water) may be applied as preventives or to help to control the disease. Spray infected plants thoroughly.

Sooty Mold

TYPE OF PROBLEM: Fungal.
SYMPTOMS: Leaves and stems are speckled or coated with a thin black film, which can be wiped off to expose healthy green leaf surfaces. Plants may also feel sticky.
PLANTS AFFECTED: A wide range of woody and herbaceous plants.
PREVENTION AND CONTROL: This fungus grows on the sticky

excretions (known as honeydew) produced by insects such as aphids, scales, and mealybugs. The fungus does not directly injure the plant, but the black coating is unsightly and may interfere with photosynthesis and reduce plant growth.

On small plants, you can wipe off the coating with a damp cloth. The best treatment is to control the insects producing the honeydew (see pages 250, 273, and 282 for aphid, mealybug, and scale controls, respectively). If the affected plants do not have an apparent insect problem, check for honeydew dripping from an overhanging plant.

Sooty mold on California laurel

Leaf Symptoms
Leaves Curled or Distorted

Disease can alter the normal pattern of leaf growth by inhibiting or stimulating cell development in unusual ways. Leaves may twist or form swollen growths called galls.

Curly Top

TYPE OF PROBLEM: Viral
SYMPTOMS: Leaves of infected plants twist and curl upward, becoming stiff and leathery. They eventually turn yellow and then brown. Leaf stems bend downward. The plant may appear stunted, and fruit production stops.
PLANTS AFFECTED: A wide range of herbaceous plants. Beets, tomatoes, beans, melons, and spinach are particularly susceptible.
PREVENTION AND CONTROL: Plant resistant cultivars. Remove surrounding weeds, such as thistles and plantain, which provide overwintering sites for disease. Leafhoppers carry the curly top virus, so keep these pests away by protecting plants with floating row cover. See page 271 for more leafhopper controls. Remove and destroy affected plants.

Curly top on tomato

Herbicide Injury

TYPE OF PROBLEM: Environmental
SYMPTOMS: Distorted, cupped, curled, or stunted foliage; yellow or white leaves; dead leaf margins; twisted stems; misshapen flowers and fruits; dropped flower buds or fruits; and underdeveloped roots are all possible symptoms of damage from herbicides.
PLANTS AFFECTED: A wide range of woody and herbaceous plants. Susceptibility varies according to type of herbicide and plant species.
PREVENTION AND CONTROL: Site home gardens away from

Herbicide injury to pepper

places (agricultural lands, municipal properties) where herbicides may be used. Ask neighboring landowners to limit herbicide use in areas adjacent to your property.

Leaf Gall

TYPE OF PROBLEM: Fungal
SYMPTOMS: Reddish or yellowish leaf spots often appear first. Infected leaves develop light green galls that later turn white and then brown. Flowers may also be damaged.
PLANTS AFFECTED: Fungal leaf galls are most common on azaleas and rhododendrons. Camellias may also get fungal leaf galls. Galls on most other plants are caused by insects or mites; see page 274 for controls.
PREVENTION AND CONTROL: Pick off and destroy infected leaves as soon as you spot the galls.

Leaf galls on azalea

Peach Leaf Curl

TYPE OF PROBLEM: Fungal
SYMPTOMS: Infected plants develop yellowish or reddish blisters on leaves, which become curled and distorted. The blisters eventually turn powdery gray. Entire leaves may turn yellow and fall early. Fruit can be deformed and may drop early. New growth can be

Peach leaf curl symptoms

stunted; infected shoot tips may die back.
PLANTS AFFECTED: Peaches and nectarines
PREVENTION AND CONTROL: Plant resistant cultivars. Remove and destroy infected leaves. Peach leaf curl is usually worst during cool, wet springs. If this disease has been a serious problem in past years, apply a dormant-season spray of lime-sulfur or Bordeaux mix. If you cannot avoid peach leaf curl on trees in the landscape, try instead growing dwarf trees in containers and move them to a covered location during wet periods in winter and spring.

Leaf Symptoms
Leaves Wilted

Leaves of diseased plants can become limp from the death of cells that move water and nutrients in the stems. Wilting is usually accompanied by other signs or symptoms.

Bacterial Wilt

TYPE OF PROBLEM: Bacterial
SYMPTOMS: Leaves appear limp and wilted. Infected stems wilt and collapse quickly. All affected parts are soft at first, but turn hard and dry. When you pull apart a cut stem, you may see long, sticky strands of whitish bacterial ooze. Spots may occur on fruit.
PLANTS AFFECTED: A wide range of herbaceous plants. Cucumbers, melons, and squash are very susceptible. Similar wilts affect tomatoes and beans.

Bacterial wilt in cucumber

PREVENTION AND CONTROL:
Plant resistant cultivars and use disease-free seed. Control cucumber beetles (see page 262) and grasshoppers (see page 267), which transmit the disease as they feed; protect plants with floating row cover. Remove and destroy infected plants.

Fusarium Wilt

TYPE OF PROBLEM: Fungal
SYMPTOMS: Wilt fungi cause leaves to yellow and leaf stems to droop, giving plants a wilted appearance. The yellow leaf patches turn brown and may spread to cover whole leaves. Leaves often fall early, and the plants will die. Symptoms usually first appear on the lower or outer parts of plants. In some cases, the symptoms are most apparent on only one side of a plant. If you cut the stem near the base, you may notice a brown discoloration in the interior.

Fusarium wilt on watermelon

PLANTS AFFECTED: A wide range of woody and herbaceous plants. Common hosts include tomatoes, peas, peppers, melons, dahlias, and mimosa trees.
PREVENTION AND CONTROL:
Fusarium and Verticillium wilt fungi cause similar symptoms. Fusarium wilt thrives in warmer areas.

Plant resistant cultivars. Crop rotation is of limited value because *Fusarium* fungi can survive in the soil a number of years even in the absence of a susceptible plant. Remove and destroy infected plants. Soil solarization may reduce the incidence of this disease.

Verticillium Wilt

TYPE OF PROBLEM: Fungal
SYMPTOMS: Wilt fungi cause leaves to yellow and leaf stems to droop, giving plants a wilted appearance. The yellow leaf patches turn brown, and may spread to cover whole leaves. Leaves often fall early, and the plants will die. Symptoms usually first appear on the lower or outer parts of the plant. The interior of the stem near the base may be discolored.
PLANTS AFFECTED: A wide range of woody and herbaceous plants. Some particularly susceptible plants include tomatoes, peppers, melons, asters,

Verticillium wilt on potato

chrysanthemums, peaches, cherries, strawberries, and maples.
PREVENTION AND CONTROL:
Verticillium and Fusarium wilt fungi cause similar symptoms. Verticillium wilt is more common in cool weather in temperate areas of the country.

There is no cure for Verticillium wilt. The most effective preventive measure is the use of wilt-resistant cultivars, when available. Crop rotation is not very effective because so many species are susceptible to Verticillium wilt. Adding compost to soil may help by boosting populations of beneficial fungi.

If you've had problems with Verticillium wilt in the past, try soil solarization to prevent recurrence. If plants become infected, bury the infected residues deeply or dispose of them in household trash.

Waterlogged Soil

TYPE OF PROBLEM: Environmental
SYMPTOMS: Because waterlogging inhibits root function, it causes essentially the same symptoms as droughty conditions do—wilting. Other common symptoms include yellowed leaves and sudden leaf drop.
PLANTS AFFECTED: A wide range of woody and herbaceous plants
PREVENTION AND CONTROL: When the soil is flooded with water, pores that previously held air become filled with water. Root cells need oxygen in order to function, and the cells may die if they are deprived of oxygen for too long. Besides causing wilting, waterlogged soils provide ideal conditions for bacteria to attack the damaged roots.

Waterlogging results if you apply too much water to the soil. Also, certain soils are naturally prone to waterlogging. Improve soil drainage by adding organic matter or making raised beds. Water plants evenly, according to their needs. Choose plants that are adapted to wet soil conditions when planting a site that is consistently soggy. Severely damaged plants may not recover and should be removed.

Flower and Fruit Symptoms
Flowers Discolored

Flower discoloration may be caused by cell death or from signs of a disease organism appearing on flower parts.

Botrytis Blight

TYPE OF PROBLEM: Fungal
SYMPTOMS: Botrytis blight generally begins on flowers, producing fluffy growth that may be white, gray, or tan. The fungus then spreads to the flower stalk, weakening the stalk and causing the flowers to droop. Affected plant parts eventually turn brown and dry. For information about Botrytis on leaves, see "Botrytis Blight" on page 312; for Botrytis infection on fruit, see "Botrytis Fruit Rot" on page 331.

PLANTS AFFECTED: A wide range of woody and herbaceous plants. The blooms of such flowers as roses, begonias, peonies, chrysanthemums, dahlias, and geraniums are particularly susceptible.
PREVENTION AND CONTROL: Provide good air circulation through pruning and site selection. Remove and destroy affected parts. Biofungicide products that contain *Bacillus subtilis* may help to limit the spread of the disease to other parts of the plant.

Brown Rot

TYPE OF PROBLEM: Fungal
SYMPTOMS: Infected flowers appear wilted and browned. Eventually they are covered with light brown spore masses, which then spread to developing fruit. Small cankers appear near

Seedlings damaged by waterlogging

Botrytis blight on marigolds

Brown rot on peach

branch tips. For more on fruit damage, see "Brown Rot" on page 332.

PLANTS AFFECTED: Peaches, cherries, plums, and other stone fruits.

PREVENTION AND CONTROL: Plant resistant cultivars. Prune trees to provide for good air circulation. Prune out and destroy damaged shoots. Pick off and clean up rotted and shriveled fruit. If brown rot has infected your fruit trees in previous seasons, preventive sprays of sulfur just before blossoms open and again after blossoming may keep the fungus from infecting the fruit. For fruit that will be stored after harvest, another spray, just before harvest, will protect fruit from brown rot during storage.

Flower Blight of Camellia

TYPE OF PROBLEM: Fungal
SYMPTOMS: Flower blight fungi produce small brown spots on petals. These spots enlarge and run together, turning whole flowers brown. Darker veins in petals give infected blossoms a netted appearance and help to distinguish this disease from symptoms of Botrytis blight on flowers.

PLANTS AFFECTED: Camellias
PREVENTION AND CONTROL: Avoid bringing the fungi into your garden by purchasing only bare-root plants; also, pick off and destroy any flower buds before planting. If disease strikes, remove and destroy all infected flowers and buds, including those that have fallen from the plants. Avoid stirring existing mulch, which may harbor disease spores; add a 1-inch layer of fresh mulch over the top to prevent their spread. Avoid watering camellias from above. If flower blight is a recurring problem, apply preventive sprays of neem oil in the spring before buds open, spraying the plants and the mulch beneath them.

Flower blight on camellia

Frost damage to magnolia blossoms

Frost Damage

TYPE OF PROBLEM: Environmental
SYMPTOMS: Exposure to frost can injure plant cells. Flowers exposed to frost may blacken at the center, or the petals may turn brown. Fruit tree blossoms damaged by frost may appear normal, but fail to produce any fruit. The tips of damaged fruit may be deformed. Many types of flowers can withstand frost with no damage. For stem symptoms, see "Frost Damage" on page 333.

PLANTS AFFECTED: A wide range of plants, including strawberries, fruit trees, magnolias, and many types of annual flowers

PREVENTION AND CONTROL: Once damage occurs, there is no control. If you expect frost, cover plants overnight; be sure to remove coverings the next morning.

Flower and Fruit Symptoms

Fruit with Spots

Disease organisms can also invade fruit, killing cells in the fleshy fruit tissues. Fruit with mild symptoms may still be harvestable, but as symptoms progress, fruit may be ruined.

Apple scab symptoms

Anthracnose

TYPE OF PROBLEM: Fungal
SYMPTOMS: Various anthracnose diseases affect fruit, producing small, dark, sunken spots. As the disease progresses, the spots may spread. Pinkish spore masses appear in the center of the spots in moist weather. Fruit eventually rots. Other plant parts are also affected by anthracnose; see "Anthracnose" on page 310 for more information.
PLANTS AFFECTED: A wide range of woody and herbaceous plants. Tomatoes as well as cucumbers and melons are often affected; similar fungi attack beans.
PREVENTION AND CONTROL: Avoid anthracnose on vegetables by selecting resistant cultivars (when available), buying healthy transplants, practicing crop rotation, and planting in well-

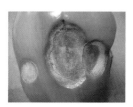

Anthracnose on pepper

drained soil. Avoid overhead watering and working among plants when they're wet. Mulch can help keep spores from splashing from the soil onto lower leaves during rain or watering. Remove and destroy infected plants, ideally before the infection spreads to fruits. Cool, wet weather favors anthracnose development; be on the lookout for symptoms when such conditions occur. Sprays of organic fungicides such as sulfur and copper may provide some protection but are rarely effective once symptoms appear on fruits. Use them as a last resort only where previous years' anthracnose infections have been severe.

Apple Scab

TYPE OF PROBLEM: Fungal.
SYMPTOMS: Fruit infected with apple scab shows green or velvety brown spots, which later turn into raised, brown, corky areas. Leaves are usually infected as well; see "Apple Scab" on page 310 for more details.

PLANTS AFFECTED: Apples and crabapples
PREVENTION AND CONTROL: Plant resistant cultivars. Rake up and dispose of fallen leaves. Apple scab is most prevalent in areas with cool, moist summers because the spores spread rapidly in wet weather. In such areas, regular sulfur or lime-sulfur sprays may prevent apple scab fungi from infecting young leaves and fruit, reducing damage and the chance of apple scab recurring later in the season.

Bacterial Canker of Tomato

TYPE OF PROBLEM: Bacterial
SYMPTOMS: Small (⅛ inch) white spots with raised, dark brown centers and distinct white or light-colored halos first appear on developing green fruits. With time these spots may lose their characteristic halos, darkening and merging into larger areas of decay. Symptoms on leaves may appear as yellowing and wilting, followed by dead spots at the margins; yellowish streaks may

Bacterial canker symptoms

also appear on leaf petioles and stems. Bacterial canker may also infect a plant's vascular system, causing wilting that is limited to one side of the plant. Slicing open the stems of such plants will reveal reddish-brown discoloration of affected tissues.

PLANTS AFFECTED: Tomatoes

PREVENTION AND CONTROL: Buy certified disease-free seed or transplants from a reputable source. Practice crop rotation and avoid planting in a site where bacterial canker occurred in the previous growing season. Do not save seed from plants showing symptoms of bacterial canker. Mulch around the base of plants to keep spores from splashing up from the soil onto leaves during rain or watering. Remove and destroy infected plants. Use a 10 percent bleach solution (1 part bleach to 9 parts water) to disinfect tools, cages, and stakes that have contacted infected plants. Copper sprays may protect healthy plants that remain after infected plants are removed; apply according to

label directions. Sprays are ineffective when symptoms of vascular infection appear.

Bacterial Speck

TYPE OF PROBLEM: Bacterial

SYMPTOMS: Small ($\frac{1}{16}$ inch), slightly raised spots on developing fruits. Unlike bacterial spot, these spots do not crack or become scaly, although they may be numerous and unsightly. Symptoms on leaves resemble those of bacterial spot (see page 311): small ($\frac{1}{8}$ to $\frac{1}{4}$ inch) black spots with faint yellow halos.

PLANTS AFFECTED: Tomatoes

PREVENTION AND CONTROL: Buy certified disease-free seed or transplants from a reputable source. Choose resistant varieties when available. Practice crop rotation and clean up crop debris and weeds that may harbor disease spores. Preventive copper sprays may give some protection if applied until developing fruits reach about one-third of their

mature size, but should only be used as a last resort if bacterial speck has been a problem in previous seasons and when cool, moist weather conditions favor this disease.

Bacterial Spot

TYPE OF PROBLEM: Bacterial

SYMPTOMS: Sunken spots; raised, scabby spots; or cracking that starts on immature (green) tomatoes. Round, green, slightly raised spots (about $\frac{1}{8}$ inch) that gradually become rough and scabby on peppers.

PLANTS AFFECTED: Tomatoes and peppers. A wide range of woody and herbaceous plants may show foliar symptoms (see page 311). A related bacterium infects peaches and other stone fruits, causing spots on leaves and fruit and twig cankers (see page 311).

PREVENTION AND CONTROL: Bacterial spot pathogens overwinter in infected plant parts and seeds, in the soil, or on

Bacterial speck symptoms

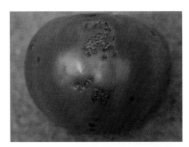

Bacterial spot on tomato fruit

contaminated tools and pots. Reduce the chances of disease by using clean seeds, rotating crops, and practicing good garden and greenhouse sanitation. Plant resistant cultivars when available. Warm, humid weather favors the development of bacterial spot; be on the lookout for symptoms when conditions are favorable and avoid working amid plants when they are wet. Use mulch to keep bacteria from splashing from soil onto plants. Remove and destroy severely infected plants.

Flower and Fruit Symptoms
Fruit with Off-Color Patches

Odd-colored patches on fruit may be caused by cultural or environmental problems, or may be signs of a pathogen.

Blossom End Rot

TYPE OF PROBLEM: Environmental
SYMPTOMS: A water-soaked spot on the end of fruit gradually enlarges and turns brown or black, with a leathery appearance. The end of the fruit will appear flattened.
PLANTS AFFECTED: Tomatoes and peppers
PREVENTION AND CONTROL: Blossom end rot is commonly from calcium deficiency. This often occurs when hot, dry weather or rapid growth (due to excess nitrogen, for example) draws extra water and nutrients to the leaves, starving fruit of this nutrient. Extended, heavy rainfall that washes calcium out of the root zone is another cause. Root damage can also interfere with calcium uptake.

To avoid blossom end rot, choose resistant varieties. Keep the soil evenly moist by watering regularly and putting down a thick layer of organic mulch. Cultivate carefully to avoid damaging roots. For beds covered with plastic mulch, check soil moisture frequently and don't let the soil dry out or overheat. If blossom end rot is a repeated problem, check pH and add lime as needed to raise pH to between 6.5 and 6.8.

Blossom end rot on tomatoes

Powdery Mildew

TYPE OF PROBLEM: Fungal
SYMPTOMS: Fruit infected with powdery mildew can crack or have raised webbing (called russeting) on their surfaces. Fruit may color slowly or not at all and may show a powdery white coating. This disease can also attack leaves; see "Powdery Mildew" on page 322.
PLANTS AFFECTED: A wide range of woody and herbaceous plants. The fruit of apples and grapes are particularly susceptible.
PREVENTION AND CONTROL: Powdery mildew fungi thrive in hot weather, especially in conjunction with cool nights. Unlike most other fungal diseases, it is actually less of a problem in rainy weather. When possible, grow resistant cultivars, and site and prune to promote good air circulation. Water (avoid wetting foliage and fruits) and apply mulch to prevent drought stress.

Powdery mildew on apples

For persistent infections, there are several organic sprays that may provide control and limit the spread of this disease; these include biofungicides containing *Bacillus subtilis,* potassium bicarbonate, or a 0.5 percent solution of baking soda (1 teaspoon baking soda in 1 quart water). As a last resort, try horticultural oil products (including neem oil), fungicidal soap, and sulfur or lime-sulfur sprays. Spray infected plants thoroughly.

Sunscald

TYPE OF PROBLEM: Environmental.

SYMPTOMS: Sunscald appears on fruit as a water-soaked, blistered spot that eventually dries out and turns brown. Sunscald can also affect leaves, starting as pale green areas that later turn brown and dry.

PLANTS AFFECTED: A wide range of woody and herbaceous plants. Fruit most commonly damaged includes tomatoes, peppers, and apples.

Sunscald damage on apple

PREVENTION AND CONTROL: Strong, direct sunlight or excessively high temperatures can cause sunscald. On tomatoes this problem commonly occurs when a disease such as leaf spot causes leaves to fall, suddenly exposing once-shaded fruit to full sunlight. Plant cultivars that are resistant to major foliage diseases. Once damage occurs, there is no control.

Flower and Fruit Symptoms
Fruit Rotted or Deformed

When fruit cells die, they can become soft, and the fruit may rot. If cell development is inhibited or stimulated, fruit may have unusual shapes.

Black Rot

TYPE OF PROBLEM: Fungal

SYMPTOMS: Purplish brown spots appear on green fruit. Infected grapes shrivel up, turn black, and cling to the bunch. Leaves and shoots can also be affected, showing circular, reddish brown spots.

PLANTS AFFECTED: Grapes; note that bulbs, tree fruits, carrots, and some other plants also suffer from a condition called black rot, but different fungi cause these diseases and symptoms, and

Black rot on grapes

treatment may not be the same as for black rot of grapes.

PREVENTION AND CONTROL: Plant resistant cultivars. Pick off and destroy infected fruit. Remove existing mulch or cover it with a fresh layer. Warm, wet weather favors the spread of black rot spores; be on the lookout for symptoms during favorable conditions. If black rot has been a problem in previous years, apply preventive sprays of Bordeaux mix or another copper-based fungicide just before and immediately after bloom.

Botrytis Fruit Rot

TYPE OF PROBLEM: Fungal

SYMPTOMS: If you have ever picked strawberries in moist spring weather, you probably have seen some berries covered with a fuzzy gray or tan mold. When you

Botrytis fruit rot on raspberry

touch an infected berry, it sends up a small cloud of spores. Other fruits, such as apples, may show an internal rot. For leaf symptoms, see "Botrytis Blight" on page 312; for Botrytis on flowers, see flower symptoms on page 326.

PLANTS AFFECTED: A wide range of woody and herbaceous plants. Fruits of strawberries, grapes, and brambles are most commonly affected.

PREVENTION AND CONTROL: Cool temperatures and high humidity promote Botrytis fruit rot. Removing infected fruit reduces the spread of the disease. Plants overstimulated with nitrogen fertilizer are most susceptible to gray mold, as are crowded plants, where air cannot circulate to quickly dry leaves, stems, and fruit.

Brown rot on plum

Brown Rot

TYPE OF PROBLEM: Fungal
SYMPTOMS: Infected fruit shows small brown spots that often enlarge to cover the surface. These patches produce masses of grayish brown spores. The fruit eventually rots and shrivels up (forming a mummy); the damaged fruit may drop or persist on the tree. Small cankers may form on branch tips. Early in the season, flowers may be infected; for more details, see "Brown Rot" on page 326.
PLANTS AFFECTED: Peaches, cherries, plums, and other stone fruits
PREVENTION AND CONTROL: Plant resistant cultivars. Prune to remove damaged shoots and to provide good air circulation. Pick off and clean up rotted and

shriveled fruit. Apply *Bacillus subtilis* to help prevent infection. If brown rot has been a serious problem in the past, spray with sulfur after blossoming to protect the fruit. Spray again just before harvest to protect fruit from brown rot in storage.

Corn Smut

TYPE OF PROBLEM: Fungal
SYMPTOMS: Smut appears as swollen, grayish white galls on any part of the plant, especially ears and tassels. These galls continue to swell, and eventually release large quantities of powdery, dark brown spores.
PLANTS AFFECTED: Corn
PREVENTION AND CONTROL: Plant resistant cultivars. Rotate crops. Clean up garden debris in fall. Remove infected plant parts as soon as you spot them.

Corn smut

Stem and Root Symptoms
Stems with Cracks, Holes, or Discolored Areas

Openings in stems include cankers caused by disease organisms. Stem cracks or cuts may also be due to damage from frost or power equipment.

Discolored or blighted areas on stems may be due to the death of cells or may be signs of a pathogen.

Cytospora canker on blue spruce

Cane Blight

TYPE OF PROBLEM: Fungal
SYMPTOMS: This disease commonly produces brownish purple spots on canes. Infected canes may wilt and die.
PLANTS AFFECTED: Black raspberries are most commonly affected, although other bramble fruits and roses may also be attacked.
PREVENTION AND CONTROL: Choose a planting site with plenty of sunshine and good air circulation. Thin canes to avoid overcrowding, but avoid prun-ing during periods of wet weather. Maintain healthy plantings and avoid overfertilization, especially with nitrogen. Remove diseased canes at ground level and destroy. The following year, spray with lime-sulfur as leaf buds begin to open in spring.

Cane blight

Cytospora Canker

TYPE OF PROBLEM: Fungal
SYMPTOMS: Cytospora canker (also known as Valsa or Leucostoma canker) causes yellowing, wilting, and dieback of new shoots. Inner bark on infected twigs may show black or reddish brown discoloration. Gummy cankers form on trunks and branches and increase in size until they girdle and kill the affected part. Note: Bacterial canker may cause symptoms similar to those of Cytospora canker; controls for this disease are the same as those for Cytospora canker.
PLANTS AFFECTED: A wide range of woody plants. Stone fruits (such as peaches and plums), apples, pears, spruces, maples, poplars, and willows are among the most susceptible plants.
PREVENTION AND CONTROL: Plant resistant cultivars when available. Vigorously growing trees are less susceptible to this disease. Prune out infected branches during dry weather;

disinfect pruners between cuts. Avoid making unnecessary wounds in the bark, which can provide an entry for the fungus. On stone fruits, it is particularly important to avoid winter damage, which can be caused by fertilizing the trees late in the season.

Frost Damage

TYPE OF PROBLEM: Environmental
SYMPTOMS: In the dead of winter, a combination of heat and cold can cause sunken areas or long cracks to form in the bark of woody plants. Damage is most common on the southwest side of a trunk. The last light of day warms the bark then the bark

Frost damage crack on maple

rapidly cools as the sun drops below the horizon. For symptoms on flowers and fruit, see "Frost Damage" on page 327.

PLANTS AFFECTED: A wide range of woody and herbaceous plants

PREVENTION AND CONTROL: Young trees that have thin bark (such as sugar maples) or trunks that are not shaded by side branches are particularly susceptible. To prevent damage to tree trunks, in fall wrap them with tree wrap or paint the trunks with white latex paint diluted with an equal amount of water to reflect heat and keep the bark temperature uniform.

Lawnmower Damage

TYPE OF PROBLEM: Cultural

SYMPTOMS: When a lawn mower hits a tree, it can cut a thin horizontal groove into the bark. Repeated damage may cause branch dieback or kill the tree.

Lawnmower damage

Lawnmowers can also damage surface roots. These wounds provide entrance points for diseases and insects. String trimmers also pose a hazard; careless use can cause the tool to strip the bark off the base of the trees, girdling and killing the plant.

PLANTS AFFECTED: Any woody plant

PREVENTION AND CONTROL: Use tools carefully around plants. Trim around trees and shrubs by hand, put plastic guards around trunks, or surround base of plants with mulch or groundcovers to eliminate the need to trim.

Lightning Damage

TYPE OF PROBLEM: Environmental

SYMPTOMS: The most common symptom is a large scar running down the trunk of the tree to the ground. In some cases, though, the only symptom you'll see is branch dieback caused by the root injury. In extreme cases, branches or the whole tree may explode.

PLANTS AFFECTED: Any woody plant, especially tall specimens

Lightning damage

PREVENTION AND CONTROL: Help trees recover by removing damaged bark or branches. Water during dry spells, and fertilize to promote vigorous growth. If you have an especially valuable tree, you might want to protect it with a lightning rod.

Sapsucker Damage

TYPE OF PROBLEM: Environmental

SYMPTOMS: Tree trunks and limbs are covered with even rows of closely spaced holes.

PLANTS AFFECTED: Any woody plants

Sapsucker damage to birch

PREVENTION AND CONTROL: Several birds in the woodpecker family feed on tree sap. These birds, known as sapsuckers, prefer trees with a high sugar content, such as sugar maples, birches, beeches, and apples. Sections of bark may fall off of severely damaged trees. The holes also provide entrance points for disease organisms and wood-boring insects. Damage is difficult to control; wrapping the trunk with tree wrap may help prevent further feeding.

Slime Flux

TYPE OF PROBLEM: Bacterial
SYMPTOMS: Slime flux (also known as bacterial wetwood) is indicated by the slimy liquid that oozes out of cracks and wounds in the bark, causing streaks on the trunk. The liquid may have a foul odor. In severe cases, shoot tips may wilt and die back.
PLANTS AFFECTED: A wide range of woody plants. Elms, maples, and poplars are particularly susceptible.
PREVENTION AND CONTROL: As long as trees are otherwise healthy, the damage caused by slime flux is cosmetic. The oozing cankers may be very unsightly. No control is available. Water and fertilize appropriately to maintain vigor; avoid injuries to the bark.

Slime flux on cottonwood

Stem and Root Symptoms
Stem Tips Stunted or Die Back

When development of a single stem is inhibited, the distances between leaves or branches shorten so the leaves or branches grow close together. The result is what appear to be whorls of leaves or broomlike growth of branches. Stem tips may die back as a result of disease problems, such as fire blight, or from physical damage to the plant.

Construction Damage

TYPE OF PROBLEM: Cultural
SYMPTOMS: Branch tips die back over the crown of the tree; overall growth is poor.
PLANTS AFFECTED: All woody plants
PREVENTION AND CONTROL: Prevent damage by fencing off the area to keep equipment from hitting the plants or compacting the soil. Once the tree is damaged, there is little you can do; cut off any damaged bark and smooth off the wound edges so they can close properly. Fertilize, if necessary, and water during dry spells to help the plant recover.

Construction damage to shade tree

Dutch Elm Disease

TYPE OF PROBLEM: Fungal
SYMPTOMS: Dutch elm disease (DED) causes leaves to wilt, yellow, and drop early. Usually, branches show symptoms and die back one at a time. Sometimes the whole tree will wilt and die suddenly.
PLANTS AFFECTED: Elm trees, particularly American elm
PREVENTION AND CONTROL: DED spores are carried by elm bark beetles or transmitted through natural root grafts. Prevent insect attacks (see page 253) and subsequent disease infection by keeping trees healthy and vigorous. Once the disease infects a tree, there is no effective organic control. Remove and immediately destroy all infected elms.

Dutch elm disease symptoms

Remove the stump, if possible, or peel the bark off to below the normal soil line to deter elm bark beetles from feeding there. (The beetles can spread the disease as they move from diseased to healthy trees.)

Fire Blight

TYPE OF PROBLEM: Bacterial
SYMPTOMS: Flowers usually show symptoms first, browning and shriveling. Leaves turn brown or black. Dead leaves remain on twigs. Symptoms progress from the tips of shoots toward the roots. Shoot tips turn black, wilt, and curl downward. Cankers form on branches. Fruit turns black and may cling to the tree.

Fire blight on pear

PLANTS AFFECTED: Many plants in the rose family, especially pears, apples, and quinces
PREVENTION AND CONTROL: Plant resistant cultivars. Do not prune susceptible woody plants too severely or overfeed them, because both practices encourage succulent, disease-susceptible growth. Prune out infected branches, along with 6 to 12 inches of healthy tissue below the infected areas; disinfect pruners in between cuts by dipping them in a 10 percent bleach solution (1 part bleach to 9 parts water). Sprays of products containing *Bacillus subtilis* may also protect against fire blight. If infections have appeared in previous seasons, apply Bordeaux mix during dormancy to help prevent recurrence.

Oak Wilt

TYPE OF PROBLEM: Fungal
SYMPTOMS: While symptoms vary according to the tree species affected, oak wilt commonly causes leaves to brown, wilt, and drop. Plants usually die within a year.
PLANTS AFFECTED: Oaks
PREVENTION AND CONTROL: Prune oaks only when they are dormant to reduce the chances of the fungus entering through the wounds. Once oak wilt begins, there is no control;

Oak wilt on northern red oak

remove and destroy infected trees. Dig a narrow, 36- to 40-inch-deep trench between infected and healthy trees to break the natural root grafts through which the fungus can spread. Backfill the trench immediately to keep the healthy roots from drying out.

Peach Rosette Mosaic Virus

TYPE OF PROBLEM: Viral
SYMPTOMS: This nepovirus (nematode-transmitted polyhedral-shaped virus) causes trees to produce shoots that have abnormally short spaces between the leaf nodes; the resulting branches appear to have rosettes of foliage. Leaves may be discolored. The tree usually dies within a few months. Infected grapes form short, crooked vines and lack overall vigor; the short distance between leaves creates an "umbrella" effect.
PLANTS AFFECTED: Peaches and, less often, plums; grapes (*Vitis labrusca* varieties), blueberries

Peach rosette mosaic virus symptoms

PREVENTION AND CONTROL:
This virus is spread by nematodes. It also infects common weeds, including dandelions and curly dock, although these hosts may not show any symptoms. Keep areas around peaches and other susceptible plants free of weeds and wild *Prunus* spp. to avoid providing sites for the virus to develop. Zinc deficiency causes symptoms similar to those of peach rosette virus. Try spraying the leaves with kelp extract. If the infected plant shows no response, remove and destroy it.

Twig Blight

TYPE OF PROBLEM: Fungal
SYMPTOMS: Infection begins on young leaves, causing tiny yellow spots. Branch tips turn reddish brown and die back. You may see a grayish band at the base of the dead shoot.

Twig blight symptoms

PLANTS AFFECTED: Many needle-leaved evergreens, including junipers and cypresses

PREVENTION AND CONTROL:
Plant resistant species and cultivars. Prune off and destroy infected shoots on a dry day.

Verticillium Wilt

TYPE OF PROBLEM: Fungal
SYMPTOMS: Infection by *Verticillium* fungi causes leaves to yellow and leaf stems to droop, giving plants a wilted appearance (see photographs on pages 321 and 325). The yellow leaf patches turn brown and may spread to cover whole leaves. Leaves often fall early, and the plants will die. Symptoms usually first appear on the lower or outer parts of plants. The interior of the stem near the base may be discolored.

Verticillium wilt on cherry

PLANTS AFFECTED: A wide range of woody and herbaceous plants. Some particularly susceptible plants include tomatoes, peppers, melons, asters, chrysanthemums, peaches, cherries, strawberries, and maples.

PREVENTION AND CONTROL:
Verticillium and Fusarium wilt fungi cause similar symptoms. Verticillium wilt is more common in cool weather in temperate areas of the country.

There is no cure for Verticillium wilt. Remove infected woody plants and replant with resistant cultivars, when available. Crop rotation is not very effective because so many species are susceptible. Soil solarization may help to control Verticillium wilt.

Winter Injury

TYPE OF PROBLEM:
Environmental
SYMPTOMS: Symptoms of cold injury can be very similar to the symptoms of sunscald: blotchy, water-soaked areas on leaves. Shoot tips often die back. For other information on leaf damage, see "Winter Injury" on page 321.
PLANTS AFFECTED: A wide range of woody and herbaceous plants

Winter injury to forsythia

PREVENTION AND CONTROL: In winter, evergreens can suffer from drying when their roots cannot get sufficient water from frozen ground. Water plants thoroughly in late fall. Spray foliage with an antitranspirant to reduce water loss. If damage has been a problem in the past, move plants to a sheltered spot or erect a barrier (such as a piece of burlap) to protect them from drying winds. Prune out damaged wood in spring; remove severely affected plants.

Stem and Root Symptoms
Stems with Parasitic Plants

Clumps of what appear to be green leaves or tangles of stringlike material on plants may actually be the living tissues of a parasitic plant.

Dodder

TYPE OF PROBLEM: Parasitic plant
SYMPTOMS: Found throughout North America, dodder grows as a tangle of orange or yellowish threads that wind around stems and other parts of host plants. The parasite draws nutrients from the host plants, weakening them. Dodder's rampant growth can rapidly smother plantings.
PLANTS AFFECTED: Many ornamentals as well as vegetables, such as potatoes and onions
PREVENTION AND CONTROL: Dodder is a parasitic plant that entwines around host plants. The parasite draws food and water from its hosts, eventually weakening and smothering the infected plants. Dodder does not have roots (except in early seedling stage), leaves, or chlorophyll. Beginning early in the season, dodder produces tiny flowers. The resulting seeds are spread by animals and tools. The best way to get rid of dodder is to prevent it from going to seed and to ruthlessly destroy it and any affected plants repeatedly throughout the season. Keep an eye out for seedlings that may develop the next season and weed them out as soon as you spot them. Grasses are not susceptible to dodder, making them a good choice for replanting of affected garden areas. Dodder cannot survive long without host plants to infest. Don't add dodder to the compost pile, or you may be spreading seeds as you spread the finished compost.

Dodder

Mistletoe

TYPE OF PROBLEM: Parasitic plant
SYMPTOMS: The mistletoe of Christmas, called leafy mistletoe, attacks mostly hardwoods in the southern parts of the country. Clusters of evergreen growth appear on the limbs of deciduous trees. Leafy mistletoe is a weak parasite, so it does little harm to the trees, besides creating a strange appearance in winter.

Another type, known as dwarf mistletoe, attacks conifers throughout the world, but most seriously threatens trees in this country on the West Coast. It weakens, deforms, and even kills trees. The parasite looks like a tuft of branches, varying in color from yellowish to brownish green.

Mistletoe

PLANTS AFFECTED: A wide range of woody plants
PREVENTION AND CONTROL: Cut off and destroy infected branches as soon as you notice them to avoid the spread of this parasite. Birds feed on mistletoe berries and subsequently spread the seeds via their droppings to new host trees.

Cedar-apple rust "horns"

Stem and Root Symptoms
Stems with Swollen Growths

Galls and other swellings on stems and roots are due to overstimulated cell development. Root swelling can interfere with water and mineral uptake, resulting in yellowing and wilting of the aboveground portions of the plants.

Black Knot

TYPE OF PROBLEM: Fungal
SYMPTOMS: Black knot appears as unsightly swellings (galls) on twigs and branches. Initially, the galls are rather subtle and velvety green in appearance, gradually increasing in size and becoming hardened and black. Tips of infected branches often die back. Severe infections can kill whole limbs, and the tree may be stunted.
PLANTS AFFECTED: Cherries and plums are most commonly affected
PREVENTION AND CONTROL: In fall or late winter, prune off infected limbs 6 to 12 inches below the knots; disinfect pruners between cuts with a 10 percent bleach solution (1 part bleach to 9 parts water). Destroy the prunings. If possible, remove any wild plum or cherry trees nearby. For persistent infections, apply two sprays of lime-sulfur, 7 days apart, before the buds begin to grow in spring. Spraying can help to limit the spread of this disease, but must be combined with conscientious removal of galls as soon as they are identified.

Black knot gall

Cedar-Apple Rust

TYPE OF PROBLEM: Fungal
SYMPTOMS: Hard, brown swellings appear on branch tips. These galls do not seriously damage red cedar trees, but they can mar the plant's appearance. Warm, moist weather in spring causes these galls to swell dramatically, and they produce gelatinous horns that release rust-colored spores. The spores then infect apple trees. For more details about this disease on apples, see "Cedar-Apple Rust" on page 312.
PLANTS AFFECTED: Eastern red cedars and other species of juniper
PREVENTION AND CONTROL: Cedar-apple rust completes its life cycle only where the fungal spores can travel back and forth between cedar and apple trees. Spores from cedar trees send spores to infect apple trees, but infections on the apple tree do not spread within the tree; they can only send the disease back to infect a cedar.

Prevention is the best control. Rust diseases thrive in moist conditions, so anything you can do to promote leaf drying will limit disease problems. Planting apple trees only if cedars are at least 4 miles away will reduce the chances of the disease spreading. If you want to grow both cedars and apple trees, plant rust-resistant species or cultivars of both plants. Prune off and destroy galls before late winter.

Crown Gall

TYPE OF PROBLEM: Bacterial
SYMPTOMS: Above the ground, infected plants may be stunted with yellowing leaves. At the soil line or just below it, this bacterial disease causes a knobby swelling (a gall) of the plant's crown that affects its ability to take up moisture and nutrients, causing the aboveground symptoms. Galls may also form on roots and on branches.
PLANTS AFFECTED: A wide range of woody and herbaceous plants. Plants commonly affected include stone fruits, grapes, brambles, euonymus, chrysanthemums, and roses.
PREVENTION AND CONTROL: This common bacterium enters plants through wounds, such as those that occur during transplanting. The bacteria may be transmitted from one plant to another on tools or via soil where infected plants have grown. The bacteria may also survive for years in the soil, waiting for a suitable host plant.

Crown gall on rose bush

Inspect nursery plants carefully before you buy to avoid infected plants. Protect healthy plants by dipping their roots in a solution of *Agrobacterium radiobacter* (sold as Galltrol-A) before planting. To control mild infections, prune off diseased growth; disinfect your pruners between cuts with a 10 percent bleach solution (1 part bleach to 9 parts water). Remove and destroy severely infected plants. Avoid replanting the area with susceptible plants.

Stem and Root Symptoms
Roots with Swollen Growths

Various diseases can cause roots to swell, but root growths may also be caused by the presence of beneficial nitrogen-fixing bacteria.

Club Root

TYPE OF PROBLEM: Fungal
SYMPTOMS: Aboveground, the plant may appear stunted, wilted, and yellowed. Belowground, infection causes the roots to swell into a gnarled mass that cannot supply water and nutrients to the plant.
PLANTS AFFECTED: Cabbage family plants, such as cabbage, cauliflower, broccoli, and Brussels sprouts
PREVENTION AND CONTROL: When possible, rotate cabbage family crops to a new location each growing season, repeating in a site only after 5 to 10 years. Once it is in the soil, club root fungus can infect wild cabbage family plants (common weeds such as wild mustard and shepherd's purse) or survive for years even in the absence of a host plant. This fungus, however, thrives only in acidic soils, so you can completely check the disease by adjusting the soil pH to 7.2 or slightly above. Soil solarization can also reduce the incidence of club root as can an early spring cover crop of winter rye, tilled into the soil 2 to 3 weeks after it germinates. Remove and destroy seriously infected plants.

Club root symptoms

Root-Knot Nematodes

TYPE OF PROBLEM: Nematodes
SYMPTOMS: The symptoms produced by root-knot nema-

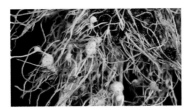
Root-knot nematode damage
to lettuce roots

todes are similar to those of other diseases and disorders that interfere with proper root function. Aboveground, plants may be yellowed and wilted; flowers and fruit are stunted or nonexistent. Belowground, however, you'll find numerous clubbed galls on the roots caused by the nematodes feeding inside. Nematode infection also increases a plant's susceptibility to infection by other diseases.

PLANTS AFFECTED: A wide range of woody and herbaceous plants. These nematodes commonly infect carrots, onions, potatoes, beans, lettuce, tomatoes, and fruit trees.

PREVENTION AND CONTROL: Plant resistant cultivars, when available. Because most garden crops are susceptible to root-knot nematode infection, regular rotation plans have little effect. Grains and grasses are nonhosts, however, and cover crops of rye, barley, oats, wheat, or sudangrass can help reduce nematode populations in the soil. Avoid spreading soil from infested to noninfested areas. Practice good weed control in and around your gardens—many common weeds are potential hosts for root-knot nematodes. Soil solarization helps to reduce nematode populations. Or try a cover crop of French or African marigolds (*Tagetes patula* or *T. erecta*) or black-eyed Susans, and turn them into the soil at the end of the season. Incorporate plenty of organic matter into the soil to promote natural nematode-ontrolling microorganisms. You can also fight nematodes by applying beneficial *Steiner-nema feltiae* nematodes to the soil.

Stem and Root Symptoms
Roots Die Back

Aboveground symptoms such as stunting and wilting may be the result of the death of cells in diseased roots.

Red Stele

TYPE OF PROBLEM: Fungal

SYMPTOMS: Symptoms include stunted growth and wilting and death of older leaves or whole plants. Infected plants bear little or no fruit. Young feeder roots die; older, infected roots have dead tips

Nitrogen-Fixing Nodules

The relationship of legumes such as peas and beans and nitrogen-fixing bacteria (*Rhizobium* spp.) is generally beneficial to both. Plants supply bacteria with nutrients; bacteria convert nitrogen from the air into a form that plants can use. The bacteria are present inside small hard nodules on the roots—they may look similar to diseased roots, but the plants will remain healthy. To promote growth of these beneficial organisms, buy the bacteria in powder form (called inoculant) and dust the seeds of appropriate crops before planting. The relationship between each garden crop and a corresponding nitrogen-fixing bacterium is fairly specific; to get the best results, it makes sense to buy the right inoculant for your crop.

Nodules on pea roots

and a reddish brown discoloration in the core of the roots.

PLANTS AFFECTED: Strawberries

PREVENTION AND CONTROL: Remove and destroy infected and surrounding plants. If red stele has been a problem in the past, prepare a new site for your strawberry bed and plant resistant cultivars.

Red stele symptoms

Root Rot

TYPE OF PROBLEM: Fungal

SYMPTOMS: Symptoms include leaves that are small, yellow or brown, and wilted. Decline may be gradual, over years, or rapid. Other symptoms, which indicate Armillaria root rot, may appear at the base of the plant. These include white mats of fungi and brownish black fungal strands on the roots or between the bark and the wood. For more information, see "Armillaria Root Rot" on the opposite page.

If you don't see any signs of fungal growth near the base of the plant, suspect other types of root rot. To check for root damage, lift the plant out of the soil and carefully wash off the soil. Look for roots that are damaged with brown or black tips.

PLANTS AFFECTED: A wide range of woody and herbaceous plants

PREVENTION AND CONTROL: These common soilborne diseases attack fully grown plants as well as seedlings. Root rots are caused by a few different types of fungi, each most prevalent in certain areas or under certain conditions. Plant resistant cultivars when available. Reduce the incidence of root rot with good cultural practices: Plant in well-drained soil, avoid overwatering, and direct surface water away from plant crowns. Incorporating compost into the soil may also help to prevent some types of root rot, and will improve soil

structure and, therefore, soil drainage. You may be able to save a diseased plant by pulling the soil away from the crown, pruning off diseased roots, and allowing the remaining exposed roots to air-dry. After working around infected plants, disinfect tools with a 10 percent bleach solution (1 part bleach to 9 parts water) to keep from spreading the disease from infected to healthy soil. Remove and destroy seriously infected plants.

Root rot symptoms

Stem and Root Symptoms
Tubers Discolored or Rotted

Disease can also cause cells of storage organs such as tubers to die, either in the ground or in storage.

Bacterial Soft Rot

TYPE OF PROBLEM: Bacterial

SYMPTOMS: In the garden or in storage, fruits or storage roots (e.g., potatoes or carrots) develop small, water-soaked spots. These areas enlarge, becoming soft, sunken, and discolored. You may notice a foul odor. Above-ground, plants may appear yellowed, stunted, and wilted.

PLANTS AFFECTED: A wide range of herbaceous plants. Vegetables with fleshy fruit or succulent stems are quite susceptible.

PREVENTION AND CONTROL: To prevent soft rots, handle fruits and vegetables (especially those you plan to store) carefully, both during and after harvest. Avoid harvesting root crops during

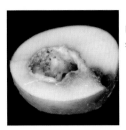

Bacterial soft rot

wet, muddy conditions. Soft rot bacteria enter wounds produced by rough handling as well as those caused when fruits, tubers, and roots are frozen or damaged by insects. Soft rots usually need a high moisture level to develop, so store produce in a cool, dry place. If you have had trouble with soft rot in past years, rotate crops to reduce the spread of the disease in the garden, remove residues of infected plants from the garden area, and incorporate compost into the soil to improve drainage and to support populations of beneficial microorganisms.

Scab

TYPE OF PROBLEM: Actinomycetes
SYMPTOMS: Scab begins as small brown spots on tubers or roots. These areas enlarge and run

Scab on potatoes

together, producing russeting and rough, corky areas on the skin. These spots are usually just on or below the surface, so the crop is still edible, although visually unappealing.
PLANTS AFFECTED: Potatoes, beets, radishes, and other root crops
PREVENTION AND CONTROL: Scab organisms thrive in light, sandy soils with a neutral or alkaline pH. Lowering the soil pH to below 5.3 will reduce the

chance of disease. Actinomycetes are decomposers involved with the breakdown of organic matter; avoid adding manure or large amounts of compost to soil where potatoes will be planted. Start with certified disease-free seed potatoes. Resistant cultivars are available but even these may develop scab when conditions favor the disease. Keep the soil evenly moist, especially while young tubers are forming.

Whole Plant Symptoms
Seedlings Die or Plants Are Stunted or Fall Over

Fungi can infect and kill a wide range of plants at the seedling stage or they can infect the roots, causing the plant to collapse. Stunted growth is due to inhibited cell development. Many viruses cause stunting, but stunted growth also may be from drought or insufficient nitrogen.

Armillaria Root Rot

TYPE OF PROBLEM: Fungal
SYMPTOMS: Common symptoms of root rot include leaves that are small, yellow or brown, and wilted. Decline may be gradual, over a period of years, or rapid. Other symptoms that may appear include white mats of fungi and brownish black fungal strands on the roots or between the bark and the wood. Honey-colored mushrooms often grow around the base of dead or dying plants. Severely damaged plants may fall over during a storm. For more on root rot, see "Root Rot" on

the opposite page.
PLANTS AFFECTED: A wide range of woody and herbaceous plants.
PREVENTION AND CONTROL: Armillaria root rot (also called shoestring root rot because of the dark fungal strands) is prevalent throughout the country, especially at sites that were recently oak forests. Avoid Armillaria root rot by planting in sites not harboring the fungus or by planting disease-resistant plants.

Maintain landscape plants appropriately to keep them

Growths caused by Armillaria fungus on apple tree trunk

healthy and, therefore, less prone to pest and disease problems that can weaken them: There is evidence that already weakened plants are more susceptible to Armillaria root rot. Plants that are resistant to this fungal disease include pears, white fir, sweet gums, and Oregon grape holly; however, resistance is variable and depends to some extent on a plant's suitability for a particular site and on the level of fungal organisms present in the soil. Once root rot has widely infected a plant's root system, the only course of action is to remove the plant and what is left of the roots.

Damping-Off

TYPE OF PROBLEM: Fungal
SYMPTOMS: Damping-off fungi can kill seedlings before they even break through the soil, but a more dramatic demonstration of this disease occurs when it strikes seedlings just an inch or so tall. The fungi rot the stems right at the soil line and,

overnight, infected seedlings topple over.
PLANTS AFFECTED: All plants
PREVENTION AND CONTROL:
Plants growing in containers are more susceptible to damping-off than are those growing outdoors in the garden. Good cultural conditions usually control it; to prevent it from attacking your seedlings, grow them in well-drained soil with plenty of light. Do not allow them to crowd each other, or the stagnant air that results will promote the growth of damping-off fungi. Avoid wetting seedlings by overhead watering; water seedling flats by setting them in a shallow tray of fresh water and then removing them when the top of the medium is moist.

A thin layer of dry material, such as sand or perlite, sprinkled on the soil surface keeps seedling stems dry at the soil line, where damping-off often strikes. Even better is a layer of fine sphagnum moss, which not only keeps the surface dry but also reduces the chance of fungal growth. After a few weeks of growth, seedling stems toughen and no longer are as susceptible to attack by damping-

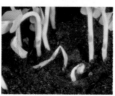

Pea seedlings infected with damping-off

off fungi. If you've had past problems with damping-off, use sterile potting mix for seed starting.

Mosaic

TYPE OF PROBLEM: Viral
SYMPTOMS: Mosaic-infected leaves are mottled with yellow, white, and light and dark green spots or streaks (see photograph on page 318). Fruit may show similar symptoms. Plants are often stunted.
PLANTS AFFECTED: A wide range of woody and herbaceous plants

Common bean mosaic symptoms

PREVENTION AND CONTROL:
Plant resistant cultivars. Mosaic viruses are mostly spread by insect pests, especially aphids and leafhoppers. If possible, deny these carriers access by covering your plants with floating row cover. For more control information on aphids and leafhoppers, see pages 250 and 271, respectively. Once plants are infected, there are no controls; remove and destroy infected plants.

PART 4

ORGANIC PEST AND DISEASE MANAGEMENT

If promoting plant health worked 100 percent of the time, you'd never need to refer to this section of this handbook. But in new gardens—and even in established organic gardens—a few pest and disease problems will sometimes reach alarming levels. Perhaps it's a new bed where the soil fertility is out of balance, or a bed that got neglected during a particularly busy few weeks, or a crop that ended up diseased after a long spell of particularly tough weather conditions. And in every region, there are a few tough pests that tend to cause problems every year, even for experienced gardeners. For these situations and problems, you'll need to employ some of the barriers, traps, repellents, biological controls, and sprays and dusts covered in this section of the book.

Choosing the Right Strategies and Products

Because of the steady increase in the number of home gardeners who choose organic methods, the range of organic strategies and products has also increased. In this section, you'll find information on practices, such as using row covers and applying parasitic nematodes to soil, to combat widespread problems, along with specific products or methods to deter a single pest, such as surrounding seedlings with collars to prevent cutworm damage.

CHOOSE THE PATH OF LEAST HARM

Keep in mind that even organically acceptable products and methods vary tremendously in their convenience and environmental impact. Always begin with the safest, least-toxic method before moving on to more toxic—and usually broader spectrum—controls. Few, if any, people, pets, wildlife, or beneficial insects will suffer ill effects from the use of row cover, kaolin clay, or other control strategies that prevent pest damage without having to actively kill the pests involved.

Researchers have learned over the years that even plant-derived sprays such as pyrethrin can pollute water, kill honeybees, or even make people sick. For example, rotenone is a plant-derived spray that is very toxic to fish, and there are unresolved questions about a potential link between Parkinson's disease and exposure to rotenone. There are no commercial rotenone products listed by the Organic Materials Review Institute (OMRI) as acceptable for use by organic growers, and Rodale recommends that rotenone never be used in organic gardens.

In this new edition of this book, the only plant-derived sprays recommended for use against pests are pyrethrin and neem, and then only as a last resort. On the disease front, there are also new, effective products for organic gardeners that are less toxic than the old standbys, sulfur and copper. Although effective against many plant diseases, sulfur and copper can have detrimental effects on plants, helpful insects, and soil. Instead, organic gardeners can now use sprays based on potassium carbonate or baking soda, as well as biological disease-fighting sprays. Overall, you'll find that the range of other options for managing pest and disease problems organically means that you'll rarely end up using the sprays of last resort.

These control methods come from a variety of sources. Some are gardening practices that have been handed down as folklore through the ages, while others are based on the latest scientific research. Regardless of the methods you choose to use to protect your plants, use care, and always follow label directions when using commercial products. You'll notice that special precautions for using some organic sprays and dusts are included in the descriptions that follow.

PLANNING YOUR STRATEGY

Since the goal in dealing with pests and diseases is always to do the least harm to your garden and the environment overall, it makes sense to start with prevention. To prevent problems, your best course of action is to *promote plant health* first and foremost. In case you missed it, turn back to Part 1, Your Healthy Garden, starting on page 1, to learn how to promote healthy plants that are naturally resistant to many pest and disease problems.

Striking a Balance

Of course you'd like to avoid pest problems in your organic garden, and the best way to do so is to remember the importance of *balance*. Most of the time, natural enemies of plant pests will keep damage levels below the point where you need to intervene. You'll find a few pests that are particularly troublesome, depending on the conditions in your yard and what you like to grow. For one gardener, slugs and snails will top the list, for another, it will be Japanese beetles. For an avid vegetable gardener, squash bugs and late blight may be the toughest problems to deal with.

Whatever your specific challenges are, your choices for taking action fall into these three basic categories:

Keeping pests away from plants. These controls exclude or remove pests from plants. Handpicking insect pests is the most basic approach; a higher-tech method is to shield plants with row cover.

Biological controls. These methods use living organisms to kill garden pests. They include encouraging beneficial insects and applying bacterial insecticides such as *Bacillus thuringiensis*.

Organic sprays and dusts. There are several types of nonsynthetic sprays, dusts, and baits that organic gardeners use to repel or poison pests. You can make some types yourself from garden and kitchen ingredients. You can buy botanical insecticides, such as neem or pyrethrin, to fight pests, and sulfur and copper sprays to prevent and limit disease problems. These sprays and dusts have varying levels of toxicity; some of them are only to be used when other strategies have proven inadequate.

Strategizing Step-by-Step

Having a system for coping with pest and disease problems is a good idea, and it's not hard to do. Here are five simple steps:

1. **Patrol your garden frequently.** There's an old proverb that says: "The best fertilizer is the footsteps of the farmer." The proverb's message is that the most successful farms—or gardens— are those that get regular care, and that includes scouting for pests. When you scout often, you're likely to spot problems early, and the sooner you spot a problem, the easier it will be to solve.

2. **Identify the cause of the problem.** In organic gardens, there's no single "pest zapper" that will solve any and all problems. So once you spot a problem, you need to figure out what's causing it. For a detailed description of how to diagnose a problem, turn to "Pinpointing Problems" on page 245.

3. **Learn the cycle.** Each pest and disease follows a specific life cycle or disease cycle, and chances are it's most vulnerable at a particular stage in the cycle. Part 3 of this book includes information on life cycles and disease cycles.

4. **Decide how serious the problem is.** If the leaves of a plant simply have a few holes in them, it may not affect yield or ruin the beauty of the plant. As long as you adjust your expectations to allow for a few imperfections, perhaps you don't need to take any action. Remember, if you wait a week or two, natural enemies of a pest may do the control work for you!

5. **Take the least harmful action first.** If a problem will threaten yields or ruin a plant,

Meshing Your Management Methods

Combining different pest management methods that are effective against individual stages in a pest's life cycle can boost your success in keeping the pest from damaging plants. The codling moth, a serious pest of apples and other fruit trees, is a good example of a pest that is vulnerable on several fronts.

In late winter, while trees are dormant, kill larvae overwintering in cocoons in the bark by scraping away loose bark and applying dormant oil sprays. Larvae overwintering in the soil litter are susceptible to attack by ground beetles, especially in orchards with cover crops, which protect the beetle populations.

In the spring, you can determine when adults begin to emerge from pupae by hanging pheromone traps among the trees to capture male moths. Large-scale orchardists can use the traps as a monitoring device, and once adults begin appearing in the traps, release parasitic *Trichogramma* wasps at 7- to 10-day intervals to attack the eggs that the adults will lay.

Most likely, some moths will still successfully mate and lay eggs, and some of those eggs will escape the parasites. However, you can deter moths from laying eggs in your trees by applying kaolin clay—the trick is to apply it before the moths begin searching for egg-laying sites and be sure the plant surfaces are fully coated (three sprays may be necessary for this). If you don't like to hassle with using a sprayer, you can instead buy small nylon bags specially designed for encasing young fruit. You'll need to bag each fruit you want to protect; the adults cannot lay eggs through the bags.

Once larvae have tunneled into fruit, they are relatively safe from control measures. However, after feeding, they will crawl down the trees to find a place to spin a cocoon. Intercept the migration by tying burlap tree bands around the trees. Check them daily and destroy the larvae.

You'll repeat the same control cycle for the second generation, and for a third generation in warmer areas. If you're diligent, you should have negligible damage from codling moths.

you'll have to decide what steps to take. For some pests, relying on a single strategy may be sufficient to prevent damage. For example, cutworm collars are reliable barriers against cutworms; once the springtime risk to new transplants has passed, cutworms usually cease to be a concern.

For other pests, especially if they are numerous, you'll need to employ several strategies at once or in succession throughout the season. See "Meshing Your Management Methods" above to find out how using several different strategies at various points throughout the life cycle of the codling moth leads to success.

As you read about various strategies, consider their advantages and disadvantages and how they fit your garden plan. Most rely on a gardener's ability to implement them completely. Of course you need to know how to set up a barrier or apply a spray properly, but you also need to keep track of pest emergence times and monitor what's happening underneath a barrier or whether a pest problem recurs after you apply a spray or dust.

Keeping Pests Away from Plants

When pests appear on plants, the most direct way to get rid of them is to pick them off. You can also handpick diseased leaves or other plant parts, limiting the ability of the infecting organism to spread further. In some cases this simple action effectively "cures" the host plants.

Physically removing pests from plants, setting up traps and barriers, and using diversionary tactics that prevent pests from reaching your plants are among the safest techniques for protecting them. In general, these methods are more often used to control insects than to control diseases.

REMOVE PESTS FROM THE SCENE

Manual controls are simple and inexpensive pest-control strategies: The only tools required—except for maybe a bucket and some dish soap—are your time and patience. And manual pest controls require that you closely examine plants, increasing the likelihood that you'll detect the early symptoms of insect or disease problems.

Handpicking

When pest populations are low and time is on your side, handpicking pests and their eggs from plants is simple and effective. Removing adult pests before they've had a chance to lay eggs prevents pest buildup and the resulting damage. Handpicking really pays off early in the season, because by removing the first generation of a pest, you're also reducing the risk that a second or third generation will be around to feed on your plants.

Protection Offered: The best candidates for handpicking are large, slow-moving pests—such as caterpillars, Colorado potato beetles, and slugs and snails—that aren't quick enough to escape. It's also easy to find and smash mealybugs, scales, and squash bugs. Scrape away easily identifiable egg masses, such as those of gypsy and tussock moths, from tree trunks or other surfaces, before the hungry larvae emerge and begin feeding. Pests that fly away when disturbed, like leafhoppers, are not easy to handpick.

What to Do: Check plants several times each week. Watch for pests that fly or crawl into your garden and for pests that emerge from the soil. It's important to distinguish pests from their natural enemies so you don't accidentally destroy the "good guys"; see "Insect Impostors" on page 297. Remember to look for pest eggs and immature insect stages. Smash pest egg masses.

Very few insects can bite into human skin, but a few, such as the striped blister beetle, can cause skin irritation if you squash them in your hands. Likewise, few plant diseases cause corresponding human illnesses. However, you can wear plastic gloves (thin surgical gloves are best) when handpicking pests if it makes you more comfortable with the job, or carry long tweezers or chopsticks.

Pests that hide or fly away can be difficult to handpick. It may help to first spray the infested plants with water to get the pests moving. For example, if you wet down squash plants before collecting squash bugs, they will either run to the topmost leaves or hide beneath those closest to the ground. In either hiding place, they are easy to find. For flying insects, use a butterfly net to catch them before and after spraying the plants with water. If you're sleuthing for cutworms, slugs and snails, weevils, and other nighttime diners, wait until just after sunset and examine plants by flashlight.

After you handpick, it's important to make sure that captured insects don't escape to feed anew. Here are some suggestions for disposal.

- Carry a container of water mixed with soap or isopropyl alcohol (a 5 percent solution). Drop pests into the water where they'll drown.

- Kill pests by leaving them overnight in a bag or jar in the freezer; then discard.

- Chickens and geese will quickly consume any insects tossed their way.

- Place the captured pests in the center of a hot compost pile—but be sure it is hot.

- Put them in your household trash—just make sure they can't escape.

- Rub or scrape infestations of scale or mealybugs from plants, or swab them with cotton soaked in alcohol or liquid dish soap.

If you're uncertain as to the identity of a captured insect, keep it for identification. You may be able to match it up with photos in this book or on Web sites (see page 397 for suggested sites). Also, the staff at your local Cooperative Extension office or state land grant university or local garden center can help you identify your captives.

You can preserve soft-bodied caterpillars by immersing them in a small container of hand sanitizer. For hard-bodied pests like beetles, simply place the sample in a pill bottle or other container to prevent it from being crushed.

Pruning

In some situations, handpicking pests isn't enough. You may have to prune away leaves or branches when pests, their eggs, and debris are heavily concentrated on one or several plant parts. Selective pruning also removes diseased leaves and keeps pathogens from spreading to other parts of the plant. Removing water sprouts and root suckers from woody plants also reduces the amount of succulent growth attractive to insects and pathogens. And pruning can expose more of a plant's foliage to air and light, which makes conditions less favorable for many fungal diseases.

One exception is virus-infected plants. Since viruses usually spread systemically within a whole plant, pruning off infected leaves or stems will not solve the problem.

Protection Offered: Control aphids, garden webworms, leafminers, and tent caterpillars by pruning infested plant parts. Pruning is also effective for removing cedar-apple rust galls from cedar trees and bagworm cocoons from evergreen trees. When powdery or downy mildew first appears on foliage, prune to prevent future infection and to improve air circulation.

Removing tomato leaves infected with blight or leaf spots can help slow the spread of the disease. Pruning infested wood can help control flatheaded borers and lilac borers.

What to Do: The kind of pruning you'll do depends on the plant and the problem. For example, many kinds of perennials and woody plants form dense clumps of foliage that benefit from thinning. This involves cutting out some of the competing shoots, promoting better air circulation, and allowing more sunlight to reach the center of the plant. On any kind of plant, you can prune off egg masses attached to foliage—just be sure the eggs are those of a plant pest.

If a plant is seriously infected by disease, it's usually best to remove the entire plant rather than try to prune it back to health. Place the infected pieces or plants in the center of a hot compost pile, or place in sealed containers and dispose of them with household trash.

If your tree has a disease that starts at the branch tips and spreads inward (such as fire blight or twig blight), you can minimize the spread of disease by pruning off the affected parts during dry weather. Cut off the infected area of the branch (blighted twigs or areas with cankers), along with 6 to 12 inches of healthy tissue. As in any pruning situation, prune back to a healthy bud or main limb; if you leave a stub of bare wood instead, it will die and become an entry point for other pests.

As you work with diseased plants, disinfect your tools between cuts by dipping them in a 10 percent bleach solution (1 part bleach to 9 parts water). Thoroughly clean up all trimmings as soon as you finish pruning, and place them in a hot (130°–140°F) compost pile or in a sealed container for disposal. Be sure to wash your hands and disinfect tools before moving from diseased to healthy plants. Always use sharp tools, which will make clean, smooth cuts that are less prone to pest attack. After any pruning, disinfect your tools, rinse them with water, and lightly oil all metal parts to prevent corrosion.

Timing is important. To allow woody plants enough time to toughen up their new growth before fall (which helps prevent diseases from gaining entry), don't stimulate them in late summer by fertilizing, watering, or pruning.

Shaking

Shaking plants to make pests fall onto the ground is one method that farmers use to monitor pest populations. In small gardens, shaking pests from infested foliage may remove enough of them to reduce damage. It takes less time than handpicking, and it can be an effective way to remove pests from hard-to-reach tree limbs.

Protection Offered: Shaking will dislodge any pest that crawls freely about on plants, including Colorado potato beetles, cucumber beetles, earwigs, Japanese beetles, and weevils.

What to Do: Shake pests from foliage early in the morning when insects are cool and sluggish. Or, capture night-feeding insects by shaking plants before sunset when temperatures begin to drop. Spread a sheet or dropcloth under trees or plants, then shake or agitate the foliage with your hands or tap woody stems and limbs with a padded stick. Scoop up fallen pests and destroy them.

Professional scouts use "beating trays" to monitor pest populations. You can construct your own beating tray to catch and control pests. Sew four small triangular pieces of material to make pockets at the four corners of a piece of white canvas or plastic roughly 3 feet square. Cut two 1 X 2's to the diagonal length of the canvas and fasten them together in the middle with a bolt and wing nut (to form a wooden X). Insert the ends of these crosspieces into the corner pockets of the fabric to make a rigid tray. Place the beating tray directly underneath plants' foliage, then shake the plants to knock pests onto the tray.

Vacuuming

Commercial growers use tractor-mounted vacuums to remove pests from strawberry plants and other crops. In the home garden, careful use of a portable, rechargeable vacuum cleaner offers similar control advantages.

Protection Offered: Vacuuming removes large leaf-eating pests like Japanese beetles and Colorado potato beetles as well as faster cucumber beetles, tarnished plant bugs, leafhoppers, and whiteflies. You can also vacuum up earwigs, sowbugs, and other pests.

What to Do: Lightly move your portable vacuum over the tops of vegetable and ornamental plants, taking care to avoid damaging tender leaves and shoots. Skim just the tops of infested plants.

That way, you'll avoid sucking up fragile beneficial wasps, which tend to remain on lower foliage. Beneficial predatory mites cling tightly to leaves and also remain unharmed.

For Japanese beetles, put a sheet or cardboard under the plants, shake the plants to make the beetles fall, and then vacuum them up.

After vacuuming, remove pests from the bag and dispose of them (see page 350 for disposal options). Don't give them a chance to escape!

Water Sprays

The physical action of a spray of water knocks pests off plants and damages them sufficiently so that they are unlikely to resume feeding.

Protection Offered: Controls small, soft-bodied insects like aphids, leafhoppers, spider mites, and thrips.

What to Do: To spray pests away with water, adjust the nozzle on your hose to provide a forceful spray that covers a large area. Hard and steady streams directed at one spot can damage foliage and flowers; move the spray back and forth among plants, being sure to reach leaf undersides.

To avoid encouraging diseases while controlling insects, refrain from spraying water during humid, wet weather.

SET UP BARRIERS

You will have fewer problems to handpick or otherwise control if you use physical barriers to keep pests, fungi, or bacteria from reaching their favorite hosts. One example is a cardboard tube slipped around the stem of a cabbage transplant to stop cutworms from munching. Many gardeners drape floating row cover over young cucumber plants to prevent cucumber beetles from feeding and transmitting bacterial wilt.

Since barriers are meant to keep pests away from your plants, they should be put in place before the pests arrive. Among the choices below are several that you can leave in place all season. You may have to remove covers when the plants outgrow them, to allow insects to pollinate flowers, or when temperatures under them become too high. When using barriers, fasten down the edges at the soil line to prevent pests from moving in.

Ant Barriers

Ants tend to gather where aphids are concentrated, since they feed on the aphid secretions. Tending them like livestock, the ants will actually carry the aphids to a food source, then tend them and protect them from predators.

Protection Offered: Ant barriers on the legs of greenhouse tables prevent ants from reaching your seedlings.

How to Use: Make a barrier by cutting a hole through the center of an aluminum pie plate; the hole should correspond in size and shape to a cross-section of a table leg. Make one barrier for each leg. Slide one pan, inverted, up each table leg. Fold each pan downward to form a cup and cover the inside of the cupped plate with a sticky coating. Seal the crack between the pie plate and the table leg with caulking or sticky coating. Renew the sticky coating when necessary. Leave the traps in place permanently to guard against ants.

Antitranspirants

Antitranspirants are commercial products usually sprayed on trees and shrubs in fall to help protect them from winter damage.

Protection Offered: Reports indicate that antitranspirants form a barrier on leaves to prevent disease organisms such as powdery mildew spores from germinating and infecting plants. Note, however, that antitranspirants are not approved and registered for use as fungicides.

How to Use: Follow label instructions for coating plants, and apply when conditions would be favorable for the spread of a disease that has previously been a problem. Avoid spraying drought-stressed plants on hot, sunny days.

Commercial Products: Moisturin, Vapor Gard, Wilt-Pruf

Fruit Barrier Bags

In small orchards, you can take the time to protect individual fruit on apple and pear trees by enclosing them in paper or nylon bags. The bags prevent insect pests from finding and damaging the fruit. You can use small paper bags, such as lunch bags, or nylon bags marketed specifically for protecting fruit.

Protection Offered: Bagging works well to control apple maggot and codling moth damage on apples and pears.

How to Use: After thinning crop, place bags over individual fruits. Avoid using plastic bags, which will overheat them. Tie bags securely to the tree limbs with string or twist ties. Remove the bags just before harvesting.

Cabbage Maggot Barriers

Adult cabbage maggot flies lay their eggs in soil at the base of young cabbage family plants. When the maggots hatch, they don't have far to travel to find their host. You can place barriers fashioned from paper or other material around seedlings as you transplant to keep egg-laying flies away from the soil around your plants.

Protection Offered: Seedling disks prevent root maggot flies from laying their eggs in the soil near susceptible seedlings like broccoli, cabbage, and cauliflower. Tar paper repels flies, offering added protection.

How to Use: Cut tar paper or other heavy, flexible paper into 6- to 8-inch circles. Or you can use heavy cloth, old carpeting, or foam rubber. Make one cut from the edge to the center. You may want to cut a small hole in the center of the circle so the paper fits snugly around the stem but lies flat on the ground. When transplanting, place one disk on the soil around each plant so that the stem is in the middle of the disk. Circles aren't magic shapes—squares work just as well. Since there will be several generations of root flies during the season, leave the covers in place until harvest.

Copper Strips

Copper repels slugs and snails. Some studies indicate that copper is effective because slugs and snails actually get an electric shock when they touch it. Their slimy coating may interact chemically with the copper, creating an electric current.

Protection Offered: Using copper strips as a permanent edging for borders or beds is an effective but potentially expensive way to keep slugs and snails away from flowers and vegetables.

How to Use: There are several ways to use copper repellent products to prevent damage.

- Bury a 3- to 4-inch-wide copper strip around the edge of the bed or border, leaving 2 to 3 inches of the copper exposed. Bend the top $\frac{1}{2}$ inch of the strip outward at a right angle to form a lip (like an upside-down L). Once the barrier is in place, you may have to trap and remove the slugs and snails that were already inside the barricaded bed.

- In the greenhouse, tack strips of copper $2\frac{1}{2}$ inches wide around bench legs.

- Place strips of copper sheeting around tree trunks to keep the slimy pests away. Cut a 2- to 3-inch-wide strip of copper several inches longer than the tree's circumference, so you can enlarge the band as the plant grows. Punch holes in the ends, then fasten the strip securely around the trunk by feeding a piece of wire through the holes and twisting it tight. Remove suckers, water sprouts, and nearby weeds that might provide alternate routes for the snails and slugs.

- Wrap copper mesh around plant pots to protect individual potted plants and trees.

Commercial Products: Snail-Barr; Slugoff; Snail and Slug Barrier

Crawling Pest Barriers

Bands of materials that are unattractive or abrasive to pests can be placed around garden plants or beds for mild infestations to keep crawling pests away. Materials such as wood ashes or crushed seashells scratch the insects' waxy coating, destroying their water balance and killing them. These materials may also deter slugs and snails. This type of barrier is less effective in wet conditions or when pest populations are high.

A substance called diatomaceous earth is also used as a barrier to crawling pests; see page 282 for more information.

Protection Offered: Barriers keep earwigs, slugs and snails, sowbugs, and soft-bodied crawling pests like caterpillars away from plants.

How to Use: Scatter a 2-inch-wide strip of wood ashes, sawdust, crushed seashells, cinders, or similar organic materials as a border around beds. Or, spread a circle of the same materials around individual plants, covering the area out to the dripline or at least within a 6-inch radius of the stem. Renew the barriers after rain.

Place a "fence" of aluminum foil around beds and gardens if you are trying to control caterpillars such as armyworms and cutworms. Bury one edge of the foil in the soil, leaving several inches extending beyond the soil surface. Fold the top edge away from the garden to form a lip (like an upside-down L) that caterpillars will find difficult to cross.

Cutworm Collars

Cutworm collars protect seedlings from cutworm damage. Cutworms are night-feeding caterpillars that spend the day just under the soil surface, resting near your plants.

Protection Offered: Cutworms will feed on tender stems of seedlings, including vegetable transplants and flower seedlings. Barriers placed around seedling stems provide protection from cutworms and other pests that crawl up the stem.

How to Use: Cut cardboard tubes from toilet paper and paper towel rolls into 2- to 3-inch sections, then place them over small seedlings while transplanting, pushing the collars into the soil. Thin, soft cardboard holds up in the garden long enough to protect your plants until they are beyond the susceptible stage. Shallow cans, paper cups, and small plastic containers (such as yogurt containers) with the bottoms cut out also make satisfactory cutworm collars, although they won't deteriorate like cardboard collars and will have to be removed later.

There are also commercially manufactured cutworm collars; use these according to label directions.

Commerical Products: Cutworm Shield

Floating Row Covers

When placed over plants, row covers don't actually float—they rest lightly on the foliage, looking like flattened sheets of cotton candy. Row covers are made of various kinds of polyethylene or spun-bonded polyesters, and they are excellent pest barriers. Since they're water- and light-permeable covers, they can be left in place over some crops from planting until harvest. You can also use floating row cover to extend the growing season, since temperatures under cover tend to be a few degrees higher than outside in spring and fall. In the Northeast, spring harvests can be gathered 5 to 10 days earlier. Row covers must be removed from time to time to allow for weeding, thinning, and other garden tasks.

Several types of floating row cover are offered in garden supply stores, ranging from lightweight materials that allow almost all air and water to pass through to heavy "garden blanket" type row covers that provide more than 10 degrees of protection from frost. However, these thicker covers also block more light and water flow, and temperatures underneath them can rise dangerously high on a warm, sunny day. For a summertime pest barrier, always choose a very lightweight row cover.

You can make your own alternatives to commercial floating row cover with mosquito netting, cheesecloth, or sheer drapery fabric. Remember that larger pores mean a greater chance that pests will penetrate your barrier, and fabric with finer pores may not offer adequate air circulation.

Protection Offered: Floating row covers protect plants from many common insect pests and other pests that fly or crawl to plants. Covers also control the plant diseases that insects transmit, and prevent rabbits, birds, groundhogs, and other animal pests from feeding on plants. One "loophole" in the protection offered by row covers is that pests that overwinter in the soil may emerge under the covers after they're put in place.

Plan to use floating row cover barriers if you have problems with aphids, asparagus beetles, cabbage root maggots, or caterpillars such as cutworms, loopers, and armyworms. Row covers also keep out Colorado potato beetles, flea beetles, leafhoppers, and Mexican bean beetles. Leave row

cover over carrots all summer to control carrot rust flies. On ornamental plants, place floating row cover over seedlings to protect them from foliage damage early in the season; remove it once the plants begin to flower and are large enough to withstand damage.

How to Use: Before covering, thoroughly weed the site. Place covers over the row immediately after planting seeds or transplants, since some insects are able to locate seeds before the plants emerge. If pests have already arrived, you'll have to eliminate them before covering. These lightweight covers are most easily installed on quiet, still days, since the slightest breeze sends them flapping away.

Lay them over the row or bed, leaving enough slack to allow plants to grow underneath. Anchor the edges with soil, rocks, boards, bricks, water-filled plastic bottles, plastic bags filled with sand or soil, or other heavy objects. You can make or buy hoop supports for delicate crops like baby lettuce that may be damaged by abrasion. Later, remove the covers temporarily to thin plants, weed, or harvest. In spring, periodically check for aphid infestations.

Remove covers permanently when plants are flowering, when plants are large enough to withstand some damage, or when the pests are no longer a threat. After using, wash covers with soapy water (add bleach to kill disease organisms) and rinse well before drying and storing. Patch holes and tears with duct tape placed on both sides. When properly stored between uses, row cover may last several years. When used all season long in hot, sunny climates, it deteriorates more quickly.

Commercial Products: Floating row cover is available under many brand names. Be sure to check the weight (thickness) of a cover before buying.

Homemade Row Covers

Before floating row covers became popular, innovative backyard gardeners built their own barriers from window screening attached to wooden frames. The list of variations for homemade barriers is limited only by your imagination. Well-constructed and sturdy homemade covers should last for many years.

Protection Offered: Rigid barriers protect crops from damage by animals and a variety of insects. They prevent insects from transmitting disease problems as well. You can use rigid barriers as defense against the same pests for which floating row cover is effective.

How to Use: Make screen cones from aluminum screening. Cut sections of screen 1½ X 2 feet. Wrap the shorter end around to form a cone, overlapping the edges. For stability, staple a wooden strip to the edge, so that it extends several inches below the base of the cone. Place cones over individual plants, inserting the wooden stakes into the soil to hold the cones in place. Sink the cone bottom into the soil so pests can't crawl under. Remove the cones when plants outgrow them or when pests are no longer a threat.

You can also make individual plant tents from window screening by folding long sheets of screening in half, then attaching triangular sections with a stapler to seal the ends.

Make permanent covers by constructing wooden frames that fit over sections of your garden. Make them wide enough to fit over your beds or rows and tall enough to accommodate plant growth for as long as you intend to keep them over the plants. Frames with the top narrower than the bottom stack easily for winter storage. Staple screening or porous fabric to the outside of the frames. Each fall, repair frames as needed, rinse them with a 10 percent bleach solution (1 part bleach to 9 parts water) to prevent disease problems, and dry thoroughly before storing.

Mulch

Mulch serves many roles in the garden. It helps protect soil from erosion and drying, it suppresses weeds, and it helps boost organic matter content as it decomposes. From a pest and disease standpoint, mulch is helpful because it forms a barrier to prevent soil that may contain disease spores from splashing up onto plant foliage. Mulch can also serve as a barrier for pests that are headed for the floor of your garden, either to lay eggs or to rest for the winter.

Common mulches include straw, grass clippings, wood chips, and various types of manufactured plastic and paper mulches.

Protection Offered: Use a black plastic mulch to discourage sowbugs and other crawling pests that can't stand the heat; black plastic also keeps leafminers from emerging from infested soil and prevents their return to the soil to pupate. Straw mulch around potatoes can reduce the risk of Colorado potato beetle problems. Covering garden and greenhouse soil with materials like newspaper or brown paper prevents thrips from reaching the soil in order to pupate. Mulching the soil surface can help protect tomato-family crops from blights and other diseases.

A thick layer of organic mulch will prevent shallow-rooted plants from being heaved out of the soil by frost action during winter, because mulch moderates changes in soil temperature.

How to Use: Spread organic mulches 1 to 2 inches thick over the soil surface. For woody plants leave an unmulched ring several inches in diameter around the main stem or trunk to prevent exces-

Reflective Mulch

Prevent damage from aphids, cucumber beetles, flea beetles, leafhoppers, thrips, and whiteflies on many types of crops in the garden and greenhouse with plastic-based reflective silver mulch. Cover beds or rows with the mulch before planting, anchor the edges with soil or weights, then cut 3- to 4-inch-diameter holes for transplants or seeds. The mulch seems to confuse the insects so that they do not land and feed. An added benefit is avoidance of the diseases—such as tomato spotted wilt virus—that these pests can transmit. Plus, the mulch reflects light back up onto crop leaves, which results in increased growth and higher yields.

sively moist conditions, which can lead to crown and trunk rots.

Plastic and paper mulches need to be weighted down with soil, boards, or other items so they can't blow away. Using these mulches does have some environmental drawbacks. Plastic mulch is a petroleum product. If you carefully roll up the plastic at the end of the season and store it in a dry place, you may be able to reuse it for several years, but eventually it must be thrown out. Biodegradable plastic mulch is designed to break down in place, but since it is a cornstarch-based product, it releases carbon dioxide as it breaks down. Paper mulch degrades, but some brands are treated with a synthetic antimicrobial substance so that they won't break down too fast.

To control rose diseases, rake debris and old mulch away from the stems in fall. Apply fresh compost or other organic mulch. In mid-winter prune as usual and apply more mulch to protect the plants from spring heaving. In spring gradually remove the mulch as temperatures increase, then apply a fresh summer mulch.

Painting

Protect fruit trees from both sunburn and flat-headed borer attack by painting the trunk with diluted white latex paint or with whitewash.

Protection Offered: The paint will reflect sunshine from the trunk, reducing the chance of sunburn or cracks from uneven trunk warming. This reduces the chance of borer damage because the adult borers typically lay eggs in cracks or wounds in bark.

How to Use: Paint the tree trunk using white latex paint diluted with equal parts of water, or use whitewash. Extend your paint barrier from 2 inches below the soil line to 24 inches up the trunk. To paint at the base of the trunk, use a hand trowel to carefully remove the soil; replace the soil after the paint dries.

Shade Cloth

Placed over rows of cool-season crops, shade cloth protects them from the scorching rays of the summer sun. It effectively extends the season for plants that normally prefer spring or fall temperatures.

Protection Offered: Because of its open weave, shade cloth offers little in the way of insect protection. It does, however, prevent injury from birds and small animals. It's most often used to protect lettuce and other cool-season crops from extreme temperatures and damage caused by direct sunlight.

How to Use: When summer temperatures reach 80°F or higher, suspend shade cloth over the crop to be protected, using stakes or other supports. Shade cloth is available in varying shade percentages that indicate the amount of light reduction; choose one that shades your crop adequately without reducing light levels to the point that plants are stretching for sunlight.

PUT OUT PEST TRAPS

Traps have two roles in managing pests: reducing pest problems directly by catching and killing pests, and serving as an early warning system for infestations. Traps like yellow sticky traps attract insects with color; other traps use chemicals produced by insects (pheromones) or plants to lure the insects to the trap. In general, using traps to monitor pest populations requires experience and training. For the most part, gardeners should use traps to lessen pest problems by capturing and killing pests, not as monitoring devices.

An older method of capturing destructive insects is trap cropping, the practice of planting crops that are known to be attractive to pests, and then harvesting them before the pests can move on to other plants.

Apple Maggot Traps

Apple maggot traps are red, apple-size spheres covered with sticky coating. The traps attract the attention of adult flies when they are ready to lay eggs. Zooming in for a landing on what they think is an apple, they become entrapped in the adhesive. You can trap enough flies on red sphere traps to control the damage they cause to fruit.

Protection Offered: Use sticky red spheres in your apple orchard to monitor the arrival and departure of apple maggot flies; this knowledge is

useful if you choose to spray your trees to control apple maggots. You can also control these pests by concentrating several traps in small areas.

How to Use: You can buy inexpensive, reusable red spheres, designed to attract apple maggot flies, from garden suppliers. They come with attached hangers for easy placement in apple trees. Or, make your own traps by painting any apple-size red ball with sticky coating. Use old red croquet, rubber, or plastic balls. Install an eye screw and insert a support wire or string for hanging. Some orchardists recommend the addition of a yellow sticky trap behind the red sphere. The red ball attracts adult flies ready to lay eggs, while the yellow trap lures newly emerged flies, which feed on apple foliage.

Hang traps in mid-June and leave them in place until after harvest. In small orchards of 10 to 15 trees, hang one trap for every dwarf tree, two to three traps for every semi-dwarf, and up to six for each full-size tree. In large orchards place one trap every 100 feet among the perimeter trees in an orchard block. Also use one or two traps per acre within the block, and put a trap in every wild or abandoned apple or crabapple tree within 400 yards of the orchard. Renew the sticky surface of the balls every 2 weeks by scraping off the accumulated insects and applying new coating. In dusty locations, renew traps more frequently.

Bait Traps

In small gardens, you can lure pests away from susceptible crops by placing attractive vegetable baits near your crops. By regularly checking the bait, you can capture and destroy pests before they move on to your crops.

Protection Offered: Carrot and potato baits trap wireworms that live in garden soil and damage plant root systems. Wireworms are a common pest in areas that were covered by sod (such as a lawn, alfalfa, cover crops, or even weeds) the previous year. Plant cull onions (onions that have sprouted in storage) to distract onion maggot flies. Inspect any plant pieces that you intend to use as trap crops to be sure they're disease free.

How to Use: Use carrots or potatoes to trap wireworms in garden soil. Insert several mature carrots every 2½ to 3 feet into the soil throughout the garden where sod was grown the previous year. Or, skewer raw potato chunks with bamboo stakes and bury them several inches deep every few feet, leaving the stakes protruding as a marker and handle. Several times each week throughout the season, pull these traps from the soil and remove the wireworms. Replace the same trap until a fresh vegetable is needed.

To control onion maggots, plant cull onions about 2 inches deep between the rows where you've sown seeds for your main onion crop. The bulbs will grow much faster than the seedlings and attract the egg-laying flies. Two weeks after the bulbs sprout, pull them out and destroy them to prevent the next generation of onion maggots from developing. This trap works best when used along with repellents such as hot pepper sprinkled on the seed rows to repel flies.

Cherry Fruit Fly Traps

Traps for cherry fruit flies differ from other yellow sticky traps in their shape and the addition of an ammonia lure.

Protection Offered: Use homemade sticky traps to catch and control adult cherry fruit flies in cherry orchards. You can also use them as monitoring tools to help you decide if and when to apply botanical insecticides.

How to Use: Paint a 10 ✕ 6-inch piece of plywood bright yellow, then cover it with sticky coating. Below it, hang a small, screen-covered jar filled with a mixture of equal parts ammonia and water, or a commercial apple maggot lure. Instead of a flat piece of plywood, you can paint the bell-shaped top half of a plastic, 2-liter soda bottle. In one study, this bottle trap was found superior to commercial designs for controlling Western cherry fruit flies.

For a small orchard, use at least four traps. Hang them 6 to 8 feet high among the leaves, preferably on the south side of the trees. Renew the bait weekly and check that the glue is still sticky. When a trap loses its stickiness, scrape off the accumulated insects and apply more glue.

Chinch Bug Traps

Chinch bugs are tiny lawn pests that destroy stems and leaves of lawn grasses. To control them in your lawn, drive them out of the sod with soapy water and into a dropcloth for counting and disposal.

Protection Offered: This type of protection works best for small areas. If you have a large lawn that is infested with chinch bugs, treatment with neem may provide more effective control.

How to Use: Mix 1 ounce of liquid dish soap in 2 gallons of water. Pour the mixture over 1 square yard of lawn. For large areas, you can use a garden hose with a siphon mixer attachment. Lay a large piece of white cloth, preferably flannel, over the treated area for 15 to 20 minutes, then pick it up. The bugs are driven out of the sod by the soapy soaking and then catch their feet on the flannel in their attempt to escape. Count them if you're monitoring the pest population, then kill them by rinsing them off the flannel into a bucket of soapy water. If there are fewer than 10 to 15 bugs per square foot, it is unlikely that they'll cause serious damage to your lawn. Water well to rinse the soap from the grass after you remove the flannel.

Earwig Traps

The same traps used to capture slugs and snails work equally well for trapping earwigs, but a different bait is used.

Protection Offered: If your garden has heavy infestations of earwigs, this simple trap may help control the population. Before you try to trap earwigs, remember that they are predators of aphids and other small garden pests; they do sometimes damage young plants, but more often are blamed for injuries caused by other night-feeding pests. Although they are scary looking, earwigs pose no threat to people.

How to Use: A low container, such as a tuna can, set into the soil so the rim is even with the soil surface and baited with fish oil or oil-soaked bread crumbs will attract large numbers of earwigs.

Japanese Beetle Traps

Japanese beetle traps rely on a combination of floral and fruit scents to attract females and a sex pheromone to trap the males. Most traps consist of some type of baffle with a bait container attached, hanging above a funnel that leads to a collection container. The beetles fly into the baffle and slide down the funnel into the container. Some traps use disposable bags; others use a permanent collection reservoir that can be emptied and reused.

Protection Offered: The effectiveness of Japanese beetle traps for home gardens is a topic of ongoing debate. Traps baited with floral lures and sexual pheromones attract lots of beetles—the problem is that they may attract more than would normally arrive. Many beetles don't actually enter the traps, and instead end up feeding on nearby plants. Japanese beetle controls work best when used by entire communities, since the adults easily migrate from one yard to the next. Unfortunately, traps that capture adult beetles don't appear to result in a corresponding drop in the number of grubs found in lawns. Adults that fail to land in a trap often wind up on the lawn, where they mate and lay eggs; the lawn area surrounding a beetle trap may have a much higher population of grubs. To control grubs, use parasitic nematodes as described on page 369.

How to Use: Follow instructions that come with commercial traps. In spring, set traps 1 to 3 feet above the ground in open, sunny areas. Place them 50 feet or more upwind from the beetle's favorite plants (these may include most of the plants in your garden). To trap beetles over large areas, place a trap every 200 feet surrounding the garden or yard. Or, use three traps for each $\frac{1}{8}$ acre of garden space. The traps should be emptied of beetles daily, since dead beetles repel the live ones from flying in. Once you put up traps, monitor the plants in your yard carefully for beetles. If you find beetles feeding in your yard, the best course of action may be to take down the traps and use other methods to combat the beetles.

Commercial Products: Bag-a-Bug; Catch-Can; and Safer traps

Light Traps

With the exception of the apple maggot fly, insects cannot see the color red. Their vision is limited to the ultraviolet (UV) to orange-red range, which is why they are attracted to blacklights (ultraviolet). Entomologists often use light traps to monitor populations of moths, which helps the scientists predict crop damage and advise growers on when to apply control measures. Such traps direct pests to a holding reservoir from which captives are collected and identified.

Protection Offered: Don't use UV light "bug zappers" in the home garden, since they attract and kill just as many beneficial insects as pests. They do provide good fly control inside barns and poultry houses and are a useful defense in orchards against codling moths when used for limited periods of time. Blacklight traps also help control the adult moths of corn earworms, European corn borers, and fall armyworms.

How to Use: Place one UV light trap near your fruit trees or corn planting. Use an automatic timer to activate the light from 11:00 p.m. to 3:00 a.m. Moth control is most effective during this time, while injury to beneficial insects is minimized.

Slug and Snail Traps

Slugs and snails are difficult to control since they feed at night and hide during the day. You can identify slug and snail damage by looking for shiny trails of slime that surround the chewed holes in leaves. Cover traps to keep pets and wildlife from lapping up their contents.

Protection Offered: Use these traps to capture slugs and snails and, occasionally, other crawling creatures, such as sowbugs.

How to Use: Garden supply stores and catalogs offer traps that feature a reservoir for bait or for a liquid in which the pests drown. Follow trap instructions and bury them partially in the soil to create a cool, damp environment that will attract these pests. You can bait the traps with beer; a mixture of yeast and water; or a commercial attractant. Use one trap for every 10 square feet of garden space. Under heavy infestation, check the traps daily to remove pests and replace bait.

You can make traps from aluminum pie plates or other recycled containers; just sink them to the brim in the soil and fill with beer. Or, cut a 1-inch hole in the side of an empty coffee can about halfway up. Bury the can so the hole is even with the soil surface and pests can enter, then fill the trap up to the hole with beer. The lid will keep rain out and allow you access to the pests trapped inside.

Slugs and snails seek out moist, shady spots in which to spend the daylight hours. Place overturned pots, boards, shingles, or even the rind from a grapefruit on soil near plants, then collect and destroy the pests early in the morning before the sun drives them elsewhere.

Pheromone Traps

When insects are ready to reproduce, they depend on chemical signals, called sex pheromones, to help them find mates. Mature females emit the pheromones, and males of the same species are able to detect them in extremely low concentrations from far away. The males follow the chemical signal in order to find receptive females.

Lures that contain pheromones are used by commercial growers to intercept and trap pests. Some products use pheromones as mating disruption lures. These products work by flooding the air with female sex pheromones, making it difficult for male insects to find the females for mating. Mating disruption lures can reduce the damage caused by pests such as codling moths, grape berry moths, and oriental fruit moths in commercial orchards. Except for codling moths, such traps are probably not effective for backyard fruit tree and vine plantings. For more information on codling moth traps, see page 32.

Commercial Products: A variety of brand name slug traps are available.

Sticky Boards

Traps covered with sticky coating strategically placed among your plants will capture sufficient numbers of certain pests to control their damage. Originally used to monitor pest population fluctuations, sticky boards work well as controls when concentrated in small areas. However, beneficial insects are also attracted to such traps, so their use can do as much harm as good.

Protection Offered: Use bright yellow traps to control aphids, cabbage root flies, carrot rust flies, cucumber beetles, fungus gnats, imported cabbageworms, onion flies, thrips, and whiteflies in the garden and greenhouse. Some growers report that blue traps are best for monitoring thrips, but not for controlling them. Use white traps to monitor European apple sawflies, flea beetles, and tarnished plant bugs.

How to Use: Sticky traps are simple affairs to mass produce at home. To make traps that will last several years, cut boards from ¼-inch plywood, masonite, or a similar material and fasten them with staples or nails to garden stakes. You can also design them to hang from wire supports. Either way, make sure the traps are at average plant height. Traps made from cardboard or paper plates will work well in a greenhouse, where they are protected from the elements.

Larger traps will catch more pests. Commercial traps are available in a range of sizes from 3 X 5 inches and up. Long, narrow, rectangular, or oval shapes may attract the most pests.

Apply sticky coating (see "Making Sticky Traps" on the opposite page) directly to your painted boards, or for easier cleanup, staple waxed paper or plastic wrap over the boards and apply the sticky coating to the paper or wrap. In either case, leave one corner uncoated for easier handling.

- To catch whiteflies and other pests, paint boards yellow (Federal Safety Yellow No. 659 from Rustoleum Company and Saturn Yellow from Day-Glo Colors are two colors most pests find attractive) before applying homemade or commercial sticky coating.

- Paint your traps a bright blue, such as cobalt or royal blue, to monitor thrips.

- Use bright white traps to monitor flea beetles or tarnished plant bugs.

Use one trap for several plants. Wait several days, then add more traps if pests continue to cause damage. For whitefly control, don't spread the traps too far apart in the garden, since these pests don't travel far from their host plants.

Place your traps near plants, but not so close that foliage gets stuck to the boards. Set traps with the sticky sides facing your plants, but out of direct sunlight. Try to avoid placing traps where the wind will blow dust and debris onto them. Occasionally disturb infested foliage with your hands to drive feeding pests into flight.

You can clean pest-covered traps with a paint scraper, or wipe insects away with a cloth soaked in baby oil or vegetable oil, before applying fresh sticky coating.

To monitor tarnished plant bugs in apple and peach trees, hang four traps per full-size tree, or one per dwarf tree. To capture flea beetles, place traps just above eggplant, tomato, or pepper foliage.

Commercial Products: A variety of commercially made yellow sticky traps are available.

Making Sticky Traps

When using sticky traps, cover them with a commercial sticky coating, such as TangleTrap, Stickem, Sticky Stuff, Tanglefoot, or Bug Gum, or make your own. Mix equal parts of petroleum jelly or mineral oil and liquid dish soap to make an inexpensive sticky coating that is easy to remove.

To capture small, lightweight pests such as aphids, thrips, and whiteflies, dilute the heavier ointments to make application easier (use 1 part sticky coating to 2 parts paint thinner). Or, buy easy-to-apply, brush-on formulas.

For heavier pests such as caterpillars that may resist being stuck, use sticky coatings at full strength.

Trap Crops

Grow pests' favorite plants to lure them away from your garden crops. Plant these trap crops around your garden or between the rows. When a trap crop becomes infested, pull it and destroy the pests. For pests that disperse quickly when disturbed, cover the trap plants with a sheet or bag before you pull them. This control method works best for pests that produce only a few generations each summer or for crops that need protection for a short, critical period in the season. A drawback is that you have to sacrifice the harvest from the trap crop and the garden space to grow it.

Protection Offered: You can use trap crops to catch a variety of insect pests. Unfortunately, trap crops may end up attracting more pests than usual to your garden. And if they're not pulled at the right time, the trap crops can provide more food for future generations of pests. Also, destroying the trap crop may mean sacrificing the beneficial insects that were attracted by the pests.

How to Use: To lure flying pests from your favorite crops, plant an attractive alternative nearby. When pests are concentrated on the trap crop, capture and destroy them, or pull and destroy the plant. To help lure the pests to the trap crop,

try spraying the crop you want to protect with kaolin clay or a hot pepper repellent as well. Try the following trap crops:

- Plant various species of flowering mustard to trap cabbageworms and harlequin bugs.

- Napa cabbage is an effective trap crop for flea beetles.

- You may want to sacrifice an early crop of radishes in order to prevent cabbage root maggot damage on broccoli, cabbage, and related vegetables.

- Tomato hornworms are attracted to dill and lovage; the trap crops lure the pest away from tomato plants.

- If you want to protect soybeans from Mexican bean beetles, plant green beans between the rows of soybeans as a trap crop.

- Chervil is irresistible to slugs; plant it among vegetables and ornamentals in slug territory.

- In the greenhouse, use pots of sprouted wheat to lure fungus gnats from your plants, then hot-compost the soil and wheat when the females have laid their eggs in it. Start a new crop of wheat every 2 weeks.

Biological Controls

Biological pest control—relying on the natural enemies of plant pests to minimize pest problems—is a phenomenon as old as the pests themselves. For organic gardeners, designing and managing gardens to shelter and encourage natural enemies is a top priority.

THE ENEMIES LIST

In a backyard garden, there's a lot more going on than meets the eye. Every day in your garden, a wide range of animals large and small, along with insects, mites, and pathogens, are helping in your efforts to prevent pests from harming your plants. The native biocontrols in your garden include:

Insects and others. Natural enemies include insects, mites, and spiders that are predators or parasites of plant pests, as well as pathogens that can infect plant pests with disease. Lady beetles and lacewings are two well-known predators of aphids and other soft-bodied pests. Predatory and parasitic insects are part of the larger community of beneficial insects that also includes pollinators such as honey bees, along with beetles and other insects that help break down organic matter in the soil. Beneficial insects and microbes play a vital role in the complex community that naturally exists in your yard.

Songbirds. Many songbirds are insect predators, too. When you consider that chickadees spend much of their time during the winter eating aphid eggs or that Baltimore orioles can eat up to 17 tent caterpillars a minute, you won't wonder why many gardeners want to attract birds to their yards. Planting trees and shrubs that provide food, shelter, and nesting sites, along with providing a source of fresh water year-round, will go a long way toward encouraging birds to visit your yard.

Toads. For consuming slugs, cutworms, and other ground-dwelling pests, nothing beats a resident toad! Be sure to provide shelter and water for these hard-working garden residents.

Microbes. Yes, even plant pests get sick, and naturally occurring bacteria, fungi, and viruses that cause disease in insects are part of the big picture of biocontrol in your backyard. Beneficial microorganisms also play a role in preventing plant disease, because the beneficial microbes compete against the plant pathogens for food, and even for space in the nutrient-rich zone surrounding plant roots. Some bacteria and fungi referred to as "antagonists" actively fight against or consume plant pathogens.

Beyond encouraging the natural biological control organisms already present in your garden, you can also purchase products that contain pest-killing bacteria, fungi, or natural substances produced by microbes. One widely used biocontrol product is BT, the bacterium *Bacillus thuringiensis,* which infects and kills a broad range of chewing caterpillar pests. Developing new biological products like these is an active area of research, so from time to time, ask your local garden center owner about new biocontrol products for home garden pests.

ENCOURAGING AND CONSERVING NATURAL ENEMIES

More beneficial organisms visit your plants than do pests, but often you won't notice the beneficials because they're small and inconspicuous. Plus, some natural enemies of garden pests are so efficient at keeping pest populations low that you may never realize that the pests are present in your garden at all. Encouraging natural enemies of plant pests isn't hard to do; it's simply a matter of learning to recognize them, avoiding garden practices that can discourage or kill them, and then supplying them with supplemental food sources, water, and sheltering refuges here and there around your garden.

Recognizing the Good Guys

Entomologists estimate that more than 90 percent of all insects are beneficial, so chances are that most of the insects you'll see in your garden are not causing your plants any harm. It pays to learn what the common natural enemies of garden pests look like, and you'll find photos and descriptions of almost 20 of these helpful insects beginning on page 293. For a quick side-by-side comparison of some of the beneficial insects that are easily mistaken for pests, see "Insect Imposters" on page 297.

Avoiding Harm

The first and most important choice for gardeners who want to encourage natural enemies and other beneficials is to avoid using toxic sprays or dusts in the garden. Even sprays such as insecticidal soap that organic gardeners commonly use can kill helpful insects. Apply insect-killing sprays only when absolutely necessary and only on the plants being attacked.

Another important point to understand is that natural enemies rarely kill 100 percent of the pests they prey upon. Those few remaining pests play an important role in maintaining the natural cycle—they will provide the next generation of beneficials

with food. In the wild, beneficials and harmful organisms often follow a natural cycle of population highs and lows. Pest numbers may rise suddenly in response to some environmental cue, such as an increase in their food supply. Populations of beneficial organisms will increase accordingly. As a result, pest numbers decline, followed by a corresponding drop in numbers of beneficials. The cycle repeats continuously each season in your garden. If you notice a certain pest population is on the rise, wait a bit to let the beneficials move in and perform, rather than reaching for a spray or dust. In many cases, a pest such as aphids won't cause any substantial harm to yarrow or other perennials, and the presence of those aphids will actually draw more predators and parasites to your garden, providing better aphid control over time.

It is important to minimize dust and provide a water source in hot, dry areas to protect beneficial insects. They are easily killed by dehydration. Hedges, windbreaks, and even fences help keep down dust. An old birdbath filled with water and rocks or gravel (to provide safe landing places for tiny insects so they won't drown) will be used by many beneficial species. Hedgerows and permanent beds protect beneficial insects while there are disruptions in the garden and often provide them with an alternate food supply of nonpest insects living in the hedge.

Once adults of beneficial species have arrived in your garden and have had a meal, the females will search for a good place to lay eggs, which later hatch into predatory larvae. Beneficial ground-dwelling insects, such as rove and ground beetles, find refuges in permanent walkways of sod, stone, or thick mulches. This provides them with a safe place to hide when plantings are being disturbed, cultivated, or harvested.

Supplemental Food

Many insect predators and parasites supplement their diets with pollen and nectar, which is a smart strategy—it helps them survive periods when their target pests are scarce. And sometimes beneficials need to feed on pollen and nectar in order to reproduce. Some parasitic wasps, for example, lay more eggs after feasting on plant nectar. Green lacewings eat aphid honeydew to boost their egg production, and syrphid flies require a meal of pollen before they can lay eggs. Thus, planting annuals, perennials, and herbs that supply pollen and nectar is a great way to boost populations of natural enemies around your yard.

Since many natural enemies are tiny insects, they need to feed from small flowers; they literally can't reach the food in larger blossoms. The best plant choices for this purpose are members of the carrot family (Apiaceae), which includes dill, fennel, lovage, and parsley. Many mint family (Labiatae) plants such as catnip, hyssop, and lemon balm are important too. Rosemary, thyme, and other herbs are attractive to both gardeners and beneficials. Members of the daisy family (Asteraceae), including coneflowers, daisies, and yarrow, are excellent sources of both pollen and nectar. Plants otherwise considered weeds might be useful food sources for natural enemies, for example corn spurry, goldenrod, lamb's-quarters, wild mustard, and Queen-Anne's lace.

One easy way to include these attractant plants is simply to mix them in among your garden crops. Or you can plant a flower border specifically designed to entice natural enemies. Once good insects are attracted to your garden, they'll often stay to control garden pests.

Cover crops are good sources of food and shelter. Buckwheat is an excellent choice, since it's easily worked into the garden season and quickly provides masses of blooms and cover to attract natural enemies. Be sure to cut down the buck-

Invite a Spider to Dine

You may be hesitant to encourage spiders in your garden, but keep in mind that garden spiders aren't interested in you—they are searching for a meal of tasty insects. Insects are the most popular items on the spiders' menu. Spiders capture their insect prey with unusual tactics. They weave various traps with the silk threads produced by spinnerets. The multipurpose silk is woven into coverings for eggs; parachutes for travel; and snares, drag lines, and webs for capturing prey.

Some spiders, including common wolf spiders, are adequately large and fast to chase down their prey. As soon as they have hold of their prey, they inject digestive fluids that liquefy the insect's tissues, then they suck the shell dry. Almost all spiders have venom, but most will not bite humans if they're not disturbed, and even if bitten, most people have little or no reaction to most spider bites.

Daddy longlegs are closely related to spiders. Often called harvestmen, they'll eat just about anything, including scraps from the kitchen table. They're most active at night, patrolling garden plants for infestations of small insect pests. Like spiders, they have eight legs. Their legs are easily shed but don't grow back. By the end of the summer, many daddy longlegs are getting about adequately on only a few legs.

Encouraging Beneficial Animals

You may not think of wild animals as helpful to your garden, but some are excellent pest-controllers. For example, in Canadian forests, shrews control larch sawflies and other pests. Lizards and toads are important natural enemies of pest insects, and snakes can help control problems with mice and voles. In many communities in Europe and North America, farmers encourage birds to control pests by placing nesting boxes around their fields. Even domesticated animals can assist in pest control. If you have a small orchard and keep chickens, let the chickens feed in the orchard. They will peck pests such as plum curculios out of dropped fruit and other ground litter.

And while birds will feast on insect pests, they may first be attracted to your yard by a well-stocked bird feeder.

Encourage or discourage large and small animals as necessary in your garden. Naturally, you'll probably want to keep out those animals that cause more damage than benefit (see "Animal Pests" on page 304). But it may be time to reconsider some of your instinctive reactions to animals. For example, snakes in the garden are usually a good thing—they're great rodent controllers! Also remember that bats are generally harmless to people, but they can consume huge numbers of mosquitoes, flies, and other pests.

If water is scarce, place small containers filled to the brim in shady locations for thirsty animals (but change the water every other day to prevent mosquito larvae from taking up residence there). Build bird-houses to attract the insect-eating birds, and place the houses along the garden's border.

wheat before it goes to seed, however, or it can become a weed problem. Try using alfalfa, buckwheat, or clover as a border around the garden (see page 7 for directions for planting cover crops).

Water

Like animals and plants, beneficial insects require water. If rain is plentiful locally, puddles of water or morning dew are probably sufficient. During a drought, provide a bug bath—a shallow container filled with water and plenty of rocks that serve as insect perches. Keep in mind, though, that any source of standing water can become a breeding ground for mosquitoes if it's not changed frequently. Avoid any possibility that mosquito larvae will hatch and mature in your bug bath by changing the water every other day. Also consider sitting a deeper water source somewhere in your yard to help encourage a toad to call your garden home.

Shelter

Beneficials need protection from wind and weather extremes, and also from dust and physical disturbance. When you are tilling, mowing, spraying, or harvesting, beneficial insects will leave your garden and seek out alternative cover. Provide them with hedgerows, flowering shrubs, cover crops, perennial borders, and mulches like newspaper or compost as resting and hiding places. To encourage soil-dwelling beneficials such as ground beetles and rove beetles, plant in permanent beds and put down stone mulches to provide lots of hiding places. Avoid excess tillage, because it will destroy or disturb beneficials. The dust cloud created by tillage eventually settles on plants and may harm the more delicate beneficials, such as parasitic wasps. Excessive tillage also alters the soil environment and may harm populations of beneficial soil microorganisms (see "Soil Tillage" on page 8).

Buying and Releasing Natural Enemies

If your native natural controls need assistance, you may choose to buy beneficial insects. Several garden supply catalogs offer beneficial insects among their products, and private insectaries offer a wide assortment. Keep in mind that you'll be competing with commercial growers and garden supply companies for what may be a limited supply of beneficials. Availability of specific species can change from year to year. Also keep in mind that most insects have the ability and instinct to disperse widely when they're released. Chances are that most of them will immediately leave your yard. Thus, while releasing beneficials won't do any harm, it may not be of significant help in managing pests in your yard and garden. Regard this as an experimental project, and see what results. If you have a home greenhouse, releasing whitefly parasites or fungus gnat predators can be effective.

Purchased beneficials need special care or they can easily die before they get a chance to do their job. Follow these steps when purchasing and releasing beneficials.

■ Become familiar with the life cycle of the target pest; know where and when to find eggs and larvae in your garden. Use garden books with good illustrations or photographs to help you.

■ Identify the natural enemies available for control of your pest and locate a source. Consult with your supplier to be certain you're buying the best biological control for the pest.

■ When the beneficials arrive, study the instructions for storage and release; each beneficial organism is unique and must be treated differently. Release them as soon as you can; if you can't release them immediately, follow the instructions for proper storage.

■ Release them at the proper rate and location. Rate of release will depend on the size of your garden or greenhouse and the severity of your pest infestation. Take a good look at the beneficials before releasing, so you don't confuse them for a pest later.

■ Once you've released beneficials, monitor their progress. If you're releasing egg parasites, watch for discolored pest eggs with odd-shaped exit holes. Parasitized larvae often become discolored and inactive. If necessary, make several releases to keep a major pest under control. Once released, some natural enemies are vigorous enough to survive from year to year. Others may require annual release if they aren't able to survive your area's climate year-round.

MITES AND NEMATODES

Tiny mites and nematodes play a powerful role in the world of biological control. Naturally occurring mites and nematodes are crucial in keeping populations of some plant pests in balance. And commercially available mites and nematodes can be very effective in managing pests in home gardens, because unlike purchased insects, the mites and nematodes that you release in your garden can't fly away.

Predatory Mites

Predatory mites are less than $\frac{1}{25}$-inch, eight-legged creatures that are related to spiders. In your garden, predatory mites live in the soil, in compost piles, and on your plants. Soil-dwelling species usually reside in the upper 2 inches of the soil, preying on other mites and insects. Species that live on garden plants consume other mites and their eggs; some types also feed on thrips. Still other species provide valuable pest control in stored grains.

Predatory mites are useful biological controls because they reproduce quickly, keeping pace with oscillating pest populations: Some are able to complete their life cycle in 1 week. If you observe mites through a magnifying glass, you can distinguish predatory mites from spider mites by the former's faster movement and oval shape. Their beneficial effects are often hardly noticed until they are killed off by pesticide sprays; the subsequent population explosion in spider mites highlights their importance.

Several species are available from insect suppliers for controlling pests in the garden, orchard, vineyard, and greenhouse. *Phytoseiulus persimilis* is the most widely sold species for spider mite control. In hot greenhouses and gardens (temperatures greater than 90°F), try *Amblyseius californicus* or *Phytoseiulus longipes*. *Galendromus (*also called *Metaseiulus) occidentalis* is an excellent hardy predator of European red mite in apple orchards and berry patches, surviving as far north as the Canadian apple-growing regions. Once established, it should only need to be re-released after a severe winter or other disruption to its population.

How to Release: Predatory mites are usually sold as a mix of several species to ensure complete control under a variety of conditions, because each species has overlapping humidity, temperature, and prey requirements. In the greenhouse or garden, order about 1,000 predatory mites for every 200 to 500 square feet. Shake the carrier and mites out among your plants; if possible apply them on the plants that are most heavily infested with pest mites. The mites are so small you may not be able to spot them in the mixture, but rest assured they will travel among your plants as necessary to find pests.

For fruit trees, if European red mite numbers are low and you just want to establish a predator population for future years, release 50 to 100 per tree; if you want to control an outbreak during the same season, release 1,000 per tree.

Nematodes

Mention nematodes and most gardeners think of the harmful types—root-knot nematodes and others that infest plant roots. But gardeners should also learn how to use beneficial nematodes such as *Steinernema carpocapsae* and *Heterorhabditis heliothidis* because they provide quick control of insect pests that spend part of their lives in garden soil.

Immature larvae of these beneficial nematodes have a protective cuticle. They aggressively search for hosts, usually in or near the soil. The nematode enters the insect host's body through natural openings, such as the mouth or spiracles, shedding the cuticle it no longer needs. Beneficial nematodes carry an intestinal bacterium that is released inside the host, paralyzing and killing it within 24 to 48 hours. Once the host is dead, the nematode completes several generations within the carcass until host tissues are depleted. Larvae then redevelop the protective cuticle and leave the carcass in search of a new host. Larvae in this protected state can survive in the soil without a host for as long as 1 year if moisture levels and temperatures remain favorable.

Nematodes require a moist, dark environment. As temperatures drop in winter, they burrow deeper in the soil and begin hibernation; as temperatures rise in spring, they move closer to the soil surface. Their return lags behind the arrival of early spring pests, so for early pest control, gardeners must reintroduce the nematodes each year.

Protection Offered: Nematodes can be used to control a wide range of pests including armyworms, black vine weevils and other root weevils, some types of borers, cutworms, flea larvae, rootknot nematodes, onion maggots, sod webworms, and white grubs.

In the laboratory, more than 250 species of pests fall prey to beneficial nematodes. Outdoors, however, uncontrolled soil temperatures and moisture reduce their efficiency. *Steinernema carpocapsae* lives closest to the soil surface and successfully controls carpenterworms, currant borers, cutworms, armyworms, earwigs, navel orangeworms, onion maggots, pillbugs, seedcorn maggots, sod webworms, sowbugs, and strawberry root weevils. A related species, *S. glaseri,* controls white grubs, and *S. riobravis* infects corn earworms, mole crickets, and citrus root weevils. *S. feltiae* nematodes are reportedly effective for control of root-knot nematodes, ring nematodes, and sting nematodes.

Heterorhabditis bacteriophora ranges deeper in soil, effectively controlling billbugs, black vine weevils, corn rootworm larvae, Japanese beetle grubs, masked chafers, mole crickets, and wireworms.

Parasitic nematodes also show promise against armyworms, cabbage root maggots, codling moth larvae, Colorado potato beetle larvae, cutworms, and rose chafers.

How to Release: Rate of application depends on the susceptibility of the target pest, its location in reference to the damaged plant, and the particular species or strain of nematode supplied. Commercial suppliers vary in the strain of nematodes they raise; you may have a choice of several strains or species. Consult with specialists at your supply source for the most appropriate species and the most efficient method of application. Always follow the supplier's label directions.

The nematodes arrive in the infective larval stage, either dehydrated or suspended in gels, sponges, or moist peat and vermiculite. It's best to release them when pest larvae are known to be present. Mix the formulations thoroughly with water, then apply to the soil with a watering can or pressure sprayer. At planting time, treat a 3-inch-wide band centered over the row. Control pests of perennial plants by spraying at the base of the plants. To control pests in sod, spray nematodes evenly over the grass with a watering can or sprayer, or pour them directly onto the grass: Use 100,000–500,000 nematodes per square yard. Water the nematodes in well; apply $\frac{1}{2}$ to 1 inch of water after spraying to soak them into the sod. Control is most successful when nematodes are applied to moist soil in the late afternoon or evening. Treatment may be less successful in lawns with thatch, which impedes the progress of the nematodes into the root zone.

Since the nematodes are susceptible to drying, control is less effective when applied directly to plants. It may take 6 weeks before you know whether treatments were effective. Parasitized hosts will appear chalky white, reddish, or gray.

To control borers in trees, mix nematodes according to label directions, and use an oil can to squirt the nematodes into the holes (about 17,000 nematodes per squirt). Or use a syringe to inject nematodes into squash vines to control squash borers or in corn silks to control corn earworms. Syringes are usually marked in cubic centimeters (cc); you'll be adding about 5,000 nematodes in 2 cc of the prepared mix.

MICROBIAL PEST CONTROL PRODUCTS

Microbial pest control products can rely on bacteria and fungi that infect pest organisms, or on the action of microbes that don't directly attack pest organisms. Instead, these microbes secrete antibiotics that are toxic to other microbial organisms.

They also compete with disease-causing pathogens for food, often winning the race without harming the host plant. This special group of microbials occurs naturally in the soil.

Using this type of product requires some understanding of both the pest and the remedy to achieve good results. For example, spraying BT (*Bacillus thuringiensis*) on your broccoli plants will effectively control imported cabbageworms. However, it will do nothing to stop aphids feeding on those same plants, because the bacteria cannot infect aphids. And while *Bacillus subtilis* is useful for helping to prevent fungal diseases such as mildew and blights, it has no effect on viruses. Always read instructions and follow them exactly when using microbial pest control products.

The specific nature of microbial products like BT means that you can use them without destroying the natural balance that exists between pests and predators. There is no danger of pollution or residual toxicity when such pesticides are properly used. Still, there may be occasions when it's best to wait and see what kind of pest–predator relationships develop before you reach for a biological pesticide. For example, if you place a bird feeder close to cabbage or broccoli, the birds may consume leaf-eating worms for you, eliminating the need for treatment with BT. Because biological insecticides are host-specific, they are not toxic to people. However, it still pays to follow proper spray procedures for best results. See page 376 for information on how and when to spray pesticides and on the best types of application equipment to use.

Remember to focus on promoting a healthy garden through good plant selection, soil management, and plant care before considering biological controls. Biological pesticides are much gentler to the environment than chemical agents, but they can still disturb the natural balance that exists on any site among soil, plants, pests, and predators.

Using microbes to control garden pests is an active area of research; be on the lookout for new microbial insecticides.

Bacillus subtilis

Like *Bacillus thuringiensis* (BT) (see below), *Bacillus subtilis* is a bacterium, but rather than killing insects, it kills or outcompetes some types of harmful fungi, including powdery mildew. Commercial products contain *B. subtilis* spores as well as a natural fungicide that the bacteria produce during fermentation.

Protection Offered: Try *B. subtilis* to help prevent fire blight, botrytis, rust, sclerotinia, powdery and downy mildews, bacterial spot, and other diseases. Trial results for this product have varied depending on the particular combination of crop, disease, and environmental conditions, so keep records of the results you have in your own garden to see when it is most effective.

Precautions: The fungicidal protein in *B. subtilis* products has no harmful effects on people, animals, or insects. Nonetheless, avoid breathing the spray when you apply it.

How to Use: Follow label directions. For greatest effectiveness, spray just before you would expect to see the first symptoms of the disease problem you're trying to avoid. Don't try to store leftover spray—the fungicidal protein in it breaks down quickly. Repeat sprays every 7 to 10 days because *B. subtilis* kills spores on leaf surfaces only; it doesn't have residual effect.

Commercial Products: Serenade

Bacillus thuringiensis (BT)

Bacillus thuringiensis, or BT, is the most widely used microbial biological control method. Scientists have identified more than 35 varieties of this bacterium; several are available to home gardeners for controlling various larval insect pests.

Protection Offered: *B.t.* var. *kurstaki* (BTK) produces crystal toxins that poison, paralyze, and kill various common pest caterpillars. After BTK is applied to plants, caterpillar pests ingest it as they feed. Although the pest may live several more days, it stops feeding, darkens in color, and eventually drops to the soil. BTK effectively controls a wide range of caterpillars including cabbage loopers, codling moth larvae, diamondback moths, gypsy moth larvae, imported cabbageworms, spruce budworms, tomato hornworms, and others. Consult the label for a complete list of susceptible pests.

B.t. var. *israelensis* (BTI) attacks larvae of black flies, fungus gnats, and mosquitoes when applied to standing water where these pests reproduce.

B.t. var. *san diego* (BTSD) controls certain leaf-feeding beetles, including black vine weevils, boll weevils, Colorado potato beetles, and elm leaf beetles. However, many commercial BTSD products are formulated by a process that involves genetically engineered organisms. Such products are not allowed under National Organic Program (NOP) standards, and gardeners who wish to avoid genetically modified organisms (GMOs) should check product labels carefully before buying a BTSD product.

Precautions: BT products are selective—they will not harm the great majority of beneficial insects in your garden. However, butterfly larvae are caterpillars and will be infected by BT. So don't spray BT indiscriminately throughout the garden: Limit applications to plants you know are infested by pests.

BT will not infect wormlike pests excluded from the label, like slugs or leafminers. BT is considered nontoxic to people.

Although it was once thought that insects would not develop resistance to microbial insecti-cides, there are confirmed reports of diamondback moths and other pests that are now resistant to BT. This is another argument for using BT with care, and only after trying methods such as delayed planting, pest barriers, or other methods for which resistance is not a factor.

How to Use: You can purchase BT in many forms, including liquids, powders, dusts, and granules. Follow label directions for either dusting on plants or preparing and applying a batch of spray solution. If sprays roll off leaves rather than adhering to them, add a few drops of liquid dish soap to the spray solution to enhance sticking.

To control mosquitoes and flies, add BTI to standing water in ponds, puddles, storm drains, and other wet areas. BTI has no harmful effects on fish or amphibians. To control fungus gnats in the greenhouse, apply BTI as a drench to soil, on benches, floors, and in large pots.

You can prepare a BT/bran bait for controlling cutworms by moistening bran with a dilute solution of BTK. Sprinkle the moist bran on the surface of beds 2 weeks before you plan to plant.

Store BT products in a cool, dry place to retain viability for several years. Use a fresh batch for each application and use it within several days. BT products break down quickly in sunlight, so several applications may be necessary to continue to control new pests as they arrive. You can prolong the effectiveness by applying sprays in the evening.

Commercial Products: A wide variety of brand-name products are available.

Beauveria bassiana

Beauveria bassiana has long been recognized as a biological control of many insect pests that spend part of their lives in the soil, particularly Colorado potato

Test for Yourself

Since many biological control products work preventively or by killing pests at a very early stage in their development, it can be hard to judge how effective they are. You won't see lots of dead insects, and you won't be able to watch injured plants making a dramatic recovery. One way to experiment when you apply a botanical control product is to leave a small portion of a bed or a plant or two untreated and see how it turns out. If it does become infested or infected, be prepared to uproot and destroy it to prevent the problem from spreading.

beetles. This fungal pathogen of insects exists naturally in garden soil, making a few insects sick each year. When environmental conditions are right and susceptible insect populations are high, outbreaks of this and other insect pathogens occur that can cause pest populations to crash almost overnight. Unfortunately, the concentrated pest population damages many plants before being controlled. With commercial products containing *B. bassiana,* you can intervene earlier to control the pest.

Protection Offered: *Beauveria bassiana* can provide control for aphids, armyworms, fire ants, diamondback moths, hairy chinch bugs, imported cabbageworms, grasshoppers, thrips, cutworms, leafhoppers, loopers, mites, whiteflies, and other insects. You can apply it to a wide range of plants including vegetables, fruit trees, vines, lawns, and ornamentals.

Precautions: This fungus can kill many kinds of natural enemies and other helpful insects, so spray only infested plants. Avoid bodies of water when spraying because the spray could be toxic to fish.

How to Use: *Beauveria bassiana* is effective as a contact spray; insects don't need to eat sprayed foliage to be infected. Prepare and apply sprays according to label directions. It works best in cool, moist conditions, and is most effective at killing young larvae.

Commercial Products: Mycotrol O; Naturalis; Botanigard

Microbial Antagonists

Microbial antagonists work not by killing plant pathogens, but by outcompeting them. For example, *Trichoderma harzianum* is a beneficial fungus that can help prevent damping-off in garden beds. The fungus forms colonies around roots of seedlings and outcompetes many pathogenic fungi that cause damping-off. In general, plants treated with *Trichoderma* also seem to produce more roots and more vigorous foliage growth. *Streptomyces griseoviridis* is a bacterium that also competes against a variety of pathogens that cause damping-off and seed rots. These products are preventive only; they will not cure plants that are already infected by damping-off.

How to Use: Apply according to label directions.

Commercial Products: Plant Shield, Mycostop, Root Shield, T-22 HC

Milky Spore

Commercial products containing milky spore bacteria, *Bacillus popilliae* and *B. lentimorubus,* are promoted as biocontrols for grubs of Japanese beetles and several related beetles. However,

Compost Tea for Disease Control

Research data indicates that compost tea can help prevent or lessen disease problems such as powdery mildew. Compost tea is not recognized as a disease suppressant under current NOP guidelines but as a home gardener you are free to experiment on your own to see what kinds of effects compost tea has on your plants.

Sometimes a single treatment of compost tea will not stop a disease from developing. Check affected plants every 3 to 4 days and repeat the application if the plants still show symptoms. Use any leftover tea to water plants growing in containers.

You can try this method at home to control damping-off and other common soilborne diseases. Mix 1 part finished compost with 6 parts water. Let the mix stand for 1 week, then strain it through a cloth, such as burlap or cheesecloth, and collect the liquid. Spray this extract undiluted on seedlings in the greenhouse or outdoors to help control many fungal pathogens and prevent infection.

results from these products have been unreliable in many areas. For better control of white grubs, use *Heterorhabditis* nematodes (see page 369) instead.

Nosema locustae

Protozoans are tiny, single-celled organisms that may have complex life cycles. *Nosema locustae* is a protozoan pathogen that infects the fat tissue of most grasshopper and cricket species. Once ingested, spores germinate in the insect's gut. The pest becomes sluggish and slowly dies or remains sufficiently ill that it no longer reproduces or causes damage. Grasshoppers that survive lay infected eggs that serve as inoculum during the following season. *Nosema* is recommended for long-term control, since mortality may take as long as 4 to 6 weeks, although some species die within a few hours. Once applied, each successive generation is reinfected by the preceding one. *Nosema* is an effective grasshopper control in large fields. It is not effective for backyard use, because grasshoppers are highly mobile and new adults will continue to migrate in. To be effective, community-wide applications are necessary.

How to Use: Apply *Nosema* products to control grasshoppers when the late nymphs are emerging. In areas with severe community-wide grasshopper problems, Cooperative Extension personnel can help you time the application. In your yard, broadcast the bait in or near areas around your yard where grasshoppers tend to hatch (grasshoppers like to lay eggs in untilled areas such as grass, pastures, or weedy ditches). The product is effective against immature grasshoppers (less than ¾ inch long) only.

Commercial Products: Nolo Bait

Organic Sprays and Dusts

Good plant care along with strategic use of traps, barriers, and biological controls will nip many plant problems in the bud. But occasionally, you'll want to expand your options to include sprays and dusts that have been accepted as part of organic gardening practices. In some cases, using one of these products can help you avoid losing your harvest or a valuable landscape plant.

HOMEMADE POTIONS

Natural sprays and dusts include commercial products that contain botanical poisons such as pyrethrin or mined minerals such as sulfur. But gardeners have long resorted to homemade sprays as well, choosing ingredients such as hot peppers, garlic, and strongly flavored herbs. The general idea is to make a pungent potion that will fool pests into turning away from their favorite plants. Some, such as hot pepper and garlic sprays, deter insect feeding and even kill some types of insects.

If you do make your own sprays, follow directions carefully, since even the safest ingredients can be used in the wrong way.

Unlike commercial pesticides, the homemade versions tend to be simple and unrefined, with a lot of room for experimenting. You may find that some concentrations work better than others; note your observations for future reference. You may find that a problem continues or reappears after a treatment. This may be because the spray kills the adult pests, but not the eggs. Or more pests may fly into your garden after you treat (this can be true of commercial products as well as homemade mixtures). So observe carefully before you decide whether or not a particular treatment worked. You may also discover that some of the mixtures have the potential to injure your plants, so be sure to test your concoctions on a few leaves before making a garden-wide application. Any damage should be apparent within a few days.

Handle with Care

In choosing a spray or dust, try first to select gentle controls such as baking soda sprays or kaolin clay that will do the least harm to beneficial garden organisms and that are the least toxic to people and pets. In all cases, use sprays and dusts with restraint. Some, especially botanical insecticides, present the same risks to the dynamic living community in your garden as do synthetic poisons. Pyrethrins and neem are botanical poisons that have broad-spectrum activity, meaning that they kill a wide variety of insects, including beneficials. Sulfur and copper products used to prevent and lessen plant disease problems are also toxic substances. Use them too freely, and you may face the problem known as pest resurgence. In other words, you kill off some pests and most of their predators, and the pests come back stronger than ever with no predators to slow them down. And, although organically acceptable botanicals like pyrethrins break down quickly after application, they are highly toxic initially. During the first few hours after they are applied, these and other naturally derived chemicals can kill large numbers of honeybees, spiders, and other beneficial organisms. When you use sprays and dusts, always follow label directions, including frequency of application; spray or dust only when the threat of disease or pests is great.

Beware These Botanicals

Historically, botanical sprays like rotenone were mainstays of organic pest control, but times have changed.

Experience and research have shown that many botanicals are very toxic not only to pests but to bees and other pollinators, birds, fish, and even people and pets. For these reasons, sprays and dusts that contain nicotine, sabadilla, ryania, or rotenone are no longer recommended for use by organic home gardeners in any circumstances. Pyrethrins and neem appear to be less hazardous, but even they should be reserved for use only as a last resort.

Many botanicals are listed as allowed with restrictions for use in organic crop production under National Organic Program (NOP) regulations; nicotine is prohibited. Certified organic growers should carefully review these regulations before using botanical poisons.

Applying Sprays and Dusts

Premixed spray products are convenient and easy to use, and many organic sprays are available in this form. It's usually more economical, though, to buy a liquid concentrate or wettable powder and mix the spray yourself.

For small jobs, use a handheld trigger sprayer. For larger spray jobs, select a pressure sprayer that you can pressurize manually through pumping. Choose a sprayer large enough to handle the area you want to cover without frequent refilling. The more times you must refill the spray reservoir, the more often you will be exposed to the spray. Carefully clean and dry the nozzle and any filters after each use. Clean your sprayer and dispose of unused spray properly, as described on the opposite page.

Reserve one sprayer for applying toxic pest and disease control products such as sulfur and pyrethrins and a separate sprayer for applying compost tea or liquid fertilizers such as fish emulsion.

With biological or botanical pesticide dusts, such as BTK or neem, use a duster designed for this purpose. Besides keeping the dust away from your face, dusting applicators put out puffs of air along with the dust, resulting in better coverage. This forms a temporary cloud around affected plant leaves, which is much more effective than sprinkling dust onto plants.

Taking Precautions

Proper application of sprays and dusts requires thoughtful preparation and careful execution. A lax approach to the treatment stage throws away the time you've spent caring for your garden, identifying pests, and selecting appropriate controls. It could also endanger you, the environment, and the plants you wish to protect.

The following guidelines will help you apply sprays and dusts safely and correctly; in addition, always follow label instructions.

Wait for calm weather. Applying any spray or dust under windy conditions can cause the material to blow or drift where it is not wanted and greatly increases the risk that you'll inhale it or get it in your eyes.

Pick and prune first. Before you apply a spray or dust, pick ripe fruits or vegetables, prune plants if appropriate, and remove weeds that provide cover for pests. Although fruits and vegetables are safe to eat within a few days after application of most botanical pesticides, it makes sense to gather up everything that's ready to eat before you spray. This also reduces your need to enter recently treated areas.

Dress properly. Wear long pants, shoes and socks, and a long-sleeved shirt. If you are applying a liquid product, wear rubber shoes or boots. Wear a face mask, such as a disposable dust mask. However, if the product label advises you not to inhale the spray vapor or mist, wear a respirator. It's a good idea to wear goggles as well, because the tissues of the eye can absorb many substances fast and easily—including spray mist. Wear rubber gloves while applying biological controls, botan-ical poisons, or any substance that could be caustic or toxic.

Precheck your equipment. Make sure spray nozzles are open and pump mechanisms are working before you load the reservoir. Otherwise, you can end up with a serious disposal problem.

Measure carefully. Mix up only as much as you will need. Work slowly and carefully so you don't spill anything during the mixing process.

Do the least harm. Apply sprays or dusts when beneficials are relatively inactive. You may need to observe insect activity patterns for a few days to discover the best time. Generally, mid-morning should be avoided, as this is prime time for honeybees and many natural enemies of plant pests. If you're only going to treat a few plants, put a row cover over them for a day or two after the spray or dust is applied to keep beneficials out of the treated area.

Make a thorough application. Treat upper and lower leaf surfaces as well as places in mulch where pests might run and hide. With commercial products, always follow label directions and apply materials at the recommended rates.

Clean up properly. The best way to dispose of any spray solution is to apply it properly, but if you do have any leftover solution, dilute it with water and place it in a bucket or other container. Rinse out equipment and allow the rinse water to drip into the bucket. Place the bucket of contaminated water in sunlight for a day or two to let the material degrade. Make sure it's inaccessible to children, pets, and wildlife while it sits—cover it with a screen if it's in an outdoor spot where animals might find it and drink from it. After it has degraded, dump the solution away from all water sources, including ponds. Return the container to storage, which should be a cool, dark place out of the reach of children. Always store pest and disease control products in their original containers. When you're finished, change your clothes and wash your hands and face. If you spilled some solution on yourself, take a shower.

HOMEMADE AND COMMERCIAL SPRAYS AND DUSTS

The sprays and dusts that organic gardeners rely on have three characteristics that distinguish them from their synthetic counterparts: (1) They are derived from natural substances, (2) they are generally less toxic to humans than synthetic pesticides, and (3) they break down to harmless substances relatively quickly in the environment. However, there is no easy way to group organic controls. Some are truly insecticidal or fungicidal, while others work by deterring pests. Some substances kill both insects and disease organisms.

Some sprays and dusts that gardeners use are known by more than one name. For example, horticultural oils used during the growing season to kill a variety of pests are also called supreme, summer, or superior oils. And some gardeners refer to spraying pyrethrins, while others call that particular botanical pesticide pyrethrum.

Inert Ingredients

Read the label on almost any pest or disease control product, and you'll find the words *inert ingredients,* a catchall term for additives that make the products easier to use. Inert ingredients keep a product stable in storage and act as "filler" material. If inert ingredients weren't added to spray concentrates, it would be almost impossible to measure the small amount of active ingredient actually required, and even more difficult to achieve the proper coverage on plants.

Inert ingredients in liquid sprays include water, alcohol, and other solvents. Powders and dusts often contain added diatomaceous earth, powdered seeds, or talc for bulk, or fuller's earth to help prevent caking. Other inert ingredients, known as surfactants, help powders mix easily with water and help sprays adhere to foliage so that pests are more likely to contact them. Inert ingredients can be toxic in and of themselves, which is one reason why legislation may be passed requiring manufacturers to disclose what inert ingredients are in a particular product.

Some pest and disease control products, like sulfur or boric acid, are packed in their pure form without inert ingredients. Others combine an active ingredient, such as pyrethrins, with an active diluting agent, such as insecticidal soap, which also acts as a synergist—a substance that enhances the effects of the active ingredient.

To figure out just how much active ingredient you are buying, read the product label for the total percentage of inert ingredients. For example, a typical insecticidal soap in a ready-to-use formula contains about 98 percent inert ingredients. Insecticidal soap in concentrated form contains a lower percentage of inert ingredients since you will be adding your own inert ingredient—water—prior to using the product.

This listing of organically acceptable controls is in alphabetical order. If you have trouble finding a control measure that you are interested in, look it up in the index.

Alcohol

Sprays of 70 percent isopropyl alcohol (rubbing alcohol) control a variety of pests on garden plants and on houseplants that have waxy foliage. However, use of isopropyl alcohol to kill pests is not allowed under NOP regulations (it *can* be used as a disinfectant).

Protection Offered: Alcohol sprays can control soft-bodied insects such as aphids, mealybugs, soft scales, and whiteflies.

Precautions: Whether applied undiluted or diluted with water, alcohol may injure foliage. Test first by applying it on a few leaves and waiting several days to see whether damage symptoms appear. If the plant passes the test, then treat the whole plant.

How to Use: Spot treat scale infestations by wiping them from your plants with a cotton ball soaked in alcohol. To make a whole-plant spray, dilute 1 to 2 cups of isopropyl alcohol with 1 quart water.

All-Purpose Insect Pest Spray

For decades the editors of *Organic Gardening* magazine have collected pest-control remedies and recipes from readers. Several ideas were repeatedly offered as safe, effective insect controls. The editors combined several of these home remedies to make an all-purpose spray out of ingredients found in most kitchens. This spray combines the repellent effects of garlic, onion, and hot pepper with the insecticidal and surfactant properties of soap. Keep in mind that sprays that contain soap may harm natural enemies and pollinating insects. Apply it only to prevent or ease a specific pest problem.

Nowadays, there are also commercial organic sprays that list garlic oil and/or hot pepper as the active ingredient (see "Garlic Oils and Extracts" on page 383 and "Hot Pepper Spray" on page 385).

Protection Offered: Home gardeners can try homemade all-purpose spray against any leaf-eating pests in the garden, and make a note of what pests are successfully controlled. Certified organic producers should check regulations before using this type of homemade spray.

Precautions: The ingredients can cause painful skin and eye irritation. When preparing and applying, wear rubber gloves and keep the mixture well away from your eyes and nose.

How to Use: Chop, grind, or liquefy one garlic bulb and one small onion. Add 1 teaspoon of powdered cayenne pepper and mix with 1 quart of water. Steep 1 hour, strain through cheesecloth, then add 1 tablespoon of liquid dish soap to the strained liquid; mix well.

Spray your plants thoroughly, including leaf undersides. Store the mixture for up to 1 week in a labeled, covered container in the refrigerator.

Bicarbonate (Baking Soda)

Bicarbonate has fungicidal properties when used as a spray on a wide range of garden plants. It is an effective protectant against many fungal diseases, and in some cases will kill organisms that have already infected plants.

Protection Offered: Research has shown that a 0.5 percent solution of baking soda will help prevent roses from being damaged by black spot. Studies also show that commercial fungicide products containing potassium bicarbonate are more effective than homemade baking soda sprays. Among the fungal diseases that bicarbonate helps to prevent or ease are powdery mildew, Alternaria blight, anthracnose, Botrytis, downy mildew, Fusarium wilt, rust, and scab.

Precautions: Bicarbonate sprays can burn foliage, especially if the spray is too concentrated. If leaves turn brown after spraying, remove them from the plant; the plant should produce healthy new foliage. Test spray to avoid such problems.

How to Use: Mix and apply commercial products according to label directions. To make a spray from common baking soda, dissolve 1 teaspoon in 1 quart warm water. Add a drop of liquid dish soap or insecticidal soap, which acts to keep the solution clinging to leaves for a longer period of time. For best effect, begin spraying plants about 2 weeks before the time when you'd expect to see symptoms, and continue spraying weekly if conditions for disease development are favorable. Spray infected plants thoroughly, being sure to cover the undersides of leaves.

Commercial Products: Bi-Carb Old Fashioned Fungicide; GreenCure; Kaligreen; Milstop

Bleach

Chlorine bleach (sodium and calcium hypochlorite) can be used as a disinfectant in the garden and greenhouse.

Protection Offered: Use bleach to disinfect greenhouse tools and benches and as a dip for cuttings taken from plants with disease symptoms. You can also use it to disinfect shovels, pruning shears, and seed-starting equipment to prevent the spread of plant pathogens.

Precautions: In diluted form, bleach is relatively safe; undiluted, it is a toxic and caustic eye and skin irritant. It breaks down rapidly in the soil, but may drive soil pH into the alkaline range. It is not selective, so it kills the beneficial organisms along with the bad.

How to Use: In the greenhouse, dip plant cuttings, before rooting, in a 10 percent bleach solution (1 part bleach to 9 parts water). In the garden, disinfect tools such as shovels, trowels, and clippers with a 10 percent bleach solution between uses if you've been working with diseased plants or digging in an area where diseased plants grew. Anytime you treat tools with a bleach solution, rinse and dry them thoroughly afterward. You can also disinfect plant cages, stakes, and row cover with a bleach solution before storing them.

Bordeaux Mix

Bordeaux mix combines copper sulfate and hydrated lime into a wettable powder that may be dusted onto plants or mixed with water and applied as a spray. It is listed as restricted by the NOP, and it is not easy to find Bordeaux mix offered for sale. Use of Bordeaux mix can result in copper accumulation in soil—enough to harm earthworms and beneficial microbes. Use it only as a last resort.

Protection Offered: Bordeaux mix acts as a fungicide with insecticidal and insect repellent properties. It can protect fruit and nut trees, vines, and some ornamentals against common plant diseases like anthracnose, bacterial leaf spots and wilts, black spot, fire blight, peach leaf curl, powdery mildew, and rust.

Precautions: Bordeaux mix can burn plant foliage. One of the safer times to apply it is just before plants leaf out in spring. Injury is most common at temperatures below 50°F and when humidity is high. Read the product label carefully before applying.

How to Use: Apply Bordeaux mix as a dust or mix it with water for spraying; follow label instructions.

Bug Juice

Long ago, backyard gardeners discovered that some insect pests wouldn't feed on plants if dead members of their species were on those plants. In the 1960s, this observation caught on as a way to repel pests, and gardeners began experimenting with solutions of pulverized pests.

The reasons why bug juice works are unknown, but one possible explanation is that substances in the crushed pests are repellent to living insects. For example, the alarm pheromones of dead beetles may discourage other beetles of the same species. Also, the substances may attract the natural enemies of the pests, which would then prey on any living pests that visit the sprayed plants.

OMRI lists bug juice as "insect extracts":

The Vinegar Option

If you've had problems with damping-off of seedlings, but you'd prefer not to use bleach, substitute vinegar instead. Wash used flats, pots, and seed-starting containers in warm soapy water first. Prepare a vinegar solution by adding 2 cups white distilled vinegar to 4 to 6 gallons water, and use it for a rinse.

Organic farms and nurseries can use hydrogen peroxide (dioxide) products such as ZeroTol for the same purpose, but must observe NOP restrictions.

Such extracts are allowed for use as pest lures or repellents, as part of insect traps, or for disease control.

Protection Offered: Gardeners report that bug juice helps reduce damage due to cabbage loopers and Colorado potato beetle and Mexican bean beetle larvae.

Precautions: There hasn't been much research conducted on bug juice. Since you're dealing with the unknown, wear a filter mask, long-sleeved shirt, rubber gloves, and long pants when mixing and spraying the juice to avoid skin contact. Don't use a kitchen blender to prepare the spray—you could contaminate your food with pathogens that may sicken you as well as the pests. Wash sprayed produce thoroughly before eating it.

How to Use: Larger pests are easier to collect than small, fast-moving types. Collect about ½ cup of the pests, especially ones that appear to be sluggish or sick. Put the insects in an old blender with about 2 cups of water and liquefy. Strain the mix, then dilute ¼ cup of this concentrate with 1 to 2 cups of water in a sprayer. You can store leftover mix in the freezer, but be sure to label it.

Use the spray to repel the same pest that is in the mixture. Spray the plants thoroughly on both sides of leaves. You can reapply once or twice a week, although some bug juice sprays are reported to be effective for as long as 2 months.

Citrus Oils

Citrus peels contain oils that are toxic to many kinds of insects. Thus, citrus oil has the potential to control many garden and home pests. *Linalool* and *d-limonene* are the active ingredients extracted from citrus waste. Linalool is an insect nerve poison that kills pests on contact; the mode of action of d-limonene remains unknown. Products containing citrus oils are labeled for use on ornamentals only, not on food crops, and they are listed as restricted by NOP standards. Use them only as a last resort.

Protection Offered: Citrus extracts are toxic to aphids, mites, leaf-eating caterpillars, fleas, fire ants, flies, roaches, and wasps.

Precautions: Although generally not harmful to humans, exposure to citrus oils may cause some animals to experience tremors and salivation.

How to Use: To control aphids and mites on ornamentals, prepare the spray solution according to label directions. Cover the leaves thoroughly, making sure to coat the undersides where many pests hide. As plants grow and as rain washes away the oils, you may need to spray at 1- to 2-week intervals to maintain the protection. Water plants well before applying the spray, and avoid applying it during hot conditions.

Commercial Products: Orange Guard; Orange Guard Fire Ant Control; Concern Citrus Home Pest Control

Copper

Copper has been used as a pesticide since the 1700s. Copper sulfate works by inactivating critical enzyme systems in fungi, algae, and other plants. Many commercial products contain copper octanoate, also called copper soap, which combines copper with a naturally occurring fatty acid. Some, but not all, copper fungicides are OMRI listed.

Protection Offered: Copper is a broad-spectrum fungicide and bactericide used to protect vegetables, ornamentals, fruits, and nuts from disease problems such as anthracnose, bacterial leaf spot, botrytis, black spot, blights, downy mildew, fire blight, peach leaf curl, powdery mildew, and Septoria leaf spot.

Precautions: Copper products are toxic to humans and other mammals; they also irritate the eyes and skin, so use adequate protection when you use these products. Copper is highly toxic to fish and aquatic invertebrates. Its toxicity is reduced when mixed with lime (Bordeaux mix; see page 380), but repeated applications of any copper product will stunt a plant. Although copper does not become concentrated in plant tissues, it persists indefinitely in the soil and can cause harm to earthworms and beneficial soil organisms.

How to Use: Copper fungicides and bactericides are available as dusts, wettable powders, liquid concentrates, or ready-to-apply formulas. Follow label directions carefully. Since copper works as a protectant, cover the entire plant surface to prevent invasion by disease organisms. Spray in the early morning in dry, bright weather so that plants have time to dry. If the solution remains on leaves too long, it may penetrate the cuticle and kill the tissue.

Commercial Products: Concern Copper Soap Fungicide; Cueva Copper Soap Fungicide; Kocide; Liqui-cop

Diatomaceous Earth

Diatomaceous earth (DE) is a nonselective dust that is thought to kill insects by wicking moisture out through the waxy coating on their bodies, so that they die of dehydration. NOP regulations allow certified organic growers to use DE with restrictions. Because DE is as lethal to beneficial insects as to pests, reserve it as a last resort for garden pest problems. Some DE products also have pyrethrins added.

Protection Offered: Dust soil with DE to control crawling pests like slugs and snails. On plant foliage, DE will kill softbodied pests like aphids, caterpillars, leafhoppers, and thrips, but will also kill a wide range of beneficial insects. It is an excellent product for use in stored grain and seeds, and for indoor flea and louse control. Farmers add DE to animal feed to control internal parasites of livestock.

Precautions: DE is considered nontoxic to mammals, but the same properties that make it lethal to pests also cause it to irritate mucous membranes. Wear a dust mask when applying DE to avoid inhaling the particles. Don't apply the dust where children are likely to encounter it. Rain will dilute or wash away DE and mix it into the soil, but the DE will retain its insecticidal properties. Don't confuse pool-grade DE with the garden variety; the type used in pools is not effective for killing insects.

How to Use: Purchase natural-grade DE as a dust and apply only in problem areas to minimize harm to beneficials. When applied around the base of susceptible seedlings like cabbage, onions, and other transplants, DE helps control root maggots and other soil-dwelling pests. For stubborn thrips infestations, dust only the undersides of affected leaves and in a circular band on the soil beneath each plant. Apply DE to the base of squash plants to help reduce squash bug problems.

Commercial Products: Perma-Guard; Safer Crawling Ant and Insect Killer

Essential Oil Sprays and Dusts

Many of the aromatic herbs are well known for their hardiness and for their lack of pest problems. Several scientific studies confirm the repellent effect of herbal extract sprays and dusts, long relied upon by organic gardeners. Researchers have also found that sprays containing essential oils can help suppress disease problems, and that they can work as nonselective herbicides, dissolving the surface waxy coating on weed plants so that they dehydrate and then die.

Protection Offered: The essential oils of sage and thyme and the alcohol extracts of such herbs as hyssop, rosemary, sage, thyme, and white clover can be used to reduce the number of pest eggs laid and the amount of feeding damage caused by a broad range of pests. Sprays made from tansy repel imported cabbageworms on cabbage, reducing the number of eggs laid on the plants. Teas made from wormwood or nasturtiums may repel aphids from fruit trees. Some gardeners have used extracts of catnip, chives, feverfew, marigolds, or rue against leaf-feeding pests. Experiment with your own herbal extracts to control leaf-eating pests in the garden.

A commercial product containing citric acid and mint oil is available for combating various bacterial and fungal diseases. Since the active ingredients are exempt from EPA registration, the label does not specify which particular diseases it helps suppress. Follow label instructions when applying. Products containing rosemary oil and other oils are labeled for use against a variety of pest insects and mites.

Commercial herbicide products containing lemongrass oil and other essential oils are labeled for use against a wide range of grasses and broadleaf weeds. You can use these herbicides in ornamental or food gardens, but keep in mind that the spray will kill almost all plant material it contacts, so careful application is required.

Precautions: Follow the same precautions as for other pesticides: Wear a mask and protective clothing to avoid inhaling the spray or getting it on your skin. Also be sure that you're using the right type of spray for the situation—never use an herbicidal essential oil spray to try to repel insects.

How to Use: For commercial products, follow label instructions. If you want to mix your own, buy essential herbal oils and dilute them with water to make sprays. Experiment with proportions, starting with a few drops of oil per cup of water.

Make your own herbal extracts by mashing or blending 1 to 2 cups of fresh leaves with 2 to 4 cups of water and leaving them to soak overnight. You can also make concentrated herbal teas by pouring

the same amount of boiling water over 2 to 4 cups fresh or 1 to 2 cups dry leaves and leaving them to steep until cool. Strain the mixture through cheesecloth and dilute the resulting liquid with 2 to 4 cups of water to make a spray. Add a few drops of liquid soap to help the spray stick to leaves.

Commercial Products: A wide variety of brand-name products is available. Read labels to see whether a particular product is formulated for insect control, disease control, or weed control.

Garlic Oils and Extracts

A homemade mix of garlic oil, mineral oil, and pure soap can be used to fight garden pests, and also has some fungicidal effect. Commercial products containing garlic oil or garlic extracts are labeled for disease control and as repellents.

Protection Offered: Garlic oil kills insects, but not selectively. Use it to prevent problems with aphids, imported cabbageworms, leafhoppers, larval mosquitoes, squash bugs, and whiteflies. It also works against some fungi and some nematodes on vegetable and fruit crops and ornamentals. Gardeners report that it has little effect against Colorado potato beetles, grapeleaf skeletonizers, grasshoppers, red ants, or sowbugs. Adult lady beetles seem unharmed by garlic oil sprays. The sprays are also reported to repel bird and animal pests.

Precautions: Some foliar injury may occur when garlic sprays include oil and/or soap. Since it is nonselective, garlic spray can kill beneficials as well as pests.

How to Use: Apply commercial products according to label directions. To make your own garlic spray, soak 3 ounces of finely minced garlic cloves in 2 teaspoons of mineral oil for at least 24 hours. Add 1 pint of water that has ¼ ounce of liquid dish soap mixed into it. Stir well and strain into a glass jar for storage. Combine 1 to

2 tablespoons of this concentrate with 1 pint of water to make a spray. Test your mixture on a few leaves to check for injury caused by the oil and soap; damage may not appear for 2 to 3 days. Spray plants thoroughly to ensure good coverage.

Commercial Products: Biolink Insect Repellant; Cropguard; Garlic Barrier; Garlic GP

Horticultural Oils

Applying light coatings of various kinds of oils to plants produces a wide range of effects—some helpful, some harmful. But in the balance, the benefits of using oils to help manage pest and disease problems (and even weeds) outweigh the drawbacks.

Oil sprays kill pests and their eggs and fungal spores by physically smothering them, blocking their access to oxygen. They also have some repellent effect.

Many horticultural oil sprays are petroleum based, and they are classified by their weight. Lightweight oils are called superior, summer, or supreme oils. They are especially effective at controlling pests because they spread thoroughly over the leaf surface. Dormant oils are heavier petroleum oils for use on dormant fruit trees and woody ornamentals.

If you wish to avoid using petroleum products in your garden, look for horticultural oils based on cottonseed or sesame oils, rather than petroleum.

Most of the horticultural oils available today are the new, lighter version, although the product names may have remained the same. Use the new oils as both a dormant and summer spray to control pests on garden and orchard plants.

Neem oil has both insecticidal and fungicidal properties; for more information on neem oil, see "Neem" on page 387.

Protection Offered: Superior oils are unique because they control a broad variety of insect pests while going easy on the beneficial insects. Oils are

effective against adelgids, aphids, mealybugs, spider mites, armored and soft scales, and whiteflies on a variety of fruit, nut, ornamental, and shade trees. Oil sprays can help prevent black spot, powdery mildew, and rust on roses and other ornamentals. Placed on wilted corn silks, vegetable oil prevents corn earworms from crawling down into the husks to feed.

Precautions: The light superior oils developed for controlling insect pests break down quickly and are less toxic to beneficials and the environment than other insecticides. They are slightly toxic to mammals and humans. They do not harm most garden plants when mixed according to label directions. (An exception among plants is blue spruce, *Picea pungens:* The oils remove the bluish frost and it may take 2 to 3 years for the normal color to return.) Among conifers, spruces and Douglas firs are more likely to suffer damage from oil sprays. If your plant is not listed on the label, it is a good idea to test the oil on a few leaves before treating the whole plant.

Don't spray water-stressed plants unless you irrigate them thoroughly before spraying. Avoid using the oils on plants weakened by disease, drying winds, or high-nitrogen applications. Don't apply if daytime temperatures are likely to exceed 85°F or nighttime temperatures are expected to fall below freezing. For conifers, also wait until any melted frost on the foliage has evaporated before applying oils, and be cautious about applying oils in late summer or early fall before the plants have hardened off for winter. Never apply oils within 1 month (before or after) of applying sprays containing sulfur.

How to Use: Horticultural oils are concentrated and must be mixed with water. The oil and water mix forms an emulsion: tiny droplets of oil suspended evenly in the water. Use a 3 percent solution for a dormant application in early spring

Fighting Weeds with Oil

There's a delicate balance between helping and harming plants by spraying them with oil, and research has shown that a combination of certain plant oils and vinegar can serve as a contact herbicide. Don't confuse *herbicidal* oils with *horticultural* oils, and be careful how you use them. Herbicidal oils are non-selective, meaning that they'll burn any foliage they're sprayed on. Natural herbicide products work well to control annual weeds along fence lines, in cracks in sidewalks and patios, and around established trees and shrubs. Brand-name products include Burnout II and AllDown, and Nature's Avenger.

---

before buds appear. Spray a 2 percent solution against insects and mites on plants in full leaf if environmental conditions are right. To make a 2 percent solution, pour ⅓ cup oil into a 1-gallon container, then fill with water to make 1 gallon of solution. For a 3 percent solution, start with ½ cup of oil. Apply successive sprays at least 6 weeks apart.

Spray early in the morning or in the evening to avoid direct sunlight. Wait 24 hours before using other sprays.

Before spraying oil on citrus crops, check with local Cooperative Extension agents for the best timing of sprays for your area and cultivars. On lemons, oils are usually applied in April and May; for other citrus crops, oils are used in late summer or fall. (Navel oranges are very susceptible to damage from oil, so do not spray them after September 1.) Avoid treating citrus trees while mature fruit is present, because fruit may drop or the color and quality may suffer.

To use vegetable oil to control corn earworms, apply a drop or two to the tip of each ear of corn after the silks have wilted.

Commercial Products: A wide range of brand-name products is available. Read labels carefully to determine how to use any particular product safely.

Hot Pepper Spray

Hot peppers owe their hot stuff to a substance called capsaicin. Black pepper, dill, ginger, and paprika also contain capsaicin. Capsaicin repels or kills many soft-bodied insects such as aphids and thrips. It appears to have little effect on most beneficial insects.

Protection Offered: Use commercial products containing capsaicin to kill and repel aphids, leafminers, leafhoppers, soft scales, spider mites, thrips, and whiteflies on vegetable crops and citrus.

Precautions: Avoid inhaling the spray or getting it in your eyes. Contact with hot peppers can irritate sensitive skin, so wear rubber gloves when handling.

How to Use: Apply commercial sprays according to label directions. The spray may be white when first applied, but the white color should disappear within a day. For directions for making a homemade spray containing hot peppers, see "All-Purpose Insect Pest Spray" on page 378.

Commercial Products: Hot Pepper Wax

Iron Phosphate Slug Baits

Commercial products containing iron phosphate mixed with a nontoxic attractant such as wheat gluten are quite effective at killing slugs and snails.

After eating the bait, slugs and snails stop feeding and die a few days later.

Precautions: Iron phosphate baits are not toxic to people or pets, but they can irritate your eyes. Wear gloves while spreading the bait and wash your hands when you're done. Warning: Many commercial slug baits are *not* iron phosphate baits. Rather, they contain metaldehyde, a toxic synthetic substance that should never be used in organic gardens.

Protection Offered: Baits containing iron phosphate kill slugs, snails, earwigs, cutworms, sow bugs, pill bugs, crickets, and ants.

How to use: Follow label instructions. For best effect, apply in the evening when it's warm and humid. Wet down the soil surface first if needed. Bait that is not eaten by slugs or snails will naturally break down in the soil over time.

Commercial Products: Sluggo; Escar-Go! Supreme

Kaolin Clay

Spraying plants with a product that contains kaolin clay puts a chalky coating on leaves and fruits, making them unappealing to pests. The coating also masks the colors of plants, which may prevent pests from recognizing the plants as their hosts. This nat-urally occurring substance helps prevent pest damage to apples, pears, and other fruit crops; in the vegetable garden, it can deter cucumber beetles, Japanese beetles, Colorado potato beetles, and other pests. Kaolin clay will also provide protection for ornamentals, but it's not often used on ornamental plants because of the whitish chalky coating.

Protection Offered: Kaolin clay helps deter damage by a wide range of pests on a wide range of crops. Trials are ongoing to gather data on the effectiveness of this clay coating against pests on specific crops. Among the pests that avoid clay-coated plants are pear psylla, tarnished plant bug, leafrollers, leafhoppers, apple maggot, Oriental fruit moth, plum curculio, codling moth, and thrips on apples, crabapples, and pears; leafhoppers on grapes; leafrollers and leafhoppers on nut trees; cucumber beetles, flea beetles, grasshoppers, and thrips on various vegetable crops; and Japanese beetles on a wide range of food crops and ornamental plants. Spraying kaolin clay can also help prevent sunburn of fruit crops and of nursery stock when transplanting.

Precautions: Kaolin clay is a dry powder, so wear a mask or respirator to avoid inhaling the dust, which could damage your lungs. Wear goggles to keep the dust out of your eyes, too.

A Starchy Solution

Starches like ordinary baking flour work to control insect pests by gumming up the leaf surfaces, trapping and holding the critters until they die. Flour is a good control for larger pests like imported cabbageworms and loopers on cabbage family crops.

A homemade potato starch spray may be effective against aphids, spider mites, thrips, and whiteflies, as well as powdery mildew on cucumbers. You can make your own potato starch spray by mixing 2 to 4 table-spoons of potato flour in 1 quart water, and adding 2 or 3 drops of liquid dish soap. Shake the mixture, and spray to cover the leaves thoroughly. You can also apply the flour as a dust. If a residue remains on ornamentals, simply wash it away with water a few days after the application.

Kaolin clay can reduce the activity of some natural enemies, especially predatory mites. In the case of mites, a flare-up of pest mites can occur after applying kaolin clay because of the adverse effect on predators. Sprays applied early in the growing season, before populations of natural enemies have increased, do the most good with the least impact on beneficials.

How to Use: Kaolin clay products are powders that do not mix easily with water. Prepare to apply it by first adding water to a backpack-type sprayer and then stir the powder into the water (consult product labels for precise amounts of water and product). If that doesn't work well, mix the clay and water first in a plastic bucket, by hand or using an electric drill with a paint mixer attachment. Spray immediately after preparing, applying to the point of runoff. For more thorough coverage, make a second pass over the plants with the coating. If necessary, stop occasionally while you work and shake your sprayer vigorously to put the clay back into suspension in the water. Reapply after rain. In most cases, the clay coating will be gone by the time you harvest a crop, but if not, simply use a soft cloth to wipe it off.

Commercial Products: Surround at Home; Surround WP

Lime-Sulfur

Adding lime to sulfur (see "Sulfur" on page 391) enhances its fungicidal properties by causing a chemical change that allows the sulfur to penetrate leaf tissue. This is an important change, since once sulfur penetrates the leaf tissue, it can kill recently germinated spores. Unfortunately, the boost in fungicidal properties also means a greater risk of damaging plants. NOP regulations allow the use of lime-sulfur with restrictions; regard it as a last resort.

Protection Offered: Applying lime-sulfur can help prevent and lessen damage from diseases like anthracnose, brown rot, leaf spot, mildew, and scab. It also helps control scales on dormant perennials, roses, evergreens, and many fruit crops. It also kills mites. However, this can be a drawback. If a lime-sulfur application kills off mite species that are natural enemies, a new pest problem may arise soon after spraying because its natural control cycle has been interrupted.

Precautions: Lime-sulfur is extremely toxic to mammals and can cause severe eye damage and skin irritation. When using it, wear rubber gloves and goggles or other face protection. Lime-sulfur is more caustic than pure sulfur, so it is more likely to damage the host plant if used improperly. If you have sprayed plants with horticultural oil, wait 2 to 3 weeks before using a sulfur product. Avoid spraying during periods when temperatures will exceed 85°F, to prevent plant damage. Lime-sulfur discolors wood and painted surfaces, so use with caution around structures.

How to Use: Buy lime-sulfur as a liquid concentrate. In early spring, spray it on dormant shrubs, like lilacs and roses, and evergreens, such as junipers. You can control powdery mildew on roses by applying lime-sulfur when the buds break in spring and by repeating the application 1 week later. Spray raspberries infected with anthracnose or blight when the buds first show silver. Spray currants and gooseberries infected with anthracnose at bud break, and repeat 10 to 15 days later.

Commercial Products: Polysul Lime Sulfur; Polysul Summer & Dormant Spray Concentrate

Neem

Extracts from the seed of the neem tree (*Azadirachta indica*) contain azadirachtin, which is poisonous to many types of insects. Products containing azadirachtin (usually simply called neem) act as a broad-spectrum repellent, growth regulator, and insect poison. Neem discourages feeding by making plants unpalatable to insects; if they still attack, it inhibits their ability to molt and lay eggs.

Unlike most botanical insecticides, neem also has somewhat of a "systemic" effect. This means that plants can take up neem extracts through their roots and leaves, spreading the material throughout the plant tissues. That's how neem can help to control pests like leafminers, which feed within leaves and are normally not bothered by sprays that only cover the outsides of the plant.

Other products contain neem oil, which has a similar effect on pests as other horticultural oils (see "Horticultural Oils" on page 384 for details). Neem oil products also help to prevent disease problems such as powdery mildew.

Protection Offered: Use neem to kill a wide range of pests on ornamentals and food crops, including ants, aphids, fruit flies, gypsy moths, leafminers, loopers, mealybugs, thrips, and whiteflies. It is effective against Colorado potato beetles, corn earworms, cucumber beetles, flea beetles, Mexican bean beetles, weevils, codling moths, Japanese beetles, and pest mites.

Precautions: Neem is almost nontoxic to mammals and is biodegradable. It is used in India as an ingredient in toothpaste, soap, cosmetics, pharmaceuticals, and cattle feed. The seeds and extracts of neem, however, are poisonous if consumed. Because neem's chemical structure is so complex, scientists hypothesize that it will take a long time for pests to develop resistance to it.

Since neem generally must be ingested for it to be toxic, its effect on spiders, honeybees, and other beneficial creatures is usually minimal. It can, however, sometimes harm parasites that prey on insects that have eaten neem-sprayed foliage. It's possible that repeated use of neem could also lead to pest resistance. To minimize the chance of affecting beneficials and encouraging pest resistance, use neem sprays only when absolutely necessary, and only on plants that you know contain pest insects. Alternating neem sprays with insecticidal soap or other treatments may be most effective.

How to Use: Follow label directions carefully. Use sprays within 8 hours of mixing. Apply to affected plants and repeat about a week later (or as soon as 4 days for heavily infested plants). Neem compounds break down fairly quickly—usually in 5 to 7 days—in sunlight and in the soil, so you may need to repeat the application during the growing season to deal with new pests that arrive throughout summer. Pests on treated plants may not show any effects right away; in fact, they may continue feeding lightly on plants until the spray takes effect. (On adult insects, in fact, you may not see any direct effect, but they may produce few or no offspring, reducing future damage.)

Neem works fastest during hot weather, so expect results within a few days in summer; spring and fall applications may take longer. Heavy rain within a few days after the application may wash the spray off the leaves; reapply if pests are still a problem.

Different brands of neem products seem to vary in effectiveness. If the product you're using seems ineffective, you may want to try another brand.

Commercial Products: A wide range of brand-name products is available. Read labels to see whether a product contains azadirachtin, neem oil, or both.

Plant Defense System Activators

When attacked by pests or disease, many plants activate their natural defense systems to help ward off the threat. Some commercial products claim to help protect plants from problems by stimulating plants to activate their natural defense systems. Among these are products containing a substance called harpin and products containing extracts from giant knotweed (*Reynoutria sachalinensis*). Some of these products have been listed by OMRI, but others have not. You'll need to read labels carefully and ask questions to decide whether these products are something you'll feel comfortable using in your garden.

Homemade compost tea sprays (see page 6) or a homemade spray made from horsetail (*Equisetum arvense*) may offer similar benefits.

If you anticipate a disease outbreak because of prevailing weather conditions, begin a preventive spray program using a protective product before you spot any symptoms. Experiment to see which plants and diseases it works best on, and keep records for future reference.

Protection Offered: Apply protective plant extracts to help prevent bacterial and fungal diseases. Different products list the specific diseases that they are effective against, and may include late blight, bacterial spot and speck, powdery mildew, downy mildew, gray mold, rust, bacterial blight, and others. Be sure to read labels to see which products have shown effectiveness for a particular crop or problem.

How to Use: Follow label directions for commercial products.

To mix a horsetail spray, buy dried horsetail from organic and biodynamic garden suppliers. In a stainless steel pot, mix ⅛ cup of dried leaves in 1 gallon of unchlorinated water. (If you have chlorinated tap water, either collect rainwater or let the tap water sit uncovered for 2 days so the chlorine will volatilize.) Bring to a boil, then let simmer for at least ½ hour. Cool and strain through cheesecloth. This mixture will keep for 1 month, stored in a glass container. Be sure to label it!

Dilute the horsetail concentrate by adding 5 to

10 parts unchlorinated water to every 1 part concentrate. Spray infected plants once every week to 2 weeks.

Commercial Products: Messenger; Regalia SC

Pyrethrins

Pyrethrum daisies (*Tanacetum cinerariifolium* and *T. coccineum)* contain several substances that kill insect pests on contact. The toxic substances in the daisies are called pyrethrins. Pyreth*roids* are synthetic versions of pyrethrins. Pyrethroids are not allowable under NOP regulations. Pyrethrins are allowed with restrictions, but should be used in home gardens only as a last resort.

Protection Offered: Pyrethrin products are broad-spectrum insect nerve poisons that will kill a range of pests on flowers, fruits, and vegetables in the garden and greenhouse. Pyrethrins are effective against chewing and sucking insects, including most aphids, cabbage loopers, celery leaftiers, codling moths, Colorado potato beetles, leafhoppers, Mexican bean beetles, spider mites, stink bugs, thrips, tomato pinworms, and whiteflies. Pyrethrins are less effective on diamondback moths, flea beetles, imported cabbageworms, pear psylla, and tarnished plant bugs.

Precautions: Pyrethrin insecticides are moderately toxic to mammals and restrictions are now being imposed on indoor use. Pyrethrins are also toxic to many natural enemies of plant pests as well as to pollinator insects.

Pyrethrin products tend to work best at the lower end of summertime temperatures and are less effective when temperatures exceed 80°F.

How to Use: To apply pyrethrins safely and effectively, wear protective clothing and follow label directions for mixing, spraying, or dusting. Two applications may be necessary for complete control.

Commercial Products: A range of pyrethrin

products is available. Note that some pyrethrin products include other active ingredients as well, such as copper or sulfur. Avoid such products unless the pest problem you're managing truly requires the application of both pyrethrins and another insecticidal or fungicidal ingredient. Be aware that many commercial products contain a synthetic synergist (a substance that enhances the effect of a spray or dust) called piperonyl butoxide (PBO). PBO is toxic in its own right, and its use is prohibited in organic production. Home gardeners should avoid using products that contain PBO.

Soap Sprays

For many years, organic gardeners used solutions of water and natural soaps for controlling garden pests. One recipe involved simmering a pot of water with chunks of Fels Naptha soap, straining it, and coating garden plants with the suds to control aphids and thrips. Since then, scientists have discovered that the salts of fatty acids found in many soaps act as selective insecticides. Insecticidal soaps control insect pests by penetrating their cuticles, which causes their cell membranes to collapse and leak, resulting in dehydration. While some insects can overcome the effects of a soap spray, others are immediately affected and die.

Protection Offered: Use insecticidal soaps to control soft-bodied insects like aphids, mealybugs, and whiteflies. They're also effective against chiggers, earwigs, fleas, mites, scales, thrips, and ticks. Generally, soap spray is not the most effective choice for killing chewing insects like caterpillars and beetles.

Fungicidal soaps are available to control powdery mildew, black spot, brown canker, leaf spot, and rust on ornamental and food plants. There are also soap products labeled for use in killing weeds.

Precautions: All soaps have phytotoxic properties, so test the kind you plan to spray on a few leaves before treating whole plants. Plants with thin cuticles, like beans, Chinese cabbage, cucumbers, ferns, gardenias, Japanese maples, nasturtiums, and young peas, are easily damaged by soap sprays. Tomatoes and potatoes are less susceptible to damage, and thick-leaved cabbages seem virtually impervious, although heavy soap use may reduce yields. A good rule is to use no more than 3 successive sprays on any plant.

Insecticidal soaps are nontoxic to humans and to other test animals, and they biodegrade rapidly in the soil. They will, however, kill beneficial insects along with the pests, so limit their use to problem areas. Herbicidal soaps will affect any plant that they are sprayed on, so use with care around valuable ornamentals.

How to Use: You can use household soaps such as Ivory Snow, Ivory Liquid, or Shaklee's Basic H to make your own insecticidal soap solution. Since manufacturers often make small changes in their soaps' contents, the effectiveness of homemade solutions may vary more than that of commercial insecticidal soaps.

Be aware that many products commonly known as soap also contain impurities, such as perfumes and whiteners, that can damage plants. For pest control, it is important to use pure soap; avoid detergents or soaps with additives.

To prepare a homemade soap solution, mix from 1 teaspoon to several tablespoons of soap per gallon of water. Start at the lower concentration and adjust the strength to maximize pest control while avoiding plant damage.

To control aphids, spray when the first aphid colonies develop in early spring and again when winged females arrive. If aphids are a continuous problem, make several applications about 2 weeks apart. To control plant bugs, spray as soon as nymphs begin feeding. To control mites, use a high-pressure spray, like that of a hose-end sprayer, that washes away many pests and kills those that remain. Repeat 7 to 10 days later to kill newly hatched mites.

You can mix soaps with other insecticides like BTK, horticultural oil, and pyrethrins to boost their toxicity, but think carefully about whether this degree of attack is truly necessary before you try a mix (premixed commercial products are also available). You can also mix homemade soap or liquid dish soap with cooking oil to boost the effectiveness of both insecticidal ingredients.

Mix 1 tablespoon of liquid dish soap and 1 cup of oil (peanut, safflower, corn, soybean, or sunflower). When you're ready to spray, mix 1 to 2½ teaspoons of the prepared base to 1 cup of water. This mixture has been used successfully to control a variety of pests on carrots, celery, cucumber, eggplant, lettuce, and peppers. However, some plants may be injured by the oil, so test the spray on a few leaves and wait several days before spraying all of your plants.

Herbicidal soaps are most effective on young weeds with tender leaf tissue. They are not very effective against mature perennial weeds, especially those with tap roots. Spray on weeds according to label directions.

Commercial Products: A wide variety of brand-name products is available. Be sure to check the label to see whether a particular soap product is labeled for pests, diseases, or weeds.

Spinosad

Spinosad is an insect toxin that's derived not from a plant, but from a type of bacterium. The actinomycete *Saccaropolyspora spinosad* produces a substance called spinosyn that is toxic when consumed by leaf-chewing caterpillars, fire ants, and some other pests. Note that although spinosad is a relatively new discovery in pest management, some pests,

including diamondback moth, have already developed resistance to it. Reserve it for use as a last resort.

Protection Offered: Use spinosad to help stop damage by caterpillars, thrips, leafminers, sawflies, flies, and ants. It works well to kill young larvae of cabbage loopers, diamondback moths, and asparagus beetles. On apple and other pome fruit trees, it helps to control codling moths, Oriental fruit moths, leafminers, and leafrollers. Spinosad is toxic to small grubs of Colorado potato beetles and some leaf-feeding beetle pests.

Precautions: Avoid applying spinosad to bodies of water. The spinosyns may be toxic to fish and will not break down in water except in direct sunlight. Spinosad also appears to be toxic to honeybees and some other types of beneficial insects.

How to Use: Mix the product according to label directions. Spray in the morning or afternoon, and reapply if needed 4 to 7 days later.

Commercial Products: Captain Jack's Deadbug Brew; Colorado Potato Beetle Beater; Entrust Naturalyte Insect Control; Green Light Lawn & Garden Spray; Monterey Garden Insect Spray. There is also a range of spinosad products specifically formulated for fire ant control.

Sulfur

Sulfur is one of the oldest pesticides known. It has been used for centuries to control plant pathogens, mites, and some insect pests. Sulfur is mined from natural deposits as a yellow solid that is almost insoluble in water. Wettable sulfur is finely ground sulfur mixed with a wetting agent to help it go into solution. Sulfur is also formulated as a finely ground dust with clay or talc added to enhance dusting qualities. NOP regulations allow the use of sulfur with restrictions.

Protection Offered: Sulfur sprays can help

prevent apple scab, brown rot of stone fruits, powdery mildews, rose black spot, rusts, and other plant diseases on ornamentals and on some food crops, including grapes, potatoes, strawberries, and tomatoes. It is also effective against mites and potato/tomato psyllids.

Precautions: Sulfur is moderately toxic to humans and other mammals. It can irritate or damage the lungs, skin, or eyes if not used carefully. Wear protective clothing when applying sulfur. Although it is more toxic to mites than to insects, sulfur is nonspecific and can kill beneficial insects, soil microorganisms, and fish. Do not apply it within 1 month of using an oil spray; use a copper fungicide instead. Sulfur spray may cause plant injury if applied when temperatures exceed 80°F. It is corrosive to metal, so use a sprayer with plastic parts; rinse equipment thoroughly after use.

How to Use: You can buy sulfur as a dry powder for dusting on plants, as a wettable formulation (also known as flowable sulfur) that mixes readily with water, or as a ready-to-use spray. Some sulfur products are colloidal, which means they have very fine particles that disperse over the leaf surfaces to provide excellent protection. Noncolloidal sulfur is made of larger particles that will leave unprotected areas on the leaf surfaces. Mix a sulfur solution according to the instructions on the label, agitating it frequently, since it tends to settle out of solution.

Commercial Products: Bonide Liquid Sulfur; Safer Garden Fungicide; That Flowable Sulfur

Tomato-Leaf Spray

Tomato and potato leaves contain significant amounts of poisonous alkaloids. Instead of acting as an insecticide, however, sprays made from tomato leaves appear to reduce pest damage by attracting natural pest enemies searching for their prey.

Protection Offered: Use tomato-leaf sprays to protect plants from aphids and to reduce corn earworm damage.

Precautions: Since alkaloids tend to be toxic to mammals, use care in handling this spray and avoid getting it on your skin. Some individuals are extremely allergic to plants in the nightshade family to which tomatoes and potatoes belong. Don't apply tomato-leaf spray on other crops in the same botanical family as tomatoes, such as peppers or eggplant, because of the risk of spreading mosaic virus.

How to Use: Finely chop 1 to 2 cups of healthy tomato leaves. Soak them overnight in 2 cups of water. In the morning, strain the slurry through cheesecloth, add about 2 more cups of water to the strained liquid, and spray, covering leaves thoroughly.

Common Insect Damage Symptoms

Use this table to narrow the list of possible culprits causing damage to your plants. Look for the damage symptoms in the left-hand column. Next, find the appropriate category of host plants, then look up the pests listed in Part 3. Your plants may be suffering from a problem not listed below, as this table is not all-inclusive.

SYMPTOMS	HOST PLANTS	INSECTS
Leaf and Foliage Damage		
Small plants cut off at soil line or consumed	Vegetables, flowers	Cutworms, earwigs, millipedes, mole crickets, slugs and snails
Large holes chewed in leaves; no excrement visible	Beans	Mexican bean beetles
	Cucumbers, corn, peanuts	Cucumber beetles
	Flowers, vegetables	Earwigs, Japanese beetles, slugs and snails
	Potatoes	Colorado potato beetles
Large holes chewed in leaves, dark green excrement often visible	Cabbage family plants	Cabage loopers, imported cabbage-worms, diamondback moths
	Tomatoes	Tomato hornworms, tomato fruitworms
	Vegetables, fruits, ornaments	Leaf beetles, woollybear caterpillars
Small, round holes (shot holes) in leaves	Cabbage family plants, potatoes, spinach, flowers	Flea beetles
Puckered, twisted leaves; sticky honeydew present	Vegetables, fruits, ornamentals	Aphids, mites
Puckered, twisted leaves; no sticky honeydew	Vegetables, fruits, ornamentals	Aphids, mites, thrips, leafhoppers, plant bugs, spittlebugs/froghoppers, nematodes
	Eggplant, potatoes, tomatoes	Potato/tomato psyllid
Skeletonized leaves	Beans	Mexican bean beetle
	Vegetables, fruits, ornamentals	Japanese beetles
	Fruit trees, roses, shade trees	Slug sawflies
Partially or fully defoliated plants	Asparagus	Asparagus beetles
	Conifers	Conifer sawflies, gypsy moths, tent caterpillars
	Deciduous trees and shrubs	Gypsy moths, May/June beetles, cankerworms, slug sawflies, tussock moths
	Flowers, vegetables	Armyworms, Asiatic garden beetles, blister beetles, climbing cutworms, leaf beetles, rose chafers, striped cucumber beetles
	Pears, cherries, plums, cotoneasters	Pear sawflies
	Squash family plants	Striped cucumber beetles

(continued)

COMMON INSECT DAMAGE SYMPTOMS—*CONTINUED*

SYMPTOMS	HOST PLANTS	INSECTS
Shoot or branch tips wilt and die	Conifers	Adelgids
	Fruit and shade trees	Oriental fruit moths
	Squash family plants	Squash bugs
	Roses	Rose midge
	Vegetables, fruits, flowers	Tarnished plant bugs and other plant bugs
Webbing on leaves, stems, and branch tips	Apples, roses, other deciduous trees and shrubs	Obliquebanded leafrollers, fruittree leafrollers, tent caterpillars, fall webworms, spider mites
Small, baglike cocoons with bits of leaves attached hanging from branches	Fruit trees, ornamental trees and shrubs	Bagworms
Mines between upper and lower leaf surfaces	Apples, roses, other deciduous trees and shrubs	Obliquebanded leafrollers (young larvae)
	Beets, chard, nightshade family plants	Leafminers
	Cabbage family plants	Diamondback moths (young larvae)
	Chrysanthemums and other ornamentals	Leafminers
	Elms, birches, alders	Leafminer sawflies
Yellow leaves	Citrus and other fruit trees	Soft scales, armored scales
	Lawn grasses	Chinch bugs
	Pears, quinces	Pear psyllas
Yellow or withered leaves	Evergreen trees and shrubs, strawberries, bramble fruits	Black vine weevil larvae
Russeted leaves	Apples, pears, tomatoes, ornamentals	Rust mites
Small, discolored spots on leaves	Vegetables, flowers	Garden fleahoppers
White, gray, or silvery speckled pattern on leaves	Vegetables, ornamentals, fruit and shade trees	Spider mites, thrips, lace bugs
Sticky honeydew on leaves	Pears, quinces	Pear psyllas
	Vegetables, fruits, ornamentals	Aphids, scales, mealybugs, whiteflies
Galls on leaves	Oaks, roses	Gall wasps
	Maples	Gall mites
Flower Damage		
Holes in flower petals or flower buds	Annual flowers, vegetables	Corn earworm, earwigs, striped cucumber beetles, tobacco budworm, woollybear caterpillars
Distorted flowers and flower buds	Vegetables, fruits, ornamentals	Aphids, thrips
Flowers partially or completely consumed	Ornamentals, vegetables	garden beetles, blister beetles, May/June beetles, Japanese beetles
	Irises, potatoes	Lily leaf beetle

SYMPTOMS	HOST PLANTS	INSECTS
Fruit Damage		
Early-dropping fruit	Apples, plums, blueberries Citrus and other tree fruits, grapes Tree fruits, blueberries, currants	Apple maggots, plum curculios Mealybugs Fruit flies
Damage around pit in fruit	Almonds, walnuts Cherries	Navel orangeworms Codling moths
Tunnels to core of fruit	Apples and other tree fruits Citrus, figs	Codling moths, Oriental fruit moths, plum curculios Navel orangeworms
Large holes or damaged areas in fruit or ears	Corn Tomatoes	Corn earworms, European corn borers, corn rootworms Tomato hornworms, tomato fruitworms
Distorted, scarred fruit	Vegetables, fruits	Tarnished plant bugs and other plant bugs, stink bugs, thrips
Poor fruit set or quality	Tomatoes, potatoes, eggplant	Tomato/potato psyllid
Russeted appearance of fruit	Apples, pears	Rust mites
Stem and Trunk Damage		
Holes bored in trunk	Apple and other fruit trees, mountain ashes, hawthorns	Roundheaded appletree borers, peachtree borers
Holes bored in stems, buds, or shoots	Corn Currants, gooseberries, raspberries, rhododendrons	European corn borer Fruit borers
Galleries bored under trunk	Elms Fruit and shade trees	Elm bark beetles Flatheaded borers, metallic wood borers, shothole borers
Plants topple over	Corn	Rootworms
Root Damage		
Holes tunneled in roots	Cabbage family plants Carrot family Gladiolus and other flower corms Irises Onions, leeks, garlic Potatoes Strawberries, grapes, raspberries, other fruits	Cabbage maggots Carrot rust flies, carrot beetles, carrot weevils Wireworms Iris borers Onion maggots Wireworms Strawberry root weevils
Knotted, lumpy roots	Beans, peas, other legumes Tomatoes, lettuce, peppers, nonlegumes	Beneficial bacteria in roots Nematodes
Chewed, stunted, withered, or damaged roots	Lawn grasses	Japanese beetles, June/May beetles, mole crickets, rose chafers, chinch bugs

GARDEN PEST AND DISEASE MANAGEMENT SUPPLIES AND PRODUCTS

Many supplies and products for natural pest and disease management are available at local garden centers. Mail-order suppliers offer an even wider range of choice. The following companies offer composting equipment, floating row covers, insect traps, biological control products, sprays and dusts, sprayers, tools, and accessories. Many also stock general gardening supplies and equipment as well.

ARBICO Organics
PO Box 8910
Tucson, AZ 85738-0910
Phone: 800-827-2847 (orders only)
Web site: www.arbico-organics.com

Biocontrol Network
5116 Williamsburg Road
Brentwood, TN 37027
Phone: 800-441-BUGS
Web site: www.biconet.com

DirtWorks
1195 Dog Team Road
New Haven, VT 05472
Phone: 802-385-1064
Web site: www.dirtworks.net

Extremely Green Gardening Company
PO Box 2021
Abington, MA 02351
Phone: 781-878-5397
Web site: www.extremelygreen.com

Gardener's Supply Company
128 Intervale Road
Burlington, VT 05401
Phone: 800-427-3363
Web site: www.gardeners.com

Gardens Alive
5100 Schenley Place
Lawrenceburg, IN 47025
Phone: 513-354-1482
Web site: www.gardensalive.com

Harmony Farm Supply
3244 Hwy. 16 North
Sebastopol, CA 95472
Phone: 707-823-9125
Web site: www.harmonyfarm.com

Johnny's Selected Seeds
955 Benton Avenue
Winslow, ME 04901
Phone: 877-564-6697
Web site: www.johnnyseeds.com

Peaceful Valley Farm and Garden Supply
PO Box 2209
125 Clydesdale Court
Grass Valley, CA 95945
Phone: 888-784-1722
Web site: www.groworganic.com

Planet Natural
1612 Gold Avenue
Bozeman, MT 59715
Phone: 800-289-6656 (orders only)
Web site: www.planetnatural.com

SOURCES

Pest and Disease ID Guides

Cebenko, Jill Jesiolowski, and Deborah L. Martin, eds. *Insect, Disease & Weed I.D. Guide*. Emmaus, PA: Rodale, 2001.

Cranshaw, Whitney. *Garden Insects of North America*. Princeton, NJ: Princeton University Press, 2004.

Dreistadt, Steve H. *Pests of Landscape Trees and Shrubs*. University of California Agriculture and Natural Resources, 2004.

Eaton, Eric R., and Kenn Kaufman. *Kaufman Field Guide to Insects of North America*. New York: Houghton Mifflin Harcourt, 2007.

Flint, Mary Louise. *Natural Enemies Handbook*. Berkeley: University of California Press, 1999.

Howard, Ronald J., J. Allan Garland, and W. Lloyd Seaman, eds. *Diseases and Pests of Vegetable Crops in Canada*. Ottowa, Ontario: Entomological Society of Canada, 1994.

Johnson, Warren T., and Howard H. Lyon. *Insects that Feed on Trees and Shrubs*. Ithaca, NY: Cornell University Press, 1991.

Sinclair, Wayne A., and Howard H. Lyon. *Diseases of Trees and Shrubs*. Ithaca, NY: Cornell University Press, 2005.

Westcott, Cynthia. *Westcott's Plant Disease Handbook*. New York: Van Nostrand Reinhold, 1979.

Pest ID and Management Web Sites

The Cooperative Extension Service in many states offers some type of pest or disease ID information on its Web site. To find the Extension Service Web site for your state, start at www.csrees.usda.gov/Extension/ and on the map of the United States, click on your home state. Also check the Web sites of the following State Extension Services, particularly those in your region.

Colorado State University Extension

http://cmg.colostate.edu/pubs.shtml#insects

Identifying Vegetable Insect Pests in Pennsylvania

http://resources.cas.psu.edu/ipm/vegpests.pdf

University of California

http://woodypests.cas.psu.edu/PestDiagnosis/index.html

University of Florida "Featured Creatures"

http://entnemdept.ufl.edu/creatures/main/search_common.htm

Univeristy of Illinois "The Bug Review"

http://urbanext.illinois.edu/bugreview/

Penn State Woody Ornamental Pest Diagnosis

http://woodypests.cas.psu.edu/PestDiagnosis/index.html

Virginia Cooperative Extension (Virginia Tech)

http://pubs.ext.vt.edu/category/agricultural-insects-pests.html

Soil Testing Information

Most state Cooperative Extension offices offer soil testing services. To find out how to submit a soil sample for testing, go to www.csrees.usda.gov/Extension/ and on the map of the United States, click on your home state.

Another option is to check the list of Extension Service and private soil testing laboratories in the United States and Canada maintained by *Organic Gardening* magazine on its Web site. Check this link: www.organicgardening.com/soiltest/

For in-depth information on soil testing, consult the online Cornell Waste Management Institute Guide to Soil Testing and Interpreting Results at http://cwmi.css.cornell.edu/guide%20to%20soil.pdf.

INDEX

Boldface page numbers indicate photographs or illustrations. <u>Underscored</u> references indicate boxed text, charts, and graphs.